Electronic Signatures Law and Regulation

AUSTRALIA
Law Book Co.
Sydney

CANADA and USA
Carswell
Toronto

HONG KONG
Sweet & Maxwell Asia

NEW ZEALAND
Brookers
Wellington

SINGAPORE and MALAYSIA
Sweet & Maxwell Asia
Singapore and Kuala Lumpur

Electronic Signatures Law and Regulation

FIRST EDITION

by

Lorna Brazell
Bird & Bird

THOMSON

™

SWEET & MAXWELL

First edition 2004

Published by
Sweet & Maxwell
100 Avenue Road
London NW3 3PF
(http://www.sweetandmaxwell.co.uk)

Typeset by Kerrypress Ltd, Luton, Bedfordshire
Printed in Great Britain by Athenaeum Press, Gateshead

No natural forests were destroyed to make this product: only farmed timber was used
and replanted

A CIP catalogue record for this book is available from the British Library

ISBN 0421 824301

The authors have asserted their rights under the Copyright, Designs and Patents Act
1988 to be identified as the authors of this work.

Preface

The law of signatures has always had a whiff of technology about it. Whether the issue be the legitimacy of using rubber stamps or pre-printed forms, or the adequacy of a mere mark, there have always been those who argue that the method used to inscribe a signature is insufficiently permanent, unique, reliable or tamper-proof to satisfy a legal requirement for a signature.

The English common law has never had much truck with technological objections. No English reported judgment has ever struck down a signature on the ground alone that inadequate technology has been used to create it. Even an X impressed with a rubber stamp can constitute a signature. Other jurisdictions, less fortunate in their traditions, have placed great store by true manuscript autographs and notarisation or similar ceremonies.

The advent of electronic communications, and the ensuing discussion over what constitutes a valid signature in the electronic environment, have magnified these differences in legal tradition. They have also exposed gaps between technologists and lawyers. Technologists, assuming that the law requires absolute certainty in an ordinary signature, have set about building elaborate systems designed to achieve this. In fact neither the law nor the marketplace demands this degree of assurance for everyday use, and so far these systems have typically been taken up only for high value transactions.

Even after harmonisation of European electronic signatures laws by the Electronic Signatures Directive, the different national approaches survive. The UK implementation of the Directive is minimalist and facilitative. Other European countries, reflecting their own traditions, have implemented the Directive in a variety of more complex and prescriptive ways.

To do justice to the topic of electronic signatures therefore requires a comparative approach, even within supposedly harmonised Europe. In this book my Bird & Bird partner Lorna Brazell has achieved this with distinction. She has covered 54 countries and territories, not merely reciting the legislation but illuminating it in the context of differing approaches to signatures.

The topic of electronic signatures ought to be simple. If each country's law were to state that a requirement for a signature is satisfied by a signature in electronic form and leave it at that, there would hardly be a book worth writing. Regrettably the laws are not so simple. The book is well worth writing, Lorna has done the subject more than justice and I commend her work to you.

Graham Smith, Bird & Bird July 2003

Contents

Preface   v
Table of Cases   xiii
Table of Statutes   xv
Table of Statutory Instruments   xvii
Table of Directives   xix
Table of Foreign Legislation   xxi

1. **Introduction**
    Identity and liability   1-004
    Certification authorities and public key infrastructure   1-005
    Historical development   1-008
    The influence of technology   1-015

2. **Legal functions and requirements of signatures**
    Introduction   2-001
    Legal effects of signatures in the law of contract   2-007
    Other jurisdictions   2-026
    Circumstances where signatures do not bind   2-030
    Signature as a form of identification   2-032
    Electronic identity   2-038
    Electronic signatures   2-044

3. **Electronic Signature Technologies**
    Introduction   3-001
    "Low tech" solutions   3-004
        Passwords   3-005
        Bitmap scan of handwritten signature   3-007
        Light pen   3-008
        Other methods   3-009
        Conclusions   3-010
    Biometrics   3-011
        Retina Scan   3-014
        Iris Scan   3-016
        Face recognition   3-018
        Fingerprints/handprints   3-019
        Hand/finger geometry   3-021
        Handwritten signature dynamics   3-022

Voice	3-023
Vein patterns	3-024
Other proposed forms of biometrics	3-025
Conclusions on biometrics	3-033
Encryption	3-035
The terms for basic cryptography	3-036
Methods	3-037
Digital signatures: what they are/how they work	3-040
Functional equivalence between electronic and handwritten signatures	3-045
Ceremony: safeguarding against undue haste or thoughtfulness	3-050
Marking version as the original	3-051
Non-repudiation	3-052

4. Structural issues

Introduction	4-001.01
Establishing identity in cross-border transactions	4-001.02
Roles within PKI	4-011
Certification practice statements	4-017
Australia: the Gatekeeper PKI framework	4-023
Victoria	4-030
New South Wales	4-031
Western Australia	4-032
Australian capital territory	4-033
The banks - project angus	4-034

5. International initiatives relating to electronic signatures

Introduction	5-001
UNCITRAL model maws	5-002
ICC general usage for internationally digitally ensured commerce(version II)	5-027
OECD ministerial declaration on authentication for electronic commerce	5-031
EU electronic signatures directive	5-033
Summary	5-039

6. Electronic signature laws of the world

Introduction	6-001
1. EUROPE	6-006
(i) Austria	6-007
(ii) Belgium	6-009
(iii) Bulgaria	6-010
(iv) Cyprus	6-013
(v) Czech Republic	6-014
(vi) Denmark	6-015
(vii) Estonia	6-017
(viii) Finland	6-020
(ix) France	6-022
(x) Germany	6-024
(xi) Greece	6-026
(xii) Guernsey	6-027

(xiii) Hungary   6-028
(xiv) Ireland   6-030
(xv) Italy   6-032
(xvi) Latvia   6-035
(xvii) Lithuania   6-037
(xviii) Luxembourg   6-039
(xix) Malta   6-041
(xx) The Netherlands   6-043
(xxi) Poland   6-045
(xxii) Portugal   6-047
(xxiii) Romania   6-051
(xxiv) Slovakia   6-053
(xxv) Slovenia   6-055
(xxvi) Spain   6-058
(xxvii) Sweden   6-060
(xxviii) Switzerland   6-061
(xxix) United Kingdom   6-062
2. ASIA/PACIFIC   6-064
(i) Australia   6-064
1. Commonwealth legislation   6-066
General   6-066
Electronic Transactions Act 1999   6-067
2. ETA Variations in each state   6-069
(ii) Bangladesh   6-071
(iii) China   6-072
(iv) Hong Kong   6-074
(v) India   6-076
(vi) Indonesia   6-078
(vii) Japan   6-079
(viii) Malaysia   6-080
(ix) New Zealand   6-081
(x) Pakistan   6-084
(xi) Philippines   6-086
(xii) Singapore   6-089
(xiii) South Korea   6-091
(xiv) Sri Lanka   6-092
(xv) Thailand   6-093
3. NORTH AMERICA   6-096
(i) Canada   6-096
(ii) Mexico   6-099
(iii) United States of America   6-101
Conclusion   6-136
Other governmental regulations concerning electronic signatures 6-137
4. LATIN AMERICA   6-138
(i) Argentina   6-138
(ii) Brazil   6-140
(iii) Chile   6-141
(iv) Colombia   6-143
(v) Ecuador   6-145

(vi) Peru   6-148
(vii) Venezuela   6-149
5. REST OF THE WORLD   6-151
(i) Russian Federation   6-151
(ii) South Africa   6-153
(iii) Israel   6-155
(iv) Turkey   6-157

7. **Practical issues**
Introduction   7-001
Cross-border transactions   7-002
Consequences of contracting cross-border without choice of
law and jurisdiction clauses   7-003
Signature policies and choice of law   7-006
Transactions with a certification service provider   7-010
Information security   7-018
Electronic record management   7-022

8. **Evidential issues**
Introduction   8-001
Burden and standard of proof   8-002
Evidential issues in real world transactions   8-003
"Traditional" signatures as evidence   8-008
Evidential issues in electronic transactions   8-010

9. **Regulatory aspects**
Introduction   9-001
1. Specific regulation of certification service providers   9-002
A. EUROPE   9-004
(i) Austria   9-005
(ii) Belgium   9-007
(iii) Bulgaria   9-009
(iv) Cyprus   9-011
(v) Czech Republic   9-012
(vi) Denmark   9-015
(vii) Estonia   9-016
(viii) Finland   9-019
(ix) France   9-020
(x) Germany   9-021
(xi) Greece   9-023
(xii) Hungary   9-024
(xiii) Ireland   9-026
(xiv) Italy   9-027
(xv) Latvia   9-028
(xvi) Lithuania   9-030
(xvii) Luxembourg   9-031
(xviii) Malta   9-033
(xix) The Netherlands   9-034
(xx) Poland   9-036
(xxi) Portugal   9-039

(xxii) Romania   9-041
(xxiii) Slovakia   9-043
(xxiv) Slovenia   9-045
(xxv) Spain   9-047
(xxvi) Sweden   9-049
(xxvii) Switzerland   9-050
(xxviii) United Kingdom   9-051
B. ASIA/PACIFIC   9-053
(i) Australia   9-053
(ii) Bangladesh   9-054
(iii) China   9-055
(iv) Hong Kong   9-056
(v) India   9-058
(vi) Indonesia   9-059
(vii) Japan   9-060
(viii) Malaysia   9-061
(ix) New Zealand   9-063
(x) Pakistan   9-064
(xi) Philippines   9-065
(xii) Singapore   9-066
(xiii) South Korea   9-068
(xiv) Sri Lanka   9-070
(xv) Thailand   9-071
C. NORTH AMERICA   9-072
(i) Canada   9-072
(ii) Mexico   9-073
(iii) United States of America   9-074
D. LATIN AMERICA   9-079
(i) Argentina   9-079
(ii) Brazil   9-081
(iii) Chile   9-082
(iv) Colombia   9-084
(v) Ecuador   9-086
(vi) Peru   9-087
(vii) Venezuela   9-088
E. REST OF THE WORLD   9-090
(i) Russian Federation   9-090
(ii) South Africa   9-091
(iii) Israel   9-092
(iv) Turkey   9-094
2. Data protection   9-095
The Directive's objects and scope   9-096
The data subject's rights and remedies   9-099
3. Regulation of encryption technologies as dual-use goods   9-100
Military roots of cryptography   9-101
Cybercrime/terrorism   9-102
Export of controls on dual-use goods   9-107
(a) At international level   9-107
(b) European Union   9-108

(c) National Legislation   9-110
(i) Australia   9-110
(ii) United Kingdom   9-111
(iii) United States   9-113

10. Standards
Overview   10-001
Assessing the security of information technology products and systems   10-005
Basic standards relating to public key infrastructure   10-007
Standards for specific technologies   10-009
Standards for the provision of certification services   10-012
Standards relating to information security   10-015
Standards for preservation of evidence   10-018

Appendices   227
Index   531

Table of Cases

A & G Construction Co. v Reid Bros Logging Co. 547 P 2d 1207 (Alaska 1976) 2-027
Actionstrength Ltd v International Glass Engineering SpA; sub nom. Actionstrength Ltd
   v International Glass Engineering IN.GL.EN SpA; Actionstrength Ltd v International
   Glass Ltd [2001] EWCA Civ 1477; [2002] 1 W.L.R. 566, CA........................2-011
Baker v Dening (1838) 8 a. & e. 94 2-022
Barclays Bank Plc v O'Brien [1994] 1 A.C. 180; [1993] 3 W.L.R. 786, HL.............2-030
Barton (Alexander) v Armstrong (Alexander Ewan) [1976] A.C. 104; [1975] 2 W.L.R. 1050,
   PC (Aus)...2-030
Bazak International Crop. v Mast Industries Inc 73 N.Y. 2d 113, 535 N.E. 2d 633
   (1989) 2-013
Beatty v First Explor. Fund 1987 & Co. (1988) 25 B.C.L.R. (2d) 377...................2-026
Bennett v Brumfitt (1867-68) L.R. 3 C.P. 28, CCP............................2-018, 5-010
Boulton v Jones (1857) 2 H. & N. 564 2-030
Brydges (Town Clerk of Cheltenham) v Dix (1891) 7 T.R.L. 397.....................2-022
Casey v Irish International Bank[1979] I.R. 364, Sup Ct (Irl)..........................2-026
Central Motors (Birmingham) Ltd v PA Wadsworth & Anr (1982) 133 N.L.I. 555 ...2-002
Clipper Maritime Ltd v Shirlstar Container Transport Ltd (The Anemone) [1987] 1 Lloyd's
   Rep. 546, QBD...2-023
Cloud Corporation v Hasbro Inc., 314 F. 3d ,289, 295 (7th Cir. 2002)..........6-107, 6-121
Cundy v Lindsay; sub nom. Lindsay v Cundy (1877-78) L.R. 3 App. Cas. 459; [1874-80] All
   E.R. Rep. 1149; (1878) 42 J.P. 483, HL...2-030
D v B (Surname: Birth Registration); sub nom. D v B (Otherwise D) (Surname: Birth
   Registration) [1979] Fam. 38; [1978] 3 W.L.R. 573; [1979], CA 2-034
Durrell v Evans (1862) 158 E.R. 848 2-019
Earl of Aylesford v Morris (1872-73) L.R. 8 Ch. App. 484, CA in Chancery 2-031
Ellis Canning Co v Bernstein (384 F Supp 1212 D Colo 1972)........................2-027
Ford & Anor v La Forrest v Ors [2001] Q.S.C. 261, 23 July 2001 6-071
Gallie v Lee *see* Saunders v Anglia Building Society 2-030
Goodman v J Eban Ltd [1954] 1 Q.B. 550; [1954] 2 W.L.R. 581, CA.2-019, 2-020, 2-022, 2-023,
   2-024, 6-013
Howley v Whipple 48 N.H. 487 (1869)..2-013
Inland Revenue Commissioners v Conbee; sub nom. Debtor (No.2021 of 1995), Re; Debtor
   (No.2022 of 1995), Re [1996] 2 All E.R. 345; [1996] B.C.C. 189, Ch D 2-023, 2-014

Jenkins v Gaisford and Thring (1863) 3 Sw. & Tr. 93...........................2-017, 2-024
Johnson v Dodgson (1837) 150 E.R. 918...2-019
Joseph Denunzio Fruit Co. v Crane 79 F. Supp. 117, 128 (S.D>Cal. 1948) 2-013, 2-027
Kelly v Ross & Ross unreported, April 29, 1980, High Court 2-027
L'Estrange v F Graucob Ltd [1934] 2 K.B. 394, KBD 2-030
Lewis v Averay (No.1) [1972] 1 Q.B. 198; [1971] 3 W.L.R. 603, CA...................2-030
McMillan Ltd v Warrior Drilling & Engineering Co.512 So.2d 14 (Ala. 1986)........2-013
McQuaid v Lynam and Lynam [1965] I.R. 564...2-026
Medical Self-Care Inc. v National Broadcasting Company Inc. 2003 U.S. Dist LEXIS 4666
    17 S.D.N.Y. Mar 31 2003...6-121
Merritt v Clason 12 Johns 102 (N.Y. 1815) 2-027
Newborne v Sensolid (Great Britain) Ltd [1954] 1 Q.B. 45; [1953] 2 W.L.R. 596, CA.2-022
Ore & Chemical Corp. v Howard Butcher Trading Corp. 455 F. Supp. 1150 (E.D.Pa.
    1978) 2-013
Phillips v Brooks Ltd [1919] 2 K.B. 243, KBD..2-030
Prairie State Grain & Elevator Co. v Wrede 217 I11. App.407 (1920).................2-027
R. v Cowper (Fitzroy) (1890) L.R. 24 Q.B.D. 533, CA 2-022
R. v More (Kevin Vincent) [1987] 1 W.L.R. 1578; [1987] 3 All E.R. 825, HL...........2-035
Saunders (Executrix of the Estate of Rose Maud Gallie) v Anglia Building Society
    (formerly Northampton Town and County Building Society) (Costs); sub nom. Gallie v
    Lee [1971] A.C. 1039; [1971] 2 W.L.R. 349, HL.....................................2-031
Shattuck v Klotzbach 2001 Mass.Super. LEXIS 642 (Super. Ct. Dec. 11 2001) .6-107, 6-122
Standard Bank London Ltd v Bank of Tokyo Ltd; Sudwestdeutsche Landesbank
    Girozentrale v Bank of Tokyo Ltd [1995] 2 Lloyd's Rep. 169; [1998] Masons C.L.R. Rep.
    126, QBD 2-029
Standard Bank London Ltd v Bank of Tokyo Ltd; Sudwestdeutsche Landesbank
    Girozentrale v Bank of Tokyo Ltd [1995] 2 Lloyd's Rep. 169; [1998] Masons C.L.R. Rep.
    126, QBD 5-009, 5-010
Thoroughgood's Case (1584) 2 Co. Rep. 9a 2-030
Walker, Re (1862) 2 Sw . & Tr. 354...2-018
Warming's Used Cars Ltd v Tucker [1956] S.A.S.R. 249...............................2-031

Table of Statutes

1677 Statute of Frauds (c.3)........2-007,
2-008, 2-010, 2-012, 2-013, 2-014,
2-015, 2-022, 5-005
    s.4 ....2-010, 2-018
    s.17 ....2-010, 2-011, 2-012
1837 Wills Act (c.26)..2-016. 2-017, 2-022
    s.9.........................2-018
    s.9(a).......................2-016
    s.9(c) 2-016
1843 Solicitors Act 2-2020
1875 Public Health Act (c.55) 2-022
1932 Solicitors Act 2-020
    s.65 2-019
1939 Import, Export and Customs
Powers (Defence) Act (c.69).....
9-111
1974 Consumer Credit Act (c.39) ..6-063
1977 Unfair Contract Terms Act
    (c.50) 7-012
    Sch.2......................7-012
1981 Forgery and Conterfeiting Act
    (c.45) 2-035
1982 Administration of Justice
    Act(c.53) 2-016
    s.17 2-016
1983 Mental Health Act (c.20)......2-016
1985 Companies Act (c.6)
    s.6.........................2-005
    s.36A(4) 2-037

1995 Civil Evidence Act (c.38) 8-006
1999 Contracts(Rights of Third Parties)
    Act (c.31) ....
    Clause.24...................7-014
    Clause.12.3 7-014
2000 Electronic Communications Act
    (c.7) 6-062, 9-104
    s.7(2).......................6-062
    s.15(2)(a)...................6-062
    s.15(2)(b) 6-062
    s.16(4) 9-052
2000 Regulation of Investigatory
Powers Act (c.23) 9-104
    Pt 111 9-104
    s.40(20 9-105
    s.49 9-105
    s.49(2)(b)(ii) 9-105
    s.49(3) 9-105
    s.49(9) 9-106
    s.50(9) 9-105
    s.51(2) 9-105
    s.53 9-106
    s.54 9-106
    s.55 9-106
    s.56(1) 9-106
    Sch.2(1)....................9-105
    Sch.2(2)-(5) 9-105
2002 Export Control Act (c.28) 9-111

Table of Statutory Instruments

1986	Insolvency Rules (SI 1986/1925)... 2-025	2002	Electronic Signatures Regulations (SI 2002/318) 6-062
	r.8.2(3) 2-024	2000	Council Regulation 1334/2000..... 5-061, 9-108
1994	Unfair Terms in Consumer Contracts Regulations (SI 1994/3159) 7-012	2000	Council Regulation 2889/2000..... 9-108
1994	Council Regulation 3381/94..9-108	2001	Council Regulation 458/2001 9-108
2000	Dual-Use Items (Export Control) Regulations (SI 2000/2620)...... 9-111		

Table of Directives

		Conditional Access Directive..9-109
		art.1...9-109
		art.2...9-109
	Dir.297/7	Distance Selling Directive..6-039
1993	Dir.93/13	Unfair Terms in Consumer Contracts Directive...........5-063, 7-012
1995	Dir.95/46	Data Protection Directive................................5-060, 9-095

Conditional Access Directive...9-109
    art.1...9-109
    art.2...9-109
Dir.297/7 Distance Selling Directive...6-039
1993 Dir.93/13 Unfair Terms in Consumer Contracts Directive...........5-063, 7-012
1995 Dir.95/46 Data Protection Directive..................................5-060, 9-095
    art.1...9-095
    art.1(1)...9-097
    art.2...9-096
    art.3...9-097
    art.6...9-097, 9-099
    art.7...9-097
    art.8...9-097
    art.10..9-098
    art.11..9-098
    art.12..9-099
    art.14..9-099
    art.22..9-098
    art.23..9-098
    art.24..9-098
1999 Dir.99/93 Electronic Signatures Directive.......1-009, 1-014, 1-016, 2-040, 3-001, 3-002, 3-003, 3-004, 3-009, 3-010, 3-013, 3-033, 4-011, 5-001, 5-032, 5-033, 5-035, 6-003, 6-004, 6-006, 6-007, 6-009, 6-010, 6-012, 6-014, 6-015, 6-017, 6-019, 6-020, 6-022, 6-024, 6-025, 6-026, 6-028, 6-029, 6-030, 6-032, 6-035, 6-037, 6-039, 6-041, 6-043, 6-045, 6-046, 6-047, 6-048, 6-049, 6-062, 6-063, 6-075, 6-084, 6-091, 6-147, 6-151, 7-005, 7-015, 9-001, 9-004, 9-008, 9-010, 9-013, 9-015, 9-017, 9-019, 9-023, 9-024, 9-027, 9-031, 9-032, 9-035, 9-041, 9-042, 9-046, 9-049, 9-099, 10-001, 10-002, 10-003, 10-004, 10-013, 10-017
    Annex 1.....5-048, 6-012, 6-036, 6-044, 6-051, 6-055, 6-056, 6-057, 6-058, 6-060, 9-051
    Annex 11....5-050, 6-011, 9-004, 9-007, 9-019, 9-020, 9-026, 9-028, 9-031, 9-036, 9-041, 9-046, 9-048, 9-049, 9-051
    Annex 111...5-056, 5-058, 5-061, 5-064, 5-067, 6-025, 6-026, 6-028, 6-046, 9-033, 10-002

Annex 1V 5-061, 5-064, 5-065, 6-007, 6-023, 6-046, 6-056
art.1 5-040
art.2...5-041, 5-060
art.2(1) 3-002
art.2(2) 3-002, 5-043
art.3 ....5-059, 5-061
art.3(1)..5-052, 5-059, 6-062
art.3(2) 5-059, 6-062
art.3(3) 5-059
art.3(4) 5-060
art.3(5) 5-053, 5-058, 5-061, 10-002
art.3(6) 5-061
art.4 5-059
art.4(1) 5-059
art.4(2) 5-060
art.5 ....5-038, 5-041, 6-009, 6-022, 6-037, 6-040, 6-056
art.5(1) 5-039, 5-046, 6-00, 6-026, 6-028
art.5(2) 5-039, 5-053, 6-026, 6-039
art.6 ....5-039, 5-062, 5-063, 9-042, 9-051
art.6(1)(a)-(c)..5-062
art.6(2) 5-062, 9-022
art.6(3) 5-062, 5-063
art.6(4) 5-063
art.7 5-064
art.7(1) 5-064
art.7(3) 5-064
art.8..5-509, 9-098
art.8(2) 5-0060
arts 9-15...5-038
2000   Dir.00/31   Information Society Services Directive
2001   Dir.01/115   Use of Electronic Invoices Directive...........................1-014
art 2 1-014

Table of Foreign Legislation

Argentina

1998 Presidential Decree No.427...9-079
    art.1 6-138
    art.2 6-138
    art.5 6-138
    art.7 6-139
    art.8 6-139
    art.9 ....6-138, 9-079
    art.10 6-139
    art.11 6-139
    art.14 6-149
    art.14(a) 9-079
    art.16 6-139
    art.19 9-080
    art.23 6-138
    art.24 6-139
    art.30 9-079
    art.39 9-080

Australia

1997 Telecommunications Act......6-066
1999 Electronic Transactions Act ..6-064,
    6-066, 6-067, 6-069, 6-070, 9-053
    s.4 ....6-670, 6-092
    s.8(1) 6-067, 6-670
    s.9(1) 6-068
    s.10 6-068
    s.10(1) 6-068
    s.11(1) 6-068
    s.11(15)......................6-068
    s.12(1) 6-068
    s.12(2) 6-068
    s.12(4) 6-068

    s.14 6-068
    s.15 6-068
2001 Customs Legislation Amendment
    and Repeal (International Trade
    Modernisation) Act 4-029
2000 Electronic Transactions
    Amendments
    Regulations(No.1) 2000
    No.101 6-067
2000 Electronic Transactions (Victoria)
    Regulations 2000(Vic)......6-069
2001 Electronic Transactions
    Regulations 2001 (NSW)...6-069
2001 Electronic Transactions (Northern
    Territory) Regulations 2001
    (NT)........................6-069
2001 Electronic Transactions
    Regulations 2001 (Tas).....6-069
2001 Electronic Transactions
    Amendments Regulations
    (No.1) 2001 No.84..........6-067
2001 Electronic Transactions
    Amendments Regulations 2001
    (No. 2) 2001 No.137........6-067
2001 Electronic
    TransactionsAmendments
    Regulations 2001 (No.3) 2001
    No.263 6-067
2002 Electronic Transactions
    Amendment (Poisons and
    Therapeutic Goods)
    Regulations 2002 (NSW)...6-069
2002 Electronic Transactions
    Regulations 2002(SA) 6-069

Austria

Austrian Civil Code 6-008
2000 Law on Electronic Signatures ......
                          6-007, 9-005
    s.3 9-005
    s.3, para.6...................9-005
    s.4(1) 6-007
    s.4(3) 6-008
    s.21..........................6-008
    s.26..........................6-008
2000 Electronic Signature Order...6-007,
    9-005, 9-006

Belgium

2000 Electronics Documents Act...6-009
    art.4(3) 6-009
    art.4(4) 6-009
    art.4(5) 6-009
2001 Certification Service Providers
    Act 9-007
    art.4(2) 9-007
    art.8(3) 9-008

Brazil

2001 Provisional Measure No.2.200 .....
                          6-140, 9-081
    art.5 9-081

Bulgaria

2001 Law on Electronic Document and
    Electronic Signature.......6-010,
    9-009
    Pt.1V 9-010
    art.4 6-011
    art.13........................6-011
    art.15........................6-010
    art.17(2) 6-011
    art.21 9-009
    art.24........................6-012
    art.26........................9-010
    art.29(2) 9-010
    arts 30-31 6-012

Canada

Canadian Evidence Act 6-096, 8-005
    s.31.1 6-097

1999 Uniform Electronic Commerce
    Act...........6-097, 6-098, 9-072
2000 Personal Information and
    Electronic Documents Act.......
                          6-096, 8-015
    s.36..........................6-096
    ss 44-46 6-096
    Sch.2 6-096
    Sch.3 6-096

Chile

2002 Law on Electronic Documents,
    Electronic Signatures and
    Certification Services......6-141,
    9-082
    art.2 6-141
    art.4 6-141
    art.5(2) 6-142
    art.8 6-141
    art.11 9-082
    art.12(c) 9-083
    art.12(e) 9-083
    art.14.................9-082, 9-083
    art.15........................6-142
    art.16........................6-142
    art.17........................9-082
    art.23........................9-082
    art.24........................9-082

China

1999 Contract Act of the People's
    Republic of China..........6-072
    art.11 6-072
2001 Digital Certificate Rules......6-073,
    9-055

Columbia

1999 Electronic Commerce Law No.
    527.................6-0143, 9-084
    art.1 6-143
    art.7 6-143
    art.11 6-144
    art.12(c) 9-084
    art.28........................6-143
    art.29 9-084
    art.35........................6-144
    art.37.............6-144, 9-085

art.43......................9-084
2000 Decree Law No.1747...9-084, 9-085

Czech Republic

2000 Law on Electronic Signatures......
    6-014
    art.5(2) 6-014
    art.6.........................9-012
    art.7.........................9-014
    art.9.........................9-012
    art.10........................9-013
    art.10(5)....................9-013
    art.10(6)....................9-013
    art.11................6-014, 9-013
    art.13(2)....................9-013
    art.16........................014
    art.16(2)....................9-014
    art.18(1)....................9-013
    art.18(2)....................9-013

Denmark

2000 Electronic Signature Law no.417.6-
    015, 9-015
    art.3(1) 6-016
    art.5........................9-015
    art.5(8)(4) 9-015
    art.10.......................9-015
    art.13.......................6-6016
    art.15(2)....................6-017
    art.16.......................9-015
    art.17(2)....................9-015

Ecuador

Consumer Protection Act ...6-147, 9-086
2002 Law on Electronic Commerce,
    Electronic Signatures and Data
    Messages No.67.....6-145, 9-086
    art.13.......................6-145
    art.16.......................6-145
    art.19.......................6-146
    art.24.......................6-146
    art.25.......................6-146
    art.26.......................6-146
    art.28.................6-147, 9-086
    art.30(h)....................9-086
    art.31.......................9-086
    art.32.......................9-086

art.34......................9-086
art.39(c) 9-086
art.42................6-147, 9-086
art.51......................6-145
art.53......................6-145

Estonia

Estonian Digital Signatures Act...6-6017
    s.2(1) 6-017
    s.2(2) 6-017
    s.2(3) 6-017
    s.3(1) 6-017. 6-018
    s.3(3) 6-018
    S.3(4) 6-018
    s.5(1) 6-019
    s.5(2) 6-019
    s.12........................9-017
    s.14........................9-017
    s.18........................9-017
    s.19(2).....................9-016
    s.20........................9-016
    s.21........................9-018
    s.22........................9-016
    s.30(2).....................9-018
2002 Identity Documents Act 2-039

Finland

2000 Electronic Service in the
    Administration.............6-020
2003 Finnish Electronic Signatures
    Act..................6-020, 9-019
    s.2(1)6-020
    s.5 6-020
    s.13........................9-019
    s.14........................9-019
    s.15........................9-019
    s.17........................6-020
    s.18........................6-020
    s.24........................9-009

France

Civil Code.........................6-022
    art.1316-4 6-022
1245 Statute of Frauds.............2-008
2000 Law no. 2000-230 6-022

Germany

German Civil Code
s.126......................6-024
1997 German Law for Electronic
Signatures 6-024
2001 Law Governing Framework
Conditions for Electronic
Signatures ...6-024, 6-025, 9-021,
9-022
s.2(8) 7-021
s.4(2) 9-021
s.4(3) 9-021
s.8 9-022
s.11(1) 9-022
s.11(2) 9-022
s.11(3) 9-022
s.12..........................9-021
s.13..........................9-022
s.13(2) 9-022
s.15..........................9-021
s.16..........................9-021
s.20..........................9-043
2001 Signatures Ordinance 6-024,
9-021, 9-022
s.4 9-022
s.8(3) 9-022
14(2)..........................6-025

Greece

2001 Presidential Decree 150/2001 ......
6-026, 9-023
art.3(1) 6-026
art.3(2) 6-026
art.4(2) 9-023
art.4(8) 6-026, 9-023

Guernsey

2000 Electronic Transactions (Guernsey)
Law 6-027
s.4 6-027
s.8(1) 6-027
S.22..........................6-027

Hong Kong

2000 Electronic Transactions
Ordinance 6-074, 9-055

s.2 6-074
s.6(1) 6-075
s.9 6-075
s.11 6-074
s.14 6-075
s.15 6-075
s.20(5) 9-057
s.22.........................9-056
s.26.........................9-057
s.34.........................9-057
s.42.........................9-057
s.46.........................9-057
s.48.........................9-056
Sch.1 6-074

Hungary

2001 Hungarian Electronic Signatures
Act 6-028
Annex 1.....................6-028
Annex 3.....................9-024
art.2(f).......................6-029
art.3(1) 6-029
art.4(2) 6-029
art.7(1) 9-024
art.8(1) 9-024
art.8(3) 9-024
art.12.......................9-025
art.14.......................9-025
art.20.......................9-024
art.21.......................9-024
art.26(2) 6-029

India

1872 Indian Evidence Act
s.85A.......................6-077
s.85B 6-077
2000 Information Technology Act ....
6-076, 9-058
s.1(4) 6-076
s.2 9-058
s.5 6-076
s.18 9-058
s.21 9-058
s.29 9-058
s.32.........................9-058
s.37 9-058
s.39 9-058
ss 73-4......................9-058

Ireland

2000 Irish Electronic Commerce
    Act 6-030, 9-026
    s.9 6-030
    s.10(1) 6-030
    s.13(2)(b) 6-030
    s.14(1) 6-031
    s.16(1) 6-031
    s.22 6-031
    s.30 9-026
    s.35 6-031

Israel

2001 Electronic Signature Law 6-155

Italy

Italian Civil Code
1228 Statute of Frauds(Verona) 2-008
1394 Statute of Frauds(Venice) 2-008
2000 Decree Law455/2000
    art.27 9-027
    art.28 9-027
2002 Decree Law10/02 9-027

Japan

2001 Japanese Law Concerning
    Electronic Signatures and
    Certification Services 6-079
    art.2(1) .9-060
    art.2(2) .9-060
    art.3 6-079
    art.4 9-060
    art.5 9-060
    art.10 9-060
    art.13 9-060
    art.17-32 9-060
    art.23 9-060

Latvia

2002 Law on Electronic Documents . . . . .
    6-035, 9-028
    art.1(4) .6-035
    art.3(2) .6-035
    art.3(4) .6-035
    art.3(6) .6-035

art.9 9-028
art.9(4) 9-028
art.10 9-028
art.13 9-028
art.14 9-028
art.16 6-035
art.17(2) .9-028
art.18 9-029
art.20-21 .9-028
art.22 9-029
art.23(12) 9-029
art.25(1) .6-037
art.55(1) .6-036
art.55(2) .6-036

Lithuania

2000 Law on Electronic Signatures . . . . . .
    6-037, 9-030
    art.1(2) .6-037
    art.2(4) .6-037
    art.4(4) .9-030
    art.4(6) .9-030
    art.6 6-038
    art.6(1) .6-037
    art.6(3) .6-038
    art.7 6-038
    art.8 6-037
    art.10 9-030
    art.12 9-030
    art.13 9-030
    art.23 9-028
    art.24 9-029

Luxembourg

Civil Code 6-039
    art.1322 .6-039
    art.1322-2 6-039
    art.1334 .6-039
2000 Law on Electronic Commerce . . . . . .
    6-039, 9-031
    art.6 6-039
    art.7 6-039
    art.13 6-042
    art.18 . . . . .6-039, 6-040
    art.21 6-040
    art.26 9-032
    art.27 9-031
    art.29 9-031

art.32........................9-032
art.32(2)c...................9-032
2001 Grand-Ducal Regulation
3(1).........................9-032
2001 Grand-Ducal Regulation
3(9).........................9-032

Malaysia

1997 Digital Signature Act ..6-080, 9-061
s.4 9-061
s.4(3) 9-061
s.6(2) 9-062
s.6(3) 9-062
s.13........................9-062
s.16........................9-061
s.19........................9-062
s.27........................9-062
ss 34-37 9-062
s.41........................6-080
s.42........................6-080
s.45........................9-062
s.46........................9-062
s.59(2).....................9-062
s.62........................6-080
s.67.................6-080, 9-061
s.76........................9-061
s.79........................9-061

Malta

2002 Maltese Electronic Commerce
Act 6-041
Pt V 9-033
art.4 6-041
art.6 6-042
art.16......................9-033
art.23......................6-043
art.25(1)...................6-041
Sch.3 9-033

Mexico

2002 Commercial Code............6-099
art.80......................6-099
art.89......................6-099
art.90......................6-099
art. 93 6-099
art.94......................6-099

Netherlands

Civil Code..........................6-043
art.15a(1)...................6-043
art.15a(2)...................6-043
art.15a(3)...................6-043
art.15a(6)...................6-044
2003 Dutch Electronic Signatures
Act 6-043
2003 Electronic Signatures Decree
200 9-034
s.2(s) 9-034
s.2(1) 9-035
s.2(q) 9-035

New Zealand

2002 Electronic Transactions Act...6-081
s.5 6-081
s.22........................6-081
ss 22-24 6-081
s.23........................6-082
s.24........................6-083
Sch.1 Pt 3 6-081

Pakistan

2002 Electronic Transactions
Ordinance 6-084
s.2(d) 6-084
s.2(h) 6-085
s.7 6-084
s.9 6-084
s.10........................6-085
s.31........................6-084
s.34........................6-085

Peru

2000 Peruvian Law of Signatures and
Digital Certificates No.27269....
9-087
art.1 6-148
art.2 6-148
art.4 6-148
art.5 6-148
art.6 6-148
art.8 9-087
art.10......................9-087
art.15......................9-087
art.16......................9-087

Philippines

2000 Electronic Commerce Act 6-086, 9-065
    s.4 6-086
    s.5(e) 6-086
    s.8 6-087
    s.9 6-088
    s.11 6-088

Poland

2002 Electronics Signatures Act ...6-045, 9-036, 9-037
    art.3(1) 6-045
    art.4(3) 6-045
    art.5(1) 6-046
    art.5(3) 6-046
    art.5(4) 6-045
    art.5(5) 6-045
    art.5(6) 6-045
    art.6(3) 6-045
    art.7 6-046
    art.8 6-046
    art.9(2) 9-036
    art.10(1) 9-036
    art.10(3) 9-036
    art.10(5) 9-037
    art.11 9-037
    art.13(1) 9-038
    art.14(1) 9-037
    art.21(1) 9-038
    art.21(4)-(7) 9-038
    art.32(2) 9-036
    art.38 9-036
    art.45 9-037
    art.47 6-045

Portugal

1999 Decree Law290-D/99 9-039
    art.5(1) 6-049
    art.9 9-039
    art.12 9-039
    art.13 9-039
    art.15(2) 9-039
    art.17 9-039
    art.27 9-030
    art.28 9-040
    art.30 9-030

    art.31 6-050
    art.33 9-040

Romania

2001 Law No.455 on Electronic Signatures 9-041
    art.3 6-051
    art.4(1) 6-051
    art.4(8) 6-052
    art.5 6-052
    art.6 6-052
    art.7 6-052
    art.9 6-052
    art.10 6-052
    art.13 9-041
    art.15(1) 9-041
    art.19(2) 9-041
    art.20 9-041
    art.21 9-041
    art.23(1) 9-041
    art.23(2) 9-041
    art.24(3) 9-041
    art.31(3) 9-042
    art.36 9-042
    art.41 9-042
    art.43 6-052
    art.44 9-042
    art.45 9-042

Russian Federation

2001 Federal Law on Electronic Digital Signature Law..............9-090
    Clause.4(1) 6-151
    Clause.6(1) 6-151
    Clause.7(2) 9-090
    Clause.8(2) 9-090
    Clause.9(2) 6-15
    Clause.9(3).................9-090
    Clause.10(1) 9-0901
    Clause.12 6-152
    Clause.13 9-090
    Clause.14 9-090
    Clause.16 6-151
    Clause.17 6-151
    Clause.18 6-152

Singapore

1998 Electronic Transactions Act ..6-089, 9-066

s.2 6-089
s.4 6-089
s.8(1) 6-089
s.8(2) 6-089
s.17 6-089
s.18(2) 6-089
s.20 6-090
s.22 6-090
ss 27-29 9-066
s.29(2)d 9-067
s.30 9-066
s.31 9-067
s.32 9-067
s.34-5 9-067
s.42 6-090
ss 42-3 9-066
s.44 9-067
s.45 9-067
s.47 6-089
s.53 9-067

Slovakia

2002 Slovakian Electronic Signature
       Act..................6-053, 9-043
       Pt.11.......................6-053
       s.1(3) 6-053
       s.4(1) 6-053
       s.4(2) 6-053
       s.10 9-043
       s.11 9-043
       s.13 9-043
       s.15 9-044
       s.17 6-054
       s.18(1) 9-044
       s.19(2)-(4) 9-044
       s.22 6-054
       s.26 6-054
       s.27 9-043

Slovenia

2000 Electronic Commerce and
       Electronic Signature Act ..6-055,
       9-045
       art.1(2) 6-055
       art.14......................6-056
       art.15......................6-056
       art.16......................6-056
       art.17......................6-057

art.18.......................9-045
art.19.......................9-045
art.20.......................9-045
art.22.......................6-057
art.23.......................6-057
art.24.......................9-045
art.26.......................9-045
art.31.......................9-046
art.35(1)....................9-045
art.38.......................6-056
art.39.......................9-046
art.41.......................9-045
art.46(1)....................9-046
art.47.......................9-046
art.48.......................6-057
art.49.......................6-057
art.52.......................6-056

South Africa

2002 Electronic Communications and
       Transactions Act No.25....6-153,
       9-091
       s.1 6-153
       s.13(1) 6-154
       s.13(2) 6-154
       s.13(3) 6-154
       s.13(4) 6-154
       s.13(5) 6-154
       s.15 6-154
       s.16 6-154
       s.19(3) 6-154
       s.24 6-154
       s.28 6-153
       s.29 9-091
       s.35 9-091
       s.38..................6-153, 9-091
       s.38(4) 9-091
       s.40 9-091
       s.81 9-091
       s.82 9-091

South Korea

1999 Digital Signature Act ..6-090, 9-068
       art.3 6-091
       art.4 9-068
       art.8 9-068
       art.14......................9-068
       art.15(1)...................9-068

art.17 9-069
art.18 9-069
art.21 9-069
art.26 9-069
art.24 . . . . .6-091, 9-069
art.31 6-091

Spain

1999 Decree Law on Electronic
      Signatures 6-058, 9-047
      art.3 6-058
      art.5.2 6-058
      art.7(4) .6-059
      art.7(5) .6-059
      art.7(6) .6-059
      art.9 9-047
      art.13 6-058
      art.15 6-059
      art.16 6-059
      art.19 9-048
      art.20(2) 9-048
      art.22 9-048
      art.23 9-048
2003 Decree Law 4-009

Sweden

2000 Qualified Electronics Signatures
      Act 6-060, 9-049
      s.2 6-060
      s.17 6-060
      s.7 6-060

Switzerland

Civil Code
      art.14(2) 6-062
      art.59a .9-050
Federal Law on Electronic Signature . .9-
050
      art.3(1) .9-050
      art.3(2) .9-050
      arts 16-18 9-050

Thailand

2001 Electronic Transactions Act . .6-093,
              6-094, 6-095, 9-070
      s.4 6-093
      s.9 6-094

United States of America

Georgia Electronic Records and
      Signatures Act 6-101
Washington Electronic Authentication
Act 6-101
Uniform Commercial Code 1-003,
              2-012, 6-118
      s.2-201 . . . . .1-003, 2-012
      s.2A-201 2-012
      art.2 . . . . .2- 2-012
      art 2A 2-012
      art 3 2-012
      art.4 2-2012
1933 Securities Act 6-119
1979 Export Administration Act . . .9-113
1995 Utah Digital Signature Act . . .1-008,
      6-101, 6-135, 9-061, 9-074, 9-075,
      9-076, 9-097, 9-078
1995 California Government Code
      s.16.5 1-009
1997 Massachusetts Electronic Records
      and Signatures Act 1-008
1998 Identity Theft Act 2-043
1999 Uniform Electronic Transactions
      Act 6-101, 6-102, 6-103, 6-104,
      6-105, 6-106, 6-118, 6-121, 122,
      123, 6-124, 6-126, 6-130, 6-131,
      6-132, 6-133, 6-134, 6-135
      s.1-206 .6-105
      s.1-207 .6-105
      s.2(2) 6-109
      s.2(7) 6-106, 6-121
      s.2(8) 6-106
      s.2(10) .6-106
      s.2(13) .6-106
      s.2(16) 6-104, 6-109, 6-118
      s.3 6-105
      s.3(b)(4) 6-132, 6-132, 6-133,
              6-143
      s.3(4) 6-105
      s.5(b) 6-108
      s.5(d) 6-108
      s.5(e) 6-108
      s.7 6-104
      s.7(a) 6-014
      s.7(b) 6-014
      s.7(c)-(d) 6-104
      s.8 6-104

s.8(a) 6-104
s.8(b)................6-104, 6-130
s.8(b)(2) 6-130
s.8(d) 6-104
s.9(b) 6-107
s.10 6-110
s.10(1) 6-110
s.10(2) 6-110
s.10(3) 6-110
s.13 6-104
s.14. 6-109
s.17 6-111
s.18 6-111
s.19 6-111

2000 Federal Electronic Signatures in
      Global and National
      Commerce...6-102, 6-103, 6-112,
       6-113, 6-114, 6-115, 6-117, 6-118,
       6-119, 6-122, 6-123, 6-124, 6-125,
       6-126, 6-127, 6-128, 6-129, 6-130,
       6-135, 6-137, 6-131, 6-132, 6-133,
             6-134, 6-135, 6-136, 6-137
      Title 1..6-113, 6-114, 6-132, 6-133
      Title 11 ....6-131,6-132, 6-133
      s.101 ..6-116, 6-118, 6-129, 6-130,
                         6-131, 6-132
      s.101(a)(1) 6-114
      s.101(c)..............6-119, 6-124
      s.101(c)(1)(B)................6-128
      s.101(c)(1)(B)(9i)(11) 6-129
      S.101(c)(1)(C) 6-126
      s.101(c)(1)(C)(i) 6-125
      s.101(c)(1)(C)(ii) 6-126
      s.101(c)(1)(D) 6-125, 6-127
      s.101(c)(1)(D)(i) 6-125
      s.101(c)(3) 6-126

s.101(c)(4) 6-127, 6-128
s.101(c)(6) 6-121
s.101(d) 6-120
s.101(d)(1)...................6-120
s.101(i) 6-117
s.102.........................6-134
s.102(a)(1)...................6-133
S.102(a)(2) 6-131, 6-134
s.102(a)(2)(A)(ii) 6-130
s.102(c)......................6-130
s.103(a)....................6-0118
s.104.........................6-129
s.104(b)..............6-114, 6-118
s.104(b)(1)..................6-109
s.104(d)......................6-119

2003 Uniform Computer Information
      Transactions Act............6-105

Venezuela

2001 Data Message and Electronic
      Signatures Law.............9-088
      art.2 6-149
      art.3 6-149
      art.6 6-149
      art.16(1)-(3) 6-149
      art.17........................6-149
      art.18........................6-150
      art.19........................6-150
      art.21........................9-088
      art.22(5) 9-088
      art.22(13)....................9-088
      art.31........................9-089
      art.35(4) 9-089
      art.37........................9-089
      art.42........................9-098
      art.43........................6-150

1

Introduction

Few areas of the law can have seen as much legislative activity world-wide in recent years **1–001** as electronic commerce in general, and the status of electronic signatures in particular. Although electronic commerce, in the form of Electronic Data Interchange (EDI), has been in use since the mid-1980s, the arrival of the Internet in the early 1990s transformed the field. EDI involved contract formation over closed systems, available only to a limited number of parties by a prior agreement, known as a Trading Partner Agreement. The mechanisms for contract formation were agreed beforehand by negotiation in the traditional way, and the electronic implementation of such a mechanism was a relatively straightforward task, subject only to the usual technical hitches arising from the use of new technologies. New legislation was unnecessary for dealing with transactions of this nature.

The Internet is an entirely different proposition. It evolved from a project of the United States military into a public global network linking both government bodies and academia in the late 1980s. After the invention of the World Wide Web in the early 1990s, the Internet left the confines of academia and the public sector and rapidly emerged as a major new locus for commercial activities of all forms, with no limitations as to who could participate beyond the requirement to be able to access a computer with a modem attached. Suddenly, communications ceased to be between parties with an existing relationship: Usenet usegroups, bulletin boards of all kinds and more recently chat rooms became methods of meeting people, for the first time. The growth of the World Wide Web provided consumers around the world with access to information, goods and services from suppliers both local and familiar and remote and unknown. As a truly global, open system the Internet changed the way transactions could be done.

Businesses rapidly began to realise the potential efficiencies and opportunities arising **1–002** from dealing with both customers and suppliers online. By 2000, some 57 per cent of medium-sized companies in the US were using the Internet for a proportion of their sales and the majority of these were also recruiting employees, procuring supplies and carrying out market research this way.[1] Since then, the number of transactions completed online has grown continuously despite the over-optimism of early expectations and the subsequent "dot.com" crash.

The issues of e-commerce as conceived in relation to "traditional" electronic communications between computers apply equally to the next generation "m-commerce", where many of the applications already in use will be transferred onto mobile devices.

Although Third Generation (3G) mobile services have been considerably slower to arrive than the network operators hoped when they bid for licences to operate them, some of the potential is beginning to be realised. Ericsson introduced the first digital signatures for secure mobile e-commerce using wireless application protocol (WAP) phones as early as *Telecom 99* in October 1999. VISA, Mastercard and a group of other organisations recently launched a Mobile Payment Forum, which will address issues of card holder authentication amongst others. Remote transacting may become even more routine in the future.

Given the distance—and boundary—free nature of communications over the Internet, electronic commerce brought complex legal issues into the mainstream of contract practice for the first time. Place and time of formation of contract, governing law and jurisdiction over disputes have always been important matters in international trade law, but this was a relatively specialised field in which a substantial proportion of contracts were individually negotiated between the parties. Never before had individuals and small enterprises around the world entered into cross-border transactions with such enthusiasm and in such numbers. Accordingly, legislators, civil servants and expert groups were extremely concerned to make sure that the uncertainties which this new medium introduced into traditional transactions were not such as to retard the growth of the new markets.

1–003   The presence of a signature in formation of a contract has less significance for English lawyers than it does for practitioners in some other jurisdictions. Under the English common law system, the attributes necessary for a legally binding contract to come into existence are an offer, acceptance of that offer, the existence of an intention on the part of the parties for form a legal relationship and some form of consideration or transfer of value between the parties. A requirement for the contract to be written down, does not feature in this list; still less is there any requirement for a signature. There are of course exceptional cases: for example, consumer credit agreements have to be signed under English law and other common law countries have similar exceptions. But most transactions do not. As a result, most common law countries have never issued a comprehensive law or regulation to establish the requirements for a *manual* signature to be legally valid. It is nonetheless usual for any contract of moderate or high value to be in writing and signed since this provides some evidence after the event as to what the agreed terms were. Where a signature is essential, specific issues—where the signature should be, what form it should take—have gradually been clarified through the case law. Uncertainty as to whether the same criteria could readily be applied to the unfamiliar technologies of electronic signatures was seen as a potentially significant barrier to the expansion of e-commerce. Although it would certainly have been possible for the courts to produce equivalent guidance through future case law, this would of course have been a slow process with potentially years of commercial uncertainty in the interim.

In other countries, the opposite situation pertains. In France, for example, any contract having a value over €800 must be in writing and signed,[2] and the United States' Uniform Commercial Code requires a party attempting to enforce a contract for the sale of goods for a price of US$500 or more to prove a memorandum in writing signed by the party against whom enforcement is sought.[3] German laws include similar provisions. Thus, for any party to a contract either governed by the laws of these countries or laws derived from them, or liable to be determined in the courts of such a country in case of dispute, the ability to conclude a contract using a legally effective electronic signature is crucial. Legal opinion crytallised around the view that a purely electronic contract would not be legally equivalent to a paper-based written document, nor would an electronic signature be legally effective as a signature. This has been confirmed in a recent decision of the French Supreme Court, which rendered a decision on April 30, 2003, regarding the probative value of an electronic signature.[4] The Supreme Court held that, "since there is a doubt relating to the identity of the proceeding act's signatory, the electronic signature should not be admitted in this particular case". In these circumstances, contract formation online would be impossible.

Identity and liability

One of the fundamental issues in carrying out transactions remotely is how to establish the identity of the other parties. It is clear that transacting with unknown persons situated in distant and unfamiliar places involves an increased risk of fraud. Traditionally, relatively complex legal mechanisms such as notarisation and legalisation of documents have been used to reduce this risk. Performing the same transactions instantaneously by electronic means requires some electronic equivalent, no ideal form of which has yet emerged. **1–004**

The most prevalent solution at present is the use of public key cryptography[5] to create a specific form of electronic signature known as a digital signature. A digital signature is created by the signer using a private cryptographic key known only to him or herself, which reduces the risk of fraud. It may be "read" using a separate second key, which is made public. Digital signatures have many advantages, including the ability to prove whether or not the message signed has been tampered with since it was signed. However, this system requires some mechanism whereby a public key can be shown to be linked to a particular person, since the key by itself does not evidence anything at all about who it is who is using the corresponding private key.

Certification authorities and public key infrastructure

The most common mechanism is the intervention of a third party, which independently verifies the identity of the holder of the keys and issues an electronic certificate confirming to the rest of the world that a particular key is associated with a particular person. The network of certifying authorities and associated certificate databases or directories is known as a *public key infrastructure* (PKI). **1–005**

One issue associated with the use of digital signatures supported by certificates of identity is whether the existence of a certificate should be required to render a digital signature legally effective. Another is whether, and if so how, the suppliers of certificates should be regulated as notaries are. Regulation may be considered desirable for several reasons, including the need to control the use of the personal data certification authorities must necessarily collect and in order to demonstrate to potential users that the authorities are trustworthy.

The need for such a public key infrastructure adds substantially to the transaction costs of a digital signature compared to a handwritten or other form of paper-based signature, and in practice despite their technical advantages take-up has been limited. It also complicates the legal landscape when it comes to apportioning the risk involved in remote electronic transactions. If three parties are involved in an electronic transaction which, had it been paper-based, would have involved only two, the possibilities as to which party may be liable in what event of default becomes more challenging. The **1–006** attraction of attempting to recover any loss from the "third party" to the transaction, the certification authority, is particularly obvious when it is a large commercial enterprise with potentially deep pockets compared to the other participants. However, the certification authority's potential exposure is an issue in itself. If a signatory loses their private key or it is stolen, it is possible in theory for the finder or thief to enter into numerous transactions by signing using the key, which as a result of the third party certificate will be accepted by the recipients as coming from the true owner of the key. In these circumstances, the potential claims a certification authority might face could be out of all proportion to the cost of the service supplied. It is therefore open to debate whether a business model with such evident limitations is likely to succeed in the longer term. Indeed, it has even been argued that the enthusiasm evinced by legislators for promoting such an unwieldy model, by giving preferential liability protection to certification authorities, may derive from an ulterior motive relating to the broader regulation of encryption technologies.[6]

1–007 Public key-based identification can also be used in a more bounded context for carrying on remote transactions between parties who are already known to each other. For example, a bank could issue public key certificates to its customers, which the customers could then use to carry out transactions with the bank across the Internet. This model is also known as "closed PKI", and curtails the risk to the certification authority which potentially arose under the open model since the only party relying on signatures forged using an hypothetical stolen key is the bank itself, which can regulate its exposure through its contracts with its customers and its own internal security procedures for detecting out-of-pattern transactions. An individual would then require a different certificate for each such relationship, but the risk associated with the loss of any one would be reduced.

A wide variety of other possible technologies for creating electronic signatures has been developed in the last decade, some free-standing and some combining other technologies, such as biometrics, with public key cryptographic methods. Biometrics have the intrinsic advantage that they are directly linked to a particular individual and a fingerprint or a retina pattern can less readily be stolen than a cryptographic key may be. In particular, the use of smart cards which use a biometric recognition criterion, such as a fingerprint, to permit the holder to access the stored private key, are widely seen as a workable solution.

Historical development

1–008 As the Internet originated in the United States both as a technical and a commercial phenomenon, it is appropriate that the legal responses to it originated there too. The American Bar Association began working to develop rules to support public key infrastructure in 1992, and in 1995 produced draft Digital Signature Guidelines, setting out in detail mechanisms for the signature of contracts digitally under a public key infrastructure of the kind outlined above. In the same year the state of Utah introduced its Digital Signature Act laying down technology-specific legal rules intended to provide legal certainty in the formation of exclusively electronic contracts. Under the Utah scheme, a government agency assumes the role of "root" certification authority, which certifies the identities of commercial certification authorities. The model also included a voluntary scheme for licensing, under which licensed certification authorities obtained benefits in the form of limited liability.

These initiatives have both been extremely influential on subsequent legislators both in the United States and elsewhere. But they have also been criticised for attempting to pre-define relationships between parties that have not yet even arisen, in contrast to existing contract laws which derive from many years' experience of the actual operation of markets.[7] In the following years, numerous governments and international bodies commissioned independent reports into how best to regulate and facilitate e-commerce. The insistence of the Utah Act on the use of a particular technology and business model was criticised as excluding the possible development of later, more advantageous technologies and models, although many commentators continued to advocate in favour of the prescriptive approach on the basis of greater legal certainty compared to the technology-neutral approach. The opposite extreme, of legislating only to remove actual barriers to electronic commerce, was adopted in some states and countries.[8] The State of California introduced an intermediate model, which has been widely imitated, setting the following criteria for legal effectiveness of a digital signature. The signature must be: unique to the person using it; capable of verification; under the sole control of the person using it; and linked to the data signed in such a manner that if the data are changed the digital signature is invalidated.[9]

In December 1996, the United Nations Commission on International Trade Law (UNCITRAL) adopted a Model Law on Electronic Commerce,[10] which included provisions relating to signature. However, the Commission concluded that the question of signature in particular required further work and set up a Working Group to draft a Model Law on Electronic Signatures. This took considerably longer to finalise, with the final text[11] and Guide to Enactment being adopted only in July 2001. The UNCITRAL solution to the issue of technology is to adopt a "two tier" approach, under which all forms of electronic signature may be legally effective provided that they meet certain functional criteria, but electronic signatures essentially based upon the public key infrastructure model are guaranteed effectiveness. This approach was intended to leave the market free to develop alternatives to the public key infrastructure if the demand exists. Many of the countries which participated in the discussions took the evolving draft into account when formulating their national legislation even before the Model Law was adopted. Between 1996 and 2001 some fifty countries worldwide introduced legislation relating to electronic signatures, and the European Union issued a Directive on a common framework for electronic signatures (the Electronic Signatures Directive),[12] which is now in the course of being implemented by its Member States.[13]

1–009

The Model Laws have therefore been an unquestionable success in bringing about a common approach to some of the issues posed by electronic commerce by a number of legislatures. The Model Laws are precisely that—models to be followed or adapted by national legislatures in preparing their own legislation. It is therefore not surprising that the national laws which have been introduced in the process of preparation of the Model Laws have almost always included some variations on the recommended approach. Nevertheless the scope and underlying principles of the various laws reflect much of the work which was carried out at UNCITRAL. The degree of consensus already achieved has spurred UNCITRAL to a yet more ambitious goal: the drafting of a Convention on Electronic Commerce, which would be binding upon all contracting parties in its entirety. However, this is still in the process of being drafted, and the process is proving slow.

The international drafting process did not include any provisions relating to the regulation of certification service providers, which has therefore been managed almost entirely at the national level. Different legislatures have taken different approaches, including requiring certification by a local certification authority, setting up licensing schemes open to all comers, or imposing strict supervision of the certification service provider's information systems, personnel and procedures by a government agency.

1–010

However, the result of these differing approaches is to make it difficult, if not impossible, for a certification service provider to comply with all of the requirements for several different jurisdictions. Certificates issued by a single certification service provider are therefore not certain to be an effective support for a digital signature worldwide. This is obviously contrary to the basic objective of enabling parties in different jurisdictions to enter into legally effective contracts without regard to jurisdictional boundaries. A variety of solutions exist, but ultimately this issue may have to be resolved by a network of international mutual recognition agreements.

In parallel with the UNCITRAL drafting process, in 1997, the International Chamber of Commerce set out a statement on *General Usage for International Digitally Ensured Commerce* (GUIDEC).[14] GUIDEC is addressed to transactions between expert commercial actors, not between business and consumers. It lays down detailed guidance for the conduct of electronic commerce which aims to:

- enhance the ability of the international business community to execute secure digital transactions;

- establish legal principles that promote trustworthy and reliable digital ensuring and certification practices;

- encourage the development of trustworthy ensuring and certification systems;

- protect users of the digital information infrastructure from fraud and errors;

- balance ensuring and certification technologies with existing policies, laws, customs and practices;

- define and clarify the duties of participants in the emerging ensuring and certification system; and

- foster global awareness of developments in ensuring and certification technology and its relationship to secure electronic commerce.[15]

1–011   The GUIDEC has also been influential on legislators, and was revised and expanded in 2001. The ICC continues to work on further framework documents to add certainty and reliability to electronic commerce.

On the policy front, the Organisation for Economic Co-operation and Development (OECD) has also taken a leading role in promoting electronic commerce. Its initial involvement was with issues of information security and policy relating to encryption technologies, both of which interlink with the use and reliability of electronic signatures.[16] The relevance of information security to electronic commerce is perhaps the more obvious of the two. Security, in respect of paper-based transactions, is a relatively simple matter: keep the originals in a safe place for production should a question arise at a later date. Where computer systems are concerned, there are questions as to what the original of an electronic document may be, and very serious concerns as to how a document may be controlled, accessed and altered. These issues arise even in connection with documents created and stored on a closed network to which a limited number of users have legitimate access. Unfortunately, but all too frequently, illegitimate users may be able to access supposedly private information systems, and potentially destroy or alter the records found there. The same concerns as to information security are greatly exacerbated where documents are transmitted over open systems. Accordingly, the growing awareness among users of the insecurity of computer systems in general and the Internet in particular has been a significant issue affecting the perception of the reliability of transacting over the Internet.

In response to the increasing importance of information stored on computer systems to governments and private organisations, both commercial and otherwise, the OECD set out Guidelines for the Security of Information Systems and Networks (the OECD Security Guidelines) in 1992. By 2002, the use of computers and networks had changed dramatically, and the OECD Security Guidelines had to be updated. As the preface to the 2002 revised version[17] put it, "ever more powerful personal computers, converging technologies and the widespread use of the Internet have replaced what were modest, stand-alone systems in predominantly closed networks. . . The Internet supports critical infrastructures such as energy, transportation and finance and plays a major part in how companies do business. . ." The new Guidelines propose that all participants adopt and promote a culture of security as a way of thinking about, assessing and acting on the operations of information systems and networks. Although like all OECD initiatives the Guidelines have no legal force, they may be influential in, for example, how a court may assess an Internet user's conduct as regards information security, which may affect the liability of any party to an electronic transaction or of third parties whose services enable the transaction to be signed. For example, a certification service provider is obliged to take reasonable care in maintaining secure systems under the UNCITRAL Model Laws.[18] **1–012**

In the interim, in March 1997 the OECD issued a further set of Guidelines, this time containing a recommended cryptography policy ("the Cryptography Guidelines").[19] Although public key cryptography has from the outset been the most widely-adopted technology for producing electronic signatures, it can also be used to transform the text of a message from a readable to an encrypted, unreadable form. In the mid-1990s the legal status of such technologies achieved a high political profile internationally due to the realisation by the United States government in particular that strong cryptographic techniques, formerly the preserve of the military and intelligence services, were reaching the public domain. The government's response was to try to control their use or, failing that, to retain the legal right to access any encrypted material either with or without the owner's consent. The United States recognised that to be effective, any control would have to be implemented internationally, since cryptographic technologies today are almost exclusively in the form of software. Once software, or an underlying algorithm, becomes available anywhere in the world there is no realistic mechanism for preventing its dissemination throughout the globe. Accordingly, the USA raised the issue for discussion at the OECD, at the same time raising the status of its representative to that of Ambassador to emphasis the seriousness with which it viewed the issue of encryption.[20] The debate was enlivened by the contributions of the somewhat anarchic Internet civil liberties community, which strongly opposed all such proposals.

The Cryptography Guidelines did not quite achieve the result the United States had been looking for. Although they envisaged that governments would indeed require lawful access to unencrypted "plaintext" or to the cryptographic keys for encrypted data, the Guidelines required that the policies implementing such access should respect a series of other principles. These included the principles that cryptographic methods should be trustworthy by their users, and that users should have available a choice of cryptographic methods. The Guidelines distinguished between cryptographic techniques and products used for producing digital signatures and those used for encrypting the text for confidentiality. Even with respect to the latter, they emphasised that market-driven development should be permitted for cryptographic technologies and that governments should show respect for privacy. They also laid down that access should only be given **1–013** where there is a legal right to possession of the plaintext, and that it must only be used for lawful purposes. The access process[21] should also be recorded, to enable judicial review if necessary.

On a more practical note, the Cryptography Guidelines recommended the establishment of international and national standards for cryptographic methods, and clear allocation of liability—to the greatest extent possible. The factors to be taken into account are: the benefits for public safety, law enforcement and national security; and the risks of misuse, the additional expense of the necessary supporting infrastructure, the prospects of technical failure and other costs. In fact, as time has passed and national security issues have focussed attention away from the Internet, consumer cryptography has come to be more readily accepted by government. In particular, the distinction between software designed to enable electronic signatures to be attached to a message and software designed to encrypt the message itself, is now fairly well understood.

1–014   Finally, in October 1998, the OECD promulgated a Ministerial Declaration on Authentication for Electronic Commerce. This committed the members of the Organisation to taking a non-discriminatory approach to electronic authentication (such as digital certificates) from other countries, encouraging efforts to develop authentication technologies and mechanisms and facilitate the use of those technologies and mechanisms for electronic commerce. The members agreed to amend, where appropriate, technology or media specific requirements in current laws or policies that may impede the use of information and communication technologies and electronic authentication mechanisms (bearing in mind in particular the UNCITRAL Model Law on electronic commerce). They also agreed to proceed with the application of electronic authentication technologies to enhance the delivery of government services and programmes to the public; and continue to work at the international level together with business, industry and user representatives concerning authentication technologies and mechanisms to facilitate global electronic commerce. In September 2002 the OECD issued a follow-up Report assessing its members' progress in implementing the agreed objectives.

Enthusiasm for the possibilities of electronic signatures amongst legislators has reached such heights that laws are now being introduce which fall little short of mandating their use. In the United States, pharmaceutical companies filing regulatory submissions with the Food and Drug Administration in electronic form are required by Chapter 21 of the Code of Federal Regulations (CFR) Part 11 to sign them using signature means which comply with strict requirements regarding their uniqueness and integrity. The European Union has introduced a Directive concerning the use of electronic invoices[22] which stipulates[23] that invoices signed using an advanced electronic signature made using a secure signature creation device and supported by a qualified certificate as defined in the Electronic Signatures Directive must be accepted by Member States (although individual Member States can choose to accept less strict conditions). It appears therefore that the original principles of the OECD regarding market-driven development in respect of cryptographic products may be overtaken by events.

The influence of technology

1–015   The technology of electronic commerce has contributed to the widespread uncertainty as to the effectiveness of electronic contracts and signatures which has caused this tidal wave of legislation and international discussion outlined above. There are few people who understand precisely or even approximately how the network of networks functions, or how the different areas of the Internet interrelate. The technology of telecommunications is equally mysterious and potentially suspect, as are the protocols which enable data to be transmitted around the globe. Even the underlying word processing function which enables electronic data messages to be composed in the first place must be taken on trust. Although on screen a contract or an e-mail appear reassuringly similar to their hard-copy equivalents, it is well understood that this is just an appearance—an output of the computer in obedience to complex instructions—and that the computer is in fact recording mysterious electrical signals undetectable and unintelligible to all but another computer. Following the success of global computer viruses such as Melissa and the "I Love You" virus, the average user is by now aware that he or she is not competent to assess whether the computer is obeying his or her instructions, or those of some more adept but hidden third party. Written or faxed communications do not inspire the same distrust. Although a fax in hard copy is merely the response of a fax machine to similar invisible and undecipherable electronic signals, traditional (public switched network rather than Internet) faxes have never been perceived to be subject to interception or a medium of fraud or simple mischief, in the same way as Internet communications are. Interception and undetectable alteration of electronic communications transmitted over the Internet is a real possibility, whereas fax alteration while the message is in transit may be possible in theory but is unlikely in reality.

As a result, the development of recognised technological standards is particularly **1–016** important in this area. Clearly, the whole objective of electronic commerce is to enable transactions to be done on a global basis. For this to be feasible, the participants need to be using reliable, interoperable technologies: an electronic signature created by one party which cannot readily be verified by another is of no value. Accordingly, electronic signatures and the associated infrastructure have been the focus of considerable debate and activity at standards organisations both nationally, regionally and internationally. At the global level, the International Telecommunications Union early on produced its X.500 series of standards which govern many aspects of the technology necessary for using digital signatures. These have been recognised by the International Standards Organisation (ISO). The Internet Engineering Task Force (IETF) has also produced a number of proposals as to how public key infrastructure should operate, which have been taken up by many organisations operating in this field. At the regional level, the European Electronic Signature Standardisation Initiative (EESSI) began work on a European standard for digital certificates in 1999 following the adoption of the European Union's Electronic Signatures Directive, culminating in the publication of a whole series of standards in 2001-2003. Part I of British Standard BS7799, relating to the security of information systems, was revised and approved as an international standard[24] by the ISO in 2002, while the US Federal Information Standards Publication (FIPS) 140-1, relating to technical standards for cryptographic products, has been taken up in a number of countries. These initiatives, although having no direct legal impact, are likely to affect the evidential issues which a court has to consider when an electronically signed document is contested in any way, as sooner or later they are bound to be.

The new technology and the opening up, or possibly abolition, of national boundaries by the advent of the Internet has even caused some jurists to begin to question conventional ways of thinking about legal constructs such as signatures. The United Nations Educational, Scientific and Cultural Organisation (UNESCO) launched a series of books on the law of cyberspace with international contributors, whose enthusiasm illustrates the perception that electronic commerce would potentially revolutionise the law just as profoundly as it was hoped it would revolutionised commerce:

"Electronic signature law invites us to revisit the law, expanding traditional concepts and, beyond this, exploding the disciplinary divisions of law. The signature, classically a question of civil contract law, veers into the field of human rights with such issues as the right to a signature, the right to eavesdrop electronically, and the protection of privacy, as well as into the field of fair trade law with the right to free competition and the issue of establishing norms."[25]

In reality, this may be something of an overstatement of the significance of electronic signatures. But its accuracy in identifying the diversity of issues upon which electronic signatures touch, either through their legal or their technological aspects, cannot be denied.

---

1.   Pam Woodall, "Untangling e-conomics: a survey of the new economy" *The Economist* September 23, 2000 at p.10.
2.   Art. 1341 of the Civil Code.
3.   U.C.C. s. 2-201 (1995).
4.   Case 00-46467, Decision of the Cour de Cassation. The underlying events took place before the implementation of the Electronic Signatures Directive in France.
5.   For a description of the technology, see Ch. 3 below at para. 3-038—3-041.
6.   Biddle, *Legislating market winners: digital signature laws and the electronic commerce marketplace,* San Diego Law Review 34:1224 (1997). The regulation of encryption technologies is discussed in Ch. 9 para. 9-100.
7.   Greenwood, *Risk and trust management techniques for an "open but bounded" public key infrastructure* 38 Jurimetrics J 277 (1998).
8.   The first being the Massachusetts Electronic Records and Signatures Act 1997.
9.   California Government Code, s. 16.5 (1995).
10.   Annex 1.
11.   Annex 2.
12.   Directive 1999/93/EC, Official Journal L13, January 19, 2000, p.12. Annex 3.
13.   It has in fact been implemented by every existing Member States and by all of the newly acceding Member States with the exception, at the time of writing, of Cyprus.
14.   The text referred to is at *http://www.iccwbo.org/home/guidec/guidectwo/foreword.asp.*
15.   GUIDEC, s. 1(2).
16.   See Chs 3 and 4 below.
17.   Recommendation of the Council Concerning Guidelines for the Security of Information Systems and Networks, adopted July 25, 2002.
18.   See Ch. 5 para. 5-024 below.
19.   Available at *http://www.oecd.org/dsti/iccp/crypto_e.html.*
20.   Since then even the US has taken a slightly more relaxed stance in that it has abandoned the export controls on cryptographic methods embedded in for example financial software. For free-standing cryptographic software, the export of packages using a key length of over 64 bits remains subject to prior review. See Ch. 9 para. 9-113.
21.   The options contemplated by the Guidelines appear to relate to key escrow and/or key recovery methods. See Ch. 9 para. 9-103 below.
22.   Directive 2001/115/EC of December 20, 2001 O.J. L 15/24 of January 17, 2002.
23.   Art. 2.
24.   ISO 17799.
25.   Y Poullet, *Some considerations on Cyberspace Law,* in *The International Dimensions of Cyberspace Law,* 2000 UNESCO Law of Cyberspace, Vol. 1 at p.147.

2

Legal functions and requirements of signatures

Introduction

The need to produce legally effective signatures in cyberspace has generated considerable confusion and anxiety. Legislators and business people worldwide have tended to approach the issue of electronic signatures from the perspective that to enable electronic commerce to function smoothly on a global basis, the law and technology should be so adapted as to provide for a form of electronic signature which would be equally recognisable and effective for all purposes in different jurisdictions. This elegantly simple objective perhaps underestimates the complexity of the problem. Signatures perform a range of functions in the real world, not all of which have legal effect. Further, signatures are treated significantly differently by different legal systems, both as regards what may be recognised as a signature and also as regards the need for formalities—sealing, witnessing, notarisation—in addition to a signature to give particular kinds of documents legal effect.

In order to understand the issues facing the project of defining a legally effective electronic signature, it is relevant to begin by looking at what signatures are and the ways they are used in the real world.

Signatures are used to conclude personal and business letters, acknowledge receipt of items of post, finalise application forms or tax returns and for dozens of other mundane purposes. Only in a minute proportion of cases is the signature checked in any way, or any attempt made to verify from whom the document in fact came.

The informality with which most signatures are executed and accepted reflects the fact that very rarely is a signature intended to convey any legal significance whatsoever. The recipient of a letter may well recognise the sender as much by the handwriting or by the matters referred to, as by the name written at the end (even where it is legible). This ambiguous status is reflected in the fact that most legal systems do not include a definition of "signature", the principal exception being France.[1]

The functions a signature may perform include:

(1)   Identifying the author or sender of a document;

(2)   Authenticating the statements made in the document, in the sense of confirming that they reflect the facts correctly;

(3)   Making manifest a declaration of will and/ or intention to be legally bound;

(4)   Representing, whether explicitly or implicitly, that the signatory was authorised to perform any legal act concerned;

(5)   As a form of ceremonial, safeguarding against undue haste or thoughtlessness;

(6)   Confirming the signatory has notice of the contents of the document;

(7)   Acknowledging or marking a particular document as the original.

It is possible to extend this list, and to sub-divide the categories, but this will suffice for present purposes. In each case, the signature demonstrates some particular association between the person signing and the document. This intention is what distinguishes a "signature" from the mere writing of the name.[2]

2–003   In any discussion of the functions performed by signatures, the term "authentication" tends to be widely used but, most unfortunately, is used in different senses. A reference to the Oxford English Dictionary illuminates why this is so. The Dictionary gives eight meanings for the term authentic, from "authoritative" (itself applicable in two separate senses of "possessing authority" and "being duly authorised") to "really proceeding from its reputed source or author" and comments that:

"the development of meaning [of this word] is involved, and influenced by medieval Latin and French. Senses 3 ['entitled to acceptance or belief as being in accordance with fact; reliable, trustworthy'] and 4 ['original, first-hand, prototypical'] seem to combine the ideas of 'authoritative' and 'original'."

In modern English usage, the most commonly used sense of "authentic" is that of "original" or "genuine", so that a process of authentication is most likely to be understood as one of establishing that a document is authentic in the sense of original or genuine, *i.e.* that it does originate from the purported signatory and has not been altered since it was signed. However, the normal American-English meaning of the term in the context of the functions of signatures, and electronic signatures in particular, is the process of signifying approval or intention to be bound, or conferring legal significance upon a document, which may be performed by appending a signature. This sense, which also appears in the Oxford English Dictionary, is the sense in which signatures are said to "authenticate" documents. The failure to distinguish these two potential meanings (let alone any of the others) is a source of potential ambiguity in much of the modern legislation relating to signature.

2–004   To the extent that a signature authenticates, manifests a will or intention, makes a representation or confirms notice, the implicit function is to prevent the signatory later denying any of these. In other words, the signature is a mechanism to prevent the signatory repudiating his or her former position. Of course, the signatory can still do this by repudiating the signature itself, on the basis that it was a forgery, or in the case of contracts may be able to repudiate the transaction as whole, on the basis that the signature, though genuine, was affixed under some misunderstanding as to what the act of signing implied, or under undue influence or duress. These possibilities will be unaffected by the form of the signature, whether in pen and ink or electronic.

The remaining functions—identification, safeguarding against thoughtlessness or conferring original status upon the document itself—do not carry this secondary implication. Identification, perhaps the best known function but highly problematic, is discussed in detail at the end of this chapter.

It is also sometimes suggested that a signature on a document has the function of guaranteeing to some extent that the document has not subsequently been altered. However, it has to be conceded that a signature performs this function extremely poorly. Many documents are signed only at the end, which in itself is no guarantee at all that every one of the preceding pages has not been changed. Signing or initialling every page of a document makes it fractionally harder to substitute a page with changed wording, but producing a facsimile of a signature is straightforward, and initials are simpler still to forge. Thus, insofar as ensuring integrity of the contents is considered to be a function of a signature on a paper-based document at all, it is a relatively minor one. If it is important for the document's integrity to be maintained, it is likely to be preserved by other mechanisms, such as the retention of contemporaneous copies by all parties to a transaction, so that any subsequent change can be identified by a comparison with an independent copy, physical access to which has been carefully controlled. In earlier times, the same function would be performed by means such as dividing the original into two parts with an uneven edge or by sealing, which were difficult to circumvent without leaving visible evidence of tampering. For valuable documents such as wills or title deeds to land, the document might be stored in safe-keeping with a bank or solicitor, to ensure both that it could be found when required and that it would be unchanged from the time of execution.

A good illustration of the number of different functions which may be performed by **2–005** signatures is their use in the commercial environment. Perhaps the example which most immediately springs to mind is the use of signatures to "sign off" a contract or other document at the conclusion of a transaction. The exact function or functions of the signature in these circumstances depends both upon the kind of transaction concerned and also upon the governing law of the transaction. In some jurisdictions, generally civil law, a signature is a necessary element to enable many contracts to be legally binding. Notably, in France any contract for the sale of goods worth €800 or more must be signed in order to be legally effective. By contrast, in common law jurisdictions a signature is very rarely required for a sale of goods but may be a requirement for a transfer of land, shares or other specific transactions. Nevertheless, many contracts of sale are signed. The function of the signature in these cases is not necessarily to render the contract itself effective but only to witness the signatory's acceptance of the terms of the contract and confirm the signatory's intention to be legally bound by those terms. The conventional wording, known formally as the *testimonium* or witness clause, which is used to conclude many contracts under English law is to the effect that

"In witness whereof the parties have entered into this Agreement this [ ] day of [ ] 200[ ]."

As this wording shows, the signatures which appear below are appended as a form of evidence that the parties have indeed agreed. Their function is therefore to evidence two matters: the identities of the parties who agreed,[3] and the fact of agreement.

These signatures may, however, also be necessary to give the agreement legal effect where one or more of the parties is a company or other legal person. This is a matter of the law of companies rather than the law of contract. A company, being purely a legal entity, cannot perform any act save through the agency of a physical actor such as a person or a computer. In order for a purported agent's act to be binding, the agent must have the necessary delegated authority. Under English law, authority to enter into a contract on behalf of a company may be express or implied.[4] Other jurisdictions may require greater formality to establish the agent's authority to act, including for example Minutes of Board Meetings at which authority was delegated signed by one or more officers of the company, an incumbency certificate establishing the present status of a representative or officer and including a specimen signature, and so on. In such cases, the requirement for and precise function of the signatures depends upon the law of the jurisdiction where the company is established and also upon the company's own internal constitution.

2–006   Further, the legal nature of the agreement may be such as to require not only signature but also additional formalities such as sealing, witnessing, notarisation and even legalisation. Once again, whether or not such formalities are required in a given case depends upon the governing law. Although there are some similarities across a range of jurisdictions—for example, transactions involving land, delegation of authority under a power of attorney or inheritance of property on death often require greater formality than ordinary transactions—the precise formalities vary considerably. A document in writing and the participation of a notary is required for agreements to make a gift in both France[5] and Germany.[6] Under most common law systems, an "agreement" or promise to make a gift would simply be unenforceable whatever form it took. Germany requires written contracts for land to use notarial form[7] (a relaxation of the previous requirement that they be publicly certified by a judge or notary), whereas signature alone is sufficient under English law. In France, mortgages need to be in the form of a deed executed in the presence of two notaries or one notary and two witnesses.[8] German law requires them to be entered in the land registry.[9] In English law, signature of the contract for sale of land must be in writing and signed by both parties, and a mortgage must be in the form of a deed though notarial supervision is not required. However, registration is required in England only for the mortgage and a form of transfer, but not the contract itself.

As can be seen, the form requirements for execution of paper-based documents are very far from being globally harmonised.

To enable all types of transactions to be completed in an exclusively electronic environment will therefore require more than simply legislating to permit electronic signatures to have legal effect. Electronic equivalents to the various other formal requirements which may apply may also be necessary.

Legal effects of signatures in the law of contract

(1) Requirement of signature

2–007   Contracts where a signature is required are very much the exception rather than the rule, under English law and most other common law systems, and the requirement for a signature originated not as a pre-requisite for the contract to be binding but for it to be enforceable in the Courts—a fine distinction.

A statutory signature requirement in respect of a contract under English law is almost always linked to a requirement that a particular document be in writing. The requirement for writing was first introduced in the 1677 Statute of Frauds, since when the law has developed organically rather than according to any clear or consistent underlying criteria.

The English Statute of Frauds 1677

The introduction of a requirement for a signature to render a contract enforceable is more **2–008** an issue of procedure than of substance. It arose in England precisely because of the limitations of legal procedure in the seventeenth century. Fraudulent claims proliferated against the background of social and political upheaval caused by the Civil War, the brief period of Parliamentary rule under Cromwell and the subsequent Restoration of the monarchy. The existing legal procedures proved wholly inadequate to cope with them.

The problems arose from two sources. First, until the sixteenth century it had been accepted that a contract could be formed by the exchange of mutual promises with no formality whatsoever. This was in keeping with historical practice across Europe. Roman law had provided for the solemnisation of contracts by the use of verbal formulae in the form of question and response: for example, *promittis? Promitto.*[10] These formulae could be spelled out in a ceremonious manner (*stipulatio*) to impress the formality of the occasion upon both participants and bystanders. But even these formalities had been abolished in 472 AD. Problems had clearly been encountered under the revised, informal system since French statutes of frauds go back to a statute of Arles in 1245. This statute limited testimonial proof of contracts to those of a value below 100 sous, and it was followed by a number of Ordonnances on the same issues. It has been suggested that the Ordonnances of 1566 and 1667 may have formed a model for the English Statute.[11] There were also statutes of frauds in Verona in 1228 and Venice in 1394.[12] In Germany, even the law itself remained largely unwritten for many centuries until the enactment in 1342 of a law that made the written law alone binding for the courts.[13]

The second problem in seventeenth century England was that the rules of legal **2–009** procedure forbade a person from testifying in any proceedings in which he or she had an interest. As a result, where a contract came into dispute the very people who were most likely to be able to shed light on the matter were prohibited from explaining the agreement to the Court. This situation derived from the medieval forms of legal action, which were linked inextricably to methods of establishing proof in order to determine which contracts might be enforceable. The principal forms included a "covenant", that is a written sealed document, and an action by "wager of law" (a method of proof using numerous witnesses under oath). Without a covenant it would be extremely difficult to enforce most types of contractual claim in the courts. Unless one party had performed their part of an oral bargain, leading to the creation of an enforceable debt, a claim for enforcement of a contract would be denied enforcement in the king's courts. Where a covenant existed, the parol evidence rule prevented litigants from questioning the document as an accurate record of the reciprocal undertakings. Although the ordinary courts began to enforce oral agreements in the sixteenth century, the suspicion of informality persisted. A decision would be reached by a jury, which was entitled to make a decision based on its own knowledge since there were few effective mechanisms for putting it in command of the facts. The result would therefore be unpredictable.

Against the background of upheaval of the seventeenth century, where old certainties **2–010** of allegiance, property ownership and even accurate knowledge of recent events had been thrown into question, the temptation for the unscrupulous to try their luck making fraudulent legal claims was evidently overwhelming.

There was thus a clear need for some provision to prevent such abuses, and this was the objective of the Statute of Frauds. The majority of the statute relates to protecting interests in property generally, and the provisions relating to contracts, sections 4 and 17, should be viewed in that context. It is unfortunate that neither section achieved its objective as a result of the poverty of the drafting. Both sections were subject to several centuries of judicial criticism as a result.[14]

Section 4 read as follows:

"No action shall be brought whereby to charge any executor or administrator upon any special promise to answer damages out of his own estate; or whereby to charge the defendant upon any special promise to answer for the debt, default or miscarriage of another person; or to charge any person upon any agreement made upon consideration of marriage; or upon any contract or sale of lands, tenements or hereditaments, or any interest in or concerning them; or upon any agreement that is not to be performed within the space of one year from the making thereof; *unless the agreement* upon which action shall be brought, *or some memorandum or note thereof, shall be in writing and signed* by the part to be charged therewith or some other person thereunto by him lawfully authorised."

2–011   The requirement then is not for the agreement itself to be written and signed, but only for "some memorandum or note thereof" to be. This threw the doors open for innumerable cases based upon the scantiest of written evidence, and the result was possibly to improve the opportunities open to fraudsters in later, more literate ages. The majority of section 4 was repealed in 1954, although the phrase relating to "any special promise to answer for the debt, default or miscarriage of another person" remains in effect.[15]

Section 17, which was wholly repealed in 1954,[16] adds one further category of contract:

"No contract for the sale of goods, wares or merchandises for the price of £10 sterling or upwards shall be allowed to be good except the buyer shall accept part of the goods so sold and actually receive the same, or give something in earnest to bind the bargain or in part payment, *or that some note or memorandum in writing of the said bargain be made and signed* by the parties to be charged by such contract or their agents thereunto lawfully authorised."

Other Statutes of Frauds

United States of America

2–012   The US law of writing and signatures derives from English common law and statutes, including most significantly the traditional English Statute of Frauds. Versions (often nearly word for word) of the English Statute of Frauds have been enacted, and remain in force, in almost every state in the US. The writing and signature requirements of the Statute of Frauds have been carried forward in the Uniform Commercial Code and other widely-adopted uniform and model laws[17] and in numerous other statutes, both federal and state, that impose writing, signature and other formal requirements on particular transactions.

An individual US state's general Statute of Frauds typically requires that certain transactions be evidenced by a "writing signed by the party to be charged." While there is a great deal of variation in individual state enactments, the following categories of promises or agreements usually fall with a state's general Statute of Frauds:

- a promise or agreement of an executor or administrator to answer for the debt of a decedent;

- a promise or agreement to be responsible for the debt of another;

- a contract in consideration of marriage;

- a promise or agreement for the sale of an interest in land
- a contract not to be performed within a year.

The Uniform Commercial Code is a uniform law that governs contracts for the sale of goods (Article 2) and leases (Article 2A), among other types of commercial transactions.[18] Section 17 of the English Statute of Frauds was carried forward in Article 2 of the UCC, which, as originally promulgated and adopted by the states,[19] provides that a contract for the sale of goods is not enforceable in the absence of "a writing sufficient to indicate that a contract for sale has been made between the parties and signed by the party against whom enforcement is sought or by his authorized agent or broker."[20] In general, contracts governed by Article 2 that are not evidenced by a writing are enforceable only to the extent of any payments that have been made and accepted or to the extent of any goods received and accepted.[21] Analogous provisions are contained in Article 2A governing lease contracts, and in other articles of the UCC.[22]

In addition to these generally applicable statutes, individual U.S. states have enacted numerous more narrowly-applicable statutes that either explicitly or implicitly require a writing or a signature, impose other formal requirements such as certification or verification, or otherwise use language that suggests a writing or signature requirement.[23]

With the development of various forms of electronic communications technology such as fax machines, telefaxes and the like, questions have periodically arisen concerning whether transactions involving the use of such technologies satisfy the writing or signature requirements of the Statute of Frauds or some similar formal requirement. In most cases involving controversy on this point, at least in commercial transactions between private parties,[24] the courts have concluded that the Statute is satisfied by electronic communications technologies. For example, US courts have ruled, both explicitly and implicitly, that the Statute of Frauds writing requirement is satisfied by communications technology such as the telegram, telex, telecopy or facsimiles.[25]

2–013

Despite precedents such as these, the emergence of the Internet as a commercial communications tool raised concerns among some commentators about whether private electronic transactions carried out on the Internet would satisfy the writing and signature requirements of the Statute of Frauds. At the same time, questions were also raised concerning the ability of parties to such transactions to assure the identity of remote participants and the security of their long-distance communications.[26] The legislatures in a number of states responded to these concerns with the enactment of electronic and digital signature statutes.

Other common law jurisdictions

Likewise the laws of the Commonwealth countries incorporated the Statute at their respective dates of independence from the United Kingdom and many retain requirements of writing and signature for certain categories of contract which derive from this source. In most cases, the English case law prior to independence will be relevant to the interpretation of present-day laws.

2–014

Civil law approach

Civil law systems also retain a patchwork of signature requirements. France also has a version of the parol evidence rule, which says that "no proof by witnesses against or beyond the contents of instruments [not] as to what is alleged to have been said previously, at the time of or since they were made shall be allowed." But this rule itself is no longer applied in commercial transactions.

2–015

Despite their intended purpose, the requirements of writing and signature have, provided fertile ground for litigants keen to escape from contracts they have entered by pleading that the contract comes within the Statute and therefore cannot be enforced unless the due formalities can be shown to have been observed. The interpretation of the English Statute has given rise to a vast collection of complex case law as the judges attempted to apply the spirit of the Act without allowing the literal wording to continue to abet potential fraudsters.

What can be a signature?

England & Wales

2–016   Case law concerning the question of what may function as a signature can be traced back to nineteenth century cases mostly concerning the execution of wills. English wills are governed by the Wills Act 1837. Making a will requires a very high level of corroboration of identity[27] such that the signature itself has become almost secondary to the surrounding circumstances. The signature must be intended by the testator as an act of execution,[28] and it must appear that he or she intended the signature to give effect to the will, which has led to wills being challenged if the signature appears elsewhere than at the foot of the document. The inevitable absence of the signatory at the point where any dispute may arise, and the social significance of the disposition of an individual's entire estate by a single document, has led to the requirement for multiple witnessing of the signature under prescribed conditions. The testator must either sign or acknowledge the signature in the presence of two witnesses present at the same time, each of whom is in a position to observe the proceeding.[29]

2–017   The corroboration provided by these additional formalities, however, has perhaps perversely led to the courts being ready to accept as signatures marks which, had they stood alone as evidence of identity or intention to execute the document, might well have been inadequate. A mark of any kind, made by the testator or by someone else, can suffice as a signature to a will if the surrounding circumstances are sufficient to demonstrate the testator's intent. The first English judge to admit such a divergence in respect of a signature not applied by the testator at all was Sir C Cresswell in deciding *Jenkins v Gaisford & Thring*, an 1863 case under the Wills Act 1837.[30] This case concerned the estate of the elderly Mr Jenkins who, as a result of his declining health, had had a stamp made on which his signature was engraved. He used this for signing documents in his later years. By the time he came to make his final will, he was no longer even wielding the stamp himself but had the "signature" affixed by his trusted agent. This was also the mode by which his will was signed, in the presence of the necessary witnesses and with all due formalities. Nonetheless, perhaps inevitably the will was challenged as not having complied with the requirement for signature. Sir Cresswell stated that

> "The word 'signed' . . . must have the same meaning whether the signature is made by the testator himself or by some other person in his presence and by his direction. . . Whether the mark was made by a pen or by some other instrument cannot make any difference, neither can it in reason make a difference that a facsimile of the whole name was impressed on the will instead of a mere mark or X."

He concluded that even though the stamp had been applied by the testator's agent the result amounted to a valid signature.

2–018   The same issue arose in *Bennett v Brumfitt*,[31] which concerned the requirements of the statute 6 Victoria governing procedures for elections, only a few years later. In deciding that case, Sir William Bovill C.J. considered whether a stamped signature would be a good signature within the Statute of Frauds 1677, section 4, and concluded that clearly it would have been. He also noted that it would have been a good signature to a will under section 9 of the Wills Act 1837. He commented once again that the ordinary mode of affixing a signature to a document is not by the hand alone but by the hand coupled with some instrument, such as a pen on pencil. The Chief Justice and his fellow judges, who concurred with his reasoning, do not appeared to have considered the issue of the increased potential for forgery by someone else producing an indistinguishable (because identical) replica of another's "signature" using their stamp, probably because the evidence in *Bennett* was that no other person had access to the stamp in question.

By this stage the formalities requirements of the Statute of Frauds were also being interpreted very loosely in the English courts, so that the "signature" need be no more than a printed name appearing anywhere on the contract or note of it, provided it is intended to authenticate the whole of the document. Thus, the requirement for signature on a contract for sale of hops was held to be satisfied in 1862 where upon conclusion of the agreement an agent printed the buyer's name at top of one copy of sale note and gave it to the buyer, and inserted the seller's name at top of other copy and gave it to the buyer. No one signed anything according to the ordinary meaning of the word. The Court held "where it is ascertained that he meant to be bound by it as a complete contract the statute is satisfied, there being the note in writing shewing the terms of the contract and recognised by him".[32]

More than 90 years after Jenkins, the suitability of a rubber stamp as a means of affixing a signature was questioned again, in *Goodman v J Eban Ltd*,[33] a case concerning the requirements of section 65 of the Solicitors' Act 1932 for a bill delivered by a solicitor to a client to be signed. This decision has been treated subsequently as the principal statement of modern English authority concerning requirements of signature. A client, J Eban Ltd, challenged a solicitor's bill on a variety of bases including that they had never instructed Mr Goodman, that the work had not been done and that he had said that any work he did for them would be free of charge. These claims perhaps set the tone for the dispute. All of these assertions were thrown out by the judge at first instance. However, the defendants appealed on the issue of the formal correctness of the bill since the signature had been applied by a rubber stamp rather than being a handwritten signature, and further the stamp was not in the solicitor's own name but his trading name (the firm was known as Goodman, Monroe & Co). The evidence showed that Mr Goodman kept the rubber stamp locked up in his own room so as to be available only for his own use.

Lord Evershed M.R. felt that the use of a rubber stamp was undesirable as a matter of practice since the aim of the Solicitors Act in requiring the signature was to ensure that the solicitor had personal responsibility for the bill, and to give the client assurance that the bill delivered was a proper bill. If matters were to be considered in isolation, he said, he should think that when Parliament required the letter to be signed it was intended that the solicitor should personally sign the bill or letter in the ordinary way by writing his name (or, where appropriate, the name of his firm) in his own hand with a pen or pencil. But he was swayed by the authorities discussed above which permitted the use of a rubber stamp as a signature.

Evershed M.R., in reaching his conclusions in *Goodman*, relied in addition upon the Oxford English Dictionary definitions, which do not appear to have changed greatly since 1954. Signature as defined merely requires the placing of a distinguishing mark upon (a thing or person). Since signing means simply placing one's name or signature so as personally to authenticate the document, it followed that a rubber stamp was sufficient.

2–019

Romer L.J. concurred on this argument (as in the overall decision), citing Stroud's Judicial Dictionary (3rd ed.) where the definition of "Signed; signature" is:

> "the writing, or otherwise affixing, of a person's name, or a mark to represent his name, by himself or by his authority with the intention of authenticating a document as being that of, or binding on, the person whose name or mark is so written or affixed".

2–020   He also observed that other parts of the Solicitors Act 1932 did require "writing under hand"—for example, by the Master of the Rolls in admitting solicitors to the Roll. The earlier Acts consolidated into the Solicitors Act 1932[34] had in fact required bills to be "subscribed by the proper hand of the attorney" which arguably would *not* have been satisfied by the affixing of a signature by rubber stamp, enabling the defendant to argue that the consolidating act ought not to be taken to have changed the law. However, Evershed M.R. observed that the formula used in the Solicitors Act, "signed by the solicitor" had also been used by Parliament in other Acts, and considered that it would therefore not be appropriate to give it any other meaning than the ordinary meaning. To hold otherwise would introduce grave doubt and uncertainty into the use of such a formula. Evershed M.R. did consider the issue of doubt arising as to whether the solicitor had personally authenticated the bill where a rubber stamp had been used, but considered this adequately met by the client's ability to enquire of the solicitor by telephone.

Denning L.J. (as he then was) dissented forcefully from the majority decision in *Goodman*, finding that in the context of the Solicitors Act a signature should be a writing or at the least a mark made by the hand of the signatory. He explained his position on the grounds that the virtue of such a signature.

> "lies in the fact that no two persons write exactly alike, and so it carries on the face of it a guarantee that the person who signs has given his personal attention to the document. A rubber stamp carries with it no such guarantee because it can be affixed by anyone. The affixing of it depends on the internal office arrangements with which the recipient has nothing to do. This is such common knowledge that a 'rubber stamp' is contemptuously used to denote the thoughtless impress of an automaton, in contrast to the reasoned attention of a sensible person."

2–021   This argument would not appear to hold a great deal of water in the case of a signature made by marking with a sign—usually a cross, as Denning L.J. noted—since, absent some distinguishing feature such as a unique colour of ink, one cross is much more like another cross than one handwritten name is like another. Where the identity of the signatory by such a mark has been called into question, extrinsic evidence has had to be admitted to link the maker with the mark.[35] This is consistent with the origin of the very term "signature", which derives from the practice in medieval times of a person indicating their agreement to a document by making on it the sign of the cross. A clerk would then write the "signatory's" name next to the cross.

The point is not perhaps too important in the discussion of a solicitor's signature, since any person who had qualified as a solicitor had by definition taken a number of examinations and would be able to write.[36] But at the level of general principle, though a cross is an acceptable signature, it is not a great guarantee of the reasoned attention of any *particular* sensible person.

2–022   Although Denning L.J.'s argument concerning the value added by a handwritten signature may not be flawless, some of his other observations are valuable. He distinguished the Statute of Frauds and Wills Act analogies relied upon by Evershed M.R. on the basis that these are very different types of document—notably, a will requires two witnesses so the form of the testator's signature is less material, while under the Statute of Frauds even headed notepaper had been found sufficient. This refusal to lump a wide disparity of forms of document together with a single form of signature equally applicable to all is perhaps reasonable in view of the different functions signatures may be performing in each case, and has perhaps led in the opposite direction to that Denning L.J. anticipated. A Law Commission report of the 1960s recommended that the weight previously placed on form requirements should be replaced by reliance instead on an analysis of the function intended by a signature and an evaluation whether this had been performed on a case by case basis, and this approach has come to be accepted. Professor Reed concluded, on evaluating the role of the signature in English law in 2000, "a signature is not a 'thing' but a process ... To the question 'what *is* a signature?', the answer is now a single word—'evidence'".[37]

This represents a decisive change of policy from the law as it was until the 1960s. Evershed MR in *Goodman v J Eban* expressed no opinion as to whether a typewritten or printed name would also fall within the Act, but in view of his reservations as to the desirability of even a stamp being used it is highly dubious that he would have permitted these. A differently constituted court of 1889 had concluded decisively that it was not.[38] The case sometimes cited as the English authority for the use of typewritten signatures does not on closer examination provide any clear statement to that effect. *Newborne v Sensolid (Great Britain) Limited*[39] concerned a contract purportedly made by a company which, as it transpired, had not in fact been incorporated at the time the contract was made. The contract bore the name of the company and below this was the manuscript signature of a Mr Newborne, the founder of the company. Upon finding that the company had not existed Mr Newborne argued that he had signed the contract as agent for the company and that in the circumstances he should stand in the shoes of the company as principal. The court rejected this, on the grounds that he had never held himself out as an agent but that so far as any contract had been formed it had been formed by the company. The conclusion therefore was that no contract had ever been made. The issue of whether the typewritten name of the company was in fact a valid signature was therefore entirely peripheral to the Court's decision; in reality it was never decided.

A printed signature at the foot of a notice had been given effect in respect of the Public Health Act 1875 even before the close of the nineteenth century,[40] albeit that in the case in question the Court also held that in fact no signature was strictly necessary anyway. Thus, although this is the case generally cited in support of the proposition that a printed signature may be a valid one, it could equally be argued that in context the case is no authority at all for the validity of a printed signature where the signature was a matter of any importance.

Following the Law Commission's recommendation, two decades passed before the **2–023** question of what might constitute a signature fell to be considered again in novel circumstances by the English courts. In *Clipper Maritime Ltd v Shirlstar Container Transport Ltd (The "Anemone")*[41] Staughton J, reached a provisional view (though he did not have to decide the point) that the answerback of a telex machine could constitute a signature since this would both indicate the origin and the approval of contents by the sender.

By the time the first cases on genuinely electronic signatures came to be decided in 1995, the approach recommended by the Law Commission had clearly prevailed. Society, and in particular commerce, had changed considerably from the *Goodman* era. In *In re a debtor (No. 2021 of 1995) Ex p. Inland Revenue Commissioners*,[42] Laddie J. mentioned without comment the fact that dividend cheques are routinely "signed" by having the company secretary's signature printed upon them, something Denning L.J. had thought too clearly unacceptable to need discussion or argument. This point was, however, the basis of Laddie J.'s subsequent decision that signature by the use of a non-human agency (here, a fax machine) is nevertheless signature for certain purposes. In practice in a vastly automated world the volume of transactions has outpaced the ability of human agents to perform all necessary steps. The banks accept and act upon cheques bearing only a printed signature; the law recognises and reflects this. Laddie J. stated that his decision was "consistent with the realities of modern technology", which perhaps was precisely what Denning L.J. was attempting to resist by insisting upon the active participation in the process of a "sensible person". For the use of a fax machine is almost an invitation to forgery: nothing is simpler than to photocopy a signature from one document onto another, and since the process of fax transmission often distorts the image in any one of several ways, the forgery is considerably less likely to be detectable than forgery of any "original" document (where the paper upon which the forgery has been performed is subject to direct observation) would be. Laddie J. was however correct in observing that the likelihood of forgery is no greater from the recipient's point of view than it is if the original is signed with a rubber stamp.

2–024   The facts of *In re a debtor (no. 2021 of 1995)* were that Laddie J. was asked to consider whether the copy of a signature which is made by a fax machine upon receipt of a transmission could amount to a signature for the purposes of the Insolvency Rules 1986. A proxy form had been sent in the post but failed to arrive in time for a creditors' meeting, so the Inland Revenue (whose proxy form it was) sent another by fax. The chairman of the meeting attempted to telephone the signatory in order to confirm his instructions but was unable to speak to the necessary person, and therefore rejected the form.

Laddie J.'s analysis included *Jenkins v Gaisford* as well as *Goodman*, but was principally directed to the wording of the rules themselves. In particular, rule 8.2(3) stated that:

> "a form of proxy shall be signed by the principal, or by some person authorised by him (either generally or with reference to a particular meeting). If the form is signed by a person other than the principal, the nature of the person's authority shall be stated. . ."

2–025   From this, Laddie J. concluded that the purpose of the signing was to provide some measure of authentication of the form, which in the nature of things could not be perfect: he pointed out that the only circumstances in which the chairman of a creditors' meeting can be certain who has signed the proxy form is where the form has been signed by the creditor (bearing some evidence of identity) in the chairman's presence. Any other signature may be a forgery, and in ordinary cases the chairman will in any event not be familiar with the "true" form of the signature he is relying upon.

Having acknowledged that printed signatures are accepted by the banks, Laddie J. went on to consider the issue of "fax from desk" technology whereby a person could create a document on a computer and cause the computer to transmit it to a fax machine bearing a bit map copy of a scanned signature. In those circumstances, the copy printed out by the receiving fax machine would be the only hard copy ever to exist and in his view would be "signed" by the sender. A proxy form created (in hard copy) by a fax machine in obedience to the instructions of the sender is no less a non-human agent applying a signature by the authority of the principal, and accordingly the proxy form the subject of the case was held to have been valid.

Other Jurisdictions

The Supreme Court of British Columbia in Canada reached the same conclusion on almost identical facts in *Beatty v First Explor. Fund 1987 & Co*,[43] relying on cases back to the nineteenth century relating to proxies communicated using telegrams and telegraphs.

2–026

The Dutch Supreme Court has likewise accepted that a writ of summons may be valid if signed and served by fax, even though the relevant statutory provisions prescribe a written signed writ.[44] However, although under Dutch law a facsimile or stamp has been accepted as a signature, in contrast to the English position a cross or fingerprint would not be.[45]

Similarly, in a 1979 Irish case a solicitor who instructed the typing of a letter setting out the terms of the memorandum on headed notepaper was held to adopt the heading as his signature.[46] This is called the "authenticated signature fiction". The writing of a name as a point of information will not suffice,[47] nor will initials added as a reference.[48]

In the United States also, over time Federal law has evolved and moved away from the focus on formalities. Signature itself is not the point; the issue is whether the other party reasonably believes that the asserted signer's intention is to authenticate[49] the writing as his own.[50] Comment 39 on the Uniform Commercial Code 1-201 states:

2–027

> "'Signed' includes any symbol executed or adopted by a party with present intention to authenticate a writing".

The incorporation here of the term "adoption" permits a party to adopt a symbol which is already on the paper. Similarly, the Restatement (Second) of Contracts, s. 134 (1981) provides that a signature may be:

> "any symbol made or adopted with an intention, actual or apparent, to authenticate the writing as that of the signer."

Subsequently, the US Courts have been fairly liberal about finding marks or symbols to be effective as signatures. A signature may be made in pencil,[51] typed,[52] stamped, printed[53] or put on by a photographic process. A taped conversation has been admitted as a signature.[54] Signature may also be effected by an agent. Courts and other authorities have focused on whether there was a reliable indication that the party to be charged intended to authenticate the communication.[55]

At this stage, therefore, the presence of a signature in legally acceptable form provides very much less confidence that the signatory had a close personal involvement with the final form of the document. The signature may be valid even though the signatory never in fact set eyes upon any hard copy document he or she is supposed to be personally responsible for. That any comfort is provided at all is as a result of the relative rarity of forgery and the confidence people have in the proper functioning of the organisations with which they deal. If a signature is available, it is taken to be more likely than not that it originated from the person whose signature it purports to be. This reduction in reliance upon formality involved in the transition reflects the enormous changes in commercial practice over the second half of the twentieth century: the advent of rapid communications have led to an expectation of rapid decision-making and action which is simply incompatible with the personal conduct of affairs, protocols and deliberations of the nineteenth and early twentieth centuries. Trust has moved from individuals to procedures.

2–028

2–029   The trustworthiness of procedures depends upon the integrity of those who carry them out. Inevitably, this will not always be sufficient to resist the temptation to abuse a position of trust or to turn a trusted procedure to personal advantage. The first English case concerning the repudiation of a form of electronic signature arose from such circumstances. In *Standard Bank London Ltd v Bank of Tokyo Ltd*,[56] decided like *In re a debtor* in 1995, three signed letters of credit were issued which emanated from the Bank of Tokyo's Kuala Lumpur branch. In fact the signatures were forged, but this was not detected by Standard Bank even though they attempted to verify the signatures using a "tested telex" mechanism. This is a telex which contains codes or tests which are secret between the sender and the recipient a form of electronic signature of the bank sending the message. The banking system makes extensive use of trusted telexes, which are meant to avoid potential arguments over authority; it is not usual to query their authenticity unless information comes to the knowledge of the recipient which might put it on notice of some irregularity. No such information reached Standard Bank in this case. It appears that the fraudsters either managed to access Bank of Tokyo's systems in order to send the telexes themselves, or tricked the Bank of Tokyo's staff into doing so. Standard Bank therefore made loans in reliance upon the letters of credit, and when these were not repaid they sued Bank of Tokyo.

Waller J. in the High Court held that Standard Bank had been entitled to rely upon the letters of credit backed by the tested telexes. The latter could not have been sent without negligence on Bank of Toyo's part, since it had complete control of the environment from which they originated, namely its own branch. The tested telex system would break down if the recipient of each telex were required to obtain further confirmation of the fact that it had been authorised. The electronic signature was sufficient on its own.

Circumstances where signatures do not bind

(2) Circumstances where signatures do not bind

2–030   Although neither writing nor a signature is required to render the majority of contracts valid and enforceable, signature of a document is nevertheless a legally important act. A party signing a contractual document containing terms is bound by them in the absence of fraud or misrepresentation.[57] This applies whether or not the party has in fact read the terms, provided that the terms were available to be read before the contract was finalised. Under English law, a party will only be excused from being bound by the effects of terms which he or she has signed under very limited circumstances. A mistake as to the identity of the counterparty may be effective,[58] but only if there are special reasons why the specific identity of the counterparty was material;[59] ordinarily, it is not.[60] However, a plea of mistake can only succeed where there has been some form of deceit. If one person makes an offer to another mistaking them for a third, but the offeree is unaware of the mistake and accepts the offer in good faith, then a binding contract arises. An offeree who is aware that the offer is not intended for them cannot bind the offeror to the mistaken offer.[61]

A separate category of mistake which may render a signed contract void is where one party is fundamentally mistaken as to the character or effect of the document signed.[62] In these circumstances the party wishing to be relieved of the contract can plead *non est factum*, *i.e.* this is not the document I believed I was signing. This plea is available only in very restricted circumstances, usually involving active fraud by a third party. The mistake must have been a serious one as to the practical effect of the document, not merely its legal character. Finally, the signer must not have been careless, as for example where a literate person signs a document known to have significant legal effect without reading it.[63]

A signed contract may also be voidable if it was signed either under undue influence exercised in the context of a relationship of trust and confidence[64] or duress[65] of any person. Finally, a contract which represents an unconscionable bargain obtained by one party exploiting a particular weakness of the other may also be set aside.[66] As for mistake, these exceptions are applicable in very limited circumstances.

Australian authorities handle the rule as to signature somewhat more leniently: if the written terms go far beyond what was actually or impliedly agreed before execution, then those terms are not adopted by the mere act of signature. In *Warming's Used Cars Ltd v Tucker*[67] the Court held that "the rights and duties of the contract fell to be determined on the oral contract unless the evidence discloses a new agreement to supersede or vary it. For that purpose it would not be sufficient for the clerk to say 'sign here'. There must be real consent to the variation."   2–031

This approach has also found favour with some English commentators. It has been argued[68] that in fact the informal deal which is reached between business people before the lawyers are permitted to get involved, which may well be the outcome of purely oral discussions sealed with a handshake, is likely to represent a legally enforceable contract. If so, then a question arises as to the relevance of the subsequent documents and signatures—particularly where they supplement or even contradict the obligations contained in the oral agreement. Arguably, the written and signed contract is a record of the planning elements of the deal, which have in the main not been considered at the negotiating stage, but should not be permitted to override the oral agreement which took priority in time. In these circumstances, signature might alternately be taken as evidence of consent to the variation of the existing contract.

Signature as a form of identification

A signature is normally the name of a person written, either in full or by the initials of the forename or names and the surname in full. When carried out by the familiar method of handwriting by the signatory, the signature identifies the signatory in two ways: by the name written, and also by the handwriting and possibly the characteristics of the pen, if the signatory can be reliably associated with a particular one. Handwriting, though a learned rather than an innate behaviour, provides some link between the marks on the document and the physical person who produced it: for example, it may demonstrate the level of literacy, or tremors due to age or illness. Graphologists claim that in addition it reveals the character of the writer. The use of a name is the first line of social identification, even though many names give very little information about the signatory. Every country has its clichéd names borne by thousands or even millions of citizens—be it "John Smith" or "Wang Li"—so that a document bearing a bare signature leaves the recipient practically none the wiser as to what person it was who signed.[69]   2–032

This raises the question of what is meant by an identity. A simple definition is a set of attributes which together uniquely identify an individual.[70] These fall into three categories: biometric (DNA, fingerprint, voice); attributed (name, address) and biographical (date and place of birth, personal history). The attributes which are relevant may differ significantly depending upon the context.

Private transactions

2–033   In the private sphere, a person's identity is a collection of information about the physical person (estimated age, gender), their personal relationships within their community and what communities they belong to (neighbourhood where they live, occupation, sports club memberships and so on). For social transactions, these attributes may be the most significant elements of the person. The details recorded in official registers such as those of births and deaths are irrelevant for most purposes. A name is simply a label by which the individual is identified, and a relatively few centuries ago was a first name only since the society of the time was organised into relatively stable small groups within which a single name was sufficient identification. Rural communities in some less developed countries still function on this basis. Surnames or family names began to be used, in the sense of being hereditary, among the nobility in about the 12th century, and gradually spread into the remainder of the population of England through the following two centuries as the need for identification among a larger group grew. By the end of the 14th century the usage of surnames covered the country as well as the towns. A surname for an individual would appear first in a clerk's records, and might be the person's father's name (patronymic), that of some other relation, the name of the place where they lived, the names of their offices or occupations, or some descriptive nick-name. Being essentially arbitrary in the first place, a surname might change several times during a person's life, and from generation to generation. The point when it became fixed and subsequently passed from father to son was quite accidental.[71] People in any case sometimes used different names from those by which they were known by the clerks. In Wales and Shetland, a large proportion of the population did not develop hereditary surnames until the 18th century, many not becoming stable until the middle of the 19th century.

The status of personal names as a matter of English law has remained equally informal. Under English law, a person's legal name is the name they are known by,[72] which ordinarily is the same in the private as well as the public sphere[73] but does not require any form of official recognition provided that their community recognises them by it. Changing one's name under English law is only a question of choosing to be known by a different name and persuading others to use it. A deed poll[74] merely announces the change of name in a formal way and can be used to change the name on passports and bank accounts,[75] but the process of making such a deed is not necessary to change the name and does not necessarily involve any verification of the previous name.

2–034   Civil law countries such as France and Spain have a considerably more centralised approach to identification, however, and in the Netherlands a name can only be changed by deposition in front of a judge. A specific reason must be given for a change of surname. In these countries, therefore, names and signatures have considerably greater value as identifiers.

Very little or none of the sort of information which makes up a personal identity may be directly relevant to a particular transaction. The cumulative evidence of a person's connectedness within a community provides confidence, however, as to their reliability or suitability to deal with.

In personal dealings with strangers, the information available for forming such a view will be severely limited both as to range and reliability since the available paths for corroborating the information the person themselves offers will be few and may also be tenuous. In these circumstances, for example, the sale of a car through a newspaper advertisement, it is unusual to accept payment by cheque because the signature, even if valid, when divorced from knowledge of the buyer's personal circumstances, is insufficient to give the level of trust necessary to handover a valuable asset. A banker's draft or cash obviates the need to know the person since the bank is universally trusted to pay upon demand provided that the draft is genuine.

Transactions between individuals and businesses
Other than for marketing purposes, a business transacting with an individual is unlikely **2–035** to be interested in the attributes which make up their personal identity. A purchase of low value goods in a shop involves simply a transfer of cash and goods. Higher value transactions generally involve either cheques or credit cards, once again bringing in the services of a bank or other financial institution as a trusted third party. In face to face transactions, the shopkeeper is able to check the customer's signature on a cheque or credit card slip by comparing it with that on the back of a card, even where the value is outside the limit of the actual guarantee. However, this is no indication of identity save insofar as the single attribute "holder of X bank account" is concerned. If the customer has succeeded in opening a bank account under an assumed name, neither shopkeeper nor bank is concerned whether the name signed on a cheque is the same as the legal name of the signer but only whether it corresponds with the name on the account and the signature reflects the sample deposited with the account opening documents. A signature on a withdrawal form from a building society account is not to a false instrument contrary to section 1 of the Forgery and Counterfeiting Act 1981 despite the fact that the name signed is not the signatory's legal name, if it was the name in which the account was opened.[76] From the shopkeeper's perspective, all that matters is that the card-issuing institution ensured that only the account holder received the unsigned card and can be trusted to sign it themselves, so that the shopkeeper is entitled to assume that any matching signature is that of the account holder.

The level of proof of identity offered by a signature is nevertheless low, since in most cases the production of a passable imitation is merely a question of obtaining a sample and copying. The real security measure in the use of cheque and credit cards is the unwillingness of the averagely honest, or timorous, citizen to attempt to commit a forgery in public, with the accompanying risk of immediate detection, exposure and shame—not to mention potential arrest. Credit card fraud is some three times more prevalent in remote transactions.

Where the signature is required to prove the signer's identity to a high level of certainty additional evidence is normally required. Verification of name and address, either in the form of a driver's licence or, better still, post such as utility bills or Council Tax statements confirm an association between a name and an address which are unlikely to be readily available to a complete fraudster.[77]

Transactions between individuals and government
Many forms of transactions with public administration require forms to be signed. The **2–036** OECD Survey on Form Requirements reports that the German Ministry of the Interior had identified more than 3,000 different instances where in practice handwritten signatures were required.[78]

Although a signature may be required, it is rarely necessary to provide any other proof of identity beyond reference to a national identity number or equivalent, such as the United Kingdom's National Insurance number (held by all residents over the age of 16[79]) or the United States' social security number. Not all British citizens have passports or driving licences, the most familiar forms of "official" identification, since each of these documents is only required for a specific, optional purpose: travelling abroad or driving a car. It is estimated that less than 25 per cent of citizens of the United States have passports, having no need of them, although the number has been rising over last decade.[80] However, the level of assurance of identity provided by a passport is also questionable, since the only evidence of identity required for an application is a birth certificate, which can be obtained in duplicate. In paper-based transactions, therefore, identity fraud may be as simple as acquiring knowledge of another person's name and national identity number. In an increasingly anonymous society, this enables substantial frauds to be perpetrated in person or through remote communications such as telephone and post. As governments worldwide begin to promote the use of the Internet as a medium for interactions with government services, the need for reliable forms of electronic identification arises.

Business transactions

2–037   Dealings in the business context often rely heavily upon unchallenged assumptions that a person able to give a company name and a business card is more likely than not to be a representative of that company—since of course the company details are verifiable from public registers, and a cross-check can be made to some extent by contacting the company and asking for confirmation that the individual is indeed authorised to represent them. The general rule, which applies in many jurisdictions, is that an organisation is responsible for the acts of its employees or agents having apparent authority. The more significant the transaction, the more care is likely to be taken to establish the identity of the counterparty. The signatures of a director and the company secretary, or two directors, are required for a company incorporated in England and Wales to execute a contract.[81] This mechanism reduces the risk of fraud by requiring a conspiracy or dishonesty on several people's parts. Further, the names of current directors and secretaries are required to be included in each company's Annual Return to the Registrar of Companies, and a director must sign a consent form to act as a director before being appointed. Thus, a specimen signature is publicly available for each officer of the company.

The process of concluding a major transaction is itself a process of establishing trust between the parties not necessarily as regards the legal identities of the parties and their representatives, but as regards the suitability of the other as an entity to do business with. Other than in a sale or purchase of a business as a whole, the parties may expect and intend to continue dealing with each other in the future. The meetings, telephone conversations and exchanges of e-mails which go into the process of agreeing a deal represent the parties' opportunity to establish how the other functions and what sort of trust the other merits. It is, in other words, a process of establishing the identity of the other akin to the process of establishing a personal community identity and based on a similar sort of personal appraisals. This process cannot entirely be substituted by purely remote, electronic communications no matter what level of assurance may be available as to the legal identity of the person communicating from each side.

Electronic identity

2–038   For several reasons, the issue of personal identity is even more problematic in the context of electronic transactions. A far greater number of transactions are likely to be with strangers and to take place remotely, removing even the limited opportunity to make a personal assessment which is provided by visual inspection. In cyberspace, there is not likely to be any way to check the extent to which a person's description of themselves reflects reality: name, age, gender and location are all to be taken on trust. The only reliable information which a correspondent has is the e-mail address (which may include an organisation name, and may be disguised by the sender) and the Internet Protocol (IP) address of the computer from which an e-mail is sent. It may be possible to work out from the IP address what network the computer is attached to, which gives some confirmation of the physical location of the user. But beyond this, none of these reveals anything at all about the person or persons operating the computer from time to time. Even an extensive correspondence does not enable one party to know more about the other than their familiarity with the language in use, the topics in which they are interested (or purporting to be) and the average turnaround time for responding to messages.

There is also the perceived greater vulnerability of cyberspace to fraud. All information in cyberspace consists solely of relatively transient electronic signals which the average person is unable to decipher, relying on the intervention of computers and software to render it intelligible. Those who have a real understanding of how the information is transferred from the mind of the sender into signals and transmitted through complex networks of telecommunications equipment and other computers eventually to end up on another screen, have an advantage over their peers which engenders distrust and anxiety. The fact that any intervention may take place in a remote location by a third party whose interest and even existence were unknown to the sender gives users of electronic communications even greater cause for concern. While electronic communications in the form of telexes and faxes have been in use for decades, the only party commonly considered to be interested in and capable of intercepting those forms of communication were the police. This was backed up by the knowledge that both faxes and telexes, once they had left the sender's machine, travelled to the recipient only over the public switched networks of the telephone operators. E-mails and other communications using the Internet, however, are known to pass through an unknown number of intervening computer systems which may as well be operated by universities or public bodies as by familiar commercial organisations.

A number of initiatives have therefore been taken around Europe to establish individual electronic identities which accurately reflect some at least of the user's critical personal details. The first, a Finnish initiative of December 1999 was a smart card combined with a paper identifier, the application of which was limited to changing the holder's registered permanent address. This optional scheme was then expanded to multiple functions (each included on the card at the holder's option) in due course. However, by November 2002 only 15,000 cards had been issued, the most popular applications being pension services and personal identity.

The European Union itself has trialled an identity smart card under a project known as **2–039** FASME: facilitating administrative services for mobile Europeans. The card is intended to assist workers moving between Member States by assisting with police registration, changes in social security, tax status and the like. Once again, the card's functionality is intended to be extended at a later stage, in this case to include private sector applications.

The most advanced initiative at the time of writing appears to be the Estonian system, under which identity cards are mandatory for all Estonian citizens and resident aliens with a visa permitting a year or more's stay.[82] The cards, which are governed by the Identity Documents Act,[83] have a fixed format combining the function of a physical identity card, with a photograph of the bearer, with a smart card function which includes a government-issued e-mail address, private key for applying digital signatures and associated certificates. However, users who have concerns about the electronic use of the card can have the certificates suspended, rendering the electronic functions invalid. The first identity cards were issued in January 2002 and 130,000 were issued in the course of the first year so that almost 10 per cent of Estonian citizens are already carrying them. The Estonian authority responsible for issuing them, the Citizenship and Migration Board, estimates that approximately 25 per cent of the population will have cards by the end of 2003.

2–040   The card's physical identity function consists of a photograph of the holder, a sample of their signature and their name, national identity code, date and place of birth, sex, citizenship and details of any residency permit. This gives a comprehensive set of attributes for establishing a legal identity. The card also identifies its own number and issue and expiry dates. This is written in natural language and machine-readable form, and is also replicated in a microchip along with the holder's private keys, certificates, unique e-mail address[84] and PIN numbers. The card includes two keys and associated certificates, one for authentication and one for digital signing. The idea of having two separate keys for closely related functions is to enhance the ceremonial significance of using the digital signature key. It is reported[85] that the European Commission is considering making the use of two certificates mandatory for compliance with the Electronic Signatures Directive. Both Estonian keys are purely personal: the national identify card does not deal with individual's roles in any organisation, authorisations or qualifications. The government's intention is that a digital signature created using the national identity card should be treated exactly as an individual handwritten signature: all-purpose, but limited to identifying the signatory.

The e-mail address is a lifetime assignment, which functions solely as a relay address to forward e-mail to a holder's own e-mail accounts.[86] These addresses are available on-line through the certification authority's directory. Encryption and signing of e-mails are at the user's own option.

2–041   The intention was to include minimal private data on the card to avoid data protection issues. The details of age, sex and place of birth and the photograph are only available to anyone in physical possession of the card, although the e-mail address, name, national identity code and certificates are published on-line.

Estonia has the advantage, as far as instituting such systems is concerned, of having a relatively small population and an almost clean slate as far as legislation is concerned, having recovered its independence only a little over a decade ago. It has also taken a pragmatic approach to the scale of its project.

The first country to attempt to issue purely electronic identity cards was Italy, which issued its first in March 2001.[87] The scheme is more ambitious than the Estonian approach, aiming to enable citizens to interact online with government departments, travel within the European Union and access medical services. The Italian cards include both a microchip and a laser optical memory band bearing identical information to reduce the risks of forgery. The cards are intended to include not only identity details but also the holder's tax code and, in future, health information and scanned fingerprints. The holder will have the right to determine what health information is included. As at November 2002 100,000 cards had been issued in a trial and the government was hoping to have issued 2 million by the end of 2003.

2–042   Trials also began in 11 towns in Belgium at the beginning of 2003 as a pilot test for the Belpic project, the ultimate objective of which is to provide all citizens with electronic identity cards similar to the Estonian model, with basic identity information, photograph and copy signature in both physical and electronic form.[88] The card is also planned to include digital certificates. France was also making serious plans to introduce an electronic identity card for citizens to use in interactions with government agencies, but the target date for full implementation was 2012.

Finally, in April 2003 the United Kingdom announced plans to issue "entitlement cards" for residents which would take the form of a passport/driver's licence card including potentially biometric means of identification. This is perceived by the government to be necessary in view of the inadequate security of all existing forms of government-issued documentation which is relied upon for identification. The United Kingdom has not had a national identity card since 1952, when the wartime scheme was repealed. Accordingly, common forms of identification, such as National Insurance Number cards, are not issued or designed with security as a feature. The introduction of photocard driving licences by the Driver and Vehicle Licensing Agency (DVLA) in the late 1990s was greeted with dismay by civil liberties groups, objecting that the information required to be included (including a holograph signature, albeit miniaturised to a point possibly beyond usefulness) went beyond that necessary for the objective. However, identity fraud is allegedy the most rapidly increasing type of fraud ever seen in the United Kingdom. CIFAS[89] Members reported just 20,000 cases in 1999, but some 75,000 in 2002. The DVLA is now participating in the European Electronic Identity/ Public Services Card network, known as the Porvoo Group.

The Porvoo group was established in April 2002 at a meeting in Porvoo in Finland as **2–043** an informal international network to promote trans-national inter-operable electronic public identities using a public key infrastructure model and smart cards. 15 countries are represented at present: Belgium, Estonia, Finland, France, Germany, Ireland, Israel, Latvia, Lithuania, Norway, Slovenia, Spain, Sweden, The Netherlands and the United Kingdom. The group recommends standardisation of the procedure for use of the cards, and guidelines for the format and content of cards, but it may be that systems will have been implemented in a number of countries before such standards have been agreed.

A single electronic identity card entitling the holder to a range of rights and benefits will of course become a major target for fraud in its own right. The universal acceptance of the social security number card as proof of identity in the United States has led to an exponential growth in false applications and forged cards leading to the passing of the 1998 Identity Theft Act. Any system which becomes operable throughout Europe will have even greater potential for abuse as the disparity of administrative systems and incompatibility of languages may render routine cross-checking impractical.

Electronic signatures

The functions of electronic signatures in general are identical to those of any other form **2–044** of signature. A *digital* signature may have additional functions, namely to authenticate the contents, assure the integrity of the message and potentially also authenticate the time of affixing the signature. In order to assist in understanding the additional expectations which are raised of digital signatures in particular, and assess the extent to which electronic signatures can perform the functions of a paper-based signature, the next chapter discusses the various technologies of electronic identification and signature.

---

1. Art. 1316-4 of the Civil Code—see *www.legifrance.gov.fr*.
2. Slade L.J. in *Central Motors (Birmingham) Ltds v PA Wadsworth & Anr (trading as Pensagain)* (1982) 133 N.L.J. 555.
3. which may well be different from the literal authorship of the document, in contrast to function (1) in the list of functions above.
4. Companies Act 1985, s. 6.
5. Art. 931, stipulating a notarial contract.
6. S. 518, requiring notarial authentication.

7. S. 313 of the Civil Code.
8. Art. 2127.
9. S. 873.
10. "Do you promise?" "I promise".
11. Rabel, *The Statute of Frauds and Comparative Legal History* (1947) 63 L.Q. Rev. 174.
12. *ibid.* at 176.
13. Wesenbery, *Neuere deutsche Privatrechtsgeschichte* (2nd ed. 1969).
14. For instance, Lord Wright summarised 250 years of cases on the subject in 1939 as "all devoted to construing badly-drawn and ill-planned sections of a statute, which was an extemporaneous excrescence on the common law". *Legal Essays and Addresses,* at p.226.
15. A decision of the House of Lords on its application was handed down as recently as April 2003: *Actionstrength Ltd v International Glass Engineering In.Gl.En. SpA & Ors.*
16. Having been replaced in 1893 by s.4 of the Sale of Goods Act.
17. The Uniform Commercial Code (UCC) is a uniform law promulgated by the Permanent Editorial Board of the UCC, a body which is comprised of representatives of the American Law Institute (ALI) and the National Conference of Commissioners on Uniform State Laws (NCCUSL). Uniform laws promulgated by these or any other such bodies are not self-executing and must be enacted in individual states in order to have the force of law. The UCC has been enacted into law in some form in 49 of the U.S. states (all but Louisiana, which has a legal system based on civil law).
18. Other articles of the UCC include, for example, Arts 3 and 4 (governing checks and other instruments), Art. 5 (concerning letters of credit) and Art. 9 (concerning secured transactions).
19. A protracted effort to revise Art. 2 and 2A of the UCC was completed in 2003. The revised text of UCC § 2-201 raises the dollar amount to $5,000 and changes the term "writing" to "record," which is broadly defined to include electronic records. The term "signed" is defined to include electronic authentication.
20. UCC s. 2-201.
21. The full text of this section provides: (1) Except as otherwise provided in this section a contract for the sale of goods for the price of $500 or more is not enforceable by way of action or defense unless there is some writing sufficient to indicate that a contract for sale has been made between the parties and signed by the party against whom enforcement is sought or by his authorized agent or broker. A writing is not insufficient because it omits or incorrectly states a term agreed upon but the contract is not enforceable under this paragraph beyond the quantity of goods shown in such writing. (2) Between merchants if within a reasonable time a writing in confirmation of the contract and sufficient against the sender is received and the party receiving it has reason to know its contents, it satisfies the requirements of subsection (1) against such party unless written notice of objection to its contents is given within 10 days after it is received. (3) A contract which does not satisfy the requirements of subsection (1) but which is valid in other respects is enforceable (a) if the goods are to be specially manufactured for the buyer and are not suitable for sale to others in the ordinary course of the seller's business and the seller, before notice of repudiation is received and under circumstances which reasonably indicate that the goods are for the buyer, has made either a substantial beginning of their manufacture or commitments for their procurement; or (b) if the party against whom enforcement is sought admits in his pleading, testimony or otherwise in court that a contract for sale was made, but the contract is not enforceable under this provision beyond the quantity of goods admitted; or (c) with respect to goods for which payment has been made and accepted or which have been received and accepted (S. 2-606).
22. *e.g.,* UCC s.2A-201.
23. A survey of one state's statutes found that "the word 'writing' appears over 2500 times, and the phrase 'in writing' accounts for over 1900 of those instances; the word 'signed' appears over 1600 times and 'signature' over 400 times; 'document' appears over 1100 times and 'memorandum' appears over 100 times; 'handwriting,' 'handwritten' and 'hand-written' appear 75 times. The related terms 'certification' and 'verification' appear over 1000 and 400 times, respectively.New Jersey Law Revision Commission, Final Report relating to Electronic Records and Signatures, at 5 (Nov. 1998), available at *http:// www.lawrev.state.nj.us/rpts/signature.pdf.*
24. A distinction should be made between the treatment of commercial transactions between private parties and those involving a governmental authority, such as the filing of a document with a government agency. Such governmental transactions often are governed by other and very specific formal requirements.
25. *e.g., Howley v Whipple,* 48 N.H. 487 (1869) (telegram); *Joseph Denunzio Fruit Co v Crane,* 79 F. Supp. 117, 128 (S.D. Cal. 1948) (teletype machine); *McMillian Ltd v Warrior Drilling & Engineering Co,* 512 So.2d 14 (Ala. 1986) (mailgram); *Ore & Chemical Corp v Howard Butcher Trading Corp,* 455 F. Supp. 1150 (E.D. Pa. 1978) (telex); *Bazak International Corp v Mast Industries,* Inc., 73 N.Y.2d 113, 535 N.E.2d 633 (1989) (facsimile).
26. *e.g.,* Daniel J. Greenwood and Ray A. Campbell, Electronic Commerce Legislation: From Written On Paper and Signed In Ink to Electric Records and Online Authentication, 53, *The Business Lawyer* 307 (American Bar Assn. Nov. 1997).
27. Wills Act 1837 s.9(a) (substituted by the Administration of Justice Act 1982 s.17). This does not apply to wills of mental patients under the Mental Health Act 1983.
28. *Re Walker* (1862) 2 Sw. & Tr. 354.
29. Wills Act 1837 s. 9(c) (substituted by the Administration of Justice Act 1982 s.17).
30. (1863) 3 Sw. & T. 93.

31. 1867 L.R. 3 C.P. 28.
32. *Durrell v Evans* (1862) 158 E.R. 848. The judge reluctantly relied upon the earlier authority *Johnson v Dodgson* (1837 150 E.R. 918 at 921).
33. [1954] Q.B. 550.
34. *inter alia* the Solicitors Act 1843 and earlier acts going back to 3 James I in 1605.
35. For example, *Baker v Dening* (1838) 8 A. & E. 94.
36. Although it is permissible even for someone who is able to write to use an X.
37. Reed C, *What is a signature?*, 2000(3) *The Journal of Information, Law and Technology (JILT)*. <http://elj.warwick.ac.uk/jilt/00-3/reed.html/*.
38. *Regina v Cowper*, 24 QBD 60.
39. [1954] 1 Q.B. 45.
40. *Brydges (Town Clerk of Cheltenham) v Dix* (1891) 7 T.L.R. 397.
41. [1987] 1 Lloyd's Rep. 546.
42. [1996] 2 All E.R. 345.
43. (1988) 25 B.C.L.R. (2d) 377.
44. Stated without case reference in Huydecoper and van Esch, *Writing and signatures: an outdated concept?* (Dutch language original in ITeR series 7, Samson Bedrijfsinformatie bv Alphen aan den Rijn, 1997) p.69.
45. Huydecoper and van Esch, *Writing and signatures: an outdated concept?* p.69
46. *Casey v Irish Intercontinental Bank* [1979] I.R. 364.
47. *McQuaid v Lynam* [1965] I.R. 564.
48. *Kelly v Ross & Ross* unreported, High Court April 29, 1980.
49. in the American sense, of adopting, rather than the more usual European usage, of verifying.
50. Farnsworth, *Contracts*, 1982 Little, Brown at [*page ref!*]
51. *Merritt v Clason* 12 Johns. 102 (N.Y. 1815).
52. *A&G Construction. Co v Reid Bros Logging Co* 547 P.2d 1207 (Alaska 1976).
53. *Prairie State Grain & Elevator Co v Wrede*, 217 Ill. App. 407 (1920).
54. *Ellis Canning Co v Bernstein* (348 F. Supp 1212 D. Colo 1972).
55. *e.g., Joseph Denunzio Fruit Co v Crane*, 79 F. Supp. 117, 128 (S.D. Cal. 1948) (the fact that parties knew each other and the codes and signals used in their telexes, coupled with the absence of an allegation that message was not genuine, was sufficient to satisfy the signature requirement).
56. [1995] C.L.C. 496; 1996 1 C.T.L.R. T-17.
57. *L'Estrange v Graucob* [1934] 2 K.B. 394.
58. *Cundy v Lindsay* (1878) 3 App. Cas. 459.
59. *Lewis v Averay* [1972] 1 Q.B. 198.
60. *Phillips v Brooks* [1919] 2 K.B. 243.
61. *Boulton v Jones* (1857) 2 H. & N. 564.
62. *Thoroughgood's Case* (1584) 2 Co. Rep. 9a.
63. *Gallie v Lee* [1971] A.C. 104 sub nom. *Saunders v Anglia Building Society*.
64. *Barclays Bank plc v O'Brien* [1994] 1 A.C. 180.
65. *Barton v Armstrong* [1976] A.C. 104.
66. *Aylesford v Morris* (1873) L.R. 8 Ch. App. 484.
67. [1956] S.A.S.R. 249.
68. Collins, *Regulating Contracts* OUP 1999.
69. This is apparently known as the "John Wilson" problem at Intel, where according to Carl Ellison a level of on-going confusion arose as there were in 2002 eight employees by that name. Ellison, *Improvements on conventional PKI wisdom*, Proceedings of the First Annual PKI Research Workshop 2002.
70. Taken from the HMG *Minimum Requirements for the Verification of the Identity of Individuals*, Office of the e-Envoy, Version 2.0 January 2003.
71. See generally P H Reaney, *The origin of English surnames* (1967).
72. *D v B (otherwise D)* [1979] 1 All E.R. 92.
73. It is however not uncommon for professional women to continue to use their maiden name in the context of their work yet be known by their husband's name in their personal sphere.
74. Halsbury's Laws Vol 35 para. 1279; the purpose of enrolment of a deed poll at the Central Office of the Supreme Court is simply a matter of providing conclusive evidence.
75. As well as persuading friends and acquaintances of the seriousness of the intention to change to an unfamiliar name.
76. *R v More* [1987] 3 All E.R. 825 HL. In that case the name in which the account was opened was the name on a cheque intercepted by the account holder.
77. Although utility bill forgery is apparently increasing due to their status as confirmation of identity, and increased availability of IT equipment makes this relatively easy (*Identity Fraud: a study* Cabinet Office, July 2002. Available at the time of writing at *http://www.homeoffice.gov.uk/comrace/entitlements/index.html*)
78. Working Party on Information Security and Privacy, *Progress achieved by OECD member countries in furtherance of the Ottawa Declaration on authentication for electronic commerce*, OECD DSTI/ICCP/REG(2001)10/FINAL, September 16, 2002 at p. 63.
79. except those who did not receive Child Benefit as a child for whatever reason and have never worked in the official economy, *Identity Fraud: a study, op. cit.*

80. Gyford, *Writing*, at *www.gyford.com/phil/writing/2003/01/31/how_many_america.php*.
81. S.36A(4) of the Companies Act 1985; this is execution by the company itself, as contrasted with execution by an agent on its behalf as discussed above.
82. This discussion is based upon the Estonian white paper "The Estonian ID Card and Digital Signature Concept" dated March 10, 2003, available at *http://www.id.ee*.
83. available in English at *http://www.legaltext.ee/text/en/X30039K7.htm*.
84. *firstname.lastname_nnnn@eesti.ee*, where nnnn is a random four digit number to deal with the problem of name duplication. The Estonian population is less than 1.5 million, so that it appears to be feasible to have a system permitting no more than 9,999 people with the same name.
85. Porvoo Group, *Report of the Seminar on Interoperable European electronic ID/ public service cards,* held on November 21-22, 2002, Dublin.
86. deleting any spam; spam is illegal in Estonia.
87. *Italy issues first electronic identity card*, article in *ITworld.com* dated March 19, 2001.
88. *Report of the seminar on interoperable European electronic identity/public service cards* held on November 20-21, 2002 in Dublin, available from *http://www.electronic-identity.org/porvoo*. This report is also the basis for the discussion of the French initiative and the activities of the Porvoo group below. Further details of the Belgian project are available from *www.globalsign.net*.
89. CIFAS is the UK's Fraud Prevention Service with Member organisations spread across banking, credit cards, asset finance, retail credit, mail order, insurance, investment management, telecommunications, factoring, and share dealing. Members share information about identified frauds in an attempt to prevent further fraud. See *www.cifas.org.uk*.

3

Electronic Signature Technologies

Introduction

3–001

The question of what may be used as an electronic signature is not a technical question but a legal one, since a technical process or data set will only function as a signature if they are recognised as such by the applicable law. Some of the legal regimes which have been introduced to govern the use of electronic signatures prescribe the use of the special category of electronic signature created using public key cryptography, namely digital signatures. Others leave the choice of technology for creating an electronic signature entirely open to the parties, although many of these give an enhanced status to signatures meeting specified criteria, generally framed to encompass digital signatures.

For example, the definition of "electronic signature" in the Electronic Signatures Directive includes any:

"data in electronic form which are attached to or logically associated with other electronic data and which serve as a method of authentication".[1]

This definition, which is similar to many of the definitions adopted in national laws around the world, is clearly very wide in scope, requiring only two criteria to be met (beyond the tautology that an electronic signature must comprise data in electronic form). The first criterion is that there must be some form of attachment to, or association with, other data—that is, the data which are being signed. The second criterion is that the signature data must serve as a method of authentication. Neither is entirely unproblematic.

3–002

First, it is not clear in the electronic context what "attached to" may mean. The electronic signals making up one part of an electronic document are not attached to the remainder of the document in any physical sense analogous to the physical bond between the ink of a handwritten signature and the paper upon which it is written. However, electronic signature data may be logically associated with the remainder of the document if they are incorporated in the document, such that a computer reading the document treats the whole as a single document. Alternatively they may be connected to it by, for example, a pointer incorporated in the document which refers the computer to an entry in a database where the signature may be found.

The second criterion is harder to interpret. As discussed above,[2] authentication is a term to which several meanings are ascribed by different users and in different contexts. It is not self-evident which meaning is intended here, and the distinction may be important. The most likely interpretation in the context of the Electronic Signatures Directive is that the data must be added by the signatory as a process of signifying approval or intention to be bound, or conferring legal significance upon the remainder of the document. In this sense, the signature "authenticates" the document by conferring upon it the status of the approved, "original" version. This meaning is preferred. The alternative, that the data must establish that they or the document which purports to be signed are authentic in the sense of original or genuine, *i.e.* that it does originate from the purported signatory and has not been altered since it was signed, would import into the definition of "electronic signature" two out of the four characteristics of an "advanced electronic signature" as defined in the Electronic Signatures Directive. The characteristics are that the signature is:

(a)   uniquely linked to the signatory;

(b)   capable of identifying the signatory;

(c)   created using means that the signatory can maintain under his sole control; and

(d)   linked to the data to which it relates in such a manner that any subsequent change of the data is detectable.[3]

3–003   These or similar criteria, which strongly imply the use of digital signatures, are also reflected in definitions of equivalent "enhanced" or "secure" electronic signatures in various national laws. If "authentication" in the definition of electronic signature requires identification of the signatory and some form of assurance as to the document being original, *i.e.* not having been changed, then elements (b) and (d) in this definition would be redundant. This interpretation of authentication in the Directive's definition of electronic signature is also consistent with the UNCITRAL definition of an electronic signature, which makes an intention to signify approval an essential element of the signature.[4]

It can be seen from this analysis, however, that the meaning of a particular definition of electronic signature in national legislation may be context-dependent, and may also depend upon what technologies the legislature had in mind in formulating their definition. Thus, technologies which may be used to create electronic signatures within the definition of one piece of legislation may not necessarily create electronic signatures within the definition of another.

That being said, this chapter reviews various different technologies which can be used to generate data which may qualify as an electronic signature, in terms of whether or not they satisfy the broad definition of the Electronic Signatures Directive. The practical question of their suitability to provide a secure and robust alternative to the traditional method of signing a paper document by hand is also addressed.

In the first section, the various "low-tech" solutions such as typing in a password are discussed, including their shortcomings. The various technologies using biometrics are then considered as a means of generating electronic signatures with a much higher degree of authenticity and security. The technology of cryptography is then examined. Finally the ability of these various technologies to perform the functions discussed in Chapter 2 is reviewed.

"Low tech" solutions

The simplest form of electronic signature would be for the signatory to type in their name, initials, or other distinguishing identifier such as a pseudonym or alias at the bottom of an electronic document. This method would satisfy the Electronic Signatures Directive's definition of an "electronic signature". However, despite its potential to come within the ambit of the Electronic Signatures Directive, this method of signing a document is inadequate for a transaction of any significance as anybody can type in the name of the purported signatory. There is no guarantee whatsoever that a message with a particular name typed at the bottom of it has actually been approved by a person of that name. Clearly, a better method is required for most purposes.

3–004

Passwords

A more secure option would be for the signatory to type in a unique password/ passphrase or Personal Identification Number (PIN) at the end of the document. PIN numbers are already widely used for transaction authentication. For example, the mechanism for credit card transactions in shops has traditionally in the United Kingdom been the customer signing a receipt so that the shopkeeper can check the signature against the signature on the back of the customer's credit card. However, this is now being replaced by systems where the customer instead has to type their PIN into a keypad on the side of the till to prove they are the credit card owner,[5] as has been the system in some countries of continental Europe for some time.

3–005

A password or PIN number has the advantage that at least, unlike a person's name, the password would not (at least to begin with) be in the public domain. It could be kept secret by encryption so that any person intercepting the message was unable (without investing significant time and effort) to find the password out. However, like all password systems there is a risk that others may discover or work out the password. Once the password is known, then a forger can produce perfect, indistinguishable electronic signatures. The risk that the password will be broken can be reduced by a number of means, including choosing an uncommon or made-up word as the password in order to reduce the vulnerability of the password to guessing. However, no password or phrase consisting solely of natural language words is resistant to a computerised 'dictionary attack'. In a dictionary attack, the computer simply tries all known words in an appropriate language, along with common names, place names and so on. A reasonably powerful computer can do this in seconds against a standard 8 character password. To be reasonably secure, a password or phrase of approximately 98 characters is necessary as this will generate a 128-bit key. The sentence "A reasonably powerful computer can achieve this in seconds against a standard 8 character password" is 98 characters, including the quotation marks. Even so, it would not be a secure passphrase as it stands because all of the words are common dictionary words.

Where a PIN is used it should ideally contain both letters and numbers and be long enough to make guessing the PIN impractical for the would-be impersonator. However, this also makes it harder to remember for the would-be signatory, and even so any PIN is vulnerable to computerised attack since the computer can simply try every possible combination of letters and numbers of the given length. A string of 98 characters consisting of random alphanumerics would be reasonably secure—but not 1 in 100 users would be able to remember it. Users would therefore write it down, and it immediately becomes insecure to any passer-by. Worse, users would almost certainly keep it in a file on

3–006

the computer. The file might be encrypted, but would be protected by a more memorable, easily crackable password. Strong technology cannot protect against the need for the system ultimately to be used and useable by mere mortals.

On its own, the use of a simple password or PIN as an electronic signature cannot be recommended for any but the smallest transaction as it does not provide a sufficient degree of certainty as to who it was that signed. Encrypted, it may be satisfactory for some transactions.

Bitmap scan of handwritten signature

3–007   A further alternative is to sign a piece of paper manually using a pen, then scan this into the computer using a standard scanning device to create an electronic "bitmap" image of the signature. This electronic file could then be attached to the document file as the electronic signature.

This method has the significant advantage that everyone is used to signing his or her name when executing a document, so it is an easy and "natural" method. Also, the traditional method of signing means that the attention of the signatory is focussed on the significance of their act in the same way as when executing a paper document—which it may not be when simply pressing a button on a computer or typing a name. However, bitmaps also have weaknesses. Once the signature exists as a bitmap, it is extremely easy to copy. Of course a handwritten signature can also be forged by those sufficiently skilled, but much less skill and effort is required to copy an electronic file. Even if a bitmap scan does not exist of a particular individual's signature, a would-be forger could obtain a copy of the subject's handwritten signature from another paper document, scan it in and pass it off as if the subject had performed the scan themselves. The ease with which this can be done means that even an encrypted version of a scanned signature carries very little assurance that the document was approved by the purported signatory.

In view of these weaknesses it is highly unlikely that such a method will become commonplace as a means of electronic signature creation, particularly as there are other methodologies involving handwritten signatures that are far more robust.[6]

Light pen

3–008   An alternative method of inputting a written signature would be to draw a bitmap using a light pen, which traces out the signature onto the screen. Whilst perhaps more convenient than scanning a written signature into the computer, this method suffers from similar drawbacks. Also, it can be quite difficult to write properly on a curved, vertical surface. However, this method has the advantage that the software which captures the signature can also capture the time at which the signature was written onto the screen. Provided that this data was incorporated into the signature image in such a way as to be unforgeable—for example, by hiding the time data among the pixels of the image undetectably[7]—such a method could avoid some of the copying concerns associated with use of a bitmap scan of a handwritten signature.

Other methods

3–009   Other methods of signifying approval or "signing" electronically are currently available on the Internet. For example, commercial websites often present customers with their terms and conditions of trading and require the user to indicate acceptance by clicking on an "I accept" or "proceed" button. In these circumstances, the click can generate a bit (1 or 0) of information which may be logically associated with the customer's order, thereby satisfying the Electronic Signatures Directive's definition of an electronic signature. Such a mechanism gives the recipient no indication of the "signatory's" identity, but is commonly used in transactions for which a credit card will be used as a payment mechanism. In these circumstances, the provision of credit card details, including the identity of the card holder, performs most of the functions more commonly associated with a signature.

Conclusions

It can readily be appreciated from the above discussion that there are a number of simple ways of creating an electronic signature which technically come within the definition in the Electronic Signatures Directive. This said, the reality is that in practice most of these methodologies fall short of providing an adequate degree of assurance as to the identity of the signatory and the authenticity of the signature, in the sense of its genuineness. They are unlikely to find widespread acceptance as appropriate methods of finalising contracts in the business-to-business environment, or in the consumer environment where higher value transactions are concerned. Accordingly, the remainder of this chapter focuses in detail on the two methodologies which do have the potential to fulfil the needs of businesses and individuals for reliable and acceptable method of electronic signature generation—biometrics and encryption.

3–010

Biometrics

Biometric devices operate by verifying the identity of a human subject by reference to one or more of the subject's unique physiological and/or behavioural features. Examples of such physiological features include: the structures of the retina at the back of the eye or the iris at the front; fingerprint patterns; and hand geometry. Behavioural features are characteristics that are learned or acquired during a subject's life, such as the mechanics of forming a handwritten signature.

3–011

Commercial biometric devices are available which can obtain data from the subject's fingerprints, irises, retina, hands, and face, together with a whole host of other parameters. Typically, such devices take a measurement of the attribute in question and reduce it to a set of numerical data values. This process is often termed "digitisation". The values are then compared with a database of biometric data, to confirm whether or not the person being scanned is recognised. Biometric devices are already being used in a wide range of applications, including law enforcement, secure electronic banking and other financial transactions, workstation access, and airport check-in systems.[8] The potential range of uses for such systems is enormous.

Biometrics are nevertheless problematic since the human body varies with age, illness and other factors. Injury may deprive a person of the feature to be measured. The interaction of the body and the measurement device can also affect measurement. A fingerprint detector may be confused by the subject pressing down hard and thereby flattening out some of the features beyond the ordinary measurement error limits, or by a cut or scar. Biometric devices are therefore subject to errors, which may be either false

3–012

positives, where someone who is not in fact authorised or recognised is accepted, or false negatives, where a legitimate user is not recognised. Most biometric devices can be set to a chosen level of sensitivity, which should generate neither too many false negatives nor too many false positives—the ratio depending upon the application. For example, for a nuclear missile bunker access system it is a much less serious problem if the system keeps legitimate personnel out on a number of occasions than it is if it lets an unauthorised person in just once. On the other hand, for a system permitting access to an airline lounge it is probably more important never to keep a legitimate, and probably stressed, customer out than it is to prevent the occasional unauthorised passenger coming in too.

This tendency to error is a disadvantage of all biometric systems for the purpose of creating electronic signatures. The best a biometric technique can deliver is a probability that the person creating the signature was or was not the purported signatory. However, it will be seen when digital signature techniques are discussed below that this probability may provide a more realistic means of achieving a satisfactory degree of assurance as to the identity of the signatory than cryptographic techniques are able to do alone.

3–013   Clearly, digitised biometric data which are associated with an electronic file as a means of authenticating it satisfy the definition of an electronic signature in the Electronic Signatures Directive. However, by themselves they do not satisfy the definition of an advanced electronic signature, and may not satisfy similar definitions of secure electronic signatures under other laws. To achieve this, for each form of biometric measurement it is envisaged that the digital data generated by the biometric device would be attached to the electronic document in such a way that if anyone tampers with the document, the biometric signature will become corrupted or changed such that the tampering can be detected. Furthermore, some mechanism is necessary to prevent an unscrupulous party simply obtaining a copy of the data generated by such a system (*e.g.* the data from an iris scan) and simply "pasting" this to the document in question, known as a "capture and replay attack". The most obvious way to achieve both of these objectives is to bind the biometric to the document signed using a digital signature technique. Another alternative is not to have the biometric data transferred beyond the reading apparatus itself (which of course would have to be physically tamper-proof), but only use it as an access means to a stored cryptographic key to be used in signing.

Where biometric data itself is used as an electronic signature, a mechanism is also needed such that the recipient of the electronically signed document can check that the electronic signature is that of a particular individual, such as a central database of biometric data. This of course brings its own problems, both in terms of security and of personal privacy.

Retina scan

3–014   The retina is the thin layer at the back of the eye which senses light and transmits impulses through the optic nerve to the brain. It has been known since the 1930s that each human being has a unique pattern of blood vessels, known as the "retinal vascular pattern", which originate in the optic nerve and disperse through the retina.[9] No two retinal vascular patterns are ever the same, even as between identical twins, and as such they provide a means of reliable personal identification. The pattern of retinal blood vessels changes little over time and so retinal scanning appears to represent one of the most stable biometric identifiers. However, eye conditions such as cataracts (which can obscure the retina) and glaucoma (where increased pressure within the eye can, amongst other things, alter the retinal vascular patterns) may interfere with the reliability of retinal scanning.

Retinal scanning systems use a camera to look through the pupil and scan the user's retina. Typically, a 360 degree circular scan is taken of the retina using a low-intensity light source and an optical coupler, to establish the blood vessel patterns present in the retina. The process typically takes around 10 seconds. This information is then reduced to a number of reference points by means of a pre-determined algorithm before being reduced to a digitised "template" which can be stored for future comparison.[10]

In existing scanning devices, the subject is required to bring their eye very close to the scanning device, and to remove spectacles or contact lenses, which has proved unpopular with some users. As a result, retinal scanning devices are now being developed which allow the scan to be performed from a distance and which are not affected by the subject wearing spectacles or contact lenses.[11] Orientation problems are minimized by using the eye's natural tendency to align itself as it focuses on an illuminated target.

Map of Retina

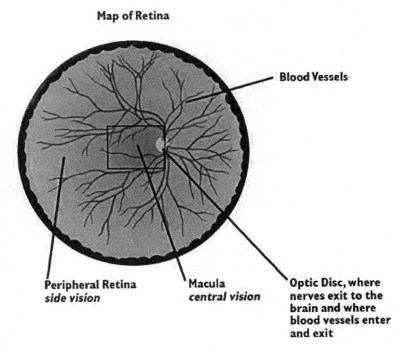

Blood Vessels

Peripheral Retina
side vision

Macula
central vision

Optic Disc, where
nerves exit to the
brain and where
blood vessels enter
and exit

Figure 1: schematic diagram of the retinal vascular pattern[12]

There is no known way to replicate a retina artificially, and it is thought that retinae **3–015** from a dead person would deteriorate too fast to be useful,[13] so no extra precautions are normally taken with retinal scans to ensure the user is a living human being.

The current market leader for retinal scanning products is Eyedentify Inc, which released the first commercial retinal scanning device (known as the Eyedentification 7.5 personal identification unit) in 1984.[14] Modern devices are small enough to be handheld and are claimed to be accurate at a distance of one metre from the user's eye.[15] The relative maturity of the technology combined with relative ease of use by a subject sitting at a computer may in time result in the more widespread use of retinal patterns as a form of electronic signature.

Iris scan

3–016   The other principal biometric method involving the eye is that of iris scanning. The iris is an internal organ, which sits behind the cornea and aqueous humour; it is visible externally as the coloured portion of the eye and consists of several layers and distinct features such as furrows, ridges, coronas, and rings.

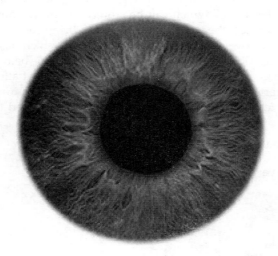

Figure 2: features of the iris[16]

The texture of the iris, which results in the patterns observed, arises from a complex fibrous structure known as the trabecular meshwork, which forms during the latter stages of gestation and all but finishes developing prior to birth. Its function is to drain the aqueous humour from the eye. It is understood that the pattern of every iris is measurably unique, even as between identical twins, and the patterns present in the iris do not change with age.[17] The trabecular meshwork is thought to deteriorate within minutes following death.[18]

The idea of using iris patterns for personal identification was first suggested by ophthalmologists in the 1960s.[19] By the 1980s the idea had received global exposure through its use in a James Bond film,[20] and in 1987 a means of iris scanning was developed and patented by ophthalmologists Flom and Safir.[21] These patents have now expired in Europe. However, in 1994 Daugman patented algorithms for iris recognition.[22] These patents[23] are the basis for the vast majority of current iris recognition systems and products.

3–017   Typically, an iris scanning system will require the user to place himself so that he can see his own eye's reflection in the device. A video camera will then capture an image of the iris. Parts of the image which do not provide meaningful data, such as the pupil, the eyelashes and so on, are masked out so as not to interfere with the encoding of the iris. Signal processing techniques (called Gabor filters) are then applied to this image to extract and encode data based on the fluctuations within the trabecular network. The user may be able to be scanned from up to two feet away or may need to be as close as a couple of inches, depending on the particular device. The user will only need to look into the device for a couple of moments.

Due to the high degree of distinctiveness and consistency over time of the trabecular network, iris scanning is an inherently accurate biometric method. It has been found to be unaffected by the user wearing spectacles or contact lenses. The iris enjoys practical advantages over other biometrics, including the ease and relative unobtrusiveness of registering its image at some distance from a subject without physical contact, its intrinsic polar geometry (which imparts a natural coordinate system and an origin of coordinates for digitisation) and the high level of randomness in its pattern. To solve the potential problem of an unscrupulous user attempting to fool a scanning device by holding up a photograph of a subject's iris, some iris scanning devices incorporate a light source and measure the resultant pupil dilation to ensure that what they are scanning is a real eye. Iris scanning systems are being introduced at airports[24] as a rapid and accurate means of identifying frequent passengers who have registered their iris scans, in an effort to streamline boarding procedures. As with retina scanning, this technology has the potential to become a frequently used method of creating an electronic signature.

Face recognition

Facial recognition is, of course, the primary means by which humans are able to identify one another, and thus photographs of faces appear on many documents relied upon to establish identity, such as passports and modern driving licenses. It is therefore perhaps surprising to learn that, whilst people are good at recognising their friends and colleagues, experiments have shown that they are in fact very poor at identifying strangers from their photographs.[25] As a result of this, automated systems have been developed to hand this task over to computers. A recent example of the use of this sort of technology this was a police operation carried out at the 2001 Superbowl XXXV, where the Tampa Police Department scanned the entire crowd using a new technology, called FaceIt, that allows snapshots of faces from the crowd to be compared to a database of criminal "mugshots". The system identified nineteen criminals using this method.

Automated facial recognition systems typically work by capturing an image of the subject's face, and then locating and matching features in a grid. Distances between eyes, nose, mouth, depth of eye sockets, and other facial elements can be measured, and this information could then be digitised into a form of electronic signature. There are many technical challenges facing such a system. The head must be within a certain number of degrees off axis from the "straight ahead" pose, and likewise may need to be a certain fixed distance from the device. There are also variables caused by facial expression, changing facial features such as facial hair and acne, and the inevitable effects of the ageing process.

Many facial recognition systems require the subject to blink or smile prior to image capture to ensure that the subject is in fact a human being and not a photograph or a mould. However, given the large number of variables and other technical challenges faced by the current technology it may be some years before this biometric method becomes refined enough to generate data which could be reliably used as an electronic signature.

One of the strongest positive aspects of facial recognition is that it is non-intrusive, and can be accomplished from a distance without requiring the subject to wait for a long period or do anything more than look at the camera. As such, it seems a suitable technology for the generation of electronic signatures. However, many people have expressed civil liberties concerns over the potential use of facial recognition cameras placed inconspicuously or surreptitiously, and this raises a concern as to whether a

3–018

person's facial recognition-based electronic signature could be captured from them without their consent or knowledge.

Fingerprints/Handprints

3–019   By far the most successful biometric products to date in terms of sales have been those based upon fingerprints. It is estimated that fingerprint recognition products account for over 70 per cent of the total sales of biometric technology.[26]

Fingerprints consist of the friction ridges and grooves that criss-cross a subject's fingers. These form a pattern of whorls, arches, loops, together with smaller features such as ridges and furrows.

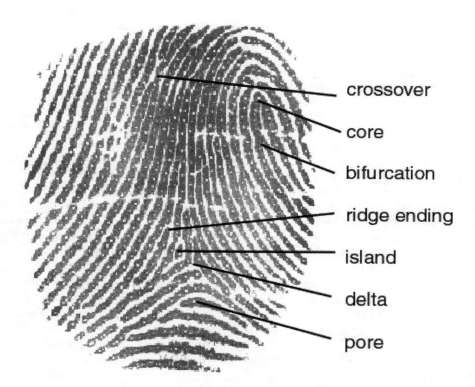

Figure 3: fingerprint patterns[27]

3–020   It is frequently said that no two fingerprints are alike. Whilst in recent years doubt has been placed on this assertion by reason of identification errors made by police experts, this has more to do with the often poor quality of prints taken from crime scenes rather than an inherent problem with using fingerprints as identifiers.

There are many historical references to the use of fingerprints as a means of personal identification, including use in a 7th century Chinese legal code as a method of identification as an alternative to a seal or signature. By the turn of the 20th Century their use had become incorporated into mainstream police practices in many jurisdictions.[28] In modern times, viable biometric systems using fingerprint technology are commonplace.

Biometric fingerprint identification systems typically involve the subject placing their finger on a small scanner. This scanner, which may take an optical, ultrasound, or other form of reading of the fingerprint geometry, is attached to a computer which takes information from the scan. The key features of the print, namely the points where the various fingerprint lines come together or change direction, together with a classification of the lines as ridges, loops, whorls and so on are reduced to a digitised form. Often no image of the fingerprint is actually created, only a set of data. Whilst the positioning and movement of the finger during the scan may affect the data output, modern systems have in-built filtering algorithms which by-and-large eliminate these effects. Obviously it helps if the finger being scanned is clean and undamaged!

Such devices are particularly suited to computer users who wish to add an electronic signature to a document created on screen. In such an environment, the fingers are likely to be free from contamination, and modern devices are so small that they can be integrated into a keyboard or a mouse. Some have been so incorporated into commercial products. For example, SecuGen Corporation have a range of computer peripherals on the market (including mice and keyboards) with fingerprint scanners built in to prevent use of the attached computer by unauthorised persons. [29] They are also very easy and convenient to use, and so their common use as a means of providing electronic signatures in the future looks promising.

Hand/finger geometry

The three-dimensional geometry of a subject's hand, based upon its size, shape, finger length/thickness and other details, provides sufficient individualised information that it can be used as a means of biometric identification. The parameters gleaned from the analysis of a subject's hand can then be digitised and used as the basis of an electronic signature.   **3–021**

Standard hand geometry biometric devices work by the subject placing their hand on a reflective surface, whereupon an image is captured using a charge coupled sensor together with an array of mirrors.

This generates three-dimensional information based on the hand's geometry. Guiding pegs are typically provided as shown to ensure that each subject places their hand in a consistent position. A method could feasibly be employed, if desired, to ensure that the subject is a living human being, though in practice commercial hand geometry devices have thus far omitted this, presumably for reasons of cost.

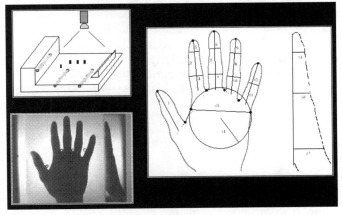

Figure 4: hand geometry measurement[30]

One major drawback of this method is that, whilst extremely diverse, the human hand is not unique. Thus, whilst hand geometry systems are employed where verification is needed,[31] it is questionable whether the data produced by a hand geometry device is suitable for use as an electronic signature. Another practical drawback is the larger size and higher cost of the device when compared with fingerprint recognition or iris scanning devices. The data may also be affected if the hand is injured or swollen, or if jewellery is worn. On the other hand, the ease of use of the system and the small amount of data required from a hand geometry scan in order to identify a user make it well suited to use with smart cards. Note that this methodology is different from vein pattern recognition, which is discussed later in this chapter.

Handwritten signature dynamics

3–022   The visual forms of handwritten signatures are without question the most commonly used form of identification, and have been so for thousands of years. Today, every credit and bank card in circulation sports a signature, and it is the principal means by which written contracts are executed. Although a forger can replicate the visual appearance of a signature, everyone has a unique way of signing a document, and the challenge for biometric systems is to capture both what is written and the way it is written. In this sense, handwritten signature capture differs from the other biometric identifiers listed above in that it is not a physiological method of subject identification, but rather a behavioural one.

The normal method of capturing biometric signature data from a subject is by means of a signature tablet—a flat surface comprising a sensor upon which the subjects "writes" their signature using a pen-like input device. These devices go beyond the simple "light pen" method described above,[32] in that as well as recording the shape of the signature, the device captures the velocity of the hand of the writer, the points where the pen was lifted off the paper, the pressure applied by the writer and other dynamics. By doing this, such devices make the biometric much harder to forge—now the forger must not only reproduce an exact likeness off his or her victim's signature, but must do so in the same *way*. It is unlikely that this will often be possible.

Products are now on the market which claim to be fraud proof and yet are able to recognise the correct subject's signature every time.[33] If these products live up to their marketing promises, then the prospects for using handwritten signature dynamics as electronic signatures look good. One key advantage is that signing a signature at the bottom of a document is a familiar and comfortable method. The method is also non-intrusive, in contrast with the eye-based methods, and thus may prove a more popular biometric amongst the public in the long run. Furthermore, unlike a password or PIN, a signature cannot be forgotten, though variability of signature due to environmental factors such as cold, and physiological factors such as age, will have to be accounted for by the signature capturing software.

Voice

3–023   Voice biometrics make use of the distinctive qualities of a person's voice, some of which are behaviourally determined and others of which are physiologically determined. Voice biometric products analyse the waveform dynamics of a short utterance by the subject which result from such features as the length of the vocal tract and the shape of the mouth and nasal cavities, together with regional accents and affectations. The sound signal is then digitised to create the data for the electronic signature.

Voice biometric capture devices are easy to use, and subjects generally feel more comfortable with speaking into a microphone than with looking into a beam of light to have their retina scanned. To prevent the use of a voice recording to fool the device, most devices require the high and low frequencies of the sound to match, which is difficult for many recording instruments to recreate well. Whether such devices could be fooled by a sufficiently practised impressionist is something of a moot point, though even an accomplished impressionist may not be able to recreate the precise dynamics of certain speakers. Conversely, the subject may be suffering from physiological problems such as a cold or laryngitis, which may result in the signature created by the biometric device being different from their usual one. Also, a person's voice changes over time, which may limit the usefulness of this technology for the purposes of electronic signature creation.

Vein patterns

A relatively recent addition to the list of biometric methodologies is the analysis of vein patterns as a means of identification. The width, location and distribution of veins are believed to be unique to an individual. Devices using vein pattern biometrics are typically hand-based, and require the subject to lay their hand on a curved reader that takes an infrared scan and digitises this information.   **3–024**

As such devices are only just coming on to the market, it is somewhat difficult to assess whether this technology would be well suited to the creation of electronic signatures. Obvious advantages include the difficulty for would-be forgers of emulating another person's vein patterns, and the fact that, as the scan operates in the infrared, external injuries would not affect the signature generated. However, it is uncertain at present what effect factors such as ageing and vascular medical problems would have. Also, current devices are rather large compared to their more established counterparts in other biometric fields. However, as the technology progresses the use of vein patterns for electronic signature generation may increase.

Other proposed forms of biometrics

A variety of other biometric methodologies have been proposed, although many of these have not yet advanced to the stage of commercial availability. These include: **3–025**

Ear lobes
The structure and shape of the external part of the ear (the "pinna") has been proposed as a biometric identifier.[34] However, ears can be totally or partially covered by hair or earrings so that measuring them for use as a biometric may be more intrusive than many of the other techniques discussed above. Identification is done by measuring the vector distances between points on the lobe. Thus far, no commercial systems using this methodology have been put onto the market.   **3–026**

Facial thermograms
Here, an infrared camera is used to capture an image of the face. The camera detects the heat patterns created by the branching of the blood vessels in the subject's face. An advantage of this technique is that the image can not be altered by plastic surgery and will   **3–027**

not change with time as the outer features of the face will do. The image can however be affected by room temperature and atmospheric change.

Keystroke dynamics

3–028   This is a method of recording not just a password, but the way that the user types the password in on a keyboard/keypad. The rhythm and keystroke times of an individual will be affected by various factors, including finger length and hand position. Net Nanny Software Inc has developed and patented a method for identifying and authenticating passwords typed on a normal computer keyboard which is incorporated in their programme "BioPassword". The user provides a series of typing samples to train the software to recognise their unique typing rhythm.

DNA typing/matching

3–029   This involves the matching of DNA samples to identify an individual by their unique genetic code or selected parts of it. A saliva sample or mouth swab is used to capture the cells necessary to perform the analysis. The process of testing currently takes a matter of days or weeks; even with the intensive research on-going in genetics, results are unlikely to be available in real-time for some years. There are also issues involving privacy, since the data collected by this method not only identifies an individual but may also reveal personal and health information. Further, identical twins are genetically identical. This technology is therefore unlikely ever to be used for generating electronic signatures.

Odour recognition

3–030   This biometrics method records the mixture of volatile chemicals which makes up each person's odour. A company in the United Kingdom, Mastiff Electronic Systems Ltd, is currently in the process of developing a product called "Scentinel", which digitally sniffs the back of a user's hand in order to verify their identity.

Palm print identification

3–031   This method uses the lines on the palm of the user's hand to verify his or her identity, in a very similar way to fingerprints. The advantages and disadvantages for such a methodology are broadly the same as those for fingerprint biometrics. NEC has developed and currently sells a range of palm identification tools under the name Automated Palmprint Identification System.

Body salt identification

3–032   There have been reports that the natural salinity level of the human body which gives it its conductivity may be used as a biometric. IBM and Massachusetts Institute of Technology (MIT) are developing a Personal Area Network (PAN) product which uses this technology. PAN is envisioned to be applied in various ways, including the passing of electronic business cards via a simple handshake and to automate and secure consumer business transactions. However, given that the level of salinity of human bodies must stay within a relatively narrow range in order for the body's metabolic processes to function correctly, it is unclear how unique the data generated by such a methodology will be.

Conclusions on biometrics

3–033   Most of the technologies above are, at least in theory, capable of producing electronic data which is uniquely linked to the signatory, which is capable of identifying the signatory, and which is created using means that the signatory can maintain under his sole control, as required for an advanced electronic signature in accordance with the Electronic Signatures Directive. Therefore, all have the potential to be used for the generation of advanced electronic signatures. However, clearly some biometric methodologies are far better suited to the task of generating an electronic signature than others. In applications designed for use by a large proportion of the public, the usage of biometrics may be limited by:

- Rejection due to personal reasons
- Cultural incompatibility
- Absence of the respective biometric
- Insufficiently unique characteristics of the respective biometric feature
- Abnormal characteristics of the respective biometric feature.[35]

The first two obstacles listed above can be reduced over time through education and through familiarity with the technology, but there will always be some users who, for whatever reason, do not wish to use biometrics. However, for the vast majority of business transactions, biometric methodologies provide a quick, relatively cheap, and easy to use means of generating an electronic signature such that (provided the data is secure, and a method of verification is available) the recipient can be confident that the document was indeed executed by the named signatory. The major problem with using biometric data as a signature in itself is how and where to store the subject's "signature" securely to enable verification. The fact that the data contains a subject's personal characteristics is naturally a cause for concern, and storing the data in a centralized database simply creates an obvious target for attack and compromise.[36]

The preferred solution is likely to be some combination of biometric systems with digital signatures. Handwritten signature dynamics, fingerprint recognition, and those methodologies based on the iris or retina look likely to be widely used for signature generation in the future, as they are easy and convenient to use, provide a high level of security due to the individuality of the characteristics, and would be easy to integrate alongside a traditional computer workstation.   **3–034**

There has been considerable work in recent years to create industry standards for biometrics and related activities.[37] Such standards should ensure consistency of approach in competing products. A standard file exchange format called CBEFF (Common Biometric Exchange File Format) has been developed to promote interoperability between different biometric platforms, and a growing number of manufacturers are developing products which comply with the Biometric Application Programming Interface, another standard developed to homogenize the interface between biometric technology modules and applications.

Encryption

Digital signatures are widely, if not universally, seen as the most effective and workable means of establishing the level of trust required between parties to business transactions. They are produced using asymmetric or "public key" cryptography. However, this is not the only kind of cryptography which may be able to be used to produce secure signatures.   **3–035**

The following section introduces the basics of cryptography before going on to discuss how digital signatures work and some of the issues surrounding their use.

The terms for basic cryptography

3–036   "Cryptography" means hidden writing: it is the art of writing messages in such ways that they cannot be read by third parties. The process of transforming a readable "plaintext'" message into an unreadable form or "cipher" is encryption. The converse, cryptanalysis, is the art of recovering the hidden meanings; the process of doing so in any given instance is decryption. (For the sake of completeness only, the correct word for the whole subject of ciphers in both directions is "cryptology"; however, in most cases where this sense is required "cryptography" is used.)

It should be remembered that cryptography is not the only means of securing the confidentiality of data or messages. Steganography involves hiding not just the contents of the message, but the fact that there is a message at all. For example, data (either plaintext or cipher) may be transmitted by changing a few pixels in a picture (still or video), such that any interceptor has no way of knowing that the data is present. To date, there have not been any specific attempts to regulate the use of steganography.

Methods

3–037   Cryptography is an art going back thousands of years; by now there are hundreds of different codes and enciphering techniques known. Caesar's code, invented by Julius Caesar, involved shifting each letter in a message three places to left or right in the alphabet. The resulting string of letters had no meaning on its face but could easily be transformed back into plaintext by a receiver knowing how the code worked. Once this method became widely known, more complex variants were developed.[38] However, the methods of cryptanalysis, such as frequency analysis of the appearances of given letters in any given language, are also well known. These methods—crucially—tend to be painstaking but mechanical, making them ideally suited for the patient idiocy of computers. Thus, the subtlest encryption techniques developed before the advent of computers, the cracking of which required all the skill and patience of a human problem-solver over many weeks, can now be done by an average PC in a matter of hours.

The only completely secure, logically uncrackable encryption method is one which has been around since long before the invention of the computer: the one-time pad. The method is extremely simple: sender and receiver both have a pad which tells them, for each letter of the message, how to transpose it to form the cipher. The letters on the pad are generated randomly. There is no pattern in the way individual letters of the alphabet appear in the cipher text, so no means of frequency analysis is going to assist the cryptanalyst in trying to decipher it. The name gives a clue as to why it is not in universal use. To be completely secure, a one-time pad can be used only once, after which another one-time pad will be needed. This method is therefore ideal for use between two people who will need to send one, vital secret message or exchange between themselves. It is of no use in repeated transactions, or with more than one person: each sender/ receiver pair has to have a unique one-time pad for each message.

3–038   The two common forms of cryptography in widespread use are *private key encryption* and *public key encryption*, otherwise known as *symmetric* and *asymmetric* encryption respectively. In both of these, a complex series of rules, or algorithm, is applied to the plaintext to produce the cipher. In each case, the algorithm calculates the transposition of each letter of the plaintext based upon a number which is called the key. A strong cryptographic algorithm should be able to be made public itself without enabling anyone to read the encrypted messages. The only way to decipher particular encrypted messages is by using the cryptographic key.

In *private key encryption*,[39] both parties use the same key to encrypt and to decrypt messages — the system is symmetric from either side. The disadvantages of this are that it is necessary for both sides to know and agree the key in advance, and to keep it completely secret thereafter. Thus, there is a need for a key exchange mechanism before the encrypted transmissions can start. Interception of the key at this stage would mean that all subsequent encrypted messages could be read. Further, even once the key has been safely exchanged there are two possible attack points for any third party trying to obtain the key. The risk of loss of key secrecy can be reduced by using the key only for one exchange of messages, or "session" but the obvious disadvantage of using this approach is the need constantly to generate new keys even for communications between the same two parties. Once more than two parties are involved, the number of keys required escalates rapidly.

Public key encryption[40] is considerably more secure since it does away with both weaknesses of private key systems. In public key systems, each party has two keys: a public key, which can be published to the world at large without the security of the method being compromised, and a private key, which must be kept to the keyholder alone at all costs. The system is therefore asymmetric. There is no need for one party to any exchange to know the other's private key in order to exchange confidential messages. The trick is that a message can be encrypted using one key and can then only be decrypted using the other. Encrypting is easy, but decrypting without the appropriate key is extremely difficult since public key algorithms are based upon tasks known to be mathematically "hard" such as factoring large numbers into their prime factors (as in the RSA algorithm) or taking discrete logarithms over a finite field (as in the Diffie-Hellman algorithm).

The keys themselves are generated using a combination of very large prime numbers **3–039** (chosen at random) and random numbers. Truly random numbers are indispensable for secure cryptographic systems, but are harder to generate than might be imagined. A poor random number generator used for this purpose may allow an attacker to optimize an exhaustive key-search attack by trying the most probable keys first. If so, the time needed to find the correct key may be orders of magnitude shorter than the predicted time based on analysis of the algorithm itself. A number of special hardware random-number generators have been developed based on various physical phenomena, such as thermal "noise" from a semiconductor diode, the instability of a free-running oscillator, or radioactive decay. In purely software systems, much simpler sources of randomness must be used. These include measuring the time between successive keystrokes, or mixing unpredictable multi-user system characteristics.

Encryption methods are always illustrated using as examples Alice and Bob, who want or need to communicate securely. In a public key cryptographic system, for Alice to send a message to Bob, she can encrypt it using Bob's public key. Bob can decrypt it using his secret private key. No one else in the world can read the message unless they have access to Bob's private key. Similarly, Bob can send a message to Alice encrypted using Alice's public key. Only Alice, or someone who has obtained her private key from her, can read the message. The system works because of the mathematical properties of the two keys;

they are complementary, so can be used to decrypt what the other has encrypted, yet the private key cannot be deduced from the public key.

Note that in the example above, Alice uses *Bob's public* key to encrypt the message, because the encryption is being performed to keep the information she is sending him secret. Digital signatures are not a method for keeping information secret, although they use the same technology.

Digital signatures: what they are/ how they work

3–040   A digital signature is a string of data which is produced using the signer's *private* key. In signing a message to Bob, Alice would use her own private key to produce the signature. She does this for a given document by using her private key to encrypt data known as the "message digest". A message digest is like the fingerprint of the message. It is calculated from the message text treating the message as a single long string of data—at the binary level, a single number. Taking that number, the computer uses a *message digest* or *hash function* to calculate a shorter string, analogous to a fingerprint of the original, which nevertheless still represents the entire data string. The message digest function must be such that no two messages will produce the same short data string, and that it would not be feasible to calculate a message to match a given hash value. A number of message digest functions have been developed which meet these criteria.[41]

The message digest is dependent upon what message Alice is sending Bob, so it is different every time. The digital signature is the message digest encrypted using Alice's private key. As a result, the digital signature has two characteristics reassuringly similar to those of a handwritten signature: it is unique to the subscriber, because it is computed using her private key, and it is different every time, because it depends upon the message. The same document signed using another private key, say Bob's, would produce a different signature.

Note that as the signature is computed using the private key, the signature can be decrypted using Alice's public key. It is not confidential. The message itself may or may not be confidential either: encrypting a message, and digitally signing one, are two entirely separate functions.

3–041   This complexity gives a digital signature some unique qualities. It cannot be copied, since a digital signature cut-and-pasted into another message will be incorrect: it will not be the number which would be produced by the alleged signatory digitally signing that second message. The recipient can check this. If Alice sends Bob a message digitally signed, Bob can decrypt the signature using the Alice's public key. He will then have a data string which is the message digest of the message Alice signed. Bob needs to know what message digest function Alice used, so he can calculate the message digest for the message on record and compare the two versions. If they match, then Bob knows for sure that the message was signed with Alice's private key and that the message has not been changed in transit.

If the two message digests are *not* then same, the Bob knows something is wrong. Either:

- the message does not in fact originate from Alice, but has been signed with someone else's private key; or

- a message was sent by Alice but the message has been changed in transit.

There is no way to tell which of these has happened, except possibly to telephone Alice.

Advantages of digital signatures

Consequently, a digital signature has a second function which is different from any function of a handwritten signature. It can be used to check the integrity of data, either transmitted or stored. For instance, an archivist may sign the data on putting it into storage. If the data is tampered with while in storage, then the new version of the data will have a different message digest. When the data is retrieved, the original digital signature can be decrypted using the archivist's public key, and the original message digest compared with the current message digest. If the two match, the message/data has not been altered. If it does not match, there has been tampering — although it will not be possible to tell what kind.

As discussed in Chapter 2, a handwritten signature on paper does not give any effective guarantee of the integrity of the document contents. This function of a digital signature is therefore closer to the function of a wax seal used to ensure the integrity of a paper document. The document was written, and then folded up and sealed before being put in a safe place. If, when the document was retrieved, the seal was found to be broken, the finder knew not to trust the contents of the document. The analogy is not exact, because careful scrutiny of a paper document might enable the finder to work out what changes had been made. There may be no way for the finder of an electronic document to find out what changes have been made; but at least they will know that the document is not to be trusted.

3–042

Of course, if the seal was not broken, the document might nonetheless have been altered by someone who had access to a method of resealing it. Similarly, if someone manages to steal the archivist's private key then they could alter the electronic records and undetectably re-sign them. No system is foolproof.

An additional possible function of digital signatures, which has no equivalent in signing technologies in the paper-based environment, is to establish the time of creation of a message or document. If a time-stamp is included in the text, so that it forms part of the message, this will also be unalterable without changing the message digest.

Limitations of digital signatures

The principal limitation on digital signatures is that the signature is not uniquely linked to Alice as such; it is only linked to Alice's private key. It can be seen that key security is paramount in public key encryption systems. If Alice leaves her private key on a floppy disk in her desk drawer, or on a file on her hard disk named "key", then anyone who finds it can digitally sign documents as coming from Alice and the digital signature will be identical to the signature Alice would have produced, in all respects. Accordingly, biometric systems are now being proposed as a secure mechanism to restrict access to private keys. If Alice's retina scan is necessary to unlock the file named "key", Bob can be fairly confident that any message digitally signed by Alice's private key really is from Alice. Smart card systems are now being implemented, for example under the European Union's FASME[42] project, whereby the smart card holds the private key but a fingerprint scan, integrated into the card itself, is necessary to access it.

3–043

The seemingly ideal solution of digital signatures suffers from drawbacks when considered in the commercial context. One problem arises from a lack of technical standardisation, so that the many cryptographic products already in circulation are not necessarily interoperable. Unless Bob's signature verification device can read Alice's digital signature, no communication is possible. A further issue is the question of how

Bob knows that the public key he has in fact corresponds to the private key held by the real-world person he knows as Alice. As in private key or symmetric encryption systems, there still needs to be a trust mechanism but in this case it is associated with identifying the holder of a particular key, not communicating the key. Solutions to this problem are discussed in Chapter 4.

There are a number of initiatives at the time of writing aiming to standardise many aspects of public key infrastructure.[43]

Choice of key length

3–044   The security of any encryption system depends upon the key length used. The "key" is in fact just a binary number. Any encryption problem can therefore be attacked by trying to guess the key, known as the "brute force" attack. A key one "bit" of information long must be either 0 or 1, so at most it can take two attempts to get it right. It will take a fast PC quite a number of hours to run through all of the possibilities for a 40 bit key, but is not impossible. The DES (Data Encryption Standard) private key system is generally used with a 56 bit key—enough to tie up a serious amount of computing power for a while but not beyond the reach of any reasonably sized business or very determined hacker. "Triple DES", where the encrypted message is itself encrypted and the resulting cryptogram encrypted again, is now being used—slowing analysis down very substantially. Pragmatically, it should be remembered that in reality there are very few problems which warrant the dedication of unlimited time and resources to solve.

The minimum length of the primes used to calculate keys in today's RSA implementations is 256 bits, which corresponds to numbers in the range 10^{75}.[44] Due to the progress in factorization algorithms used to break RSA, it is currently recommended to use 384, 512, or even 1024-bit primes. Seriously paranoid users, however, and even encryption service providers, now opt for 2,056 bit keys: a length such that it will take the combined current computing power of the world several thousand years of continuous searching to guess the right key. These are considered to be effectively unbreakable for the moment. But the advent of developments in semiconductor technology, such as the change over from existing processors to vector processing or Dynamic Associative Access Memory, may bring further strides forward in the ability of computers to perform the enormous number of calculations needed to test every possible key.[45] In computing, it has so far proved relatively accurate to assume that what technology can do, the next generation of technology will always be able to undo.[46]

Functional equivalence between electronic and handwritten signatures

3–045   None of the electronic signature technologies discussed above display identical qualities to handwritten signatures, which affects their ability to perform the functions for which handwritten signatures are used. By way of reminder, these include: identifying the author or sender of a document; authenticating the statements made in the document, in the sense of confirming that they reflect the facts correctly; making manifest a declaration of will or intention to be legally bound; representing, whether explicitly or implicitly, that the signatory was authorised to perform any legal act concerned; safeguarding against undue haste or thoughtlessness; confirming the signatory has notice of the contents of the document; and acknowledging or marking a particular document as the original.

Handwritten signatures (or marks legally treated as equivalent) are suitable for all of these functions since they are easy to use, durable (to the same extent as the document signed), directly discernible and individual, in the sense that they are inherently linked to a particular person. Their legal significance is also very familiar so that the act of signing is generally understood to be important.

The world of electronic communications is different in that hardly any users have any real grasp of what happens when they press a key on a computer keyboard, and most have none at all of the particular software they rely upon to process a personal identification number (PIN) or other signature mechanism. Electronic documents can be durable but different precautions to be applied to ensure their preservation than those familiar for paper-based documents. In particular, software and the hardware upon which it runs become obsolete within a few years of their initial release, so that even though a floppy or optical disc may endure for decades, the information stored on it may be inaccessible in practice after no more than 5-10 years. This is significant since an electronic signature is not directly discernible, needing the mediation of hardware and software to be revealed. This also reduces the extent to which it is possible to be confident about what is actually stored, since the retrieval and translation onto screen could be subject to the intervention and distortion of a malicious third party. Finally, electronic signatures other than those based upon unique biometric characteristics are not individual, in that they are linked not to a person but to a code, cryptographic key or other item of information.

3–046

Identification

Very "low tech" mechanisms such as a typed name or scanned bitmap signature can identify the signatory, but are subject to a high risk of forgery. Biometrics are singularly appropriate to perform the function of identification since they are uniquely linked to an individual and impossible to forge, provided that some mechanism is available for storing biometric data (templates) securely to enable them to be checked without making them vulnerable to being stolen.

Digital signatures, on the other hand, are by themselves singularly inappropriate for identifying a signatory; they can only identify a particular key. Some other mechanism is required to establish who is wielding that key.

3–047

Authenticating statements made

This function of a signature relates not so much to the signature mechanism as the context in which the signature is applied. A signature is functioning here as a gesture of confirmation, so that any gesture could suffice provided that the recipient could be confident that it was made with this intention. Websites commonly achieve this by requiring the browser to click a button marked "I accept", having been warned that by doing so they are accepting given terms and conditions. The button click is an active gesture of acceptance, and likely to be enforceable in most jurisdictions as a signature for this functional purpose. It does not, of course, by itself communicate who it is that accepts. For this, a biometric appears to be the only effective mechanism to date.

3–048

Making manifest a declaration of will or intention to be legally bound/ Making a representation of authorisation/ Confirming the signatory has notice of the contents

These functions, like that of authenticating, are a gesture of acceptance, approval or affirmation and accordingly can be achieved by any form of electronic signature discussed in this chapter, provided that the context makes clear that the gesture indicates the intention. Once again, the issue of who it is who will be bound or makes the representation is not communicated.

3–049

Ceremony: safeguarding against undue haste or thoughtlessness

3–050   Most electronic signature techniques lack the formality inherent in wielding pen over paper so may not be suitable to the ceremonial or reflective function of a handwritten signature. This may be different if biometric access means are used, since these require some positive gesture on the part of the signatory—looking into the retina scanner, positioning the hand or finger in the correct way on a geometry or print scanner—which is eminently suitable to remind them of the significance of the signature to be produced.

Marking a version as the original

3–051   Affixation of any form of electronic signature can be used to denote a particular version as the original with as much assurance as would be provided by affixing a handwritten signature. In the "low tech" and biometric cases, however, the mark will only be reliable if the "original" is then removed from network access and kept in physical safety, exactly as is the case with a paper-based original document.

Digital signatures have their major advantage in respect of this function, and it is this which has given them their widespread dominance among systems in actual use. A digital signature can guarantee the integrity of a document, and this can be used to denote the status of a particular copy as an authentic copy of the "original" without the need to resort to physical safe-keeping. There are of course issues around what exactly is meant by an original of an electronic document, since the version sent to a counterparty bearing an electronic signature is only a copy, possibly reassembled from more than one piece, of the document created by the signatory's computer in the act of signing, as likewise will be the version stored on the signatory's own hard drive. However, this concern is in practice irrelevant if the technology of signing incorporates a guarantee of the integrity of every copy.

Non-repudiation

3–052   It is widely believed that a digital signature reduces the freedom of the signatory to repudiate an electronic signature on any grounds other than those equally available in respect of handwritten signatures, namely mistake, duress and the like. However, this is not the case because of the digital signature's inability to identify the signatory. A digital signature proves only what key was used to sign. This gap between signature and signatory leads to a need for legal assignment of responsibility for the consequences of signature, which is addressed in the UNCITRAL Model Law on Electronic Signatures.[47] A biometric, on the other hand, may provide genuine non-repudiability.

As this review shows, digital signatures have no particular advantage over other forms of electronic signature in respect of many of the functions for which a handwritten signature is used, and in particular are significantly flawed when it comes to the function of identifying the signatory with confidence. In order to produce an electronic signature which can perform all of the functions of a handwritten signature, a combination of biometric and digital signature technology is required.

---

1.   Art. 2(1).
2.   Ch. 2, para. 2–003

3. Electronic Signatures Directive, Art. 2(2).
4. See Ch. 5, para, 5–013 below.
5. "Now the PIN is mightier than the pen" BBC News website, May 19, 2003: *http://news.bbc.co.uk/1/hi/ technology/3039619.stm.*
6. See para. 3–022 below.
7. This technique is known as steganography.
8. For a full discussion of actual and proposed applications of biometric technology, the reader is referred to "Biometric—Advanced Identity Verification", Julian Ashbourn (2000), Ch. 2. Publisher: Springer-Verlag London Ltd.
9. "A New Scientific Method of Identification" Simon and Goldstein (1935), New York State Journal of Medicine, vol. 35(18) pp. 901–6.
10. "Biometric—Advanced Identity Verification", Julian Ashbourn (2000), p. 55.
11. For example, see the aspheric lens array device produced by Retinal Technologies LLC at *www.retinaltech.com/technology.html.*
12. Image courtesy of *http://www.vitreo-retinal.com.*
13. National Centre for State Courts Biometric Website *http://ctl.ncsc.dni.us/biomet[2]0web/BMIndex.html.*
14. National Centre for State Courts Biometric Website.
15. For example, the aspheric lens array device produced by Retinal Technologies LLC.
16. Image courtesy of EyeTicket Corp.
17. "Biometric—Advanced Identity Verification", Julian Ashbourn (2000), p. 52, Springer-Verlag London Ltd.
18. "Who Are You Really", T Sigmon, *Virginia.edu*, Vol. III, no. 1, Spring 1999.
19. For example, F.H. Alder, "Physiology of the Eye", Clinical Application, fourth ed. London (1965).
20. *Never Say Never Again*, 1983; the villain uses a scan of the President's right eye to foil a passkey system.
21. L. Flom and A Safir, "Iris Recognition System", US Patent 4,641,349 1987.
22. J. Daugman, "Biometric Personal Identification System Based on Iris Analysis", US Patent 5,291,560, 1994. See also Daugman's article "High Confidence Visual Recognition of Persons by a Test of Statistical Independence", *IEEE Transactions on Pattern Analysis and Machine Intelligence*, Vol. 15, No. 11, November 1993.
23. Now owned by Iridian Technologies Inc.
24. For example, Schipol airport in Amsterdam.
25. Kemp, Towell, Pike, "When Seeing Should Not Be Believing: Photographs, Credit Cards and Fraud", *Applied Cognitive Psychology*, v.11, no.3, (1997), p. 211-222.
26. R. Anderson, "Security Engineering", (2001) John Wiley & Sons, Inc. p. 265.
27. Image courtesy of *www.finger-scan.com.*
28. R. Anderson, "Security Engineering", (2001) John Wiley & Sons, Inc, p. 266, Publisher: John Wiley & Sons, Inc.
29. see *www.secugen.com.*
30. Image courtesy of *http://bias.csr.unibo.it.*
31. "Biometric—Advanced Identity Verification", Julian Ashbourn (2000), p. 51, Springer-Verlag, London Ltd.
32. Para. 3–008.
33. See, for example, Cyber-SIGN Inc's range of products at *www.cybersign.com.*
34. See, for example, "Biometric Security Solutions" J. Vacca, *www.informIT.com*, October 25, 2002.
35. "Use of Biometrics for User Verification in Electronic Signature Smartcards", B Sturif 2000. In Smart Card Programming and Security—Proceedings of the International Conference on Research in Smart Cards (E-smart) (Cannes, France, September 2001), pp. 220-228.
36. "A Practical Guide to Biometric Security Technology", S Liu and M Silverman. IEEE Computer Society, IT Pro-Security, Jan-Feb 2001, *http://www.computer.org/itpro/homepage/Jan_Feb/security3.htm.*
37. For detailed information on Biometrics Standards activities, see the Biometrics Consortium's Standards website: *http://www.biometrics.org/html/standards.html.*
38. A thorough discussion of the evolution of cryptography is given in David Kahn's book *The Codebreakers* (Simon & Schuster, 1996 revised edition).
39. For example, using the Data Encryption Standard (DES) of the United States, the International Data Encryption Algorithm (IDEA) from Switzerland, algorithms RC4 and RC5, and so on.
40. The best known public key algorithm is the RSA (Rivest, Shamir, Adelman) now licensed by RSA Data Security in the United States. The widely used PGP (Pretty Good Privacy) encryption software, developed and released onto the Internet by Phil Zimmerman, uses the RSA algorithm.
41. Examples would be MD5, RIPEM 160 or the Secure Hash Standard.
42. Facilitating Administrative Services Access for Mobile Europeans, a project concluded in 2001 which aimed at enabling EU citizens resident in countries other than their home country to access local services more readily.
43. See Ch. 10.
44. That is, a 1 followed by 75 zeros.
45. "A Perfect Match", David Kestenbaum, *New Scientist* April 18, 1998, p. 36.
46. The development of quantum cryptography, which is allegedly logically unbreakable provided that the current understanding of quantum mechanics is correct, may change this.
47. See Ch. 5 below.

4

Structural issues

Introduction

4–001.01 Before looking at how legislators have addressed electronic signatures, it is necessary to understand how PKI is made up and the basic relationships within it. This will provide the context for many of the proposals made both at international and national level, discussed in Chapter 5 and 6 respectively.

Establishing identity in cross-border transactions

4–001.02 A paper-based signature on a document requires no apparent infrastructure beyond the provision of paper, pen and ink. However, where the parties have no pre-existing relationship and the transaction is material, a mechanism is required to establish each party's identity to the satisfaction of the other. In a paper-based transaction in such circumstances, this could be managed by, for example, having the signatures of each party notarised. Each party would in principle be able to rely on the fact that the signature it received was the genuine signature of the other party because an independent third party, the notary, had checked the identity of the signatory against identifying documents such as a passport and had verified the signature against the specimen given in that document. The notary could also be required to establish the signatory's authority to sign.

This mechanism is not infallible: for example, the notary may be bribed, or the passport may be forged and the notary not detect the forgery. But it is considered to be sufficient evidence of authenticity for most transactions. Every jurisdiction has its own system for accrediting and regulating the activities of notaries, which is generally little known to anyone outside the notarial profession. Notaries are nevertheless trusted because it is known that they are regulated in the performance of their duties. In effect, they are trusted not only for their own integrity and effectiveness, but also because the system, ultimately the state, is trusted to make sure that they are reliable.

4–002 Where the document is to be relied upon outside the notary's jurisdiction, the affixation of an apostille under the Hague Convention may also be necessary. An apostille involves the notary's seal and signature being certified by the national government or equivalent authority. If the jurisdictions concerned are not parties to the Hague Convention then legalisation by the overseas jurisdiction's consulate in the notary's jurisdiction, is necessary. However, both these mechanisms are solely concerned to verify the notary's status. Neither involves any additional verification of identity or of signature of the party over and above that performed by the notary.

Electronic signatures can only come into existence in the context of a considerably more elaborate technological environment: at the minimum, a computer. Where the document to be signed is one to which more than one entity is a party, means for sending and receiving electronic data messages are also necessary. The context to which most of the law and regulation discussed in this book relates is that of open systems such as the Internet. In this context the communications infrastructure is complex, involving a worldwide network of computers linked by a physical communications infrastructure of undersea cables, satellite links and so on as well as by the communications protocols which enable data messages to be correctly addressed, routed and delivered.

For electronic signatures to be used over such a network between parties with no or a limited pre-existing relationship some mechanism is required to establish the link between the signature creation or verification data—be they biometric, cryptographic or otherwise—and the signatory. As in the paper-based environment, this is not difficult on a small scale. Within a community of any kind, such as a university, village or company, the pool of possible correspondents is either known or easily ascertained. If someone receives an e-mail purporting to be from Jan in accounts, it is simple to check that the accounts department does employ a person called Jan. There is unlikely to be any reason to disbelieve her assertion that particular verification data—say, a public key—are hers. Alternatively, if an e-mail comes from the finance manager enclosing a public key which he certifies to be Jan's, likewise there is unlikely to be reason not to accept this. Up to a certain scale, informal mechanisms such as this are entirely adequate. **4–003**

The model does not scale well, however. Above a certain size, any organisation will employ more than one Jan, and there will come a point at which the layers of management are too complex for the recipient of an e-mail to be confident that a sender purporting to be a finance manager actually is.

Web of trust

One option is to create a "web of trust". This involves individuals digitally signing each other's certificates of identity to confirm who holds the certified keys. A stranger could then examine the certificate and, if they know and trust any of the signatories, can choose to trust that the keys are actually associated with the person named as the certificate holder.[1] This system is broadly equivalent to the real world dealings that businesses have with regular customers and indeed acquaintances have with each other. However, it takes a lot of exchanges of information before any sufficient quantity of trust has spread through a given community (customers, suppliers, service providers) to enable everyday commercial transactions. **4–004**

Public key infrastructure

A form of notarial model is therefore being transposed into the electronic environment. The model is not exact, and indeed a number of variations are being developed. The commonest form consists of a hierarchy of certification authorities. Consider the example of a large organisation. At the local level, there needs to be a certification authority which is able to verify Jan's identity and certify that she owns a particular public key. This function might be performed by the head of the accounts group, who knows Jan **4–005** personally. The head of accounts issues and signs a certificate to this effect. However, the identity and trustworthiness of this certification authority must also be certified, perhaps by the Finance Director or head of Human Resources, who would issue a certificate confirming that the public key attached is that of the head of the accounts group. This certificate is signed by the Finance Director, who will be more widely known in the organisation. Ultimately, a "root" authority must certify the correspondence between the Finance Director and his or her public key. This might be the Chairman of the Board of Directors, whose word is taken to be universally trusted. The result is a chain of certificates confirming incontestably that a particular public key corresponds to Jan. The length of the chain depends upon the size and structure of the organisation.

This structure also provides a solution to the problem of lack of uniqueness of names. The head of accounts may well only be certifying one Jan, even if there are a dozen in the organisation. Jan becomes reliably identifiable as "Jan (accounts)". If the organisation is international, she may be "Jan (accounts)(Canada)". Of course, if there are several Jans in one group, a further solution is needed which might be "Jan Jones (accounts)(Canada)" or ultimately "Jan Jones1 (accounts)(Canada)". But there is no issue of confusion provided that Jan is given a unique identifier by her local certification authority, since she will always be identified by reference to that group.

The hierarchy of certification authorities is known as a *public key infrastructure* or *PKI*. A PKI can function at an organisational level, a national level or an international level. Outside the organisational context however, the issue of appropriate root authorities is more complex. The issue is how to ensure that certification service providers are in fact trustworthy.

4–006   Within the banking community, Identrus has been set up as an certification service provider whose trustworthiness is assured by the participating banks' knowledge of their respective customers and control of its operations.[2] Financial institutions in the Identrus system serve as Identrus Certificate Authorities, establishing the identities of their corporate customers and certifying them as trusted trading partners on the Internet. Once certified by an Identrus Certificate Authority, one trading partner can conclusively identify any other Identrus trading partner easily and with assurance. The fact that he/she is a certified member of Identrus makes the trading partner viable in the global trust system.

Banks have long been familiar with trust issues; other commercial organisations are less so. Accordingly, many governments have responded by laying down detailed regulations governing how certification service providers must operate, including supervision of all certification service providers by a state agency to make sure that the information systems being used are secure, the personnel being employed are properly qualified and have no criminal record, and the procedures being used are comprehensive and reliable. A further level of assurance is provided under some legislation by providing for some certification service providers to become accredited, upon demonstrating that their systems and procedures reach a prescribed level of reliability and security. Under such a system, users of certification services are not required to assess for themselves the trustworthiness of a given certification service provider; they can instead rely upon the national government to set appropriate standards and oversee compliance with them, as they do when dealing with notaries.

4–007   Alternatively, commercial certification authorities may be left to try to establish trust in the marketplace. In the interim, signatories bear the risk that their signatures will not be accepted by a counterparty on the grounds that there is insufficient assurance as to its authenticity in view of the unknown status of the certifier. Relying parties who choose nonetheless to rely risk the possibility that the signature may later be successfully repudiated, as not originating with the purported signatory after all. For example, a relying party which has no knowledge of a particular certification service provider cannot be confident that the certificate may not have been issued to someone other than the named holder as a result of inadequacies in the certification service provider's registration procedures. The only way for a potential relying party to try to assess an unknown certification service provider's trustworthiness is by reference to a *certification practice statement*. These are discussed in more detail below.

Both approaches are being used in different jurisdictions. In some cases, both approaches are being used within the same jurisdiction for different purposes. In both Canada and Australia the government has established a PKI for the purpose of enabling electronic transactions with government, although commercial certification authorities are generally unregulated. The Australian Gatekeeper hierarchy is described in detail by way of example below.

Limitations of PKI

Despite its potential, establishing a PKI is not a universal panacea.[3] For a start, establishing such a network involves very substantial expenditure, in information systems, technology and procedures for keeping the contents of those systems secure, procedures and processes for issuing and publishing certificates, mechanisms for announcing the revocation or suspension of certificates and so on. All of this must add to the transaction costs of using electronic signatures. There is a serious question as to whether any of this investment is actually warranted for its assumed purpose: to enable global e-commerce. Global e-commerce is already a reality in a number of ways: electronic data interchange (EDI) systems have been in operation over closed networks for many years; consumers buy and sell through retailers such as *Amazon.com* or auction sites such as *e-Bay.com* without worrying about electronic signatures and PKI. And companies transact major contracts using faxed signatures or even trusted telex systems.

Second, the PKI model, like the notary model upon which it is based, only removes the risks of remote transactions in very limited aspects. There is a world of difference between knowing someone's legal identity, which the basic PKI model can do for you, and deciding that they are sufficiently trustworthy to divulge to them one's credit card details. There are many people to whom one might not trust this information despite, or perhaps because of, knowing their identity beyond a reasonable doubt. There is the further issue of whether a given name equates to a particular person, or merely one of the set of people who share that name. The certificate may correctly inform the world that a particular public key is held by a particular person. But until users become familiar with dealing with people using hierarchical identifiers, there are bound to be incidents where the relying party relies upon a certified signature believing it to be the signature of a different (trusted) person of the same name.

Third, knowing the identity legitimately associated with a particular public key does not provide any assurance whatsoever that the corresponding private key is in fact being used by the rightful owner. PKI cannot solve this problem; it comes down to a question of the security users provide for their own private keys. This underlies one of the difficult legal issues of electronic signatures which use non-biometric methods, such as public key cryptography. Should a signature created with the private key belonging to a particular individual be attributed to that individual even if in fact it was not created by the individual but by someone else, or even by a virus, who or which has by whatever means

4–008

4–009

obtained the key? The UNCITRAL Model Law proposes this solution for certain circumstances,[4] but it is far from being generally accepted.[5]

Simple distributed security infrastructure

4–010   An alternative model is the Simple Distributed Security Infrastructure (SDSI), advocated by amongst others the Massachusetts Institute of Technology's Computer Science department, including one of the developers of the RSA algorithm for public key cryptography. This model was developed in response to frustration at the extremely slow growth of global PKIs, and represents a group-based variant of the web-of-trust approach. Thus, the key-identity correspondence is made and verified within a local group, such as a company; anyone within that group can certify anyone else within the group to external correspondents. Trust is focussed on the group, since the correctness of any certificate depends upon the reliability of the group's identity verification method. The result is a hierarchy which operates from the bottom up: small organisations may link into larger groupings, such as chambers of commerce, which in turn link into larger (say national) groupings, which may ultimately link to international groupings. However, this model was proposed for the first time only in 1996 and it is not clear whether it will ever break through into commercial reality given the massive support subsequently given to the development of classic PKI by much of the recent legislation worldwide.

Roles within PKI

4–011   The PKIs which are now being established around the world encompass more roles than simply the issuance of certificates. A registration authority validates and/or verifies the identity of an applicant for a certificate. The registration authority may also issue the certificate, or may confirm the identity and public key details to a separate certification authority. Other roles include time-stamping electronic documents to provide reliable evidence of the date and time of creation; generating key pairs for use in digital signing, and trusted archive services (sometimes known, confusingly, as e-notaries) for retaining secure, unaltered and accessible copies of electronically signed documents.

   Some of these peripheral activities have become relevant to the legal effectiveness of signatures through the requirements that have been included in some countries' legislation. The European Electronic Signatures Directive uses the generic description "certification service provider" to refer to any organisation carrying out one or more of these roles. This term is adopted hereafter for describing PKI participants unless it is clear that only a single role is involved.

Registration authorities

4–012   Registration authorities have two possible functions. The first is validation—to establish that there is such a person or entity as that who or which purports to be applying for a certificate. Verification—that the public key proferred does indeed correspond with that person or entity—is logically a second stage. The evidence required for each of these functions is often identical, however.

   Establishing the existence of a claimed identity will involve the applicant, whether a natural or a legal person, providing sufficient evidence to a CA as to who they are and how that identity fits into the community. The form of evidence required will depend upon the level of assurance to which the identity needs to be verified.[6] For low value certificates, low assurance is required: a personal statement, credit card and evidence of address may suffice. For greater certainty the evidence required might include, for natural persons, a personal interview and presentation of a passport, driver's licence, birth certificate or other evidence. The passport and birth certificate contribute to establishing the existence of the identity; all three contribute to verifying that the applicant holds that identity. Many jurisdictions have enacted requirements that a registration authority see the applicant face to face and examine a passport or national identity card before a certificate is issued which can be used to support legally effective electronic signatures. Third party corroboration, from a trustworthy third party such as a family doctor or lawyer, could also be required, but this does not feature in any of the legislation surveyed in this book.

For legal persons, evidence of legal establishment such as a certificate of incorporation **4–013** for a registered company, a partnership deed for a partnership, or equivalent for other forms of incorporated or unincorporated body will validate identity. A business licence, in jurisdictions where these are necessary in order to trade, would fairly reliably verify the holder's identity.

Depending upon the functions for which a signature is to be used, additional evidence could be required to prove residence at a claimed address, or that the entity is in fact engaged in the activities it claims. For example, membership of trade associations, chambers of commerce or similar organisations could be demonstrated.

A registration authority may also provide *attribute authority services* if it verifies not only the applicant's identity but other qualities such as professional qualifications, business licences or status or authorisation level within an organisation.

Certification authorities

A certification authority issues certificates linking a particular identity to a particular **4–014** signature verification mechanism, such as a public key. This may involve a number of functions, including in particular:

- establishing that the applicant ("subscriber") has signature creation means corresponding to the signature verification means to be certified;

- verifying the information which the applicant wishes to include in the certificate; and

- ensuring that the applicant understands the mechanism for using the signature and certificate and the potential liabilities of so doing.

Certification authorities may also provide *directory* services, maintaining directories of the certificates they have issued to enable third parties to cross-check that the certificate originates from the authority. A critical function, which is likely to be performed by the certification authority, is the publication of a *certificate revocation list* showing any certificate which has been revoked or suspended before its expiry date.

Certification authorities also often maintain repositories which hold copies of their subscriber agreements, certification practice statements, certificate policies, relying party agreements and similar materials. The role of these documents is discussed below.

Time stamping

An unavoidable issue arising from the trusted third party business model is the status of **4–015** an electronic signature which is supported by a certificate which has been revoked. In many jurisdictions, legal effectiveness is dependent upon support at the time of signing by a valid certificate. Thus, to determine whether or not a particular signature was effective, it will be necessary to show conclusively whether the certificate was still valid at the time when the signature was produced. This will necessitate independent evidence of the time at which the signature was created. Such evidence may be provided by a time stamp, which consists of binding a particular time to the signed document by adding a time record and digitally signing the resulting extended document with the time stamping authority's own private key.

Trusted archival/ e-notary services

4–016   A major issue in electronic transacting is that of record keeping. Electronic documents are potentially subject to undetectable alteration, and in addition may become unreadable after only a short period, due to obsolescence of technology. There is therefore a need for reliable archival services. An alternative approach to this problem as regards the signatures themselves would be independent verification of the parties' signatures at or slightly after the time of signing combined with an independent party keeping a record of the result of this verification for future reference.

Certification practice statements

4–017   A certification practice statement is a document which sets out the procedures and systems the certification service provider uses in order to provide its services. Many follow the format of a document, the *Internet Public Key Infrastructure Certificate Policy and Certification Practices Framework*, produced by the Internet Engineering Task Force (IETF), known as RFC 2527.[7] This sets out in detail the areas that a certification practice statement should cover, although it does not lay down requirements for what practices or procedures a certification service provider should actually use. In effect, RFC 2527 is a checklist for users setting out the questions they may want to know the answers to.

The legal issues to be covered include statements of the certification service provider's obligations, and the obligations it wishes to impose upon subscribers and relying parties; its position as regards liability for loss; its policies as regards confidentiality; compliance audits for any standards which are incorporated and so on. The certification practice statement should also spell out the governing law and any dispute resolution procedures applicable to the certification service provider's activities, notice provisions and other boilerplate to enable the contracts based upon the statement to be administered smoothly.

The confidentiality provisions should include definitions of which information is to be treated as confidential and which not, as well as the certification service provider's policy on release of information to the police or other authorities.

4–018   RFC 2527 recommends that a certification practice statement should include an obligation on the certificate subscriber to ensure that information in a certificate application is accurate, that the private key is kept secure, that the private key and certificate are used only for the purposes specified, and to notify the certification service provider as soon as the private key's secrecy is considered to have been potentially compromised. A relying party should be obliged to check whether the certificate has been revoked or suspended, to rely upon the certificate only for the purposes for which it was issued, to verify that a signature has been properly executed and to accept any liability caps or warranties asserted by the certification service provider.

Liability limits should be spelled out in detail, including any limits as to the kinds of damage (direct/ indirect, special, consequential loss) for which the certification service provider may be liable, any limitations on that liability in terms of financial caps per certificate or per transaction, and exclusions for losses due to third party fraud, Acts of God, force majeure and the like.

The statement should also include clear information as to the frequency of publication of any certificate revocation list. This highlights, once again, the difference between online transactions and those in the real world: the importance of timing. In paper-based transactions, the time at which a signature took place is rarely, if ever, significant to within 24 hours. A court may want to know at a later stage whether a document was signed today or yesterday, but except in cases of fraud is not generally interested as to whether the signature was alleged to have been formed at 11 a.m. or 11.15 a.m. In the online context, security compromise may be able to happen at any moment whether the subscriber is logged on or not, and certificate revocation or expiry may likewise take place at a time which is apparently random in the time zone of the relying party even if it is a logical moment in the time zone of the certification service provider. So the potential validity or otherwise of a certificate also varies from moment to moment, and the exact timing of any related act—signing or verification—may be relevant in every transaction.

The statement should spell out both how identification and authentication is done on **4–019** initial registration, how the identity of a person making a request for revocation or suspension of a signature will be verified and also how the certification service provider deals with reissuance of certificates after either routine lapse of a certificate or upon revocation. This will also include how the certification service provider deals with giving holders unique identifiers which are not simply their names (as discussed in paragraphs 4–003—4–005). The conventions they use for assigning these should be spelt out—in particular whether or not the names will be meaningful and how disputes over them will be resolved.

Legal entities will be represented in signing documents by individuals. The certification practice statement should explain how an individual's status as a representative of an organisation will be verified.

The certification practice statement may also deal with the certification service provider's arrangements for storing its records relating to certificates issued and revoked for future reference.

RFC 2527 also recommends that a certification practice statement include details of the **4–020** certification service provider's policy for termination of its business. In practice, termination other than through takeover or merger will result in the certificate records being lost unless some other agency is available to take over their maintenance. For this reason many legislatures have included in their electronic signature legislation provisions for the state to act as archive of last resort for the records of any national certification service provider which ceases operations. However, the accessibility in perpetuity of evidence to demonstrate the validity of any given signature is unlikely to be a major issue for many subscribers. The courts of all nations are accustomed to resolving disputes without access to all of the facts.

Actual certification practice statements range from a page or two to over 100 pages, depending upon the degree of transparency a particular certification service provider wishes to give.

Limitations of the use of certification practice statements
The existence and diversity of certification practice statements highlights one of the **4–021** intrinsic difficulties with the use of electronic signatures. At one level or another, the user is required to make choices, and take responsibility for those choices, which are far more

onerous than the level of engagement which is required to participate in a paper-based transaction. Clearly, a one-page certification practice statement simply does not include sufficient information for the informed user to make a realistic assessment of the trustworthiness of the services on offer.[8] On the other hand, a document such as VeriSign's 96 page epic contains most (though not necessarily all) of that information, but it is completely unrealistic to imagine that the average user is going to read even one such document, let alone go to the effort of comparing it with equivalents in order to assess which service is more trustworthy— even if this mechanism were in fact reliably effective. The procedures described may be more than adequate but actual compliance is the real issue.

Certificate policies

4–022   A certificate policy is a named set of rules that indicates the applicability of a certificate to a particular community and/ or class of application with common security requirements. For example, it might specify what information must be contained in the certificate and whether a certain type of certificate is appropriate for the authentication of EDI transactions for trading goods within a particular price range. It also sets out what principles the certification service provider will apply in issuing a particular category of certificate. Most certification service providers have detailed certificate policies, which set out the obligations and warranties given by all parties to the certificate (subscriber, issuing authority and relying party).

Ideally, certificate policies should be standardised globally. Once all certificates of a given type are in a standard format containing standard information, this will assist in rendering automated methods for procedures such as signature verification interoperable between certification service providers and across national boundaries.

Australia: the Gatekeeper PKI framework

4–023   The Australian Gatekeeper PKI framework is described below as an illustration of the complexity of PKI systems. It was one of the earliest to be established, and incorporates the world's largest Government-to-business rollout of digital certificates.[9] The Gatekeeper framework is not established by Commonwealth legislation but administratively through Head Agreements which the National Office for the Information Economy (NOIE) signs, on behalf of the Commonwealth, with each Gatekeeper-accredited certification authority and/or registration authority. Gatekeeper Head Agreements both contractually bind certification/registration authorities and govern the basis of their accreditation as such.

Issues addressed in the Head Agreements include:[10]

(a)   the approved documents, policies and criteria which the certification/ registration authority may use with its customers;

(b)   the types of certificates issued;

(c)   the apportionment of liability between the certification/ registration authority and the Government;

(d)   the rights of the Government to undertake compliance and privacy audits;

(e)   procedures for updating the approved documents; and

(f)   the basis on which the Government may terminate the certification/ registration authority's Gatekeeper accreditation.

If a certification/ registration authority is in breach of any of its obligations under the Head Agreement, it can lose its accreditation.

A requirement under the Head Agreement, and part of the accreditation process, is the preparation by certification authorities of standard documentation, such as contracts with the subscribers to whom it issues certificates. This includes Certificate Policies and Certification Practice Statement, which are incorporated by reference into the Head Agreement and each of the agreements referred to below.

The certification authority must:

(g)   submit its certificate policies to NOIE for approval;

(h)   provide authentication services to Subscribers in accordance with its Accredited Documentation; and

(i)   provide NOIE with a copy of every contract it enters into with a Government Agency.

Under the Gatekeeper framework, for a Government Agency to take advantage of **4–024** authentication services, every employee who will digitally sign messages on behalf of the Agency must have their own key pair and corresponding digital signature certificate. To enable this, an Agency which wishes to use Gatekeeper must enter into a services agreement with a certification authority. While the Head Agreement does not directly regulate the terms of contracts between a certification authority and an Agency, each contract must be approved by NOIE.

Other contractual arrangements under the Gatekeeper framework include:

(j)   Non-individual subscriber agreement—every employee of an Agency must sign a Subscriber Agreement and the Agency must warrant that it will be responsible for all use of employee's certificates;

(k)   Australian Business Number Digital Signature Certificates (ABN-DSC) Subscriber Agreement—an Agency must nominate Authorised Officers who are to have their own certificates. Authorised Officers each execute an ABN-DSC Subscriber Agreement and are issued with a certificate. Once an Authorised Officer has been issued with a certificate, they are able to authorise, by digitally signing an email, the issuance of certificates to other employees in the Agency;

(l)   Individual Subscriber Agreement—used by persons external to Government Agencies who wish to deal electronically with Government Agencies; and

(m)   Relying Party Agreement—this is an agreement which a person who wishes to access a digital certificate kept by a certification authority enters into with the certification authority each time they seek access for verification purposes of a Subscriber's certificate. In practice, it is unlikely that a Relying Party will have an opportunity to negotiate the terms of the agreement because the terms will be taken to have been accepted by the Relying Party as a "clickwrap" agreement over the Internet when accessing the web site to verify a signature against a certificate. Note that the relationship between the Subscriber and the Relying Party is not regulated by the certification authority or the Gatekeeper framework.

As at June 2003, eight organisations had obtained Gatekeeper accreditation.[11]

In addition to promoting Gatekeeper in Australia, NOIE has also been involved in developing a cross–recognition policy to encourage PKI interoperability, both in Australia and overseas.[12] The policy proposes cross-recognition of PKI domains as the mechanism to facilitate (though not guarantee) recognition of digital signature certificates and is consistent with the Asia-Pacific Economic Corporation (*APEC*) paper *Achieving Interoperability in PKI*.[13]

Actual use by Australian Governments

4–025 On April 22, 2003, The Australian newspaper reported[14] that the uptake of Gatekeeper by government agencies was almost zero, with the Australian Taxation Office the only Department to "fully adopt it". It was reported that a primary criticism of the Gatekeeper strategy is that it is "too expensive and difficult" for agencies to implement, with only larger organisations able to justify the expense. The "only agency ready to implement Gatekeeper in the near future" was the Australian Customs Service.

There are other Commonwealth Government Agencies which utilise Gatekeeper, including the Health Insurance Commission and the Department of Employment and Workplace Relations. At a State and Territory level, however, the uptake of Gatekeeper or PKI generally has been slow, with few State Government Agencies actively pursuing the implementation of a PKI strategy as part of their overall business strategies.

Australian Taxation Office (ATO)[15]

4–026 Under The New Tax System legislation, which introduced a goods and services tax (*GST*) into Australia from July 1, 2000, businesses with a turnover of more than AU$20 million are required to deal with the ATO online using public key certificates. In addition, any entity with an Australian Business Number (*ABN*) may nominate to submit its GST returns electronically, may apply for a digital certificate from the ATO.

As mentioned above, the ATO's implementation of an electronic commerce platform, the Electronic Commerce Interface (*ECI*), in June 2000 is seen as the world's largest Government-to-business rollout of digital certificates. It enables all Australian businesses, small and large, to lodge their Business Activity Statements directly via the Internet, is available 24 hours per day, seven days per week and will eventually support a range of high volume business transactions with the ATO. The ATO is a Gatekeeper-accredited Certification Authority and Registration Authority. While the ECI uses PKI endorsed by Gatekeeper,[16] the ATO-issued digital certificates are part of a closed PKI and are for use with the ATO only.[17] Only some ATO online applications support ABN-DSCs issued by another Gatekeeper accredited supplier.

With the introduction of the GST in 2000, some 300,000 digital certificates were issued to businesses, and more than 65,000 businesses downloaded certificates for active use.[18]

Fedlink

4–027 In 1997, the Commonwealth Government, announced the establishment of "Fedlink", a means of providing secure electronic communications between government agencies.[19] The initiative is managed by NOIE and is based on encrypting network data packets and linking agents using a virtual private network over the internet.

Fedlink went live in July 2001 and, as at June 2003, 20 Commonwealth Agencies are connected to it.

Health Insurance Commission (HIC)[20]

HIC is Commonwealth statutory authority established in 1974. It is currently responsible **4–028** for administering government health programs such as Medicare, which enables the free treatment as a public patient in a public hospital and free or subsidised medical treatment outside of hospital.

HIC utilises PKI in a number of ways to facilitate the secure transmission of patient information, such as patient referrals from general practitioners to specialists. HIC has established the Health eSignature Authority Pty Limited (*HeSA*) to facilitate the introduction of PKI across Australia's health industry. HeSA is a wholly owned proprietary company of HIC whose primary function is to act as the Registration Authority within the Australian healthcare industry, with SecureNet Limited acting as the Certification Authority. HeSA obtained Gatekeeper accreditation on January 19, 2001.

HIC funds the initial registration costs of PKI for general practitioners, specialists, pharmacists and other health professionals who wish to utilise the system to securely transmit patient related information. Other health related information being transmitted electronically utilising PKI includes the exchange of admission and discharge information between doctors and hospitals and for the payment of patient-billed and direct-billed claims under the Medicare system.

HIC also utilises PKI for all new electronic data interchange and its e-business solutions.

Australian Customs Service (Customs)[21]

Customs utilises Gatekeeper PKI for all EDI emails sent and received by the Customs **4–029** Connect Facility (*CCF*), the communications gateway for all of its electronic business transactions. CCF is part of Customs' Integrated Cargo System, Release 1 of which relates to document consignment reporting by air express couriers. Customs uses digital signatures and certificates for security and authentication purposes to ensure that there is a legally verifiable trail to enable identification of people who communicate with Customs.

The use of digital signatures and certificates when communicating electronically with Customs, together with Customs' re-engineering of its cargo management systems and processes, has also required amendments to the Customs Act.[22]

While each State and Territory Government has an online presence, with many using the medium to enable the payment of various government fees and fines (which utilises SSL encryption), few appear to be actively using digital signatures and certificates in their dealings with the public.

Victoria

The Transport Accident Commission (*TAC*) of Victoria is one of the few State government **4–030** entities in Australia which utilises digital signatures and certificates in the normal course of its business. TAC is a Victorian Government-owned organisation whose role includes paying for the treatment of and benefits for people injured in transport accidents, promoting road safety in Victoria and improving Victoria's trauma system.

TAC first implemented a Gatekeeper ABN-DSC certificate model in 2001. As at June 2003, TAC has issued Gatekeeper ABN-DSC certificates to all of its employees and is actively encouraging third parties with whom it does business to obtain a Gatekeeper certificate to enable secure electronic communication with TAC. To date, TAC has managed the issuing of approximately 45 Gatekeeper certificates to third parties who deal with TAC.

New South Wales

4–031   The NSW government is implementing a licensing project[23] to reduce red tape for business and produce savings to the government of around A$70 million in infrastructure costs. Under the project, the 200 different business and occupational licences administered by 28 NSW government agencies will come together under a single system featuring online access. As part of the new system, digital certificates, including Gatekeeper certificates, will be used for authentication purposes.[24]

Western Australia

4–032   The Government Electronic Market (GEM)[25] is a comprehensive Western Australian online government buying service, providing an end-to-end online system where government buyers can browse and search the supplier registry, browse supplier catalogues, request information and quotations, place orders and have them approved online by their agency, receipt orders, and arrange payment to suppliers. GEM was developed in a manner consistent with Australian Procurement and Construction Council's "Government Framework for National Cooperation on Electronic Procurement",[26] which notes[27] that digital signatures and certificates, including under the Gatekeeper framework, is one method of authenticating the other party to an electronic transaction.

Australian Capital Territory

4–033   "Canberra Connect", the ACT Government's web portal, uses digital certificates issued by VeriSign Australia to give its customers confidence that it is indeed Canberra Connect with whom they are dealing online.[28]

The Banks— Project Angus

4–034   Project Angus involves four of the largest Australian banks which have been working for a number of years to establish a system whereby they could issue digital certificates which are interoperable with international banking systems and exist within the Identrus electronic trusts and payment scheme.[29] Following an announcement by the Minister for Communications on March 22, 2001,[30] digital signature certificates issued by Australian banks to businesses as part of "Project Angus" are now accepted by Government agencies and regarded as ABN-DSCs. In practice, this will minimise the number of digital certificates required by organisations who deal with the banks and with Government as an organisation with a bank issued certificate will not have to get a Gatekeeper ABN-DSC as well.

ANZ Bank launched its Identrus application on March 3, 2003. ANZ utilises digital certificates stored on smart cards, which its customers can use when dealing with the bank online. In time, ANZ customers may be able to use the digital certificate issued to deal online with ANZ with other organisations, including the Government.[31]

The National Australia Bank currently uses digital certificates in a different way. NAB provides comfort to its online customers that their transactions are with the NAB by asking customers to check each time they engage in online banking that a valid digital certificate for National Internet Banking has been issued at the time of the transaction.[32]

1. This "web of trust" approach is explained in more detail in *PGP: Pretty Good Privacy* by Simson Garfinkel (O=Reilly & Associates, Inc, 1995).
2. See generally *www.identrus.com*.
3. See discussion in Ellison & Schneier, *Ten Risks of PKI: what you're not being told about Public Key Infrastructure* at *http://www.counterpane.com/pki-risks-ft.txt*.
4. See Ch. 5, para. 5–008.
5. See for example the Spanish Decree-Law of June 2003 at Ch. 6, para. 6–058, which opts for the opposite solution that the purported signatory is not bound unless the transaction is in fact in its interests.
6. The United Kingdom government's *Minimum Requirement for the verification of the identity of individuals* sets out three possible levels of assurance which could be required: on the balance of probabilities, substantial assurance or beyond reasonable doubt. Version 2.0, January 2003.
7. Available at *http://www.ietf.org/rfc/rfc2527.txt*.
8. The ICC is nevertheless working to develop a one page Model PKI Disclosure Statement, to enable simple and rapid comparisons of certification practices of different certification service providers by users.
9. The Australian Tax Office's Electronic Commerce Interface, discussed below.
10. A model Head Agreement is available at *http://www.noie.gov.au/projects/confidence/ ra[2]0head[2]0agreement.htm*.
11. See *http://www.noie.gov.au*.
12. See *http://www.noie.gov.au/projects/confidence/Securing/Gatekeeper/cross_recognition_policy_v2_1.doc*.
13. Available at *http://www.apectelwg.org/apecdata/telwg/eaTG/eatf06.html*.
14. See *http://news.com.au/common/story_page/0,4057,6313537[2]55E15306,00.html*.
15. See *http://www.ato.gov.au*.
16. John Rimmer, CEO, National Office for the Information Economy, Speech—*Electronic Government in Australia's Information Economy* Technology in Government Week, Ottawa Canada, October 15, 2001, available at *http://www.noie.gov.au/publications/speeches/Rimmer/Canada_Oct01.htm*.
17. K Boyle 'An Introduction to Gatekeeper: The Governments Public Key Infrastructure' *Journal of Law and Information Science*, Vol. 11, No. 1, January 2000, pp. 38-54 at p. 46.
18. John Rimmer, CEO, National Office for the Information Economy, Speech *op cit*.
19. See *http://www.fedlink.gov.au/*.
20. See *http://www.hic.gov.au*.
21. See *http://www.customs.gov.au*.
22. See, for example, *Customs Legislation Amendment and Repeal (International Trade Modernisation) Act 2001 (Cth)* and Sch. 3 to *Customs Legislation Amendment Act (No.1) 2002 (Cth)*.
23. See *http://www.oit.nsw.gov.au/pages/5.4.3.nswglp.htm*.
24. See *http://www.oit.nsw.gov.au/pdf/5.4.44.Technical-Overview.pdf*.
25. *http:// www.gem.wa.gov.au/text/index.jsp*.
26. Available at *http://www.apcc.gov.au/apcc/docs/NationalFramework3August01.pdf*.
27. See p. 11.
28. See *http://www.canberraconnect.act.gov.au/legal/privacystatement.html*.
29. See *http://www.identrus.com*.
30. See *Boost for Business to Government E-commerce* media release, available at *http://www.dcita.gov.au/Article/ 0,,0_1-2_15-3_371-4_15597,00.html*.
31. See *http://www.anz.com/TrustCentre/FAQs.asp*.
32. See *http://www.national.com.au/Internet_Banking/0,,13893,00.html*.

5

International initiatives relating to electronic signatures

Introduction

5–001　A number of international organisations have produced materials addressing the problems of authentication, non-repudiation and integrity of electronic messages in the context of electronic commerce. The majority of these are recommendations or guidance only; the only international instrument having binding legal effect to date is the European Union's Electronic Signatures Directive. However, this is limited in its effect to the Member States of the European Union for the time being.[1] Initiatives of UNCITRAL, OECD and International Chamber of Commerce (ICC) may lack legal authority but have a significant persuasive effect among a much broader international community. This chapter begins by examining what has taken place in these fora and the influence they have had, before going on to review in detail the development and terms of the Electronic Signatures Directive.

UNCITRAL Model Laws

5–002　UNCITRAL is a body of the United Nations which develops legislative texts in the area of trade law representing, so far as is possible, an international consensus. The majority of resulting texts are not binding upon any state, but are part of a process of gradual harmonisation of laws. States which chose to incorporate a Model Law may adopt all or part, and may modify elements as they see fit in order to achieve their national legislative objectives. The result of this flexibility is of course a lower level of harmonisation than might be achieved by the use of a convention or treaty. However, the advantage is that a degree of harmonisation is reached among a greater number of states than would be likely to sign up to and implement a "one size fits all" fixed and binding wording. The UNCITRAL Model Laws are influential among the entire membership of the United Nations so that an understanding of their provisions is particularly valuable in understanding the approaches of legislators from outside Europe and North America.

Model Law on Electronic Commerce
The UNCITRAL Model Law on Electronic Commerce was originally adopted by the   **5–003**
Commission at its 29th session in 1996, after several years of discussions by the Working
Group on Electronic Commerce. The aim was to offer national legislators a set of
internationally acceptable rules as to how a secure legal environment could be created for
electronic commerce. One aspect of this is the question of what form a contract must take.

(1) Form
The Model Law was intended to be technologically neutral, and its approach to formal   **5–004**
requirements such as that a document must be in writing or signed was to adopt an
approach based on functional equivalence. Accordingly, Article 5 provides that
information shall not be denied legal effect, validity or enforceability solely on the
grounds that it is in the form of a data message, defined as:

> "information generated, sent or received or stored by electronic, optical or similar
> means including, but not limited to, electronic data exchange (EDI), electronic mail,
> telegram, telex or telecopy."[2]

Article 6 provides that a data message may satisfy a legal requirement for information to
be "in writing" if the information is accessible so as to be usable for subsequent reference.
Article 7 deals with signature of electronic documents. It specifies:

Article 7

(1) Where the law requires a signature of a person, that requirement is met in relation   **5–005**
to a data message if:

    a. A method is used to identify that person and to indicate that person's
approval of the information contained in the data message; and

    b. That method is as reliable as was appropriate for the purpose for which the
data message was generated or communicated, in the light of all the
circumstances, including any relevant agreement.

(2) Paragraph (1) applies whether the requirement therein is in the form of an
obligation or whether the law simply provides consequences for the absence of a
signature.

(3) The provisions of this article do not apply to the following:

    a. . . .[3]

This article was based upon the recognition of certain functions of a signature in a
paper-based environment, namely: to identify a person; to provide certainty as to the
personal involvement of that person in the act of signing; and to associate that person
with the content of a document. The objective was to establish general conditions under
which data messages would be regarded as authenticated with sufficient credibility for
their purpose and would be enforceable in the face of signature requirements. However,
the difficulty with this article is that the test set out in paragraph (1)b is a test which
appears to require hindsight since the appropriateness of the level of reliability of the
chosen method will ultimately fall to be decided by a court. Beforehand, the parties can
only make an agreement as to what level of reliability they consider appropriate in all the
circumstances, and hope that this will be the decisive factor in any tribunal's assessment.

While in the paper-based environment one party may be misinformed of the other party's identity or intentions when signing a document, but not of the effectiveness of the mechanism being used, the Model Law affirms the uncertainty it was intended to address by potentially leaving both parties uncertain of the mechanism. Of course, it could be argued that in these circumstances it is in both parties' interests to ensure that the method is as reliable as the transaction can possibly warrant. But it is equally likely that, like the Statute of Frauds,[4] the article provides a loophole for those looking to leave a way out from under their obligations by arguing (for example) that alternative, more reliable methods were readily available. Where both parties are within a single jurisdiction and familiar with its courts' approach, they may be able to assess reasonably well how the test will operate. But the principal concern in relation to electronic transactions is the enforceability of cross-border transactions, which may prove, upon analysis in the event of a dispute, to be governed by the laws of a jurisdiction where neither party is based, in which case both parties may be at risk. Alternately, if the governing law is the home law of one party the other party will be likely to have less familiarity with the approach taken and may perceive itself to be at a potential disadvantage as a result.

5–006   The Working Group also produced a Guide to Enactment of the UNCITRAL Model Law on Electronic Commerce, as a non-binding note of guidance for governments. This specifies a list of factors which a tribunal attempting to assess the appropriateness of the level of reliability of a method shall take into account in forming its decision. Though long, the list is not exhaustive. The factors include:

(1)   the sophistication of the equipment used by each of the parties;

(2)   the nature of their trade activity;

(3)   the frequency at which commercial transactions take place between the parties;

(4)   the kind and size of the transaction;

(5)   the function of signature requirements in a given statutory and regulatory environment;

(6)   the capability of communication systems;

(7)   compliance with authentication procedures set forth by intermediaries;

(8)   the range of authentication procedures made available by any intermediary;

(9)   compliance with trade custom and practice;

(10)   the existence of insurance coverage mechanisms against unauthorised messages;

(11)   the importance and value of the information contained in the data message;

(12)   the availability of alternative methods of identification and the cost of implementation;

(13)   the degree of acceptance or non-acceptance of the method of identification in the relevant industry or field both at the time the method was agreed upon and the time when the data message was communicated; and

(14)   any other relevant factor.[5]

Some of these are capable of being assessed differently in hindsight. For example, the importance and value of the information may appear significantly greater some years after the event, when the deal has proved to generate substantial profits for both parties, than it did when the parties agreed to an essentially speculative venture. Likewise, given the rate of advance of computer and communications technology, a court reviewing the parties' equipment several years down the line may form a negative view simply because the systems used, though perhaps not far behind the cutting edge in their day, sound antiquated from a more privileged modern standpoint.

(2)   Other provisions

The Model Law on Electronic Commerce also deals with the dynamic aspects of contract **5–007** formation: offer, acceptance, time of sending and time of receipt of data messages, acknowledgment of receipt and so on. The Model Law specifies that offer and acceptance may be expressed by means of data messages, and the addressee of a data message is not permitted to deny legal effect to a statement solely on the grounds that it is in the form of a data message.[6]

Perhaps the most important aspect of these provisions for present purposes is Article 13, which deals with the attribution of data messages. Clearly, many electronic transactions will take place between companies or other legal persons which can only act through the agency of human representatives or computers programmed to communicate automatically. A question therefore potentially arises as to when a message originating from somewhere within an organisation can be taken to be the official communication of the organisation or not.

Article 13 provides that a data message is that of the originator (of the message) if sent **5–008** by the originator itself. The originator is defined as a person by whom or on whose behalf the data message purports to have been sent or generated prior to storage, but it does not include a person acting as an intermediary.[7] This deals with transactions with natural persons. By Article 13(2), a data message is deemed to be that of the originator if it was sent either by a person who had the authority to act on behalf of the originator in respect of that data message, or by an information system programmed by or on behalf of the originator to operate automatically. Further, by Article 13(3) the recipient is entitled to regard a data message as being that of the originator and to act on that assumption if either:

(a)   the addressee properly applied a procedure previously agreed with the originator to ascertain whether the data message was that of the originator, or

(b)   the message resulted from the actions of a person whose relationship with the originator or any agent of the originator enabled the person to gain access to a method used by the originator to identify data messages as its own.

This latter provision is potentially controversial. In the context of electronic commerce, one method likely to be used by an originator to identify data messages as its own is some form of electronic signature. This might be in the form of a digital signature, generated by a private key (which may be either personal or representative of a particular office, such as Company Secretary or Chief Technical Officer) stored on the originator's computer system. A number of employees and contractors are likely to have access to the originator's computer system as a result of their relationship with the originator. However, a relatively limited subset of these will in fact be authorised to send data messages on behalf of the originator. If any employee or contractor is able to access the data message identification method, then the recipient of that data message will be entitled to assume that it comes from the originator and to act on that assumption even if in fact the data message was not authorised. It will not be apparent on the basis of the signature, which is of course identical whoever is wielding the private key.[8] But the content of the message might be such as to cause suspicion. For example, a data message sent by a company to its bank ordering the transfer of additional monies to the account of a junior IT employee ought to cause some alarm bells to ring—and probably in the real world the bank would query such an order. But under a law implementing Article 13(3)(b), the bank does not necessarily (subject to Article 13(4)(b), discussed below) have to: the company is liable for the loss caused as a result of the security lapse which enabled the employee to access the signature means.

5–009   This mechanism is the analogue of the ordinary position under English law that a third party dealing with a company is entitled to treat as authorised to represent the company anyone who has "ostensible authority". In other words, a party is not required to dig deep into the company's Memorandum and Articles of Association and consult the Board of Directors before agreeing to deal with a particular Director who holds herself out as authorised to bind the company. The company bears the risk that its senior employees, who may credibly present themselves to third parties as authorised, may abuse their positions to their own advantage. However, in the electronic context at least at present it is unlikely to be the senior employees who have sufficient IT expertise to abuse their rights to use the computer system. It is more likely that more junior staff will have the necessary skills. Thus, under any implementation of this provision a company now bears the risk of a much wider, and perhaps intrinsically less trustworthy, category of employees and contractors abusing their positions.

Essentially, this provision encodes the decision of the English High Court in *Standard Bank London Ltd v Bank of Tokyo Ltd*[9] that the holder of a method of producing a non-repudiable 'signature' is responsible for all uses of it by people with legitimate access to the system, whether that use is authorised or not. This is not surprising given that the original of the provision was the UNCITRAL Model Law on International Credit Transfers,[10] where the equivalent obligations of the sender of a payment order are set out. The facts in the *Standard Bank* case concerned a payment instruction sent by tested telex.

5–010   This situation and the potential liabilities arising from it do indeed seem onerous upon the supposed originator since, at first sight, there appears to be a marked contrast with the treatment of traditional handwritten signatures. The decision was justified by Waller J. in *Standard Bank* on the grounds that the Bank of Tokyo had complete control over its environment and therefore Standard Bank had no duty to enquire into the authenticity of each transaction instruction it received: a fraudulent instruction could not be sent unless Bank of Tokyo were negligent to some degree. Although the facts of this case took place in circumstances of a closed banking system with secure links between the participants, the underlying rationale is equally applicable to communications over an open system provided that the signature mechanism being used is proof against third party manipulation in transit. A digital signature should provide such a mechanism; there is therefore no injustice in requiring the signatory to take responsibility for the use of their private key in the circumstances set out in the Article. The simplest[11] alternative would be not to permit legal effect to signatures capable of being produced by mechanical means. Such a position would be consistent with the English court decisions in both *Bennett v Brumfitt* and *Goodman v J Eban*,[12] where the respective Courts, in approving signatures produced by a rubber stamp, relied heavily on the evidence that the signatory in both cases had kept the necessary mechanism strictly secure and accessible only by themselves. However, it is precisely this restrictive approach which national legislatures have been attempting to roll back. The UNCITRAL approach leaves the risk of liability upon the party in the best position to guard against misuse of a signature mechanism, which must be the fairest solution.

If less secure signature means are being used, then the proposed allocation of liability may not be so readily justified. But arguably a party which opts to use an insecure means of signature cannot reasonably expect a counterparty to accept the risk of fraud. The outcome is likely to be that signatures produced by obviously insecure means will not be acceptable for transactions of any significance in any jurisdiction applying this principle.

The addressee of the message does not get the benefit of Article 3(3) if they receive **5–011** actual notice from the originator that the message is not in fact from the originator a sufficient time before acting in reliance upon it. The draconian effect of Article 13(3)(b) is also potentially mitigated for the originator of a data message by Article 13(4)(b), which provides that the addressee does not get the benefit of that assumption if they knew or should have known had they exercised reasonable care or used any agreed procedure, that the data message was not that of the originator. Thus, to continue the example above, if the junior IT employee sends a signed data message authorising the transfer of £1m to her account, the bank ought to find out by exercising reasonable care to scrutinise out-of-pattern transactions that this message is not that of the purported originator. Alternatively, if there is an agreed mechanism (such as a telephone call to an agreed contact person) for checking the authenticity of data messages, then the bank will be liable for the company's loss if it simply carries out the transfer without first making the call. But if there is no agreed mechanism and the junior employee is sufficiently cautious in the amount and timing of each transfer she causes to be authorised, then the bank may have no cause for alarm and the company will be liable.

Article 13 also deals with transmission errors. If the addressee ought to have spotted (using reasonable care) that the message contained an error then they are not entitled to act on the assumption that the data message is what the originator intended to send.[13] Finally, an addressee which receives duplicate messages which it ought to have known, by the exercise of reasonable care or the use of any agreed procedure, were simply duplicates and not to be treated as separate messages, then they are not entitled to act on the assumption that they are separate messages.[14]

Model Law on Electronic Signatures
Despite its name, the Model Law on Electronic Signatures ("the Model Law") is in reality **5–012** based on the assumption that the technology most likely to be in issue is public key cryptography. Accordingly, the issues it addresses are those typically encountered in dealings based upon a public key infrastructure, namely the use of digital signatures and the certification of public keys for verification of them. This restricted approach was the subject of repeated debate in the drafting process but was repeatedly concluded to be the most rational approach in view of the emerging dominance of digital signatures in the marketplace at the time.

Nevertheless, the Model Law was also intended to be suitable for facilitating the use of other signature technologies including biometrics, PIN numbers and the like.[15] It aims to lay down practical standards against which the technical reliability of electronic signatures can be measured. It is therefore a supplement to Article 7 of the Model Law on Electronic Commerce, the idea being that a signature which complies with the Model Law on Signatures will certainly meet the test laid down in that article for legal validity. This approach does not deny validity to other forms of signature but merely leaves them to be considered by the relevant authorities on a case by case basis. The Guide to Enactment of the UNCITRAL Model Law on Electronic Signatures describes it as a "modest but significant addition".[16]

5–013   Work on drafting this Model Law and accompanying Guide began in 1996 after the adoption of the Model Law on Electronic Commerce, and was completed in July 2001. It was conceived as an independent document despite its close relationship with the Model Law on Electronic Commerce, since that had already been enacted, or was in the process of being, in a number of States. The complication of expanding the existing Model Law at such a late stage was not considered necessary. To ensure consistency, however, the basic articles (scope, definitions, interpretation and variation by agreement) of the Model Law on Electronic Commerce have been repeated in the Model Law on Electronic Signatures. Thus, an electronic signature is:

> "Data in electronic form in, affixed to or logically associated with a data message, which may be used to identify the signatory in relation to the data message and indicates the signatory's approval of the information contained in the data message."[17]

A certificate is:

> "A data message or other record confirming the link between a signatory and signature creation data."[18]

Signature creation data may be, for example, a private key from the signatory's public-private key pair or it could be a digitised biometric scan result.

The Working Group seems to have had more difficulty reaching a consensus on this Model Law than on its broader predecessor. Within the Commission there were differing views as to whether the Model Law should address only the business model in which digital signatures are backed by certificates, typically issued by third parties, or should have a broader approach. Ultimately, the limited approach was adopted.

5–014   The Model Law focuses on the three principal functions relating to key pairs for asymmetric encryption: key issuing, certification and reliance, although the Working Group recognised that more than one of these functions may be carried out by the same party. In taking this approach, it concurs with the common law attitude that a signature is not a thing having any significance in isolation: it is an element of proof, such that the processes surrounding its creation are in practice the real guarantee of reliability.

The detailed issues which the Model Law aims to address relating to this business model include:[19]

- the legal basis supporting the certification processes, including emerging digital authentication and certification technology;

- the applicability of the certification process;

- the allocation of risk and liabilities of users, providers and third parties in the context of the use of certification authorities;

- the specific issues of certification through the use of registries; and incorporation by reference.[20]

In fact, nothing in the Model Law appears to address the issue of certification through the use of registries, which would have brought in the difficult issues of regulation of certification service providers and whether or not a contract can exist between the certification service provider and a relying third party. These are left to national law. The drafters also recognised that in practice an electronic signature is being expected to perform more functions than those performed by a handwritten signature alone.

The core of the Model Law is Article 6. Article 6(1) restates the test of reliability test of **5–015** Article 7 of the Model Law on Electronic Commerce, that a signature should be produced by means which are "as reliable as appropriate for the purpose... in the light of all the circumstances". Article 6(3) goes on to set out the requirements for a signature to be considered to satisfy the requirement:

(3)   An electronic signature is considered to be reliable for the purpose of satisfying the requirement referred to in paragraph (1) if:

(a)   the signature creation data are, within the context in which they are used, linked to the signatory and to no other person;

(b)   the signature creation data were, at the time of signing, under the control of the signatory and no other person;

(c)   any alteration to the electronic signature, made after the time of signing, is detectable; and

(d)   where a purpose of the legal requirement for a signature is to provide assurance as to the integrity of the information to which it relates, any alteration made to that information after the time of signing is detectable.

The provisions do not give rise to an irrebuttable presumption of validity of a signature created in accordance with these requirements, however. Paragraph (4)(b) of Article 6 expressly reserves any party's right to adduce evidence of the non-reliability of an electronic signature. For example, as discussed above in the context of Article 13 of the Model Law on Electronic Commerce, technology alone does not provide an assurance as to who controlled the signature creation data when they were used. Biometric access devices may assist in evidencing compliance with this criterion. Paragraph (4)(b) may also be interpreted as preserving the existing legal grounds, such as mistake or duress, for the challenge of a signature even though it was in fact made by the purported signatory.

The effect of introducing this test of the sufficiency of an electronic signature is to create **5–016** a two-tier system for electronic signatures. Signatures which pass the test will definitely be sufficiently reliable, subject to any challenge under Article 6(4)(b); other signatures may or may not be, depending upon the circumstances of their use in accordance with the general principle set out in Article 7 of the previous Model Law. This approach, which retains the approach widely used in respect of paper-based signatures of testing each according to the circumstance, has also been adopted in the Electronic Signatures Directive.

The Model Law goes on to set out criteria against which to assess the conduct of the three notional parties to an electronic signature. They are minimum codes of conduct since the rapid rate of change in both technical, commercial and regulatory environments during the drafting process made a consensus difficult to achieve. The basic requirement is that each participant should exercise a reasonable level of care—a very flexible test which will enable courts faced with particular facts to assess how much care was reasonable in the circumstances. The test will need to be applied objectively to ensure that parties have a degree of certainty in advance as to whether their particular level of care was sufficient. In each case, failure to meet the specified criteria may lead to the party in question being liable for any loss, the details of how or to what extent being left to enacting States.

1. The signatory (Article 8)

5–017   The signatory is expected to exercise reasonable care to avoid unauthorised use of the signature creation device. This must include taking physical care of portable devices; controlling access to electronically stored data and potentially limiting access to the physical interfaces with the computer system on which they are stored. If the signature is supported by a certificate, the signatory should exercise reasonable care to ensure the accuracy and completeness of all material representations made by the signatory in connections with the certificate which are relevant throughout the certificate's life-cycle (from application to revocation or expiry) or included in it. The information to be included are such matters as the holder's name, address, authority or qualification, the details of the certification service provider, the public key and so on. Since the accuracy and completeness of all such information is likely to be within the signatory's direct knowledge at all times, the only aspect as to which reasonable care is likely to be necessary in practice is making sure that the certification service provider is notified promptly of any changes, rather than in checking the data themselves.

Where the signatory knows that the signature device has been compromised, or knows of circumstances which give rise to a substantial risk that the signature creation device may have been compromised, the signatory should give notice without undue delay to any person who may reasonably be expected to rely on, or to provide services in support of, the electronic signature.

2. The relying party (Article 11)

5–018   The concept of relying party is broad and could in some circumstances include the certification service provider or even the signatory. A relying party, even if they transact in the capacity of a consumer, is expected to take reasonable steps to verify the reliability of an electronic signature. No mechanism is suggested for verification, but verification in the context of a digital signature may mean no more than that the recipient decrypts the digital signature using the purported signatory's public key, computes the message digest of the message received and compares the two. Any party relying on another form of electronic signature may be expected as a minimum to obtain confirmation from the purported originator that they had sent a message signed in the form received. For prudence, it might be as well to obtain this confirmation through a medium other than e-mail since an e-mail confirmation does not necessarily amount to independent confirmation. If the signature is supported by a certificate, the relying party should, before relying upon it, take reasonable steps to verify the validity, suspension or revocation of the certificate and observe any limitation (for example, as to the value limit for the signature, or the signatory's authority in any context) laid down in the certificate.

The Model Law is expressly without prejudice to any other legislation governing the protection of consumers.

5–019   The Model Law again leaves the specific details of what consequences should flow from a failure to comply with these requirements to the enacting states. A particular issue would be whether the relying party who fails to perform any checks should assume any liability if carrying out reasonable checks would not have revealed that the signature or certificate was invalid, even though in fact it was. This will be up to the Courts of any enacting States to determine unless specific provisions are added at national level.

3. The certification service provider (Articles 9 and 10).

Given its objectives, it is not surprising that the Model Law goes into the conduct of certification service providers in considerably more detail than it provides for the other two parties.

Article 9 lays down the basic criteria a certification service provider must meet. The first is that the certification service provider should use trustworthy systems, procedures and human resources. The question of what trustworthy means is the subject of a separate article (Article 10, discussed below) in its own right.

Article 9 also requires the certification service provider to act in accordance with any representations that it makes with respect to its policies and practices, such as through a certification practice statement.[21] Certification service providers should also exercise reasonable care to ensure the accuracy and completeness of all material representations it makes in connection with a certificate which either are included in the certificate or are relevant throughout the certificate's lifecycle.

The article lays down minimum requirements for what information must be provided in the certificate itself, and also for further information which may either be included in the certificate or made available elsewhere. For example, the certificate may include the uniform resource locator (url) of a website where the data can be found. Indeed, in view of the context envisioned for many electronic signatures to be used, it is open to argument as to whether indicating a telephone number or even a means for obtaining a paper-based copy of this information would be sufficient or not.

The certificate itself should provide reasonably accessible means which enable a relying party to ascertain from the certificate:

- the identity of the certification service provider;

- that the signatory identified had control of the signature creation data at the time that the certificate was issued; and

- that the signature creation data were valid at or before the time of issue.

Note that the certificate does not and cannot make any representation as to who had control of the signature creation data at the time the certificate was created.

The required further information (again to be provided by reasonably accessible means) are:

- the method used to identify the signatory;

- any limitations on the purpose or value for which the signature creation data may be used;

- that the signature creation data are valid and have not been compromised;

- any limit on scope or extent of liability undertaken by the certification service provider;

- whether there is a mechanism for the signatory to give notice of any compromise or possible compromise of the signature creation data (which may not be relevant for "one-time" or low cost, low risk certificates); and

- whether a timely revocation service is offered.

Note that there is no obligation for the certification service provider to offer a timely revocation service or provide a mechanism for the signatory to give notice of compromise of the signature creation data. The article merely requires relying parties to be informed whether or not these exist, leaving the relying party to choose whether or not to rely upon a signature in the case where there is no way of finding out about any compromise which may have occurred. However, in the absence of some such mechanism the certification service provider cannot give the required information as to whether or not the signature creation data are valid and have not been compromised—which in any case only be made to the best of the certification service provider's knowledge and belief. National implementations of this article have tended not to leave the possibility of not providing such a mechanism open.

5–023   The certification service provider will be liable for any loss resulting from its failure to meet these criteria. The Model Law does not contain any indication of what factors should be taken into account in assessing any loss resulting from a certification service provider's failure to meet its requirements. This is left up to national law, although the Guide to Enactment explains that it was not intended to impose absolute liability upon the certification service providers: they should for example be able to prove contributory fault on the part of either signatory or relying party. Once again, a non-exhaustive list is provided for consideration in the Guide to Enactment, consisting of:

(a)   the cost of obtaining the certificate;

(b)   the nature of the information being certified;

(c)   the existence and extent of any limitation on the purpose for which the certificate may be used;

(d)   the existence of any statement limiting the scope or extent of the certification service provider's liability; and

(e)   any contributory conduct by the relying party.[22]

For example, the relying party's failure to check the validity of the certificate, or the fact that the relying party had possession of facts which would have given a reasonable person grounds for suspicion may contribute to the relying party's exposure to liability and concomitantly reduce the certification service provider's.

Trustworthiness

5–024   Article 10 sets out seven factors which may be taken into account in assessing a certification service provider's trustworthiness. In practice there are only six meaningful factors since the last is "any other relevant factor." Note that these factors are entirely optional; a particular jurisdiction may choose to consider some, all or none of them (in which case it is to be hoped that it would substitute for them alternative factors for the guidance of parties and the courts). The list therefore comprises a tentative suggestion as to the minimum criteria by which a certification service provider ought to be assessed. No standards are set; procedural matters of that level of detail are intentionally reserved to the enacting States.

The specific factors included in the Article are:

(a)   the certification service provider's financial and human resources, including existence of assets;

(b)   quality of hardware and software systems;

(c)   procedures for processing of certificates and applications for certificates, and retention of records;

(d)   availability of information to signatories identified in certificates and to potential relying parties;

(e)   regularity and extent of audit by an independent body; and

(f)   the existence of a declaration by the State, an accreditation body or the certification service provider regarding compliance with or existence of the foregoing.

The Guide to Enactment of the Model Law lists an overlapping but significantly different set of factors to be taken into account for the same purpose.[23] The first, tellingly, is independence. Since the Model Law is not intended to impose the business model where the certification authority is a third party, this factor could not appear as a necessary condition for a certification service provider to be deemed trustworthy. However, the Working Group clearly had it in mind as a highly desirable criterion. The full list comprises: **5–025**

(1)   independence;

(2)   financial resources and ability to bear the risk of being held liable for loss;

(3)   expertise in public key technology and familiarity with proper security procedures;

(4)   longevity;

(5)   approval of hardware and software;

(6)   maintenance of an audit trail and audit by an independent entity;

(7)   existence of a contingency plan for disaster recovery;

(8)   personnel selection and management;

(9)   protection arrangements for the certification authority's own private key;

(10)   internal security;

(11)   arrangements for termination of operations, including notice to users;

(12)   warranties and representations (given or excluded);

(13)   limitation of liability;

(14)   insurance;

(15)   inter-operability with other certification authorities;

(16)   revocation procedures.

The inclusion of longevity is interesting. It suggests that the Working Group had in mind that certification services would preferably be provided by established and supposedly enduring organisations rather than new businesses springing up to offer these services. The most successful model to date in terms of active usage has of course been that of Identrus, a public key-based signature and certification scheme set up by the international banking community. However, the other contender is VeriSign Inc, a company which came into existence only on being spun out of the cryptography company RSA Data Security Inc in the mid-1990s.

It is also curious that inter-operability with other certification authorities is listed as a factor to be considered in assessing trustworthiness. It is clearly a factor affecting the usefulness of the authority's certificates, but does not appear to have any direct relationship to trustworthiness.

5–026   The other major issue addressed by the Model Law is that of recognition of foreign certificates and electronic signatures, which is the subject of Article 12. The essence of this Article is non-discrimination on the grounds of location. Paragraph (1) provides that neither the geographic location where the certificate is issued nor the signature created or used, nor the geographic place of business of either issuer or signatory may be taken into account in determining whether the certificate is valid. Instead the sole criterion for either a foreign certificate or foreign signature having legal effect should be whether they offer a substantially equivalent level of reliability to a domestic certificate or signature of the same type. In turn, equivalence of reliability is to be assessed by reference to recognised international standards, which may be either technical, legal or commercial, and "any other relevant factors". The Guide to Enactment explains that this was directed in particular at the factors listed in Articles 6, 9 and 10. Article 12 does however provide an exception: the parties can between themselves agree to the use of a particular type of electronic signature or certificate provided that the agreement would be valid or effective under the applicable law.

National laws implementing the Model Law have not been consistent in their treatment of foreign-based certificates or certification service providers, despite the fact that most countries appear to recognise the criticality of international recognition.

The Model Laws being finished, the Working Group which prepared them began work in 2002 on a draft Convention on Electronic Contracting. This would, unlike the Model Laws, be binding upon signatories, but at the time of writing the draft appears to be a long way from completion.

ICC General Usage for Internationally Digitally Ensured Commerce (version II)

5–027   The objective of the ICC's Usage for Internationally Digitally Ensured Commerce (GUIDEC) is to establish best practice for electronic transactions across large-scale public networks in such a way as to allocate risk and liability equitably among transacting parties in accordance with existing business practice. This is of course a significant factor to be taken into account by a tribunal in assessing the appropriateness of reliability of an electronic signature method, under Article 7 of the Model Law on Electronic Commerce.

The first version of the GUIDEC was published in November 1997 as part of the ICC's Electronic Commerce Project. A second version was released in October 2001, carrying on from the original: it retains most of the issues discussed in the previous version but attempts to go further in the field of application (for example, the possible role of the new technologies of biometrics), and contains several new definitions and best practices.

As might be expected from a project of the ICC, the GUIDEC is aimed only at international business transactions and assumes that the parties are expert commercial actors. Like the Model Laws, it covers the rights and responsibilities of subscribers, certifiers and relying parties. Also like the Model Laws, it primarily considers PKI based systems using digital signatures, but states that most of its principles will apply for other technologies as well.

The proposed best practices break into two sections: authenticating a message, and certification. Authentication is defined for the purposes of the document as recording or adopting a digital seal or symbol associated with a message with the present intention of identifying oneself with the message, which accords with the normal American usage.[24]

(1)   The signatory

With respect to authentication, the best practices attribute loss resulting from a forgery of a digital signature or alteration of a document, which occurs because the purported signatory has failed to safeguard their key or otherwise, to the purported signatory.[25] A signatory using a device to sign is expressly required to exercise *as a minimum* reasonable care to prevent its unauthorised use.[26] Reasonableness is a standard well understood in common law jurisdictions, though less so in civil law countries, where the concept of the orderly businessman may be a more appropriate referent. However, the GUIDEC commentary helpfully sets out the basic requirements which the reasonable or orderly businessperson might be expected to meet. This includes keeping the signature device in a location to which physical access is limited and carefully controlled—the lamentably common practice of private keys being kept on floppy disks in the users' desk drawers is clearly not adequate. Access by a password or phrase, biometrically or by other secure mechanism is recommended. Authentication by a suitably authorised agent, however, is accepted—although the commentary recommends that the person transacting with the agent should obtain a certificate "or other, more reliable proof" of agency.[27] The drafters also provide that the recipient of a message can request further assurances of its validity if not satisfied that the method used was appropriate under the circumstances of the transaction. This could include requiring the message to be re-authenticated using a technologically more reliable method.[28] Where doubt is being cast on a signature *ab initio* the provision of a faxed or even hard copy manuscript signature may be the most prudent approach.

(2)   The certification service provider

Certification occupies considerably more space. Principally, the rights and responsibilities of the certifier are set out. The certifier's obligation is in effect to let the relying parties know what information it has or has not verified, and its certification practice, to enable the relying parties to carry out their own risk assessment.[29] The certifier is also obliged to keep records for a reasonable period of time—which the drafters suggest should be the same as those laid down by limitation provisions and professional rules for equivalent paper documents.[30] This sensible suggestion has been adopted in only a small number of national laws.

Upon ceasing business, the records must be transferred to a qualified successor.[31] This provision is obvious good sense and, in these days of abrupt insolvencies of venerable institutions and frequent takeovers and mergers, more pragmatic than the suggestion in the Guide to Enactment of the UNCITRAL Model Law that an organisation's longevity should be a factor in assessing its trustworthiness,[32] but unfortunately incapable of being a legal requirement since once the certifier has gone out of business it is likely to be extremely difficult, to say the least, under most legal systems to impose any sanctions upon any participant for a failure to comply. Many jurisdictions have enacted a variant of this under which a certification service provider which is about to go out of business must give notice of that fact to the national registry of certification service providers to enable

5–028

5–029

the records to be preserved and transferred to either a successor certification service provider or the registry itself.

The certifier is also required not to act where it has any conflict of interest, a requirement not laid down in the Model Laws, and to refrain from contributing to any breach of duty by a subscriber.[33] Further, it must revoke a certificate if it confirms either that a material fact in the certificate is false, or that its information system has been compromised such that the certificate's reliability is affected. It is proposed that it should be able to but not have to suspend the certificate while investigating, although this would be a matter for the contract between the certifier and its subscribers.[34] These latter proposals have been widely enacted.

(3) The relying party

5–030   The relying party is entitled to rely upon a valid certificate unless they have notice that the certifier has failed to satisfy a material requirement of authenticated message practice such as those set out above.[35] Since the reference is only to valid certificates, it is to be assumed that the relying party checks any revocation list or other form of notice as to the status of the certificate before proceeding.[36] This provision is not intended to override any legal provisions relating to fraud, negligence and similar doctrines.

Although the GUIDEC has no legal force in any country, it does set out the sort of practices which a prudent businessperson would be expected to follow by the most senior international business forum. As such, it is likely to be very influential with national courts in assessing whether or not a party to a disputed transaction has behaved reasonably and exercised appropriate control over the mechanism of the transaction. Of course, the GUIDEC recognises that many transactions simply may not be of sufficient value or other significance to warrant invoking all of the safeguards it recommends, and no doubt a court faced with a dispute over a relatively minor transaction would acknowledge the same. But where a serious dispute takes place, the GUIDEC approach may well be persuasive.

OECD Ministerial Declaration on Authentication for Electronic Commerce

5–031   Following the OECD's 1998 Ottawa Conference on "A Borderless World: realising the potential of global electronic commerce" the Ministers of the member countries of the OECD made a declaration of a series of intentions regarding electronic authentication. Probably the most significant is their intention to take a non-discriminatory approach to electronic authentication from other countries. They also declared the intention to encourage efforts to develop authentication technologies and mechanisms and facilitate the use of those technologies and mechanisms for electronic commerce; amend, where appropriate, technology or media specific requirements in current laws or policies that may impede the use of information and communication technologies and electronic authentication mechanisms (bearing in mind in particular the UNCITRAL Model Law on electronic commerce); proceed with the application of electronic authentication technologies to enhance the delivery of government services and programmes to the public; and continue to work at the international level together with business, industry and user representatives concerning authentication technologies and mechanisms to facilitate global electronic commerce.[37]

Although none of these commitments is ground-breaking in itself, the list as a whole is an ambitious one. Further, the membership of the OECD is an interesting mix, including a number of European countries including Switzerland, Iceland and Norway, as well as Turkey, Japan, South Korea, Australia and New Zealand, Canada and the United States. This Declaration is therefore a significant plank in building a global consensus on electronic signatures, and in particular the commitment to take a non-discriminatory approach to overseas forms of electronic authentication should be a major contributor towards the use of electronic signatures in cross-border transactions.

The Declaration was followed up by a survey in 2001 by the OECD's Working Party for Information Security and Privacy, assessing the progress which member states had made in the intervening four years in implementing the Declaration. The review was released in September 2002.[38] It established that many countries are still developing laws and policies in the light of evolving technologies and of the work at international level, so that a further review will still be needed at some future stage. On the issue of international recognition, the survey did not find any country which had an express policy of discrimination against foreign authentication, but commented that the criteria laid down for recognition of signatures of foreign origin may be interpreted differently in different jurisdictions despite being expressed generically. Further, accreditation requirements for certification service providers are likely to vary from country to country which may act as an effective barrier to the recognition of foreign certificates. There were regional standardisation initiatives in progress (European Union, Asia-Pacific Economic Cooperation (APEC)) and bilateral collaboration between the United Kingdom and Canada aimed at facilitating interoperability of the two countries' systems. The report observed, however, that these were not sufficient to respond to the requirements of a wider international approach. It recommended the establishment of an international framework for information exchange and study. **5–032**

The study also reviewed Members' governments' activities aimed at applying authentication technologies to delivery of government services. All 28 of the countries which responded to the survey had started either planning or implementing some initiative such as tax or VAT services being delivered electronically. It is hoped that the introduction of such services may act as a driver to encourage increased use of electronic signatures in the private sector also.

EU Electronic Signatures Directive

Origins

In September 1996, the European Parliament invited the European Commission to prepare legal provisions relating to information security and confidentiality, digital identification and the protection of privacy.[39] The European Council followed suit in November 1996, inviting both the Commission and the Member States to prepare consistent measures on the integrity and authenticity of electronically transmitted documents.[40] The result was a first discussion paper, *Towards a European Framework for Digital Signatures and Encryption*, published in October 1997,[41] at the same time as the Commission was formulating the Directive on Electronic Commerce.[42] As the title betrays, although the paper makes passing reference to the possibility of other solutions, at the time the Commission was thinking only in terms of public key cryptography, prompted by the legislation which had already been passed in Germany[43] and Italy[44] on digital signatures. The possibility that other Member States would follow suit and introduce their own, potentially incompatible legislation governing digital signatures and encryption, leading to a further obstacle to the proper functioning of the Internal Market, was the motivation for addressing the whole area at Community level. **5–033**

The discussion paper reviewed the basic parties involved in a public key digital signature system, and highlighted in particular the range of trusted third party functions which could be involved—time stamping, key management and so on—distinguishing these from the core role of a certification authority: authenticating the ownership and characteristics of a public key so that it can be trusted. The paper acknowledges both the hierarchical approach to certification, along the lines of the X.500 standards developed by the International Telecommunications Union (ITU),[45] and also the "web of trust" approach adopted by the Pretty Good Privacy community. The question of whether a certification authority should be able to "self-certify" or not was raised but not conclusively answered. The paper did conclude that contrary to the existing common approach of Germany and Italy both licensed and unlicensed certification authorities ought to be able to operate in the market.

5–034   The original objective was to provide mutual recognition of certificates issued in one Member State by the courts and authorities of another. The Commission foresaw national structures coordinated by a mechanism at European level, with the Community then taking the lead in any negotiations with third countries over mutual recognition of their respective certificates. It also considered the possibility of a harmonisation of European certification services for issue, evaluation and procedures to reduce the uncertainties and mistrust which could arise in dealings with entities operating under unknown rules. The Commission also felt that the rules on certification authorities' liability should be clear to encourage reliance upon their services—although a better reason for this might be to encourage potential service providers to come forwards, in view of the otherwise apparently open-ended liability they could face.

As regards signatures themselves, the Commission identified the problems of thoughtless signing and of associating a given key, which indubitably made a given signature, with a particular person, who may or may not have been wielding that key at the time. Issues were identified with the rules of evidence in some Member States whereby a digital signature would simply not be admissible in Court proceedings as not complying with a requirement for writing. The idea that each person has just one handwritten signature, copies of which can be distinguished more readily than can forged digital signatures, was accepted.

Legislative history

5–035   This paper was followed in October 1998 by a draft proposal for a Directive on a common framework for electronic signatures.[46] In this, the emphasis is on the importance of interoperability and the role of voluntary accreditation schemes in establishing the level of trust necessary for certification authorities to function in open environments. This framework was perceived as the establishing foundation upon which electronic signatures might flourish. The draft was intended to have no effect within closed environments such as EDI systems, which are governed exclusively by the agreements between the parties and therefore have no need of legal harmonisation. To encourage the provision of certification services Member States were barred from requiring a certification service provider to be authorised before offering its services.

The draft followed the UNCITRAL principle that a signature should not be denied legal validity solely on the grounds that it is in the form of electronic data, but went on to specify (in its own terminology) that neither the lack of a qualified certificate, nor the lack of a certificate from an accredited certification service provider nor the use of a certificate from a certification service provider from another Member State should be a bar to recognition. Nevertheless, it went beyond the UNCITRAL Model Law in proposing a category of qualified certificates which would confer upon electronic signatures associated with them have the same status in law as handwritten signatures. This version of the "two tier" approach was intended to maximise the market's freedom to find new solutions and the Courts' ability to give these effect, while also providing a mechanism upon which parties could rely with confidence from the outset as having definite legal effect—subject to any challenge on grounds such as fraud, mistake, duress or undue influence.[47]

The draft also proposed liability rules for certification service providers, and looked hopefully towards the possibility of agreeing multilateral rules on mutual recognition of certification services. The issue of privacy and data protection, always a major concern in Europe, led to the inclusion of a provision requiring Member States to permit certificates to be issued under a pseudonym of the subscriber, a provision which was not contemplated in the UNCITRAL discussions. The draft was carefully written *not* to interfere with any aspect of contract law or other legal requirements for signatures.   **5–036**

The importance attributed to this proposal is evident from the speed with which it managed to pass through the various legislative stages. Several of the bodies which scrutinised the draft commented on the fact that the plethora of international initiatives then underway could result in conflicts between the various sets of rules resulting. It was reviewed by the Economic and Social Committee within two months, and by Committee of the Regions and the European Parliament on January 13, 1999. The latter passed the proposal subject to a number of amendments, all of which were relatively minor in substance. The Commission accepted more than two thirds of the amendments, rejecting proposals to require certification service providers to be independent (on the grounds that the term is ambiguous), and to reiterate the need for respect for existing data protection and privacy laws (on the grounds that these in any case must be respected). The amendments accepted included deletion of the reference to digital signatures as the most recognised form of electronic signature, and other references to the signature being digital.

The Economic and Social Committee expressed serious reservations as to the prospect of unaccredited certification service providers being able to issue certificates which might be given legal validity. They wanted accreditation to be subject to public supervision. The Committee also wanted recognition of certificates from certification service providers established in non-Member States to be limited to those countries which granted mutual recognition to certificates from Community certification service providers. However, the opinion of this Committee, though influential, is not binding on the Commission and the Committee has no power to veto proposed legislation. The comments do not appear to have been acted upon.   **5–037**

The Committee of the Regions' principal comment was to highlight the possible significance of electronic signatures in the relationship between individuals and public administration, in view of initiatives then being taken such as the Italian smart card electronic identity. A recital to this effect was added as a result.

The Commission having amended its proposal as required by the Parliament, the Council reached a Common Position on the amended draft on June 28, 1999 and the Parliament approved it on October 27, 1999, just over a year after the publication of the first draft.

The final form of the Directive
The Directive as passed consists of 15 Articles, of which 8 deal with substantive matters, and 28 recitals which explain the context and intent of the text. The remainder, Articles 9   **5–038**

to 15, concern implementation and notification of existing provisions by Member States, entry into force and the establishment of a reporting Committee which is intended to review the operation of the Directive and report to the Parliament and Council by July 19, 2003.[48]

The context of the text is, as discussed above, the concern that divergent rules relating to the legal recognition of electronic signatures in Member States and the accreditation of certification service providers may create a significant barrier to the use of electronic communications and electronic commerce. The technological roots of the Directive in digital signatures in particular remain in recital 5, which discusses the interoperability and free movement issue, but confirms that its provisions are without prejudice to the laws relating to dual-use goods. These laws are relevant as they relate to the export of products capable of both military and civilian application. Cryptography software and products are therefore covered by them in principle.[49] Thereafter, recital 8 confirms the Directive's intent to be technologically neutral in the face of the pace of technological development and the global character of the Internet.

The substantive articles, apart from defining all of the necessary terms, deal with the scope of the Directive, market access by and liability of certification service providers, internal market principles, the legal effects of electronic signatures, international (i.e. cross-border) aspects and data protection. They do not lay down any requirements for the regulation of certification service providers. This is left to Member States' national law.

Summary

5–039   In summary, Article 5 of the Directive establishes two levels of electronic signature. Electronic signatures, without qualification, may or may not have legal effect or be admissible in Court according to the national laws of each Member State. An electronic signature does not qualify for automatic legal recognition merely by virtue of being electronic in form. Conversely, Member States are not permitted to deny either legal effect or admissibility solely on the grounds that the signature is electronic and not an advanced electronic signature.[50]

Member States must ensure that advanced electronic signatures created by a secure signature creation device (as defined in the Directive) and supported by a qualified certificate (also defined) satisfy any legal requirements of a signature in relation to electronic data in the same manner as handwritten signatures do in relation to paper-based data and that they will be admissible in legal proceedings.[51] This provision sets out a series of separate criteria to be satisfied by an electronic signature in order to obtain the benefit of legal certainty. There is no term in the Directive itself for a signature which satisfies these requirements, but it is a convenient shorthand to refer to it as a qualified signature. The definitions of these criteria— advanced electronic signature, secure signature-creation-device and qualified certificate— along with the liability of certification service providers and the criteria a certification service provider must meet to issue qualified certificates, make up the bulk of the Directive.

The Directive, unlike the UNCITRAL Model Law or the ICC GUIDEC, does not attempt to regulate the conduct of either the signatory or the relying party. There are however recommendations as to how a signature should be securely verified, and the liability of a certification service provider to a relying party is only to one whose reliance was reasonable. This is discussed in the context of Article 6 below.

(i)   Article 1: Scope

This article states the facilitatory, as opposed to mandatory, nature of the Directive. It recognises that in some Member States electronic signatures may already be recognised, and so aims only to facilitate the use of electronic signature and contribute to their legal recognition. This is achieved by establishing a legal framework for electronic signatures and for certain certification services, in order to ensure the proper functioning of the internal market.

Recital 16 clarifies that no such framework is considered necessary for electronic signatures used exclusively within systems based on voluntary agreements under private law between a specified number of participants, which should be respected to the extent permitted by existing national law. In other words, Article 1 is not to be interpreted to interfere with the operation of closed systems such as EDI. However, the recital does go on to state that "the legal effectiveness of electronic signatures used in such systems and their admissibility as evidence in legal proceedings should be recognised". Thus, the *framework* elements of the Directive are not intended to apply to closed systems but the provisions giving legal effect to electronic signatures and requiring them to be acknowledged by national courts as admissible evidence, are.

Article 1 also expressly excludes from the scope of the Directive any aspect of contract formation or validity or other form requirements prescribed by national law. Nor does the Directive affect any rules or limits contained in national or Community law governing the use of documents.

(ii)   Article 5: Legal effects of electronic signatures
Since this Article is the heart of the Directive it is set out here in full, with defined terms indicated in italics.

1.   Member States shall ensure that *advanced electronic signatures* which are based on a *qualified certificate* and which are created by a *secure signature-creation-device*:

(a)   satisfy the legal requirements of a signature in relation to data in electronic form in the same manner as a handwritten signature satisfies those requirements in relation to paper-based data; and

(b)   are admissible as evidence in legal proceedings.

2.   Member States shall ensure that an *electronic signature* is not denied legal effectiveness and admissibility as evidence in legal proceedings solely on the grounds that it is:

-   in electronic form, or

-   not based upon a qualified certificate, or

-   not based upon a qualified certificate issued by an accredited *certification-service-provider*, or

-   not created by a secure signature-creation-device.

The relevant definitions, which are given in Article 2, control the interpretation of the Article. Since the definition of advanced electronic signature is dependent upon the definition of electronic signature, this will be examined first.

Electronic signature
An electronic signature is:

"data in electronic form which are attached to or logically associated with other electronic data and which serve as a method of authentication"

This is an extremely broad definition.[52] There are no limits on the data itself, which may be anything from a single bit (0 or 1 being the smallest unit of information which an electronic system can recognise)[53] through to a digital signature consisting of thousands of bits and created using advanced technology. The data may represent in ASCI code the letters of the signatory's name, initials or a user identifier for a computer system, a scanned bitmap of the signatory's handwritten signature or a biometric identifier. All that is required is that the data, whatever they may be, are fulfilling the functions of a signature, namely to authenticate the message or other data with which they are associated.

There must be some form of attachment to or association with other data—that is, the data which are being signed. It is not clear in the electronic context what "attached to" may mean. The electronic signals making up one part of a file are not attached to the remainder of the file in any physical sense analogous to the physical bond between the ink of a handwritten signature and the paper upon which it is written. However, electronic signature data may be logically associated with the remainder of the file if they are either incorporated in the file, such that a computer reading the file treats the whole as a single document, or connected to it by, for example, a pointer incorporated in the file which refers the computer to an entry in a database where the signature may be found.

5–043　　The signature data must serve as a method of authentication. The most likely interpretation of "authentication" in this context is that the data must be added by the signatory as a process of signifying approval or intention to be bound, or conferring binding legal significance upon the remainder of the document. This meaning is preferred. The alternative interpretation is that the data must establish that they or the document, which purports to be signed, are authentic in the sense of original or genuine, *i.e.* that it validates the identity of the purported signatory and has not been altered since it was signed. To adopt this interpretation would import into the definition of electronic signature two out of the four required characteristics of an advanced electronic signature, namely that it be capable of identifying the signatory and be linked to the data to which it relates in such a manner that any subsequent chance of the data is detectable.[54] These elements would then be redundant in the definition of advanced electronic signature. This interpretation of authentication in the Directive's definition of electronic signature is also consistent with the UNCITRAL definition of an electronic signature, which makes an intention to signify approval an essential element of the signature.[55] However, the expert group of the European Electronic Signature Standardisation Initiative concluded[56] that only the validation of claimed identity aspect was required. In their view some additional indication of approval is required, such as express text in the document itself or by reference to a signature policy. Some clarification by national courts or ultimately the European Court of Justice may ultimately be required on this point.

5–044　　A single "1" may therefore be able to authenticate a document provided that it is appended to the document with that purpose. Of course, it may not be self-evident from a "1" that this is its purpose unless there is some external reason so to believe—for example, that the signatory clicks on a particular button on a website which is marked "I have read and agree to the terms and conditions above". Nor does the "1" in itself identify the signatory in any way. But the same points are true of the "X" traditionally used by illiterates as a signature: a cross in the margin of a document might ordinarily indicate disagreement with the text, it is the context which makes an "X" a signature.

Advanced electronic signature
An advanced electronic signature means an electronic signature which is: **5–045**

"(a) uniquely linked to the signatory;

(b) capable of identifying the signatory;

(c) created using means that the signatory can maintain under his sole control; and

(d) linked to the data to which it relates in such a manner that any subsequent change of the data is detectable."

An advanced electronic signature therefore has to meet a very much stricter set of requirements than an electronic signature. The definition is similar to the ISO 7498 definition of a digital signature, which includes not only signatures created by public key cryptographic methods but also symmetric cryptographic methods associated with tamper-proof signature creation and verification devices. The single bit of data fails all four branches of the test. A bitmap of a handwritten signature would arguably pass the first two limbs but not the last two, since a signature which has been scanned and transmitted once can be replicated exactly and attached to any subsequent document by anyone who obtains a copy. Nor does the presence of the scanned signature assist at all in proving whether there has been any subsequent alteration. Likewise biometric identifiers, once created, can be duplicated for subsequent use.

It is arguable that even a digital signature on its own, while clearly meeting the second,   **5–046**
third and fourth criteria, does not qualify under the first branch of the test. This is because the signature is not uniquely linked to the signatory: it is uniquely linked only to the signatory's private key. In the real world, no one is ever going to keep their private key in their head, inaccessible to all others. The number is simply too long. So in practice private keys will be stored: in computer memories, on floppy disks, on smart cards. These are the 'means that the signatory can maintain under his sole control' referred to in the third branch of the test, but it is this control issue which will be the source of any disputes as to whether or not a signature has been validly given or not.[57] Given the presence of this third limb, it is likely that the first criterion will be taken only to refer to the existence of some unique logical link between the signature and the signatory, such as the existence of a certificate stating that any digital signature produced with the associated private key is that of the signatory.

The presence of the fourth limb of the test implies the use of digital signatures for the present since this, in combination with the message digest function, is the only technology currently able to detect subsequent changes to the signed data. Thus, whatever data is used as the signature itself, it will still have to be bound to the signed data using a digital signature technique in order to produce an advanced electronic signature.

To obtain the benefit of Article 5(1), an advanced electronic signature must be based on a qualified certificate. A qualified certificate is a particular species of certificate, which is itself a defined term.

Certificate
A certificate is defined as: **5–047**

"an electronic attestation which links signature-verification data to a person and confirms the identity of that person."

This would include an e-mail sent by one private individual to another stating:

> "the attached is Jane Smith's public key. Jane is a friend of mine from school who is now working in information technology and wanted to get in touch with you."

Under the Directive, as under the UNCITRAL Model Law, such a certificate may be sufficient for the recipient to rely on depending upon the circumstances. If Jane simply wants to share some observations on a topic of mutual interest, or even sell the recipient a secondhand book on the same, then the recipient would certainly be justified in accepting this e-mail as sufficient evidence of her identity and public key. If Jane is CEO of a multinational who is proposing a takeover of the recipient's business, possibly it would be reasonable to proceed with a little more circumspection before accepting a contract signed with the private key corresponding to this public one.

The definition would of course also cover standardised certificates such as the ITU X.509 format.

The definition of qualified certificate follows on from this definition.

Qualified certificate

5–048   Qualified certificates must comply with a substantial list of requirements. These are set out in Annex I of the Directive, and introduce further defined terms. The certificate must contain:

(a)   an indication that the certificate is issued as a qualified certificate;

(b)   the identification of the *certification-service-provider* and the State in which it is established;

(c)   the name of the *signatory* or a pseudonym, which shall be identified as such;

(d)   the provision for a specific attribute of the signatory to be included if relevant, depending on the purpose for which the certificate is intended;

(e)   *signature-verification data* which correspond to *signature-creation data* under the control of the signatory;

(f)   an indication of the beginning and end of the period of validity of the certificate;

(g)   the identity code of the certificate;

(h)   the advanced electronic signature of the certification-service-provider issuing it;

(i)   limitations on the scope of use of the certificate, if applicable; and

(j)   limits on the value of transactions for which the certificate can be used, if applicable.

5–049   This is a straightforward list of the minimum requirements to make a certificate intended to have legal effect transparent to the holder and to third parties who may want to rely upon the signature in question. It does not include all of the information which Article 9 of the UNCITRAL Model Law on Electronic Signatures would require to be made available to a relying party. For example, the method used to identify the signatory; any limit on scope or extent of liability undertaken by the certification service provider; whether there is a mechanism for the signatory to give notice of any compromise or possible compromise of the signature creation data; and whether a timely revocation service is offered, are not required. A relying party who is familiar with European law will be aware that provision of a mechanism to give notice and a timely revocation service are both requirements under Annex II, but the remaining proposals of the Model Law are not included anywhere.

Note that unlike the Model Law's proposals this information must be contained in the certificate itself: it cannot be necessary for a potential relying party to refer elsewhere, such as a website, in order to obtain it.

Certification-service-provider

This is another very broad definition. A certification-service-provider is: **5–050**

> "an entity or a legal or natural person who issues certificates or provides other services related to electronic signatures."

There is no limit on what services may bring an organisation or person within the definition, provided that they relate to electronic signatures. Registration services stopping short of actual issuance of certificates, time-stamping, directory services and others will fall within it. There is also no requirement that a certification-service-provider meet any standard with respect to any of their activities. The sender of the Jane Smith e-mail above is a certification service provider within this definition.

In order to issue qualified certificates, a certification-service-provider must comply with a lengthy set of requirements set out in Annex II of the Directive. These lay down the standards to which its technical and management systems must adhere. The issuing certification service provider must:

(a)   demonstrate the reliability necessary for providing certification services;

(b)   ensure the operation of a prompt and secure directory and a secure and immediate revocation service;

(c)   ensure that the date and time when a certificate is issued or revoked can be determined precisely;

(d)   verify, by appropriate means in accordance with national law, the identity and, if applicable, any specific attributes of the person to which a qualified certificate is issued;

(e)   employ personnel who possess the expert knowledge, experience and qualifications necessary for the services provided, in particular competence at managerial level, experience in electronic signature technology and familiarity with proper security procedures; they must also apply administrative and management procedures which are adequate and correspond to recognised standards;

(f)   use trustworthy systems and products which are protected against modification and ensure the technical and cryptographic security of the process supported by them;

(g)   take measures against forgery of certificates and, in cases where the certification-service-provider generates signature-creation data, guarantee confidentiality during the process of generating such data;

(h)   maintain sufficient financial resources to operate in conformity with the requirements laid down in the Directive, in particular to bear the risk of liability for damages, for example, by obtaining appropriate insurance;

(i)   record all relevant information concerning a qualified certificate for an appropriate period of time, in particular for the purpose of providing evidence of certification for the purposes of legal proceedings. Such recording may be done electronically;

(j)   not store or copy signature-creation data of the person to whom the certification-services-provider provided key management services;

(k)   before entering into a contractual relationship with a person seeking a certificate to support his electronic signature, inform that person by a durable means of communication of the precise terms and conditions regarding the use of the certificate, including:

- any limitations on its use,

- the existence of a voluntary accreditations scheme and

- procedures for complaints and dispute settlement.

   Such information, which may be transmitted electronically, must be in writing and in readily understandable language. Relevant parts of this information must also be made available on request to third-parties relying on the certificate;

(l)   use trustworthy systems to store certificates in a verifiable form so that:

- only authorised persons can make entries and changes;

- information can be checked for authenticity;

- certificates are publicly available for retrieval in only those cases for which the certificate-holder's consent has been obtained; and

- any technical changes compromising these security requirements are apparent to the operator.

5–051   This list meets the stipulation of Article 9 of the UNCITRAL Model Law, that the certification service provider should use trustworthy systems, procedures and human resources. It also includes most of the factors which Article 10 of the Model Law lays down for assessing a certification service provider's trustworthiness—although two factors are not explicitly present: an independent audit; and any form of accreditation or State supervision.

Point (e) in the list requires a certification service provider which wishes to issue qualified certificates to correspond to "recognised standards" as regards its administrative and management procedures. This reference leaves the certification service provider the choice of whether to comply with particular national or international standards, but imposes the need to comply with at least one whether or not it actually becomes accredited. However, the easiest way to demonstrate compliance is to obtain the recognition of the body responsible for the standard. Since standards of this nature ordinarily require an audit of activities within their scope, and accordingly require records to be kept, this requirement goes some way towards meeting the Model Law's stipulation of independent audit—since the latter did not specify what it was that was to be audited.

Although point (k) in the list requires the certification service provider to inform a prospective subscriber of the existence of any accreditation scheme before entering into a contract, it does *not* require the certification service provider to be accredited itself: if the certification service provider is not accredited, the consumer is to be given the option of making an informed choice instead to go to an accredited body. Accreditation must be, in principle at least, voluntary. Voluntary accreditation is also a defined term as discussed below.

Most of the list are self-explanatory, but two give pause for thought. Point (a) requires **5–052** the certification service provider to *demonstrate* its reliability. This suggests a need to establish to some external body that it is reliable. Member States are not permitted to require a certification service provider to be registered, licensed or accredited before beginning operations,[58] although they are required to establish a supervision system. This requirement therefore permits Member States' supervision to include an element of standard setting and enforcement at least for certification service providers which wish to issue qualified certificates.

Point (l) requires the certification service provider to store certificates in a verifiable form so that the information can be checked for *authenticity*. It is not entirely clear what is meant by authenticity in this context. Pure information, as opposed to a document in which it is contained, may be accurate or inaccurate, complete or partial but it is difficult to think of a sense in which it can be authentic or inauthentic—unless perhaps it is meant that the check is to establish whether it is in fact the information which was provided by the subscriber and not some subset or variant of it. However, this interpretation would not make sense in the context since it is the certificate which is to be stored and not the materials provided by the subscriber from which the information must have been drawn.

The requirement of point (f) for trustworthiness of a certification service provider's systems will be presumed to be met if the systems comply with a standard recognised by the European Commission and published in the Official Journal.[59] None had yet been published at the time of writing but a major standards project was in progress. It is discussed in Chapter 10.

Voluntary accreditation
A voluntary accreditation is: **5–053**

"any permission, setting out rights and obligations specific to the provision of certification services, to be granted upon request by the certification-service-provider concerned, by the public or private body charged with the elaboration of, and supervision of compliance with, such rights and obligations, where the certification-service-provider is not entitled to exercise the rights stemming from the permission until it has received the decision by the body."

In other words, a certification service provider can choose whether or not to apply for accreditation under any accreditation scheme (which may be run by the state or privately). In order to become accredited, it will need to meet the criteria laid down for the scheme. It may not describe itself as accredited, however, or use any associated quality mark unless and until the supervising body for the scheme has accepted its application. However, bear in mind that Article 5(2) specifies that failure to become accredited cannot be used as a basis for denying legal effectiveness to the signatures supported by certificates it has issued.

Signatory

5–054   A signatory is defined as:

> "a person who holds a signature creation device and acts either on his own behalf or on behalf of the natural or legal person or entity he represents."

At first sight this definition might appear to undo the effect of the broad definition of electronic signature, but in fact the term signatory appears in the rest of the Directive only in the context of certification. The reference to acting on behalf of another, and in particular a legal person or entity, was inserted by the European Parliament.

Signature-creation   data/Signature-creation   device/Signature-verification   data/Signature-verification device

5–055   These four definitions relate to any data or device used by the signatory to create or verify an electronic signature.

The data must be unique, although the definition of signature-creation-data goes on to state that codes as well as private cryptographic keys will be included. There is a potential contradiction here. As regards codes, it is unlikely that any code will ever be unique since it will probably consist of alphanumeric symbols in one of the world's recognised writing systems. Particularly where the latin alphabet and Arabic numerals are used, any given code is statistically bound to be selected by more than one person worldwide. Uniqueness is in any case incapable of proof in any dispute since the keys or codes in use by all other users worldwide or even within the European Union or a given Member State will not be available for the comparison to be drawn. Even in respect of cryptographic keys, the best that a signatory can do is to state that their key pair was generated at random and privately, and to the best of their knowledge and belief no other person is using an identical pair. In these circumstances, it is unlikely that "unique" will be given any strict interpretation in these definitions.

The devices used to implement the signature creation data—that is, create signatures— or signature verification data—that is, verify signatures—may be either configured software or hardware. This could include a program on a computer (PC, laptop, palmtop or even mobile phone), a smart card or other device.

Note that neither the data nor the device need be such that the signature generated is unique nor that it cannot be obtained by others.

Secure-signature-creation device

5–056   There are four requirements for a signature creation device to qualify as a secure-signature-creation device, and these are set out in Annex III to the Directive. The device:

> "must, by appropriate technical and procedural means, ensure at the least that:
>
> (a)   the signature-creation-data used for signature generation can practically occur only once, and that their secrecy is reasonably assured;
>
> (b)   the signature-creation-data used for signature generation cannot, with reasonable assurance, be derived and the signature is protected against forgery using currently available technology;
>
> (c)   the signature-creation-data used for signature generation can be reliably protected by the legitimate signatory against the use of others."

The inclusion of "at the least" indicates that these are minimum criteria. Nevertheless, the standard laid down is a high one, although the use of "reasonably" leaves some room for debate. The device must invoke both technical and procedural means, which can be read to suggest that the signatory, or their IT support, cannot simply delegate all responsibility for the creation of the signature to the computer but must pass some threshold procedural requirement, such as entering a password or biometric identifier, to access the signature creation step.

Clause (a) appears to suggest that the secure signature creation device is responsible for generating the signature creation data as well as the signature, and for safeguarding them afterwards. The former would be inconsistent with the obvious meaning of the name of the device and the wording of the definition of *signature-creation device,* which specifies that the device's function is to *implement* the signature creation data rather than to generate them. However, it is difficult to see how a secure-signature-creation device can perform the function of "ensuring that the signature-creation-data used for signature generation can practically occur only once" if it does not generate them. A smart card, for example, which stores a signatory's private key, does not ensure that the key data occur only once; nor does a computer program which uses the key to generate a digital signature unless it generates a new key pair at the time of signing every time—which would render the system of certification by third parties useless. This provision would therefore seem to require the secure-signature-creation device to perform some sort of check upon the data that are being used, perhaps by checking the bit length in order to ensure that it is long enough that statistically it is unlikely to be in use by another person. This was almost certainly not what the drafters intended. The intention was probably that the device would produce a *signature* which could occur only once—the signed message digest being unique to the message signed.

The device must also be sufficiently well-protected to maintain the secrecy of the key   **5–057** pair against outside access threats, either by "eavesdropping" techniques such as side-channel attacks, or by simply copying the whole device.

Clause (b) requires a key mechanism to be used such that the signature-creation-data cannot be derived with reasonable assurance. The wording does not specify from what the signature-creation data might be derived, but there are two obvious options: the signature, and the signature-verification data. The former is clearly essential for the signature to be secure from forgery, as the second half of the clause requires. The latter makes sense in the context of public key cryptography since the essence of the asymmetry is that the private key cannot be derived from the public one. Both are probably intended. Clearly, the cryptographic and message digest algorithms chosen must be suitable to achieve these criteria. This can be assured by selecting from those algorithms which meet recognised technical standards.

The second half of the clause is potentially ambiguous in that it is not clear whether it is the protection from forgery which must use currently available technology, or whether the protection should be against any forgery capable of being carried out using currently available technology. However, since the only protection that the device can logically offer to provide is at the level offered by currently available technology, the clause is probably meant to require secure-signature-creation devices to protect the signature from all currently available technological means of forgery. Note that this section of the clause is completely unqualified and thus appears to require absolute protection rather than 'the best that can reasonably be implemented' or similar. This again makes sense principally in the context of cryptography, either symmetric or asymmetric, since these are the systems which use keys substantially proof against brute force attacks.

5–058   It is also not clear whether the potential for forgery by currently available technology is assessed at the time of manufacture or sale of the device, or the time at which it is used to create a signature. The literal interpretation is that the assessment is at the time of signature, since it is at the point of signature that the device is required to be secure in order for the signature produced to be an advanced electronic signature. However, this is contradicted by Article 3(5), which states that all the requirements of Annex III will be presumed to be met by a device if it complies with a standard recognised by the European Commission and published in the Official Journal. The term secure-signature-creation device should therefore be treated as a label rather than a literal description. A number of types of existing device may be able to meet such requirements: smart cards, PCMCIA cards for personal computers, and Personal Digital Assistants, for example, but the standards with which they should comply to be assured of doing so have yet to be adopted. This is expected to follow on from the Electronic Signature Committee's report of July 2003. The determination of whether or not a particular manufacturer's device does comply will be carried out by designated bodies in one or more Member States, each of which already has a nationally recognised accreditation body for accrediting certification bodies for particular products and management systems, themselves operating in accordance with European Norm 45010-12

Clause (c) requires the device to ensure that the data can be reliably protected against the use of others. What degree of reliability is required is not defined: it is unlikely to be absolute, since this is not yet physically attainable, but a degree of assurance is clearly required. Where the signature is being generated on a computer attached to a network, this may require access control to the file where the signature-creation-data are stored even as against the system administrator, who would normally have access to otherwise private files. Certainly the signature-creation data should be password protected as a minimum, and procedural controls implemented to ensure that the password is an effective one (an alphanumeric combination as opposed to a birthday, for example) and changed periodically. The same precautions should be applied to a smart card, since once in unauthorised hands most simple passwords can be guessed relatively quickly, albeit with computer assistance. Ideally, the password should be technologically protected against an exhaustive search attack of trying all possible combinations of letters and numbers.

Further, the device:

> "must not alter the data to be signed or prevent such data from being presented to the signatory prior to the signature process."

This last requirement simply stipulates that the signing process must be transparent, so that the signatory can see what the data are that they are signing and the data remain unchanged by the process of signing. The concern being addressed is the presence in electronic documents of data which are not ordinarily presented on screen. In reality, such data are unlikely to be accessed by the average user even without any technical barrier preventing them from doing so. No signature creation mechanism which did not meet this criterion could function effectively to produce a legal signature.

(iii)   Articles 3, 4 and 8: Market access, data protection and the internal market

5–059   These three articles define Member States' powers and responsibilities with regard to the regulation and supervision of certification service providers and electronic signature products.

Article 3 lays out the extent to which Member States are permitted to control access to their market of anyone wishing to provide certification services. The regimes introduced by Germany and Italy prior to the passing of the Directive both required certification service providers to be registered; the Directive expressly prohibits any requirement of prior authorisation[60] or other measures having the same effect[61] or any limits on the provision of services by certification service providers established in another Member State.[62] Member States' intervention is strictly restricted to the establishment of voluntary accreditation schemes[63] and the establishment of an appropriate system for supervision of certain certification service providers which are located within their territory and issue qualified certificates to the public.[64]

Certification service providers which either do not issue qualified certificates, or issue them only within some closed scheme—an internal certification authority for a government department, company, a university or a professional institute, for example—are not subject to supervision.

Voluntary accreditation schemes must, further, be objective, transparent, proportionate and non-discriminatory. They must be open to an unlimited number of certification service providers unless a numerical limit is imposed for reasons falling outwith the scope of the Directive. Recital 13 states that the existence of such schemes is not to be allowed to reduce competition for certification services, and recital 14 emphasises that the schemes must be truly voluntary so that non-participation does not exclude certification service providers from the marketplace.

5–060 Member States are required to ensure that both certification service providers and the national bodies responsible for accreditation and supervision comply with the requirements of the Data Protection Directive.[65] The issuing of certificates is necessarily going to entail processing and retaining a significant volume of personal data concerning the subscribers. Certification service providers which issue certificates to the public are prohibited from collecting data other than directly from the data subject (i.e. the prospective subscriber) or with his or her explicit consent, and even then only insofar as it is necessary for the purposes of issuing and maintaining the certificate.[66] This would appear to go beyond the requirements of the Data Protection Directive, which permits most forms of processing provided that the conditions laid down in Schedules 2 and 3 are met.[67] Article 8(2) contains no proviso of this sort. The Article on a whole would therefore appear to constrain certification service providers from offering other services which require the use of personal data, or requiring them to collect the same data separately in respect of any services other than certificate issuance and maintenance.

Member States must also designate appropriate bodies to ascertain whether secure signature creation devices meet the requirements of Annex III, but must recognise the findings of any body designated by another Member State.[68] This is intended to prevent the situation arising where a supplier of secure signature creation devices has to have its device approved in every Member State; a single approval will be effective throughout.

Likewise, Member States are required to permit electronic signature products to circulate freely in the internal market.[69] An electronic signature product is defined[70] as:

"hardware or software, or relevant components thereof, which are intended to be used by a certification-service-provider for the provision of electronic-signature services or are intended to be used for the creation or verification of electronic signatures."

5–061 This definition is as broad in effect as the definition of electronic signature. Electronic signature programs such as those embedded in Netscape Navigator and the various e-mail programs available, or smart cards for the storage of private signature keys and biometric devices giving access to a signature function will all come within it. Article 3(5) permits the Commission to publish in the Official Journal the reference numbers of generally recognised standards for electronic signature products.

A specific provision requiring Member States to permit free circulation of such products would appear superfluous in the light of Article 28 of the Treaty of Rome, but may have been considered necessary due to the application to cryptographic products of Council Regulation 1334/2000 establishing a Community-wide regime for the control of export of dual-use goods.[71] However, even under this regime no licences are required for movement of cryptographic goods within the European Union so the inclusion of this reminder in the Directive represents an abundance of caution on the part of the legislators.

Member States are permitted to add further requirements to those in the Directive for electronic signatures which are to be used in the public sector, provided that the additional requirements are:

- objective, transparent, proportionate and non-discriminatory;

- relate only to the specific characteristics of the application concerned; and

- do not constitute an obstacle to cross-border services for citizens.

Typical additional requirements might be those for use in tax matters or social security.

Article 3 also covers future policy. Article 3(6) requires the Member States to work with the Commission to promote the development and use of signature verification devices in the light of the recommendations for secure signature verification in Annex IV of the Directive and also in the interests of consumers.

(iv)   Article 6: liability

5–062 Certification service providers which issue qualified certificates will be liable for any damage caused to any entity, legal or natural person who reasonably relies on a qualified certificate either:

- as regards the accuracy at the time of issue of all information in it (including the fact that it contains all the information prescribed for a qualified certificate);

- for assurance that at the time of issue the signatory did indeed hold the certification creation data corresponding to the signature verification data given or indicated in the certificate;

- for assurance that, where the certification service provider has generated both signature creation and verification data, they can be used in a complementary manner;[72] or

- as not having been revoked.[73]

In each case the certification service provider can escape liability only by proving that it has not acted negligently. This apparent reversal of the burden of proof reflects the expectation that certification service providers may be the target of claims by an unpredictable number of third parties in respect of each certificate they issue. It in effect enables the certification service provider to raise a shield against all such claims provided it maintains adequate systems, procedures and records to be able to demonstrate that it reached a suitable standard of care. This is an onerous requirement, given the complex nature of a certification service provider's operations, but is intended to make the business of qualified certification service provision more attractive. Certification service providers issuing unqualified certificates do not get the benefit of this provision.

Certification service providers are however permitted to limit their liability, either as to scope of use[74] or value of transaction,[75] on the face of the qualified certificates they issue provided that the limitation is recognisable to third parties. Where such a limitation has been included clearly on the certificate and a third party nevertheless relies on the certificate outside that scope, the certification service provider will not face any liability either relating to use outside the scope of use or beyond the specified maximum value. However, certification service providers still face the risk that the limits they impose upon their certificates could, where the signatory deals as a consumer, be found to be unfair contract terms and void as a result of the Unfair Terms in Consumer Contracts Directive.[76]

5–063

The issue of when reliance on a qualified certificate will be reasonable or not is not addressed. Clearly, reliance on a certificate beyond its defined scope of use or specified value limit will not be reasonable, but there is nothing in the Directive to indicate whether or not a relying party will be expected to carry out any of the checks recommended in Annex IV or otherwise attempt to verify the position, in order to be able to claim damages from the certification service provider. In the light of the best practice laid down by the ICC's GUIDEC some courts may be prepared to find that at least minimum precautions ought to be taken. However, the aim of the Directive is to facilitate and encourage increased usage of electronic signatures, so the omission of any defined risk to relying parties could be seen as an element of that encouragement. Given that the Directive, unlike GUIDEC, encompasses the use of electronic signatures by consumers as well as between businesses, certification service providers would be well advised to make sure that all certificates issued clearly state an intended scope of use and value limits, since these may in practice be the only limits which can be placed on reliance on a qualified certificate.

Article 6 does not address certification service providers' liability in respect of unqualified certificates. This leaves Member States entirely free to make whatever provision they see fit.

(v)   Article 7: international aspects

Article 7 deals with the treatment of certification service providers established outside the European Union, and the treatment in third countries of Community undertakings with respect to their access to those markets.

5–064

The Directive anticipates the need to enter into bilateral or multilateral agreements with third countries in order to enable the mutual recognition of certificates for cross-border trade. As a preliminary step, Article 7(1) requires Member States to give legal equivalence to certificates issued by certification service providers established outside the European Union provided that either:

(a)   the certification service provider fulfils the requirements laid down in Annex III and is accredited under an EU voluntary accreditation scheme; or

(b)   the certificate is guaranteed by an EU certification service provider which meets the requirements of Annex III; or

(c)   the certificate or the certification service provider is recognised under a bilateral or multilateral international agreement.

With this in mind, the Article also authorises the Commission to propose to the Council negotiating mandates for such bi- or multi-lateral agreements either to achieve the effective implementation of standards and international agreements,[77] or to assist any EU undertaking which is unable to obtain market access in a third country.[78]

To date no such agreements have been finalised and there are none presently under negotiation.

(vi)   Annex IV: Secure signature verification

5–065   Recommendations for secure signature verification are set out in Annex IV to the Directive but no mandatory requirements are imposed. Essentially, the Member States are left to specify, or not, how signatures should be verified.

The recommendations are curiously drafted in the passive voice, with the effect that they do not presuppose who it is that will do the verification. It need not be the relying party, therefore. All that is required is that *someone or something* ensures with reasonable certainty the seven recommendations are met. This was probably intentional on the part of the drafters, in that these recommendations are linked with (though not limited to) the Community's concern to protect consumers. The objective may be that devices be developed which enable the checks to be made without the consumer actually having to take any active role in the matter, and the use of these should meet any criteria of reasonable reliance. What is reasonable certainty would appear therefore to be limited to the technological possibilities without regard to extrinsic factors such as the importance of the document signed, by value or otherwise, since this will not be within a device's ability to assess.

The checks which need to be carried out are:

(a)   the data used for verifying the signature correspond to the data displayed to the verifier;

(b)   the signature is reliably verified and the result of that verification is correctly displayed;

(c)   the verifier can, as necessary, reliably establish the content of the signed data;

(d)   the authenticity and validity of the certificate required at the time of signature are reliably verified;

(e)   the result of verification and the signatory's identity are correctly displayed;

(f)   the use of a pseudonym is clearly indicated; and

(g)   any security-relevant changes can be detected.

5–066   In point (c), the term "verified" must be read in the context of digital signatures to mean that a digital signature is decrypted and the resulting message digest is compared with the message digest for the message as received. The result of the verification will be either that the two match, in which case the signature is verified as being that of the sender on the message as received, or that they do not, in which case the either the message or the signature is incorrect. As with the UNCITRAL Model Law version of this provision, it is not at all clear what steps will amount to verification in respect of any kind of electronic signature other than a digital one, but resort may have to be had to non-Internet forms of communication for the purpose.

Where signature verification is performed by a device, the net effect is that the holder of the device will be told:

●   who signed,

●   whether they used a pseudonym,

- that all checks were successful (or not) and

- whether or not any changes have been made to the data.

These displays will confirm (without necessarily saying so to the user) that:

- the signature was made with the private key corresponding to the public key indicated in the supporting certificate, which was the key which is displayed to the user,

- the certificate was authentic and valid when the signature was made and

- the fact of any changes to the data would have been picked up.

The first point to be ensured reflects once again the concern over the ability of electronic documents to incorporate data which is not visible to the ordinary user. Here, the process of verification is required to include an affirmation that the key which was used to verify the signature is the same as the key which is displayed to the user, *i.e.* that there is no second, hidden key perhaps belonging to a third party which is in fact the key which was used to unlock the signature. However, any person able to include such a hidden key in a valid and authentic certificate might also be able to instruct the receiving device to display a "yes, the key used is the key on display" message despite it not being the case. This does not add a great deal of additional security.   **5–067**

The only other instrument issued to date on the operation of the European electronic signature framework is a Commission Decision[79] on the minimum criteria to be taken into account by Member States when designating bodies to assess the conformity of particular signature creation devices with the requirements laid down in Annex III for secure signature-creation-devices. This merely stipulated that the body and staff must not engage in any activity which may conflict with their independence of judgment and clarity and must be financially independent. Conformity assessment should be transparent, and staff's remuneration must not depend on the number of assessments carried out. The body must be able to perform assessments with a high degree of professional integrity, reliability and sufficient technical competence.

---

1. From May 1, 2004, this will include Cyprus, Malta and six additional countries from Central and Eastern Europe.
2. Art. 2.
3. Since the law is a model for enactment in different countries, the list and scope of exceptions to the application of the law (if any) are left to each legislature to complete.
4. See Ch. 2 above.
5. *Guide to Enactment of the UNCITRAL Model Law on Electronic Commerce*, paras 53, 56-8.
6. Art. 11 and 12.
7. Art. 2(c).
8. See Ch. 2, para. 2–029.
9. [1995] C.L.C. 496; 1996 1 C.T.L.R. T-17, discussed at Ch. 2, para. 2–029 above.
10. Guide to Enactment of the Model Law, n. 83.
11. Though not the only alternative—see Ch. 6 at para. on the implementation under Spanish law.
12. See Ch. 2 at paras 2–018—2–019.
13. Art. 13(5).
14. Art. 13(6).
15. See discussion in Ch. 3 above.
16. para. 4.
17. Art. 2(a) Model Law on Electronic Signatures.
18. Art. 2(b) *ibid*.
19. Guide to Enactment of the Model Law, para. 12.
20. Art. 5bis was added to the Model Law on Electronic Commerce in 1998 to enable incorporation by reference.

21. See Ch. 4, para. 4–017.
22. *Guide to Enactment of the Model Law on Electronic Signatures,* para. 141.
23. Guide to Enactment, para. 61.
24. GUIDEC version II, Glossary.
25. *ibid.* s. IX(2).
26. *ibid.* s. IX(6).
27. *ibid.* s. IX(3).
28. *ibid.* s. IX(4).
29. *ibid.* s. X(2) and (4).
30. *ibid.* s. X(6).
31. *ibid.* s. X(7).
32. see para. 5–025 above.
33. *ibid,* s. X(3).
34. *ibid* s. X(10).
35. *ibid* s. X(1).
36. *ibid,* Glossary 23.
37. SG/EC(98)14/FINAL, *http://www.olis.oecd.org/olis/1998doc.nsf/linkto/sc-ec(98)14-final.*
38. Working Party on Information Security and Privacy, *Progress achieved by OECD member countries in furtherance of the Ottawa Declaration on authentication for electronic commerce, OECD DSTI/ICCP/REG(2001)10/FINAL,* September 16, 2002.
39. Resolution A4-244/96, September 9, 1996, O.J. 320 p. 163.
40. Resolution 96/C 376/01 November 21, 1996, O.J. C376.
41. COM (97) 503 Final.
42. Directive 2000/31, O.J. L 178/1.
43. Gesetz zur digitalen Signatur, August 1, 1997.
44. Schema di Regalomento "Atti, documenti e contratti in forma elettronica" August 5, 1997.
45. See para. 10–010 below.
46. COM (1998) 297 final, O.J. C325/5, October 23, 1998.
47. See Ch. 2
48. Unfortunately the report was not yet publicly available at the time of writing.
49. See s. 3 of Ch. 9 below.
50. Art. 5(2).
51. Art. 5 (1).
52. The interpretation of this definition was discussed in Ch. 3 but is repeated here for ease of reference.
53. Arguably a single bit is excluded since the definition refers to *data* which is a plural word, the singular being *datum,* but under the normal English rules of statutory construction at least, the plural includes the singular.
54. Electronic Signatures Directive Art. 2(2).
55. See para. 5–013 above.
56. Final Report of the EESSI Expert Team, July 1999.
57. Evidential and procedural issues are discussed at Ch. 8 below.
58. Recital 12 and Art. 3(1).
59. Art. 3(5).
60. Art. 3(1).
61. Recital 10.
62. Art. 4(1).
63. Art. 3(2).
64. Art. 3(3).
65. Directive 95/46/EU of October 24, 1995, O.J. L 281 p. 31
66. Art. 8(2).
67. See Ch. 9.
68. Art. 3(4).
69. Art. 4(2).
70. Art. 2.
71. Discussed at Ch. 9 below.
72. Art. 6 (1)(a)-(c).
73. Art. 6(2).
74. Art. 6(3).
75. Art. 6(4).
76. Directive 93/13/EEC of April 5, 1993, O.J. L 95 April 21, p. 29.
77. Art. 7(2).
78. Art. 7(3).
79. of November 6, 2000 c (2000) 3179, O.J. L289/42, November 16, 2000.

6

Electronic signature laws of the world

Introduction

In the late 1990s the status of electronic signatures was difficult to ascertain in a number of countries, simply because the issue had not come up or been adjudicated. As discussed in Chapter 2, requirements for documents to be signed originate in concerns as to the availability of reliable evidence for a court to use as the basis for resolving a later dispute, and are commonly associated with requirements for the document itself to be in writing. There was perceived in many countries to be an issue as to whether an electronic document qualified as a document in writing, and concerns were raised over signatures in two similar respects. First, would an electronic signature be admissible in evidence in court proceedings at all? This is discussed in more detail in Chapter 8. And secondly, would an electronic signature be recognised as having the same legal effect as a handwritten or other physical form of signature?

6–001

The concern as to whether or not documents and signatures in electronic form would be admissible in evidence may have been unnecessary. In a September 2002 report by the OECD Working Party on Information Security and Privacy, 27 countries stated that their courts were allowing electronic signatures to be admissible even before half those countries had passed specific electronic signature legislation.[1] Nevertheless, many countries have chosen to address this issue expressly in their subsequent legislation.

The second issue as to the legal effect of electronic signatures might likewise have been resolved through case law given sufficient time. However, the issue was seen as too critical and too immediate to be left to the slow grinding of the courts. Legislators worldwide opted instead to pass laws to ensure that electronic commerce could continue without unnecessary uncertainty over form requirements such as signatures. The difficulty was to know what form of law to adopt, when the Internet was still a very new locus for commerce and diverse business models were still evolving.

6–002

The Internet Law and Policy Forum (ILPF) carried out a survey[2] of existing electronic signature initiatives in September 2000 which identified a number of trends amongst those laws, regulations and guidelines then in existence.

Perhaps the most significant was that while almost all of the laws reviewed gave basic legal effect to electronic signatures independent of the technology used to produce them, many reserved important legal effects, such as presumptions of validity, to signatures supported by a certificate issued by a certification service provider which was licensed or accredited in some way or otherwise met certain standards. Thus, although the principle of technology neutrality may have triumphed in much of the legislation over the technology prescriptive approach, advocated by early commentators in the field, the business model of third party certification has also won a leading role. The regulation of certification service providers is therefore inextricably linked with the legal effectiveness of electronic signatures in many jurisdictions. This can include quasi-compulsory licensing or accreditation systems, strict and detailed regulations of the financial provisions to be made by certification service providers, specifications as to the qualifications and records of employees and so on. Compliance with these requirements is commonly rewarded by favourable treatment in the form of limitations of liability for loss or damage to third parties caused by reliance on a certificate. These regulatory aspects are reviewed in Chapter 9.

6–003 The second observation made by the survey's authors was that in most of the countries legislating for electronic signature effectiveness, detailed technical standards were not yet in place. Where standards were in the process of adoption, the survey's authors had difficulty in ascertaining whether those standards were truly international or not. The standards efforts have continued in the years since the ILPF survey, at both international, regional and national levels. At the time of writing the European Union is on the brink of adopting a complete set of standards for use in its Member States, but these are not effective elsewhere in the world. Convergence is clearly recognised as a necessary endpoint, but it may not be achieved for some time to come. The current position is reviewed in Chapter 10.

The survey also pointed out a divergence between policy approaches reflected in the legislation, in part due to the fact that the technology of electronic signatures was still evolving. The three basic legislative approaches are minimalist, prescriptive or "two tier". Minimalist laws aim to do no more than remove any obstacles or uncertainty which might otherwise affect the use of electronic signatures. This includes clarifying the evidential status of electronic signatures and records, including the factors which may need to be assessed in determining whether or not the signatory intended the signature to have legal effect. This was the approach favoured at federal level in Australia, Canada and the United States and by the United Kingdom.

The prescriptive approach aims to specify in detail a particular technology and procedure which will provide the equivalent certainty to existing paper-based transaction mechanisms. Public key cryptography for the production of digital signatures is universally approved by counties adopting the prescriptive approach, and the public key infrastructure also tends to be closely regulated. This was the approach initially adopted by Malaysia, Singapore, Italy and Germany, although the latter have now amended their pre-existing regimes to comply with the Electronic Signatures Directive.

6–004 The third approach is the "two tier" mechanism which, having been adopted in the UNCITRAL Model Law on Electronic Signatures and the Electronic Signatures Directive, is now in effect the "approved" approach at the international level. This involves conferring definite legal effect upon a class of electronic signatures for which the criteria are specified in detail, but removing any presumption of invalidity which might otherwise have been applied to all other forms of electronic signature. It is not inevitable, but common, that the criteria this privileged class of electronic signature must meet reflect the specific functions of public key cryptography. In effect, digital signatures and any others which are able to meet their criteria are given legal effect; all other forms are left to take their chances in the courts depending upon the facts of any given case. This approach aims to permit the continued development of new and potentially superior technologies, although tilting the pitch in favour of public key cryptography since the legal effect of a signature made using any new technology will be uncertain until its adequacy has been expressly approved by the courts. This is a powerful incentive to use digital signatures.

Beyond these basic policy approaches, there are also issues as to the reach of electronic signature legislation. Should the legislation override existing contractual frameworks within which electronic signatures are being used, such as EDI arrangements, or should it be limited to transactions across truly open networks? Should electronic signatures be used for communications with public administration, and if so should special criteria be applied? Do laws need to address the evidential issues for electronic documents in general, or the formation of contracts electronically? The laws discussed below give different answers to each of these questions, so that electronic signature legislation appears in a wide variety of different contexts. Where the law governing electronic signatures is very broad in scope, only the electronic signature issues will be described; otherwise, the context as a whole is given.

The legislators have also had to consider what additional presumptions should be attributed to an electronic signature, if any. Some, such as Malaysia, have ascribed to an electronic signature a legal presumption as to the identity of the signatory and their intent to sign. Alternatively, digitally signed documents may be given the same status as notarised, or sealed or sworn documents. These approaches raise the puzzling question as to why electronic signatures should be treated more favourably than handwritten ones. These concepts were probably introduced in the belief that, as their proponents claim, digital signatures are actually more reliable than a handwritten signature for some purposes. However, this assertion is dangerously simplistic; a number of assumptions are involved about electronic business practices and the context of signing. **6–005**

An interesting omission from most of the legislation is the possibility that, unlike a handwritten signature, an electronic signature could exist in isolation from a particular individual but relate instead to a particular office or function. Provided that the organisation concerned exercised strict control over access to the signature creation means, in principle a company or association could have its own signature. This was the case historically in the United Kingdom with state indicia of authority such as the Great Seal, which could be wielded (with the sovereign's permission) by anyone to the same legal effect. However, to permit such handling of electronic signatures for private entities would have been inconsistent with past approaches to company seals, which are perhaps the closest equivalent to an "authority" signature, and which had to be affixed along with the signature of an office holder.

It will be appreciated that the originals of the majority of the legislation discussed here are in languages other than English. In many instances, this discussion is based upon available translations, the accuracy of which has not been verified. Further, the author's own translations were used for any secondary legislation in French and for the laws of Latin America. Special competence is not claimed in any of the relevant languages: *caveat lector!*

1. EUROPE

The vast majority of countries of Europe have enacted measures, most though not all of which are intended to implement the Electronic Signatures Directive. Accordingly, each **6–006** takes the "two-tier" approach or a variant upon it. The discussion in each case in this section focuses upon those areas where the transposition appears not to be exact, or additional requirements or recommendations have been included. Any matter not mentioned can be taken to be in accordance with the Directive. It is interesting to note how each legislature has attempted to interpret the term "authentication" in implementing into national law the definition of an electronic signature in the Directive. Since there is no definition of "authentication", as used in that definition, in the Electronic Signatures Directive, it is arguable either way (as discussed in Chapter 3) whether or not the term authentication was intended to include integrity-checking, identification of the signatory or source of the document or both. This must also await clarification, either in the national courts or at the European Court of Justice.

In addition to the present and future members of the European Union, this section reviews the status of electronic signatures in Switzerland since it is an important jurisdiction for many international transactions. Perhaps the most minimalist approach of all is that adopted in Guernsey, which therefore is also included.

(i)   Austria

6–007   Austria passed its Law on Electronic Signatures[3] in July 1999, even before the Electronic Signatures Directive upon which it is based, and which it is intended to implement, had been finally approved by the European Parliament. It came into effect on January 1, 2000 and has since been amended three times in the course of 2000-2001. A further Order, the Electronic Signature Order,[4] was adopted in February 2000 spelling out the technical security requirements for secure electronic signatures (the Austrian term for what the Directive calls advanced electronic signatures).

The Law on Electronic Signatures transposes the substantive elements of the Electronic Signatures Directive, including Annex IV on signature verification procedures, very closely. It applies to transactions over open systems and can also apply to closed system transactions if the parties so agree. Electronic signatures in accordance with the law are also effective for transactions with public administration without any variation. Austria has transposed the definitions laid down by the Electronic Signature Directive almost exactly, and likewise enacted Article 5.1 giving legal effect to advanced electronic signatures by direct transposition.[5]

6–008   A document signed with a secure electronic signature is also given the benefit of the presumption of authenticity which applies under the Austrian Civil Code to signed private deeds.[6] However, neither of these provisions applies if there has been a security breach. The parties can also agree not to permit legal effect to be given to electronic signatures, and future legislation can also exclude the use of electronic signatures.

Signatories are obliged under the Austrian Law to keep their signature creation data safe, prevent access to them and to refrain from passing them on.[7] A signatory who loses their signature creation data or has reason to believe that their secrecy may have been compromised is obliged to request the revocation of the supporting certificate immediately. Revocation must take place within three hours during office hours, and an automatic suspension mechanism has to be available out of hours. Misuse of another's signature creation data without their knowledge and consent is an administrative offence punishable by a fine of up to 56,000 shillings (€4070).[8]

Austrian law did not formerly require written signatures for most purposes so the effect of the Law has not been revolutionary. Where a degree of formality was previously required by law, such as in transactions relating to family law or inheritances, sureties, documents requiring official authentication, judicial or notarial legalisation (for example for entry into the Land or Companies' Registers),[9] these formalities are still necessary so that a document simply signed, electronically or otherwise, will not be adequate. Filing of lawsuits in electronic form was introduced in 1989

There are no provisions relating to the use of electronic signatures by public bodies.

(ii)   Belgium

Belgium passed an Act on October 20, 2000 bringing electronic signatures into legal effect for judicial and extra-judicial proceedings ("the Electronic Documents Act").   **6–009**

The Electronic Documents Act provides that a collection of electronic data which is linked to a particular person and confirming that the integrity of the signed document has been maintained can satisfy the requirement for a signature. The Act also provides that e-mail can satisfy a requirement for a document to be in writing, and documents such as notices may also be by e-mail if the proposed recipient has given an e-mail address as a contact means. This Act did not attempt to deal with any of the details of advanced electronic signatures or certificates.

A further Law of July 9, 2001 lays down rules governing the legal framework of electronic signatures and certification services. This law incorporates the definitions and Annexes from the Electronic Signatures Directive and transposes Article 5 precisely.[10] Other than an additional stipulation that the holder of signature creation data is solely responsible for their confidentiality, and clarification that no-one can be forced to conclude legal acts by electronic means, the law contains no additional provisions relating to the effect of electronic signatures. There is a reservation however that further regulations may be imposed for the use of electronic signatures in the public sector.[11]

The silence of the law implies that it is universally applicable, to closed as well as open systems and, pending the additional regulations foreshadowed, to transactions with public administration as well as private transactions. There are no express reservations as to areas of law in which electronic signatures are not capable of being used.

(iii) Bulgaria

Bulgaria passed its Law on Electronic Document and Electronic Signature in May 2001 and the Law came into force later that year. The Law regulates electronic documents and   **6–010**
signatures save for those transactions where a specific written form is required by law or bearer documents such as bills of lading. It therefore appears to cover closed as well as open systems. The Law addresses the issues of technology, legal effect and data protection of the Electronic Signatures Directive, but it is not a simple transposition of the whole. Elements of the UNCITRAL Model Law on Electronic Commerce are also included on matters such as time and place of receipt of electronic statements (data messages). In particular Article 13 of the Model Law is incorporated.[12]

The Law specifies three categories of electronic signature. The basic definition of an electronic signature appears to be based on the definition in the UNCITRAL Model Laws, in that it should be data which is linked to an electronic statement, which identifies the signatory, indicates their consent to the content of the statement and is agreed between the parties to be sufficiently secure having regard to the purpose of the message. However, the definition goes beyond that in the Model Laws or the Electronic Signature

Directive in requiring the electronic signature to protect the content of the electronic statement to which it is attached from any subsequent change. Although the Law purports to be technologically neutral, this last requirement is at present only achievable by digital signatures.

6–011   Advanced electronic signatures under the Law are essentially digital signatures since the definition requires the signature to be a transformed version of the statement being signed, the transformation being done using an algorithm "including the use of the private key of an asymmetric cryptosystem". A supplementary regulation will define the permitted algorithms. The required means of creation of an advanced electronic signature are based on the definition of a secure signature creation device in Annex II of the Electronic Signature Directive.

Both basic and advanced electronic signatures are given the same legal effect as a handwritten signature under the Law,[13] except where the owner[14] or addressee of the statement is a state or municipal authority. An advanced electronic signature must be verified using a mechanism which guarantees that the private key used to sign corresponds to the public key and this information is given to the relying party.[15] An advanced electronic signature may be supported by a certificate issued by a certification service provider.

A universal electronic signature, the third category, has the effect of a handwritten signature towards everyone and is an advanced electronic signature supported by a certificate issued by a registered certification service provider.

None of the categories of electronic signature is given the benefit of any additional presumptions. Nor are the admissibility provisions of the Electronic Signatures Directive incorporated; it is to be presumed that the Bulgarian law of evidence would admit electronic documents and signatures into evidence without special provisions.

6–012   The requirements for advanced electronic signature certificates are substantially similar to Annex I of the Electronic Signatures Directive, with the additional provision that certificates will be valid for three years unless otherwise agreed.[16]

The owner or signatory may be liable to third parties where the signature is not created securely or revocation of the certificate is not requested on learning of a potential compromise of the private key data, as well as to third parties and the certification service provider for any false statements in the certificate.[17]

The Law also provides for mutual recognition of certificate issued by overseas certification service providers on less strict conditions than those laid down in the Electronic Signature Directive: in addition to certificates guaranteed by a Bulgarian accredited certification service provider and certificates recognised under international agreements, Bulgaria will recognise certificates issued by certification service providers which meet the requirements of the Law and are recognised in their home countries. However, this is subject to determination by the State Telecommunications Commission, which will then publish the public key of such a certification service provider in its register.

Signatories who fail to abide by the conditions laid down in the Law may be liable to administrative fines of up to 100,000 BGL (€51,356).

(iv) Cyprus

6–013   A draft law on digital signatures was in preparation in the course of 2002 as well as legislation to adjust the laws of evidence to permit the introduction of evidence in court based on electronic documents.[18] This is expected to be introduced into Parliament for enactment by the end of 2003.[19]

In the interim, should any issues come before the Cypriot courts concerning the admissibility or legal effect of an electronic signature, the principles of English common law will be applied since the Cypriot legal system is based upon the common law as it stood at independence in 1960. In view of the decisions of the English High Court in *Goodman v J Eban Ltd* and *In re a Debtor (No. 2021 of 1995)* ex p. *Commissioners of the Inland Revenue*,[20] it is probable that an electronic signature would be found effective as a matter of Cypriot law provided that the circumstances of its creation and affixation could be established with appropriate evidence.

(v) Czech Republic

The Czech law on Electronic Signatures came into effect on October 1, 2000. The Law **6–014** closely follows the terminology and approach of the Electronic Signature Directive, with occasional additions, such as definition of a data message, from the UNCITRAL Model Laws. It is generally applicable in all areas of law, to public administration[21] and to open and closed systems.

The definition of electronic signature has been transposed as requiring an electronic signature to enable the identity of the signatory to be identified, which may be more limited than the definition in the Directive, which requires it to serve as a method of authentication.

A signatory is responsible for the safekeeping of signature creation data for the production of advanced electronic signatures, and must notify any certification service provider which has issued a qualified certificate of any compromise of them. Failure to do so may result in liability. However, a party relying on an advanced electronic signature supported by a qualified certificate will bear any loss resulting from their reliance if they failed to take all acts necessary to verify that the signature was valid and the certificate had not been rendered invalid.[22] This appears to be stricter than the provision of the Electronic Signature Directive, which only requires a relying party's reliance to be reasonable to enable them to claim damages from the certification service provider.

The Act also lays down rules for secure signature creation devices, requiring among other things that the use of the device must be password protected and must notify the user as to what they are doing, *i.e.* creating a legally binding signature.

No additional presumptions are attached to the use of electronic signatures.

The Law also amends a variety of other Czech legislation to permit the use of electronic forms of communication in tax filings, administrative, civil and criminal proceedings. The Czech Industrial Property Office reported that it had begun to accept filings signed with qualified electronic signatures in the course of 2002.[23]

(vi) Denmark

Danish Law no. 417 of May 31, 2000 enacted the Electronic Signatures Directive; it came **6–015** into force on October 1, 2000. The provisions reflect the Directive very closely with some relatively minor additions. The Law applies to all areas of law and to open and closed systems, but is not effective in Greenland or the Faroe Islands.

The definition of electronic signature used in the Law arguably goes beyond the very basic version in the Electronic Signatures Directive in that to be an electronic signature under the Danish Law requires the data to be used to check that the data signed originate from the person indicated as signatory and that the data have not been changed.[24] These requirements reflect the Danish government's understanding of the meaning of "authentication" in the definition in the Directive.[25] The definition of advanced electronic signature then repeats these two requirements and adds the remaining elements from the Directive's definition of an advanced electronic signature.

6–016   The Law gives express legal effect, where an electronic message is required to be signed, to advanced electronic signatures created with a secure signature creation device[26] and supported by a qualified certificate as stipulated in the Directive, provided that where messages to or from public authorities are concerned there is no law or regulation prescribing otherwise.[27] This excludes the electronic signing of paper documents, but this may not be very important in practice.

The Law is silent as to the effect in law of other electronic signatures, but as Danish law did not previously include any general requirements for signatures in the commercial context[28] there is no apparent need for any active endorsement of electronic signatures' effectiveness. Similarly, electronic signatures are admissible in evidence without any change to the existing law.

No additional presumptions are applied when an electronic signature is used.

Following the implementation of this Act, the Danish government entered into an agreement in March 2003 with TDC for the supply of national digital signatures. These signatures were criticised for not meeting the highest standards contemplated by the EU but, as the Ministry of Science, Technology and Innovation has pointed out, in practice handwritten signatures are also subject to well-founded criticism as regards their lack of security.

(vii) Estonia

6–017   The Estonian Digital Signatures Act was passed in March 2000 and entered into force in December 2000. It has since been amended several times, most recently in July 2002. It covers the conditions of use of digital signatures. It is an original Act in several ways, not evidently derived from any of the preceding international initiatives. The Act's approach is prescriptive. The choice of technology is expressly limited to digital signatures[29] which alone are given equivalence of effect to handwritten signatures,[30] so the Act alone does not comply with at least the technology-neutrality requirements of the Electronic Signatures Directive. Unless Estonian law is already permissive of the use of other forms of electronic signature and does not deny these legal effect, the Act may need to be amended when Estonia accedes to the European Union in 2004.

The Act applies to the use of digital signatures in public law generally and to their use in private law transactions by the agreement of the parties. This is inconsistent with the Directive unless under Estonian law agreement of the parties is also required for the use of handwritten signatures. However, it clearly permits the use of digital signatures in closed networks.

A digital signature is defined as a data unit created using a private key to which there is a corresponding public key, which a signatory uses to indicate his or her connection to a document.[31] It must further enable unique identification of the person in whose name the signature is given, and the manner of using the signature must enable determination of the time at which the signature is given and link the signature to data in such a way that any subsequent change of the data or the meaning thereof is detectable.[32] It is difficult to see how the meaning of the data could be changed while leaving the data itself unchanged, but this merely makes one of the two redundant without making the definition any harder to satisfy.

A digital signature which is proved to meet the definition has the same legal effect as a handwritten signature subject to any restrictions imposed by other laws.[33] This approach, requiring the party relying on it to prove that the signature it meets the definition, imposes an additional burden on parties transacting electronically over and above those carried by parties transacting on paper. No special presumptions are applied to the use of a digital signature.

6–018

The Act specifically provides that an apparent signatory may repudiate a signature by proving that the private key was used without the consent of the holder of the corresponding certificate.[34] However, if the misuse was due to the certificate holder's intent or gross negligence, then the certificate holder will be liable to compensate any relying party.

Certificates are defined as documents which are issued in order to enable a digital signature to be given and in which a public key is uniquely linked to a natural person.[35] This is restrictive compared to the definition of a certificate in the Electronic Signatures Directive, but as no distinction is drawn between basic and qualified certificates, the proper point of comparison should perhaps be with the definition of a qualified certificate. The requirement that only natural persons should have keys is in keeping with the principles of the Directive since a legal person can only act through natural persons.

6–019

The Act specifies the data to be included in certificates, which is similar to that required for a qualified certificate with the omission of the public key of the certification service provider and the fact that the certificate is issued as a qualified certificate.[36]

Certificates issued by foreign certification service providers can be recognised under the circumstances specified in the Directive.

In addition, there are equivalent sections dealing with time stamping services.

(viii)   Finland

The Finnish legal system already permitted the use of electronic signatures in the private sector and their admission in evidence, and Finland's preference was for a minimalist approach of removing obstacles to their use case by case as any issue might arise. However, in order to be seen to comply with the Electronic Signatures Directive a new Finnish Electronic Signatures Act, closely modelled on the Directive, was brought into effect on February 1, 2003. Not all of the Directive has been transposed precisely. There are minor changes in the definition of an electronic signature, to specify that it serves as a means of authenticating the identity of the signatory.[37] The criteria for a secure signature creation device include the requirement that the signature creation data can be protected against use by others, but without the qualification "reliably".[38]

6–020

The new Act regulates the use of electronic signatures other than in public administration, which is the subject of a separate Act on Electronic Service in the Administration which came into force on January 1, 2000.

At least advanced electronic signatures in accordance with the Act will be valid for any transaction which by law requires a document to be signed.[39] As Finnish law does not require any particular formality for most forms of contract, ordinary electronic signatures will be as effective as other signatures for those circumstances and, since this provision is not exclusive, may also be valid for transactions requiring a signature by law.

A signatory is liable for damage caused by unauthorised use of the signature creation data for an advanced electronic signature supported by a qualified certificate up to the

6–021

point where the certification service provider receives a request to revoke the certificate provided that one of the following conditions is met:

(1)   the signatory gave the signature creation data to another;

(2)   the signatory's negligence, which was more than trivial, caused the signature creation data to come into another's possession; or

(3)   having otherwise lost control of the signature creation data the signatory failed to request revocation of the certificate.[40]

No special presumptions are applied to the use of any form of electronic signature.

The Finnish Communications Regulatory Authority is responsible for designating inspection bodies to assess whether a device meets the requirements for a secure signature creation device.

The Act on Electronic Service in the Administration also regulates the use of electronic signatures and the issuing of certificates, within the sphere of public administration, but uses different definitions and the provisions governing certification are also different. A Bill is apparently under consideration to update this Act.

(ix)   France

6–022   France was one of the countries which initially imposed the strongest restrictions on its citizens' access to cryptographic products, but has been relaxing its stance progressively over a number of years. In particular, the restriction on the strength of a commercially distributed cryptographic device to those having a key length of 56 (later 128) bits was lifted in respect of devices being used only for electronic signature purposes in 1996. This paved the way for the widespread use of electronic signatures, once they had been given full legal recognition.

French law traditionally adopted a restrictive attitude towards giving signatures evidential weight, and an initial report by the Conseil d'Etat concluded that the Civil Code did not readily accommodate electronic signatures.

Law no. 2000-230 adapting the law of evidence to information technology and electronic signatures was passed in March 2000. The Law amended article 1316-4 of the Civil Code to include a new definition of the function of a signature,[41] and went on to provide that any form of data may be admitted in evidence on condition that the person from which it emanates can be properly identified and that it is created and saved under conditions such as to guarantee its integrity. In other words, electronic documents and signatures, whatever technology is employed, may be recognised as written documents as evidence of a transaction. This was an important development in French law since the Civil Code contains a substantial number of references to transactions having to be in writing, going back to a 1566 Ordinance of Moulins establishing the pre-eminence of written over oral evidence. It was always possible for parties to a private contract to agree the probative effect of an electronic document, but under the new law, written evidence continues to be pre-eminent but will automatically be recognised equally in electronic form or on a paper support. Should there be a conflict of evidence between these two forms, it will be up to the judge to determine by any available means which is the most accurate.[42]

6–023   The Law delegated to the Conseil d'Etat the power to fix the conditions under which an electronic signature will be presumed reliable once the identity of the signatory and the integrity of the signed communication are assured. This decree, no. 2001-272, was passed on March 30, 2001. It reflects aspects of the Electronic Signatures Directive. A signature is presumed reliable if it was created with a secure signature creation device and based on a qualified certificate. The definition of advanced ("secure") electronic signature is imported from the Electronic Signatures Directive, save that the ability of an advanced electronic signature to identify the signatory is omitted. This has no effect on the conformity of the law to the Directive since it is anyway a separate requirement for legal effectiveness under article 1316-4. Article 2 of the decree confers a presumption of legal effectiveness on an advanced electronic signature under the conditions stipulated in Article 5 of the Directive. The presumption of reliability of any electronic signature is capable of being rebutted by appropriate evidence.

The law does not expressly refuse legal effect to other forms of electronic signature; these merely do not benefit from the presumption of reliability conferred upon secure electronic signatures attached in the circumstances specified in the law. It remains to be seen whether the French Courts will be prepared to rely upon forms of electronic signature which do not have express legislative sanction.

The decree requires secure signature creation devices to be certified to conform to the requirements of the law. Under a further decree, 2002-535 of April 19, 2002, conditions for certifying the security of secure signature creation or verification devices are laid down. Compliance is to be measured by reference to international standards by either a French compliance authority accredited by the Central Directorate for IT Systems (DCSSI) or by another European Union compliance authority approved by the DCSSI. Further, it provides for the possibility of certified signature verification devices where these comply with the recommendations in Annex IV of the Directive.[43]

(x)   Germany

The passing of the highly prescriptive German Law for Electronic Signatures in 1997 was   **6–024** one of the factors motivating the European Commission to introduce the Electronic Signatures Directive. That law has now been superseded by the Law Governing Framework Conditions for Electronic Signatures ("the Framework Law"), which came into force on May 22, 2001.[44] This Law is supplemented by a number of pieces of secondary legislation, in particular the Signature Ordinance of November 22, 2001 and a law adjusting section 126 of the German Civil Code to the effects of electronic communication and commerce.[45] It is the latter which provides that a qualified electronic signature (as defined in the Framework Law) can be used where the Civil Code formerly required a handwritten signature, except for certain documents such as guarantees. The collection of provisions retains an essentially prescriptive approach; the status of other forms of electronic signature remains unclear. However, as a matter of the general German law writing and signature are not required for the majority of transactions (although there are many exceptions, such as transactions dealing in real property or consumer credit transactions). Although public procurement contracts often include a signature requirement, it is likely that in future qualified electronic signatures will be accepted. Thus, the uncertainty as to effect may not be material in practice in most circumstances.

The Framework Law governs conditions for electronic signatures. It contains legal provisions for qualified electronic signatures. Qualified electronic signatures are defined as advanced electronic signatures which are supported by a valid qualified certificate and have been produced using a secure signature creation device. Qualified certificates may be valid for up to 5 years.[46] The law stipulates that compliance with additional conditions may be required for the use of qualified electronic signatures for public administrative activities (f.e. "qualified electronic signatures with provider accreditation").[47]

The Law introduces definitions relating to time stamping, in addition to those set out in the Electronic Signatures Directive.

6–025 The Framework Law contemplates that key pairs will be created only by a certification service provider using a secure signature creation device, which reflects one potential meaning of the term as used in the Directive, but also provides that the keys once created will be transferred to a secure signature creation device, which reflects the other. The latter meaning—of a device which is used to create a signature—is a more natural interpretation of the phrase but the German Law correctly implements the implication of Annex 3 of the Directive in requiring that secure signature creation devices ensure that a particular set of signature creation data can occur only once.[48]

The third act concerning the amendment of the law of administrative procedure, which came into effect in February 2003, governs the use of electronic signatures in public administration in general. Sec. 3a (2) provides that in general a qualified electronic signature (as defined in the Framework Law) can be used where a handwritten signature was required formerly.

(xi) Greece

6–026 Presidential Decree 150/2001 was issued in June 2001 to implement the Electronic Signatures Directive. It exemplifies the minimalist approach to compliance with European Union requirements: it transposes the definitions and essential provisions from the Directive exactly.

Article 3(1) of the Decree implements Article 5.1 of the Directive, giving advanced electronic signatures which are based on a qualified certificate and created by a secure signature creation device equivalent status to handwritten signatures, where required by Greek law or procedure. No additional presumptions are added, and conversely the Decree has no effect on any provision which stipulates the use of a particular form.[49]

Other electronic signatures are dealt with in Article 3(2) in the terms required by Article 5.2 of the Directive. The Annexes to the Directive are likewise transposed as Annexes to the Decree.

The supervisory authority under the Decree is the National Telecommunications and Post Commission,[50] which is producing regulations governing the assessment of secure signature creation devices with the requirements of Annex III.

(xii) Guernsey

6–027 The Electronic Transactions (Guernsey) Law was passed in June 2000. It takes an approach as close as imaginable to the minimalist extreme without simply leaving all of the issues to be decided by the Courts. There is no definition of electronic signature as such. "Signature in electronic form" is defined in section 22 as:

> "a signature wholly or partly in electronic form attached to or logically associated with information in electronic or non-electronic form."

thereby contemplating the novel possibility that paper-based documents may be electronically signed. The definition leaves the whole burden of determining what is meant by signature, attachment and logical association to the Courts.

The Law contains only two further statements relating to signatures. Section 4 aims to remove barriers to the use of electronic form:

"a signature, seal, attestation or notarisation shall not be denied legal effect, validity, enforceability or admissibility solely because it is in electronic form."

This leaves the way open for barring admissibility on other grounds, such as unreliability in all the circumstances, but does not permit a court simply to refuse to contemplate an electronic signature.

Section 8(1) states that:

"if a law, whether statutory or customary, requires. . .a signature, a signature in electronic form satisfies the law."

This appears simply to be a restatement in the positive of the effect of section 4.

(xiii) Hungary

The Hungarian Electronic Signature Act was passed in May 2001 and came into force in September 2001. In addition to the formality of signatures, it also covers time stamping and other aspects of electronic documents, such as their admissibility in evidence in general, and the use of electronic signatures in public administration. This Act takes the opposite approach to the majority in that it appears to apply to the use of electronic signatures in closed networks unless the participants agree otherwise.[51] However, marriage, family and guardianship law are all excluded from the effect of the Act.   **6–028**

The Act is basically modelled on the Electronic Signatures Directive and uses definitions clearly based upon those in the Directive. Nevertheless, a number of material changes and additions have been made. The definition of electronic signature has been narrowed to require an electronic signature to be *inseparably* attached to an electronic document[52] rather than merely "attached". While this may be desirable, it may also be technically infeasible—even a digital signature can be cut off from the document signed. On the other hand, the definition of a signature creation device in the Hungarian Act is arguably clearer than the wording of the Directive as it has been expanded to clarify that the use of a signature creation device to implement signature creation data means creating an electronic signature. The definition of secure signature creation device from Annex III of the Directive has accordingly been modified in Annex I of the Hungarian Act to remove the ambiguous reference to ensuring the signature creation data can practically occur only once.

The definition of signatory has also been amended, to specify that a signatory is a person linked to particular signature creation data by a certification service provider's directory. This is more restrictive than the Directive and would exclude arrangements such as the PGP-style web of trust approach.

A definition of "qualified electronic signature" has been introduced to cover the signatures specified in Article 5(1) of the Directive.

The legal effect given to electronic signatures under the Act is broader than that required under the Directive since, having prohibited denying them effect on the sole   **6–029** basis of their being electronic in Article 3(1) the Act goes on to provide a presumption of integrity to any electronic document, other than a contract or deed, which has been electronically signed[53]—without apparently any requirement that the electronic signature be an advanced electronic signature. However, the presumption is then stated not to apply if otherwise proven by the verification of the signature. Signature verification is clearly conceived as a function using cryptographic methods, so it may be that the presumption is only intended to apply to signatures produced using such methods. The presumption is also sensibly inapplicable to printouts of the electronically signed documents.

The Act also provides for recognition of certificates issued by certification service providers anywhere in the European Union upon Hungary's accession,[54] and extends the prohibition on recognition of electronic signatures in Article 3(1) to all certificates wherever issued.

Once a certificate has been issued, the holder must notify the certification service provider immediately if any of the data provided changes, the signature creation data are compromised, litigation relating to a signed document is started or any irregularity comes to his or her knowledge. Failure to do so renders the holder of the certificate liable for any damage.[55]

(xiv)   Ireland

6–030   The Irish Electronic Commerce Act 2000, as its title implies, is a broad Act dealing with issues of time and place of dispatch and receipt of data messages in addition to implementing the Electronic Signatures Directive. It transposes the bulk of the latter's provisions very precisely but then tailoring their application in the following ways.

The Act does not currently affect the existing laws relating to wills, trusts or enduring powers of attorney, real property or court documents, affidavits and declarations,[56] although power is delegated to the Minister for Public Enterprise to extend it by regulations to these areas if after consultation he or she is of the opinion that technology has sufficiently advanced and access is sufficiently widely available.

All forms of electronic information are confirmed to be admissible in evidence and capable of legal effect.[57] However, information required to be given by way of application, claim or notice may only be given to a private party in electronic form if the proposed recipient consents to it being given in that form. Similarly, if a signature is required by law and the recipient is private party, their consent is required to it being given in electronic form.[58]

6–031   Additional conditions may be imposed by public bodies for the use of electronic signatures in dealings with them. Advanced electronic signatures may also be used to witness the signing of electronic documents by advanced electronic signatures[59] and where documents are required to be sealed, once again subject to the consent of a recipient who is a private party.[60]

The prohibition on refusing electronic documents and signatures admissibility in legal proceedings is extended to include a prohibition on their admissibility on the grounds that they are not originals, if they are in fact the best evidence the party producing them could be expected to obtain.[61]

No additional presumptions are applied where electronic signatures are used. Forgery of and tampering with electronic signatures and certificates are made criminal offences.[62]

(xv) Italy

Italy was the first country in Europe to pass legislation relating to electronic signatures, with its Digital Signature Law No. 59 of March 15, 1997, implemented by Regulations in November 1997.[63] Decree No. 445 consolidating the law on electronic documents including the use of digital signatures was passed in December 2000. The introduction of the Digital Signature Law was a factor motivating the European Commission to propose harmonised, technology neutral legislation for the whole of the European Union. Accordingly, although many of the provisions of the existing law were the same as or very similar to the Electronic Signatures Directive, the legislation had to be updated in January 2002 by Legislative Decree 10/02[64] to bring it in line with the Directive by recognising the potential legal effect and admissibility in evidence of forms of electronic signature other than digital signatures.[65] A further set of Regulations was promulgated in April 2003 by Presidential Decree 137/03[66] co-ordinating law provisions concerning electronic signatures, according to art. 13 Legislative Decree 10/02. **6–032**

The much-revised Decree 445/2000 covers the use of electronic signatures in both private transactions and public administration.[67] As well as electronic signatures, it covers a number of other matters including the legal effect of transmission and receipt of electronic documents, the regulation of certification service providers, legalisation of signatures and identity cards.

Electronic documents are given evidential effect under section 2712 of the Italian Civil Code. This means that they are taken as final evidence of the things represented unless their accuracy is disowned by the maker in which case the judge is free to form his judgment on the basis of other forms of evidence, including presumptions. An electronic document signed with an advanced electronic signature (as well as any qualified electronic signature, *i.e.* the digital signature) created using a secure signature creation device and based on a qualified certificate issued by a registered certification service provider is taken to be truthful evidence of identity of the signatory unless proved otherwise. Forms of electronic signature other than advanced electronic signatures according to the Directive shall not be denied legal effect, but will be given evidential weight by the court subject to their objective characteristics of quality and security. They also satisfy the requirement of articles 2214 and following of the Civil Code. [68] **6–033**

To be legally effective in the same way as a manuscript signature, seal, stamp or other mark, a digital signature must identify unequivocally the person who is signing and be associated with the document signed, although it need not be part of it. [69] This provision does not appear to have been amended to provide legal effect to other forms of electronic signature. The certification service provider which has certified the signature as that of the signatory must also be identified.

Where asymmetric cryptographic methods are being used, the keyholder is obliged to adopt all necessary organisational measures and appropriate technologies to prevent third parties from causing any relevant damage.[70] **6–034**

If a digital signature is affixed in the presence of a notary public then the document is treated as a notarised document. This procedure also requires the notary to confirm that the document reflects the signatory's will and does not breach any existing law.

A certificate may not be valid for longer than three years.

Electronic signatures are acceptable for use with public administration provided that a digital signature supported by a qualified certificate and created using a secure signature creation device is used, with the signatory being identified in addition by either an electronic ID certificate, which are introduced under the same piece of legislation, or using their Italian national services card.[71]

The compliance of secure signature creation devices with the requirements of the Directive is assessed by the National Scheme for the Evaluation and Certification of Security in the field of Information and Communication Technology.

(xvi)   Latvia

6–035   The Latvian Saeima (Parliament) adopted a Law on Electronic Documents in October 2002, which came into effect as regards transactions between private parties, whether in closed or open systems, in January 2003. Public bodies will not be obliged to accept electronic documents until January 2004. Further, the Law does not apply to transfers of land, guarantees, documents relating to family or succession law or documents for which the existing law prescribes a certification procedure.[72]

The Law is closely based upon the Electronic Signatures Directive although not identical to it. For instance, the definition of an electronic signature includes an interpretation of "authentication" as a requirement that the signature must both ensure the authenticity of the document and certify the identity of the signatory.[73] There is no prohibition on denying electronic signatures other than advanced electronic signatures (labelled "safe electronic signatures" in the Law) legal effect on the basis of their electronic form, although all electronic signatures are made admissible in evidence.[74] This may be an equally effective way to leave it up to the Latvian Courts to decide upon the legal effect, if any, of all electronic signatures other than advanced ones.

Safe electronic signatures are also given the same effect as a seal, provided that a time stamp is also applied.[75]

6–036   Interestingly, the Law provides that paper copies of electronic documents are also legally effective provided that they have been certified as correct copies and the person relying on the copy is able to present the electronic version upon request, and vice versa.[76]

The requirements for qualified certificates are drawn from those in Annex I of the Directive, although the requirement for inclusion of the start date for validity of the certificate is omitted and the requirement to include any limitations on the scope of the certificate is optional rather than compulsory, as it would be under the Directive.[77] It is of course in the interests of certification service providers to include any such restrictions in the certificates they issue, so the latter is unlikely to be a significant issue.

A signatory has an obligation to give a reliable certification service provider (as defined) truthful information and to ensure that its signature creation data are not used without its knowledge. If the signatory has any reason to suppose that the data have been compromised, it must inform the reliable certification service provider without delay. Similarly, if the information in the certificate changes the certificate holder must request its cancellation without delay.[78] Failure to comply with these obligations may render the signatory liable for any losses by relying parties.

(xvii)   Lithuania

6–037   A Law on Electronic Signatures was adopted in July 2000 and came into effect later the same month. However, it was not implemented in practice until January 1, 2002. The Law was then further amended in June 2002 to clarify the position where by law both a signature and a seal are required on a document.

The Law adopts the two tier approach of the Electronic Signatures Directive in an uncluttered fashion. It covers correspondence between government institutions, private law contracts made over either open or closed networks, and authentication of identity of people and servers on the world wide web. It expressly did not relate to the use of encryption to ensure the confidentiality of information.[79] It aimed for technology neutrality in view of the potential emergence of biometrics as an alternative to digital signatures, although it then stipulates that an electronic signature must be created using the signature creation data from the data to be signed.[80] This appears to contemplate a message digest function with encryption.

The definitions and principles have been adopted from the Electronic Signatures Directive. The Law hedges the position on interpretation of "authentication" in the definition of electronic signature by providing that the signature data may be attached to the signed data for the purpose of confirming the authenticity of the signed data and/or the identity of the signatory.[81] Advanced electronic signatures as defined in the Directive are named secure electronic signatures under the Law, but the definition is identical. Article 5 of the Directive on the legal effect of basic and certain advanced electronic signatures is transposed exactly into the Law.[82] No additional presumptions arise from the use of electronic signatures.

Signatories are made responsible for the creation and safekeeping of their signature   **6–038** creation data and may be liable for any damage caused by misuse of it.[83] Interestingly, signature creation data are made non-transferable to any other natural person,[84] which may reduce the risk of signature repudiation. Transferability of signature creation data is clearly a very bad idea, and in practice may not be possible in other jurisdictions on the basis that certification service providers would be unwilling to certify "second hand" signature creation data.

Upon applying for a certificate, the signatory must provide documentary proof of their identity and also any authority to sign on behalf of a company or other legal person, specifying the limits of that authority. However, a relying party must verify the signature and specific procedures for so doing are to be laid down by the supervision institution;[85] the consequences of failure to do so are that damage resulting from the failure is the relying party's responsibility.

Although the basic principles of the Directive are included within this Law, much of the detail as to how it is to operate in practice is left to secondary legislation to be introduced by the supervisory authority.

(xviii)   Luxembourg

Luxembourg implemented the Electronic Signatures Directive in part through its Law of   **6–039** August 14, 2000 on electronic commerce and in part through Regulations of June 1 and December 28, 2001. The Law of August 14, 2000, which also implements the Distance Selling Directive[86] and certain elements of the Information Society Services Directive,[87] implements the provisions of the Directive through transposing them into law but also amends the Civil Code to add a definition of signature to Article 1322 (governing legal requirements for proof of a signature) which, like the French definition, requires a signature to identify the signatory and manifest their approval of the contents of the act. It specifies that the signature can be handwritten or electronic.

An electronic signature is defined as being data in electronic form which are attached in an inseparable fashion to the document and guarantee the integrity of the contents.[88] However, it then goes on to specify that an electronic signature created using a secure signature creation device which the signatory can keep under their sole control and supported by a qualified certificate will satisfy the definition.[89] Other electronic signatures will be assessed on a case by case basis in accordance with Article 5(2) of the Directive. The requirement for electronic documents to be created and stored in circumstances guaranteeing their integrity which was imposed under the French legislation in order for electronic documents to be treated as originals, is also imposed here.[90] However, if the original no longer exists copies made by the person responsible for its safekeeping will have the same probative value as the documents of which they are assumed to be copies unless there is proof to the contrary, provided they have been produced in the context of a properly monitored procedure.[91]

6–040   Article 5 of the Directive is transposed exactly, with the addition that no person can be required to sign electronically.[92] No additional presumptions apply to the use of electronic signatures.

Once signature creation data have been created the holder is solely responsible for their use which will be presumed to have been by the holder unless proved otherwise. The certificate holder must notify the certification service provider as soon as any of the information in the certificate changes, and have the certificate revoked if the signature creation data are compromised.[93]

The requirements for qualified certificates, which are not permitted to subsist for more than 3 years, are set out in the Regulations.[94] The law also amends the Criminal Code to add provisions for offences such as forging electronic signatures or using stolen keys to commit theft.

(xix)   Malta

6–041   The Maltese Electronic Commerce Act (Cap. 426) was brought into force on May 10, 2002. It is a comprehensive law, modelled on the UNCITRAL Model Law for Electronic Transactions and the EU E-Commerce and Electronic Signatures Directives, with the objective of making electronic transactions legally equivalent to paper based ones, and setting up the regulatory framework for the provision of electronic signature certification and other services. It also covers offences of computer misuse.

The law does not cover the making of wills, trusts or powers of attorney, affidavits or court procedures, provisions of the laws of persons or taxes, sureties.[95] It appears to apply equally to open and closed networks, and to communications between private parties or with public administration, although the Minister is given power to make regulations specifying additional requirements for the use of electronic signatures in communications in the public sector.[96]

Most, but not all, of the definitions relating to electronic signatures have been transposed directly from the Electronic Signatures Directive. Signature creation data are not defined, the Act treating signature creation devices as the sole regulated entities.

6–042   Electronic signatures are deemed to satisfy any requirement under Maltese law for a signature and shall not be denied legal effect for being in electronic form or not created using a secure signature creation device and backed by a qualified certificate, given by an accredited certification service provider or otherwise. An advanced electronic signature created using a secure signature creation device and based upon a qualified certificate is presumed to be the signature of the signatory.[97] The Act does not specify whether or not this presumption is rebuttable.

There are no provisions in the Act relating to procedures for verifying electronic signature, or liabilities of signatories to third parties for failure to keep signature creation data secure, nor is power expressly delegated for such provisions to be introduced by regulations.

The Act also introduces a number of offences for the misuse of signature creation devices, fraudulent use of certificates or electronic signatures, forgery of certificates and so on.[98] These are punishable by a fine of up to 100,000 liri (€232,379) and up to 6 months' imprisonment.

(xx) The Netherlands

The Dutch Electronic Signatures Act of May 8, 2003[99] transposed the Electronic Signatures **6–043** Directive into effect in Dutch law by amending various existing statutes, in particular the Civil Code and the Telecommunications Act. It came into effect on publication.

Electronic documents and signatures were in any event admissible under Dutch law. The Act therefore takes a minimalist approach to implementing the Directive. It covers all areas of law save the law of property unless the nature of the legal act to be signed or the legal relationship dictates otherwise. It therefore appears to cover closed as well as open networks and communications between private parties or with public administration.

Electronic signatures are not denied effect on the grounds of being electronic in form[100] but must meet the UNCITRAL Model Law on Electronic Commerce test of being sufficiently reliable for the purpose for which the electronic data are used in all the circumstances.[101] This is not inconsistent with the Directive since it does not amount to a refusal of recognition on the sole grounds of electronic form.

Electronic signatures which meet the definition of advanced electronic signature in the **6–044** Directive and which are based on a qualified certificate[102] and created using a signature creation device which the signatory can maintain under his or her sole control are assumed to meet the requirements of the reliability test, and therefore are given legal effect equivalent to a handwritten signature. The parties are however free to agree their own signature mechanisms.[103] Electronic signatures do not get the benefit of any additional legal presumptions.

The specific requirements for qualified certificates are set out in the Decree and conform closely to the specifications of Annex I of the Directive.

The Decree also covers the requirements for a body to be designated for certifying compliance or otherwise of signature creation devices with the required standards.

Overseas certificates are recognised under the circumstances laid down in the Directive.

No provisions are included on signature verification procedure.

(xxi) Poland

Poland passed an Act on Electronic Signatures on September 18, 2001 which came into **6–045** effect in June 2002.[104] The Prime Minister symbolically used the first Polish electronic signature to sign a letter to the Marshall of the Sejm (Parliament) in February 2003.[105]

The Act transposes the Electronic Signatures Directive and also regulates the provision of time-stamping services. The interpretation of authentication in the definition of electronic signature is that it means to identify the signatory.[106]

Certificates from foreign certification service providers if they are accredited or included within the Polish register of' qualified certification service providers.[107] This is in addition to the usual provision for guarantee by a local (*i.e.* after Poland's accession, EU) certification service provider or mutual recognition of certificates by international agreement.[108]

6–046   The Act deals with the legal effect of electronic signatures in precise detail. For example, in addition to specifying (as required by the Electronic Signatures Directive) legal effect equivalent to a handwritten signature for a secure electronic signature supported by a valid qualified certificate, the Act specifies that such a signature made while the certificate is suspended shall take effect from the time of repeal of such suspension.[109] Further, the signature must also ensure unique identification of the certificate in such a way that any later change to that identification can be detected.[110] There appears to be an irrebuttable presumption that an electronic signature verified by a valid qualified certificate has been made by the signatory, which puts a heavy burden on the holder of such a certificate to ensure that it is not misused.[111] On the other hand, the penalty for using someone else's secure electronic signature is punishable by a fine and/or up to 3 years' imprisonment.[112]

Time-stamping by a qualified certification service provider raises the presumption that the electronic signature was created no later than the time at which the time stamp was applied. The presumption lasts until expiry of the certificate supporting the time-stamp verification data, but can be renewed by repeated time-stamping.[113] This approves later time-stamping of existing signatures.

Ordinary electronic signatures are not to be denied legal effect on that basis, as required by the Directive.[114]

The definition of secure signature creation device is expanded from Annex III of the Directive to include in addition a requirement to warn the user that continuing will generate an electronic signature.[115] Annex IV of the Directive is enacted in the form of requirements for secure signature verification devices.

(xxii)   Portugal

6–047   Portugal passed electronic signature legislation, Decree-Law 290-D/99, in August 1999, before the Electronic Signatures Directive was passed by the European Parliament. It was based on the proposal for a Directive in the form it had reached at that stage, so largely (though not completely) complies with the Directive's provisions. However, the law in its original form was technology-specific in that it expressly focused on digital signatures, although it claimed also to be applicable also to other forms of electronic signature which complied with digital signature security requirements. The law was amended to bring it into conformity with the Directive in April 2003,[116] in particular to replace references to digital signatures with references to qualified electronic signatures or qualified electronic signatures certified by an accredited certifying entity. References hereafter are to the Decree-Law as amended.

The amended law is still not a simple transposition of the Directive, however. The definition[117] of electronic signature is:

"the result of electronic data processing likely to be the subject of an exclusive and individual right and to be used to make the author of the electronic document known."

The requirement here for the signature to be the result of electronic data processing excludes a simple "click", and the requirement that the processing be the subject of an exclusive and individual right is very much more restrictive than the definition in the Directive. Note also the interpretation of "authentication".

6–048   These differences follow through into the definition of advanced electronic signature, which then diverges further from the Directive's definition. The Portuguese law incorporates exactly two of the four elements of the Directive's definition of an advanced electronic signature (that it be created using means that the signatory can maintain under his sole control, and linked to the data in such a manner that subsequent changes are detectable) but does not incorporate the other two precisely. In the Portuguese law, an advanced electronic signature is one which clearly identifies the signatory as the author of the document, which approximates rather than equates to the Directive's requirement that it be capable of identifying the signatory. However, the final requirement in the Directive, that the advanced electronic signature be uniquely linked to the signatory, appears not in the definition of advanced electronic signature in the Portuguese law but in Article 7, relating to the use of qualified electronic signatures. Instead, the definition of advanced electronic signature in the Portuguese law adds a requirement that the placing of the advanced electronic signature on the document depend solely on the will of the author.

A revised definition of digital signature is retained, and a qualified electronic signature is then defined as:

"a digital signature or another type of advanced electronic signature that meets the security requirements similar to those of a digital signature, based on a qualified certificate and created by means of a secure signature creation device."

However, this probably complies with the requirements of the Directive since an **6–049** advanced electronic signature in accordance with the Directive's requirements is likely to meet the Portuguese "security requirements similar to those of a digital signature". Documents so signed, where the certificate is issued by an accredited certifying entity, are given equivalent evidential value to private signed documents under article 376 of the Civil Code.[118] In addition, the parties can agree another type of electronic signature as evidence of authorship and integrity. Other documents are simply assessed under the general terms of the law.[119] This is not quite effective to implement the non-discrimination requirement of Article 5(1) of the Directive, since it provides another ground for dispute and the potential need for additional evidence to prove whether or not the parties had so agreed, before an electronic signature may be given legal effect.

The use of a qualified electronic signature also has the benefit of a number of presumptions under Article 7, provided that the certificate on which it is based is valid at the time. These are that:

- the person who placed the signature on the document was the holder of the signature or, where the signatory is a legal person, an authorised representative of the signatory;

- the signature was placed with the intention of signing; and

- the document has not been altered since it was signed.

If the certificate is revoked, expired or suspended at the time or the signature does not comply with its conditions, then the signature is treated as absent.[120] This is not consistent with the Directive's requirement that a signature not be denied legal effect merely because it is not based upon a qualified certificate.

The law covers the use of electronic signatures in both open and closed networks, and between private parties and in public administration. Public bodies may use qualified electronic signatures to issue electronic documents.[121]

Qualified certificates are required to contain information as laid out in Annex I of the **6–050** Directive with the omission of the certifying entity's own advanced electronic signature.

However, they are unlikely to be very effective without this since the relying party will be unable to ascertain whether they are valid (by tracing the certification service provider's own signing certificate) or not.

Certificate holders must take all necessary technical and organisation steps to prevent loss and damage to third parties and protect confidentiality of information transmitted. If the signature creation data are compromised, the holder must request revocation of the certificate with all due diligence and speed, and cease using the signature creation data.[122]

Finally, qualified certificates issued by foreign certification service providers will be recognised in Portugal in the circumstances laid down in the Directive.

(xxiii)   Romania

6–051   Romania passed its Law No. 455 on Electronic Signatures on July 18, 2001[123] and the Law came into effect on November 1, 2001. It incorporates elements of the UNCITRAL Model Laws as well as implementing the Electronic Signatures Directive.

The Law takes a form of minimalist approach, stipulating at the outset that nothing it contains should be construed as constraining the independent will and contractual freedom of the parties.[124] It applies in all areas of law, public and private transactions and open and closed networks.

The definitions used are largely those from the Directive, although an advanced electronic signature is named an extended electronic signature and definitions of data in electronic form and document in electronic form are also provided. Notably, the definition of data in electronic form requires the data to be:

"supplied in a conventional form appropriate for creating, processing, sending, receiving or storing that information by electronic means."[125]

The requirement of a conventional form may be ambiguous but is also a sensible incentive to citizens to use widely available word-processing, cryptographic and other data manipulation methods, since data in a form which can only be accessed using a package known to a very few are unlikely to have great evidential value after the elapse of a number of years. The suggestion that the data be supplied in a form in which they may be created is difficult to give any meaningful interpretation to.

6–052   The provisions on the effects of electronic documents and signatures relate to the state of the law previously applying in Romania. An electronic document signed with an electronic signature (whether or not extended) which is created using a secure signature creation device and based on a valid qualified certificate is given the same effect as a document under private signature.[126] If the receiving party acknowledges an electronically signed document, whether or not the additional criteria are met, then the document has the same effects as an authentic document as between those parties.[127] A document signed with an extended electronic signature based on a qualified certificate and created using a secure signature creation device satisfies a requirement for written proof or validity (where writing is required by the law).[128] The relying party has the burden of proving that the signature was an extended electronic signature, but this is presumed if it was based on a qualified certificate issued by an accredited certification service provider.[129] Similarly, a party relying on a qualified certificate has the burden of proving that the certification service provider met the requirements for issuing qualified certificates, which is presumed if the provider is accredited.[130]

Certificate holders must apply promptly for revocation of the certificate if the signature creation data are lost of compromised, or any information contained in the certificate ceases to be valid.[131] However, no liability is stipulated for failure to do so.

Foreign-issued certificates will be recognised under the circumstances laid down in the Directive.

The Directive's definition of a secure signature creation device is clarified in the Romanian Law by specifying that the signature must be protected against forgery by means currently available *at the time it is generated*,[132] which is likely to mean that secure signature creation devices will necessarily have a relatively short shelf-life as the suppliers, who will no doubt be warranting that their products meet these criteria, will have to upgrade their products constantly as hacking technology improves.

(xxiv) Slovakia

The Slovakian Electronic Signature Act was passed in March 2002 and came fully into effect in September 2002. It applies to the use of electronic signatures in both open and closed networks, although participants in closed networks can agree otherwise.[133] It also permits the use of advanced electronic signatures in communications with public bodies, where permitted by the law.[134] It incorporates many aspects of the Electronic Signatures Directive but has been extensively revised and expanded. **6–053**

The Act, despite its title, in fact relates only to digital signatures and is therefore not technologically neutral as required by the Electronic Signatures Directive. An electronic signature is defined as:

"data affixed to or logically associated with an electronic document which shall meet the following requirements:

(a) they are incapable of being created without knowing the private key and electronic document;

(b) they are capable of being used based on the data and the public key corresponding to the private key used to generate the data to verify that an electronic document which they are affixed to or logically associated with is identical with the electronic document used to generate the data."

This interprets "authentication" as checking the integrity of the message signed. A valid advanced electronic signature is then defined as an electronic signature, created with a secure signature creation device, such that the signatory can be reliably identified, and supported by a qualified certificate which is valid at the time of the signature, where the electronic document concerned has not subsequently been changed.[135] This confers legal effect upon the matter signed to the extent that written form was required for that purpose.[136] There is no provision defining a valid electronic signature, or prohibiting denial of legal effect based upon a signature being in electronic form. It may be that this is unnecessary under the ordinary rules of evidence in Slovakian law.

Certificate holders may be liable for damage resulting from any failure to exercise due care of their private keys, for any misrepresentation in applying for a certificate or failure to request revocation if the key is compromised.[137] Unauthorised use of a private key by a legal person may be punished with a fine imposed by the National Security Bureau (NSB) of up to SK1m (€24,430), and by a natural person SK100,000 (€2,443).[138] **6–054**

Foreign certificates may be recognised if their validity is verifiable in Slovakia and the issuing certification service provider is either registered or accredited in Slovakia, or guaranteed by a Slovakian certification service provider or under an international mutual recognition agreement.[139] Upon Slovakia's accession to the European Union certificates issued by EU certification service providers will become equivalent to those issued in Slovakia.

(xxv)   Slovenia

6–055   Slovenia passed its Electronic Commerce and Electronic Signature Act in June 2000 and the Act came into force later that year. The Act was based on the UNCITRAL Model Law and the Electronic Signatures Directive and intended to regulate electronic commerce and the use of electronic signatures in legal affairs. It does not apply to closed systems save insofar as the electronic signatures and data therein benefit from the prohibition on denying legal effect to such solely on the grounds of their being in electronic form.[140] The Act generally aims only to remove obstacles to electronic commerce; parties' freedom to contract is expressly preserved.

6–056   The definition of electronic signature from the Directive has been clarified to state that the signature data must serve as a method of authentication of the data signed and also of identification of the signatory. The definition of advanced electronic signature has been narrowed to specify that an advanced electronic signature can only be created using a secure signature creation device. Additional definitions—for example of electronic message (which includes EDI and e-mail) and of sender, addressee and recipient of an electronic message—are included.

Chapter III, which deals with electronic signatures, transposes Article 5 of the Directive on legal effect of electronic signatures, exactly.[141] However, electronic signatures do not benefit from any additional presumptions and until further legislation is introduced the Act has no effect where notarial verification of a signature is required under the existing law.[142] The Act deals with the issue of electronic archiving by the simple though not necessarily adequate expedient of requiring parties which store electronically signed documents also to store the complementary signature verification data and devices for as long as the documents are stored.[143]

Parties relying upon advanced electronic signatures must verify them in accordance with Annex IV of the Directive.[144]

6–057   The use of signature creation data or devices without the knowledge of the signatory or holder of any certificate is prohibited and may be subject to a fine between 50,000 and 150,000 Tolars (€218.75-656.25).[145] A certificate holder must use reasonable care to keep their signature creation data safe and prevent unauthorised access, and can be subject to the same fine for failing to do so or failing to notify the certification service provide promptly if the data are compromised in any way or the information in the certificate changes.[146] Unusually, the Act contemplates a certificate including information about a third party not a certificate holder. Such a person also has a right to demand revocation of the certificate, presumably on the basis that the information has changed.[147] Revocation is effective against third parties from the moment of publication.

Foreign certificates may be recognised under the circumstances laid down in the Electronic Signatures Directive.

(xxvi)   Spain

6–058   Spain passed a Decree Law on Electronic Signatures in September 1999, before the Electronic Signatures Directive had been finally approved by the European Parliament and Council. A further Decree Law was therefore passed in June 2003[148] bringing the existing framework into conformity with the Directive and also making provision for the Spanish electronic identity card system. The law relates to the use of electronic signatures in open and closed networks, public and private transactions. Electronic signatures used in public agencies may in addition require time-stamping.

The new Law defines an electronic signature as data in electronic form, attached to or logically associated with other data which may be used as a method of identifying the signatory. An advanced electronic signature is defined in accordance with the Directive. A definition of "recognised electronic signature" is introduced which equates to a qualified electronic signature in other laws, *i.e.* an advanced electronic signature based upon a qualified certificate and created using a secure signature creation device. These are given equivalent effect to handwritten signatures; Article 5.2 is also transposed. No special presumptions are applied to the use of an electronic signature. Backups of electronically signed documents are admissible in evidence.[149]

The law includes specific provisions on the use of certificates by legal persons. Custody of the signature creation data corresponding to the certified signature verification data is made the responsibility of the natural person using the certificate, who is to be identified in the certificate. If the representative uses the certificate outside the permitted limits, the legal person will be bound only if they adopt the acts as their own or the acts are to their benefit.[150] This provision is an attempt to address the situation covered by Article 13 of the UNCITRAL Model Law, allocating responsibility between the sender and recipient of an unauthorised communication. However, the Spanish solution is in effect the opposite of the UNCITRAL approach, so that the risk is on the recipient whose only recourse is to claim against the physical person who holds the signature creation data—a remedy which may be of little use where the loss caused is substantial. The only exceptions to this provision are the signatures used by certification service providers to sign certificates or signatures used in public administration.[151]

6–059

Qualified certificates may not be valid for more than four years. Foreign certificates will be recognised under the circumstances laid down in the Electronic Signatures Directive.

The National Electronic Identity Card introduced under Article 15 will accredit electronically the holder's identity and permit electronic signature of documents. In producing them, the Department of the Interior will be required to comply with the criteria for certification service providers issuing qualified certificates. The technology used for the card is intended to be so far as possible compatible with different accepted forms of electronic signature product.[152]

(xxvii) Sweden

The Qualified Electronic Signatures Act was passed in November 2000 and entered into force on January 1, 2001 to implement the Electronic Signatures Directive. It takes a minimalist approach to so doing. For instance, it relates only to qualified electronic signatures; no legislation was considered necessary regarding unqualified electronic signatures since there are in any event no rules of evidence in Sweden which would prevent electronic documents or signatures being admissible in Court. Requirements of form are also rare in private transactions, the main exceptions being transactions involving real property, consumer credit and provision of financial services.

6–060

A qualified electronic signature is an advanced electronic signature created by a secure signature creation device and based on a qualified certificate.[153] Such signatures meet any (rare) requirement under Swedish law for a handwritten signature, where the requirement "may be satisfied by electronic means".[154] It is not clear where this may apply – it would be surprising if any section of existing Swedish law specifies that a requirement for handwritten signature can be satisfied by electronic means. Additional requirements may be specified for communication with or between government authorities.

The Swedish law recognises qualified certificates issued by certification service providers established anywhere in the European Economic Area and permitted to issue such certificates there.[155] Curiously, there are no provisions for mutual recognition of certificates from third countries under mutual recognition agreements. This may go without saying.

A further Act was passed in 2001 dealing with the conformity of secure signature creation devices to the requirements laid down in the Directive.

(xxviii)   Switzerland

6–061   Not being a member of the European Union, Switzerland is not obliged to implement the Electronic Signatures Directive. Further, the position of Switzerland is complicated, being an essentially federal state with each canton having the power to make its own laws. However, the general principle of contracting under Swiss law is that the parties are entirely free to choose the form of contract, which may be oral, paper-based or electronic. There are various requirements for specific kinds of contracts to be in writing and signed by hand, such as sale or purchase of land, a promise of a gift, a guarantee or a will and consumer credit. In these cases, the signature must be made by the party personally unless specified otherwise. The law does permit a signature on a bond issue, which is likely to require large numbers of documents, to be created by printing.

Similarly, the principles of evidence permit the admission of electronic documents and signatures into legal proceedings without the need for legislation, to be given such effect as the judge may see fit.

There is currently no Federal law on electronic signatures in effect, although a draft has been circulated for consultation. It may be passed in the course of 2003. The draft Federal Law is intended broadly to comply with the EU Directive. Article 3(1) sets out the conditions which a Swiss organisation must meet in order to be recognised as a certification service provider, and Article 3(2) sets out the equivalent conditions for foreign companies.

The draft law covers private contracting rather than communications with or within public administration. Legal effect is to be conferred on a certified electronic signature issued in the name of a natural person and certified by a recognised certification service provider not by this law but by a new Article 14(2)bis of the Civil Code.

(xxix)   United Kingdom

6–062   The use of electronic signatures in the United Kingdom is governed by the Electronic Communications Act 2000, in force to the extent relevant here since May 2000, and the Electronic Signatures Regulations 2002.[156] These came into force in March 2002.

The Electronic Communications Act takes a minimalist approach, not specifying any level of legal effect for any category of electronic signature. It was arguably unnecessary to take any steps to implement Article 5 in the light of the evolution of the case law[157] up to that date. Instead, the Act merely deals with the status of electronic signatures and supporting certificates in evidence. The definition of electronic signature in the Act[158] is very similar to that in the Electronic Signatures Directive although not a simple transposition. However, in terms of substance the only divergence is the addition in the definition in the Act of the purpose of establishing the integrity of a communication or data.

The Act expressly provides[159] that electronic signatures and the certification by any person of such a signature are each admissible in evidence in relation to any question as to the authenticity or integrity of the communication or data signed.[160] Authenticity is defined for this purpose[161] as any of the identity of the originator, the accuracy of any time or date on the document or data or whether the document was intended to have legal effect. Integrity means[162] whether there has been any tampering with, or other modification to, the data.

It is not clear why it was felt necessary to introduce these provisions, since the general position under English law is that any form of evidence is admissible if it assists the court in determining any fact in issue. Clearly, where the source, accuracy or purpose of an electronic document is in issue an electronic signature may assist the court in coming to a finding on any of these matters. A digital signature may also assist the court in determining integrity. A certificate may assist the court in establishing the source of a signature. Thus, it is probable that both signatures and certificates would have been admissible evidence in any event.

There is also the outside possibility that in prescribing the purposes for which an electronic signature may be admitted in evidence the Act may raise doubts as to whether an electronic signature may be admitted for other evidential purposes—such as confirming that any statements in the document reflect the facts correctly; confirming the signatory has notice of the contents of the document; or acknowledging or marking a particular version of the document as the original. No doubt this will be clarified by case law in due course.   **6–063**

There are no provisions regarding recognition of foreign certificates or certification service providers, since the law does not require the use of a certificate for an electronic signature to be given legal effect, let along any particular category of electronic signature deriving from any particular source.

At the time of writing the government is in the process of amending certain existing legislation such as the Consumer Credit Act 1974, for compliance with the Electronic Commerce Directive's requirement to allow contracts to be concluded by electronic means. The Consumer Credit Act, which governs credit and hire contracts with consumers up to the value of £25,000, is one of the few United Kingdom statutes which currently includes substantial requirements as to the form of the contract. Notably, one of the issues raised in the consultation process[163] is the relevance of signatures in the context of electronic transactions since one of the major functions of the signature under the existing Act is to bring the consumer's mind to focus on the significance of the act they are performing, in other words the ceremonial function, which could be implemented in a completely different way in the electronic environment.

2. ASIA / PACIFIC

(i) Australia

In Australia, there is no legislation requiring or governing the use of cryptographic signatures. The *Electronic Transactions Act 1999* (Cth) (*ETA*) does, however, provide that an   **6–064** electronic signature will have the same legal effect as a handwritten one for the purposes of Commonwealth legislation but does not specify any particular method of signing something electronically.

The effectiveness of a particular method of signing electronically is dependent on whether that method meets the requirements of the ETA (which, together with the State based regimes, is discussed below), one of which is that the method used be appropriately reliable for the circumstances.[164] To address this issue, amongst others, some Government agencies have implemented systems which utilise digital signatures for the purposes of identifying and then verifying the person or organisation with whom it is dealing. In many instances, this is supported by the Gatekeeper framework, which is overseen by Australia's National Office for the Information Economy (*NOIE*).

6–065   While the Federal Government in particular is encouraging the use of digital signatures and certificates utilising the Gatekeeper framework, the commercial uptake of digital signatures and certificates has been slow. In particular, while there is commercial use of digital signatures and certificates for internet based purchases and similar server based transactions, the use of the more sophisticated public key infrastructure and similar technology is limited.

This section discusses the current legislative position in Australia, at both a Commonwealth and State level, and some of the ways in which digital signatures and certificates are currently being used in Australia.

1.   Commonwealth legislation

(i)   Australia

General

6–066   At a Federal level, the primary legislation dealing with electronic signatures and authentication issues is the ETA referred to above. Other Federal legislation which has an impact on the use of cryptographic technology includes the Customs Act, which restricts the movement of certain encryption technologies outside of Australia, and the Telecommunications Act 1997 (Cth), which requires that telecommunications carriers and carriage service providers possess interception capabilities.

Electronic Transactions Act 1999

6–067   The Commonwealth introduced its *Electronic Transactions Act* in 1999 to give legal efficacy to electronic signatures. It was assented to on December 10, 1999 and commenced on March 15, 2000. The ETA is based on the UNCITRAL Model Law on Electronic Commerce of 1996 and was developed by the Commonwealth in cooperation with the Australian State and Territory Governments to attempt to develop a national uniform legislative scheme to facilitate the use of electronic transactions. Each State and Territory has also enacted equivalent legislation for their jurisdiction. This State and Territory legislation is discussed further below. While the Commonwealth ETA is part of the national uniform scheme, it operates independently of the State and Territory legislation.

The ETA creates a light-handed regulatory regime for the use of electronic communications in transactions by business and the community in dealings with the Government and currently applies to all laws of the Commonwealth, unless they are specifically excluded from the application of the ETA. The legislation is purposely technology neutral, in that it does not endorse any particular type of electronic signature, so that it will not need to be revised to take account of technological changes.

The ETA has broadly removed the legal impediments that may have prevented a person using electronic communications to satisfy obligations under Commonwealth law and specifically states[165] that, for the purposes of a law of the Commonwealth, a transaction is not invalid because it took place by means of one or more electronic transactions, unless specifically stated otherwise. This provision does not apply, however, to transactions or laws of the Commonwealth which are listed in regulations to the ETA.[166]

It also provides[167] that, if information is required to be given in writing, it can be given by way of an electronic communication where:

(a) at the time that it was given, it was reasonable to expect that the information would be readily accessible for subsequent reference; and

(b) if the information is required by a Commonwealth entity that has particular technological requirements, those requirements are met; and

(c) if the Commonwealth entity has any requirements for particular action to verify the receipt of the information, those requirements are met; and

(d) if the information is required to be given to a person who is not a Commonwealth entity, the person consents to the information being given by electronic communication.

Under Section 10 of the ETA, an electronic signature is recognised as equivalent to a handwritten one for the purposes of a Commonwealth law, provided that certain conditions are met. The requirements will be taken to be met if:[168]   **6–068**

(a) a method is used to identify the person and to indicate the person's approval of the information communicated; and

(b) having regard to the relevant circumstances the method used was as reliable as was appropriate for the purposes for which the information was communicated; and

(c) if a Commonwealth entity has certain technological requirements, those requirements are met; and

(d) if not a commonwealth entity, the person to whom the signature is required to be given consents to the requirement being met in the manner stated in (a).

The ETA also specifies requirements for:

(a) the electronic production of a document,[169] other than migration and citizenship document, which are not able to be produced electronically;[170]

(b) the electronic recording of information;[171]

(c) retention of a written document;[172]

(d) retention of electronic communications;[173]

(e)   the time and place of dispatch and receipt of electronic communications;[174] and

(f)   attribution of electronic communications.[175]

2.   ETA – Variations in each State

6–069   As noted above, under Australia's Federal system of government, each State and Territory has introduced its own version of the ETA. The State and Territory Acts are important since most contracts in Australia are governed by the law of a State or Territory, rather than Commonwealth law.

The State and Territory legislation is substantially the same as the Commonwealth legislation, with the primary differences being the removal of references to copyright, immigration and Commonwealth Evidence law and other specific requirements of Commonwealth entities or responsibilities. Specific State legislation is also excluded from the operation of the relevant State Act in a similar manner to the exclusion of operation of the Commonwealth Act.[176]

The State and Territory legislation is listed in the following table.

State	Name of Act	Commencement Date
New South Wales	*Electronic Transactions Act 2000*	December 7, 2001
Victoria	*Electronic Transactions (Victoria) Act 2000*	September 1, 2000
Tasmania	*Electronic Transactions Act 2000*	June 1, 2001
ACT	*Electronic Transactions Act 2001*	July 1, 2001
Northern Territory	*Electronic Transactions (Northern Territory) Act 2000*	June 13, 2001
Queensland	*Electronic Transactions (Queensland) Act 2001*	November 1, 2002
Western Australia	*Electronic Transactions Act 2003*	May 2, 2003
South Australia	*Electronic Transactions Act 2000*	November 1, 2002

6–070   There has been minimal judicial consideration in Australia of either the Commonwealth, State or Territory ETAs. In the only case reported to have considered the ETAs to date, the Queensland Supreme Court[177] and Court of Appeal[178] confirmed that, pursuant to Sections 4 and 8(1) of the *Electronic Transactions Act 1999* (Cth), the acceptance of an offer by email is capable of creating legal relations. In the case, a party to court proceedings was found to have accepted the other parties' separate offers to settle the matter when it sent email replies to each of them to the effect that it was prepared to accept their respective offers.

(ii) Bangladesh

6–071   Bangladesh has not yet introduced any law relating to electronic signatures but its Law Commission did produce a draft Information Technology Act in 2002.[179] This was based upon the Singaporean and Indian laws and intended to conform with the UNCITRAL Model Law on electronic commerce.

The proposed law, which would recognise digital signatures but no other form of electronic signature, would apply to all fields of law except negotiable instruments, wills, trusts, contracts for sale of land and conveyances of land, powers of attorney and documents of title. A number of offences would be introduced relating to forgery of digital signatures and false certificates, as well as computer hacking, spreading viruses and the like.

The timetable for the passage of this Bill through Parliament is not known.

(iii) China[180]

In March, 1999, the National People's Congress published a new *Contract Act of the* **6—072** *People's Republic of China* ("the Contract Act"). Article 11 of the Contract Act provides that:

"A writing means a memorandum of contract, letter or electronic message (including telegram, telex, facsimile, electronic data exchange and electronic mail), etc. which is capable of expressing its contents in a tangible form"

This clearly recognizes electronic messages as a form of writing. However there are no other provisions in the Contract Act to govern how an electronic contract may perform the functions of a paper-based document. According to China's current evidence rules, e-mail and other e-records are only classified as "audio-visual material," they cannot stand as independent evidence but must be supported by other forms of circumstantial evidence. So it may be difficult for parties to persuade the judge to enforce a contract entered into by e-mail or other e-message. Legal uncertainty regarding the enforceability of contracts has therefore not been solved.

At provincial level, Hainan Province led the way with Digital Certificate Rules released **6—073** on August 9, 2001,[181] and Guangdong province enacted comprehensive legislation in March 2003. This specified that digital signatures have legal effect, as well as providing rules for the formation of contracts over the Internet. However, there is an issue as to whether government officials will register or approve electronic contracts (as is necessary for certain contracts under Chinese national law) because of the uncertainty of their status, and that of any signatures, pending national legislation.

Shanghai province has also apparently considered introducing legislation in this area, but has not published any acts up to now.

In May 2002 the SLGI began drafting a law on Electronic Signatures (the Statute). In the process of drafting, there are some debates on the scope of the Statute. First, whether the electronic signatures should include seals. In China, individuals and enterprises as well as government agencies are used to using a seal or a seal in combination with a personal signature. So if the Statute does not cover the use of seals its application will be limited. The second issue is whether the Statute will apply to the government administration affairs, includes intra-documents exchanges and public service businesses between government and citizen. One of the purposes of the Statute is to enhance the use of electronic documents in all communication (include public and private), or to carry out the strategy. But some professionals worry about conflicts between legal principles on e-government affairs and on e-business. In addition to the scope issues, there are other delicate issues to be solved, such as how to implement the technology-neutral principle. This statute is on the legislative agenda of the State Council for 2003–04.

(iv) Hong Kong

The Hong Kong Electronic Transactions Ordinance[182] was passed in January 2000. It **6—074** concerns digital signature technology, since the Hong Kong government concluded that this was the only technically mature technology which provides a security service of an adequate quality. This may have the effect of precluding other forms of technology from development and use in Hong Kong.

The Ordinance applies generally subject to a number of exceptions, including wills, trusts, mortgages or transfers of land, negotiable instruments and instruments requiring to be stamped.[183] This list may be extended by the Secretary for Commerce, Industry and Technology from time to time by publishing an order in the Hong Kong Gazette.[184]

The Ordinance uses a broad definition of electronic signature but goes on to give a technically precise definition of a digital signature as one generated using an asymmetric cryptosystem and enabling the recipient to determine whether the signature was generated using the private key that corresponds to the signer's public key; and whether the initial electronic record has been altered since signature.[185]

6–075   Digital signatures are given legal effect provided that they are supported by a recognised certificate and generated within the validity of that certificate,[186] and, where the giving of notices, etc. is concerned, the person intended to rely upon the signature has consented (which may be express or inferred) to a digital signature being used.[187] No additional presumptions apply to the use of a digital signature.

A certificate is required to identify the issuing certification authority, name *or* identify the person to whom it is issued, contain the holder's public key and be signed by a responsible officer of the issuing authority. This definition is almost as minimalist as the definition of certificate in the Electronic Signatures Directive, providing little more than a single pointer to the authority which may be able to provide evidence to assist in determining how reliable the signature is.

Electronic signatures other than digital signatures are recognised only insofar as any other Ordinance specifies or leaves it to the discretion of a person for the purpose.[188] Electronic records are not to be denied admissibility in evidence on the sole grounds of being in electronic form.[189]

There are no provisions relating to certificates issued by foreign certification authorities where the foreign certification authority has not applied for recognition, so the question of recognition of such certificates remains to be determined by the Courts but it is unlikely that any will be so recognised, in view of the detailed prescriptive nature of the Ordinance. There are also no obligations on subscribers to protect their private keys and no liability is prescribed for a failure to do so.

(v)   India

6–076   India passed its Information Technology Act, after long debate, in June 2000 and it came into effect later that year. It is entirely technology-specific, not including even a definition of electronic signature in the general sense, and highly prescriptive in approach.

The Act covers the use of digital signatures on documents other than wills, trusts, powers of attorney, negotiable instruments and contracts for sale of land or conveyances of land.[190] In principle it applies to public administration as to private transactions, though in practice further conditions will apply and the administration cannot be required to accept electronic forms. However, the first digital signature was symbolically applied in 2002 to an e-mail sent by the Communications Minister to the Prime Minister.[191]

Digital signatures can be used to authenticate electronic records, and by section 5, where any law requires a document to be signed that requirement is satisfied by the affixing of a digital signature in a prescribed manner. A digital signature of a party to an agreement which appears on the agreement is presumed to have been affixed by the party.[192] The details of the type of digital signature, manner and format of affixing, how the signatory is to be identified and the processes and procedures for ensuring adequate integrity, security and confidentiality of electronic records were thereby left to secondary legislation. Rules were brought into effect in October 2000.

A secure digital signature is a digital signature which at the time it was created can be   6–077
verified, by the application of a security procedure agreed to by the parties concerned, to have been unique to the subscriber affixing it, capable of identifying them and created in a manner or using means under the exclusive control of the subscriber, which also is linked to the electronic record to which it relates in such a manner that if the electronic record were altered the signature would be invalidated. Once again, the procedure was to be laid down by rules under the Act which would take into account the nature of the transaction, sophistication of the parties' technological capacity, availability of alternatives and similar factors as suggested in the Guide to Enactment of the UNCITRAL Model Law. Secure digital signatures have the benefit of rebuttable presumptions to the effect that the signature was affixed by the subscriber with the intention of signing or approving the electronic record.[193]

The Controller of Certifying Authorities can recognise foreign certifying authorities, and acts as a repository for all digital signature certificates issued under the Act.

A digital signature certificate holder must exercise reasonable care to retain control of their private key and take all steps to prevent its disclosure.[194] This is a strict requirement which would appear to be automatically violated if in fact any third party ever does succeed in obtaining someone else's private key. However, the subscriber ceases to be liable for damage occurring after he or she has communicated the fact of the compromise of the key to the certifying authority.

The Act also amends the Indian Evidence Act 1872 to include provisions on the admissibility of computer evidence in legal proceedings.[195]

(vi) Indonesia

A draft Electronic Transactions and Electronic Signatures Bill was prepared in 2002 but   6–078
was still in draft form at the end of the year.

(vii) Japan

The Japanese Law Concerning Electronic Signatures and Certification Services came into   6–079
effect in April 2001. It does not apply to government, for which a separate project is in progress which is hoped to come into effect in the course of 2003.

The Law uses a restrictive definition of electronic signature which requires the signature not only to identify the signatory but also to be able to confirm whether or not any alteration of the signed record has taken place. This would therefore appear to require digital signatures.

Private electromagnetic records are presumed authentic if signed with an electronic signature which, if the necessary codes have been properly controlled, only the principal can perform.[196] It is not clear whether this amounts to recognition of an electronic signature as conferring legal effect upon a document, or solely to authenticating records in the sense of establishing that they have not been changed. It is also noteworthy that there is no provision in the Law relating to electronic seals, although this was considered when the Law was being drafted as seals are still commonly used, either alone or with handwritten signatures, in paper-based transactions in Japan.

A user who makes a false application to an accredited certification service provider and gets a false certificate may be imprisoned for up to three years or fined up to 2m yen (€15,109). The Law contains no provisions mandating the use of certificates.

(viii) Malaysia

6–080   Malaysia enacted its Digital Signature Act in 1997. The Act, which came into effect on October 1, 1998, was amended in 2001. As can be seen from the title, the approach is technology-specific and the Act prescribes the method of use of digital signatures in great detail.

Digitally signed documents are deemed valid and enforceable, and a digital signature created in accordance with the Act is a legally binding signature.[197] A digital signature affixed with the intention of signing and supported and verified by a certificate issued by a licensed certification authority is presumed to be that of the subscriber listed in the certificate and to have been affixed with the intention of signing. The digital signature is presumed to have been created before it was time-stamped if it has been time-stamped by a recognised time-stamp service using a trustworthy system. Finally, the recipient is also presumed not to have had any notice of any breach of duty by the subscriber or that their possession of the private key was not rightful.[198]

Rightfully hold a private key means:

"to be able to utilise a private key-

   (a)   which the holder or the holder's agent have not disclosed to any person in contravention of this Act; and

   (b)   which the holder has not obtained through theft, deceit, eavesdropping or other unlawful means."

A subscriber has a corresponding duty to exercise reasonable care to retain control of their private key and prevent its disclosure.[199] The subscriber, by accepting an issued certificate, represents to all who reasonably rely upon the information in it that they rightfully hold the private key corresponding to the certified public key and that all material representations made to the issuing licensed certification authority, or made in the certificate, are true. The subscriber must indemnify the certification authority for any loss or damages caused by any false and material representation of any fact or failure to disclose any such.[200] The Act makes a private key personal property.

(ix) New Zealand

6–081   The Electronic Transactions Act was passed in October 2002 but at the time of writing was not yet in force as the necessary Regulations were still being drafted.

The Act takes a minimalist approach, governing only the use of electronic signatures where the use of a signature is required by statute or regulation. Since most contracts under New Zealand law are not made pursuant to a legal requirement of this sort, and indeed generally do not require a signature, the Act has no effect upon private parties' choice of form of signature. Further, various kinds of documents are expressly excluded from the Act, including negotiable instruments, wills, trusts, powers of attorney, affidavits, notices to the public, bills of lading and safety information relating to goods or services.[201]

The Act is technology neutral. The definition of electronic signature is simply:

"in relation to information in electronic form . . . a method used to identify a person and to indicate that person's approval of that information."[202]

Sections 22 to 24 specify the circumstances in which legal requirements for signature can be met using an electronic signature. A legal requirement for a signature other than the signature of a witness can be met using an electronic signature if three requirements are met:

- the electronic signature adequately identifies the signatory and indicates the signatory's approval of the document to which the signature relates;

- the signature is as reliable as appropriate given the purpose for which, and the circumstances in which, the signature is required; and

- where information which must be given to a person is required to be signed, the recipient must have consented to receiving the electronic signature, rather than a traditional paper-based signature.[203]

The Act does not deal with attribution, which is left to the same common law rules that apply to paper based signatures. In all cases, where the signature relates to information which must be given to a person as a legal requirement, an electronic signature may only be used if the prospective recipient consents.   **6–082**

A significant number of statutes require a signature or a corporate seal to be witnessed. Witnesses may witness a document using an electronic signature, if:

- where a signature is being witnessed, that signature is also an electronic signature; and

- the electronic signature of the witness meets requirements that correspond to those for a primary signature in Section 22.[204]

Section 24 establishes a rebuttable presumption that certain electronic signatures are reliable. It is not intended to be limited to public-private key methods but may in fact be until new technology develops. The presumption arises if: **6–083**

- the means of creating the electronic signature are

  - linked to the signatory and to no other person;

  - under the control of the signatory and of no other person;

- any alteration to the electronic signature made after the time of signing is detectable;

- where the purpose of the legal requirement for a signature is to provide assurance as to the integrity of the information to which it relates, any alteration made to that information after the time of signing is detectable.

Even if these requirements are not met, an electronic signature may still be valid if proved to have been as reliable as appropriate for the purpose.

(x) Pakistan

6–084 An Electronic Transactions Ordinance was promulgated in September 2002 under the Provisional Constitution of 1999. It confirms the efficacy of electronic documents and signatures in all circumstances except for negotiable instruments, powers of attorney, trusts, wills or contracts for sale or conveyances of land.[205]

It is intended to be technologically neutral and minimalist. An electronic signature can be any letters, numbers, symbols, images, characters or combination in electronic form provided that they are applied to an electronic document with the intention of authenticating or approving the same in order to establish authenticity (defined in the sense of attribution to a particular person or information system), integrity or both. It then uses, as one definition of an advanced electronic signature, a definition identical to that in the Electronic Signatures Directive. The other definition is an electronic signature provided by an accredited certification service provider and itself accredited as being capable of establishing authenticity and integrity of an electronic document.[206]

Both forms of electronic signature are given legal effect where a signature is required by law,[207] but advanced electronic signatures also benefit from the rebuttable presumption:

- that the electronic document so signed is authentic and has integrity; or

- that the signature is the signature of the person to whom it correlates and was affixed with the intention of signing or approving the relevant document which has not since been altered.[208]

6–085 The use of "or" in this provision suggests that only one of these presumptions may be raised in respect of any given document, but there is no logical basis for refusing to raise the other and it may simply be that the legislators had different scenarios in mind such that only one presumption was expected to be relevant at any one time.

Certificates may relate either to an electronic signature or to an electronic document, in which latter case it certifies the authenticity and integrity of the information contained.[209]

The surprising advantages are conferred on electronic transactions of not requiring witnessing or notarisation or being stampable until the Provincial Governments have implemented measures for recovery of stamp duty through electronic means.[210] This could be a significant incentive for businesses to take up electronic forms of transacting.

It is an offence, publishable by up to 7 years' imprisonment and/or a fine of up to 10m rupees (€157,486), for a subscriber to provide false information in an application for a certificate, to fail to notify the certification service provider if the information in a certificate ceases to be true or to knowingly cause or allow a certificate or electronic signature to be used in any fraudulent or unlawful manner.[211]

(xi) Philippines

6–086 The Philippines Electronic Commerce Act of 2000[212] came into effect in June 2000. It applies to the use of data messages and electronic documents in both commercial and non-commercial dealings domestically and internationally,[213] and the bulk of the text relates to the formation of electronic contracts. However, it also provides for the use of electronic signatures on all kinds of documents including transactions with government.[214]

The Act appears to have been drafted with the intent of being technologically neutral. The definition of electronic signature is an unusual one, it refers to:

"any distinctive mark, characteristic and/or sound in electronic form, representing the identity of a person and attached to or logically associated with the electronic data message or electronic document or any methodology or procedures employed or adopted by a person and executed or adopted by such person with the intention of authenticating or approving an electronic data message or electronic document."[215]

This would encompass a recorded voice message or a ritualised gesture, since the definition does not appear to require a signature in the form of a methodology or procedure to be recorded in any form (electronic or otherwise) or attached to or logically associated with the electronic document. This may not have been the legislators' intention, since the term being defined would as a matter of the ordinary meaning of the words appear to require at the least that there be some electronic signal. The definition is then used in the context that it is "on" an electronic document, which implies that a record must exist. These issues will remain to be worked out by the Filipino Courts. On its face, it is the broadest and most flexible definition of electronic signature in any of the legislation surveyed here.   **6–087**

An electronic signature is given legal recognition only when it can be proved that:

"a prescribed procedure, not alterable by the parties interested in the electronic document, existed under which:

(a)   a method is used to identify the party sought to be bound and to indicate said party's access to the electronic document necessary for his consent or approval through the electronic signature;

(b)   said method is reliable and appropriate for the purpose for which the electronic document was generated or communicated, in the light of all the circumstances including any relevant agreement;

(c)   it is necessary for the party sought to be bound, in order to proceed further with the transaction, to have executed or provided the electronic signature; and

(d)   the other party is authorized and enabled to verify the electronic signature and to make the decision to proceed with the transaction authenticated by the same."[216]

This does not equate to the usual description of a mechanism of applying a digital signature; it appears more consistent with some form of website-based transaction where by technical means a party cannot proceed with a transaction without having entered a password and clicked a button to continue. It is not at all clear what it may mean for the counterparty to be authorised to verify the electronic signature.

The express requirement for proof, and that for authentication of electronic signatures in data messages or electronic documents set out in section 11, sits oddly with section 9, which gives all electronic signatures the benefit of a presumption that the electronic   **6–088** signature is the signature of the person to whom it correlates and that it was affixed by that person with the intention of signing or approving the electronic document unless the relying party knows or has notice of any defects in the signature or reliance on it is not reasonable in the circumstances. The former presumption would appear redundant when the signature is only to be given legal effect if it can be proved that the signatory was identified by a reliable method under the prescribed procedure. One possible consistent interpretation is that the presumption is not that the signature relates to the person, but that an electronic mark or signal is to be treated as a signature. However, this might likewise be considered redundant in view of the second presumption

New rules of evidence to implement the Act were brought into effect by the Supreme Court of the Philippines in August 2001.[217] These make electronic signatures and digital signatures authenticated in a prescribed manner admissible in evidence as the functional equivalent of the signature of a person on a written document.[218] The prescribed manner is effectively by evidence of a method or process being used to generate a digital signature or otherwise by means satisfactory to the judge. The concept of certificates is introduced by the rules in that where an authenticated digital signature is supported by a certificate the accuracy of the contents of the certificate, and the identity of its stated issuing authority are presumed as is also that the associated message has not be changed from the time of signing, which is presumed to have been during the validity of the certificate.[219] These presumptions are rebuttable by evidence on affidavit or under cross examination. The Court will assess the evidential weight to be given to electronic records by reference to a set of factors which include a comprehensive examination of the security of all relevant information systems.[220]

The Rules also make audio, video and photographic evidence of events, acts and transaction admissible subject to confirmation by testimony.[221]

(xii)   Singapore

6–089   Singapore was one of the first countries to introduce electronic commerce legislation, with its Electronic Transactions Act of July 1998. It applies to signatures of all documents except wills, negotiable instruments, trusts and powers of attorney, contracts for disposition of an interest in land or documents of title.[222] Government bodies are entitled to accept electronically signed documents, although they may stipulate what kind.[223]

The Act takes the "two tier" approach. It includes an express provision that a click on a website may be treated as an electronic signature,[224] which is otherwise defined as:

> "any letters, characters, numbers or other symbols in digital form attached to or logically associated with an electronic record and executed or adopted with the intention of authenticating or approving the electronic record."[225]

By section 8(1), an electronic signature satisfies any rule of law requiring a signature or providing certain consequences if a document is not signed.

A further category, secure electronic signature, is also defined. A secure electronic signature is one which can be verified to have been, at the time it was made, unique to and capable of identifying the person using it, created in a manner or using a means under the sole control of the person using it and linked to the electronic record to which it relates in a manner such that if the record was changed the electronic signature would be invalidated.[226] This is identical to, and may, in draft have been, the source of, the definition of advanced electronic signature used in the Electronic Signatures Directive.

Secure electronic signatures are presumed, subject to evidence to the contrary, to be the signature of the person to whom they correlate and to have been affixed with the intention of signing or approving the record in question.[227]

Digital signatures are then addressed expressly. A digital signature may be a secure electronic signature provided that the signature was created during the operational period of a valid certificate and is verified by reference to the public key included in the certificate. The certificate must be considered trustworthy either if it was issued by a certification authority in Singapore licensed by the Controller of Certification Authorities,[228] or a foreign certification authority recognised by the Controller of Certification Authorities, or a Singaporean public body. Alternatively the signature may be trustworthy because the parties had expressly agreed to use digital signatures as a security procedure and the public key of the sender is used to verify it.[229]   **6–090**

Reliance on a digital signature may nevertheless be unreasonable, in which case the relying party bears the risk. Circumstances making reliance unreasonable include knowledge or notice of facts listed in or referred to in the certificate itself (such as a recommended reliance limit, which all certificates issued by licensed certification authorities must contain), the value or importance of the signed record or trade usage.[230] Certification is anticipated only in relation to digital signatures.

(xiii)   South Korea

South Korea passed a Digital Signature Act[231] in February 1999 and it came into force in July 1999. It applies to all areas of law, open as well as closed networks and the use of electronic signatures by government as well as by private parties.   **6–091**

As the title suggests, it recognises only digital signatures, which are defined as information, which is unique to an electronic message, created by a private key using an asymmetric cryptosystem such that the identity of the person generating the electronic message and any possible alteration thereof can be verified. Digital signatures are given legal effect as either a signature or a signature-seal, provided they are created by a private key corresponding to the public key listed in a certificate issued by a licensed certification authority. Further, the signature is presumed to be the signature of the person to whom the relevant electronic message relates, and the message is presumed not to have been altered since signature.[232]

The contents of a certificate are prescribed under the Act and are broadly the same as those in the European Electronic Signatures Directive. Similarly, the Act imposes data protection obligations which are very similar to those under the Directive.[233]

The fraudulent use or disclosure of anyone else's private key is prohibited, as is obtaining a certificate in someone else's name on pain of up to 3 years' imprisonment or a fine of up to 30m Won (€22,389).[234]

There are no provisions for recognition of foreign certification authorities or their certificates save by bilateral government agreement.

(xiv)   Sri Lanka

Sri Lanka was considering introducing legislation dealing with electronic transactions in the autumn of 2002 but at the time of writing had not yet done so. The proposed legislation was said to be based upon the Australian Act of 1999. Since Sri Lanka is a common law jurisdiction electronic signatures may already be legally effective provided   **6–092** that adequate evidence can be produced to convince a court that the alleged signatory did affix the signature and intended by so doing to demonstrate their intention of adopting or agreeing to be bound by the contents of the signed document.

(xv) Thailand

6–093   The Thai Electronic Transactions Act was passed in October 2001, after several years in draft form and much debate, and came into effect in April 2002. It is based on the two UNCITRAL Model Laws, and governs private transactions subject to a list of exceptions provided by a separate Royal Decree, and to consumer protection law. It may also be extended to transactions with public administration by a further Royal Decree.

   The Act adopts the two tier approach. It includes a broad definition of electronic signature:

> "letters, characters, numbers, sound or any other symbols created by electronic means and attached to a data message for establishing the association of a particular person with the data message for the purposes of identifying the signatory and indicating that such person has approved and agreed to be bound by the data message."[235]

6–094   The Act provides that electronic documents are admissible in evidence in court and that electronic signatures within the above definition can be legally effective as signatures provided that the method used was as reliable as was appropriate in the circumstances. This is a direct transposition of Article 7 of the Model Law on Electronic Commerce.

   The Act goes on to state at section 9 that a signature shall be deemed reliable if:

(1)   "the signature creation data are, within the context in which they are used, linked to the signatory and to no other person;

(2)   the signature creation data were, at the time of signing, under the control of the signatory and no other person;

(3)   any alteration to the electronic signature made after the time of signing can be detected; and

(4)   where it is a purpose of the legal requirement for signature to provide assurance as to the integrity of the information to which the signature relates, any alteration to the information after the time of signing is also detectable."

6–095   At present only digital signatures can meet the third and fourth elements of this test; accordingly, only digital signatures are considered reliable.[236] However, Thai law does not require the majority of contracts to be in writing or signed to be enforceable. Exceptions include sales of real property, hire purchase agreements, loans of over 50 Baht and contracts for sale of goods over 500 Baht.[237]

   Electronic documents are subject to a similar assessment in their use as evidence as to whether the storage method used was suitably reliable to ensure the information's integrity and subsequent display.

   Foreign signatures are recognised if created by a system as trustworthy as those required by the Thai Act.[238]

3. NORTH AMERICA

(i) Canada

The federal Personal Information Protection and Electronic Documents Act came into **6–096** effect in May 2000. The Act applies the two tier approach to the enablement of electronic filing of documents and the use of signatures under federal law. It also amends the Canada Evidence Act to govern the use of electronic signatures in evidence.

The Act defines an electronic signature in very broad terms as a signature consisting of one or more letters, characters, numbers or other symbols in digital form incorporated in, attached to or associated with an electronic document. A secure electronic signature is one which results from the application of a technology or process prescribed by regulations.

Secure electronic signatures can be used by ministers or public officers to sign any document for which a signature is required under federal law[239] or in any circumstance where specified federal laws[240] require a seal to be affixed. Ordinary electronic signatures can be used for all purposes where the same federal law requires a signature, except where a statement is required to be made under oath, certified to be true accurate or complete or witnessed. In those circumstances a secure electronic signature must be used (in the case of witnessing, by both the maker of the statement and the witnesses) for the signature requirement to be met.[241]

An electronic document may satisfy any requirement of the specified federal laws for **6–097** an original document if it contains a secure electronic signature, added when the electronic document was first generated in its final form, which can be used to verify that the electronic document has not been changed since that time.

Various amendments were made to the Canada Evidence Act at the same time, adding new sections 31.1-8 relating to the use of electronic documents in evidence. A person seeking to rely upon an electronic document in evidence has the burden of proving that it is that which it purports to be. Its admissibility may be established by reference to standards, procedures or practices concerning the manner of storage. The integrity of an electronic documents system is proven either:

- by evidence that the computer system was operating properly at all material times or, if not, that any malfunction did not affect the integrity of the electronic document, or

- by evidence that the document was recorded by a party with an adverse interest to the party seeking to rely upon it, or that it was recorded or stored in the ordinary course of business by a third party who did not record or store it under the control of the party seeking to rely upon it.[242]

The Uniform Law Conference of Canada and the Federal Justice Department adopted a Uniform Electronic Commerce Act (UECA) in September 1999.[243] This Act is not binding in any legal jurisdiction but is intended as a model to be followed by the governments of Canada's provinces in introducing their own electronic commerce legislation. The Act is minimalist and technology neutral, proposing a definition of electronic signature which is simply "information in electronic form that a person has created or adopted in order to sign a document and that is in, attached to or associated with the document."

The Act is not intended to apply to wills, trusts, powers of attorney which affect the financial affairs or personal care of an individual, documents which create or transfer an interest in land or negotiable instruments. Enacting governments can amend this list.

6–098   The Act provides that where existing or future legislation uses terms such as "in writing" or "signature" this does not by itself prohibit the use of electronic documents. It proposes that electronic signatures shall satisfy any requirement under applicable law for a signature, subject to the enacting government's power to specify that:

- the electronic signature shall be reliable for the purpose of identifying the person, and

- the association of the electronic signature with the relevant electronic document shall be reliable for the purpose for which the electronic document was made,

in each case in the light of all the circumstances, including any relevant agreement and the time the electronic signature was made.[244] The enacting government may also consent to the use of electronic signatures in communications with government. If the government does consent, the electronic document must meet any standards and requirements as to method and reliability of signature which have been established by the whole or part of the government. No special presumptions apply to the use of electronic signatures.

Since UECA was adopted, the governments of all of Canada's provinces have adopted electronic commerce legislation, most of which (other than the Quebec Act) are based upon UECA though some, such as Manitoba, are more minimalist still. Quebec's Act is based upon the UNCITRAL Model Law on Electronic Commerce.

(ii)   Mexico

6–099   Mexico passed amendments to its Commercial Code in 2002 which enable contracts to be formed electronically[245] and electronic documents to be used in evidence. The approach to date is minimalist.

The amendments incorporate features of the UNCITRAL Model Laws regulating electronic transactions, such as presumptions as to the place and time of receipt of data messages. There is also a presumption that a data message originates with a person if it has been sent using a medium of identification such as cryptographic keys or a password.[246]

The amendment to Article 93 of the Commercial Code gives the contacting parties the right to use electronic signatures provided that the signature is attributable to the party to be bound and also accessible for subsequent consultation. This would appear to require an electronic signature to be sufficiently non-forgeable that the signatory can be identified with certainty for the purpose of the contract, but there are no other qualifications, such as the use of certificates, stipulated. Where the law requires a contract or other document to be notarised, both the parties and the notary may communicate by data messages in which case the notary should ensure that they retain under their own control a complete copy of the signed document for subsequent consultation.[247]

6–100   The Federal Code has also been amended by the introduction of new Article 1834 *bis*. Article 1834 provides that contracts which are required by law to be in writing must be signed by all parties upon whom any obligation is imposed by the contract. Article 1834 *bis* confirms that the signatures required by the preceding article will be considered complied with if electronic, optical or other technological media are used provided, once again, that the signature is attributable to the party to be bound and also accessible for subsequent consultation.

It appears, however, that the need to use printouts of electronic documents to provide evidence of electronic contracts and signatures in court has led to some confusion and further amendments may be necessary before electronic contracting can be relied upon under Mexican law.[248]

(iii)   United States of America

Introduction

The law applicable to electronic signatures and records in the US is drawn from numerous **6–101** sources, including state common law, statutes and regulations, with an overlay of federal statutes and regulatory requirements. While there was some uncertainty regarding the legal validity of electronic signatures prior to 2000, those questions have largely been resolved by electronic signature enactments on both the federal and state level. At the same time, government regulatory provisions remain in place that may still place particular requirements on the use of electronic records and signatures.

US law on electronic signatures generally

Prior to 2002, some states enacted electronic signature laws which applied broadly to all commercial transactions, while others had more limited applicability application. For example, the Utah[249] and Washington[250] digital signature statutes afforded transactions effectuated with PKI technology legal equivalence with transactions using traditional paper and signature technology. They also created a PKI regime, authorizing the Secretary of State to license PKI certification authorities. In contrast, electronic signatures statutes such as that enacted in Georgia,[251] did not specify a particular technology but broadened the definitions of "writing" and "signature" to encompass electronic forms of communication.[252]

The Uniform Electronic Transactions Act and the Federal Electronic Signatures in Global and National Commerce Act

Concerns about the enforceability of electronic transactions, as well as the perceived **6–102** growth in inconsistent state enactments of electronic and digital signature laws such as those noted above, prompted the National Conference of Commissioners on Uniform State Laws (NCCUSL) in 1997 to embark upon a project to draft a uniform act dealing with the validity of electronic records and electronic signatures. The resulting Uniform Electronic Transactions Act (UETA) was promulgated by NCCUSL in 1999 and has since been adopted in some form in 41 states and the District of Columbia.[253]

At the same time that NCCUSL embarked upon the UETA project, the US Congress began to express concern that uncertainty concerning the legal status of electronic transactions could hamper the growth of electronic commerce. Proceeding on a parallel track to the UETA drafting project, the Congress sought to enact federal legislation that would similarly validate the use of Internet and other electronic communications technologies. The resulting federal Electronic Signatures in Global and National Commerce Act (E-Sign) was enacted and signed into law in June 2000.[254]

As will be more fully discussed below, UETA and E-Sign are inextricably linked. One of **6–103** the stated purposes of E-Sign is to serve as an interim measure, giving the individual US states time to adopt UETA.[255] Thus, E-Sign contains a unique preemption provision. E-Sign validates the use of electronic records and signatures in certain transactions and pre-empts any state law to the contrary. But, E-Sign also provides that states may "supersede" E-Sign by enacting the official text of UETA. The preemption provision in E-Sign unquestionably has accelerated the widespread adoption of UETA.

It is important to note that while UETA and E-Sign share a common general purpose they are not identical in their scope or provisions. Due in part to constitutional limitations on federal legislative authority, the scope of E-Sign is narrower that than of UETA. For example, E-Sign applies to transactions in or affecting interstate or foreign *commerce*, while UETA expressly extends to governmental transactions.[256] On the other hand, E-Sign contains certain provisions, most notably its "consumer consent" provisions that are not included in UETA.[257]

Despite the widespread adoption of UETA, the federal statute will continue to be important because unanswered questions concerning the operation of its preemption provisions may affect the applicability of individual state enactments of UETA and other digital and electronic signature statutes.

The next sections provide a broad overview and analysis of comparable provisions of UETA and E-Sign.

Uniform Electronic Transactions Act (UETA)

(a) Purpose and general scope

6–104   The purpose of UETA is to "remove barriers to electronic commerce by validating and effectuating electronic records and signatures."[258] UETA is intended to be a procedural rather than substantive statute, and defers to existing substantive law on such matters as the meaning and effect of the term "sign," the "method and manner of displaying, transmitting and formatting information" in certain contexts, rules of attribution and the law of mistake.[259]

UETA applies to electronic records and signatures "relating to a transaction."[260] A "transaction" is defined as "an action or set of actions occurring between two or more persons relating to the conduct of business, commercial, or governmental affairs."[261]

Sections 7 and 8 of UETA contain its central, operating principles. Section 7 states the general rule in both negative and positive terms. It provides that an electronic signature or an electronic record "may not be denied legal effect or enforceability solely because it is in electronic form."[262] The same rule applies to the use of electronic records used in the formation of a contract,[263] and Section 13 extends the rule further to the admissibility into evidence of electronic records and signatures.[264]

In addition, any laws requiring a record to be "in writing" or requiring a "signature," are satisfied by an electronic record or an electronic signature respectively.[265] Section 8 deals with the provision of information in electronic form, stating the general rule that electronic records may satisfy requirements for providing, sending, posting or displaying information.[266] Section 8 includes an important caveat, however: such requirements are satisfied by an electronic record that is "capable of retention by the recipient at the time of receipt."[267] This requirement is not satisfied if the recipient's ability to print or store the record is inhibited by either the party sending the record or that party's "information processing system," and in such circumstances the record may not be enforced against the recipient.[268]

Section 8 also states a rule that applies to formal requirements related to writing and signature requirements, such as display, formatting and delivery requirements.[269] Laws specifying such requirements are preserved, but may be varied by agreement if the underlying law permits variation by agreement.[270]

(b) Exclusions

6–105   UETA expressly excludes several classes of transactions from its scope, to the extent that they are governed by other law:

- the creation and execution of wills, codicils, or testamentary trusts;

- transactions governed by the UCC (other than sections 1-207, 1-206, and Articles 2 and 2A), discussed below; and

- transactions governed by the Uniform Computer Information Transactions Act.[271]

The exclusion for transactions governed by the UCC reflects the fact that it was anticipated that UCC provisions regarding the validation of electronic transactions would be separately considered and enacted as amendments to most articles of the UCC.[272] But the specific references to sections 1-107 and 1-206, and to Articles 2 and 2A, means that UETA validates electronic contracting in transactions involving the sale of goods and leases.[273]

Section 3 contemplates that individual states might wish to add to the list of excluded transactions. Thus, subsection 3(4) contains bracketed text referring to "other laws, if any, identified by State." The official Comment to this section explains that this provision is intended to afford individual states the opportunity to add additional exclusions, although they are strongly discouraged from doing so. Comment 9 includes a list and accompanying discussion of categories of transactions that the Drafting Committee considered and decided not to exclude from the scope of UETA. These include trusts, powers of attorney, real estate transactions and consumer protection statutes. Thus, unless a state specifically references additional statutes in this (or another) UETA section or otherwise excludes these documents or transactions from the scope of its UETA enactment, the enumerated categories fall within UETA's scope and may be subject to its enabling provisions.

(c) Electronic records and signatures

Much of the work of validating electronic transactions is accomplished in the definitions section of UETA, in particular in the definitions of the terms "record," "electronic record" and "electronic signature." These definitions are very broad and technology-neutral. **6–106**

A "record" is defined in section 2(13) as "information that is inscribed on a tangible medium or that is stored in an electronic or other medium and is retrievable in perceivable form." "Information" is similarly broadly defined as "data, text, images, sounds, codes, computer programs, software databases, or the like."[274] The definition of an "electronic record" is simply a list of the various ways in which a record in electronic form may be found. An "electronic record" is defined as "a record created, generated, sent, communication, received, or stored by electronic means."[275]

An "electronic signature" is defined in section 2(8) as "an electronic sound, symbol, or process attached to or logically associated with a record and executed or adopted by a person with the intent to sign the record." This definition parallels the definition of a traditional signature in the UCC, but substitutes for the traditional concept of "marking" a document the electronic version of marking: attachment or "logical association." Accordingly, either a digital signature using PKI technology or a name typed at the end of an electronic message may satisfy the logical association requirement, provided that "in each case the signer executed or adopted the symbol with the intent to sign." Thus, a name typed at the end of an e-mail message may constitute a "signature," provided the requisite intent to authenticate is shown.[276] **6–107**

Attribution and effect of signatures is addressed in section 9. An electronic record or signature may be attributed to a person "if it was the act of the person," a fact which may be proved "in any manner." Specifically, attribution may be shown by demonstrating "the efficacy of any security procedure" that a party has utilized to determine attribution. Specific reference is made in the Comment, by way of example, to "click-through" agreements, where proof of the ability to track the source of a "click-through" may be necessary to attribute a "click" to a particular source. Once a signature has been attributed to a person, the effect of that signature is determined "from the context and surrounding circumstances," including any agreement of the parties and any other applicable law.[277]

(d)   Principle of voluntariness

6–108   Section 5(a) of UETA states that UETA is intended to be an enabling statute, to permit, but not require, the use of electronic records and signatures. Thus, UETA is applicable to transactions in which the parties have agreed to transact electronically.[278] An explicit agreement is not required; whether the parties have so agreed is to be determined by the context of the transaction and the circumstances surrounding it, including the conduct of the parties.[279]

An agreement to conduct transactions electronically can be limited to a single transaction. A party may refuse to conduct other or subsequent transactions electronically, and the right to do so is not waivable by agreement.[280] The effect of UETA's provisions may be varied by agreement unless UETA otherwise provides.[281]

(e)   Automated transactions and electronic agents

6–109   UETA references the novel concept of an electronic agent capable of executing binding electronic contracts on behalf of its human principals.[282] An electronic agent is defined as an electronic or other automated process that independently takes some action or responds to an "electronic record or performance" without review by a person.[283] An automated transaction is defined as one which is effectuated by electronic means or records, and in which review by an individual does not take place in the ordinary course of formation or performance of the contract or the fulfillment of a contract obligation.[284] A transaction that is automated with respect to only one of the parties falls within the definition. Thus, the online ordering of a book by an individual who inputs the order via the bookseller's web site, with the confirmation of the order on the part of the bookseller (and probably its execution as well) taking place automatically, would be included.[285]

By including electronic agents within its scope, UETA renounces any claim that lack of human intent at the time of contract formation prevents contract formation. When contracting via the use of "e-bots," "the requisite intent to contract flows from the programming and use of the machine."[286]

(f)   Mistake

6–110   UETA section 10 addresses concerns over the applicability of the law of mistake to automated electronic transactions. This section provides a limited set of rules to address errors that may occur where there is a "change or error" in the transmission of information in an electronic transaction. Under these rules, where there is a security procedure that the parties have agreed will govern the transaction, a party conforming to the security procedure may avoid the effect of an error if the nonconforming party could have detected the error by conformity with the procedure.[287] The foregoing rule applies to transactions generally, but there is a second rule that applies only to individuals and thus will likely apply only in consumer transactions. Where an individual is a party to an automated transaction, that individual may avoid the result of an electronic error he or she has made in dealing with the other party's electronic agent, if the agent did not provide an opportunity for error correction. The individual must promptly notify the other party of the error and not profit from it.[288] If neither of these rules applies to the particular electronic error in question, then the general law of contract, "including the law of mistake," applies to the transaction.[289]

(g) Government records

UETA Sections 17, 18 and 19 are "bracketed" optional provisions that cover the use of electronic records and signatures by state government bodies. While the general provisions of UETA will apply to a state government entity acting as a commercial party (*e.g.*, in its procurement transactions with non-government parties),[290] these provisions give state governments flexibility in defining whether, and under what circumstances, they will use electronic records and signatures. The fact that these provisions were designated as optional reflects the drafters' recognition of state-specific conditions, including the economic cost to procure and implement appropriate technology, that may impact a state's ability to adopt electronic methods in government transactions.

6–111

Private parties should bear in mind state government requirements when considering all aspects of an electronic transaction. Thus, while the parties to a transaction may choose to execute an electronic agreement, the parties' agreement to do so does not obligate a state to accept that electronic transaction for certain purposes. For example, parties may agree to execute a deed electronically and under UETA that deed will be legally valid, but a state or county recording office is not required to accept the electronic deed for filing unless local law provides for such a filing.[291] The result is that while the deed may be a valid transaction between the parties, they may have difficulty in obtaining the benefit of filing that deed in the land records (*i.e.*, providing constructive notice of the transaction to other parties).[292] Therefore, until such time as individual states have modernized their systems to provide for electronic filing of documents such as deeds, the use of electronic records and signatures in certain types of transactions may be possible but impractical.

Federal Electronic Signatures in Global and National Commerce Act (E-Sign)

Even as NCCUSL's UETA drafting project was completed and enacted into law in a number of states, the US Congress moved forward with legislation containing very similar provisions broadly validating the use of electronic records and signatures in "interstate and foreign commerce."[293]

6–112

(a) Purpose and general scope

The Electronic Signatures in Global and National Commerce Act (E-Sign)[294] took effect in the United States on October 1, 2000.[295] E-Sign is crafted to give electronic signatures, contracts, and other electronically generated documents, the same force of law as their paper-based counterparts. Technology neutral in nature, E-sign validates, but does not mandate, the use of electronic signatures, electronic records, and electronic agents. E-Sign federally legislates uniformity in the law governing electronic signatures and electronic records in transactions in interstate and foreign commerce and creates a standardized legal regime that preempts inconsistent state laws.[296]

6–113

E-Sign is subdivided into three Titles: "Electronic Records and Signatures in Commerce;"[297] "Transferable Records;"[298] and "Promotion of International Electronic Commerce."[299] The provisions that generally validate electronic records and signatures are contained in Title I.

(b) General rule of validity; principle of voluntariness

6–114   The general rule of validity established in Title I is similar to that established by UETA. Section 101(a)(1) provides that a record, contract, or signature may not be denied legal status or effect on the basis of its electronic form, nor may a contract be denied legal effect on the basis that electronic instruments were used in its formation.

E-Sign does not alter the existing rights or obligations of the parties under any law or regulation.[300] E-Sign expressly states that its provisions have no bearing on the actual content or timing of electronic consumer disclosures, which remain governed by existing law.[301] Thus, for example, a requirement that a consumer be provided with certain information about interest rates in connection with an automobile loan is not affected, nor is a provision requiring that such information be given within a certain time period. Section 104(b) further protects the rule-making authority of federal and state regulatory agencies.[302] The Act seeks to facilitate the use of electronic instruments by upholding their legal effect regardless of the methods selected.

6–115   E-Sign is does not mandate the use of any specific technological process to conduct or validate electronic transactions. On the contrary, E-Sign prohibits any state or federal statue, regulation or rule from requiring a particular technology for electronic transactions.[303] This technology neutral approach allows businesses to customize their business transaction methods and security procedures. Consent to create an electronic contract is voluntary under the Act, leaving the interested parties free to define which procedures will create an authentic signature or contract. But special provisions apply to the consent of a consumer to transact electronically where there is a pre-existing legal requirement that information be "provided or made available" to a consumer.[304]

(c)   General scope, inclusions and exclusions

6–116   The rule of validity contained at section 101 of the Act is intended to govern "any transaction in or affecting interstate or foreign commerce."[305] In particular, "transaction" is defined to include consumer, commercial, and business agreements concerning the sale, lease, exchange, licensing, or other disposition of personal property, services, or any combination thereof.[306]

Express inclusions

6–117   E-Sign expressly includes the sale, lease, exchange, or disposition of any interest in real property[307] and Section 101(i) also states the express intent of Congress that the provisions of E-Sign apply to the business of insurance.[308] Thus, E-Sign enables consumers and businesses to seal multi-million dollar mergers, buy insurance, open brokerage accounts, apply for loans, or close mortgages online with assurance that such transactions are valid and enforceable.

Express exclusions

6–118   Subsection 103(a) of E-Sign expressly exempts transactions governed by trusts and estates law; family law; or the Uniform Commercial Code, other than by sections 1-107, 1-206 and Articles 2 and 2A. Accordingly, section 101 of the Act does not apply to the creation and execution of wills, codicils, or testamentary trusts; nor does it apply to adoption, divorce, or other matters of family law. These exceptions are based on those found in UETA, although some of these transactions would not, in any event, fall within the general scope of E-Sign, not being transactions in interstate or foreign commerce.

Section 103(b) further exempts the following additional categories of transactions from the provisions of E-Sign:

- court orders, notices or documents required to be executed in connection with court proceedings (including briefs, pleadings, and other writings);

- notices of cancellation or termination of essential utility services (including water, heat, and power);[309]

- any notice of default, acceleration, repossession, foreclosure, eviction, or the right to cure, relative to the primary residence of an individual;

- any notice of cancellation or termination of health insurance or life insurance benefits (excluding annuities);

- any notice relating to product recalls or product failures that risk endangering health or safety; or

- any document that is required to accompany the transportation or handling of hazardous materials, such as pesticides or other dangerous materials.

With the exception of transactions governed by the Uniform Commercial Code, certain articles of which had been or were in the process of being amended to address issues involving electronic transactions, the common thread shared by each of these exceptions is the heightened importance of their subject matter. These exceptions were added to the legislation largely to address concerns raised by consumer groups that electronic communications are not sufficiently reliable, nor is the access to electronic communications by all segments of the population sufficiently certain, to replace current paper-based practices with respect to certain particularly critical kinds of documents.[310]

Regulatory exclusions

In addition to the express exclusions, E-Sign provides that any federal regulatory agency may, following notice to the public and an opportunity for public comment, exempt a category or type of record from the consumer consent requirements provided at section 101(c). This right, however, may only be exercised where the exemption "is necessary to eliminate a substantial burden on electronic commerce and will not increase the material risk of harm to consumers."[311]   **6–119**

In a similar vein, section 104(d)(2) directs the Securities and Exchange Commission (SEC) to issue a regulation or order expressly exempting certain records from the consumer disclosure provisions contained in section 101(c). This section was inserted to address concerns that E-Sign not interfere with the electronic delivery of prospectuses related to the issuance of securities. In July 2000, the SEC issued interim final rule 160 under the *Securities Act of 1933*.[312] The interim final rule permits a registered investment company to provide its prospectus and supplemental sales literature on its web site or by other electronic means without first obtaining investor consent to the electronic format.

(d)   Document retention

Remaining technology neutral in its approach, E-Sign sets standards of accuracy and accessibility for the electronic retention of contracts and records. Under section 101(d), electronic document retention will satisfy any law requiring that a contract or other record be retained, provided that the electronic document is accurate and remains accessible to all entitled to view or reproduce the document. An electronic record may further be used to comply with a legal obligation to provide, make available, or retain a document in its original form, where the requirements of section 101(d)(1) are otherwise met. Also, a rule compelling retention of a cheque will be satisfied where the information on the front and   **6–120** back of the cheque is retained in an electronic record that complies with section 101(d). If, however, the electronic record is not in a form capable of being retained and "accurately reproduced," the Act allows the legal effect and validity of that record to be denied.[313]

(e)   Electronic records and signatures under federal E-Sign

Records

6–121   E-Sign, tracking UETA, defines a "record" as "information that is inscribed on a tangible medium or that is stored in an electronic or other medium and is retrievable in perceivable form."[314] An "electronic record" is defined as "a contract or other record created, generated, sent, communicated, received, or stored by electronic means."[315] This broad language has been held to include e-mail communications and a downloadable software license agreement.[316]

Section 101(c)(6) of the Act further provides that neither an oral communication nor a recording of an oral communication shall qualify as an electronic record, except as otherwise provided under applicable law. Among other reasons, section 101(c)(6) was included to prevent oral communications from becoming a substitute for written notice to consumers.

Signatures

6–122   E-Sign broadly defines an "electronic signature" as "an electronic sound, symbol, or process, attached to or logically associated with a contract or other record and executed or adopted by a person with the intent to sign the record."[317] This reflects Congress's acceptance of the approach embodied in UETA; namely, that the private sector is free to determine the specifics of electronic signatures in the laboratory of the marketplace.[318]

Captured within the meaning of the Act, both the "click" in a click wrap agreement and the press of a key in a telephone keypad agreement (*e.g.*, "press 1 to agree or 2 to return to the main menu") may constitute a signature. Typing one's name at the foot of an e-mail also may be a valid signature, provided the requisite intent to authenticate is present.[319]

In contrast to UETA, E-Sign does not contain language dealing with the authenticity of signatures, nor does it provide any standards attributing responsibility if an electronic signature is forged or stolen.

(f)   Electronic agents

6–123   Like UETA, E-Sign expressly recognizes the ability of an "electronic agent" to execute binding contracts but adds the proviso that the actions of the electronic agent must be "legally attributable" to the party to be bound.[320]

(g)   Consumer consent provisions

6–124   E-Sign's consumer consent provisions are perhaps misnamed, as these provisions do not apply to all transactions with consumers. Only in circumstances in which existing law requires a party to provide or make available information in writing to a consumer does E-Sign demand that the obligated party obtain affirmative consumer consent to the use of electronic records in the manner specified in section 101(c). If existing law requires that information be provided to a consumer, E-Sign requires the obligated party to comply with its detailed specification and disclosure requirements. Unlike under UETA, a non-electronic consent to receive such information is not a valid consent under E-Sign.[321] This is perhaps the most significant difference between the two laws.

Giving Consumer Consent

The Act contains several consumer disclosure provisions that must be satisfied before consumer consent may be procured. For instance, section 101(c)(1)(C)(i) requires that the consumer be provided with a statement of the software and hardware system requirements needed to access and retain the records. In addition, prior to obtaining consent, the obligated party must provide the consumer with a "clear and conspicuous" statement informing the consumer of:

6–125

- any right of the consumer to receive the record in non-electronic form, how the consumer might request a hard copy of the record, and any associated fees;

- the consumer's right to withdraw consent, the procedures used to withdraw consent, and the consequences of such a withdrawal (including fees, termination of the agreement, etc.);

- whether the consent in question applies to a particular transaction or to an identified category of records; and

- the procedures for updating consumer contact information.[322]

E-Sign further demands that consumer consent be renewed where a material change is made to the hardware and/or software requirements previously consented to. Specifically, renewed consent must be obtained where modifications are made to system requirements such that it creates a "material risk" that a consumer will no longer be able to receive, access, or store the information.[323] Before renewing consent, section 101(c)(1)(D)(i) requires that the consumer be provided with a statement detailing the revised system requirements and advising that, under the circumstances, the consumer may withdraw consent without the imposition of any consequence not previously disclosed. The revision notice issued under section 101(c)(1)(D) must again comply with section 101(c)(1)(C), and consent (or confirmation of consent) must be secured in electronic format.[324]

In a deliberate departure from the approach adopted in UETA, E-Sign effectively requires consumer consent in electronic form. Pursuant to section 101(c)(1)(C)(ii), the obligated party must obtain the consumer's consent (or confirmation of consent) in a manner that "reasonably demonstrates" the consumer's ability to access the information in the necessary electronic form. The term "reasonably demonstrates," however, is not further defined, leaving both consumers and businesses without a real-world model to follow in complying with E-Sign's consumer consent provisions.

6–126

Although the requirements appear extensive, E-Sign contains a savings clause at section 101(c)(3) which expressly states that a failure to obtain electronic assent in accordance with section 101(c)(1)(C)(ii) may not form the sole basis for denying the legal effect of an electronic consumer contract. However, E-Sign is silent on the enforceability of transactions where other electronic consent requirements are left unsatisfied.

Withdrawing Consumer Consent

Although E-Sign makes clear the right of the consumer to withdraw consent, it does not define when consent has been withdrawn. By requiring obligated parties to inform consumers of the procedures used to withdraw consent, E-Sign anticipates that withdrawals will involve an affirmative act on the part of the consumer.[325] Notwithstanding repeated references to the circumstances surrounding withdrawal of consumer consent, the Act expressly envisions only two types of withdrawals:

6–127

- withdrawal of a prior consent;[326]

- the consumer's right to claim withdrawal of consent where the obligated party fails to renew consent pursuant to section 101(c)(1)(D) of the Act.[327]

It is less certain under what circumstances an obliged party may presume withdrawal of consent where there are reasonable indicators that such withdrawal may have occurred.[328] Guidance may be found in the fact that E-Sign does not expressly compel a company to continuously and actively monitor the consumer's ability to receive information electronically. Apart from obtaining initial and renewed consent as prescribed by the Act, the obligated party bears no responsibility for monitoring consumer accessibility. Rather, the burden falls on the consumer to maintain access to the Internet, the appropriate computer equipment, and a viable e-mail account. In any event, it seems unlikely that a single delivery failure will constitute withdrawal of consumer consent.[329]

6–128   Alternatively, it may be that when obtaining consumer consent pursuant to section 101(c)(1)(B), the references contained in the "clear and conspicuous" statement should not be limited to mere statements of the right to withdraw, the procedures, and the penalties that may attach. Subsection 101(c)(1)(B)(i)(II) requires that the obligated party inform the consumer of any "conditions, consequences (which may include termination of the parties' relationship) or fees in the event of such withdrawal." Thus, one viable solution to the issue of constructive withdrawal would be for the obligated party to supply consumers with a clear "Terms of Service" statement setting forth the circumstances under which withdrawal will be deemed to have occurred.

Finally, section 101(c)(4) deals with the prospective effect of a consumer's withdrawal of consent. Specifically, E-Sign provides that withdrawal of consumer consent shall not affect the legal validity of the electronic records provided or made available to the consumer prior to "implementation" of the consumer's withdrawal.[330] E-Sign further states that withdrawal of consumer consent becomes effective within a "reasonable period of time" after the provider receives the withdrawal.[331] Although this provision is largely uncontroversial, it is unclear what constitutes a "reasonable period of time" after which the consumer's withdrawal of consent would be considered effective.

(h)   Government regulations

6–129   Section 104 of E-Sign defines the authority of federal and state regulatory agencies to interpret E-Sign with respect to the filing and submission of documents to those agencies, as well as any record-keeping requirements that they may impose on regulated parties. The provisions of this section reflect the concern of some of the sponsors of the legislation that regulators would be inclined to undermine its general purpose through the use of their existing regulatory authority.[332] Subsection 104(b)(1) grants agencies that are "responsible for rulemaking under any other statute" the authority to interpret section 101 of E-Sign "with respect to such statute."[333] Section 104 constrains that interpretive authority, however, by generally prohibiting interpretations that are inconsistent with section 101 or that "add to [its] requirements,"[334] or that impose or reimpose an obligation to use a record that is "in a tangible printed or paper form."[335] The authority of such agencies to regulate filings "in accordance with specified standards or formats" is preserved.[336] In addition, limited authority is given to deviate from the general rule of section 101 where there is a "substantial justification" for the deviation and certain other requirements are met.[337]

(i) Pre-emption of state laws

The approach of E-Sign is to regulate, as an overlay to existing legislation, a broad and **6–130**
wide-ranging facilitation of electronic commerce. In service of that purpose, E-Sign
preempts any contrary state statute, state regulation, "or other rule of law."[338] E-Sign's
complementary purpose is to encourage individual states to enact uniform local
legislation on the same subject, *i.e.*, UETA. Thus, having preempted contrary state
enactments, E-Sign permits a state to supersede its provisions by enacting a state statute
that "constitutes an enactment or adoption" of the official version of UETA. Several
provisos apply, however. The inclusion of any exceptions to the scope of UETA that are
enacted by the state "shall be preempted to the extent such exception is inconsistent with
this title or title II, or would not be permitted" under section 102(a)(2)(A)(ii), which
requires non-UETA state enactments to be technology neutral.[339]

In order to prevent states from circumventing the requirements of the Act, states are
further prohibited under section 102(c) ("Prevention of Circumvention") from imposing
non-electronic delivery method requirements under section 8(b)(2) of UETA. As noted
above in the discussion of UETA, section 8(b) of UETA preserves laws that require
information to be posted, displayed, communicated or transferred in a specific manner,
such as a requirement that notice be delivered by First Class Mail, or a requirement that
a notice be printed in 20 point bold type. This subsection of E-Sign prohibits the use of
section 8(b)(2) as a "back door" to impose non-electronic delivery requirements that
would effectively thwart the general rule enabling electronic transactions.

As an alternative to enacting UETA, subsection 102(a)(2) provides that a state may **6–131**
"modify, limit, or supercede" the general rule of section 101 where the state law satisfies
three conditions: First, the alternative procedures or requirements proposed by the state
law relating to the validity or enforceability of electronic contracts and other records must
be consistent with Titles I and II of E-Sign. Second, the state law must remain technology
neutral.[340] Lastly, if enacted after the date of enactment of E-Sign, the state law must make
specific reference to E-Sign.[341]

Arguably the most complex area of E-Sign, the preemption provisions contained in the
Act raise questions regarding the applicable law in states that passed UETA prior to the
introduction of E-Sign, as well as regarding those that enact UETA with material or minor
variations from the approved text, and even those that enact the official text of UETA
without change.[342]

(j) Post E-Sign enactments

The simplest case for analysis of preemption is presented by a state that enacts the official **6–132**
version of UETA, without variation, subsequent to the enactment of E-Sign. Where a state
adopts the official version of UETA without modification, state law will supersede E-Sign
pursuant to section 101 of the Act. Even in such situations, however, questions have arisen
concerning the extent to which E-Sign is superseded. Some of the Congressional sponsors
of E-Sign have stated, post-enactment, that they intended the consumer consent
provisions of E-Sign to survive state enactments of UETA unless the state "affirmatively
and expressly" displaces them.[343] Under this construction of E-Sign, in states that have
enacted the official text of UETA without modification, the consumer consent provisions
continue to apply. At least one state has affirmatively enacted the consumer consent
provisions in E-Sign into its enactment of UETA.[344]

Issues also arise if the official text of UETA is modified, even where the modifications
are invited by UETA itself. Subsection 3(b)(4) of UETA permits a state to exempt specific
categories of transactions governed by other laws from falling under UETA's rules.

Section 102(a)(1) of E-Sign contains language intended to close the perceived loophole created by this subsection of UETA. Such exemptions, E-Sign provides, are preempted to the extent that they are inconsistent with Title I or Title II of E-Sign or are not technology neutral.

6–133   One category of exemptions that would appear to satisfy the proviso in E-Sign that modifications of UETA not be inconsistent with E-Sign, are the exemptions contained in E-Sign itself for court documents, utility cancellation and foreclosure notices and the like.[345] Thus, some states have utilized section 3(b)(4) to mirror these E-Sign exemptions.[346]

There is significant uncertainty as to what other exemptions are "inconsistent with" Titles I and II of E-Sign. Other than adding the additional exemptions in E-Sign itself, the option to create an exception pursuant to section 3(b)(4) may, as a practical matter, prove illusory.[347] Under section 102(a)(1) if a state enacts an "inconsistent" exemption, the exemption is subject to being declared inoperative but the remainder of a state enactment of UETA would not, under the limiting language of this subjection, be preempted.[348]

6–134   If a state goes beyond merely adding additional exemptions under section 3(b)(4) and adopts UETA with major modifications but still retains its critical provisions, additional questions arise as to the scope of E-Sign's preemptive effect. Some commentators interpret the Act to mean that any change to the final version of UETA will invalidate the state law in its entirety, allowing E-Sign to remain in effect.[349] But other commentators argue that there must be more than a de minimus variation to the text of UETA before E-Sign will continue to preempt state law.[350]

Another approach to evaluating the superceding effect of a modified enactment of UETA involves the independent evaluation of both the conforming and nonconforming UETA provisions against the alternative test in section 102(a)(2) of the Act. Using this approach, each state provision that parallels the official version of UETA or satisfies the neutrality test of E-Sign would supplant any corresponding provision in E-Sign. Likewise, any state law provision that falls short of the Act's standard as set forth in section 102 would be preempted by its analogous provision in E-Sign.

A similar method of comparison presumably would be involved in determining the status of a state electronic signature enactment that is not a variant of UETA. However, as of June 2003, it does not appear that any state has enacted broad electronic signature legislation that is not an enactment of UETA. Therefore, E-Sign appears to have significantly achieved its intended purpose of compelling states to enact at least some version of UETA in preference to any other form of electronic signature law.

(k) Relationship to pre-existing state electronic signature laws, including digital signature laws

6–135   As noted above, E-Sign was in part a Congressional reaction to concerns that inconsistent state electronic and digital signature laws would impede electronic commerce. One source of concern in that regard was non-uniform enactments of UETA. Also of particular concern to Congress were certain state enactments that were not technology neutral[351] and others that were technologically neutral on their face, but which nonetheless required that electronic signatures satisfy specific criteria in order to be considered legally effective.[352]

It is generally conceded that technology-specific statutes such as that enacted in Utah are preempted by E-Sign because they "accord greater legal status or effect to" transactions effectuated with digital signature technology such as PKI.[353] It is interesting to note in this regard that Utah has retained its existing digital signature law while also enacting UETA in 2000.[354] New York has not enacted UETA but amended its non-UETA electronic records and signatures act in 2002 to eliminate the non-technology neutral provisions.[355]

Conclusion

The unique preemption provisions of the federal E-Sign enactment have created a **6–136** situation of significant legal complexity in determining precisely what law applies to the use of electronic signatures and records in a transaction governed by US law. At the same time, these enactments share a core of common principles that broadly and generally validate the use of electronic records and signatures in most transactions between commercial parties. As a result, identification of the validating law is likely to be of only academic interest in the vast majority of commercial transactions. Caution should be exercised, however, with respect to two situations in particular. First, in consumer transactions that may fall under the consumer consent provisions of federal E-Sign, careful adherence to the consent procedures will be necessary. Second, in commercial transactions where filing with a state or local government agency is anticipated, consideration must be given to satisfying any local, paper-based requirements.

Other governmental regulations concerning electronic signatures and records

The federal government had begun to implement electronic processes long before the **6–137** enactment of E-Sign, and some of those pre-E-Sign regulations remain in effect. Among those regulations is the 1997 Federal Food and Drug Administration (FDA) Final Rule establishing criteria for FDA acceptance of electronic records and signatures.[356] The adoption of the Rule was the culmination of a process that began when representatives of the pharmaceutical industry sought FDA approval for the submission of electronic documents to the agency.

The FDA Rule covers electronic records that are "created, modified, maintained, archived, retrieved or transmitted" in response to any records requirements that are contained in agency regulations or required under FDA regulatory statutes. The Rule authorizes the use of electronic records provided the party using such records establishes procedures and controls that ensure their authenticity, integrity and confidentiality, as well as "ensure that the signer cannot readily repudiate the signed record as non-genuine." The general provisions applicable to electronic signatures require that: (1) the electronic signature is unique to a single individual; (2) the organization utilizing the signature verifies the identity of the signer prior to assigning, certifying or otherwise sanctioning an individual's electronic signature and (3) the parties using electronic signatures certify to the FDA that the electronic signatures are intended to be the legally binding equivalent of traditional handwritten signatures. In addition to these broad requirements, the Rule contains specific requirements for procedures and controls for "closed systems" (systems in which system access is controlled by the individuals responsible for the content of electronic records on the system) and "open systems" (systems in which access is not controlled by such individuals). The requirements include provision for audit trails, access control, and written compliance policies. Explicit recognition is given to electronic signatures using biometric technology.

Since the adoption of the Rule the FDA has issued several draft guidance documents setting forth agency interpretations and implementations of the Rule. However in a Draft

Guidance issued in February 2003 the agency withdrew those prior documents as part of an effort to reexamine, and possibly revise, the Rule, in response to concerns that in its current form the Rule unnecessarily restricts the use of electronic technology, increases the costs of compliance and stifles innovation.[357] The agency also expressed its intention, pending the re-examination and revision process, to interpret the Rule narrowly and exercise enforcement discretion with respect to certain of the Rule requirements.

4.LATIN AMERICA

(i) Argentina

6–138 Argentina was one of the first countries to introduce electronic signature legislation, with its Presidential Decree No. 427/98 of 1998 on digital signatures. The Decree applies to all areas of law except for inheritance and family law, and any other acts excluded either as a matter of law or by agreement of the parties. Digital signatures may be used by all branches of public administration under the Decree as well as by private parties.

Electronic signatures other than digital are defined but given no express legal effect, although their potential validity is contemplated as this may need to be established by the person seeking to rely upon it.[358] Digital signatures are defined as signatures created using private signature creation data which the signatory maintains under its absolute control, and which can be verified by third parties enabling them simultaneously to identify the signatory and detect any tampering with the signed document.[359] The Decree gives the same legal effect to digital signatures as to manuscript signatures,[360] provided that the signature was created during the period of validity of a valid digital certificate issued by a licensed certification authority and is properly verified by reference to the public key specified in the certificate.[361] The signature will not be valid if it is used for purposes other than those for which the certificate was issued or for a transaction whose value exceeds any limit in the certificate.[362]

6–139 A digital signature is presumed to have been made by the holder of a corresponding digital certificate unless the opposite is proven, and a digitally signed communication is presumed to have been sent by the signatory.[363] To be valid, a digital certificate must contain as a minimum: the identity of the holder and the issuing certification authority; the period of its validity; a unique identification number; a means of verifying whether or not it has been revoked; the information (public key) necessary for verifying the holder's digital signature; and identification of the certification policies under which it was issued.[364] The certificate holder must use a technically dependable signature creation device, keep its private key under its exclusive control, report any change in the data in the certificate without delay, and request revocation of its certificate as soon as it becomes aware of any possible compromise to the private key.

An unusual provision is included in Article 24 on the rights of the subscriber, which is the right not to receive any commercial publicity of any kind through a licensed certification authority. This provision appears very forward-looking given the date of the Decree, and could usefully be incorporated in other electronic commerce legislation if any effective enforcement mechanism is devised.

Under the decree, a digitally signed electronic document is presumed to be unaltered unless the contrary is proved[365] and is given evidential effect either in its original form or as an electronic copy.[366]

Certificates issued by foreign certification authorities may be recognised under any international mutual recognition agreement, or if an Argentinian licensed certification authority guarantees the certificate's validity and effect.[367] If so, the guaranteeing authority is liable for any damage due to a default of the foreign certification authority.

(ii) Brazil

Brazil launched a public key infrastructure system in February 2002, based upon its **6–140** Provisional Measure No. 2.200 of June 2001. This is intended to ensure that electronic documents may be digitally signed with legal effect in communications with both private parties and public administration. Further legislation dealing with electronic signatures in general is under consideration by Congress at the time of writing.[368]

(iii) Chile

Chile enacted a Law on Electronic Documents, Electronic Signature and Certification **6–141** Services of such Signatures in April 2002.[367] The Law was implemented by Regulations in August that year. The law does not apply to the laws of family and succession, or to any legal act for which there are requirements of formality which cannot be satisfied by an electronic document including where the personal appearance of one or both parties is required. It is applicable to open and closed networks, and to private transactions and transactions with and within public administration, although only advanced electronic signatures may be used in signing documents effective as public instruments.[370]

The Law adopts the two tier approach. Electronic signatures are any sound, symbol or electronic process which allows the recipient of an electronic document formally to identity its author. Advanced electronic signatures are electronic signatures which are certified by an accredited certification service provider and created using technologies which are under the exclusive control of the user in such a manner that the signature can only be linked to the user and any subsequent changes to the document can be detected. [371] The drafters clearly have public key cryptography and digital signatures in mind in this definition.

Ordinary electronic signatures are legally effective in the same way as handwritten **6–142** signatures if functionally equivalent to handwritten signatures, and are admissible in evidence. However, advanced electronic signatures have the advantage in all private transactions of being deemed effective as a matter of law without any further evidence being required.[372] Otherwise, an electronic signature's probative value is assessed in accordance with the ordinary principles of evidence.

Certificates must include as a minimum a unique identification code, details of the certification service provider and its advanced electronic signature, the name and e-mail address of the subscriber and the certificate's period of validity.[373] Certificates may not be valid for a period more than three years,[374] and may contain additional limitations on their scope of use. A certificate holder must give complete and truthful information to the certification service provider and keep it up to date, and must observe the certification service provider's certificate security system.

(iv) Colombia

Colombia's Electronic Commerce Law 527 of 1999 is closely based upon the UNCITRAL **6–143** Model Laws. The law applies to closed as well as open systems, including fax or telex. It does not apply to government acts such as international treaties. An additional and unusual exception is the exclusion of the use of electronic documents for the provision of written warnings required to be printed on hazardous goods.[375]

It applies a two tier approach to electronic signatures. Digital signatures are given the benefit of a presumption of intent to approve the document signed, and have the same effect as manuscript signatures provided that they are unique to the user, capable of verification, under the user's exclusive control and connected with the message in such a way that any alteration to the message invalidates the signature.[376]

The Law also implements the provisions of Article 7 of the UNCITRAL Model Law such that any other form of signature may be effective in connection with a data message provided that the method of signing enables the signatory to be identified and indicates the signatory's approval of the document, and is as reliable as is appropriate for the purpose for which the document was produced.[377] As the form of this provision implies, there is no definition of electronic signature as such.

6–144   Electronic documents are admissible in evidence, but their evidential weight must be assessed sceptically by the Court bearing in mind factors such as the reliability of the method by which the document was generated, communicated or stored, and the reliability of any method used to determine the integrity of the document and the identity of the creator.[378] A similar provision applies to categorising data messages as original records.

A certificate must include a serial number, the name, title and address of the subscriber, and of the certification service provider, the subscriber's public key and the period of validity of the certificate.[379]

A subscriber must request revocation timeously if the private key is lost or compromised. Failure to do so results in the subscriber being solely responsible for any consequent loss or damage.[380]

The Law also governs electronic commerce issues such as the presumptions as to by whom a data message was sent, time of sending or receipt of data messages, acknowledgment of receipt, storage of electronic documents and so on.

(v) Ecuador

6–145   The Ecuadorean approach[381] to electronic signature is relatively minimalist. The law permits any electronic data attached to a data message which enables the signatory to indicate their approval of the message and be identified to be used to sign with legal effect.[382] Parties can agree the use of particular forms of electronic signature. The law applies to all areas of law and to public administration[383] as well as private transactions.

To be valid a signature must be individual, exclusively linked to the signatory, created and verifiable by reliable means and permit the identity of the signatory to be verified unmistakably.[384] This last requirement is to be carried out using technical verification devices as provided by regulations under the law. There is no requirement to be able to establish lack of alteration of the message, so that some forms of signature other than digital may come within the definition. An electronically signed data message is presumed to be signed with legal intent.[385] An electronic signature certified by an accredited information certification company carries a presumption of identity of the signatory and of integrity.[386]

6–146   Interestingly, the law provides for the duration of electronic signatures—indefinite— and their extinction on death, incapacity (which includes abduction or kidnap) or dissolution of the holder, or by Court Order. However, the extinction of an electronic signature does not exempt the holder from obligations previously contracted by its use.[387]

Electronic certificates, on the other hand, are only extinguished on request, extinction of the signature of the holder or by expiry of their period of validity.[388] A certificate may be suspended if the information contained in it proves to be false or the holder proves to have breached the terms of the subscriber agreement,[389] and will be revoked by the National Council of Telecommunications if the certification service provider ceases operations and its certificates are not taken over by another, or the certification service provider is pronounced bankrupt.[390]

The law lays down the same requirements for the contents of certificates as are specified in the Electronic Signatures Directive, including name and address of holder and of certification company, period of validity, unique serial number of the certificate, method of signature verification, any limitations or restrictions on use of the certificate and the electronic signature of the certification company.[391]   **6–147**

Electronic documents and signatures are admissible in evidence but will be given weight according to the security and reliability of the storage medium. A supporting certificate can be admitted in evidence in support, but ultimately technical expert evidence and the judge's discretion will decide.[392]

Subscriber agreements are subject to the Ecuadorean Consumer Protection Act.[393]

Electronic signatures created abroad will be recognised as valid in Ecuador provided that they comply with the provisions of the Ecuadorean law and its regulations.[394]

The law also covers matters relating to electronic commerce generally.

(vi) Peru

Peruvian Law no. 27269 was passed in May 2000, governing Signatures and Digital Certificates. The law appears to be of completely general application. Although apparently technology neutral, the definition of electronic signature—any electronic symbol utilised or adopted by a party with the intention of authenticating a document which complies with all or some of the characteristic functions of a manuscript signature —includes the requirements to identify the signatory and guarantee the authentication and integrity of the signed document.[395] This would appear at present to require the use of digital signatures. Electronic signatures as defined are given equivalent legal effect to manuscript signatures.   **6–148**

Digital signatures are separately defined as electronic signatures created using a public key cryptographic method, but are not given the benefit of any additional recognition or presumptions. Use of a digital signature requires the use of a certificate; the subscriber must give true and complete information to the certification service provider.[396]

Digital certificates must contain data identifying the subscriber and the certification company, the holder's public key and the methodology to verify the subscriber's digital signature, a serial number for the certificate and the validity of the certificate (presumed to mean the period of validity).[397]

Foreign certificates are recognised only under a guarantee arrangement with a domestic certification company.

(vii) Venezuela

The Venezuelan Data Message and Electronic Signatures Law[398] was passed on February 10, 2001. It is expressed to be technology neutral, and defines an electronic signature as   **6–149** data created or utilised by the signatory associated with a data message which enables attribution of responsibility to the signatory.[399] In principle, electronic signatures can be used in public administration as well as private transactions.[400]

Electronic signatures are given the ability to satisfy a legal requirement for a signature in the same way as a handwritten signature,[401] provided that the data used for generating the signature can be produced once only, its confidentiality is reasonably assured, it is sufficiently secure as not to be forgeable as regards the current level of technology and it does not alter the integrity of the data message.[402] However, an electronic signature which does not fulfil these requirements may still be given such legal effect as is appropriate.[403]

6–150   An electronic signature supported by a certificate provided by a certification service provider is deemed to comply with the requirements above.[404] The certificate must contain the identity and addresses (real and electronic) of the subscriber, the identity of the certification service provider, both by address and by assigned identification code, the period of validity of the certificate, the subscriber's electronic signature and any limits on the scope of use of the certificate or liability of the certification service provider.[405] There is a requirement that the subscriber's electronic signature itself appear in the certificate, which is feasible for cut-and-pasted bitmaps or typed names, but infeasible for digital signatures since by definition the signature only comes into being when a particular message is signed. It is likely that this requirement will need to be changed.

Electronic documents and printed copies of them are made admissible in evidence subject to the tests laid down in the Civil Code of Procedure.

The holder of an electronic signature must diligently keep the signature from unauthorised use and notify the certification service provider as soon as it finds out that the signature has been compromised. Failure to do so results in liability for any unauthorised use of the signature.[406] The holder of a certificate can request cancellation or suspension of the certificate, which may also be suspended by order of a competent legal authority, if any of the data supplied in the application is verified to be false, if the subscriber breaches any major obligation of the subscriber agreement or on any breach of the certification service provider's system security which may affect the integrity and reliability of the certificate.[407]

5.   REST OF THE WORLD

(i)   Russian Federation

6–151   The current Electronic Digital Signature Law was enacted in December 2001 and approved by the President in January 2002. It applies to all areas of civil law, closed as well as open networks[408] and to public administration as well as private transactions.[409] Digital signatures are given equal status to handwritten signatures provided that the signature's authenticity is confirmed and the signature is used within any limits in a certificate issued by an official from a certification centre, which is valid at the point of verification (or, if evidence is available, at the moment of signing).[410] No electronic signature not meeting these conditions is given any recognition. Digital signatures can also be used to authenticate paper documents transferred into electronic form. No special presumptions arise.

A certificate must include a certificate identity number, with start and end dates for its period of validity; the subscriber's name or pseudonym (which must be identified as such); the subscriber's public key; the name of the algorithm being used; the name and address of the certification centre and information concerning the scope of use of the certificate.[411] Details of the subscriber's attributes, such as authority limits or qualifications, may also be included. All information to be included in the certificate must be verified by presentation of appropriate documents.[412] The certificate may be either paper or electronic in form; if the latter, it must be signed with a valid digital signature of the official of the certification centre.

The certificate holder must keep the private key secret and not use the signature keys **6–152** knowing they have been compromised and must demand immediate suspension of the certificate.[413] Failure to abide by this clause may result in liability for any losses caused.

Foreign digital signatures which comply with the requirements of the home country's electronic signature laws will be recognised in Russia. This does not abrogate the need to comply with other Russian laws concerning notarisation or the affixing of apostilles.[414]

(ii) South Africa

South Africa's Electronic Communications and Transactions Act[415] became law in August **6–153** 2002. It is a broad Act covering not only requirements of writing and signature but also domain name registration, consumer and data protection, provision of authentication[416], or cryptography (encryption) services and cyber crime. It applies to the public administration as well as to private transactions, potentially subject to specific requirements.[417]

As regards electronic signatures, the Act applies the two-tier approach so that the basic definition of electronic signature is very simple—data attached to, incorporated in, or logically associated with, other data and which is intended by the user to serve as a signature—but a separate category of advanced electronic signature is also defined. Advanced electronic signatures must be uniquely linked to and capable of identifying the user based on a face-to-face identification, created using means under the user's sole control and which are linked to the data or data message to which it relates in such a manner that any subsequent change of the data is detectable.[418] This definition currently mandates digital signatures.

Advanced electronic signatures are given automatic legal effect where a signature is **6–154** required by law; they also meet any legal requirement for a signature. Basic electronic signatures are not denied legal effect merely on the grounds that they are in electronic form.[419] In fact the Act stipulates that if the parties to a transaction have not required an electronic signature to be used a data message may still have legal effect provided some means other than an electronic signature can be used to evidence the parties' intent.[420] Where an electronic signature is to be used but the parties have not agreed the type, the signature will be effective provided that the UNCITRAL Article 7 requirements are met, namely that a method is used to identify the person and indicate that person's approval of the information communicated and that method is as reliable as was appropriate for the purpose in all the relevant circumstances.[421]

An advanced electronic signature also satisfies any legal requirement for a document to be notarised, acknowledged, verified or made under oath,[422] or sealed.[423] They are presumed valid and to have been applied properly absent evidence to the contrary.[424]

The Act also provides for the admissibility in evidence of data messages, as originals or otherwise, and sets out factors to be considered in assessing their weight.[425]

(iii) Israel

Israel's Electronic Signature Law was passed in March 2001 and it came into effect in **6–155** October of that year. It applies to all signature requirements except those relating to wills, certain trust statements, notary documents, power-of-attorney documents, certain real estate applications, surrogate applications, parental consent for adoption, banking documents between banks and clients, and depositions on which a signature is required by law. It applies equally to open or closed systems, and in principle (though subject to special conditions) to the transmission of electronically signed messages to or from governmental entities. Special conditions for transmission of messages to the Israeli Securities Authority have already been prescribed.

The Israeli law distinguishes three types of electronic signatures. A Secure Electronic Signature is essentially a digital signature. It must be unique to the owner of a signing device enabling apparent identification of such owner; be created using a signing device that can be maintained under the sole control of such owner; and enable identification of any change to the electronic document subsequent to signing.

An electronic message signed with a Secure Electronic Signature is admissible in any legal procedure and will constitute *prima facie* evidence that the signature is indeed that of the owner of a signing device and that the electronic message is that signed by the owner of same. Regulations enacted under the Law specify criteria according to which Electronic Signatures are considered "Secure Electronic Signatures".

6–156   A Certified Electronic Signature is a Secure Electronic Signature for which a Certification Authority has issued an electronic certificate regarding the signature verification device used to verify such signature. A Certified Electronic Signature is the highest level of authentication and admissibility the law attributes to an electronic signature. It is the only type of electronic signature that may be used to sign documents for which there is a mandatory legal requirement for a signature.

A Simple Electronic Signature is the most basic type of electronic signature and includes any electronic data or electronic sign attached to or associated with an electronic document. Electronic Signatures do not benefit from any evidential or other validity presumptions.

The owner of any electronic signing device is required to take all reasonable steps to protect the signing device and to prevent its unauthorized use. In addition, immediately upon discovery that the signing device has been compromised, the owner is required to notify anyone who might reasonably rely on its electronic signature. By complying with these requirements, the owner of a signing device will avoid liability for any damage caused by unauthorized use of its signing device.

In addition, the owner of a Certified Electronic Signature signing device is required to provide the Certification Authority, upon request, with information that is, to the best of its knowledge, correct and complete, as required by the Certification Authority for carrying out its duties and obligations and to notify the Certification Authority that issued the electronic certificate immediately upon discovery that its signing device has been compromised. Failure to do so may render the signatory liable for any damage caused by unauthorized use of its signing device.

Israel is also working on projects to issue national identity cards to all citizens and the implementation of an electronic signature system in the military, which are hoped to encourage the general take up and use of electronic signatures.

(iv)   Turkey

6–157   The Turkish government is, at the time of writing, in the process of preparing a draft electronic signature law based upon the Electronic Signatures Directive.[426] The proposal would give secure electronic signatures based upon qualified certificates the same effect as handwritten signatures, subject to a list of exceptions.

---

1.   *Progress achieved by OECD Member Countries in furtherance of the Ottawa declaration on authentication for electronic commerce* DSTI/ICCP/REG(2001)10/FINAL, at p. 9.
2.   Kuner *et al.*, *An analysis of international electronic and digital signature implementation initiatives* available at *www.ilpf.org/groups/analysis.IEDSII.htm.*
3.   Bundesgesetz über Elektronische Signaturen.
4.   Verordnung des Budeskanzilers über Elektronische Signaturen.
5.   S. 4(1) of the Law on Electronic Signatures.
6.   S. 4(3).
7.   S. 21.
8.   S. 26.
9.   This list is not complete.
10. Art. 4(4) and (5).
11. Art. 4(3).
12. Art. 15.
13. Art. 13.
14. The person on whose behalf the statement has been signed (Art. 4).
15. Art. 17(2).
16. Art. 24.
17. Arts 30-31.
18. National Report of Cyprus to the 15th Colloquy on IT and Law in Europe: "E-justice: interoperability of systems" presented in Macolin (Switzerland) under the aegis of the Council of Europe in March 2002.
19. Personal communication, Dr K Chrystostomides of Chrysostomides & Co.
20. Discussed in Ch. 2 at para. 2–023.
21. which, however, is restricted to the use of advanced electronic signatures supported by qualified certificates issued by accredited certification service providers: Art. 11.
22. Art. 5(2).
23. *Introductory word of the President of the Industrial Property Office* in 2002 Annual Report, at http://www.upv.cz/rocenky/2002/ann_rep02a.pdf.
24. Art. 3(1).
25. Explanatory notes to the draft Law at p. 40. Danish Ministry of Science Technology and Innovation 2000. Available at *http://www.videnskabministeriet.dk.*
26. Which must be tested and verified before it can be marketed and used as such: Art. 15(2).
27. Art. 13.
28. Explanatory notes to the draft Law, at p. 32, Danish Ministry of Science Technology and Innovation 2000.
29. S. 2(2).
30. S. 3(1).
31. S. 2(1) and (2).
32. S. 2(3).
33. S. 3(1).
34. S. 3(3) and (4).
35. S. 5(1).
36. S. 5(2).
37. S. 2(1).
38. S. 5.
39. S. 18.
40. S. 17.
41. to identify the signatory and manifest their consent to the obligations attendant on the act.
42. Speech of Mme Guigou introducing the law to the National Assembly, February 29, 2000, Art. B16–22 of the Civil Code.
43. Art. 5.
44. Signaturgesetz, or SigG, p. 876 Official Journal no. 22 dated May 16, 2001.
45. Formvorschriftenpassungsgesetz of August 1, 2001.
46. Signature Ordinance 14(2).
47. Art. 1 (3).
48. See discussion at para. 5–056 of Ch. (5) above.
49. Art. 1(2).
50. Art. 4(8).
51. Art. 1(2).
52. Art. 2(f).
53. Art. 4(2).

54. Art. 26(2).
55. Art. 13 (1) and (2).
56. S. 10(1).
57. S. 9.
58. S. 13(2)(b).
59. S. 14(1).
60. S. 16(1).
61. S. 22.
62. S. 35.
63. Presidential Decree No. 513.
64. Published in *Gazzetta Ufficiale* n. 39 of February 15, 2002.
65. In fact the Italian Supreme Court had already admitted in evidence digital data notwithstanding the lack of an advanced electronic signature to guarantee its integrity, as arguably required by clause 5(2) of Decree No. 513 (*Case no. 11445/2001, Corte di Cassazione* reported in [2002] C.T.L.R. 65). But this interpretation of Decree 513 may have been over-ruled by the revised wording included in Decree 445.
66. Published in *Gazzetta Ufficiale* n. 138 of June 17, 2003—in effect from July 2, 2003.
67. Art. 2, Decree 445/2000.
68. Art. 10(1)-(3) Decree No. 445 as amended.
69. Art. 23 Decree 445/2000.
70. Art. 29— bis (1).
71. Art. 38 Decree No. 445 as amended.
72. Art. 3(6).
73. Art. 1(4).
74. Art. 3(4).
75. Art. 3(2).
76. Art. 55(1) and (2).
77. Art. 16.
78. Art. 25(1).
79. Art. 1(2).
80. Art. 6(1).
81. Art. 2(4).
82. Art. 8.
83. Art. 6.
84. Art. 6(3).
85. Art. 7.
86. Directive 297/7/EEC of May 20, 1997.
87. Directive 2000/31/EEC.
88. Art. 6 of the Law of August 14, 2000.
89. Art. 18.
90. Art. 7, inserting art. 1322-2 into the Civil Code.
91. Art. 13, inserting replacement Art. 1334 in the Civil Code.
92. Art. 18.
93. Art. 21.
94. Regs 2 and 3.
95. Art. 4.
96. Art. 25(1)(c).
97. Art. 6.
98. Art. 23.
99. Bulletin of Acts and Decrees of the Kingdom of the Netherlands, Vol. 2003, 199.
100. New Art. 15a(2) and (3) of Title 1 Book 3 Dutch Civil Code, as amended.
101. New Art. 15a(1).
102. As specified in art. 1.1 of the Telecommunications Law.
103. New Art. 15a(6).
104. Journal of Laws (Dziennik Ustaw) 130 2001, 1450.
105. Press release of the Chancellery of the Prime Minister of the Republic of Poland, February 1, 2003.
106. Art. 3(1).
107. Art. 4(3).
108. Art. 5(4), (5) and (6).
109. Art. 5(1).
110. Art. 5(3).
111. Art. 6(3).
112. Art. 47.
113. Art. 7.
114. Art. 8.
115. Art. 18(1).
116. Legislative Decree No. 62/6003, Diario da Republica I Series A No. 79.

117. All definitions are in Art. 2 of the amended Decree.
118. Art. 3(2).
119. Art. 3(5).
120. Art. 7(4).
121. Art. 5(1).
122. Art. 31.
123. Official Gazette 429, July 31, 2001.
124. Art. 3.
125. Art. 4(1).
126. Art. 5.
127. Art. 6.
128. Art. 7. This suggests that under Romanian law ordinary "private signatures" do not confer admissibility upon documents. But this point has not been checked.
129. Art. 9.
130. Art. 10.
131. Art. 43.
132. Art. 4(8).
133. S. 1(3).
134. Art. 5.
135. S. 4(1) and (2).
136. Pt. II.
137. S. 22.
138. S. 26.
139. Art. 17.
140. Art. 1(2).
141. Arts. 14 and 15.
142. Art. 52.
143. Art. 16; see also Ch. 10 para. 10–018.
144. Art. 38.
145. Arts. 17 and 49.
146. Arts. 22 and 48.
147. Art. 23.
148. coming into effect in September 2003.
149. Art. 3.
150. Art. 7(4).
151. Art. 7(5) and (6).
152. Art. 16.
153. S. 2.
154. S. 17.
155. S. 7.
156. The Electronic Signatures Regulations 2002, S.I. 2002 No. 318.
157. See Ch. 2 para. 2–019.
158. S. 7(2).
159. Electronic Communications Act (2000 Ch 7) S. 7(1).
160. There is no suggestion that a signature will only be admissible if supported by a certificate, contrary to the interpretation given in Mason, *The evidential issues relating to electronic signatures I*, Computer Law and Security Report 18(3) (2002) 175.
161. S. 15(2)(a).
162. S. 15(2)(b).
163. *Review of the Consumer Credit Act 1974* DTi No. CCP 015/02, December 2002.
164. S. 10, *Electronic Transactions Act 1999* (Cth).
165. S. 8(1) *Electronic Transactions Act 1999* (Cth).
166. See *Electronic Transactions Amendments Regulations 2000*, as amended by *Electronic Transactions Amendments Regulations 2000 (No. 1)* 2000 No. 101, *Electronic Transactions Amendments Regulations 2001 (No. 1)* 2001 No. 84, *Electronic Transactions Amendments Regulations 2001 (No.2)* 2001 No. 137 and *Electronic Transactions Amendments Regulations 2001 (No. 3)* 2001 No. 263.
167. S. 9(1) *Electronic Transactions Act 1999* (Cth).
168. S. 10(1) *Electronic Transactions Act 1999* (Cth).
169. S. 11(1) *Electronic Transactions Act 1999* (Cth).
170. S. 11(5) and Sch. 1 of *Electronic Transactions Act 1999* (Cth).
171. S. 12(1)*Electronic Transactions Act 1999* (Cth).
172. S. 12 (2) *Electronic Transactions Act 1999* (Cth).
173. S. 12(4) *Electronic Transactions Act 1999* (Cth).
174. S. 14 *Electronic Transactions Act 1999* (Cth).
175. S. 15 *Electronic Transactions Act 1999* (Cth).

176. See, for example, *Electronic Transactions Regulation 2001* (NSW), *Electronic Transactions Amendment (Poisons and Therapeutic Goods) Regulation 2002* (NSW), *Electronic Transactions (Victoria) Regulations 2000* (Vic), *Electronic Transactions (Northern Territory) Regulations 2001* (NT), *Electronic Transactions Regulations 2002* (SA) and *Electronic Transactions Regulations 2001* (Tas).
177. *Ford & Anor v La Forrest & Ors* [2001] Q.S.C. 261 (July 23, 2001). Available at *http://www.austlii.edu.au/au/cases/qld/QSC/2001/261.html*.
178. *La Forrest v Ford La Forrest v Ford & Ors* [2001] Q.C.A. 455 (October 23, 2001). Available at *http://www.austlii.edu.au/au/cases/qld/QCA/2001/455.html*.
179. The following discussion is based upon the Bangladesh Law Commission's Working Paper on the law of information technology.
180. Discussion based upon personal communications from and a paper prepared by Professor Fuping Gao of the East China University of Politics and Law, Shanghai, Temple International and Comparative Law Journal (Fall, 2003).
181. available at *http://itb.hainan.gov.cn/read_law.php?law_class=5&id=112*.
182. Ch. 553, Hong Kong Gazette 1/2000.
183. Sch. 1.
184. S. 11. The Electronic Transactions (Exclusion Order (553B) includes a list of specified exclusions which is updated from time to time.
185. S. 2.
186. S. 6(1).
187. S. 15.
188. S. 14.
189. S. 9.
190. S. 1(4).
191. India report, [2002] C.T.L.R. 5 N88.
192. Indian Evidence Act 1872, new s. 85A.
193. Indian Evidence Act 1872, new s. 85B.
194. S. 42.
195. Second Sch.
196. Art. 3
197. S. 62
198. S. 67.
199. S. 43.
200. S. 41. This indemnity cannot be disclaimed or limited by contract.
201. Sch. Pt. 3
202. S. 5.
203. S. 22.
204. S. 23.
205. S. 31.
206. S. 2(d).
207. S. 7.
208. S. 9.
209. S. 2(h).
210. S. 10.
211. S. 34.
212. Republic Act 8792.
213. S. 4.
214. Government agencies were required to promulgate guidelines by June 2002 as to the type of electronic signature required and how it is to be affixed to any document. S. 27.
215. S. 5(e).
216. S. 8.
217. A.M.No. 01-7-01-SC.
218. R. 6(1).
219. R. 6(4).
220. R. 7.
221. R. 11.
222. S. 4.
223. S. 47.
224. S. 8(2). The relying party must show that a procedure existed by which it was necessary for a party in order to proceed further with a transaction to have executed a symbol or security procedure.
225. S. 2.
226. S. 17.
227. S. 18(2).
228. who has the power to lay down regulations for licensed authorities as to standards to be maintained, qualifications of employees, accounts and audit and so on. S. 42.
229. S. 20.

230. S. 22.
231. Act No. 5792.
232. Art. 3.
233. Art. 24.
234. Art. 31.
235. S. 4.
236. Pitiyasak, *Electronic Contracts: Contract law of Thailand, England and UNCITRAL compared* [2003] C.T.L.R. 1: 16.
237. Thai Civil and Commercail Code, ss. 456, 528, 572 and 653.
238. S. 31(3).
239. S. 36.
240. Set out in Schs 2 and 3 of the Act.
241. Ss. 44-46.
242. Canada Evidence Act new s. 31.1.
243. The Uniform Law Conference of Canada was founded in 1918 to assist in harmonising laws throughout the country. The main work of the Civil Section is reflected in "uniform statutes", which the Section adopts and recommends for enactment by all relevant governments in Canada.
244. S. 10.
245. Arts. 80, 89.
246. Art. 90.
247. Art. 94.
248. Tejada, *Amendments to Mexican Legislation on Electronic Transactions* on *legal500.com/devs/mexico/pr/mxpr_007.htm* at January 2003.
249. Utah Digital Signatures Act, Utah Code Ann. §§ 46-3-101 *et seq.*
250. Washington Electronic Authentication Act, Wash. Rev. Code §§ 19.34.010 *et seq.*
251. Georgia Electronic Records and Signatures Act, Ga. Code Ann. §§ 10-12-1 *et seq.*
252. For example, the Georgia statute broadly defines an electronic signature for almost all purposes as including a "secure electronic signature" but is not limited to such signatures. Ga. Code Ann. § 10-12-3.
253. The Official Text of the Uniform Electronic Transactions Act (1999) is available at *http://www.law.upenn.edu/bll/ulc/fnact99/1990s/ueta99.htm.*
254. The Electronic Signatures in Global and National Commerce Act, Pub. L. 106-229, codified at 15 U.S.C. § 7001 *et seq.*
255. Statement of Senator Bliley, 146 Cong. Rec. H4351, 4353 (June 14, 2000) and see 15 U.S.C. § 7002(a)(1).
256. Compare 15 U.S.C. § 7001(a) with UETA §. 2(16) (defining "transaction" to include business, commercial or governmental transactions). See further discussion below.
257. 15 U.S.C. § 7001(c), discussed more fully below.
258. UETA Prefatory Note.
259. UETA Prefatory Note, b. Procedural Approach.
260. UETA Prefatory Note, a. Scope of the Act and Procedural Approach.
261. UETA 2(16). The inclusion of transactions involving "governmental affairs" is a significant expansion of UETA's scope in comparison to federal E-Sign. See discussion below of 15 U.S.C. § 7006(13) (definition of "transaction" that does not extend to transactions with and within state governments).
262. UETA § 7(a).
263. UETA § 7(b).
264. UETA § 13.
265. UETA § 7(c)-(d).
266. UETA § 8.
267. UETA § 8(a).
268. UETA § 8(a) & (b).
269. UETA § 8(b) refers to laws that require "a record (i) to be posted or displayed in a certain manner, (ii) to be sent, communicated, or transmitted by a specified method, or (iii) to contain information that is formatted in a certain manner." Thus, for example, if a law requires delivery of a notice by first class US mail, that requirement would be unaffected by UETA. See UETA § 8, Comment 4.
270. UETA 8(d).
271. The Uniform Computer Information Transactions Act (UCITA) is a NCCUSL uniform act covering transactions in "computer information," *e.g.*, software licensing and development agreements and subscriber agreements with online information providers, etc. As of June 2003, UCITA has been enacted in only two US states, Maryland and Virginia.
272. The official Comment to UETA s.3 notes that it is beyond the scope of the UETA project to consider the desirability of validating electronic transactions with respect to the check collection and electronics fund transfer systems governed by Arts 3, 4 and 4A. Arts 5 (Letters of Credit), 8 (Investment Securities) and 9 (Secured Transactions) are excluded because of ongoing or completed revision projects that took such issues into account.
273. As noted above, the recent revisions of Arts 2 and 2A address electronic contracting, but UETA will apply to existing enactments of the unrevised versions of these articles.
274. UETA § 2(10).

275. UETA § 2(7).
276. See, *Shattuck v. Klotzbach*, 2001 Mass. Super. LEXIS 642 (Super. Ct. Dec. 11, 2001) (construing the Maine Statute of Frauds; holding that a jury could properly find an intent to authenticate in a party's "deliberate choice to type his name" at the end of e-mails); *Cloud Corporation v Hasbro Inc.*, 314 F.3d 289, 295 (7th Cir. 2002) (citing *Shattuck v Klotzbach* in concluding, in a transaction that pre-dated E-Sign, that the "sender's name on an e-mail satisfies the signature requirement of the statute of frauds"; commenting that E-Sign would have been "conclusive" on this point had it been applicable).
277. UETA § 9(b).
278. UETA § 5(b).
279. UETA § 5(b).
280. UETA § 5(c).
281. UETA § 5(d).
282. UETA § 14.
283. UETA § 2(16).
284. UETA § 2(2).
285. UETA § 2(2), Comment 2.
286. UETA § 14, Comment 1.
287. UETA § 10(1).
288. UETA § 10(2).
289. UETA § 10(3).
290. UETA § 18, Comment 1.
291. See, *e.g.*, California Attorney General Opinion No. 02-112 (Sept. 4, 2002) (concluding that the recording offices in only two California counties have the statutory authority to implement electronic recording systems, and specifically concluding that neither UETA nor federal E-Sign provide such authority).
292. Comment 3. to UETA § 3 points out this issue.
293. Congressional authority to regulate commerce is, in general, limited to "interstate and foreign commerce" by the constraints of the US Constitution. See US Const. Art. I, sec. 8, cl. 3; *Gibbons v Ogden*, 9 Wheat 1 (1824). As a practical matter, most commercial transactions are in, or affect, interstate or foreign commerce.
294. Pub. L. 106-229, codified at 15 U.S.C. § 7001 *et seq.*
295. See 15 U.S.C. § 7001 Note. The effective date of the records retention provisions in 15 U.S.C. § 7001(d) was delayed, however, until March 1, 2001.
296. For a thorough treatment of the legislative history of the E-Sign Act, see T.E. Crocker, "The E-Sign Act: In Facilitation of E-Commerce" (2001) 3 Mealey's Cyber Tech & E-Commerce Report 1.
297. 15 U.S.C. § 7001-7006.
298. 15 U.S.C. § 7021.
299. 15 U.S.C. § 7031.
300. 15 U.S.C. § 7001(c)(2).
301. 15 U.S.C. § 7001(c)(2)(A).
302. 15 U.S.C. § 7004(b).
303. 15 U.S.C. § 7002(a)(2)(A)(ii).
304. See further discussion below.
305. 15 U.S.C. § 7001(a)
306. 15 U.S.C. § 7006(13)(A). "Transaction" is defined in 15 U.S.C. 7006(13) as "an action or set of actions relating to the conduct of business, consumer, or commercial affairs between two or more persons," a definition that does not to include governmental transaction. Note that the E-Sign definition of "transaction" differs significantly from the definition in UETA 2(16) ("an action...relating to the conduct of business, commercial and governmental affairs").
307. 15 U.S.C. § 7006(13)(B).
308. Although normally the sole province of the states, federal law preempts state insurance law if Congress clearly states that its intent is to do so: McCarran-Ferguson Act, 15 U.S.C. § 1011 *et seq.* E-Sign's express coverage of the insurance business is balanced by an exculpatory provision in S. 101(j) that is applicable only to insurance agents and brokers who act under the direction of a party to enter into a contract by means of electronic record or signature.
309. 15 U.S.C. § 7003(b)(2)(A). "The exclusion. . .does not apply to notices for other broadly used important consumer services, such as telephone, cable television, and Internet services, etc. Electronic cancellation or termination notices may be used in association with those other services." 146 CONG. REC. S5281, 5286 (2000) (Abraham Explanatory Statement).
310. See, *e.g.*, National Consumer Law Center, Request for Comments on Cancellation or Termination of Utility Services Exceptions to the Electronic Signatures in Global and National Commerce Act (March 31, 2000), available at *http://www.nclc.org/initiatives/energy_and_utility/content/test033103.pdf.*
311. 15 U.S.C. § 7004(d)(1).
312. For a text of Rule 160, see Release No. 33-7877, IC-24582 (July 27, 2000) available at <*http://www.sec.gov/rules/final/33-7877.htm*> (lasted visited May 5, 2003).
313. 15 U.S.C. § 7001(e).
314. 15 U.S.C. § 7006(9).

315. 15 U.S.C. § 7006(4). Note that UETA § 2(7) omits the phrase "a contract or." It does not appear that any difference in the scope of the two definitions was intended.
316. See *Specht v Netscape Communications Corp., Inc.*, 306 F.3d 17, 27 n. 11 (2d Cir. 2002) (parties could not dispute that downloadable software license agreement is a "written provision" satisfying the Federal Arbitration Act because the "point has been settled by" federal E-sign); *Medical Self-Care, Inc v National Broadcasting Company, Inc.*, 2003 U.S. Dist. LEXIS 4666 *17 (S.D.N.Y. March 31, 2003) ("a decision not to consider an e-mail a writing is arguably foreclosed" by federal E-Sign). See also *Cloud Corporation v Hasbro, Inc*).
317. 15 U.S.C. § 7006(5).
318. See The Electronic in Global and National Commerce Act: Hearings on H.R. 1714 Before the Subcomm. on Telecommunications, Trade, and Consumer Protection of the House Commerce Comm., 106th Cong. 19, 30 (1999).
319. See *Shattuck v Klotzbach,; Cloud Corporation v Hasbro Inc*. See also D.W. Carstens, "Contracts Have a New Look Thanks to E-Signature Act" (July 31, 2000) Texas Lawyer at 54; H. Ominsky, "Oops! I Just Clicked My Life Away" (July 26, 2000) *The Legal Intelligencer* at 7; M.J. Hays, "The E-Sign Act of 2000: A Triumph of Function over Form in American Contract Law" (June 2001) 76:4 *Notre Dame Law Review* at 1196.
320. 15 U.S.C. § 7001(h) & id. § 7006(3) (defining "electronic agent").
321. UETA provides that an agreement to transact electronically may be determined from the parties' conduct and the circumstances surrounding the transaction. UETA § 5(b). E-Sign requires that the consumer consent, or confirm consent, electronically. 15 U.S.C. § 7001(c)(1)(C)(ii).
322. 15 U.S.C. § 7001(c)(1)(B).
323. 15 U.S.C. § 7001(c)(1)(D).
324. 15 U.S.C. § 7001(c)(1)(D)(ii).
325. 15 U.S.C. § 7001(c)(1)(B)(iii).
326. 15 U.S.C. § 7001(c).
327. 15 U.S.C. § 7001(c)(4). S. 101(c)(4) provides that a consumer may elect to treat a failure to renew consent as a withdrawal of consent for the purposes of that paragraph.
328. Consider, for example, an e-mail notification to consumer that is "bounced" and the company is notified that no such e-mail address exists.
329. Compare the Federal Reserve Board's "Redelivery Requirement" in its interim regulations implementing the Truth in Lending Act (Regulation Z) and other laws. These provide that if a creditor or lender gains knowledge that a consumer has not received an electronic communication, the creditor or lender is under a good faith duty to take "reasonable steps" to attempt redelivery of the message "using information in its files" (12 C.F.R. §226.36(e) (2001)).
330. 15 U.S.C. § 7001(c)(4).
331. Id.
332. See, *e.g.*, 146 Cong. Rec. S5281, 5286 (2000) (Statement of Senator Abraham).
333. 15 U.S.C. § 7004(b)(1). Presumably, in the case of state regulatory agencies, rulemaking authority with respect to "any other statute" refers to any other *federal* statute, although that limitation is not explicit in the language of the statute.
334. 15 U.S.C. § 7004(b)(2)(A) & (B).
335. 15 U.S.C. § 7004(c). However, an agency may require a record to be retained in "tangible printed or paper form" if there is a "compelling government interest relating to law enforcement or national security" and "imposing such requirement is essential" to that interest. Id. § 7004(b)(3)(B)(i) & (ii).
336. 15 U.S.C. § 7004(a).
337. 15 U.S.C. § 7004(b)(2)(A), (B) & (C).
338. See 15 U.S.C. § 7001(a) which states that § 101 of E-Sign applies "notwithstanding any statute, regulation, or other rule of law (other than this title and title II of this chapter). . ."
339. 15 U.S.C. § 7002(a)(1), cross-referencing id. § 7002(a)(2)(A)(ii), which prohibits provisions that "require, or accord greater legal status or effect to, the implementation or application of a specific technology or technical specification for performing the functions of creating, storing, generating, receiving, communicating, or authenticating electronic records or electronic signatures."
340. 15 U.S.C. § 7002(a)(2)(A).
341. 15 U.S.C. § 7002(a)(2)(B).
342. These issues are extensively discussed in P.B. Fry, "A Preliminary Analysis of Federal and State Electronic Commerce Laws," available at *http://www.nccusl.org/nccusl/uniformact_articles/uniformacts-article-ueta.asp*.
343. See: 146 CONG. REC. S5165, 5320 (2000) (Hollings, Wyden and Sarbanes Statement).
344. See New Jersey Statutes 12A:12-21, incorporating the provisions of 15 U.S.C. § 7001(c).
345. 15 U.S.C. § 7002(b)(1), id. §7002(b)(2)(A) through (D) and id. §7002(b)(3).
346. See, *e.g.*, New Jersey Statutes 12A:12-3c.
347. For example, under a broad interpretation, all laws not affirmatively containing the detailed provisions found in Title I would be inconsistent with Title I.
348. S. 102(a)(1) provides that preemption exists only "to the extent that" such exception is inconsistent with Titles I and II of the Act.
349. See R.T. Nimmer, "Electronic Signatures and Records, A New Perspective", 17 Computer & Internet L. at 17.
350. See T.E. Crocker, "The E-Sign Act: In Facilitation of E-Commerce", 2 Cyber Tech Litigation Report at 23.

351. *e.g.*, Utah Digital Signature Act is codified at Utah Code Ann. § 46-3-1-1 *et seq.*
352. *e.g.*, New York's Electronic Signatures and Records Act, which, prior to being amended in 2002, did not expressly require the use of a certain technology, but defined an electronic signature in such a manner that the requirements can only be satisfied by a handful of technologies available on the market today, most significantly PKI.
353. *e.g.*, P.B. Fry, "A Preliminary Analysis of Federal and State Electronic Commerce Laws"; Alston & Bird LLP, How the New E-Sign Act Will Affect E-Commerce, available at *http://www.gigalaw.com/articles/2000-all/alston-2000-06-all.html.*
354. UETA is codified at Utah Code Ann. § 46-4-501 *et seq.*; the Utah Digital Signature Act is codified at Utah Code Ann. § 46-3-1-1 *et seq.*
355. L.2002, Ch. 314, amending the New York Electronic Signatures and Records Act, codified at N.Y. Tech. Law. § 101 *et seq.*
356. 62 Fed. Reg. 13430 (March 20, 1997) effective Aug. 20, 1997, codified at 21 C.F.R. §§ 11.1— 11.300.
357. See Draft Guidance for Industry, Pt. 11, Electronic Records; Electronic Signatures—Scope and Application (February 2003), available at *http://www.21cfrpart11.com/files/fda_docs/guide_doc_scope_appFeb2003.pdf.*
358. Art. 5.
359. Art. 1.
360. Art. 2.
361. Art. 9.
362. Art. 23.
363. Arts 7 and 10.
364. Art. 14.
365. Art. 8.
366. Art. 11.
367. Art. 16.
368. Barretto Ferreira da Silva and de Freitas e Ferreira, *Multilateral Bodies get to grips with e-commerce,* in World e-Business Law Report May 15, 2003.
369. Law no. 19, 799.
370. Arts 4 and 8.
371. Art. 2.
372. Art. 5(2).
373. Art. 15.
374. Art. 16.
375. Art. 1, Law 527 of 1999.
376. Art. 28.
377. Art. 7.
378. Art. 11.
379. Art. 35.
380. Art. 37.
381. Law Governing Electronic Commerce, Electronic Signatures and Data Messages No. 67 of April 2002.
382. Arts 13 and 14.
383. Art. 51.
384. Art. 15.
385. Art. 16.
386. Art. 53.
387. Art. 19.
388. Art. 24.
389. Art. 25.
390. Art. 26.
391. Art. 22.
392. Art. 42.
393. Art. 34.
394. Art. 28.
395. Arts 1 and 2.
396. Arts 4 and 5.
397. Art. 6.
398. Decree No. 1.204; Official Gazette 37.148 of February 28, 2001.
399. Art. 2.
400. Art. 3.
401. Art. 6.
402. Art. 16(1)-(3).
403. Art. 17.
404. Art. 18.
405. Art. 43.
406. Art. 19.
407. Art. 42.

408. Cl. 17.
409. Cl. 16.
410. Cl. 4(1).
411. Cl. 6(1).
412. Cl. 9(2).
413. Cl. 12.
414. Cl. 18.
415. No. 25 of 2002.
416. Authentication is defined as the process of identifying the holder of an electronic signature to others.
417. S. 28.
418. S. 1 definition and s. 38.
419. S. 13((1) and (2).
420. S. 13(5).
421. Ss. 13(3) and 24.
422. S. 16.
423. S. 19(3).
424. S. 13(4).
425. S. 15.
426. Information derived from an article by Levent Berber, Paksoy & Co in Istanbul published in World eBusiness Law Report (*http://www.worldebusinessllawreport.com*) on March 18, 2003.

7

Practical issues

Introduction

7–001 This chapter looks at four practical aspects of electronic contracting in the light of the issues raised by the diversity of national laws surveyed in Chapter 6.

The issue which springs first to mind is the question of what happens when a contract involves parties in different jurisdictions, which will far more often be the case in contracts made over the Internet than it might have been in the purely paper-based environment.

Second, the issues potentially raised in connection with the contracts made with or sought to be imposed by certification service providers are reviewed.

The third issue is that of information security, which arises under certification service provider contracts as a potential obligation of certificate holders but is also a source of risk for certification service providers and subscribers alike. The level of information security maintained by all parties is also likely to be a central evidential issue in many disputes concerning electronic signatures.

Finally, the question of electronic document management after signature is highlighted briefly. This is raised in this chapter as a preliminary to the discussion of evidential issues generally in Chapter 8, since many of the issues raised in Chapter 8 will only be able to be assessed by a court if a party's document management system can provide adequate information as to the document's storage history.

Cross-border transactions

7–002 The wide variations in the provisions relating to the recognition of electronic signatures in different countries make it particularly critical to include appropriate choice of law and jurisdiction clauses in any contract which is proposed to be signed electronically. Failure to do so leaves the contracting parties at the mercy of the rules governing conflict of laws and choice of jurisdiction in each of the countries which may have a connection with the transaction.

The inclusion of choice of law and jurisdiction clauses enables the parties to be certain that the form of signature used will be recognised and given effect (all other things being equal), and to choose a law which requires a level of surrounding formalities which the parties feel appropriate. A survey of the laws described in Chapters 6 and 9 shows that the technological requirements for the signature itself are disparate enough, but the requirements for the operation of certification service providers, the contents of certificates and even the verification of signatures are at least as variable. The more complex the regulations with which a certification service provider may have to comply in order for its certificates to be recognised as effective, the more grounds there are for a party wishing to avoid a contract at a later stage to argue that the certificate did not meet all the stipulated criteria. The value of such arguments will of course depend upon the attitude taken by the relevant courts. If the national supervisory agency's word that the certification service provider was adequately reliable is taken as final, then such objections may not be worth raising. Accordingly, even if the parties opt to choose a jurisdiction where certification is required, there may still be a number of factors affecting which jurisdiction may be preferred.

Finally, the courts' approach to electronic evidence will be a material factor in choice of jurisdiction. Few of the laws addressing admissibility of electronic documents and signatures give any clear indication as to how these will be assessed, although some include guidelines as to the factors the court should take into account. These factors generally relate to the security of the participants' information systems, an area in which neither courts nor users in general have as yet great expertise although this may have to change as more and more evidence is stored in electronic form.[1] How such guidelines are applied in practice still remains, in most cases, to be seen.

Consequences of contracting cross-border without choice of law and jurisdiction clauses

The governing law will determine: 7–003

- whether any signature was required in the first place in a particular kind of contract and,
- if so,
    - whether any form of electronic signature will be recognised and
    - if so what form.

Which courts have jurisdiction will determine the rules of evidence and procedure by which the dispute will be resolved, including whether or not electronic documents and signatures can be admitted in evidence and what, if any, additional evidence may need to be adduced as to the reliability of any computer systems involved.

In the absence of a choice of law clause, the applicable law is commonly ascertained by evaluating the jurisdiction with which a contract is most closely connected. Similarly, courts may commonly found jurisdiction on factors such as where the supplier and the purchaser are respectively based, or where the contract was performed. The outcomes of the two analyses do not have to be the same: one country's courts may have jurisdiction over an agreement which is subject to the laws of another.

By way of illustration, a claim may be brought in the courts of England and Wales if the claim:

- is for a remedy against a person domiciled within the jurisdiction, or

- is a claim for an injunction requiring a defendant to do or refrain from doing an act within the jurisdiction, or

- relates to a contract which

  - was made within, or by or through an agent trading or residing in, the jurisdiction, or

  - is governed by English law or

  - has a jurisdiction clause giving the English courts the right to determine any dispute.[2]

Other jurisdictions likewise have their own rules to determine when their courts may hear a dispute.[3] It is not unusual for the application of more than one set of rules to result in more than one country potentially having jurisdiction over a single dispute, since for example one may seize jurisdiction based on the domicile of the defendant whereas another founds its jurisdiction on the territory within which the contact was to be performed. Which courts ultimately hear the dispute may then depend upon which party takes the initiative in bringing the matter before the courts, save in Europe where the Brussels and Lugano Conventions provide a mechanism for determining the outcome.

7–004   It is immediately evident that this may lead to a variety of problems. Many jurisdictions require an electronic signature to be in a particular form to be effective. Often, though not always, this is linked to a requirement that the identity of the signatory be certified in a particular form by a third party certification service provider meeting particular standards or accredited by a particular national supervisory body. A contract governed by a law requiring such forms but signed with an electronic signature not complying with any one of the requirements, risks being found wholly ineffective.

Most countries' laws provide for the possibility of recognition of certificates issued by foreign certification service providers, but this possibility is often linked to a requirement for the certificate to be guaranteed by a domestic certification service provider. Accordingly, a network of mutual recognition agreements established between certification service providers from different countries may eventually result in subscribers in any country being able to obtain a certificate locally which will be recognised in any jurisdiction with which they do business.[4] But this desirable situation is some years away.

7–005   Until that time, absent a choice of law clause the only way to be certain that an electronic signature will be recognised in the territory of the other party to a contract will be to obtain a certificate from a certification service provider based in that country. This in itself may be problematic in practice since many countries' laws require a certification service provider to identify a subscriber through face-to-face identification. Even where this is not a legal requirement, certification service providers commonly impose such a requirement as part of their Certification Practice Statement.[5] The result could be in many cases that the would-be subscriber has to travel to the certification service provider's home territory in order to prove identity. If so, the proposed benefits of electronic contracting remotely will be completely undermined. If one party must travel to the other's jurisdiction to obtain a certificate enabling them to sign, then the transaction may as well take place face to face with the contract being drawn up on paper.

Nevertheless, such difficulties are not insuperable for business to business transactions, since businessmen commonly travel in order to make contacts, promote sales or scrutinise potential suppliers for example. The number of countries where a small business may wish to transact is likely to be limited, and obtaining local certificates for each of them, though a nuisance, may prove no more of an obstacle than obtaining export licenses and visas. Where consumers are concerned, there is no question of their obtaining multiple nationally-recognised certificates to ensure that any signature they append to a contract will be legally effective. The reality, however, is that the vast majority of consumer transactions over the Internet are likely to be of a value below that which would warrant conventional court proceedings even if something does go wrong. A number of online dispute resolution services have been set up which may help to deal with such cases.

Within the European Union, this issue should in principle be resolved by the standardisation of certificate qualified requirements of the Electronic Signatures Directive.[6] Elsewhere, however, except in contracting with parties based in states whose electronic signature recognition is independent of recognition or accreditation requirements for certification service providers, signatories may have to apply the "belt and braces" approach of entering into an electronic contract electronically signed as a statement of intent but confirm the transaction on the basis of paper documents, faxed and/or posted.

Signature policies and choice of law

The disadvantage of choosing the law of a forum which has not opted for the prescriptive approach is that there is less certainty as to whether any particular form of signature will be recognised as valid. A possible solution to this is to incorporate a *signature policy* into the agreement. A signature policy is a set of detailed rules, as to how the signature will be created (what devices, syntax and algorithms), the relevance of any certificate or other indicator of identity of the signer, and how the signature should be verified including whether there is a need to maintain time-stamped records of signature validation data. The European Electronic Signature Standardisation Initiative has produced two reports on signature policies for different contexts.[7] It is of course also prudent to agree exactly what level of commitment is indicated by a signature.

7–006

Such a policy performs several functions. It gives the parties certainty as between themselves as to how the signature is to be executed, and it provides evidence for a court in the event of any dispute as to what mechanism the parties considered adequately reliable for the purpose at the time of the transaction. Where the reliability test under Article 7 of the UNCITRAL Model Law on Electronic Commerce has been enacted in any form,[8] this may provide additional confidence that the signature will be given effect by the court. It also precludes the possibility that some ill-chosen expression in the course of e-mail correspondence may be asserted to have amounted to a contractual commitment.[9]

Finally, an agreed signature policy can materially lessen the risk of repudiation for the relying party. Four basic grounds for repudiation can be identified:

- the signature (and any supporting certificate) are genuine but the purported signatory did not cause the signature to be affixed. This could arise either where someone accessed the signature creation data and certificate without authority, or even deciphered them from previous communications;

- the signature is genuine but was not affixed with the intention of being legally bound;

- the signature is genuine but was affixed outside the period of validity or scope of use of any supporting certificate;

- the signature is false. The purported signatory did not cause the signature to be affixed and it is not their signature—an impostor has caused a certificate to be issued in the purported signatory's name.

The risk (for the relying party) that any of these will be successfully invoked can be limited by requiring the primary signature—that of the party to be bound—to be witnessed by a second signatory exactly as in paper-based transactions. The second signatory may be either a witness or a notary, but either way the effect will be to make it much more difficult for the signatory to deny that the document was signed and signed with appropriate intention. Conversely, a fraudster who has unlawfully obtained one set of signature creation data will be unable to forge binding documents without both knowing of the need for the second signature and whose it was to be. However, the use of such a mechanism complicates the transaction beyond the norm for many day-to-day matters and may prove unacceptable.

7–007   Absent an agreed signature policy, the potential application of the reliability test raises concern since, once again, it is not yet known how courts will assess reliability. It is possible to formulate only rough ideas as to when formality, and hence a substantial level of reliability, may be considered appropriate.

As a starting point, many jurisdictions have excluded electronic signatures from having legal effectiveness altogether for the validation of the most formal documents: wills, trusts, powers of attorney, sales of land and so on. These classes of transactions commonly require a high level of formality for their conclusion in the paper-based environment whatever the monetary value concerned: independent witnessing, judicial authentication or notarisation and so on. This suggests, perhaps contrary to the impression given by some commentators, that those transactions for which electronic signatures can be legally effective do not intrinsically require a level of reliability as great as the formalities stipulated by law to accompany the execution of such documents.

A high level of reliability may nevertheless be dictated by other circumstances, such as a high monetary value. As discussed in Chapter 2, high value paper-based business-to-business transactions are frequently accompanied by a significant level of formality not as a matter of applicable law but as a requirement of the parties' own constitutions. A similar level of reliability, in terms of verification of the identity of the signatory and their authorisation level, is therefore likely to be considered by a court as the minimum level which is reasonable in concluding an equivalent transaction electronically. In any event, an organisation's own constitution will no doubt continue to govern the mechanisms for execution of significant contracts whether concluded on paper or electronically.

7–008   Where individuals are concerned, the approximate level of reliability which is likely to be required by a court is relatively easy to assess for very low value and very high value transactions. Where the value of the contract is trivial, any form of electronic data attached to indicate acceptance is likely to be accepted. Determining where the lower threshold lies, below which a relatively unreliable signature would normally suffice, will involve considering the level at which formality begins to be an issue as a matter of national law. For any jurisdiction which has a value limit below which a contract may be legally binding despite not being recorded in writing at all, contracts below that cannot reasonably require highly reliable electronic signatures. If writing and signature are not necessary, then it should not be possible to challenge the validity of a contract by reference to the absence of a complex form of validation of identity by a trusted third party. A click on a button marked "I accept", or the typing of a name in a box on an order form, should be a sufficiently reliable electronic signature for such purposes. This is of course a separate issue from the confidence a seller may require before shipping goods in reliance on such a contract. But for low value transactions of this kind payment is frequently by credit card, in which case the provision of credit card details[10] and shipment to the billing address registered for that card give at least as much confidence as any form of signature.

The upper limit may be likewise assessed from any value at which a private individual concluding a contract ceases to be treated as a consumer, where national law applies such limits. A rule of thumb in countries where there is no such consumer protection threshold might be the value of a substantial fraction of the national average annual wage—which of course will vary widely from country to country. An individual, whether contracting in their private capacity or in the course of trade, can reasonably be expected to be circumspect in concluding a contract at or above 50 per cent of the average national earnings figure. To conclude such a contract electronically, a secure and reliable means of identification should be required for both parties, which in the current state of technology may involve the use of digital signatures with third party certification of means, such as a public key, for verifying a signature as that of the purported counterparty. Of course, the transaction costs involved may well persuade the parties to rely on the tried and trusted paper format instead.

The appropriate standard of reliability is likely to be most difficult to predict in transactions whose value falls between these limits. The level of reliability which is appropriate will vary on a continuum, so that transactions only slightly above the lower threshold should require only slightly more reliability than clicking a button, while those only slightly below the upper limit may be required to be practically as secure as those at or above it. Obviously, the parties to any transaction will want to err on the side of certainty and therefore apply a level of reliability higher than that which the court may consider the minimum. But in many cases this need not mean invoking the full paraphernalia of public key cryptography, secure computer systems and third party certification. An agreement between the parties as to what form of signature they consider appropriately reliable prior to entering the transaction must be persuasive unless the agreed mechanism is self-evidently inadequate in the light of the information available to the parties at the time. To avoid the risk that a court may be influenced by hindsight as to the level which ought to have been considered appropriate, the parties could even recite the information which they had available and which they took into account in setting the level. There will of course be cases where the courts conclude that the parties' assessment was unreasonable. But it is to be hoped that as electronic communications and transactions become more familiar, the anxiety which underlies the present rash of worldwide legislation may diminish and the standards applicable to electronic signatures become more transparent and predictable. **7–009**

Transactions with a certification service provider

The dominance of the trusted third party business model in legislation has led to the emergence of a new industry of certification service provision. The viability of such a business is critically dependent on the certification service provider's ability to manage its exposure, when it has no way of knowing what transactions a certificate holder may enter into or what reliance may be placed in such transactions upon the certificates it has issued. Whenever a transaction goes wrong, the certification service provider is at risk of a claim, justifiable or not, being brought against them by a party which has suffered loss. **7–010**

The total value of the exposure may not be quantifiable, but the probability of claims being made is high.

In addition, a certification service provider may be liable in negligence in a number of circumstances. This could arise through the certification service provider's failure to take proper care in any one of a variety of ways:

- verifying the identity of an applicant for a certificate,

- failing to provide appropriate technological security measures to prevent access to its information systems by outsiders,

- management failure enabling unauthorised employees or contractors to access the system and issue a false certificate,

- failure to transmit an issued certificate through a secure medium to the subscriber.

Errors in issuing certificates are bound to occur. In a notorious incident in 2001, VeriSign issued two code-signing certificates in the name of Microsoft Corporation to a third party, who then held them until an audit uncovered the error two months later.[11] Even after that, unless and until the parties relying on the certificate checked the certificate revocation list and discovered that it had been revoked, the certificate could reasonably be treated as valid. Since at the time of the incident VeriSign Class 3 certificates did not include the url from which potential relying parties could obtain the relevant certificate revocation list, and Microsoft did not issue software which independently obtained the address, third parties could reasonably have gone on relying on the certificate for some time thereafter.

Three principal mechanisms are available for limiting risk in these circumstances, all of which are likely to be used by all certification service providers.

7–011   The key mechanism for a certification service provider to manage its risk is the imposition of limits on the scope and value of use of the certificates it issues. Many of the laws surveyed expressly acknowledge the effectiveness of such limits, provided that they are clearly visible to potential relying parties on the face of the certificate. Provided that the number of high-value certificates a certification service provider issues is relatively small, its overall exposure will be kept within manageable limits.

Once certificates have been in widespread use for some time it may also become possible for certification service provider to establish a pattern of use of certificates, which could be combined with actuarial evaluations such as those used by the insurance and pensions industries to estimate the total value of transactions potentially certified at any one time. This should enable certification service providers to insure appropriately against their risks of loss through fraud or accident. Many of the jurisdictions which have opted for the prescriptive/ regulated approach have imposed insurance requirements upon certification service providers operating within their territory, albeit with widely variable levels of cover.

In addition, certification service providers are tending to include extensive provisions in agreements with subscribers and relying parties which, not surprisingly, attempt to shift the risk to those parties. The agreement typically states that the certification service provider will follow its own certification practice statement and attempts to disclaim any liability provided it has done so. Any liability a certification service provider does accept is likely to be quite limited.[12]

Subscribers

Subscriber contracts are rarely negotiable, although some certification service providers **7–012** offer a range of possible subscription arrangements. Whichever model is chosen is likely to incorporate the certification service provider's Certification Practice Statement. This will commonly include a limitation of liability to a particular value per incident, and will also exclude all economic losses such as loss of profits, business, savings.

The effectiveness of any form of exclusion or limitation of liability clause will depend upon any applicable specific regulation regarding unfair or onerous terms in contracts, which arise in particular where one party may be dealing as a consumer. Many jurisdictions' laws specify that subscriber contracts are subject to any applicable consumer protection law. Under English law, the Unfair Contract Terms Act 1977 (UCTA) may affect subscriber contracts with either individuals or businesses, and where dealings with consumers are concerned the Unfair Terms in Consumer Contracts Regulations 1994 (UTCCR) will also apply. The latter implemented Directive 93/13/EC of April 5, 1993 on unfair terms in consumer contracts, and therefore the same principles apply in any Member State of the European Union.

The effect of UCTA is to render any exclusion clause void unless it is *reasonable*, the assessment of which depends upon a series of factors set out in Schedule 2 of the Act. These factors include the relative bargaining strength of each party, whether the contract was concluded upon one party's standard terms, whether an alternative source of the same goods or services was available to the other party which did not include a similar limitation, which party might most readily insure itself against the relevant risks and so on. Since, as noted above, certification service providers will invariably obtain insurance, a clause attempting to exclude all liability is unlikely to be reasonable. However, in view of the potential for multiple claims to arise as a result of any security lapse in respect of a single certificate, limitation to a realistic upper value per incident and/or a cumulative total may be reasonable and therefore effective. The UTCCR imposes a similar test of "fairness" upon exclusion clauses.

Subscriber agreements also tend to include:

- intended, permitted and prohibited uses of the certificate;

- warranties by the subscriber that they are in fact the person identified or are authorised as represented in the certificate;

- an agreement to comply with the limitations, if any, stipulated by the contract; and

- the standard of care which the subscriber is expected to use to avoid loss or compromise of the signature creation data.

VeriSign's certification practice statement, incorporated by reference to its subscriber **7–013** contracts, specifies the security measures which the subscriber must take, and includes a right to audit either by itself or through a third party auditor. For Class 1 certificates VeriSign requires[13] only the use of commercially reasonable measures for the physical protection of the Subscriber's workstation and the use of a password (which should be at least 8 characters other than the user's name and containing at least one letter and one number) to activate the private key. This is not a very high level of security: such a password is crackable by a palmtop in a matter of minutes by simply trying all possible combinations of letters and numbers at this length. For class 3 certificates, the requirement includes the use of a smart card, other cryptographic hardware device or biometric access device possibly in association with a password, as well as the physical protection of the workstation. As this example shows, parties wishing to carry out high value electronic transactions based on electronic signatures will need to adjust to a very different approach to computer use from that which most current users are accustomed to.

System security is generally not addressed. In principle each party might require the right to audit or even carry out penetration testing of the counterparty's systems. However, few subscribers are likely to have either the expertise or the resources to do so; any organisation sufficiently sophisticated to include such a requirement may not require third party certification. Further, the value of a certificate is rarely likely to be sufficient to warrant the cost.

Instead, the certification service provider simply disclaims any liability for losses arising if the subscriber fails to meet prescribed standards for the protection of their private keys, throwing the question back to the courts as and when any dispute arises over a signature of sufficient value. So far, no such cases have arisen. On the analysis above as to the limits of value for which it is reasonable to use solely an electronic signature, it is possible that no such disputes will arise. As and when one does, however, the courts will need to consider the intrinsic vulnerability of key protection mechanisms such as smart cards and passwords and rule as to what level of information security will in fact have to be achieved by subscribers.

7–014   Finally, a subscriber agreement needs to address what will happen if the certification service provider ceases operations. Access to the certificate revocation list may need to remain available for a number of years after the expiry of a certificate in case of disputes arising during and after the period of contracts signed while the certificate was valid. The subscriber may need the right to transfer all records relating to their certificates to another certification service provider and may require sufficient notice of a termination of services to enable them to arrange this. Alternatively, if the certification service provider's certification practice statement includes some automatic transfer arrangement in these circumstances, the subscriber may want the right to object.

Comodo Ltd (Comodo) includes an unusual provision in its subscriber agreements. The agreement states that the subscriber shall be solely responsible for any transactions of any kind entered into between the subscriber and any third party using or acting in reliance on the subscription service, and that the subscriber acknowledged that Comodo itself shall not be a party to or be responsible in any way for, any such transaction.[14] The agreement also expressly excludes any rights accruing to third parties under the Contracts (Rights of Third Parties) Act 1999.[15] These provisions may be intended to permit Comodo to call upon the subscriber to indemnify it if a claim is later made by a relying party against Comodo. However, there is no such provision in the express indemnities provided by the subscriber under the agreement, which are limited to losses arising as a result of the subscriber's breach of the agreement,[16] so its effectiveness must be open to doubt.

Relying parties

7–015   The relationship between the certification service provider and relying parties is more problematic, in that there is unlikely to be direct contact between them up to the point where the relying parties decide whether or not to rely upon a given certificate. Tort, and specifically negligence, may therefore be the basis upon which any claims are brought. Under English law, a claim may be brought against a certification service provider if it has a duty of care to any person and has failed to apply an adequate standard of care, resulting in loss. Ordinarily, the claimant has the legal burden of proving both that a duty was owed and that the standard of care taken was inadequate. However, in the provision of certification services it is self-evident that a certification service provider owes a duty of care towards anyone who may rely upon their certificate in deciding to accept a particular electronic signature in a particular transaction, since the very purpose for which the certificate is issued is to encourage such reliance. The only issue in dispute is likely to be what was the appropriate standard of care.

The most likely reference point for a court attempting to establish what standard of care ought to have been applied is, first, the certification service provider's own Certification Practice Statement and, secondly, Certification Practice Statements of other industry players in order to check whether the standards proposed by the defendant were in accordance with industry practice. A certification service provider which lays down and adheres to a reasonable standard of care should not be liable to third parties for loss. In principle, therefore, the certification service provider's exposure is within its own control. However, until some judicial decisions have been handed down as to what standard is reasonable, uncertainty will remain. Current certification service providers have responded by setting extremely high standards for the competence and reliability of the staff they employ, the accessibility of their computer systems and the meticulousness of their procedures. While this may be appropriate where unlimited or very high value certificates are concerned, the effect may be to raise the standard of care required throughout the industry even where the certificates in question are of relatively low value.

Where qualified certificates issued under the provisions of the Electronic Signatures Directive are concerned, the liability regime established under that Directive will apply. This limits the certification service provider's liability provided it can demonstrate that it was not negligent. Although this reversal of the normal burden of proof is unusual from a legal standpoint, it makes sense from the pragmatic perspective since a certification service provider will in any event be retaining records of its operations in order to meet any claims under its subscriber contracts, and in many cases also as a requirement of national law. The certification service provider, therefore, should not face any undue difficulty in demonstrating the standards it purports to apply, and whether or not these standards were in fact met. In contrast, it would be impossible under most legal systems for the relying party to get access to the information necessary to establish what in fact took place.

Relying party agreements

Certification service providers commonly attempt to constrain the extent to which they   **7–016**
may be liable for a relying party's loss as a matter of tort by requiring a relying party to enter a Relying Party Agreement before status information on a given certificate will be provided. The consideration for the contract is simply the provision of the relevant information. The contract typically provides that the certification service provider's liability for any signatures and transactions certified is limited according to the class of the certificate in question.

Taking VeriSign as the example once again, a total liability limit for any class 1 certificate is set at US$100 in aggregate.[17] In effect, VeriSign is disclaiming any liability whatsoever to any particular relying party, since it would take very few claims to reach this limit. A reasonable relying party, who cannot determine whether any claims have already been made, should only proceed on the basis they will not be compensated by VeriSign. For class 2 certificates, the aggregate limit is US$5,000, while for Class 3, the highest level, it is US$100,000. Given that Class 3 is VeriSign's most secure and most carefully verified certificate, this is still a very low limit. However, it is understandable that VeriSign does not want to face unlimited claims. The contract also includes an express notice to the relying party that a private key used to create an electronic signature may have been stolen and used to forge the signature. In other words, reliance should not be based purely on the existence of even a valid certificate.

7–017   Such contracts may well be enforceable in all cases where the relying party attempts to verify the status of the certificate before relying upon it: either the relying party accepts the contract and is bound by it, or does not accept the contract but is then consciously relying on the certificate without having verified it, and in the awareness that the certification service provider does not consent to their so relying. The issue as to whether the contract is effective remains open, however, when the relying party chooses to rely upon the certificate without attempting to verify its status, and so remains unaware of the certification service provider's terms and conditions. Many jurisdictions have included a requirement for any limit on value or scope of use of a certificate to be included in the certificate itself, and some also require any limitations of liability to be so stated. Certificates in X.509 standard format[18] can include a User Notice which might incorporate this information. This approach should give the certification service provider the greatest possible confidence that a relying party is bound by at least these terms.[19] The certification service provider could even set up the certificate in such a way that the relying party must acknowledge the terms and conditions have been accepted, before proceeding. Although this still depends upon the relying party actually accessing the certificate, a relying party who does not attempt to do so is almost certainly not acting reasonably in relying upon it.[20]

Provided the relying party does access the certificate, then the terms and conditions could be incorporated by such a mechanism. Even if the terms and conditions are not in fact incorporated in the certificate itself but are merely incorporated by reference, provided their existence is drawn to the relying party's attention in a sufficiently clear and effective way before the contract is formed, they may be construed to form part of a contract between the certification service provider and relying party under both common law and civil law principles of contract.[21] Terms and conditions not drawn to the relying party's attention are unlikely to be binding upon them.

Information security

7–018   Where an electronic signature is disputed, the security of all parties' information systems is likely to be in issue. For example, a court attempting to assess whether or not the signatory had taken reasonable care of their signature creation data, as required either under contract or as a matter of national law, is likely to try to establish the standard of care of the reasonable person in the signatory's position. This issue may involve an examination of the signatory's choice of PIN or any password, and the management of access to the information system.

Liability provisions such as those contemplated by Article 13 of the UNCITRAL Model Law on Electronic Commerce,[22] where enacted, will also focus attention on the security of a party's information systems. The issue in such a dispute will be whether a signed but repudiated message was in fact sent by a person whose relationship with the originator enabled their access to the signature creation data or device, and when and how the relying party was notified of the falsity of the message.

In many organisations a user is required to enter a user name and password to log into the system once a day but thereafter is permitted to leave the computer active whether present at their desk or not. During any period when the terminal is unattended, it may be possible for any passer-by to access the system. Really secure systems would require all legitimate users to log on to an electronic signature application in a secure way (perhaps using a password or biometric access) for each and every use, and log off again afterwards. However, ordinary users will immediately look for means to circumvent this sort of additional discipline.

Smart card access to a signature application may also pose security problems. Signature creation data kept on a smart card become potentially vulnerable as soon as the card is misplaced or stolen, for example through a "side channel attack".[23] In this scenario, the signatory may be liable for any abuse of the signature creation data at least until they have notified any certification service provider that the data have been compromised. It would be interesting, in this context, to know the average time between loss of a credit card and notification being given to the credit card company.

Further, it is not unusual for departing employees to retain access to systems because their user names and passwords are not revoked, and long-standing employees may build up extensive access rights to a system without any proper record being kept, as accesses are never revoked but new ones added for some good (but possibly temporary) reason from time to time. Unless an audit is carried out of user names and access privileges is carried out periodically, it may turn out that a security breach such as an unauthorised access to signature creation data could have been caused by any number of people who have left the company over a period of years. In all such circumstances, the party which appears to have signed may be liable for loss caused by the unauthorised signature.

The security of information systems is also a major issue as regards certification service provider liability. Any certification service provider whose systems can be broken into may find it has issued certificates to unknown persons with unlimited liability to third parties who rely upon them in good faith. Unauthorised changes to a certificate revocation list are also likely to result in the certification service provider being liable for any losses resulting.

Finally, in considering the weight to be placed upon any form of electronic record as evidence, the physical and electronic security of the information management system in which it is stored is bound to be a highly relevant factor.

The standard of security which organisations can be expected to achieve is not yet clearly defined. Information security has become a material concern worldwide only in recent years, and the majority of existing information systems are not built on any formal security model.[24] The advent of the Internet led to many sources of data, which formerly would have been protected by simple restrictions on physical access, becoming digitised, connected to the Internet for the purpose of e-mail or otherwise, and therefore potentially vulnerable to exploitation through remote access. Further, more and more businesses have employees interacting with their computer systems remotely, through dial-in connections from home or when travelling, or directly over the Internet. As a result, networks are considerably more open and outward facing than they were in the 1980s. Unless managed extremely carefully this leads to an increasing number of potential vulnerabilities in every such system. These and similar concerns have led to a number of international initiatives relating to the protection of computer systems and the data stored in them.

The OECD first issued Guidelines for the Security of Information Systems and Networks in 1992, but technology and the ways in which it is being used had evolved sufficiently by 2002 for the Guidelines to have to be updated. Accordingly, new Guidelines were adopted as a Recommendation to member countries in July 2002.[25]

7–019

7–020

The new Guidelines set out nine principles to be acted upon by all those, at government, organisation or individual level, who develop, own, provide, manage, service or use information systems in order to maximise their security:

1) All participants need to be aware of the need for security of information systems and networks and what, appropriate to their personal role, they can do to enhance security.

2) All participants should be responsible for the security of information systems and networks, and be accountable within their role.

3) Participants should respond to security incidents in a timely and co-operative manner, which should include sharing information about threats and vulnerabilities.

4) Participants should also respect the legitimate interests of others, and strive to develop and adopt best practices.

5) Security should be implemented in a manner consistent with the values recognised by democratic societies, including the freedom to exchange thoughts and ideas, the confidentiality of information and communication.

6) Participants should conduct risk assessments. The Guidelines do not specify how frequent these need to be, but focuses on the broad basis which should be employed to encompass key internal and external factors including third party services with security implications.

7) Security should be incorporated as an essential element of information systems and networks.

8) Participants should adopt a comprehensive approach to security management based upon the assessed risks. The management should include forward-looking responses to emerging threats and address prevention, detection and response to incidents. Audit is also recommended. Once again, the level of security management required should be commensurate to the participant's role.

9) Participants should continually reassess the security and make appropriate modifications to all aspects to deal with evolving risks.

7–021 In order to apply the principles effectively, the Guidelines require that security thinking becomes ingrained in every user of a system. In contrast, at present the majority of users of computer networks see the computer databases and applications with which they work as invisible tools which either perform as required or do not, but either way are very much someone else's responsibility to maintain and protect. Changing that attitude is likely to take significant time and effort since users in general will never attain a level of understanding of how the information system operates sufficient to feel that they can make a material difference to its security and be motivated to take the necessary care. It is therefore a question of changing the culture of computer users to increase awareness of the impact their use can have upon the system's security and the importance of appropriate use. This is unlikely to reach a high priority in any company unless and until the company suffers a major security breach and loses material information or money as a result. To this extent, therefore, security thinking is likely to remain an "after the fact" issue for many users for a long time to come.

There is a natural inclination to see information security as a criminal issue, and indeed the Council of Europe adopted a Convention on Cybercrime in 2001 which was intended to approximate members' laws on a range of offences against the confidentiality, integrity and availability of data.[26] The European Commission has subsequently produced a Proposal for a Council Framework Decision on attacks against information systems, which would harmonise Member States' criminal laws relating to serious attacks.[27] Notably, this proposal seeks to criminalise only attacks with intent to cause harm, gain an economic benefit or against protected information systems. However, the Commission's commentary points out that a high proportion of users leave themselves exposed by not having adequate or even any technical protection such that criminal penalties need to be imposed for intrusion even where, as it were, the door has been left open. As with property offences in the real world, the existence of criminal penalties may discourage intrusion to some extent, but is no substitute for active measures to prevent it.

The basic requirements of international information security standard ISO17799 are described briefly in Chapter 10.

Electronic record management

Record management is another issue which needs to be reconsidered in dealing with electronically signed documents since these may need to be stored in a tamper-proof, reliable and accessible form for reference many years after the original signatures were applied.   **7–022**

Bare assertion that a document has not been changed is unlikely to be sufficient in view of the perceived (and currently actual) insecurity of information systems. A court may want to see an audit trail to establish that the "original" was correctly stored, and that there has been no later possibility of tampering, or that all subsequent changes were documented. It is, in principle, easy to establish that a particular electronic record is complete and accurate by implementing appropriate procedures for access to and management of the information system upon which the records are stored. In practice, ensuring that this information is continuously and accurately recorded about a system which is in daily use by a large number of users with different access permissions, will take considerable organisation and on-going vigilance on the part of the system administrators. Technical standards designed to ensure that the system and the organisation which runs it are properly managed to achieve this are discussed in Chapter 10. It should be borne in mind, however, that save in cases where the information system can be demonstrated to be substantially insecure, the court may still accept an electronic document at its face value unless there is some genuine reason for believing that it may in fact have been altered. The decision as to the strength of security to apply to particular information systems should therefore be a cost-benefit based one. The costs of implementing effective security may simply not be justified for certain kinds of information. Other records, the integrity of which is critical to the organisation, may securely be stored in limited access databases or even on a standalone system access to which is physically and/or electronically restricted and meticulously logged, rather than commit the information holder to the attempt to render an entire computer system invulnerable.

Digital signatures can be used as guarantees of the integrity of stored electronic documents, as discussed in Chapter 3. However, a digital signature has a limited "shelf life" in that any cryptographic system becomes insecure as cracking technology improves.

As a result, documents may need to be periodically re-signed with updated technology in order to ensure that an acceptable level of confidence in their integrity can be warranted. This, too, will need to be recorded, and the audit logs likewise securely stored for future reference.

7–023   A further problem in the realm of electronic records is the preservation of records over time. Any electronic record will need to be migrated from one format or storage medium to another as technologies evolve. Migration of records risks the loss of information contained in the original record, and needs to be accurately documented to enable a court reviewing the documents at a later stage to have confidence that they reflect the original sufficiently accurately and completely for the purpose for which they are being invoked.

Finally, storage systems typically use some method of compressing the electronic file so that it takes up less storage space on the disk or tape—potentially introducing yet further loss of information. The impact of such losses depends entirely upon the kind of document concerned. For the majority of purely text documents, it is unlikely to have any great impact upon the court's ability to rely on the information concerned. However, where images are included distortions of colour or loss of resolution in a migration process may ultimately render the document considerably less informative than the original version. These issues need to be addressed at the point when an electronically signed document is committed to storage rather than years later when one party or the other is seeking to rely upon it in a dispute—which may be too late.

---

1.   See section on information security at para. 7–018 below.
2.   CPR r. 6.20.
3.   The overlap of these rules with the Brussels and Rome Conventions in Europe and the European Union Directive on Electronic Commerce is discussed in Ch. 6 of Smith, *Internet Law and Regulation* 3rd ed., Sweet & Maxwell 2002.
4.   ViTAS, a Voluntary Trust-service Approval Schemes common interest group was set up to explore the possibility of such a network in Europe in December 2002. See *http://www.tscheme.com/ViTAS/main.html*.
5.   See Ch. 4, para. 4–017.
6.   See Ch. 5, para. 5–038.
7.   TR 102 038: XML format for signature policies and TR 102 041: Signature Policies Report. See discussion of EESSI in Ch. 10, para. 5–015.
8.   See Ch. 5, para. 5–015.
9.   As electronic transactions have become more familiar, some companies are adding to the disclaimers automatically appended to any outgoing e-mail the statement that 'this e-mail does not constitute acceptance of any contract unless expressly so stated'.
10. Increasingly commonly including a security reference number, which is in effect a form of password.
11. Lemos,   *Microsoft   warns   of   hijacked   certificates   at   http://news.com.com/2100-1001-254586.html?legacy=cnet&tag=tp_pr*.
12. See for example VeriSign's Certification Practice Statement at *http://www.verisign.com/repository/CPS/*, Telstra's at *http://www.itrust.telstra.com/TTS_ABN-DSC_CP_v20.pdf* or Comodo's at *www.comodogroup.com/repository/Comodo_WT_CPS_v2.0.pdf*.
13. Certification Practice Statement, s. 6.2.7.
14. Comodo's IdAuthority Express Credentials Subscriber Agreement and Free Secure Email Certificate Subscriber   Agreement,   in   each   case   at   4.2.5   (*www.comodogroup.com/repository/docs/ideauthority_express_subscriber_agreement and secure_email_subscriber_agreement*).
15. *ibid.* cl. 24.
16. *ibid.* cl. 12.3.
17. VeriSign Relying Party Agreement Cl. 4.
18. See Ch. 10, para. 10–010.
19. Provided that the terms are themselves legally acceptable. Not all may be. For example, the GlobalSign relying party agreement attempts to bring a contract with a relying party into existence when the relying party uses any information provided by GlobalSign through its website. This would appear excessively broad, since the relying party might refer to the website only for introductory information as to who GlobalSign are and how electronic signatures work, but would purportedly still be bound when they subsequently rely upon a GlobalSign certificate.
20. A show of hands among the audience at a recent lecture on electronic signatures appeared to show that only 10 per cent of users actually do make any attempt to verify certificates, however.

21. Larose, *Brief essay on the notion of and rules relating to incorporation by reference in civil law systems,* 38 Jurimetrics J 295 (1998).
22. See Ch. 5, para. 5–008.
23. This involves measuring the electrical and other physical signals, such as heat, emitted by the card while it performs different computations. These can be used to deduce information about the codes it is using.
24. Schneier, *Secrets and Lies: Digital Security in a Networked World* at p. 133. John Wiley, 2000.
25. OECD Guidelines for the Security of Information Systems and Networks: Towards a culture of security, Recommendation of the Council at its 1037th meeting July 25, 2002.
26. *http://conventions.coe.int/Treaty/EN/CadreListeTraites.htm.*
27. COM/2002/0173 final, OJ C 203 E of August 27, 2002, p. 109.

8

Evidential issues

Introduction

8–001 Regardless of its theoretical legal effect, the litmus test of effectiveness of an electronic signature is whether it will be relied upon as valuable evidence by a court in the case of any dispute.

The issue of the admissibility of electronic documents and signatures in evidence has generally been addressed in legislation by those of the jurisdictions surveyed in this book which considered that evidence in electronic form was otherwise likely to be refused admission in legal proceedings. The provisions are commonly to the effect that electronic documents and signatures "shall not be refused admission solely on the basis that they are electronic in form".

Such provisions leave open, however, the possibility that a court may decide not to admit electronic evidence on grounds other than its electronic form. These could include the belief that the electronic signature was simply too unreliable to assist the court in coming to a decision. In order to illustrate why admissibility was perceived to be a problem and may still be an issue in some cases, this chapter begins with a basic review of the principles of evidence and discusses their application to electronic documents and signatures. The issues likely to arise in respect of disputed electronic signatures are then reviewed, and the kinds of evidence which may require to be adduced. Since very few cases have as yet been heard in which electronic signatures have been in issue, this discussion is essentially speculative at this point.

Burden and standard of proof

8–002 Each party to a legal action attempts to persuade the court of the merits of their case by adducing relevant evidence - that is, information in the form of oral testimony, documents or objects (referred to as "real evidence") - to convince the court of the truth of facts which, if accepted, will tend to persuade the court to their favoured conclusion. As a minimum, the court will need to make a finding one way or the other upon certain essential facts in order to decide the case. There may also be surrounding facts which, though not in themselves determinative, assist the Court in coming to a conclusion upon the essential facts. Failure to assert and prove every possible fact in support of a claim or defence is not necessarily fatal to the case, however.

In common law legal systems at least, the *legal* burden of proof of any particular fact lies upon the party which affirmatively asserts that fact. In theory, only the party bringing the claim needs to assert, and therefore prove, any facts: they bear the legal burden of proof. A defendant may choose to rely solely upon a bare denial of the claim, trusting that the claimant will fail to establish the truth of the facts essential to the success of the claim, to the necessary standard of proof. In practice in most cases, the safer course for a defendant will be to allege facts tending to prove that the claimant's contentions are incorrect. Both parties are therefore likely to have an *evidential* burden of proof of their own version of the essential facts.

There are exceptions to this basic rule as to which party has the burden of proof. One common exception is where the truth or falsity of one party's contention lies within the particular knowledge of the other party. If so, that other party may instead have a burden of disproving the contention. But this exception is not universally acknowledged.

The standard to which a given fact must be proved is, in civil cases, that the fact is likely to be true on the balance of probabilities. In other words the court must be convinced that the fact asserted is more likely to be true than not. In criminal cases, such as a prosecution for theft accomplished by the forgery of an electronic signature, the fact must be proved true beyond reasonable doubt.

Evidential issues in real world transactions

(1)   Admissibility of evidence

Not all evidence is admissible in legal proceedings. Adversarial systems view the oral testimony of a witness who has first-hand knowledge of the facts as the best form of evidence, where available. This is founded upon the presumption that despite all witnesses' possible tendency to give a partial account of the truth (even if not necessarily lying), cross-examination in public will enable the court to discover the full facts.   **8–003**

Documentary evidence has traditionally been viewed as a less reliable form of evidence for several reasons. First, it is often hearsay evidence, that is, information at second-hand from the event, since the document itself has no knowledge of the facts it records: it passively records what it is "told". Hearsay evidence in whatever form has tended to be viewed with suspicion simply by virtue of being indirect, and in many jurisdictions is subject to severe restrictions on its admissibility. This disadvantage is compounded by the fact that even the best drafted document can, taken on its own, be ambiguous.[1]

Further, documents may seamlessly incorporate information received by the author from sources other than their own first-hand knowledge. Such information tends to suffer from the "Chinese whispers" effect of a cumulative distortion of the original. Worse still, documents can be forged or tampered with. Accordingly, documents were originally admitted in evidence in the United Kingdom only if a witness was available who could testify as to the provenance of the document and what it recorded. A document as such was considered reliable only if it was an original record, had not been altered in any way, and was not counterfeit. This is one traditional meaning of the term "authentic".

Clearly, copies of documents are even more prone to suspicion, because of the potential for tampering with them during the copying process. A copy of an original or authentic   **8–004** document was formerly inadmissible in legal proceedings if the original still existed on the basis that a copy was not the best available evidence of the record which the original held. At one time it was thought that if the original document had been intentionally destroyed, that raised a presumption of suspicion and it was not clear that the court could admit the copy document in evidence at all. However, it is now accepted by the English courts at least that even if the original was intentionally destroyed, provided that the destruction took place in non-suspicious circumstances – for example, pursuant to a standard document retention policy - then the copy can be admitted in evidence.[2]

The advent of many forms of reprographic copying, and its ubiquity for normal business use, have led to the further relaxation of this rule so that a copy may now be as admissible as the original provided that the reliability of the copying or conversion process can also be demonstrated. Accordingly, the main concern in disputes over paper-based transactions is to remove any possibility of suspicion from the destruction of the originals and creation of the copies, whether electronic or paper based.

8–005   The requirement for a witness to testify in respect of each and every admissible document has also been substantially eroded over time. This began with the recognition in the late nineteenth century that it was impractical and substantially unnecessary to call a clerk to testify as to the origin of each and every entry in a bank's books. The books, being the critical records upon which the bank's business was transacted, were considered to be sufficiently reliable to stand alone as evidence of the matters they contained. In civil proceedings in the English High Court today, the authenticity of any document produced by a party in the course of the disclosure exercise[3] is deemed admitted by the other party unless a notice is served requiring the document's authenticity to be proved at trial.[4] As a result, the vast majority of documents are admitted and assessed without any formal testimony in support as such, although witnesses may address the interpretation or the weight to be given to a particular document.

The hearsay rule is still applied with its full rigour or with limited, specific exceptions in some other common law jurisdictions, however. Where this is the case, evidence is required to demonstrate the authenticity and reliability of any document for that document to be admitted into evidence,[5] and additional procedural requirements such as notice to the opponent may be imposed. Business records are often treated as an exception to the hearsay rule,[6] since they may be the only useful source of evidence of the day-to-day activities of a business.

(2)   Weight

8–006   Once a piece of evidence has been accepted to be admissible, a second issue falls to be considered. This is the question of how much weight the court should place upon the evidence in making its final assessment of the fact in issue: whether it should trust the evidence implicitly, or treat it as mildly persuasive, or largely disregard it as being potentially unreliable.[7] When the traditional rule disallowing hearsay evidence was abolished in respect of English proceedings, it was replaced by guidelines for the courts to assess the weight to be given to such evidence.[8] These are:

"(a)   whether it would have been reasonable and practicable for the party by whom the evidence was adduced to have produced the maker of the original statement as a witness;

(b)   whether the original statement was made contemporaneously with the occurrence or existence of the matters stated;

(c)   whether the evidence involves multiple hearsay;

(d)   whether any person involved had any motive to conceal or misrepresent matters;

(e)   whether the original statement was an edited account, or was made in collaboration with another or for a particular purpose;

(f)   whether the circumstances in which the evidence is adduced as hearsay are such as to suggest an attempt to prevent proper evaluation of its weight."

In considering what weight to place upon a particular document as evidence, the court will attempt to evaluate the purpose of the message or document, the intended use of the information it contains and the nature and degree of risk or opportunity for fraud.

Two factors that will affect the weight that any court will attach to any document are the possibility of alteration and the loss of context. Paper documents are very rarely challenged on the basis that they have been altered, although forensic techniques such as dating of the ink and the paper, assessment of the physical marks on the paper by electrostatic methods and other methods are available for ascertaining whether tampering has occurred, and are called upon from time to time. Where a signature is concerned, a comparison of the appearance to any other available sample is carried out, often unconsciously, by any reader seeing both samples. An expert in handwriting analysis can sometimes form an opinion on the authenticity of a signature by detailed comparison of small details of the two.

The second factor, loss of context can affect the confidence with which witnesses can testify to the document. Anyone would have difficulty several years after the event in putting any single document out of the totality of their files accurately into its correct sequence. The chances of identifying what was attached to a particular copy are even slighter. This may be an issue in many kinds of disputes. For example, where one party attempts to repudiate an electronic signature alleging that it was not created using a means appropriately reliable for its purpose in the light of the context of the transaction, the question of what information each party had available at the time becomes relevant. **8–007**

Just how reliable the document needs to be depends on the importance of the information it contains to the issues under consideration, and the availability or otherwise of other sources of evidence on the issue. Perfection is not necessary in every case. Where there is some possibility that a document could have been altered, this does not mean that the court will assume that it has been. Courts are used to making decision based upon incomplete evidence, and likewise to treating individual elements of the evidence as only partially persuasive.

"Traditional" signatures as evidence

Where signatures are concerned, the facts to be established will generally be **8–008**

- whether the signature was in fact made by the purported signatory, and

- if so, what his or her intention was in signing.

A signature by itself is not necessarily a very compelling form of evidence on either of these. The common law courts have been prepared over the years to accept many forms of signature, from the traditional "X" or thumbprint of the illiterate through to fax copies or signatures applied by a printing process,[9] neither of which gives great assurance as to the identity of the person who caused it to be applied Even full handwritten signatures may be of little assistance: some are elaborate, often illegible flourishes in which only a letter or two may be decipherable. One person may sign in a different form on different occasions.

Civil law systems therefore rely in a range of transaction types upon having signatures authenticated by a notary, whose function is to verify the identity of the person signing and certify that the signature does indeed originate from that person. In some transactions, the notary may also be called upon to ascertain the authority of a person to sign a particular document. The signature itself has no material value absent these surrounding proofs. It is the professional status of the notary which is a guarantee of authenticity to the relying party or the court, rather than any characteristic of the signature itself.

8–009   In common law systems, where additional assurance is required that a signature will not be repudiated at a later date, a similar mechanism is employed by having the signature witnessed. A witness does not necessarily verify the signatory's identity unless they happen to be a person who knows them, but does provide a source of independent evidence of the event. The signatory will have greater difficulty denying that they signed, in the face of independent testimony as to how the signature came to be on the document, than they will have if a document was signed in private. Oral testimony by witnesses as to the circumstances of the document being finalised is likely to be admissible in court if the signature's authenticity is challenged, and to carry substantial weight.

However, where remote communications such as post or fax are used, not infrequently the alleged signatory may be the only party present at signature. If so, the relying party may have to prove the authenticity of the signature by forensic analysis of the ink, to give an approximate date, and the visual similarity of the signature to other specimens of the same. If this is sufficient to satisfy the Court that the purported signatory did indeed appear to have signed the document, then the signatory would in practice have the evidential burden of proving that the document, whether hard copy or electronic, in fact left their presence (if it had ever been in it) unsigned. This is likely to be difficult to establish unless some positive evidence is available, for example to show that the purported signatory was not present at the alleged place and time of signing, or to raise a genuine basis for suspicion of forgery.

The exact nature of a signatory's intent in signing has never been susceptible of proof from the mere presence of a signature. The context of the signature may assist, if the *testimonium* is unambiguous and was visible to the signatory at the time. The function of the notary in civil law systems sometimes includes ensuring that the signatory understands the significance of their act. This provides independent evidence of the signatory's intention. Similar evidence can be provided by the witnesses to a signature under the common law approach, but at least as great assurance would be derived from the fact that witnesses were involved at all: the use of such a relatively elaborate mechanism in itself demonstrates that the signing of the document was seen as a significant transaction.

Evidential issues in electronic transactions

8–010   The basic facts in issue in any dispute over an electronic signature are likely to be the same as those in a paper-based transaction: whether the alleged signatory did in fact sign the document and, if so, what was intended by that act.

In the electronic context, however, courts are much less familiar with the form of the evidence and so additional questions may need to be considered to enable them to assess its proper weight. At the extremes, there are two possible approaches to this. One is that the court assumes that an electronic document is reliable unless evidence is adduced to show otherwise. The other, which has been assumed by many commentators, is that electronic evidence in general will be treated as wholly unreliable, and hence potentially inadmissible, unless sufficient evidence can be adduced to convince the court that it is in fact useful. This approach is consistent with the historical treatment of paper-based documents, and may well be taken by at least some courts.

Admissibility

A number of additional issues may arise which could be used to challenge the admissibility of electronic records. As noted above in the context of paper documents, courts have traditionally placed reliance on the question of whether a document presented to them is an original. However, for most documents forming the basis of an electronically signed transaction, it will not be at all clear what (if anything) constitutes the "original" document. The image seen by the writer on screen is only a representation of the electromagnetic signals passing through the computer at any one instant, and if saved, is stored in a different form from that represented to the viewer. It is therefore questionable whether any electronic document can comply with a "best evidence" requirement. On the same grounds, writers and courts in some, principally civil law jurisdictions, concluded that an electronic document did not meet a legal requirement for "writing" where this was stipulated in law since the electronic document itself consists not of marks recognisable as letters and numbers but of electromagnetic charges in a computer memory or on a storage medium: either way, invisible and unreadable to the naked eye.

8–011

The ease of apparently undetectable alteration of electronic documents is also a cause for treating them with general suspicion.

The principle of the admissibility of electronic records in evidence has therefore formed a substantial part of the wave of legislation surveyed in Chapter 6 above. Electronic records are now becoming admissible for the first time in a wide range of jurisdictions.

Even so, where doubt can be thrown upon the reliability of the relevant computer system, corroborative evidence may still be required to establish that the system was functioning correctly at all pertinent times. Alternatively, if a malfunction can be shown to have occurred, evidence may be required as to whether and if so how the records would have been affected. This can require witness evidence from the system administrator or other person familiar with how the computer would normally operate and the effect any malfunction might be expected to have had upon the record in question. Where the effect is material, the record could be ruled inadmissible on that basis. Technical standards for record management may introduce some greater certainty in this respect. Examples are identified in Chapter 10.

Weight

In assessing the weight to be placed upon electronic documents, a court may require supporting evidence in order to assess how reliable they are. Further, the courts' unfamiliarity with the technology involved in signing and recording electronically may also lead to limited weight being placed upon electronic documents in general until their authenticity and integrity have been thoroughly established. Both of these requirements may of course be satisfied by the same evidence.

8–012

As stated above, the factor that usually causes most immediate concern with electronic documents is the possibility of alteration, due to the ease with which undetectable alterations can be made to any digital record. If the court thinks that the record may have been altered, for example by unauthorised access in storage or as a side-effect of a routine migration to a new medium, it will attach little or no weight to it. This is a question of proving the adequacy and correct operation of the record management system which has been implemented[10] and the credibility of the evidence adduced in support of a particular record's integrity.

Loss of context issues apply equally as much in the electronic context as in the paper-based. In a situation where the court is reconstructing exactly what information someone had access to at the time, an electronic record management or archive system will need to incorporate a sufficient audit trail and indexing system to be able to pinpoint where each document fitted in, and where other related documents came from and went to. Compliance with recognised technical standards for information security and electronic record management systems is likely to assist in reassuring the Court on both counts.

Finally, electronic documents are still hearsay and may be subject to additional procedural requirements on that basis in some jurisdictions.

Burden of proof

8–013   The burden of proof in a transaction using electronic methods is the same as that in a paper-based transaction: each party must prove any facts it asserts.

It has been argued that Article 13 of the UNCITRAL Model Law on Electronic Commerce proposes a shift in the burden of proof in respect of attribution of data messages from the relying party to the sending (originating) party.[11] As discussed in Chapter 5, Article 13(3) states that the addressee of a data message is entitled to regard a data message as being that of the originator and to act on that assumption if . . . the data message as received by the addressee resulted from the actions of a person whose relationship with the originator or with any agent of the originator enabled that person to gain access to a method used by the originator to identify data messages as its own. Article 13(4) provides two exceptions to this, where the addressee either had notice that the signature was not authorised or knew or should have known that it was not that of the originator.

The effect of enacting this article is not to shift the burden of proof but to raise an irrebuttable presumption in favour of the addressee that a signature originating from a party's computer system as a result of the action of a person whose access to the system is authorised, can be treated as the signature of that party unless one of the exceptions in Article 13(4) applies. The provision does not give the apparent signatory the option of repudiating the signature vis-à-vis the addressee by proving that it was not authorised. The signatory's only remedy would be to bring a claim against the person who caused the unauthorised signature to be sent. This may be of little value in practice.

Evidence requirements for repudiation of signatures

(1)   The signature is genuine but not authorised

8–014   Where Article 13 of the UNCITRAL Model Law has not been incorporated into national law, the purported signatory may need to be able to demonstrate to the court how the signature came to be affixed. This will require evidence as to the operation of the information system from which the signature originated at the time when the signature was created.

If the signature was produced by an intruder, intrusion detection systems may be able to establish this. Intrusion detection systems have been in use for some time, but are far from universal and are not necessarily intended to prevent intrusions: detection may be the sole objective. The use of intrusion detection systems as sources of evidence is a relatively new concern, and only even more recently taken into account by suppliers of such systems. In 1997, an expert subgroup on intrusion detection systems commented[12] that systems then current were not designed to collect and protect the integrity of the type of information required to conduct law enforcement, nor were employees of network users normally told how to respond to intrusions and capture the necessary information. Nevertheless, the logs which some such systems record of activity on a network can provide a source of information to those sufficiently conversant with the system's set-up and objectives, from which some inferences may be drawn as to when an attack took place and what effects it had. However, as with any other form of evidence it will be necessary to convince a court that the logs are sufficiently reliable to be relied upon. This may mean producing evidence that the logs have not been corrupted or tampered with, and that they are accurate in that the system was functioning normally at the time of interest. It may also be necessary to adduce expert evidence to assist in the interpretation of the data.

Without evidence of an intrusion or how the signature came to be affixed, the purported signatory may be reduced to trying to establish that no authorised person did affix the signature while simultaneously arguing that its information security is of a sufficiently high standard that it should not be considered negligent given that (*ex hypothesi*) an unauthorised person appears to have succeeded in accessing it.

The standard of care which participants maintain in respect to the security of their information systems are therefore likely to be central in any dispute of this nature. The information security recommendations of the OECD[13] are at too high a level to be taken into account in court proceedings in determining whether either party should be liable for a loss that has occurred as a result of a security breach. However, the emergence of international and national technical standards for computer security may, once they have reached a threshold level of acceptance, have such an effect. Compliance with technical standards is of course voluntary. The standard which a court imposes may not ultimately be that laid down in recognised standards, since the latter are aimed at improving information security management beyond the average. Nevertheless, they provide a benchmark against which a court can review a party's conduct in attempting to assess whether or not the standards they have attempted to achieve and had achieved in practice were sufficient to avoid a finding of negligence. For instance, the Canadian Personal Information and Electronic Documents Act 2000 states expressly:

8–015

"For the purpose of determining under any rule of law whether an electronic document is admissible, evidence may be presented in respect of any standard, procedure, usage or practice concerning the manner in which electronic documents are to be recorded or stored, having regard to the type of business, enterprise or endeavour that used, recorded or stored the electronic document and the nature and purpose of the electronic document."[14]

Individuals transacting as consumers are unlikely to be expected to maintain such standards of information security, but may reasonably be expected to take minimum precautions such as disconnecting a computer from the Internet when not in use—exactly contrary to current trends.

It is of course open to the purported signatory to allege that the signature (and, presumably, entire communication) originated outside the purported signatory's information system. It should not be forgotten that any cryptographic system, including a public key encryption to create a digital signature, can be broken though this could take significant computing power. However, this argument is also unattractive without some real evidence of the actual source of the forged message, since it appears wholly self-serving.

(2)   No intention of being legally bound.

8–016   It may perhaps be credible, particularly where one party deals as a consumer, that a party could affix an electronic signature to a document without fully realising the effect of their action. The repudiating signatory would need to produce evidence to show, for example, that the software which caused a signature to be affixed either had no advance screen warning that the effect of clicking "Sign" would be to create a legally effective signature, or that the screen layout was sufficiently confusing that the signatory could genuinely have been mistaken as to the function the software was going to perform. It is unlikely that many packages with such an inadequacy would survive very long in the marketplace, but there will always be users whose lack of familiarity with operating a computer is such that genuine confusion arises.

An alternative scenario is the insertion by a fraudster into the system of a document which is then substituted at the point of signature for the document which the signatory intended to sign. This could be done using a piece of software known as a Trojan Horse.[15] In this case, the signature is genuine but the resulting document genuinely is not signed with the intention of being legally bound. The repudiating signatory will need to be able to demonstrate that a Trojan Horse exists which is capable of this, and that there is reason to believe it had entered the information system.[16]

(3)   Certificate invalid/ transaction outside valid scope

8–017   The relying party can reasonably be expected to check that the purported signature was, if required for legal effect, supported by a valid certificate and being used within its scope. If the signatory can establish that in fact it was not, then the issue arises as to whether or not the relying party could or should have been aware of this.

The information on the face of the certificate could potentially be tampered with in transit by an interceptor, but this should be revealed by the relying party checking the certification service provider's digital signature and/or directory. Where the certificate has been revoked or suspended before its expiry date, then circumstances may arise where the relying party could have had no way of knowing of the certificate's invalidity. The time limit, if any, within which certificate revocation or suspension must be requested and published may be material in some cases. Here, the times of sending and receipt of the revocation/ suspension request and update of the list will be significant, so that time-stamping all such requests and retaining records of publication times will be important sources of future evidence.

(4)   The signature is false

8–018   Different evidential issues are likely to arise where the purported signatory alleges that a third party has effectively stolen their identity by persuading or tricking a certification service provider into issuing a certificate in support of the signature creation data in the wrong name. Proof of this proposition would require the alleged signatory to demonstrate that the certification service provider had issued a certificate in reliance on false data, or had inadequate technical or procedural security systems such that a third party had succeeded in causing a certificate to be issued without the certification service provider becoming aware. This may be difficult in jurisdictions where there is no procedure for obtaining information from parties to a dispute or third parties.

In England and Wales, an application can be made for an order that a third party disclose specified documents, such as the data provided in support of the certificate application, if these are likely to resolve a dispute one way or the other.[17] Alternatively, the third party could be sued for negligence in allowing their systems to be abused in such as way as to enable the false certificate to be issued.

The position of the relying party
No matter what the weaknesses of the signatory's system, it will not always be reasonable for the relying party to rely upon a signature. Ideally, the relying party should check, and be able to prove that they checked, that: **8–019**

- the certificate does indeed certify the expected person as holder of the relevant private key,

- the certificate is valid for the transaction in question at the relevant time,

- the certification service provider's own signature was authentic and valid at the time when the certificate was issued

- the certificate revocation list is authentic, in that it is signed by the certification service provider's own electronic signature certified with a root certificate;

- the certificate revocation list is the current version.

In practice, this "due diligence" will often be done automatically by a verification device. If so, evidence could be required that the device correctly performed the necessary checks, adding yet another level of documentary and technical evidence which may need to be amassed and adduced in support of any single electronically signed transaction.

---

1. A document may not be hearsay if it is not being adduced in order to prove the truth of the statements it contains. A signature on a contract, for example, is adduced to prove that the contract was signed when it may not be in doubt that the signatory's name is that which is written. In this case the signature could be real, rather than documentary, evidence. See discussion in Smith, *Internet Law and Regulation* (3rd ed.) at para. 10-136.
2. *R v Wayte* (1983) 76 Cr. App. R. 110, CA.
3. Required by CPR Pt 31.
4. CPR Pt. 32.19.
5. See for example, Ch. 9, Canadian Department of Justice Report 1999.
6. For example the Canada Evidence Act, s. 30 permits their use.
7. Reliability needs to be assessed independently of the authenticity of the document. For example, a document could be an authentic record made by a witness who was biased, or simply mistaken.
8. Ss. 1 and 4 of the Civil Evidence Act 1995, respectively.
9. As discussed in Ch. 2 above.
10. As discussed in Ch. 7, para. 7–022.
11. McCullagh and Caelli, *Non-repudiation in the digital environment*, in First Monday 5(8) *http://firstmonday.org/ issues/issue5_8/mccullagh/index.html*.
12. US National Security Telecommunications Advisory Committee Network Group Intrusion Detection Subgroup, report at *http://www.nstac.org FIDSGREP.pdf*.
13. See Ch. 7 para. 7.018.
14. S. 31.5.
15. Described in Schneier, *Secrets and Lies* at p. 264.
16. The software is likely to have deleted itself after executing.
17. Formerly known as *Norwich Pharmacal* Order; now covered by CPR 31.18.

9

Regulatory aspects

Introduction

9–001 As will be seen from the review of national legislation in this chapter, three years after the ILPF carried out its survey of electronic signature laws, the business model of third party certification of keys is if anything further entrenched. The European Union's Electronic Signatures Directive, which endorses this approach, has been implemented by all but one of the 23 existing and acceding Member States. Although only a minority of countries which have enacted legislation include a requirement for certification service providers to be licensed before beginning operations, many require them to be registered and to submit to some form of technical and procedural audit by a supervising agency. However, the specific arrangements for supervising, licensing or accrediting certification service providers vary from country to country, and in many cases proposed detailed regulations have not yet been issued.

The regulation of data protection is also an area having a direct impact upon certification service providers which provide certification services to individuals. Registration and certificate issuing and revocation operations necessarily involve the collection of personal data about subscribers. Although data protection standards vary very widely around the world, there appears to be a greater consensus that data held online should be subject to controls as to its collection and subsequent use.

Finally, there are regulatory issues associated with the use and supply of cryptographic products. These derive from the original use of cryptography as a means of maintaining secrecy, and particularly its use in espionage. As a result of its potential for such uses, cryptographic products are classified as "dual-use" goods, *i.e.* those having potential for military as well as civilian uses. Although the products being developed specifically for use in producing electronic signatures are not always capable of being used for confidentiality purposes, nevertheless many such products will fall within the definitions of dual use goods and suppliers may therefore need to comply with the relevant export and supply regulations.

1. Specific regulation of certification service providers

9–002 No legally binding instruments have yet been signed on this issue at the international level, and there are no proposals for any to be introduced.

The question of whether or not to impose public supervision on certification service providers, and if so of what nature, closely relates to the question of whether or not to provide certification service providers with any form of statutory ceiling on their potential liability to third parties which rely upon the certificates they issue. This was initially viewed as a possible necessity to permit certification services to emerge into the marketplace, and the subject of much discussion. The contrary view is that a business which cannot internalize its own costs without legislative protection should not be artificially promoted over other potential market solutions.[1] The effect of legislative protection for certification service providers is to shift the risk of a transaction onto the relying party – but this may be a more logical approach, since it is the relying party who makes the decision as to how much reliance to place upon a particular certificate. In any event, certification service providers in most systems have the discretion as to the value limits for which their certificates can be used. Article 9 of the UNCITRAL Model Law, which sets standards of conduct, does not address the extent of liability a certification service provider should face for failing to meet its criteria, but the Guide to Enactment does include the existence and extent of any limitation on the purpose for which the certificate may be used and the existence of any statement limiting the scope or extent of the certification service provider's liability among the factors which may be taken into account. The issue of liability protection is therefore complex, and a variety of approaches has emerged.

Most national laws introducing electronic signature regimes have provided for some **9–003** form of government registration or supervision of certification service provider operations. Variables include minimum capital or insurance requirements, the need for external security audits, limitations on permitted employees by reference to criminal record, technical qualifications or both, administrative and criminal penalties for the issuance of false certificates, which may apply not only to the certification service provider itself but also to individual directors or officers, and so on.

Accreditation or licensing arrangements are also diverse. Although the variables in terms of the burden upon participating certification service providers are usually similar, the benefits of accreditation or licensing range from the ability to issue certificates at all through exclusive rights to issue certificates conferring legal effect upon the supported certificates, to the benefit of limited liability in respect of certificates issued. For instance, Article 10 of the UNCITRAL Model Law on Electronic Signatures lists accreditation as one of the factors to be taken into account in assessing whether or not a certification service provider uses trustworthy systems. This is one of the criteria a certification service provider must fulfil in order to limit its exposure to liability for third party losses, although the extent of the limit is left to enacting states to decide.

The following review does not attempt to set out the complete regulatory requirements of each of the countries surveyed; to do so would occupy a substantial tome. Each jurisidiction is reviewed briefly, the principal provisions of note described and any particularly unusual provisions are highlighted.

A. EUROPE

The two benefits associated with qualified certificates under the Electronic Signature **9–004** Directive are the legal effectiveness of supported signatures, and the right of the certification service provider to limit its liability for third party losses. The Directive expressly prohibits Member States from making either of these benefits contingent upon the licensing or accreditation of certification service providers. However, Annex II (a) of the Directive does require certification service providers wishing to issue qualified certificates to demonstrate the reliability necessary for providing certification services; demonstration implies some external observer with the authority to confirm or deny that the necessary standard has been achieved. In practice almost all current and future Member States have established some system of supervision, whether by a government agency or through an industry scheme of self-regulation.

(i)   Austria

9–005   The Law on Electronic Signatures includes various provisions relating to the regulation of certification service providers. A further Order, the Electronic Signature Order,[2] was adopted in February 2000 spelling out the technical, organisational and personnel requirements for certification service providers.

No prior registration or licence is required, but notification to the supervisory body is necessary including a copy of a security policy and certification policy. The supervisory body must also be notified immediately of any security breach.[3] Specific requirements for a minimum financial resource of €300,000 and minimum insurance of €1 million have been imposed; minimum training requirements for technical staff of a one year training course or three years' professional experience are required, and staff cannot be employed who have a previous conviction for an offence against property carrying a sentence of a year or an offence against documents or evidence carrying a sentence of 3 months or more.

The supervisory body nominated is the Telekom Control Kommission, which has responsibility for making sure that when a certification services provider ceases operations its revocation service is continued by another. Certification services providers have the burden of proof, if a claim is made against them, of showing that they were not at fault, once the injured party has shown that there is a probability that the certification service provider had breached its duty to supply correct information or failed to maintain appropriate security.[4] The supervisory body also has responsibility for managing a voluntary accreditation scheme and maintaining a directory of accredited certification service providers online.

9–006   Before a qualified certificate is issued the registration or certification body must see an official form of identification including a photograph of the applicant. A signatory can request that additional information about them such as a power of attorney be included in any qualified certificate but must prove the existence of the power rigorously.

Certification service providers must keep a certificate revocation list online at all times, and must keep records of their security measures which must be verifiable at all times. The circumstances in which certificates must be revoked are specified.

The Secure Information Technology Centre, A-SIT, has been recognised as a body able to confirm the compliance of secure signature creation devices with the requirements of the Directive.[5] A-Trust[6] and Datakom Austria GbH have been recognised as certification services providers capable of issuing qualified certificates in accordance with the Electronic Signatures Order.

(ii)   Belgium

9–007   Belgium passed an Act on July 9, 2001 bringing a regulatory framework for certification service providers into effect ("the Certification Service Providers Act").

Certification services providers wishing to issue qualified certificates must notify the Ministry of Economic Affairs before beginning operations,[7] giving contact information and evidence of insurance cover. Thereafter, the Ministry is responsible for supervising the certification service provider. It can at any time of its own motion or in response to a complaint examine the certification service provider's records and premises and, if appropriate, notify it that it does not meet the legal requirements. Unless the certification service provider then ceases operations the Ministry can bring court proceedings to stop it.

The Certification Service Providers Act transposed the requirements of Annex II for certification service providers issuing qualified certificates.

Where a certificate is issued to a legal person, the certification service provider must **9–008** maintain a register of the identities and attributes of the natural persons who can represent the legal person and use the relevant signatures.[8] Certificates must be revoked in specified circumstances, such as upon request or death of the holder or by Court order.

The liability regime for certification service providers issuing qualified certificates is exactly that laid down by the Electronic Signature Directive. A certification service provider is required to keep its records for 30 years, which corresponds to the limitation period for claims involving real property.

A voluntary system of accreditation is contemplated by the Act for certification service providers which are competent to issue qualified certificates and use approved secure-signature-creation-devices. Specific provisions for the scheme, BE.SIGN, which is also to be run by a Technical Committee under the Ministry for Economic Affairs, were laid down by further regulations.[9] Accreditation is subject to an audit and evidence of financial and administrative independence. It lasts up to three years and is renewable. Falsely claiming to be accredited may be an offence punishable by a fine of up to €50,000 or 3 months' imprisonment.

(iii)   Bulgaria

The conditions to be met by all certification service providers in Bulgaria under the Law **9–009** on Electronic Documents and Electronic Signatures are substantially similar to those set out in Annex II of the Electronic Signature Directive for certification service providers issuing qualified certificates.[10] There is no requirement for a certification service provider to be registered but they must notify the Communications Regulation Commission (CRC)[11] upon beginning activities. The notification must include details of insurance cover and certification practice. For the purpose of supervision, the CRC has right of access to information concerning certification service providers' systems and staff, as well as to their information systems. An industry-led accreditation system is envisaged.

The Law does not specify how the certification service provider is to verify the identity of a subscriber, but does specify that it must enter into a written contract with every subscriber.

Each certification service provider must maintain a registry of issued certificates but **9–010** does not appear to have to maintain a certificate revocation list. Instead, the certificate is made inaccessible. A certification service provider which has reason to believe that a certificate ought to be revoked may suspend the certificate for up to 48 hours, and must suspend when asked to do so by the owner or signatory, the CRC or a person who in the circumstances is clearly likely to know of reason for the certificate to be revoked.[12] This provision would appear to derive from the ICC GUIDEC.

The liability provisions of the Law concerning certification service providers[13] are based on the Electronic Signature Directive, so limited scope and value certificates are permitted, but the certification service provider's right to exclude or limit liability through contract is negated by making such contracts invalid.[14] The Law in addition provides for the certificate owner to be liable for a failure on the part of the signatory either to keep the signature creation data secure as required by the certification service provider, or to notify the certification service provider promptly on learning of a compromise of a private key. Both owner and signatory are liable to the certification service provider for any loss as a result of the provision of false data or the concealment of data. The CRC is proposing to introduce further regulations governing the activities and liabilities of certification service providers in more detail.

Certification service providers which fail to abide by the conditions laid down in the Law may be liable to administrative fines of up to 100,000 BGL (~€51,356).

(iv) Cyprus

9–011   There are no present regulations in effect in Cyprus specific to certification service providers.

(v) Czech Republic

9–012   The Czech Electronic Signature Act contains considerable detail on the regulation of certification service providers, and a further Regulation was introduced in October 2001 spelling out the matters to be addressed by certification service providers in their certification and system security policies.

Certification service providers issuing qualified certificates are required to ensure that the information contained in certificates they issue is accurate, true and complete including verifying the identity of the subscribers "by appropriate resources". They must maintain a certification revocation list remotely accessible by at least two independent means, and store all relevant records, which include precise times of issuance and invalidity of certificates, in electronic form for at least 10 years from the expiry of a qualified certificate.[15] Certificates must be revoked in circumstances such as death of the signatory or imposition by a court on the signatory of limitations to their competence to perform legal acts. Supervision of certification service providers is by the Bureau of Personal Data Protection (BFPD).

Any certification service provider which, having been accredited by the BFPD[16] has its accreditation withdrawn must so inform all those to whom it supplies services and state the fact in its registers. A certification service provider which is not accredited but intends to issue qualified certificates must give the BFPD 30 days' notice before beginning to do so. The Law also imposes an express confidentiality requirement on employees and former employees of certification service providers which issue qualified certificates.

9–013   As well as supervising the activities of certification service providers, the BFPD is also responsible for managing the accreditation scheme.[17] The BFPD must also take over the management of subsisting valid qualified certificates if the certification service provider which issued them ceases operations without having been able to transfer its activities to another certification service provider.[18] It has the power to impose fines of up to CZK10m (€316,635) for a first breach by a certification service provider of its obligations, and up to CZK20m (€633,270) for a second breach within a year.[19]

Only entities which have their registered office in the Czech Republic are eligible for accreditation,[20] and accredited certification service providers may not undertake any activity other than certification services unless they operate as an attorney, notary or "expert".[21] Public authorities may only use advanced electronic signatures which are supported by a qualified certificate issued by an accredited certification service provider.[22] This provision would appear to be contrary to the non-discrimination on the grounds of nationality provisions of the Treaty of Rome,[23] and may have to be amended once the Czech Republic has acceded to the European Union.

Foreign certification service provider may however apply to the BFPD for their certificates to be recognised as qualified certificates under the Law.[24] The provisions of the Electronic Signature Directive on mutual recognition and guarantee by a national certification service provider have also been incorporated.[25]   **9–014**

Certification service provider's liability can be limited by issuing limited scope or value qualified certificates, but a certification service provider will be liable for damage caused by breach of its statutory obligations.[26]

(vi)   Denmark

Certification authorities operating under the Electronic Signature Law, which is all those issuing certificates to the public, are required to retain all relevant information relating to all certificates they issue for an appropriate period of time. Six years is specified as the minimum, but there is no upper limit.[27] It is therefore incumbent upon the certification authorities to make a judgment as to when information can safely be disposed of after the expiry of the 6 years.   **9–015**

The liability limitations of the Electronic Signature Directive are included, but the principle of liability for losses due to inaccuracy of a certificate, failure to revoke and so on cannot be altered by agreement with "the injured person". This appears to restrict the use of relying party agreements to disclaim all liability.

An Order of May 2000[28] sets out requirements for certification authorities' security procedures, the procedures to be used for verifying the identity of subscribers and the provision of directory and revocation services.

Supervision of certification authorities is allocated to the National Telecom Agency, which must be notified before any certification authority begins issuing qualified certificates.[29] The notification must include details of the certification authority's activities and systems and also statements from both the management and an external public accountant as auditor[30] that the company's overall data, system and operation security comply with the requirements of the Act,[31] and this report must be updated annually. However any change to any of the notified data must itself be notified within eight days of the change taking place. The Agency can also order a system auditor to provide information on a certification service provider without the certification service provider's consent.

The possibility of a voluntary accreditation scheme is contemplated by the Law[32] but no provisions are made.

(vii)   Estonia

The Digital Signatures Act specifies the principles by which certification service providers must operate,[33] which are very detailed. Employees must have no criminal records; a   **9–016** certification service provider must maintain a system for 24 hour acceptance of applications for suspension and 24 hour access to the certificate revocation list. All certification service providers must undergo an annual audit of their information systems.[34]

The certification service provider must verify the identity of an Estonian applicant for a certificate other than by checking that name and personal identification code of the applicant correspond. An applicant who does not have a personal identification code must submit their date of birth, which will have to be verified before the certificate can be issued, presumably either from a birth certificate or passport. The certification service provider must verify the accuracy of this data.

9–017 Certification service providers must currently be Estonian companies or public agencies,[35] and must be registered with the Ministry of Transport and Communications before beginning operations. Presumably the nationality restriction will be lifted upon accession to the European Union. They must also have their public keys approved by it and submit an annual information systems audit report to it. They must carry insurance and publish the conditions of that insurance on the Internet. Certificates issued by foreign certification service providers can be recognised under the circumstances specified in the Directive.

A certification service provider must suspend or revoke a certificate in specified circumstances.[36] Suspension is required, among other cases, where the certification service provider has reason to believe that data in the certificate is incorrect; where the private key may have been compromised; or upon request by the certificate holder, the data protection supervision authority or the police or a court. Certificates must be revoked if: the holder so requests; the key has been compromised; the holder dies or loses legal capacity; where data in the certificate is false; or the certification service provider ceases business. It must be possible to apply for suspension of a certificate 24 hours per day, and the certificate revocation list must also be permanently available.

9–018 There are no provisions for limiting certification service providers' liability. Documentation concerning services provided must be kept until a certification service provider ceases activities and then transferred to the state register of certificates.[37] The Ministry of Transport and Communications must be notified promptly of a decision to terminate service provision, and subscribers must be notified at least one month beforehand.

Certification service providers may not employ anyone who has a criminal record for an intentionally committed offence.[38]

In addition, there are equivalent sections dealing with the establishment and supervision of time stamping service providers.

(viii) Finland

9–019 The Finnish Communications Regulatory Authority (FCRA) is responsible for supervising the operations of certification service providers, which must notify it in writing before beginning to issue qualified certificates. FCRA has the right to have a certification service provider's systems inspected for compliance with the Act on Electronic Signatures.[39] Certification service providers issuing qualified certificates to the public must comply with the conditions of Annex II of the Electronic Signature Directive.

Certificates issued as qualified certificates by certification service providers situated outside Finland will be recognized under the conditions specified in the Electronic Signature Directive.

Qualified certificates must be revoked on request of the subscriber, and may be revoked for "another special reason".[40] The signatory must be informed of the revocation. A certificate register and revocation list available to parties relying on qualified certificates 24 hours per day must be maintained, the information being kept for 10 years after the certificate ceases to be valid.[41] The limitation of liability provisions of the Electronic Signature Directive are incorporated.

Separate provisions apply to certification service providers providing certification services to public administration.

(ix) France

The elements of the Directive relating to issues such as the liability of certification service providers and signatories do not appear to have been implemented in France at the time of writing. However, certification service providers issuing qualified certificates must comply with the requirements of Annex II of the Directive and may demand recognition for such compliance with an approved accreditation body.[42] A complex hierarchy of supervision and accreditation is in place, under the supervision of the Central Directorate for IT Systems and, as regards accreditation, the French Accreditation Committee "Cofrac". An Arret was issued on May 31, 2002 on accreditation of certification service providers. A Decree of April 18, 2001 governs evaluation of security of products and services.

9–020

(x) Germany

Under the Framework Law and Signatures Ordinance, very detailed provisions are laid down for the regulation of certification service providers. Failure to comply with these provisions can lead to the imposition of a fine. However, a certification service provider is defined as an entity issuing qualified certificates or time-stamps,[43] so it would appear that the regulatory framework does not apply to certification service providers not issuing qualified certificates.

9–021

Although no approval is required, only those who can prove that they have the necessary reliability and specialized knowledge may operate as a certification service provider.[44] The Regulierungsbehörde, a government agency under the Economics Ministry, must be notified of beginning operations as a certification service provider, including proof that these criteria are fulfilled.[45] Thereafter certification service providers must co-operate with the Regulierungsbehörde, including permitting access to premises during normal operating hours and providing documents for inspection.[46] All certification service providers must also carry at least €250,000 insurance cover.[47]

A voluntary accreditation system is also established, under which a certification service provider's own qualified electronic signature is certified by the competent authority for the accreditation system.[48] Accreditation is by the Regulierungsbehörde, upon demonstrating compliance with detailed technical and administrative security requirements, and entitles the certification service provider to a quality "seal". The Regulierungsbehörde acts as the root certification authority as it issues the qualified certificates the accredited certification service providers need in order to issue certificates. Electronic signatures supported by a certificate from an accredited certification service provider are called "qualified electronic signatures with provider accreditation".[49]

9–022   A certification service provider must identify an applicant for a certificate by inspection of a national identity card, passport or document offering an equivalent level of security —any of which may be substituted by an electronic document signed with a qualified electronic signature.[50] The certification service provider must keep its records relating to qualified certificates for five years after they cease to be valid, but an accredited certification service provider must keep them for 30 years post expiry or revocation.[51]

The criteria stipulated for invalidating a qualified certificate are relatively limited: only upon request by the holder or their representative (upon appropriate verification of authority to revoke), upon ceasing operations,[52] if the certificate is found to have been based on false data or if ordered to do so by the competent authority.[53] The possibility that a certification service provider might come to be aware that signature creation data had been compromised does not appear to be contemplated. In those circumstances, presumably the certification service provider would have to contact the signatory and request that they request the certificate to be revoked, unless permitted to revoke the certificate unilaterally under the subscriber agreement. However, unlike Article 6(2) of the Directive the Framework Law does not appear to hold a certification service provider liable for failure to revoke a certificate. There is no provision for liability of the signatory within the Law.

The liability regime for certification service providers is restricted to breaches of their obligations under the Law or Ordinance and further restricted to exclude damages altogether if either:

- the relying party knew or must have known that the information in a certificate was faulty;[54] or

- the certification service provider was not at fault; or

- to the extent that any limits on use of the certificate were exceeded.[55]

A certification service provider which ceases operations must report this to the Regulierungsbehörde without delay and ensure that its certificates and related records are taken over by another certification service provider. If no other certification-service-provider takes over the documentation, the Regulierungsbehörde shall do so.[56] Subscribers concerned must also be notified;[57] they are not given the option to object under the law, though this may of course be a term of the subscriber agreement.

(xi)   Greece

9–023   The supervisory authority for certification service providers under Presidential Decree 150/2001 is the National Telecommunications and Post Commission (EETT),[58] which is also responsible for certifying the compliance of secure signature creation devices with the requirements of the Decree.[59] All certification service providers based in Greece must notify EETT before beginning activities. However, no licence is required. Thereafter, they must submit an annual report to EETT specifying in particular any complaints they have received or other problems, and are subject to inspection by EETT, and must also notify it of ceasing operations.

Liability is regulated in accordance with the limitations permitted by the Electronic Signature Directive. EETT is producing regulations governing a voluntary accreditation scheme and the supervision of inspection of certification service providers established in Greece. Falsely claiming to be accredited can result in a fine of up to €300,000.

Foreign certification service providers are recognized in the circumstances laid down in the Electronic Signature Directive.

(xii)   Hungary

A certification service provider based in Hungary and intending to provide advanced or qualified signature services must notify the Communication Inspectorate 30 days in advance.[60] To provide qualified certificates a certification service provider requires a certificate confirming that it has been registered by the Inspectorate as meeting the personnel, technical and other conditions[61] necessary to provide this service.[62] These include appropriately technically qualified staff, with no criminal record, evidence of liability insurance and necessary financial resources. A registered certification service provider can include the fact of its registration in the qualified certificates it issues,[63] but remains subject to on-site inspection at least once a year by the Communications Inspectorate of documents, data carriers, work processes and so on.[64] Employees must provide data and statements upon request. Failure to comply with the Act can lead to a certification service provider being struck off the register, fined and having its certificates revoked.[65]

9–024

The certification service provider's liability provisions accord closely with the Directive; liability is contingent upon the certification service provider having failed to comply with its obligations under the Act, so can presumably be avoided by demonstrating compliance.

All certification service providers are required to keep their records relating to a certificate for at least 5 years after the certificate's period of validity or, where any legal dispute relating to the signature or a document signed with it is in progress, until a final judgment has been given.

9–025

The identity of a subscriber must be established by reference to an ID card, passport, driving licence or other suitable document, which must be checked against the issuing authorities' records.[66]

The circumstances where a certification service provider can suspend or revoke a signature are spelt out in Article 14, including an order of the Communications Inspectorate. Cessation of business can only take place once ongoing certificates and their records have been transferred to an equivalent certification service provider, failing which the Communications Inspectorate will revoke all its current certificates and publicise this fact.

If a certification service provider breaches the law repeatedly not only the organisation but also its senior executives may be fined. The fines laid down under the Act to be imposed on a certification service provider are between 10,000 and 10m forints (~€41—41,000), and on a senior executive between HUF50,000 and 1m (~€205—205,000).

(xiii)   Ireland

No prior notification or permission is required for the provision of certification services in Ireland under the Electronic Commerce Act. Supervision of certification service providers which issue qualified certificates, and any voluntary accreditation scheme, is ultimately the responsibility of the Ministry for Communications, Marine and Natural Resources, but no regulations appear to have been introduced to date.

9–026

The liability provisions of the Electronic Signature Directive are incorporated at Section 30.

(xiv)   Italy

9–027   Technical rules on digital signatures were promulgated on February 8, 1999, by Decree of the Ministers Counsel President,[67] and updated in January 2002 by Legislative Decree 10/02,[68] which regulate the activities of certification service providers.

There is no requirement for a body wishing to provide certification services to obtain prior authorization, but supervision on qualified certification services providers is carried out by the Innovation and Technologies Department of the Presidential Council of Ministers[69] which must be notified before operations begin. There is also an accreditation system, to which qualified certification services providers may apply. The Innovation and Technologies Department publishes a list of approved certification service providers, which is updated as soon as a certification service provider's status changes. Italy has been running a PKI infrastructure for longer than any of the other European countries and has already a number of approved certification service providers on the relevant public list.

The technical rules cover the security of certification service providers' systems for key creation and administering the certificate register, the circumstances in which certificates must be suspended or revoked, the operating procedures and recovery plans to be observed and the content and format for certificates. Qualified certification service providers must prove their financial reliability,[70] while to obtain accreditation qualified certification services providers must meet the capital requirements for authorised banking enterprises of a minimum of €6,455,711.[71] They must keep the records of a certificate for at least 10 years.

The liability limitation provisions of the Electronic Signature Directive have now been incorporated precisely.[72]

(xv)   Latvia

9–028   The Law on Electronic Documents does not require certification services to be subject to any prior approval or accreditation, but a category of reliable certification service providers is established being those which meet specified requirements. Most of these are drawn from the requirements of Annex II of the Directive, but not all of those requirements are included: there is no general requirement to demonstrate a particular level of reliability, to verify subscribers' identities and attributes, to take measures against forgery of certificates or guarantee the confidentiality of signature creation data which a service provider generates.[73] However, each of these requirements is included elsewhere in the law: verification of identity is required before a qualified certificate may be granted,[74] measures against counterfeiting and to ensure confidentiality of signature creation data are among the responsibilities of a reliable certification service provider set out in Article 23.

In order to qualify as a reliable certification service provider, the certification service provider must be accredited by the State Data Inspectorate,[75] which is also responsible for supervising all reliable certification service providers.[76] Accreditation is upon submission of a certification practice statement, sample subscriber agreement and details of information systems and operating procedures.[77] Independent testing of the security of the information systems by an approved expert is required as a precondition to accreditation.[78] Reliable certification service providers are also required to carry adequate insurance of at least a minimum to be set by regulations.[79]

Qualified certificates may be cancelled or suspended.[80] Cancellation must be without delay if the signatory requests, or the certification service provider is notified of the signatory's death or any other change in the information in the certificate, or the information in the certificate is false or misleading, or upon order by a court. Suspension is upon either request by the signatory in writing, by court order or if the certification service provider has reason to believe that either the signatory is dead or the information in the certificate false or misleading. In the last two instances, suspension is pending investigation.[81]

9–029

If a certificate is maliciously or negligently cancelled or suspended, the certification service provider is liable for any losses caused. Similarly, the certification service provider appears to be liable for losses caused to third parties by reasonable reliance upon the accuracy of a certificate; the Electronic Signature Directive provisions for limiting this in the situation where the certification service provider can prove it was not negligent do not appear to have been incorporated. However, a certification service provider will not be liable for reliance upon a certificate beyond its specified limits.[82]

Upon ceasing operations, a reliable certification service provider must transfer its data and information systems to another reliable certification service provider by agreement or, if this is not possible, to the State Archives.[83] Signatories can transfer their own data to another reliable certification service provider in these circumstances.

No period is specified for the retention of signature or certificate records.

(xvi) Lithuania

The Law on Electronic Signatures, adopted in July 2000, was not implemented in practice until January 1, 2002 since the infrastructure was not in place pending a decision as to whether certification service providers should be state-controlled. Ultimately, this was eschewed in favour of private service providers.

9–030

Certification service providers which wish to issue qualified certificates are required to register with the State's nominated supervisory body,[84] but the requirements for registration are left to secondary legislation, as are the details of record-retention time. A voluntary accreditation is also contemplated.

Certification service providers must enter a written contract with potential subscribers before issuing any certificate. Documents confirming the subscriber's identity must also be submitted. The certification service provider must maintain a certificate registry 24 hours per day.[85]

Certificates must be suspended if the signatory or a law enforcement agency so requests, or if the certification service provider learns either that data in the certificate is false or that the keys have been compromised.[86] They must be revoked upon request of the signatory or the legal person represented by the signatory, or on loss by the signatory of the keys, legal capacity or life, if the data in the application for the certificate are found to be false, or if the limitations of the certificate are exceeded or the signatory otherwise breaches the law relating to signatures or the contract.[87]

A certification service provider which is proposing to cease operations must inform all its subscribers and the supervisory body at least one month before doing so. Before ceasing operations the provider must then transfer all of its certificates and records either to a stipulated successor or to the supervisory body.[88]

(xvii)   Luxembourg

9–031   The Law on Electronic Commerce provides for supervision of certification service providers which issue qualified certificates by the National Accreditation and Monitoring Authority (NAMA), which must be notified that their operations conform with the requirements of the law.[89] It is not specified that this notification must be in advance. NAMA has a right of inspection to enable it to perform its supervisory functions.

The Law includes a limitation on the liability of certification service providers in accordance with the Electronic Signature Directive,[90] although this is expressed to be without prejudice to Luxembourg's Consumer Protection Law.

Under the Regulation of June 2001, certification service providers which wish to issue qualified certificates must comply with the requirements of Annex II of the Electronic Signature Directive.[91] A specific requirement of confidentiality is imposed upon certification service providers, their directors and employees, the breach of which is an offence.

9–032   Certification service providers must keep a record of subsisting certificates, which for qualified certificates must be kept for at least 10 years from the date of issue,[92] and revoke or suspend certificates in specified circumstances.[93] Their liability mirrors that in the Directive, including the limitation that liability is only vis-à-vis parties which reasonably rely on a certificate.

Provisions for a voluntary accreditation system are set out in the Regulations.[94] NAMA must be informed within a reasonable time of any intent by an accredited certification service provider to cease providing certification services.[95] On ceasing operations, all current certificates and associated records must be transferred to another certification service provider, save that individual certificate holders must be notified of their right to refuse the transfer. If a holder fails to indicate express acceptance then the certificate is revoked instead.[96]

NAMA also responsible for approving laboratories for certifying the compliance of secure signature creation devices with the Regulations.

(xviii)   Malta

9–033   Part V of the Maltese Electronic Commerce Act sets up the regulatory framework for the provision of electronic signature certification and other services.

No prior authorisation is required for certification service providers, but there is a voluntary accreditation scheme supervised by the Malta Communications Authority (MCA) which is also responsible for supervising certification service providers generally.[97] Certification service providers issuing qualified certificates must comply with the principles of Annex III of the Directive, which are transposed as Schedule 3 of the Act. Certification service providers are liable for any damage caused to any third party who reasonably relies on a qualified certificate, save where that reliance goes beyond the limits on the scope or value for which the certificate is issued or the certification service provider can show that it did not act negligently. The Minister responsible for communications is given the power to prescribe the powers and functions of the MCA as supervisory authority, which could include further specifications as to the operation of certification service providers.

(xix)   The Netherlands

The specific requirements for certification service providers which issue qualified **9–034** certificates are set out in the Electronic Signatures Decree 200 of May 8, 2003 and conform closely to the specifications of Annex II of the Directive.

No registration is required for a certification service provider which does not issue qualified certificates to the public; certification service providers which do, must be registered and thereafter are supervised by the Board of the Independent Mail and Telecom Authority.

A certification service provider which wishes to issue qualified certificates to the public must be independent of all secure signature product suppliers and must give a declaration that neither the certification service provider itself nor any director or employee responsible for processing confidential data has been convicted of an offence penalised with six months' imprisonment in the Netherlands, Netherlands Antilles or Aruba.[98]

The Dutch Decree requires a certification service provider to identify prospective **9–035** qualified certificate subscribers on the basis of valid documents specified in the Compulsory Identification Act. The certification service provider must also be able to identify the time of issue and withdrawal of qualified certificates to within one minute, and to keep records relating to them (in particular those which may be required to prove the certification in legal proceedings), for at least seven years. A certificate directory must be maintained in electronic form which includes all certificates current and having expired or been withdrawn in the preceding six months.[99]

A certification service provider is also required to take such measures that upon termination of its services the qualified certificates it has issued are taken over by another registered certification service provider and subscribers are informed. Even if no other certification service provider takes over, the certification service provider must make sure that the certificate list continues to be published for at least six months after it has ceased operations.[100]

A certification service provider which issues qualified certificates is entitled to the limitations of liability to relying parties precisely as set out in the Electronic Signature Directive.

An industry-led regulation scheme, TTML Cooperation, has been set up which has been involved in discussions with the United Kingdom's tScheme over possible mutual recognition arrangements.

(xx)   Poland

The Polish Electronic Signature Act defines a certification service provider as either an **9–036** entrepreneur within the meaning of the Polish Economic Activity law (as amended), the National Bank of Poland or a public authority.[101] Any person or organisation which has a criminal conviction for offences of forgery, money laundering, insider dealing, economic relations or tax offences may not operate as a certification service provider.[102]

The organizational, insurance and technical requirements for certification service providers able to issue qualified certificates are to be laid down in detail by Regulation; the Act stipulates the list of requirements of Annex II of the Electronic Signature Directive.[103] Certification service providers wishing to issue qualified certificates must be registered with the Minister for the Economy; the data required for the application are set out in the Act. The Minister or a body nominated by him or her will inspect the systems and make a decision within two months. Thereafter the Minister supervises through a system of inspections, the inspectors being authorised to enter certification service providers' premises and inspect their systems and records as well as questioning employees.[104] Any irregularities identified must be corrected on pain of a cash penalty of up to 50,000 Polish ztoty (~€11,724).[105] No accreditation scheme appears to be established.

Both certification service providers and their employees are subject to a requirement of confidentiality in respect of data provided to the certification service provider in connection with a subscription, which in the case of employees lasts 10 years from the date of termination of the employment.[106]

9–037   A certification service provider must verify the identity of a prospective subscriber, which may (but does not have to) include requiring a notarially-established proof of identity before issuing a certificate of identity.[107] A subscriber contract must be entered into in writing or will be invalid. Certification service providers have a specially defined function of *electronic authentication* for signing certificates. However, upon unraveling the definitions, this appears to equate to the use of what would be an advanced electronic signature (called in the Polish Act a secure electronic signature) save that it is not uniquely linked to a natural person.[108]

Certification service providers will be liable for relying party losses resulting from failure to comply with their obligations unless able to show that this was not due to negligence. They will not be liable for losses due to the relying party exceeding the scope of use of the certificate. Further, certification service providers are not to be held liable for losses arising from false data in the certificate which was supplied by the subscriber.[109] Certification service providers are nevertheless obliged to carry insurance conforming to a regulation issued by the Minister in charge of Financial Institutions.[110] Failure to do so may result in a fine of up to 1m Polish ztoty (~€235,000).[111]

9–038   The list of circumstances in which a qualified certificate must be revoked (after a suspension of 7 days for investigations)[112] includes: upon request by the signatory or person on whose behalf they sign, or the Minister for Economy; where false or obsolete data were given by the subscriber; where the signatory loses legal capacity; or where the certification service provider ceases operations without their affairs being taken over by another.[113] However, the certification service provider's liability for damage expressly survives the revocation.

Certification service providers must keep records directly relating to the provision of certification services for 20 years after the completion of the document or data concerned.[114] On termination of operations, these records must be transferred to a body indicated by the Minister for the Economy. For storing these records the Minister is permitted to charge €1 per file—it is not clear to whom, nor whether this is a one-off or recurrent charge. The latter would appear more realistic.

(xxi)   Portugal

9–039   Under Decree 290-D/99 there is no prior registration or licensing requirement for certification service providers, unless a certifying entity intends to issue qualified certificates in which case it must be registered.[115] Certifying entity is defined very broadly, to include among the usual functions entities which only ensure the publicity of certificates. A certifying entity must have sufficient capital (not less than €200,000). In addition, certification service providers must carry civil responsibility insurance in accordance with Administrative rule 1370/2000.[116]

Directors, employees, agents and representatives of a certifying entity must be of good standing, which is defined as excluding various forms of criminal conviction in Portugal or abroad, bankruptcy/ insolvency or breach of any regulatory provisions relating to certification or notarial services, judicial administration, public registers or libraries.[117]

There is also provision for voluntary accreditation, which lasts up to three years but may be renewed indefinitely. To be accredited the certifying entity must demonstrate absolute integrity and independence in the conduct of their business and use technical and human resources meeting standards laid down by regulation.[118] A list of materials to be provided in support of an application for accreditation (or renewal) is laid down in Article 13. Accreditation is subject to supervision, including inspection, by the accrediting agency. All certifying entities are required to have a security audit every year.[119]

Certifying entities issuing qualified certificates are required to comply with a list of criteria closely approximating those of Annex II of the Directive, with minor omissions. For example, the requirement to retain records relating to qualified certificates issued is implemented only as a requirement to retain the certificates themselves. The retention period is 20 years. There is no prohibition on retaining a subscriber's private key. There are also some additions, such as the requirement to inform subscribers of the procedures for signature and signature verification, and the desirability of re-signing documents in some circumstances.[120]

The certificate list must be kept permanently up to date and accessible to any person wishing to consult it. This could be interpreted to preclude the imposition of terms for such consultation, such as acceptance of a relying party agreement.

Qualified certificates must be suspended on request of the holder (properly identified) or if there are reasonable grounds to believe that the certificate was issued based on false or misleading information, or is no longer accurate or the signature creation data may have been compromised. They must be revoked on the same grounds, and when the certifying entity ceases trading or by order of the supervising agency. Suspension and revocation have effect as against third parties from the date of registration.[121]

Three months' advance notice must be given to the accrediting authority and subscribers of any intention of voluntary termination of operations by any certifying entity issuing qualified certificates. Any risk of insolvency must be notified to the accrediting authority immediately. This is to enable the accrediting authority to arrange the transfer of records to another verifying entity or, if this is not possible, to revoke the certificates and store the relevant data.[122]

9–040

(xxii) Romania

Under the Law on Electronic Signatures there is no prior authorization requirement but all prospective certification service providers must notify the supervising authority 30 days before beginning operations[123] giving complete details of their security and certification procedures, and subsequent changes to these must be notified 10 days before being implemented.

Obligations of confidentiality are imposed on all certification service providers and their employees, without limit in time.[124] Paper copies of all qualified certificates issued must be kept for at least 10 years and the information on which the certificate was based must be kept (though not necessarily on paper) for evidential purposes for 10 years after the certificate has expired;[125] a fine of up to ROL250m (~€660) may be imposed for failing to keep it for 5 years.[126] The Directive's requirement that information stored must be able to be checked for "authenticity" has here been transposed expressly as "accuracy". In

9–041

addition to the criteria to be met by certification service providers issuing qualified certificates specified by Annex II of the Directive, the Romanian Law requires them to use only secure signature creation devices.[127]

Certification service providers are required to maintain a permanently accessible electronic register of certificates, but are given a generous 24 hours to suspend any certificate after the moment they learn or should and could have learned, of a request from the signatory, a court ruling, or a change in the facts contained in the certificate. 24 hours is also permitted for revocations on request or death of the signatory, a final court ruling, proof beyond reasonable doubt of faulty or fake information in the application for a certificate, compromise of the certificate or fraudulent use of it.[128] These provisions appear to leave considerably more leeway for invalid or potentially invalid certificates to remain in effect in Romania where they would have been suspended or revoked in other jurisdictions.

30 days' advance notice must be given to the supervisory body and subscribers of an intent to cease certification-related activities and upon ceasing operations, a certification service provide should transfer its subsisting certificates to another provided that the certificate holders explicitly agree to the transfer. Any certificate whose holder does not agree must be revoked.[129]

9–042 Supervision by the appointed authority may include inspection of the premises and documents of the certification service providers, including sealing off any equipment necessary for up to 15 days.[130]

The terms of the voluntary accreditation scheme are to be issued in regulations by the appointed authority.[131] Foreign certification service providers are entitled to apply for accreditation after which their certificates will be given effect as qualified certificates. The international recognition provisions of the Electronic Signatures Directive are included, but no provision has been made for automatic recognition of other EU certification service providers upon accession.

Certification service providers will be liable for losses caused to third parties in the circumstances specified in Article 6 of the Directive but a high standard of care is imposed in that liability ensues unless the certification service provider proves that it could not prevent the damage occurring despite its best efforts.[132] This appears to be a stricter requirement than merely not being negligent as the Directive requires. Further, a detailed system of fines is provided for failure to comply with the requirements.[133]

(xxiii) Slovakia

9–043 Prior authorisation is not necessary under the Electronic Signature Act for the provision of certification services, but all certification authorities (*not* necessarily all certification service providers) are subject to supervision by the National Security Bureau (NSB). The Act distinguishes certification authorities as a separate class of certification service providers, being those which issue, validate and revoke certificates, maintain certificate archives and perform related certification functions. Those services provided by certification service providers and not within this list are the publication of certificate revocation lists, confirmation of the existence and validity of certificates and provision of directory access to issued certificates for reference. Accredited certification services also include time stamping.

Before beginning to provide services a certification authority must publish its certification guidelines, technical specifications, limitations of service provision, charges and accreditation status and also give 30 days' advance notice to the NSB. Likewise, 6 months' notice of ceasing operations must be given, both to the NSB and subscribers.[134] The NSB is responsible for supervision of all matters relating to electronic signatures including accreditation, the mode and frequency of publication of qualified-certificate revocation lists, and the making of regulations governing the mode and procedure of use of electronic signatures in commerce and communications with public authorities.[135] Its powers of supervision include the right of access to premises, records and IT systems for the purpose of inspection.[136]

Accreditation requires, among other things, an annual external security audit of the authority's operations and a current statement of the criminal records of any authorised representative. **9–044**

There is no provision for suspension of certificates, but certificates must be revoked if the certification authority finds non-fulfilment of any requirement under which the certificate was issued, becomes aware of any misrepresentation of information, the death or dissolution of the certificate holder or that the private key is known to anyone other than the holder, or by Court order.[137] Each certification authority is permitted to set its own time limit for revocation. Documents relating to any revoked certificate must be kept for 10 years.[138]

The Act appears to impose absolute liability on certification authorities (other than accredited certification authorities) for any breach of their obligations. An accredited certification authority can escape liability under this provision if it proves that the obligations were not breached, and will also not be liable for loss arising from reliance on a qualified certificate beyond its scope of use or limit of value.[139]

(xxiv) Slovenia

Certification service providers do not need any permit for beginning operations under the Electronic Commerce and Electronic Signature Act, but must give 8 days' notice to the Ministry of Economy, which must include details of their internal procedures and infrastructure. Similarly, the Ministry must be informed of any changes or of ceasing to operate.[140] **9–045**

A certificate must be revoked promptly in specified circumstances, including if the holder or his trustee so requests, if the holder loses legal capacity, if the data in the certificate or upon the basis of which it was issued are found to be false, if the signature creation data are compromised.[141] If a certification service provider ceases operations without revoking its certificates, the Ministry must do so. Revocation is effective as against third parties from the moment it is published or otherwise brought to a relying party's notice.[142]

Records relating to ordinary (not qualified) certificates must be kept for at least 5 years after revocation.[143] Where qualified certificates are concerned, the records must be kept for:

> "as long as the data, signed with the electronic signature to which the qualified certificate is referred, will be stored, but at least for five years from the issuance of the certificate".[144]

This provision may be difficult for a certification service provider to comply with since they will have no way of knowing how long data signed with any particular key may be stored. If the certification service provider knows that a certificate is being issued for use **9–046** with transactions such as sale and purchase of land where a long limitation period may apply, it may be on notice that the records have to be kept for a considerable period.

Before issuing a qualified certificate to a person the certification service provider must verify the subscriber's identity using a form of identity document including a photograph (for natural persons) or officially verified documents (for legal persons).[145]

The requirements of Annex II of the Directive for certification service providers to issue qualified certificates are all incorporated in the Act in various places. Further regulations are to be produced governing the details of qualifications and systems required.

Supervision of certification service providers by the Ministry of Economy includes the power to send inspectors to the certification service provider's premises to inspect its documents, systems and procedures and to confiscate documentation for up to 15 days.[146] Failure to comply with the Act may lead to a fine of up to 5m tolars (€21,600).[147] However, certification service providers may limit their liability to relying parties in respect of qualified certificates in accordance with the provision of the Electronic Signature Directive.[148] There are no provisions relating to liability in respect of ordinary certificates.

The voluntary accreditation scheme is run by the national Telecommunications Agency, and is open to foreign certification service providers although it appears that they require the request of a Slovenian accredited certification service provider for their admission to the register.[149] However, qualifying certificates issued by EU certification service providers are treated exactly as domestic qualified certificates.[150]

(xxv) Spain

9–047   The new Decree-Law on electronic signatures applies to certification service providers located in Spain and also to the services of certification service providers located elsewhere which are offered through a permanent establishment in Spain. No prior authorization is required for offering such services, but systems of supervision by the Department of Science and Industry and of accreditation are envisaged. The Department of Science and Industry must be notified upon a certification service provider beginning operations.[151]

Certificates must be suspended in specified circumstances such as on request or by Court order.[152] Certification service providers must publish the suspension or expiration of a certificate immediately upon becoming aware of reason to suspend, and keep this information available until the end of the period at which the certificate would have expired. The certification service provider must verify the applicant's identity (in person, where natural persons are concerned) and the correctness of all information in the certificate before issuing it.

9–048   All certification service providers are required to formulate and publish a certification practice statement.[153] In addition to this and the criteria laid down in Annex II of the Directive, certification service providers which issue qualified certificates must carry a guarantee or insurance of at least €3m[154] to meet their potential liabilities for damage caused by reliance on their certificates. Provision is made for certification service providers' liability in various circumstances such as breach of obligation or delay in publishing certificate revocation, and the liability regime is expressly subject to the law on unfair terms in consumer contracts.[155] However, provided it has acted with due diligence the certification service provider will not be liable if the certificate holder has provided incomplete or false information (although the certification service provider should independently verify any data which is available from public records), or has failed to notify the certification service provider of any changes. Further, the certification service provider will not be liable if the signatory has been negligent in keeping their signature creation data secure or has used them after expiry of the certificate or beyond the limits of value or scope of use. Finally, the certification service provider will not be liable if the relying party is negligent by failing to abide by the restrictions in the certificate or its expiry or revocation.[156]

Supervision of certification service providers by the Department of Science and Industry will include on-site inspection, with which certification service providers must cooperate. Fines of up to €600,000 can be imposed for serious breaches of the obligations in Annex II of the Directive and a further €6,000 per day for failure to implement agreed remedies.

(xxvi)   Sweden

The Qualified Electronic Signatures Act takes a position of minimum regulation necessary to comply with the Electronic Signature Directive. In order to issue qualified certificates, certification service providers must meet the criteria set out in Annex II of the Directive and notify the supervisory authority, the National Post and Telecom Agency, before beginning. Certificates must be revoked immediately upon the request of the signatory or "where there are other grounds for doing so".   **9–049**

Certification service providers are liable for damages due to reliance on their certificates unless they can show they were not negligent. There is no liability for loss due to reliance on a certificate beyond its scope. However, the Act also restricts the certification service providers' ability to include exclusion clauses in relying party agreements by simply stating that they shall not apply to the party to whose detriment they are.[157]

(xxvii)   Switzerland

Pending the passing of a Federal Law on Electronic Signature, a temporary bye-law has been passed which regulates the provision of certification services, with accreditation being conferred by the Accreditation Service of the Federal Office. However, at the time of writing there are currently no public certification service providers operating in Switzerland since SwissKey ceased trading at the end of 2001.   **9–050**

The draft Federal Law is intended broadly to comply with the EU Directive. Article 3(1) sets out the conditions which a Swiss organisation must meet in order to be recognised as a certification service provider, and Article 3(2) sets out the equivalent conditions for foreign companies.

The liability of certification service providers is proposed at articles 16-18, but a new article 59a, is to be introduced into the Civil Code making the owner of a signature key liable in damages to any third party which relies on their certificate. Only if the owner can prove that they kept the key confidential will they be excused from this.

(xxviii)   United Kingdom

The regulatory regime in the United Kingdom is possibly the most limited in the European Union. There is no obligation upon certification service providers to be registered or approved before beginning operations, whether or not they issue qualified certificates, nor is there any obligation to notify after beginning operations although the   **9–051**

Secretary of State for Trade and Industry is required to keep a register of those certification service providers which issue qualified certificates to the public, of which he or she is aware.[158] Where the Secretary of State becomes aware of any conduct of such a certification service provider which appears detrimental to the interests of either subscribers or relying parties, he or she may publish evidence of this. No other state supervision is contemplated.

Certification service providers' liability is provided for in the same circumstances as those set out in Article 6 of the Directive, with the addition of liability for failure to include in a qualified certificate all of the information stipulated in Annex I of the Directive.[159] This may have been considered necessary since a certificate which does not meet the requirements for a qualified certificate is arguably not a qualified certificate and an advanced electronic signature based upon it may not obtain the benefit of legal effect which is intended. A duty of care is imposed upon certification service providers which issue qualified certificates with respect to parties relying upon certificates they have issued, clarifying that as a matter of law a certification service provider will be liable at least in tort for any damage such a party suffers. The standard of care required may be tested by reference to the standards imposed upon certification service providers by Annex II of the Directive.[160] It is also specified that the certification service provider has to prove absence of negligence even if there is no proof that the certification service provider was negligent.

9–052   The accreditation system established in the UK is known as the tScheme,[161] which is an industry-run scheme set up by a consortium of industry bodies including the Confederation of British Industry and the Computer Services and Software Industry Association. Under section 16(4) of the Electronic Communications Act 2000, the government is prepared to leave the administration of accreditation to the tScheme for 5 years. If the scheme is functioning effectively at the end of that time the government's power to establish its own accreditation scheme under the Act will lapse.

Accreditation under the scheme enables a certification service provider to display a quality mark showing that their services have been approved. Assessment for approval under the tScheme is delegated to a list of approved assessors of which the applicant chooses one. The assessment is then repeated on a yearly basis for so long as the certification service provider wishes to remain a member of the scheme,[162] and the tScheme is contractually entitled to inspect the certification service provider's premises, staff and documents.[163] There is however no mention of access to the certification service provider's computer systems. Failure to meet the required standards can lead to withdrawal of the right to display the quality mark, subject to a right of appeal to an independent expert appointed (in default of agreement by the parties) by the British Computer Society.[164]

B.   ASIA / PACIFIC

(i)   Australia

9–053   The Electronic Transactions Act 1999 does not include any provisions relating to the regulation of certification service providers.

(ii)   Bangladesh

9–054   The draft Information Technology Act produced in 2002 would establish a licensing regime for certification service providers, including the potential recognition of foreign certification service providers. The timetable for the introduction of this Bill to Parliament is not known.

(iii)   China[165]

There are no regulations concerning certification authorities at state level, but certification service providers have been being set up to provide trust services to individuals or entities in Shanghai, Beijing, Guangzhou, Shenzhen, Hainan and other cities since the end of 1999. At the same time, banks and other financial industries have set up certification service provider systems to provide trust services to their clients.[166]   **9–055**

Some provincial governments have enacted regulations to govern certification services. Hainan Province led the way with Digital Certificate Rules released on August 9, 2001,[167] and Guangdong province enacted comprehensive legislation in March 2003. The rules require certification service providers to be licensed by the provincial industry regulator, the Administration for Industry and Commerce, as are all businesses in China. Further, before issuing a certificate to a subscriber the certification service provider must verify both their legal capacity and their creditworthiness.[168]

(iv)   Hong Kong

Unrecognised certification authorities are permitted to operate under the Electronic Transactions Ordinance, but the certificates they issue will not confer legal effect on the digital signatures certified unless the common law permits. A recognized certification authority can apply[169] to have its certificates recognized, which will confer legal effect on the digital signatures they support.   **9–056**

Recognition is thus voluntary, but highly desirable.[170] A certification authority must apply to the Director of Information Technology Services for recognition setting out its financial status, its arrangements for any potential liabilities, security arrangements and the procedures it uses to issue certificates. The application must also confirm that the authority and its officers are fit and proper persons.[171] An audit report prepared by someone acceptable to the Director is required unless the Director waives this, which he may if the certification authority is established abroad with a status comparable to that of a Hong Kong recognised certification authority—including recognition by the competent authority of domicile.[172]

To be recognised, a certification authority other than the Hong Kong Postmaster General[173] must use trustworthy systems, maintain an online publicly accessible directory of certificates, and comply with a code of practice issued by the Director of Information Technology Services. "Trustworthy" is defined in section 2 as: **9–057**

"computer hardware, software and procedures that-

   (a)   are reasonably secure from intrusion and misuse;

   (b)   are at a reasonable level in respect of availability, reliability and ensuring a correct mode of operations for a reasonable period of time;

   (c)   are reasonably suited for performing their intended function; and

   (d)   adhere to generally accepted security principles."

Once recognised, a certification authority's exposure is limited to any reliance limit specified in a certificate[174] (unless recognition is suspended or revoked under section 26) provided that they have complied with all material provisions of the Ordinance and the code of practice and have not been negligent—even where loss is caused by false or forged digital signatures cased upon certificates which they have issued. Continued recognition is subject to providing an annual compliance report by an approved person.

Section 46 of the Ordinance imposes an obligation of secrecy upon certification authorities and their employees in respect of the information provided by subscribers, except as regards criminal proceedings. Disclosure in breach of this provision can attract up to 6 months' imprisonment and a fine.

(v) India

9–058   Under the Information Technology Act, the operation of certification service providers is heavily regulated down to a fine level of detail such as the form in which applications for a certificate must be made. Certifying authorities must be licensed by the Controller of Certifying Authorities,[175] which can specify, amongst a long list of others, the standards to be maintained by certifying authorities, employees' qualifications, form for accounts and auditing. The Controller is also responsible for supervising their activities, including inspecting their computer systems when he has reasonable cause to suspect that the Act is being contravened,[176] and resolving conflicts of interest, and certifying their public keys.[177]

The Act caps the fees which may be charged for the issue of a digital signature certificate at 25,000 rupees (~€480).

A certifying authority may suspend a certificate for up to 15 days upon request of the subscriber or their authorised agent, or if it is of the opinion that the certificate should be suspended in the public interest.[178] No limitations are placed upon the factors which might cause a certifying authority to form such an opinion. It may revoke a certificate on request or death, dissolution or insolvency of the subscriber, or if it is of the opinion that a material fact represented in the certificate is false or has been concealed, another requirement for issuance was not satisfied, or its own private key or security system has been materially compromised.[179] However, the subscriber has a right to an opportunity to be heard before their certificate is revoked. There is no provision for suspension pending any representations by the subscriber, which may lead to potentially invalid certificates remaining in effect for a considerable time.

There are no special provisions governing certification service providers' liability or any limitations upon it.

Publishing false certificates is punishable by up to two years' imprisonment or a fine of 10,000 rupees (~€192).[180]

(vi) Indonesia

9–059   A draft Electronic Transactions and Electronic Signatures Bill was prepared in 2002 but was still in draft form at the end of the year.

(vii) Japan

9–060   The Japanese Law Concerning Electronic Signatures and Certification Services defines a certification service as a service of confirming that the item used to confirm that the user has performed an electronic signature—*i.e.* a public key—belongs to the user.[181]

There are no requirements for licensing or authorisation to begin functioning as a certification service provider, but certification service providers (including foreign entities) may apply to the Ministry of International Trade and Industry or Ministry of Posts and Telecommunications, to be accredited as designated certification service providers. To become accredited, they (including individual directors) must have no criminal record for an imprisonable offence either in Japan or elsewhere, and have not incurred a penalty or had an accreditation revoked under this Law within the last two years.[182] In addition, foreign certification service providers may be recognised under a bilateral or multilateral agreement. Accreditation requires conformity with the prescribed standards for hardware and software and for ascertaining the identity of the subscriber. Once accredited a certification service provider can use an accreditation mark on its certificates.[183] If an accredited certification service provider intends to cease operations it must give the relevant Minister immediate notice of the decision.[184]

Accredited certification service providers are subject to investigation including on-site inspections by a person or body designated by the relevant Ministry, which may be a private entity. The directors and employees of such an entity are deemed public officials for the purpose of the investigation and are subject to a duty of confidentiality.[185] The regulation of such entities occupies a significant proportion of the Law.[186]

There are no provisions limiting the liability of certification service providers, whether accredited or otherwise.

(viii) Malaysia

The Malaysian Digital Signature Act of 1997 was a very early example of national electronic signature legislation. It takes the prescriptive, regulatory approach and appears in many respects to have been based upon the seminal Utah Digital Signature Act. **9–061**

All certification authorities (defined as persons which issue certificates) need to be licensed by the Controller of Certification Authorities under section 4 of the Act on pain of a fine of up to 500,000 ringgit (€119,700). However, the Minister can exempt an entity from the licensing requirement on application from a certification authority operating solely within an organization, or such other classes of person as the Minister considers fit.[187] A significant level of regulation applies to both licensed and unlicensed certification authorities.

A certificate issued by an unlicensed certification authority (which is not permitted to call itself a certification authority)[188] may still be sufficient since a digital signature may be valid without any certification at all. An unlicensed a certification authority will not benefit from the limits on liability provided to licensed certification authorities, and the signature will not benefit from the presumption of validity for digital signatures affixed with the intention of signing and supported by certificates issued by licensed certification authorities.[189] Unlicensed certification authorities are subject to investigation by the Controller in the same manner as licensed certification authorities,[190] and to the same prohibition on conducting their business in such a manner as to create an "unreasonable risk of loss" (undefined). The penalty for so doing appears to be limited to the publication of an advisory statement by the Controller.[191]

Licensed certification authorities must use trustworthy systems,[192] which must be independently audited annually either by an accountant or computer security expert. By issuing a certificate a licensed certification service provider is taken to give various warranties to subscribers and relying parties as to the completeness and accuracy of the information in the certificate.[193] Licensed certification authorities must include a **9–062** recommended reliance limit in the certificates which they issue, but as a result benefit from limitations on their liability to that limit. Licensed certification authorities also cannot be held liable for losses due to false or forged signatures if they have complied with the Act, or for punitive or exemplary damages or damages for pain or suffering.[194]

The definition of certify in the Malaysian Act includes a duty upon the certifier to apprise themselves of all material facts, and certificates may only be issued upon taking all reasonable measures to check the proper identification of the subscriber.[195] This imposes a duty of active investigation of potential subscribers upon certification service providers operating in Malaysia. Once the certificate has been issued, the certification authority must have the application certified by a notary public.[196]

Unusually, a licensed certification authority may hold a subscriber's private key and use it as a fiduciary with the subscriber's prior written approval.[197] A certification authority may suspend a certificate for 48 hours on request of the subscriber or a person in a position such that they are likely to know of any compromise to the keys, or by order of the Controller.[198] A certificate may be revoked again on request, but subject to confirming that the requestor is the subscriber or an authorised agent. A certificate must also be revoked on the subscriber's death or dissolution, or if the certificate becomes unreliable. The validity of certificates is limited to three years.[199]

The Government can recognise foreign certification authorities if they satisfy the requirements of the Act, in which case the benefits of licensing apply equally to them.[200]

There are also provisions concerning the regulation of repository services and date or time-stamping services.[201]

(ix) New Zealand

9–063   There are no provisions in the New Zealand legislation relating to the supervision or accreditation of certification service providers, or the apportionment of liability.

(x) Pakistan

9–064   No prior notification or approval is required for certification service providers to begin operations in Pakistan, but they are prohibited from claiming to be accredited unless they hold a valid accreditation certificate from the Certification Council, which is established for this purpose.[202] The Certification Council will produce regulations setting out the terms and conditions for accreditation and act as a repository for all accreditation certificates and also certificates and certification practice statements issued by accredited certification service providers. It is also able to recognize or accredit foreign certification service providers.[203]

If a certification service provider issues a false certificate or fails to revoke one on finding (or when it ought reasonably to have known from the circumstances) that it is false commits an offence for which it may have to pay compensation and its officers may be imprisoned or fined.[204]

There are no provisions for any limitations on certification service providers' liability, but the Certification Council is empowered to make regulations to this effect.[205]

(xi) Philippines

9–065   The Philippines Act does not include any regulatory framework for certification service providers, leaving all issues as regards certification—which is not required by the Act—

to the contracts between providers and their subscribers, and as regards third parties to the general principles of tort.

(xii)   Singapore

The Singaporean Electronic Transactions Act specifies the duties of certification authorities in detail,[206] including the requirement to use trustworthy systems and minimum checks to be carried out before issuing a certificate to a prospective subscriber. A Controller of Certification Authorities is appointed for the purpose of overseeing and licensing certification authorities. The Act itself does not specify that certification authorities must be licensed, but the Controller is empowered to make regulations concerning licensing. The Controller may also recognize foreign certification authorities.[207]

9–066

The Act specifies that reliance on certificates is foreseeable, prefiguring liability by certification authorities in tort for any damage caused to third parties by such reliance. By issuing a certificate the certification authority is taken to represent to third parties that the information in the certificate is accurate and the certification authority has no knowledge of any material fact which would affect the reliability of the representations in the certificate.[208] Creation or publication of a certificate for an unlawful purpose is an offence attracting a prison sentence of up to two years, and/or a fine up to S$20,000 (€10,233).

Section 29(2)(d) requires a certification authority to confirm that the subscriber rightfully holds the private key corresponding to the public key to be listed in the certificate, unless it has a certification practice statement with which it has complied. This suggests that in these circumstances the certification authority must generate the key pair itself, since there is no obvious means by which the concept of rightful ownership can otherwise be applied to personally generated keys. A certification authority must suspend a certificate upon request by a person the authority reasonably believes to be the subscriber, their duly authorised agent or a person acting on their behalf. Similarly, a certificate must be revoked on request, although the certification authority must confirm that the requestor is the subscriber or an authorised agent. A certificate must also be revoked upon the death or dissolution of the signatory.[209] The authority must also revoke upon confirming that any material fact in the certificate is false, or a requirement for issuance was not satisfied, or upon any material compromise of its own key or systems. In either case, the authority must publish a signed notice of the suspension or revocation immediately in its repository.[210] There is no independent requirement to suspend or revoke based upon the certification authority's own information concerning the subscriber's key security.

9–067

A licensed certification authority must specify a recommended reliance limit in the certificates it issues.[211] It is then not liable for reliance beyond that limit, whatever the circumstances, or for loss due to reliance on a false or forged digital signature provided the certification authority had complied with the Act.[212]

The Controller has power to investigate any certification authority, including access to the premises, records and computer systems it uses. Certification authorities must assist in any such investigation upon pain of a fine of up to S$20,000 and/or 12 months' imprisonment.[213] Curiously, the investigators are subject to an obligation of confidentiality in respect of the information they access but there is no equivalent express provision in respect of the certification authorities' own personnel.

(xiii)   South Korea

9–068   The South Korea Digital Signature Act does not expressly prohibit certification authorities providing services without being licensed, but makes no provision for their certificates to have any effect.

Licensing and supervision of certification authorities is by the Minister of Information and Communication, which has investigatory powers of entry to premises and examination of systems, books and records for this purpose.[214] Licensed certification authorities are required to use a public key which is certified by the Korean Information Security Agency (KISA).[215] A certification practice statement must be filed with the Minister before beginning operations. No entity any of whose officers are bankrupt, lacks legal capacity, has had a sentence of imprisonment less than two years ago or is still under a suspended sentence or has been an officer of a certification authority whose licence was revoked less than two years ago, may be licensed.

Once licensed, certification authorities are prohibited from discriminating against subscribers or refusing to provide certification services without a valid reason. However, they must verify an applicant's identity taking into account the scope of intended use of the certificate.[216]

9–069   The Minister also supervises mergers, acquisitions and suspension or cessation of business by licensed certification authorities. On ceasing business a certification authority must transfer its existing certificates and records to another licensed certification authority or, if this cannot be done, to KISA. Subscribers must be given 60 days' notice.

It is left to the individual certification authorities to decide how long a certificate may be valid. A certificate may be suspended by request of the subscriber or his or her agent, for up to six months, and must be revoked upon request by the same, or upon the certification authority becoming aware that the subscriber has died, been judicially declared missing or dissolved, that the private key has been compromised or that the certificate was issued through fraud or otherwise wrongfully.[217] A licensed certification authority may hold a subscriber's private key by their request.

Certification records must be retained for at least 10 years after expiry of the relevant certificate.[218] A licensed certification authority is liable for damages incurred either by subscribers or relying parties unless resulting from force majeure or the relying party's intent or negligence.[219]

Data protection provisions prohibit the collection of personal data beyond the minimum necessary for carrying out certification services, and to data collected with the data subject's consent. The information can only be used or disclosed for any purpose other than certification practice when required by law or with the data subject's consent.[220]

(xiv)   Sri Lanka

9–070   Sri Lanka not yet introduced any relevant legislation at the time of writing.

(xv)   Thailand

9–071   The Thai Act itself does not include any requirement for electronic transaction service providers to be registered or even notified to the government, but does provide for possible secondary legislation in the form of a Royal Decree to introduce such requirements. Once such requirements are introduced, failure to notify, register or obtain a licence will be publishable by imprisonment and/or a fine of up to 200,000 Baht (~€4,239), which may be applied not only to the enterprise but to its managing directors or other senior officers. Further, an Electronic Transactions Commission was established by the Act which is responsible for monitoring the operations of businesses providing electronic transactions services.

C. NORTH AMERICA

(i) Canada

There are no provisions at Federal level relating to the establishment or supervision of certification service providers.   **9–072**

There is also nothing in the Uniform Electronic Commerce Act dealing with any regulation of certification service providers, since the Act does not contemplate the business model of third party certification for electronic signatures. The national government has however established a public key infrastructure allowing the provision of electronic commerce and confidentiality services to public servants. There was also a proposal in 1998 that certification authorities should not be permitted to operate in Canada unless they provide access for the police to plaintext when served with a Court Order, but this does not appear in the Act.

(ii) Mexico

There is no specific legislation to date in Mexico dealing with the regulation of certification service providers.   **9–073**

(iii) United States of America

There are no provisions at Federal level relating to the regulation of certification service providers. However, many states have enacted their own electronic signature legislation, often incorporating detailed provisions concerning certification service providers either directly or through implementing rules. There is a wide range of approaches, which space does not permit to be addressed in their entirety. The most comprehensive and restrictive is the Utah Digital Signature Act (the Utah Act),[221] which is therefore discussed below by way of example. Since enactment of the Utah Act, some other states have enacted legislation substantially based on or derived from the Utah model; others have chosen more liberal approaches.   **9–074**

Most, but not all, of the obligations imposed on a certification service provider under the Utah Act apply only to licensed certification service providers; becoming licensed is optional.

In issuing a certificate a licensed certification service provider must confirm that the prospective subscriber is the person to be listed in the certificate, that the prospective subscriber rightfully holds the private key to be listed in the certificate and that the information in the certificate is accurate after due diligence.[222] This requirement cannot be waived or disclaimed.[223] Licensed certification service providers must also undertake to revoke certificates within one day upon receiving a confirmed request for revocation.[224]   **9–075**

Licensed certification service providers are also required to use only trustworthy systems and to disclose their certification practice statements.[225]

Failure to comply with these requirements could result in an investigation by the agency responsible for carrying out and enforcing the Utah Act (the Division). Depending upon the result of the investigation, licence restrictions could be imposed, the licence could be revoked or, ultimately, the certification service provider could be prosecuted.[226]

Licensed or unlicensed certification service providers which conduct their business in a manner that creates "an unreasonable risk of loss" to subscribers, relying parties or repositories could be subject to injunctive or other civil relief as requested by the Division (though there is no private right of action under this provision).[227] What constitutes an unreasonable risk of loss is not defined.

9–076   A licensed certification service provider is deemed to give various statutory warranties to subscribers upon issuing a certificate. These include that the certificate contains no information known to the certification service provider to be false and that the certificate satisfies all material requirements of the Utah Act.[228]

A licensed certification service provider is also deemed to make various statutory representations unless agreed otherwise: that it will act promptly to suspend or revoke a certificate and that it will notify the subscriber within a reasonable time of any facts known to it which significantly affect the validity or reliability of the certificate.[229] The certification service provider represents to all parties who reasonably rely on the certificate that the information in the certificate which is listed as confirmed by the certification service provider is accurate, that all information foreseeably material to the reliability of the certificate is stated or incorporated by reference, and that the subscriber has accepted the certificate.[230]

By accepting a certificate, subscribers undertake to indemnify the issuing certification service provider for loss or damage caused by an intentional or negligent material misrepresentation or failure to disclose.[231] Whether this indemnity will in practice be adequate is a separate question.

9–077   Under the Utah Digital Signature Administrative Rules (the Utah Rules), certification service providers are required to maintain records to show their compliance with the Utah Act and regarding the issuance, acceptance and any suspension or revocation of a certificate for at least ten years after the certificate is revoked or expires. The consequence of failing to comply with this rule is not specified.

A certification service provider must give subscribers at least 90 days' written notice[232] and the Division at least two months' written notice[233] before ceasing to act as a certification service provider and pay reasonable restitution to subscribers for revoking unexpired certificates. These time limits may be modified by contract, to a minimum of ten days' written notice before ceasing to act.[234]

9–078   A certification service provider which serves as a repository for publishing the certificates it issues, for posting notices of suspended or revoked certificates and for posting certification authority disclosure records, will be subject to the liability provisions concerning repositories. These provide that "a repository is liable for a loss incurred by a person reasonably relying on a digital signature verified by the public key listed in a suspended or revoked certificate if: (a) the loss was incurred more than one business day after receipt by the repository of a request to publish notice of the suspension or revocation; and (b) the repository had failed to publish the notice of suspension or revocation when the person relied on the digital signature."[235] This potential liability cannot be disclaimed by contract.[236]

A *recognized* repository's exposure is limited in various circumstances, including where the loss arises from a misrepresentation in a certificate published by a licensed certification service provider, for accurately reporting information which a licensed certification service provider has published, and to the amount specified in the certificate as the recommended reliance limit.[237]

A licensed certification service provider is not liable for damages above any amount specified in the certificate as its recommended reliance limit,[238] or for punitive or exemplary damages, lost profits, saving, or opportunity; or pain or suffering.[239] Nor is a certification service provider liable for any loss caused by reliance on a false or forged digital signature or a subscriber if the certification service provider complied with all material requirements of the Utah Act.[240] Liability is also limited to the cases where the relying party's reliance was reasonable.[241]

D.   LATIN AMERICA

(i)   Argentina

The Argentinian law does not require prior licensing for an entity to function as a   **9–079**
certification authority as such, but only digital certificates issued by licensed certification authorities are valid and so support valid digital signatures.[242]

The system of licensing of certification authorities is overseen by an Application Authority which also has responsibility for laying down operating and technical standards for the Argentinian PKI.[243] These are to be devised by a PKI Commission, whose members are appointed for a five year period.

To be licensed, a certification authority must be Argentinian and comply with regulations laid down by the Licensing Authority including submission of a manual of procedures and details of its information systems and security arrangements. It must obtain only those personal data which are necessary for the issue of a certificate, keep any not included in the certificate confidential and retain data relating to a certificate for 10 years after its revocation or expiry. It must maintain a certificate revocation list permanently accessible on the Internet or other publicly accessible network and must also keep accessible its certification policies and practice statement, which must be approved by the Licensing Authority. It must use trustworthy information systems, employ personnel having the specialist knowledge and expertise in both technical (including security) and managerial matters, and keep its own private key within its exclusive control.

Certification authorities are subject to a periodic audit of the reliability and quality of   **9–080**
their information systems, their compliance with their certification practice statements and the integrity, confidentiality and availability of their records, either by the Application Authority or third parties authorised by it.

For a breach of its obligations, a licensed certification authority can be fined between A$10,000 and A$500,000, as well as having its licence revoked for security lapses, issuing false certificates, an unauthorised transfer of its licence or insolvency.

A licensed certification authoritiy's liability is excluded where the certificate is used outside its terms and conditions, or if the certificate is used in an unauthorised way or for inaccuracies in the data provided to it by the subscriber provided that it has taken all reasonable measures to verify the data.[244]

A licensed certification authority must inform a subscriber of the terms of use of a certificate and its own procedures, before issuing the certificate. The relationship between certification authority and subscriber is regulated by the terms of the contract between them, subject to the terms of the Decree. It must revoke a certificate upon request of the holder, or if it appears that the certificate was issued based upon false information, or upon any conditions specified in its certification policy, or by order of the Administrative Authority or the court.[245]

(ii)   Brazil

9–081   Brazil launched a public key infrastructure system in February 2002, based upon its Provisional Measure No. 2.200 of June 2001. This is intended to ensure that electronic documents may be digitally signed with legal effect in communications both between private parties and with public administration. The Provisional Measure established a Governing Committee, which will make policy and adopt regulations laying down the licensing arrangements and operational requirements for certification authorities.[246]

There is also a root certification authority which in turn will register certification companies, whose operations will be supervised by the National Institute of Information Technology (NIIT). NIIT will lay down regulations specifying the procedures and checks to be used by certification companies in order to become accredited. A highly prescriptive system appears to be envisaged, with a detailed regulatory and supervision regime for certification authorities.

Registration with the root certification authority is a pre-condition to issuing digital certificates, and a certification authority's operational rules will have to be approved by the root authority.

(iii)   Chile

9–082   Under the Chilean Law on Electronic Documents and Signatures and Certification Services, certification services may only be provided by legal, not natural, persons, but may be either domestic or foreign, although the latter may need to be guaranteed by a domestic certification service provider.[247] To be accredited, the service provider must also: be registered with the Ministry for the Economy, Reconstruction and Development, which is responsible for supervising the activities of certification service providers; be domiciled in Chile; be able to show the necessary means and resources to grant certificates; and maintain insurance against damages for civil responsibility of at least US$115,000.[248] Certification service providers are also subject to Chilean law on consumer and data protection.

A certification authority will in general be liable in damages for loss resulting from their services unless they can show that they acted with proper diligence. However, a certification authority will not be liable for loss due to:

- the undue or fraudulent use of a certificate; or

- use in excess of any limit recognizably included in the certificate.[249]

Certificates can be valid for up to three years, but must be revoked on request or death/ dissolution of the holder, by judicial order or on breach by the subscriber of its obligations under Article 24, namely to submit true and complete information in support of the application for a certificate and to keep it up to date, and to keep the certificate secure. The certificate also ceases to be effective if the certification service provider's accreditation is revoked. A certificate holder has the right to be informed immediately if this occurs, and to have the data they provide to the certification authority kept confidential.[250] However, no penalties are specified for a certification service provider which fails to comply with these obligations.

An additional requirement is imposed on a certifying authority granting a certificate to support an advanced electronic signature, to verify the subscriber's identity for certain using a method including the personal appearance of the subscriber before the certification authority or a notary or court official.[251] The certifying authority will not be liable for damages arising from misuse of the certificate, but may otherwise be liable for damages for any loss resulting from the performance of their services unless they can show that they were not negligent.[252]

9–083

On ceasing operations, a certification authority must transfer the records of the current certificates it has issued to another certification authority and inform all subscribers at least two months beforehand. If any subscriber objects to the transfer, the relevant certificate expires.[253]

Accreditation requires demonstrating that the certification service provider has suitable information systems, human resources and software and provides a reliable certificate revocation list. An Accreditation Company is charged with accreditation and supervision of accredited certification service providers.

(iv)   Colombia

The Colombian Law 527 of 1999 governs the regulation of certification service providers in general, and a further Decree, 1747 of 2000, lays down detailed provisions relating to certification service providers' operations and audits.

9–084

Only legal persons can function as certification service providers, and must be authorized by the supervising authority of Industry and Commerce. Authorisation requires demonstrating adequate financial and technical capacity. Further, no administrative or legal representative must have been convicted of an imprisonable offence other than a political crime, or suspended from practice of their profession for ethical reasons.[254]

Foreign certification service providers' certificates may be recognised by a reciprocal agreement with a Colombian certification service provider.[255] The supervising authority of Industry and Commerce is responsible for accreditation and supervision, and accordingly has the right to audit. The supervising authority's permission is also necessary for a certification service provider to cease operations.[256]

Certification service providers must retain records relating to certificates they issue for the period of time stipulated in the law regulating relevant area of business.

Decree 1747 of 2000 also gives the supervising authority the power to determine the technical standards to which certification service providers must conform in matters such as certificate formats, information system security and key pair generation.

9–085

A certificate will be revoked on the subscriber's request, death or liquidation, upon finding that the information contained in the certificate is false, if the certification service provider's own security system is compromised, upon the certification service provider ceasing operations (of which 90 days' notice must be given to subscribers) or by judicial order.[257] Revocation must be published immediately, and the subscriber informed within 24 hours.

There are no provisions limiting certification service providers' liability; certification service providers are expressly liable for all damage which they cause in the exercise of their activities.[258]

(v) Ecuador

9–086 Certification service providers must be authorized in order to operate in Ecuador under the Law on Electronic Commerce, Signatures and Data Messages.[259] The National Council of Telecommunications, CONATEL, is responsible for authorising and supervising certification service providers, including by audit,[260] and is also given the power to lay down regulations governing the recognition in Ecuador of certificates issued by foreign certification service providers.[261] It can issue administrative penalties of up to US$6,000 for breach of regulations.[262]

Accredited certification service providers must be able to demonstrate financial, technical and logistic reliability, and must maintain a certificate status list. A certification service provider must carry a guarantee to cover its potential liabilities for breach of its obligations under the law which, where it issues certificates with a limited value of use, must be not less than 5per cent of the total value of certificates issued.[263]

An accredited certification service provider is liable for any damage as a result of its breach of its obligations under the law or of its negligence, as well as for use of a certificate outside its value range unless the limit was indicated clearly in the certificate itself.[264] The burden of proof is on the certification service provider in respect of all claims to limited liability. If the certification service provider's guarantee is inadequate to cover its liabilities it must draw upon its share capital.

A foreign accredited certification service provider may have its certificates recognised in Ecuador if an Ecuadorean certification company guarantees the certificates.

A certification service provider must keep all personal data of its subscribers confidential.[265] At least 90 days' notice must be given to CONATEL of an intention to cease operations. Subscriber agreements are subject to the Ecuadorean Consumer Protection Act.[266]

(vi) Peru

9–087 A system of registration of certification companies is contemplated by the Peruvian law on Signatures and Digital Certificates, but this does not appear to include the detailed supervision and audit contemplated by many other Latin American countries' legislation.

An administrative authority is to be specified by decree which will register certification service providers. The authority is intended to function at least as a directory identifying certification service providers.[267] There is no reference to any system of licensing or accreditation. However, additional functions may be specified for the administrative authority in the decree which establishes it, and as a minimum the registration authority is given the power to approve methods of electronic signature other than digital signature as complying with the requirement of the law[268] so something more than a purely informational service would appear to be contemplated.

Certification companies are permitted to obtain personal data only directly from their subscribers, and must keep it confidential unless ordered to disclose it by court order.[269] A certificate must be revoked if the certificate company discovers that the information it contains is false or has been modified, or if the holder dies or breaches any term of the subscriber agreement.[270] A certificate can also be cancelled on request of the holder.

There are no provisions relating to the liability of certification service providers.

(vii) Venezuela

9–088 The Venezuelan Data Message and Electronic Signatures Law governs the regulation of certification service providers.

A system of accreditation of certification service providers is supervised by a government agency, the Superintendent of Electronic Certification Services in the Department of Science and Technology,[271] which also supervises certification service provider activities, including by inspection of operations, and mediates disputes between certification service providers and their users.[272] It is also responsible for coordination with national or international agencies.

There is no obligation for certification service providers to be accredited before beginning operations.[273] Certification service providers must however be registered. Certification service providers must maintain an appropriate financial and technical capability, including a "quick and sure" certificate suspension or revocation mechanism, a free access certificate revocation list and certificate issuance mechanisms which comply with international standards. Falsely claiming to be accredited can incur a fine of up to 5,000 tax units.

Accreditation does not provide any benefits in terms of reduced liability; rather, an **9–089** accredited certification service provider must provide a guarantee to the supervisory agency to cover all damages either contractual or otherwise of both signatories and parties which rely upon a certificate in good faith, which arise from any deceitful act or culpable omission by the employees or agents of the certification service provider. There is no exclusion of any other form of liability. Certification service providers may be companies established under Venezuelan or foreign laws.[274]

Certification service providers must verify subscribers' identities before issuing a certificate, and also provide a medium for subscribers to notify any unauthorised use of a certificate. They must guarantee the integrity, availability and accessibility of their registry information and also maintain a certificate revocation list. There is no limit put upon the time permitted for updating this, however.

The holder of a certificate can request cancellation or suspension of the certificate, which may also be suspended by order of a competent legal authority, if any of the data supplied in the application is verified to be false, if the subscriber breaches any major obligation of the subscriber agreement or on any breach of the certification service provider's system security which may affect the integrity and reliability of the certificate.[275]

Any certification service provider must also notify the supervisory agency of an intention to cease operations 30 days before it takes place. The supervisory agency will then direct such measures as may be necessary to publicise the fact of termination and to guarantee the conservation of necessary information.[276] Certification service providers must ordinarily keep records relating to the certificates they have issued for ten years after the expiry of the certificate.[277]

E.   REST OF THE WORLD

(i)   Russian Federation

Certification centres which wish to operate in Russia must be licensed under the Federal **9–090** Law on Electronic Digital Signatures prior to beginning operations.[278] They must possess the financial resources necessary to bear civil liability towards relying parties for losses suffered as a result of inaccurate information in certificates; these are to be laid down by regulations. Certification centres are subject to supervision by a federal agency, to which they must submit a copy of the certificate for their own signature for authentication of certificates, in both electronic and paper form, for entry in the register.[279]

A certification centre must provide a copy of each certificate it issues authenticated with the manual signature of the signatory and an official of the centre, to the signatory on issue. It retains an identical copy itself.[280] If the technology used loses its certification, all certificates issued under it must be annulled. Licensed certification centres must be insured against any civil damages which arise as a result of inaccurate data being attributed to a digital signature.

Certificates must be suspended on request by the signatory, or upon instruction by any person or body which has the legal right to give such instructions (which presumably includes the supervisory agency or the Courts). A maximum period for effecting suspension is to be set by regulations.[281] Certificates will be annulled on expiry, on written application by the signatory or if the certification centre is reliably informed that a document used as a basis for issuing the certificate has lost its validity.[282] The certificate's annulment must then be entered in the certificate register.

The certification centre must store records relating to the certificate for the period stipulated under Russian law for document retention in the class of business for which the certificate is to be used, followed by five years' archival storage.[283] Upon ceasing operations, all certificates not transferred to another certification centre are annulled and transferred to the supervisory agency for storage.

(ii)   South Africa

9–091   Cryptography providers are required by the Electronic Communications Transactions Act to be registered with the Department of Communications.[284]

Certification service providers who do not provide encryption services are not required to be registered but may apply for voluntary accreditation by the Director-General of Communications.[285] If not accredited, they are not subject to any form of supervision. Accreditation does not affect the status of any signature supported by a certificate issued.

If accredited, they are then referred to in the Act as authentication service providers. Accreditation is subject to satisfying the Director-General that the hardware and software systems and procedures are reasonably secure from intrusion and misuse, provide a reasonable level of availability, reliability and correct operation, are reasonably suited to performing their intended functions and adhere to generally accepted security procedures. They must also demonstrate the quality of their financial and human resources and external audit.[286] The Director-General may promulgate regulations stipulating matters such as the technical requirements for certificates, the responsibilities and liability of certification service providers, the records to be kept and for how long they must be kept, certificate suspension and revocation requirements.[287] The Minister may also recognise foreign accreditations.[288] Accredited or recognised authentication service providers are subject to inspection by the cyber inspectors of the Department of Communications, which include the power to search premises and information systems and request records.[289]

There are no provisions in the Act limiting the liability of any category of certification service provider.

(iii)   Israel

9–092   Only a Certification Authority approved by the Israeli Certification Authority Registrar (an organ of the Ministry of Justice) can issue an electronic certificate required for the creation of a Certified Electronic Signature. Among the provisions that have to be fulfilled by an applicant to be registered as a Certification Authority by the Israeli Certification Authority Registrar are that:

(1)   the applicant is a citizen or resident of Israel, a company incorporated in Israel or a Public Corporation or other Public Entity established by law, whose place of business or activity is in Israel and among whose objectives is conducting business or activity as a Certification Authority;

(2)   the applicant possesses trustworthy hardware and software systems that provide reasonable protection from penetration, disruption, interference, or damage to a computer or to computer material and provide a reasonable level of availability and reliability;

(3)   the applicant has filed a bank guarantee or other suitable guarantee or insured itself, as prescribed by the Registrar, to ensure compensation for anyone suffering damage due to an act or omission of the Certification Authority;

(4)   the applicant has registered its Electronic Certificate databases as databases under the Protection of Privacy Law, 5741-1981; and

(5)   neither the applicant nor its intended manager has been convicted of any crime and, if the applicant is a corporation, no acting director or controlling shareholder has been convicted of a crime.

The Registrar may impose additional terms for registration.

The Law also allows the Certification Authority Registrar to recognize as a Certification Authority any non-Israeli authority, provided that the Registrar finds that it fulfills conditions similar to those required by the Law.

A Certification Authority must not issue an electronic certificate unless it has taken **9–093** reasonable measures to identify the requestor of such certificate, to check his/its signature verification device, and to ensure that the information in the application for issuance of a certificate is accurate and complete. In addition, a Certification Authority is required to maintain a database of the electronic certificates it issues, as well as a database of revoked electronic certificates.

A registered Certification Authority will not be held liable for any damage caused by reliance on an electronic certificate that it has issued, if it shows that all reasonable measures have been taken to assure the fulfillment of its obligations.

The circumstances in which a certificate should be revoked are specified, including upon request by or death or liquidation of the owner of the Certificate, immediately following receipt and verification of the requestor's identity; immediately upon discovery that any of the information in the Certificate is incorrect or that the Certificate or owner's signing device is no longer reliable for any other reason; or immediately upon discovery of any material fault with the Certification Authority's own Secure Electronic Signature or hardware or software.

Upon revocation of an Electronic Certificate, a Certification Authority shall immediately notify the owner of the Certificate thereof and shall record the revocation in a database.

Regulations enacted under the Law specify standards by which Certification Authority systems are deemed "trustworthy."

(iv)   Turkey

9–094   The Turkish government is at the time of writing in the process of preparing a draft electronic signature law. Certification service providers would be required to notify the Telecommunication Authority before beginning their activities, and would be liable for damage caused to any third party which reasonably relies upon a certificate it has issued, unless the provider can show that it was not negligent.

2.   Data protection

9–095   Certification service providers will necessarily obtain, process and store personal data about all of their subscribers. This is not subject to specific regulation in the United States, but in many other jurisdictions the amassing of such collections of data has caused concern in the context of certification service provision. Why this should be the case in countries which do not otherwise strongly regulate the use of personal data is not clear.

Within the European Union, the Data Protection Directive 1995[290] applies to all certification service providers. It is designed to secure a common level of protection of privacy for personal information throughout the Member States of the Union. Member States were required to adapt their respective national laws to conform to the Directive by July 1998. The Directive allows latitude for Member States to derogate from the Directive's terms in some respects, and the Directive itself is capable of alternative interpretations,

The Directive's objects and scope

9–096   Article 1 of the Directive states that the Directive has two related objects, namely:

–   the protection of the fundamental rights and freedoms of natural persons, and in particular their right to privacy, with respect to the processing of personal data; and

–   the prevention of restrictions on or prohibition of the free flow of personal data between Member States for reasons connected with such protection.

The Directive sets a high standard of protection, and creates a general right of informational privacy. This amounts to a civil right to object to, and to be compensated for, the unfair use of personal information which either:

–   is processed wholly or partly by automatic means; or

–   forms part of, or is intended to form part of, a filing system as defined by the Directive and is processed otherwise than by automatic means.

Article 2 of the Directive sets out definitions of terms.

"Personal data" means any information relating to an identified or identifiable natural person, and an identifiable person is one who can be identified directly or indirectly. This can include an e-mail address as much as a physical address.

"Processing" is so widely defined under the Directive as to include almost any information related activity, including use, misuse, storage or destruction of personal data as defined.

"Controller" means a person who determines the purposes and means of processing.

The Directive applies to processing of personal data wholly or partly by automatic means. It is therefore bound to apply to all activities of certification service providers operating within the European Union.[291]

Chapter II of the Directive, which deals with general rules on lawfulness of processing of personal data, includes under Article 6 principles relating to data quality. Article 7 sets out mandatory requirements for legitimate processing. These may be summarised as:

9–097

- data subject's consent given;

- processing necessary for formation or performance of a contract with a data subject or to comply with a data subject's request;

- processing necessary to comply with controller's legal obligations;

- processing necessary to protect vital interests of data subjects;

- processing necessary for performance by a controller or by a disclosee of a public interest or officially authorised task; or

- processing necessary to pursuit of controller's or a disclosee's or a third party's legitimate interests, except where such interests are overridden by the data subject's interests or fundamental rights and freedoms protected under Article 1(1).

Compliance with this basic rule should be easy for certification service providers which will only be collecting data under a contract with the data subject, and where personal data are used solely for the purpose for which they were collected, confidentially and fairly. The information should also be kept up to date, and should be made available to the respective data subjects on request. In appropriate circumstances, the information may be disclosed to tax authorities or to the police in order to comply with the controller's legal obligations. None of this seems to be in principle objectionable, once the concept of responsible and proper use of personal information is accepted.

Special rules are applied by Article 8 of the Data Protection Directive to categories of sensitive data, namely data revealing racial or ethnic origin, religious or political beliefs or trade union membership, or concerning the health or sex life of a data subject. It is possible to imagine circumstances which exaggerate the difficulty of dealing with information which discloses racial or ethnic origin, as for example names, but there are sufficient exemptions and qualifications in the Article to protect controllers against liability for these extreme interpretations and to allow Member States to legislate appropriately for such protection.

A certification service provider which wishes to use the information it collects for purposes other than performing the subscriber contract may still be able to do so with the subscriber's consent. Processing with the data subject's unambiguous consent is broad. Such consent need not necessarily be written, although clearly from the data processor's point of view written consent is preferable as being less open to later challenge, but whether written or otherwise the consent must be freely given and be an informed

9–098

indication of wishes signifying consent. If the certification service provider is unable to rely on data subject consent, it must look to one or more of the alternative grounds for legitimate processing referred to above. If none of those grounds is available, the certification service provider may risk failing to comply with the Directive by continuing to process the data, and could be exposed to potential liability, remedies and sanctions under Article 22, 23 and 24.

Articles 10 and 11 provide alternative rules for information being provided to the data subject in cases of collection of data from the data subject and for information where the data have not been obtained from the data subject. In both cases, the information required to be given to the data subject centres round the identity of the controller, the purposes of processing for which the data are intended, further information necessary to guarantee fair processing, such as categories of recipients of the data, and the existence of rights of access and rectification. However, collection by certification service providers other than directly from the data subject is prohibited by Article 8 of the Electronic Signatures Directive.

The data subject's rights and remedies

9–099 Article 12 gives a data subject rights of access to any data kept about them. Under Article 14, the data subject has the right, on compelling legitimate grounds, to object to processing except where otherwise provided by national legislation, and a right to object to processing for direct marketing purposes. Refusal to correct, suppress or block the processing of inaccurate personal data would be contrary to the data quality provisions of Article 6 and so presumably could be compelling legitimate grounds justifying an objection to continued processing.

Chapter III, on judicial remedies, liability and penalties, gives the data subject a right to compensation for damage suffered from unlawful processing or any act incompatible with national provisions implementing the Directive. The right to compensation under the Directive may extend to losses arising from the transfer of personal data to a third country, if the transfer does not comply with the Directive's provisions on the transfer of personal data to third countries set out in Chapter IV. This may be applicable to any certification service provider which has operations in more than one country, one or more of which is outside the European Union.

Despite the existence of this comprehensive data protection regime, concerns were expressed by the United Kingdom's Data Protection Registrar in her Twelfth Annual Report, in 1996, as to amassing of personal data by and supervision of certification service providers. Possibly in response to such concerns, the Electronic Signatures Directive includes[292] a restriction prohibiting certification service providers from collecting personal data except directly from the data subject or with the explicit consent of the data subject, and even then only insofar as it is necessary for the purposes of issuing and maintaining the certificate. The data may only be collected insofar as it is necessary for the purposes of issuing and maintaining a certificate, unless the data subject gives explicit consent. The regime applicable to certification service providers is therefore considerably more restrictive than that applicable to other data controllers or processors.

Outside Europe, a number of countries have included some data protection provisions in their laws governing electronic signatures and the operation of certification service providers. These are noted in the respective sections on national regulation of certification service providers above.

3. Regulation of encryption technologies as dual-use goods

Two major objections have been brought to bear on the issue of civilian access to and use   **9–100**
of encryption technology.

Military roots of cryptography

Firstly, despite the demise of the Cold War, governments still tend to harbour an anxious   **9–101**
and proprietary attitude towards encryption, which has for centuries been a key weapon
in military intelligence and counter-intelligence. It is now widely known that the breaking
of the advanced German Enigma codes by the British intelligence team under Alan Turing
at Bletchley Park was a material factor in enabling the Allied Forces to gain the advantage
in World War II. With the advent of modern computers, code-breaking became a very
much less skilled exercise, since the patience and phenomenal power of modern
computers is ideally suited to the tedious task of trying every possible code against a
given ciphertext in order to determine whether any leads to a meaningful plain text. Of
course, computers have also enabled enormous advances in cryptographic theory, and
there is so far no encryption method in existence which cannot be cracked if sufficient
time and computing resources are devoted to it. However, technology of this strength is
not something governments are happy to see in widespread use. The whole value of
possessing a strong cryptographic method is that of having an advantage over the enemy,
who cannot read the communications one encrypts while only being able to use less
strong, and therefore potentially breakable, encryption for its own communications. Once
strong cryptography is in widespread use among civilians, the chances of any country
being able to maintain this sort of advantage is materially reduced.

Cybercrime/terrorism

The second principal justification for government restrictions on encryption technology is   **9–102**
that if strong encryption is freely available, the fight against crime and terrorism will be
severely handicapped. The authorities fear that the traditional means of gathering
intelligence about criminal activities—telephone taps and so on[293]—will become obsolete
in the face of sophisticated criminal or other anti-social organisations able freely to
communicate across open networks without fear of their messages, even if intercepted,
being understood.

This justification is flawed in two respects. First, strong public key encryption is already
widely available,[294] such that any illegal organisation wishing to make use of it is either
already in a position to do so, or insufficiently competent to warrant concern. These
organisations are unlikely to cease to use encryption merely because it had been declared
illegal. Further, given the possible use of steganography[295] instead of or in addition to
encryption, the prohibition of encryption will do little to reduce the effectiveness of the
truly professional criminal or terrorist's armoury.

Second, there is minimal evidence that encryption of communications by anti-social
elements has had any substantial impact on the efficiency of the crime investigation and
prevention agencies. At the OECD ad-hoc meeting of experts on cryptography in 1996, the
US representative stated that out of 350 cases involving computer evidence, encryption
had been relevant in only 2 per cent—that is, 7 cases. It is in any case often possible to

obtain access to encrypted data without cracking the encryption algorithm—for example, unencrypted copies of the data may be present on the suspected criminal's computer, or copies of the key may be kept on floppy discs. An alternative avenue to obtaining access could be exploitation of the adverse inference as to the contents of encrypted files which may be drawn if the key is *not* made available. In many cases, this may suffice to encourage assistance with investigations; the possibility of shifting the burden of proof to the Defendant to prove that the encrypted material was not relevant could even be considered.[296]

9–103   Nevertheless, inspired to a degree by the attitude adopted by the US government in the 1990s, many governments attempt to regulate the availability and manner of use of encryption technology, or to ensure that there will be means of accessing even encrypted communications. A number of options have been proposed.

Key escrow is a system under which all legitimate users of encryption would deposit a copy of their private key with an escrow agent.[297] This may be an external "trusted third party", where communication between companies or other organisations is concerned, or within a single organisation it may be an additional function of the system administrator in respect of keys for use with corporate data or communications. It may or may not be the same entity as that which generates the keys for use in the first place.

The point of both of these approaches is to enable a higher authority to obtain access to the keys without having to get them out of the user directly. In the public sphere, those seeking access would be the intelligence and law enforcement agencies; in a corporate setting, the senior levels of the organisation. Access would be given possibly after obtaining a warrant from the courts, or through some other administrative procedure (the potential insufficiency and invalidity of which is a source of extreme concern to those who see no reason to give the government access to their communications).

9–104   Key escrow arrangements have a number of disadvantages:

–   the increased vulnerability of having multiple users' keys held in a single place,

–   users loss of control over key management;

–   the increased number of communication paths required for dealings with the archived key;

–   the inherent distrust of consumers and users generally for any potential imposed third party; and

–   the high entry cost of setting up such an arrangement in the first place.

Against these, there is the advantage of simplicity: if copies of the keys are being kept, then there are no issues relating to lack of interoperability of IT environments or non-standard storage schemes frustrating attempts at key recovery. An even simpler possibility is that of a "Trusted First Party"—which in essence is simply a legal mechanism whereby the government could force the data holder to deliver up the key through a system of subpoenas.

In the United Kingdom, this issue was originally proposed to be handled as part of the Electronic Communications Act 2000, under which it was proposed to give the Government access to stored keys, either from trusted third parties or users. This was strongly opposed by the majority of respondents to the initial Government consultation paper and so it was removed from the draft of that Act. However, a "Trusted First Party" mechanism has instead been introduced as part of the Regulation of Investigatory Powers Act 2000 (RIP Act).

The relevant portion of this Act is Part III, which despite having been on the statute book for nearly three years is still not in force. It relates to protected (*i.e.* encrypted) information which comes into any person's possession through the exercise of a statutory power to seize or otherwise interfere with documents or to intercept communications, or has otherwise come by lawful means into the possession of any of the intelligence services, the police or customs and excise.

The RIP Act gives these various authorities—the police, armed forces, customs and excise—the power to serve a notice, a "section 49 notice", on any person who is believed on reasonable grounds to have a means of accessing the information, requiring them either to produce a copy of the information in intelligible form or, if stipulated in the notice, the key.[298] Such a stipulation may only be given by a senior police officer, an officer of the rank of brigadier or above or the Commissioners of Customs and Excise.[299] Written permission from a judge is required only exceptionally[300] since in almost all cases in which information might lawfully come into a person's possession, the Secretary of State or another civil authority has the power to authorise the giving of a section 49 notice.[301]   **9–105**

Failing having either of these, the person subjected to the notice must instead give any information in their possession which would facilitate the obtaining or discovery of the key or the deciphering of the information.[302]

For such a notice to be given, the disclosure of the information must be necessary and the imposition of the notice a proportionate way of obtaining the disclosure. It is not necessary for the service of the notice to be the *only* way of obtaining the information: it need only be not reasonably practicable to obtain the information by other means, for the keyholder to be required by notice to co-operate. Further, the grounds upon which the disclosure may be considered to be necessary are extremely broad: it may be in the interests of national security, for the purpose of preventing or detecting crime, in the interests of the economic well-being of the United Kingdom or necessary for the purpose of securing the effective exercise or proper performance by any public authority of any statutory power or duty.[303] There are rules governing the situation where the keys belong to a commercial organisation with several keyholders; essentially, the notice must be served on an appropriately senior officer or employee.

The section does not apply to keys which are intended to be used only for the purpose of generating electronic signatures[304] and have in fact only been used for that purpose.[305] However, in any other circumstances, failure to comply with a section 49 notice is an offence punishable by up to two years' imprisonment unless the respondent can show that they were not in possession of the key after the time when the notice was given and until compliance with the notice was required. Late disclosure is a defence provided that the respondent can show it was not reasonably practicable to disclose within the stipulated time.[306]   **9–106**

It is also an offence under the Act for the recipient of a section 49 notice which stipulates secrecy to tip off any other person as to the fact that the notice has been given, its contents and anything done in pursuance of it.[307] Breach of such a secrecy requirement other than by the automatic operation of key-compromise software is also punishable by up to two years' imprisonment.

The authorities which are empowered to give section 49 notices are required to ensure that keys disclosed under such notices are used only for obtaining access to information which did or could have formed grounds for the giving of a notice. Any use made of a key must be proportionate to the end for which it is obtained, and the key must be stored securely while in their possession. A person who makes a disclosure under a section 49 notice or whose information is so disclosed, and to whom loss is caused by a breach of the authorities duties of safeguarding the key and the use made of it, may bring an action against the authority.[308]

The Government's position is that these powers are intended only to maintain the effectiveness of the existing legislation, in the face of new technologies. However, there is at the time of writing no date set by which they will be brought into effect.

Export controls on dual-use goods

(a) At international level

9–107   The major international instrument dealing with the regulation of transactions in encryption products is the Wassenaar Arrangement, which came into force on 1 November 1996.[309] The Arrangement is the successor to the old COCOM, the Coordinating Committee for Multilateral Exports Control; 33 states are party to it. It aims to promote transparency and responsibility with respect to transfers of potentially military technologies, and to enhance cooperation to prevent the acquisition of armaments and sensitive dual-use goods for military end-uses by regions or states which are causing the Participating States concern. The Arrangement applies to both conventional arms and dual-use goods. The provisions of this Arrangement are reflected in the export controls imposed by the European Union (discussed below) and the various other signatories.

The Arrangement was amended in December 1998 to loosen the controls in respect of private key encryption software which:

- uses a key length of less than 64 bits: and

- is generally available to the public through "over the counter" or equivalent channels,

as long as the cryptographic function cannot easily be changed by the user. This is likely to include most commercial encryption products already in circulation, many of which use keys of this sort of length or less. In addition, cryptographic products designed solely for authentication or digital signatures and products for the protection of copyright-protected data are excluded from the control scheme.

(b) European Union

9–108   EC Council Regulation Council Regulation (EC) No. 1334/2000 of June 22, 2000[310] establishes a Community-wide regime for the control of export of dual-use goods. It replaced Council Regulation 3381/94 on the same, reflecting the changes to the Wassenaar Arrangement. The most significant change from the previous regime is that "export" now includes transmission of software or technology by electronic media, fax or telephone to a destination outside the Community. Oral transmission of technology by telephone is covered only where the technology is contained in a document the relevant part of which is read out over the telephone, or is described over the telephone in such a way as to achieve substantially the same result.[311]

Subsequent amendments[312] have updated the control list to which Regulation (EC) No 1334/2000 applies.

The Dual-Use list in the Regulation agrees broadly with the agreed Dual-Use list from the Wassenaar Arrangement, as it is intended to do. Cryptographic products, including software, are included in the list and thus (subject to some stated exceptions not relevant to use of encryption by Internet users) in principle require a licence for export from the European Union. No licences are required for movement of cryptographic goods within the Union, so that as stated above cryptographic products intended solely for digital signatures or authentication are now excluded altogether.

The only other piece of European legislation with relevance to encryption products is the European Commission's Conditional Access Directive.[313] This takes pains to point out that it is not directly concerned with the legal status of encryption technology as such. Rather, it aims to provide a framework for the use of encryption as a mechanism whereby services which depend for their remuneration on limiting access should be able to be certain of achieving effective limitation—that is, ensuring that access to their services is conditional upon meeting the subscription conditions. This is the foundation for providers of on-line services such as digital radio services or video on demand to broadcast commercially over the Internet.   **9–109**

The Directive requires Member States to prohibit the commercial sale, installation or use of "illicit devices", that is, equipment or software designed or adapted to give access to a protected service in an intelligible form without the authorisation of the service provider.[314] It does not include any express regulation of encrypting mechanisms or devices except to ban Member States from restricting free movement of conditional access devices.[315]

The European Commission's explanatory notes accompanying the adopted Directive hint that this Directive may form the model for a broader international instrument on the control of illicit devices, but as with most international agreements this is likely to take some time.

(c)   National legislation

(i)   Australia

There are restrictions on exporting designated types of cryptographic algorithms and key lengths from Australia. These are described in the *Defence and Strategic Goods List (DSGL)* pursuant the *Customs (Prohibited Exports) Regulations 1958*.[316]   **9–110**

An export permit or licence[317] is required for:

(a)   symmetric algorithms employing a key length in excess of 56 bits; or

(b)   asymmetric algorithms, where security of the algorithm is based on factorisation of integers in excess of 512 bits; or

(c)   discrete logarithms in a multiplicative group with a finite field size greater than 512 bits; or

(d)   discrete logarithms in other groups in excess of 112 bits.

However, the export licensing requirements do **not** apply to cryptographic technology used *only* for authentication and digital signatures. There are also exceptions for personal use and retail cryptographic products with key lengths less than 64 bits.

There are currently no restrictions upon the importation of cryptography technology into Australia, although taxes and duties may be payable in respect of any such import.

(ii) United Kingdom

9–111   The United Kingdom passed a new Export Control Act[318] in 2002 to replace the antiquated Import, Export and Customs Powers (Defence) Act 1939 and consolidate the existing primary and secondary legislation governing the control of exports. Once it comes into force, it will govern the procedures for obtaining export licences for encryption products and software from the United Kingdom. The express intention is to make the decision making procedures in respect of applications for export licences more transparent. In practice, the Arms Export Licensing Criteria introduced in October 2000 remain in effect under the new Act until amended. The new Act also covers the export of technology through the provision of technical assistance in addition to the straightforward sale of goods; this is intended to permit the implementation of the European Union's Joint Action of June 22, 2000[319] concerning the use of technical assistance related to military end-uses. There are no restrictions on most cryptographic items being transferred to other Member States of the EU, although records must be kept of items which are transferred.

The new EC Council Regulation discussed above had already been implemented through the Dual-Use Items (Export Control) Regulations 2000; these Regulations continue in effect under the new Act until new secondary legislation is approved by Parliament. Annex 1 of the Regulations contains the General Software Note which gives a general exception in respect of software generally available without restriction at retail points and through mail order, etc. or otherwise "in the public domain" (by which is meant publicly available, rather than that the term of copyright has expired).

9–112   Other specific technologies are also excepted by Annex 1: certain personalised smart cards; equipment for radio broadcasting or pay-TV which includes decryption technology for audio/ video or management functions; mobile telephones for civil use; decryption functions to allow the execution of copy-protected software, as long as these are not accessible to the user.

New secondary legislation is in draft at the time of writing.

Since the EU Regulation is directly effective upon all Member States, the remaining Member States of the European Union have more or less equivalent restrictions on export for encryption software.

(iii) United States

9–113   The Export Administration Act of 1979, as amended, lapsed in August 2001. In the absence of an Export Administration Act, the US dual-use export control system depends on the President's invocation of emergency powers under the International Emergency Economic Powers Act. The Administration has expressed an intention to introduce a new Export Administration Act but this has not yet been introduced into Congress. In the interim a web of regulations is promulgated and administered by the Bureau of Industry and Security at the Department of Commerce (BIS).[320] Since 2002, when the US updated its system to comply with the revisions to the Wassenaar Arrangement, mass market encryption products using symmetric encryption algorithms with key lengths exceeding 64 bits are eligible for export and reexport after a 30-day review by BIS and the ENC Encryption Request Coordinator. There are no post-export reporting requirements or licensing requirements related to the export or re-export of these mass market encryption products once this review is completed.

Similarly, all encryption source code that would be considered publicly available such as source code posted to the Internet and the corresponding object code may be exported and re-exported, once notification (or a copy of the source code) is provided to BIS and the ENC Encryption Request Coordinator. Otherwise, a licence is required before any encryption product is exported to any country other than Canada or, in the case of a limited set of products, the European Union (including the newly acceding countries).

---

1.   Biddle, *Legislating market winners: digital signature laws and the electronic commerce marketplace*, 1997, *San Diego Law Review* 34: 1225.
2.   Verordnung des Budeskanzilers über Elektronische Signaturen.
3.   S. 3, para. 6.
4.   Art. 23.
5.   Ordinance BGBI 2000/31.
6.   A-Trust Gesellschaft für Sicherheitssysteme im elektronischen Datenverkehr GmnH.
7.   Art. 4(2).
8.   Art. 8(3).
9.   Arrete royale of December 6, 2002.
10.   Art. 21.
11.   which is the current supervisory body for certification service providers, replacing the State Telecommunications Commission as originally specified in the Act (Art. 32).
12.   Art. 26.
13.   Pt IV.
14.   Art. 29(2).
15.   Art. 6.
16.   The supervisory body nominated by the Law: Art. 9. It is also responsible for certifying compliance of secure signature creation devices with the legal requirements: Reg. 8.
17.   Art. 10.
18.   Art. 13(2).
19.   Art. 18(1) and (2).
20.   Art. 10(5).
21.   Art. 10(6).
22.   Art. 11.
23.   Treaty of Rome, Art. 6.
24.   Art. 16(2).
25.   Art. 16.
26.   Art. 7.
27.   Art. 10.
28.   Executive Order (Bekg. No. 923) of May 10, 2000.
29.   Art. 16.
30.   Art. 5.
31.   Art. 17(2).
32.   Art. 5(8)(4).
33.   Ss. 20 and 22.
34.   S. 19(2).
35.   S. 18. A private company must have a minimum capitalisation of 400,000 kroons (€25,559).
36.   Ss. 12 and 14.
37.   S. 30(2).
38.   S. 21.
39.   S. 24.
40.   S. 13.
41.   Ss. 14 and 15.
42.   Art. 7, Decree no. 2001-272 of March 30, 2001.
43.   S. 2(8).
44.   S. 4(2).
45.   S. 4(3).
46.   S. 20. The right not to incriminate oneself is expressly preserved, however.
47.   S. 12.
48.   Ss. 15 and 16.
49.   S. 15(1).
50.   Signature Ordinance 3.
51.   Signature Ordinance, Ss. 4 and 8(3).
52.   unless transferring current certificates to another certification service provider.

53. S. 8
54. S. 11(1).
55. S. 11(2) and (3).
56. S. 13 (2).
57. S. 13.
58. Art. 4(8).
59. Art. 4(2).
60. Art. 7(1) Electronic Signature Act 2001.
61. Annex 3, which conforms with Annex II of the Electronic Signature Directive.
62. Art. 8(1).
63. Art. 8(3).
64. Art. 20.
65. Art. 21.
66. Art. 12.
67. Published in *Gazzetta Ufficiale* no. 87, of April 15, 1999.
68. As far as we examined Decree 10/02 no amendments to Decree of February 8, 1999 are contained therein.
69. This Department replaced the former Authority in charge, *i.e.* Authority for Information Technology in Public Administration (AIPA).
70. Art. 27, para. 2 of Decree n. 445 of December 28, 2000, published in *Gazzetta Ufficiale* n. 42 of January 20, 2001 as amended by Presidential Decree no. 137 of April 7, 2003.
71. Art. 28, para. 3 of Decree n. 445/2000 as amended by Presidential Decree no. 137 of April 7, 2003.
72. Art. 28 bis Decree 445/00, as amended by Decree 10 of January 23, 2002.
73. Art. 9.
74. Art. 17(2); the identification must take place face to face according to Art. 23(4).
75. Art. 9(4).
76. Arts 20-21.
77. Art. 10.
78. Art. 13.
79. Art. 14.
80. Art. 18.
81. Art. 23(12).
82. Art. 24.
83. Art. 22.
84. Art. 10.
85. Art. 12.
86. Art. 4(4).
87. Art. 4(6).
88. Art. 13.
89. Art. 29 Law.
90. Art. 27.
91. Grand-Ducal Regulation 3(1) of June 1, 2001.
92. Grand-Ducal Regulation 3(9).
93. Art. 26 Law.
94. Regs 2 and 3.
95. Art. 32 Law.
96. Art. 32(2)(c).
97. Art. 16.
98. Decree 200, 2(s).
99. Decree 200, 2(l).
100. Decree 200, 2(q).
101. The National Bank and public authorities are the certification service providers solely for the public sector: Art. 9(2).
102. Art. 10(3).
103. Art. 10(1).
104. Art. 38.
105. Art. 32(2).
106. Art. 12(2).
107. Art. 14(1).
108. Art. 3(19).
109. Art. 11.
110. Art. 10(5).
111. Art. 45.
112. Art. 21(4)-(7).
113. Art. 21(1).
114. Art. 13(1).
115. Art. 9.

116. Art. 17.
117. Art. 15(2).
118. Art. 12.
119. Art. 33.
120. Art. 28.
121. Art. 30.
122. Art. 27.
123. Art. 13.
124. Art. 15(1).
125. Arts 19(2) and 20(h).
126. Art. 45(h).
127. Art. 21.
128. Art. 23(1) and (2).
129. Art. 24(3)c.
130. Art. 31(3).
131. Art. 36.
132. Art. 41.
133. Arts 44 and 45.
134. Art. 20(3).
135. Ss. 10, 13 and 27. Regulation 542/2002 was promulgated in October 2002 governing these last.
136. S. 11.
137. S. 15.
138. S. 18(1).
139. S. 19(2)-(4).
140. Arts 18 and 19.
141. Art. 20.
142. Art. 24.
143. Art. 26.
144. Art. 35(1).
145. Art. 31.
146. Art. 41.
147. Art. 47.
148. Art. 39.
149. Art. 42.
150. Art. 46(1).
151. Art. 30(2).
152. Art. 9.
153. Art. 19.
154. subject to variation by royal Decree. A sum of €6m was proposed in the draft published in 2002. Art. 20(2).
155. Art. 22.
156. Art. 23.
157. Art. 15.
158. Reg. 3.
159. which is incorporated as Sch. 1 to the Regulations.
160. which is incorporated as Sch. 2 to the Regulations.
161. *www.tscheme.org*.
162. tScheme Model Agreement cl. 6 and 10, available from tScheme's website at *www.tscheme.org*.
163. tScheme Model Agreement cl. 13.
164. tScheme Model Agreement cl. 24.
165. Discussion based upon a paper prepared by Professor Fuping Gao of the East China University of Politics and Law, Shanghai, Temple International and Comparative Law Journal (fall, 2003).
166. Twelve banks, including the People's Bank of China, set up the China Financial Certification Authority (CFCA, 2000) to provide CA service to its clients; there are also others, for example, the China Telecommunication Certification Authorities, 1999, etc.
167. available at *http://itb.hainan.gov.cn/read_law.php?law_class=5&id=112*.
168. Guangdong report based in part upon World eBusiness Law Report of March 13, 2003, submitted by Andrew Zeng, Beijing.
169. S. 22
170. A false representation that a certification is recognised can attract up to 6 months' imprisonment: s. 48.
171. Factors listed in s. 21(5) include any convictions for dishonesty, or insolvency.
172. S. 20(5)
173. which is a recognised certification authority by virtue of s. 34, without reference to the Director.
174. S. 42
175. Ss. 21 and 32.
176. S. 29.
177. Ss. 2 and 18.

178. S. 37.
179. S. 39.
180. Ss. 73-4.
181. Art. 2(1) and (2).
182. Arts 4 and 5.
183. Art. 13.
184. Art. 10.
185. Art. 23.
186. Arts 17-32 inclusive.
187. S. 4(3).
188. S. 16.
189. S. 67.
190. S. 76.
191. S. 79.
192. S. 27.
193. Ss. 34-37.
194. S. 13.
195. S. 6(2).
196. S. 6(3).
197. S. 45.
198. S. 46.
199. S. 59(2).
200. S. 19.
201. Pt VI, s. 68-70.
202. S. 18, Ordinance No. LJ of 2002.
203. S. 21(2).
204. S. 35.
205. S. 43(2)(i).
206. Ss. 27-29.
207. Ss. 42-3.
208. S. 30.
209. Ss. 31 and 32.
210. Ss. 34-5.
211. S. 44.
212. S. 45.
213. S. 53.
214. Art. 14.
215. Arts 4 and 8.
216. Art. 15(1).
217. Arts 17 and 18.
218. Art. 21.
219. Art. 26.
220. Art. 24.
221. Utah Code Ann. §§ 46-3-101 to -504.
222. Utah Code Ann. § 46-3-302(1).
223. Utah Code Ann. § 46-3-302(1)(c).
224. Utah Code Ann. § 46-3-307(2).
225. Utah Code Ann. § 46-3-301.
226. Utah Code Ann. § 46-3-203.
227. Utah Code Ann. § 46-3-204.
228. Utah Code Ann. § 46-3-303(1)(a).
229. Utah Code Ann. § 46-3-303(2).
230. Utah Code Ann. § 46-3-302(3).
231. Utah Code Ann. § 46-3-304(4)(a).
232. Utah Rule 154-10-304.
233. Utah Admin. R. 154-10-304(4).
234. Utah Admin. R. 154-10-304(3).
235. Utah Code Ann. § 46-3-502(1).
236. Utah Code Ann. § 46-3-502(1).
237. Utah Code Ann. § 46-3-502(2)(a)(ii).
238. Utah Code Ann. § 46-3-309(2)(b).
239. Utah Code Ann. § 46-3-309(2)(c).
240. Utah Code Ann. § 46-3-309(2)(a).
241. Utah Code Ann. § 46-3-402.
242. Art. 14(a) and 9.
243. Art. 30.

244. Art. 39.
245. Art. 19.
246. Art. 5.
247. Art. 11.
248. Arts 11 and 17.
249. Art. 14.
250. Art. 23.
251. Art. 12(e).
252. Art. 14.
253. Art. 12(c).
254. Art. 29.
255. Art. 43.
256. Art. 34.
257. Art. 37.
258. Decree 1427 of 2000, heading Responsibility.
259. Art. 28.
260. Art. 39(c).
261. Art. 28.
262. Art. 41.
263. Art. 30(h).
264. Art. 31.
265. Art. 32.
266. Art. 34.
267. Art. 15.
268. Art. 16 Third.
269. Art. 8.
270. Art. 10.
271. Art. 21.
272. Art. 22(5) and (13).
273. Although the provisions stipulating the contents of certificates appear to require the certification service provider to be at lest registered with the supervisory agency in order to obtain a unique identification code.
274. Art. 31.
275. Art. 42.
276. Art. 37.
277. Art. 35(4).
278. Cl. 8(2).
279. Cl. 10(1)
280. Cl. 9(3).
281. Cl. 13.
282. Cl. 14.
283. Cl. 7(2).
284. S. 29.
285. S. 35.
286. S. 38.
287. S. 38(4).
288. S. 40.
289. Ss. 81 and 82.
290. Directive 95/46/EC of October 24, 1995, O.J. L 281, November 23, 1995 at p. 31.
291. Art. 3.
292. Art. 8.
293. The Secure Electronic Commerce Statement places considerable emphasis on the importance of the lawful interception of communication in in law enforcement—apparently around 2,600 warrants for such interception were issued during 1996 and 1997 (see para. 13).
294. The author of the Pretty Good Privacy code, Phil Zimmerman, deliberately released this onto the Internet in accordance with his views on the citizen's right to privacy—and was accordingly prosecuted. However, the code is now freely available around the world.
295. The concealment of a message among other data, for example by changing a few pixels in a picture. There should be no reason for an interceptor to suspect that a message is there. However, it helps to have some plausible reason for sending the particular picture.
296. For further cases and examples, see *http://guru.cosc.georgetown.edu/~denning/crypto/cases.html*.
297. A more secure alternative is to split the key into several parts and leave one with each of several agents. This is known as dispersion.
298. RIP Act s. 49(2).
299. S. 51(2). The person giving the direction must believe there are special circumstances requiring disclosure of the key rather than just the information, and that to require disclosure of the key is proportionate. There is no requirement for this belief to be reasonable.

300. RIP Act, Sch. 2(1).
301. Sch. 2(2)-(5).
302. RIP Act s. 50(9).
303. RIP Act s. 49(3) and 49(2)(b)(ii).
304. Defined in S. 56(1). The definition is very similar to that in the Electronic Communications Act.
305. RIP Act, s. 49(9).
306. RIP Act, s. 53.
307. RIP Act, s. 54.
308. RIP Act, s. 55.
309. Text available at *http://wassenaar.org*; the relevant sections are the General Software Note and related materials.
310. Official Journal L 159, June 30, 2000, p. 1.
311. Art. 2.
312. Council Regulation (EC) No. 2889/2000 of December 22, 2000 (relating to nuclear fuels) and Council Regulation (EC) No. 458/2001 of March 6, 2001 (relating to computers).
313. Published in the Official Journal at O.J. L 320/54 of November 28, 1998.
314. Definition in Art. 1; prohibition in Art. 3.
315. Art. 2.
316. The Customs legislation and regulations relevant to this issue reflects Australia's status as a signatory to international agreements, including the Wassenaar Arrangement on Export Controls for Conventional Arms and Dual Use Goods and Technologies.
317. Applications for an export licence or permit for cryptographic technology which is on the DSGL are to be made to the Department of Defence (Strategic Trade Policy and Operations Section).
318. 2002 Ch. 28.
319. 2000/401/CFSP.
320. Export Administration Regulations, codified at 15 Code of Federal Regulations, Ch. 7.

10

Standards

Overview

Standards are agreed technical specifications which ensure interoperability between all **10–001** equipment and processes which conform to them. They are necessarily voluntary, but in the field of telecommunications, in particular, compliance is in reality essential in order for networks and systems operated in different countries to communicate effectively and for equipment such as mobile handsets to be able to be used worldwide. From the commercial perspective, the development of international standards enables manufacturers from one country to supply products for use by the network operators of another without the need to develop additional conversion or connection equipment. Standards will have to be agreed for many elements of electronic signature technology before international mutual recognition is likely to be achieved in practice.

It is therefore not surprising that even before the advent of the UNCITRAL Model Laws or the Electronic Signature Directive, the International Telecommunications Union (ITU) had begun to work on the development of standards for electronic signature technology. This had resulted in the standard known as X.509, which specifies the format and content for a certificate for use in a public key system. X.509 has been taken up widely, and is likely to be the format used for the majority of key certificates in practice. It will therefore be reviewed in more detail below. The ITU has also developed an associated set of standards for an authentication framework using these certificates (ISO/IEC 9594-8), for message digest functions and for hardware tokens such as smart cards for the secure storage and usage of private keys (ISO/IEC 7816).

Similarly, the Internet Engineering Task Force, an international grouping of network designers, suppliers and researchers concerned with the evolution and operation of the Internet, began work on a PKI K.509 (PKIX) set of standards as early as autumn 1995, from which several widely used standards have emerged.

The importance of standards was acknowledged in both the UNCITRAL Model Law on **10–002** Electronic Signatures and the Electronic Signatures Directive. Article 12 of the Model Law specified that certificates issued by foreign certification service providers were to be recognised as the equivalent of national certification service providers of the same type if they were as reliable—reliability being assessed by reference to recognised international standards, among other things. The Electronic Signatures Directive states at Article 3(5) that all the criteria of Annex III for a secure-signature-creation-device will be presumed to be met by a device if it complies with a standard recognised by the European Commission and published in the Official Journal.

The rash of national legislation relating to the legal effect of electronic signatures made the need for standards more critical. Even though many of the national laws passed are technology neutral, nevertheless there is a premium to be had in knowing for certain that the particular technology used will confer legal effect upon the resulting signature. The relatively broad acceptance and recognition of digital signatures at the end of the 1990s gave this technology a substantial edge over most alternative possibilities since it had been impliedly approved by the drafters both of the UNCITRAL Model Law and of the Electronic Signatures Directive, as well as a number of national and, in the United States, state legislatures. Accordingly, it was an obvious requirement that technical standards should be introduced which would remove any remaining uncertainty affecting the use of digital signatures. In particular, standards for signature format, certificate revocation list contents and structure, certificate verification processes and time stamping services needed to be agreed to ensure that so far as possible signed documents and signature creation and verification devices should be interoperable. Without this, the technical difficulties inherent in each stage of a signature creation and verification process, where the parties concerned were each operating a different manufacturer's equipment, would, by themselves, be sufficient to act as a significant barrier to the use of electronic signatures, regardless of their theoretical legal standing.

In addition, recognised standards can help to generate the trust which users, both subscribers and relying parties, need to have in the certification service providers in order for the system to function effectively. This involves both internal information security and the processes for verifying the identity of subscribers and maintaining certificate verification mechanisms. There may also be a need for technical standards to address the issue of long term storage and accessibility of electronically signed documents in archive. Given, in addition, the potential evidential relevance of standard compliance in ascertaining liability of one or other party to an electronic transaction,[1] standards are more closely related to a number of aspects of the legal effectiveness of electronic signatures than they are to most other legal issues.

10–003   In view of this, it is unfortunate that there are as yet very few truly international standards applicable to the electronic signature infrastructure. In the light of divergent national technical standards, initiatives have been taken in the Asia-Pacific Economic Co-operation (APEC) and in the European Union to develop appropriate standards for use on a regional basis, and it is to be hoped that the current information sharing between these two groups will assist ultimately in harmonising into a single set of global standards. However, past experience in the telecommunications industry suggests that this convergence may take some time despite its evident desirability. Since a lot of effort and capital is invested in agreeing a "local" standard, once it is in place there is sizeable resistance to any subsequent modification. In telecommunications, this led to a period when (for example) European mobile telephones could not operate in the United States and vice versa. However, the industry may have learned from these experiences to standardise with the global markets in mind. At present the work towards international standardisation is at a relatively preliminary stage, such as creating mappings between standard certificate policies.[2]

The following sections review what aspects of electronic signature infrastructure and technology may need to be standardised, and the particular standards which either are already recognised relating to those aspects or, in Europe in particular, are being proposed for recognition by the European Commission for compliance with the various requirements of the Electronic Signatures Directive. In view of the Directive's wide-ranging technical requirements, the European Electronic Signature Standardisation Initiative (EESSI) was set up contemporaneously with the finalisation of the Directive. It appointed an Expert Team, comprising technical and legal experts from industry and academia which carried out a study as to what standardisation activities would be required in support of the Directive's implementation. This team reviewed existing laws and standards relevant to the Directive and delivered its final report in July 1999.[3]

The report recommended an initial focus purely on asymmetric cryptographic **10–004** techniques with the use of existing recognised international standards wherever possible in preference to the development of new standards. However, by carrying out a detailed mapping of the existing information security standards and the leading model certification practice statement outline (RFC 2527, discussed below) it identified areas where these did not fully meet the requirements of the Directive.

This report has led to a joint effort by the European Telecommunications Standardisation Institute (ETSI) and European Committee for Standardisation (CEN) which are in the process of finalising standards intended to cover almost every aspect of electronic signatures and the provision of certification services in Europe. Their work is to be reviewed by the Electronic Signature Committee established under the Directive, which was due to report by July 19, 2003—shortly after the time of writing. It is expected that the outcome of that review will lead to the European Commission publishing the reference numbers of the approved standards in the Official Journal. Once this has taken place, it will be possible to state with certainty what secure signature creation devices meet the criteria of the Directive for generating advanced electronic signatures.

Assessing the security of information technology products and systems

In order to understand the terminology of information technology standards, it is **10–005** necessary to begin by considering how products will be assessed for compliance. This has in itself been the subject of a global harmonisation effort. In 1995 the United Kingdom, France, Germany and the Netherlands agreed Information Security Evaluation Criteria (ITSEC) relating to the design and implementation of secure information systems, which was widely adopted. It specifies 7 levels of security, E0 to E5 and E698, of which E0 represents no security and E698 the highest level of confidence. These correspond reasonably well to the functionality requirements of the longer-standing US Trusted Computer System Evaluation Criteria[4] D to A1. The criteria are applied to assess whether the system functions as required, whether the chosen functions work together synergistically, what vulnerabilities it has and how well it withstands direct attack. However, the flaw in these ratings as indicia of security is that they apply functional tests rather than security tests: the criteria asked, "does this product have a mandatory access control", rather than "is it secure"? As a result, manufacturers could claim compliance with a particular level simply by including an appropriate list of features in a stand-alone version, which would not provide nearly equivalent security if the same elements were networked. For example, Microsoft's NT operating system had a respectable C2 security rating—which applied only if the operating system was running on a standalone Compaq 386 PC without a network card, with the floppy disk drive irreversibly closed with epoxy resin.[5] Clearly, no real world user will ever use the operating system with these constraints. Outside the specified constraints, the security classification no longer applies.

The US security evaluation criteria were subsequently amended to try to tackle the networked environment, but more recently have been replaced altogether by the Common Criteria for Information Technology Security Evaluation ("the Common Criteria").[6] This international system permits certification of particular products in one country to be recognised in the other participating countries. Participants include Australia, Canada, Finland, France, Germany, Greece, Italy, the Netherlands, New Zealand, Norway, Spain, the United Kingdom and the United States. The Common Criteria is a catalogue of security concepts which users can use to develop a *protection profile* setting out their particular security needs. Individual products can then be designed according to the profile. The design methodology and resulting product may be tested by a government-approved certification laboratory against that profile and their security rated accordingly as complying to one of the Evaluation Assurance Levels (EALs). In total, the Common Criteria amount to 618 pages of guidance as to how to protect information from unauthorised disclosure, modification or loss of use, although it does not claim to be comprehensive.[7] Nevertheless, it still recognises that information systems in operation may interact with other software and hardware in unexpected ways, so that even a highly secure system may develop unforeseen vulnerabilities which may require further modification.

10–006   The Common Criteria set out functions to be included in a protection profile, such as non-repudiation of origin functions, with several levels of security for each function. For non-repudiation, the product may permit the user to request evidence of the origin of the information, and the audit side of the product may record information such as the identity of the user who requested evidence of origin, identification of the information, destination and the evidence provided.[8] Similar optional levels of feature security and audit record apply to securing data against change *in situ*, identification and authentication of users and their security attributes (privileges, role), the ability of users to interact with the system anonymously or pseudonymously.[9]

Seven EALs are specified, balancing the level of assurance of security obtained against the cost and feasibility of acquiring that degree of assurance. EAL1 is the least and EAL7 the most secure. In contrast to the preceding sets of security evaluation criteria, the lowest level in this system does not represent a total lack of security: EAL1 is intended to give some confidence in correct operation such as to support the contention that due care has been exercised with respect to the protection of personal data, for example.[10] EAL3 and 4 are the highest levels likely to be required for standard commercial products; levels above this include an analysis of the effectiveness of the developer's covert channel analysis and require some specialist security engineering techniques. EAL7 is intended for use in extremely high risk situations, such as military applications, or where the high value of the assets to be protected justifies higher costs of evaluation and testing.[11]

A number of protection profiles have been developed by industry using the Common Criteria, for various aspects of the electronic signature generation and certification process.

Basic standards relating to public key infrastructure

10–007   There have been a number of standards developed concerning the operation of public key infrastructures, several of which have been approved by the ISO. The most fundamental is ISO/IEC 7498, which describes a Basic Reference Model of Security Architecture for Open Systems. This defines a digital signature and non-repudiation. ISO/IEC 10181-4 and 13888 refine and extend the concepts of non-repudiation services described in the previous standard to include the generation, storage and verification of evidence. Several digital signature mechanisms are set out in ISO/IEC 14888 on digital signature security techniques, including the verification of a digital signature.

At the national level, in 1995 the American Bar Association developed public key infrastructure assessment guidelines, which came before any of the state or national legislation on the subject. Being the first statement of norms for the operation of digital signatures, these guidelines have been widely influential.

More recently, the Australian Government has been active in developing standards and taking other steps to encourage the uptake on electronic signatures and digital certificates in Australia. It has produced PKI Criteria for Accreditation of Certification Authorities, and Standards Australia International Limited,[12] a commercial organisation which develops and publishes technical and business standards, has also developed a number of Standards specifically related to the implementation and use of digital signatures and certificates in Australia. These include:[13]

(a)   MP 75 – 1996, which describes the national Public Key Authentication Framework ("PKAF"); and

(b)   the AS 4539 series of PKAF related Standards:

    (i)   General (4 "General" documents);

    (ii)   PKAF Architecture;

    (iii) X.509 supported algorithms profile; and

    (iv) Assurance framework—Certification Authorities.

PKAF is a framework for the generation, distribution and management of public key **10–008** certificates. PKAF sets out a certification hierarchy containing Certification Authorities, Registration Authorities and users.

While the standards published by Standards Australia (which includes international standards adopted in Australia) are not legal documents in themselves, some of them are referred to in Federal or State legislation, at which time they become mandatory. Approximately 2,400 of Standards Australia's standards are currently mandatory.[14]

The Canadian Government likewise has a set of detailed PKI Certificate policies.

The EESSI Expert Group also recommended a baseline Certificate Policy for all certification service providers issuing qualified certificates. In the event three standards for use in Europe and a report on international harmonisation have been produced by ETSI:

• TS 101 456: Policy requirement for certification authorities issuing qualified certificates

• TS 102 023: Policy requirements for time-stamping authorities

• TS 102 042: Policy requirements for certification authorities issuing public key certificates

• TR 102 040: International Harmonization of Policy Requirements for certification authorities issuing Certificates.

In addition, ETSI produced TR 102 030 on the provision of harmonized Trust Service Provider status information. This report gives information about a recommended national supervisory system, which would maintain a list of approved certification service providers, their respective approved services and the histories of the services' approval status. Copies of each of these standards (TS) and related reports (TR) are available from the ETSI website at *http://portal.etsi.org/esi/el-sign.asp#Workplan*.

Standards for specific technologies

10–009 Electronic signature technology, beyond the more basic forms such as appending typed or scanned signatures, involves numerous stages. For cryptographic methods:

- a secure cryptographic algorithm must be selected,

- cryptographic keys must be generated, stored and accessed,

- a certificate may need to be generated identifying the key holder and the certification service provider,

- message digest function algorithms must be chosen,

- message digest function values (*i.e.* message digests) must be calculated,

- the digital signature itself must calculated, which may involve padding the message digest function result up to a certain length,

- the recipient must (in an asymmetric system)

    - obtain the sender's public key,

    - verify, by consulting the certificate itself and the current certificate revocation list, that the certificate is still valid,

    - decrypt the signature to obtain the message digest of the original message, and

    - re-calculate the message digest of the message as received.

Standards can be specified for each of these functions. In the United States, Federal Information Standards Publication (FIPS) 140-1, issued by the National Institute of Standards, specifies the overall requirements for the design and implementation of cryptographic modules, at four security levels, effectively independent of the module's application. This standard is used in Canada and other countries as well as the United States. The EESSI expert group recommended the use of FIPS 140-1 concurrently with a suitable protection profile under the Common Criteria for Information Security Technology Evaluation for all cryptographic modules in Europe. As part of the EESSI project, CEN has developed such a profile for signature devices for use by certification service providers in issuing qualified certificates.[15] The smart card industry has developed a separate protection profile for smart cards, which are widely envisaged as being fundamental to the eventual acceptance and routine use of electronic signatures through providing secure storage for signature data.

The EESSI Expert Group also recommended standards for the syntax and encoding of electronic signatures, supporting multiple signers and role signatures which should be verifiable long after their initial use. This recommendation has resulted in:

- SR 002 176 Algorithms and Parameters for Secure Electronic Signatures

- TS 101 733: Electronic Signature Formats

- TS 101 903: XML Advanced Electronic Signatures

- TS 101 861: Time Stamping Profile

A further recommendation was that a profile should be developed for qualified **10–010** certificates to be based on the X.509 standard. Clearly, a signature or a certificate in a non-standard format will be of very little use outside a limited group of users applying the same format, since the recipient may not be able to read it using a standard-compliant verification device designed with a different format in mind. ISO-ITU Recommendation X.509 is therefore perhaps the most fundamental of the electronic signature standards. It defines the framework for public key certificates and attribute certificates and for the provision of authentication services by a directory, consisting of a collection of information processing systems together with the directory information they individually hold. It covers both simple authentication, such as the use of a password, and authentication using strong cryptography. The current version of this Recommendation is that which was approved in March 2000.

The Recommendation describes what format certificates must be in, in order to comply, and how compliant certificates can be issued, managed, used and revoked. It does *not* cover the means the certification authority uses to ensure that the subscriber is in fact in possession of the private key corresponding to the certified public key, or to verify the identity of the subscriber.

X.509 compliant certificates must include as a minimum the subscriber's *distinguished* **10–011** *name* and public key. The use of distinguished names, which are defined in another ITU standard X.501, is intended to avoid the problem which arises through many individuals having identical names. A distinguished name is an identifier assigned by a naming authority, which may be a certification service provider. The distinguished name must be unique to the subscriber as between all subscribers to that certification service provider. Distinguished Name (DN) attributes uniquely identify a user or group so that it can be located in the directory server. A DN customarily contains at least three attributes: a user's name or user ID; an organization name; and a country designation. Most companies use many more attributes in order to store additional user and group information. Thus, although two users may have identical distinguished names, those names plus the information as to which certification service provider issued a certificate gives each user a genuinely unique identifier. The certificate may also include the certification authority's unique identifier for that subscriber, a certificate number and version number, the identifier for the algorithm used to sign the certificate, the period of validity of the certificate, as well as other extensions defined by the issuing authority such as the limits on usage of the certificate and the certificate policy or policies under which the certificate was issued.

The standard spells out in great detail how each possible item of information which may be included in a certificate should be formatted and the circumstances in which it can be used. Similarly, the format and access requirements for certificate revocation lists are detailed, and rules for generating and processing them. It describes the use of certificates in transactions, pointing out that time-stamping of each stage of a transaction may be required for the relying party to be able to prove that its reliance was appropriate at the time at which it checked the certificate validity. Of course, this assumes that a universal reference time is used since otherwise disputes are likely to arise over time zones.

The resulting European proposed standard is ETSI TS 101 862: Qualified Certificate Profile.

The Working Committee of CEN has submitted a number of CEN Workshop Agreements (CWA) relating to the technology for creating and verifying electronic signatures:

- CWA 14168: Secure Signature-Creation Devices, version "EAL 4"

- CWA 14169: Secure Signature-Creation Devices, version "EAL 4+"

- CWA 14170: Security Requirements for Signature Creation Applications

- CWA 14171: Procedures for Electronic Signature Verification

- CWA 14172-4: EESSI Conformity Assessment Guidance: Part 4—Signature creation applications and procedures for electronic signature verification

- CWA 14172-5: EESSI Conformity Assessment Guidance: Part 5—Secure signature creation devices

- CWA 14355: Guidelines for the implementation of Secure Signature-Creation devices

These are available through the CEN website.[16]

For biometric applications, standards are needed for the biometric readers as regards the data they measure, for formats for data recordal and the algorithms digitising the data read, for attaching the digitised data to the data message (possibly in the form of a digital signature) and so on. As mentioned in Chapter 3, some standards are in development.

Standards for the provision of certification services

10–012 In addition to purely technical standards, certification service providers and, in some circumstances, signatories will need to be able to show that their procedures were adequate and that these were strictly adhered to. The provisions of some certification practice statements such as those of VeriSign or the Korean Information Security Agency include impressive procedures for verifying the identity[17] and authorisation level of any person who attempts to gain physical access to the most secure areas of the information systems, but these are irrelevant if in fact in practice they are routinely or even occasionally ignored or circumvented.

The basic and best known standard for the management of service quality is ISO 9000. This is a very general standard for the management of service organisations across all industries, and is therefore relevant to certification service providers in the absence of local or international standards dealing more specifically with certification services. The principles of ISO 9000 are applicable to any complex organisation which needs to be assured of maintaining minimum levels of quality in performing its operations, and of keeping adequate records of how those procedures were adhered to. The ISO's Quality Management System (QMS) is a collection of processes, documents, resources and monitoring systems which must be established, documented and maintained. For example, the organisation needs to draw up a quality policy, which will identify the main goals of the QMS, and set out quality objectives. There should then be a quality manual which describes the areas of the business that the QMS relates to, set out all of the quality procedures or where to find them. This, along with all other QMS related documents, must be legible, identified as such, kept scrupulously up to date and distributed to everyone who might need it. Obsolete documents need to be identified and protected from unintended use.

The quality process needs active management, which should be at a senior level to ensure that it is taken seriously throughout the organisation. The standards assign senior management the job of making sure customer requirements are understood and met, with the goal of improving customer satisfaction. They are responsible for setting a quality policy appropriate to the organisation's purpose, including a commitment to meet legal and regulatory requirements, and ensuring this is communicated throughout the organisation. Measurable objectives supporting the policy need to be set. Management must then undertake regular reviews of the QMS and its functioning, and keep records to show this has been done.

The organisation also needs proper resourcing to meet the standards—human resource issues are particularly pertinent in relation to certification service providers, but the standards also refer to building, workspace, equipment and support services.

Product realisation—the work of developing, manufacturing and delivering a finished **10–013** good or service—needs a comprehensive approach from concept to product including finding out what customers actually want in the first place, keeping a dialogue going to monitor customer feedback, setting appropriate product verification, monitoring, inspection and test activities. All of these—the proposed ideal and the actual practice— need to be recorded meticulously to enable management to review the process meaningfully, and also to demonstrate that the standards are being adhered to. At the end of the day the standard is about management which, as discussed in the context of information security standards, is the most difficult aspect of any operation. The key is to demonstrate that the organisation takes quality seriously—for example, where a review identifies any problem there should be a track record showing that the management ordered corrective actions, and that these were addressed to the real problems not just getting rid of the symptoms.

The standard which it is necessary to achieve depends upon the function of the certificates being issued and the legal requirements for these. The Electronic Signatures Directive places no special requirements upon certification service providers unless they propose to issue qualified certificates. Nevertheless, certificates are unlikely to acquire market reputation unless the certification service provider operates reasonably secure computer systems and takes adequate steps to verify subscriber identities. Consequently, basic information security standards are relevant to all certification service providers. A protection profile using the Common Criteria has been developed for certification services in the United States. The Expert Team designated to assess what standards are required for the European Electronic Signature Standardisation initiative recommended that a protection profile of this sort should also be developed for European certification service providers.[18]

Certification service providers issuing qualified certificates in Europe must also as a **10–014** minimum provide prompt and secure directory and revocation services and use appropriate means for verifying subscribers' identities. Some certification service providers will in addition provide services such as time stamping which support but are not legally essential to electronic signatures.

The EESSI Expert team recommended profiles for public key infrastructure operational management protocols based on the Internet Engineering Task Force's PKI-X RFC documents. In response to this, ETSI submitted the following technical reports:

- TR 102 038: XML format for signature policies

- TR 102 041: Signature Policies Report

- TR 102 044: Identification of requirements for attribute certification

Also relevant are the following CEN Workshop Agreements:

- CWA 14172-1: EESSI Conformity Assessment Guidance: Part 1—General

- CWA 14172-2: EESSI Conformity Assessment Guidance: Part 2—Certification Authority services and processes

Standards relating to information security

10–015 At a more general level, compliance with technical standards will provide some assurance as to the security of information systems, both those of the certification service provider and those of the signatory. These include technical measures such as firewalls, intrusion detection systems, virus checking software, physical access control measures and the like, as well as management procedures to ensure that the system is accessed only by authorised users and only within authorisation limits appropriate to the users' present requirements.

The most widely recognised standard in this field is ISO 17799: Code of Practice for Information Security Management. This standard derives from the British Standard for information security management systems, BS7799, which was introduced in 1998. Part 1 of the standard, providing a comprehensive set of controls comprising best practice in information security, was adopted as international standard, ISO 17799, in December 2000. Sadly, according to the Department of Trade and Industry annual survey only 25 per cent of British businesses surveyed in that year were aware of it, and only 6 per cent could quote the number. The British Standard was revised in 2002.

The controls laid down by the standard echo the ideas in ISO 9000. They include the drawing up of an information security policy document, the allocation of information security responsibility, the provision of information security education and training, means for reporting security incidents and business continuity management. The factors essential to success include making the security policy and activities reflect business objectives, visible support and commitment from senior management, effective marketing of security to all managers and employees, distributing guidance on information security policy to all employees and contractors, and a comprehensive and balanced system of measurement to evaluate performance and feed back suggestions for improvement.

10–016 The essence of the standard is that an organisation should take information security seriously, to the extent that it is as well integrated into the organisation's functioning as are more traditional core activities such as research or marketing. Just as an organisation will keep informed as to the latest advances in the technologies its products use, so it should also keep informed on developments in information security—both those being used to exploit any vulnerabilities and those available to resist attack. Further, any security incident should be treated as a learning opportunity rather than a source of embarrassment to be suppressed. None of the recommendations in the standard are surprising; but all of them require responsibility to be taken for the detailed aspects of keeping information secure as much as is done for physical assets. As both the OECD and the European Commission have observed, this is something few organisations presently do.

The standard does not assume that the organisation's information systems have been designed with security in mind; its objective is to ensure that the systems which are actually in use are managed as securely as possible. This should include taking external expert advice, and having security policies and arrangements independently reviewed. On the other hand, third party access to an organisation's information systems should be minimised, and where it is necessary should be managed in such a way as to minimise the risk. In order to achieve this, information should be classified as to its appropriate level of protection and personnel should be subject to identity and qualification verification both on joining the organisation and upon job transfer to any role involving the handling of sensitive information.

There is a separate Part 2 to British Standard 7799 which sets out a management model **10–017** —"Plan—Do—Check—Act"—intended to reflect the current version of the OECD Guidelines on Information Security as regards risk assessment, security design, implementation and management.

The EESSI project also produced two documents relating to trustworthy systems:

- CWA 14167-1: Security Requirements for Trustworthy Systems Managing Certificates for Electronic Signatures: Part 1 - System Security Requirements

- CWA 14172-3: EESSI Conformity Assessment Guidance: Part 3—Trustworthy systems managing certificates for electronic signatures

Following a meeting of the Electronic Signature Committee in June 2003, these are both anticipated to be formally recognised as approved standards by the European Commission under the Electronic Signatures Directive in the course of 2003.

There are various other information security standards and guidelines. At the international level, IISO Technical Report 13335 gives guidelines for the management of information technology security, and the Information Systems Audit and Control Federation has produced Control Objectives for Information and Related Technologies.

Standards for preservation of evidence

The difficulty of convincing a court of the reliability of electronic evidence has not escaped **10–018** the notice of the standards organisations. A number of solutions have been proposed, which can broadly be categorized as:

- preserving the original technology used to create or store the records;

- emulating the original technology on new platforms;

- migrating the software necessary to retrieve, deliver, and use the records;

- migrating the records into up-to-date formats; and

- converting records to standard forms.

The first of these has the advantage that there will in principle be no change in the records or the technological context in which they exist. This should minimise the issues as regards integrity and authenticity. On the other hand, maintaining these old technologies and formats will become more complex and more impractical over time as support for obsolete technologies disappears.

The British Standards Institute produced DISC PD 5000 in 1999, aimed precisely at establishing the proper procedures for maintaining an adequate audit trail to enable electronic records to be admissible in evidence.

10–019   Standards Australia has produced Australian Standard AS 4390, which consists of six parts covering general issues, responsibilities for recordkeeping, strategies, control, appraisal and disposal, and storage. It uses a continuum management model, for planning the management of records covering the whole extent of a record's existence, to establish a regime of records management beginning at the design stage of electronic recordkeeping systems.

Similarly, the National Standards of Canada has produced a standard[19] covering the use of microfilm and electronic images as documentary evidence.

The ISO has approved as a standard a reference model for an Open Archival Information System.[20]

Standards in this area are, of course, relevant to all electronically signed documents and the audit trails which are maintained concerning them, though not to the processes by which they are generated. However, their provisions are likely to be found especially persuasive by courts unfamiliar with electronic documents and therefore less confident of forming an independent view of the evidence's reliability. These standards therefore should be of interest to any organisation moving towards transacting and recording electronically.

---

1.   See Ch. 8 paras 8–012, 8–015.
2.   Spencer, *Trip report for APEC TEL* August 26, 2002, *www.cio.gov/fpkisc/library/trip_report_apectel.pdf*.
3.   *http://www.ict.etsi.org/EESSI/Documents/Final-Report.pdf*.
4.   Otherwise known as the "Orange Book".
5.   According to Schneier, *Secrets and Lies* p. 132.
6.   ISO standard 15408 version 2.1.
7.   For example, it does not directly address control of electromagnetic emanation from IT products, which can be used by attackers to work out certain elements of the system's operation (Common Criteria (1b)). However, it does include physical access constraints which may achieve much of the same effect since many electromagnetic signals have limited range.
8.   Common Criteria Pt. 2: Security Functional requirements, s. 4.1: Communications.
9.   the latter enabling a user to act without his or her identity being transparent to other users, while still being potentially accountable for his or her actions: Common Criteria Pt. 2. s. 9: Privacy.
10. Common Criteria Pt. 3: Security Assurance Requirements, s. 6.2.1: Evaluation assurance levels.
11. Common Criteria Pt. 3 s. 6.2.7.
12. See *http://www.standards.com.au*.
13. For a full listing of Standards Australia PKAF and other information security related standards, see *http://www.standards.com.au*.
14. See *http://www.standards.com.au/STANDARDS/INFO/ALLABTSTNDRDS/ALLABTSTNDRDS.HTM#0*.
15. CEN Workshop Agreement 14167-2: Security Requirements for Trustworthy Systems Managing Certificates for Electronic Signatures: Pt 2—Cryptographic Module for CSP Signing Operations—Protection Profile (MCSO-PP).
16. *http://www.cenorm.be/isss/CWAs/cwalist.htm*.
17. The KISA Certification Practice Statement includes a requirement for biometric verification of identity by two measures, one of which is the person's physical weight—not easily assessed by a would-be intruder through any of the standard approaches or even by eye. It may however require relatively frequent updating of the Agency's records.
18. Final Report July 1999, 5.2.2.
19. CAN/CGSB-7211-93.
20. Available at *www.classic.ccsds.org/documents/p2/CCSDS-650.0-R-1.pdf*.

Appendices

Appendix 1: Czech Republic—Electronic Signatures Act Part 1
Appendix 2: Finland—Electronic Signatures Act
Appendix 3: Germany—Law Governing Framework Conditions for Electronic Signatures
Appendix 4: Ireland—Electronic Commerce Act Parts 1–3
Appendix 5: Latvia—Law on Electronic Commerce
Appendix 6: Luxembourg—Law on Electronic Commerce ss.1 and 2; Regulation of June 1, 2003 Chs I–VII
Appendix 7: Malta—Electronic Commerce Act Parts I–V
Appendix 8: Poland—Act on Electronic Signatures Act Part 1
Appendix 9: Slovakia—Electronic Signatures of June 2003
Appendix 10: Spain—Law on Electronic Signatures of June 2003
Appendix 11: UK—E-commerce Act ss.7 and 15: Electronic Signatures Legislation

Czech Republic

Electronic Signature Act

PART I

Electronic Signature

ARTICLE 1

Purpose of the Act
This Act regulates the use of electronic signatures, the provision of related services, the monitoring of obligations set out hereby and sanctions for breaches of obligations set out hereby.

ARTICLE 2

Definition of terms
For the purposes hereof,

a 'electronic signature' shall refer to data in electronic form which are attached to a data message or which are logically associated therewith and which enables the identity of the signatory in relation to the data message to be verified;

b 'advanced electronic signature' shall mean an electronic signature which complies with the following requirements:

   i is uniquely linked to the signatory;

   ii allows identification of the signatory in relation to the data message;

   iii was created and attached to the data message by means of resources which the signatory is able to keep under his exclusive control;

   iv is attached to the data message to which it is related in such a way that it is possible to detect any subsequent change in the data;

c   'data message' shall mean electronic data which may be transmitted by electronic communication resources and which may be stored in recording media used in the processing and transfer of data by electronic means;

d   'signatory' shall mean a natural person who has a resource for the signature creation device and acts in his own name or on behalf of another natural or legal person;

e   'certification service provider' shall mean an entity issuing certificates and keeps records thereof, or which provides other services related to electronic signatures;

f   'accredited certification service provider' shall mean a provider of certification services to whom accreditation hereunder has been granted;

g   'certificate' shall mean a data message which is issued by a provider of certification services, which links data for the verification of signatures with the signatory and which enables the identity of this person to be verified;

h   'qualified certificate' shall mean a certificate which has all of the prerequisites set out hereby and which was issued by a provider of certification services which complies with the conditions set out hereby for certification service providers issuing qualified certificates;

i   'signature creation data' shall mean unique data which the signatory' uses to create an electronic signature;

j   'signature verification data' shall mean unique data which are used for the verification of an electronic signature;

k   'signature creation device' shall mean technical equipment or program resources which are used for the creation of electronic signatures;

l   'signature verification device' shall mean technical equipment or program resources which are used for the verification of electronic signatures;

m   'secure signature creation device' shall mean a signature creation device which complies with the requirements set out hereby;

n   'secure signature verification device' shall mean a signature verification device which complies with the requirements set out hereby;

o   'electronic signature product' shall mean technical equipment or program resources or components thereof which are used to procure certification services or for the creation or verification of electronic signatures;

p   'accreditation' shall mean certification that the certification service provider complies with the conditions set out hereby for the performance of the activity of an accredited certification service provider.

ARTICLE 3

Compliance with requirements for signature

1   A data message is signed insofar as it is furnished with an electronic signature.

2   The use of an advanced electronic signature based on a qualified certificate and created by means of a secure signature creation device allows verification that the person specified on this qualified certificate has signed the data message.

ARTICLE 4

Conformity to the original
The use of an advanced electronic signature guarantees that, if there is a violation of the content of the data message from the moment when it was signed, it will be possible to discover this violation.

ARTICLE 5

Obligations of the signatory

1   The signatory is obliged

a   to handle the resources, as well as the data for creation of an advanced electronic signature, with the necessary care so as to prevent the unauthorized use thereof;

b   to notify without delay the certification service provider which has issued the person with a qualified certificate of the fact that there is a risk of the abuse of its data for the creation of an advanced electronic signature;

c   to submit accurate, true and complete information to the certification service provider in relation to the qualified certificate;

2   The signatory shall be liable for damage caused by a breach of obligations under paragraph (1), pursuant to statutory provisions (1). However, the signatory shall be exempted from liability if he or she can prove that the person who incurred damage did not perform all acts necessary in order to verify to himself or herself that the advanced electronic signature was valid and that its qualified certificate had not been rendered invalid.

ARTICLE 6

Obligations of a certification service provider issuing qualified certificates

1   A certification service provider issuing qualified certificates is obliged

a   to ensure that the certificates which it issued as being qualified contain all of the prerequisites set out hereby for qualified certificates;

b   to ensure that the information specified in the qualified certificates is accurate, true and complete;

c   prior to the issue of a qualified certificate, to safely verify, by means of the appropriate resources, the identity of the person to whom it is issuing the qualified certificate and, if applicable, that person's special symbols, if the purpose of the qualified certificate so requires;

d to ascertain whether, at the time of issue of the qualified certificate, the signatory had data for the signature creation data corresponding to the data for the signature verification data contained in the qualified certificate;

e to ensure that every person can assure himself or herself of the identity of the certification service provider and its qualified certificate;

f to ensure the operation of a safe and publicly accessible register of qualified certificates issued, with remote access, and to update the information contained therein immediately upon every change;

g to ensure the operation of a safe and publicly accessible register of qualified certificates which have been rendered invalid, with remote access;

h to ensure that the date and time, including statement of the hour, minute and second, when the qualified certificate was issued or rendered invalid can be accurately determined and that this information is available to third parties;

i to receive into employment or a similar relationship persons who have the professional knowledge, experience and qualification necessary for the services provided, and who are familiar with the relevant safety procedures;

j to use safe systems and instruments of electronic signature product and to ensure sufficient safety of the procedures which support these systems and instruments; an electronic-signature product is safe insofar as it complies with the requirements set out hereby and by the procedural declaration; this must be verified by the Bureau of Personal Data Protection (hereinafter referred to as "Bureau");

k to adopt appropriate measures to prevent the abuse and forgery of qualified certificates and to ensure the concealment of data for the creation of advanced electronic signatures in the case that the certification service provider allows a signatory to create them within the framework of the services provided;

l to have at its disposal sufficient funds for operation in compliance with the requirements set out herein and with regard to the risk of liability for damage;

m to store all information and documentation on the qualified certificates issued for a period of at least 10 years from the expiration of the validity of the qualified certificate; the information and documentation must be stored in electronic form;

n prior to the conclusion of a contractual relationship with a person who applies for the issue of a qualified certificate, to inform that person in writing of the precise conditions for the use of the qualified certificate, including any restrictions in its use, and on the conditions governing complaints; the provider is also obliged to inform this person of whether or not the provider is accredited by the Bureau under Article 10; this information may be conveyed by electronic means; upon request, the substantial parts of this information must be available to third parties who are dependent upon this qualified certificate;

o   to use a safe system for the storage of qualified certificates in a verifiable form in such a way that records or changes thereto might be made only by authorized persons, that it is possible to check the correctness of the records and that any technical changes or program changes that violate these safety requirements are detectable.

2   A certification service provider issuing qualified certificates issues qualified certificates to the signatory on the basis of a contract. The contract must be in writing or otherwise it is invalid.

3   A certification service provider issuing qualified certificates may not store and copy data for the creation of an advanced electronic signature of persons to whom the provider provides its certification services.

4   If accreditation has been withdrawn from a certification service provider issuing qualified certificates by the Bureau, the provider is obliged to inform those parties to whom it provides its certification services of this fact, and to state this fact in the registers specified under paragraph (1)(f) and (g).

5   If the certification service provider is not accredited by the Bureau, it is obliged to declare to the Bureau, at least 30 days prior to the issue of its first qualified certificate, that it will be issuing qualified certificates.

6   If, in a qualified certificate, a certification service provider issuing qualified certificates has specified a restriction in the use of this certificate, including restrictions on the value of the transaction for which the qualified certificate may be used, these restrictions must be recognizable by third parties.

7   A certification service provider issuing qualified certificates must, without delay, terminate the validity of a certificate if the signatory so requests or in the case that the certificate was issued on the basis of untrue or erroneous data.

8   A certification service provider must also terminate the validity of a qualified certificate if it discovers demonstrably that the signatory has died or that a court has deprived this person of his or her competence to perform legal acts or has imposed limitations on this competence (2), or if the information on the basis of which the certificate was issued has ceased to apply.

9   Operational documentation must be kept on all activity of a provider of certification issuing qualified certificates. This documentation must contain the following information:

a   the contract with the signatory for the issue of the qualified certificate;

b   the issued qualified certificate;

c   copies of the submitted personal documents of signatory;

d   confirmation of the receipt of the qualified certificate by the signatory;

e   precise time determination of the validity period of the issued qualified certificate.

10   Employees of the certification service provider issuing qualified certificates, and any other natural persons who come into contact with personal information and data for the signature creation data of signatory, are obliged to maintain confidentiality concerning personal data, data for the signature creation data and

safety precautions the dissemination of which might jeopardize the safeguarding of personal information and data for the signature creation data. The confidentiality obligation survives the termination of employment or the relevant work.

ARTICLE 7

Liability for damage

1   The certification service provider issuing qualified certificates shall be liable for damage caused by a breach of obligations set out hereby under statutory provisions (3).

2   The certification service provider shall not be liable for damage, ensuing from the use of a qualified certificate, which has occurred as a result of the failure to comply with restrictions on its use.

ARTICLE 8

Personal data protection
The protection of personal data shall be governed by statutory legislation (4).

ARTICLE 9

Accreditation and supervision

1   The granting of accreditation for operation as an accredited certification service provider, as well as supervision of compliance with this Act, is a matter for the competence of the Bureau.

2   The Bureau shall

    a   grant and withdraw accreditation for operation as an accredited certification service provider to entities operating on the territory of the Czechlands;

    b   exercise supervision of the activities of accredited certification service provider and certification service providers issuing qualified certificates, and shall impose upon them remedial measures and fines for breaches of obligations hereunder;

    c   keep a record of accreditation granted and of changes thereto, and shall keep a record of the certification service providers which have informed the Bureau that they are issuing qualified certificates;

    d   regularly publish a review of accreditations granted and a review of certification service providers issuing qualified certificates, in a manner that allows remote access;

    e   evaluate the compliance of electronic signature products with the requirements set out hereby and by the procedural declaration;

   f   fulfill other obligations set out hereby (for example, Article 10(7), Article 13(2) and Article 16(2)).

3   For the purpose of exercising supervision, an accredited certification service provider issuing qualified certificates is obliged to allow authorized employees of the Bureau access, to such an extent as is absolutely necessary, to its business and operational premises, upon request to present documentation, records, documents, written materials and other materials related to its activity, to allow them access, to such an extent as is absolutely necessary, to its information system and to provide information and all necessary co-operation.

4   Unless this Act sets out otherwise, while exercising supervision the Bureau shall proceed in accordance with the statutory legislation (5).

ARTICLE 10

Conditions for the granting of accreditation for the provision of certification services

1   Every certification service provider must apply to the Bureau for a grant of accreditation for the performance of the activity of an accredited certification service provider. The submission of the application for accreditation is subject to an administrative fee (6).

2   In the application for accreditation under paragraph (1), the applicant must provide evidence of

   a   the business name, registered office and identification number of the applicant;

   b   a document of authorization to carry on entrepreneurial activity and, in the case of a person registered in the Commercial Register, an extract from the Commercial Register no older than 3 months;

   c   the extract from the Criminal Register of the entrepreneur/natural person or of the statutory representatives of the legal person in the case that the applicant is a legal person, no older than 3 months;

   d   the material, personnel and organizational prerequisites for the activity of a certification service provider issuing qualified certificates under Article 6 hereof;

   e   information on whether the applicant is already issuing or intends to issue qualified certificates;

   f   a document of the payment of the administrative fee.

3   If the application does not contain all of the required information, the Bureau shall interrupt the proceedings and shall call upon the applicant to complete the application within a specified time period. If the applicant fails to do so within the allocated time period, the Bureau shall stop the proceedings. In this case, the administrative fee shall not be returned.

4   If the applicant satisfies all the conditions prescribed hereby for the granting of accreditation, the Bureau shall issue a decision whereby it shall grant accreditation to the applicant. In the opposite case, the Bureau shall reject the application for grant of accreditation.

5   An accredited certification service provider must have its registered office on the territory of the Czechlands.

6   Besides the activities specified herein, an accredited certification service provider may operate without the consent of the Bureau only as an attorney, notary or expert (7).

7   Verification by the Bureau of the qualified certificate of the certification service provider forms part of the decision of the Bureau.

ARTICLE 11

untitled

In the area of organs of public authority, only advanced electronic signatures and qualified certificates issued by an accredited certification service provider may be used.

ARTICLE 12

Requirements for a qualified certificate

1   A qualified certificate must contain

   a   designation that it is issued as a qualified certificate hereunder;

   b   the business name of the certification service provider and its registered office, and specification that the certificate was issued in the Czech Republic;

   c   the name and surname of the signatory, or that person's pseudonym with appropriate designation that it is a pseudonym;

   d   special symbols of the signatory if the purpose of the qualified certificate so requires;

   e   signature verification data, which correspond to the data for the signature creation data which are under control of the signatory;

   f   the advanced electronic signature of the certification service provider which is issuing the qualified certificate;

   g   the number of the qualified certificate, which is unique in the case of the certification service provider in question;

   h   the commencement and expiration of the validity of the qualified certificate;

   i   if applicable, information on whether the use of the qualified certificate is restricted by nature and extent to certain uses only;

   j   if applicable, restrictions on the values of transactions for which the qualified certificate may be used.

2   The qualified certificate may contain other personal data only with the permission of the signatory.

ARTICLE 13

Obligations of an accredited certification service provider upon termination of activity

1   An accredited certification service provider must announce its intention to terminate its activity to the Bureau at least 3 months prior to the planned date of termination of the activity, and must use its utmost efforts to ensure that the valid qualified certificates are taken over by another accredited certification service provider. The accredited certification service provider must also demonstrably inform every signatory to whom it provides its certification services of its intention to terminate its activity, at least 2 months in advance.

2   If an accredited certification service provider is unable to ensure that another accredited certification service provider take over the valid qualified certificates, it is obliged to inform the Bureau thereof in time. In such a case, the Bureau shall take over the recording of qualified certificates issued and shall notify the signatory thereof.

3   The provisions of paragraphs (1) and (2) shall also apply, as appropriate, in the case when an accredited certification service provider becomes extinct, dies or ceases to perform its activity without fulfilling the announcement obligation under paragraph (1).

ARTICLE 14

Remedial measures

1   If the Bureau discovers that an accredited certification service provider or certification service provider issuing qualified certificates is in breach of obligations set out hereby, it will enjoin it to arrange for remedy within a stipulated time period and, if applicable, shall determine what measures for the removal of the deficiencies this certification service provider is obliged to adopt.

2   If an accredited certification service provider commits a serious breach of obligations set out hereby, or if it fails to remove deficiencies discovered by the Bureau within the allocated time period, the Bureau is entitled to withdraw its accreditation.

3   If the Bureau decides on the withdrawal of accreditation, it may simultaneously terminate the validity of qualified certificates issued by the certification service provider within the validity period of the accreditation.

ARTICLE 15

Cancellation of a qualified certificate

1   The Bureau may order a certification service provider to invalidate the qualification certificate of a signatory as a preliminary measure (8) if there exists a justifiable suspicion that the qualified certificate was forged, or if it was issued on the basis of untrue information. An order for the invalidation of the qualified certificate may also be issued if it is discovered that the signatory is using a

resource for the signature creation device, which contains safety deficiencies which could enable the forgery of advanced electronic signatures or the changing of the signed data.

2   The register of certificates under Article 6(1)(g) must contain precise specification of the time from when the certificate was invalidated. It is not permitted to restore invalidated certificates to operation and use them.

ARTICLE 16

Recognition of foreign certificates

1   A certificate which is issued by a foreign certification service provider as qualified as set forth hereunder may be used as a qualified certificate if it is recognized by a certification service provider issuing qualified certificates hereunder, and on the condition that this certification service provider guarantees the correctness and validity of the qualified certificate issued abroad to the same extent as it does its own qualified certificates.

2   A certificate which is issued by a foreign certification service provider as qualified as set forth hereunder is recognized as a qualified certificate if this follows from a decision of the Bureau or from international agreements, or if an agreement on mutual recognition of certificates has been entered into between the relevant foreign organ or foreign certification service provider and the Bureau.

ARTICLE 17

Resources for the safe creation and verification of advanced electronic signatures

1   A resource for the secure signature creation device must, by means of appropriate technical and program resources and procedures, at least ensure that

   a   the data for the signature creation data, can appear only once, and that the concealment thereof is secured as is necessary;

   b   it is not possible, when the requisite security is applied, to infer the data for the signature creation data from knowledge of the manner of its creation, and that the signature is protected against forgery with the use of existing available technology;

   c   the data for the signature creation data can be reliably protected by the signatory from abuse by a third party.

2   Resources for the secure signature creation device may not alter data that are signed, nor may they prevent this data from being presented to the signatory prior to the actual process of signing.

3   A resource for the secure signature creation device must, by means of appropriate technical and program resources and procedures, at least ensure that

   a   the data used for verification of a signature corresponds to the data displayed to the person performing the verification;

b   the signature is reliably verified and the result of this verification is duly displayed;

c   the verifying person is able to reliably ascertain the content of the signed data;

d   the correctness and validity of the certificate is reliably ascertained during verification of the signature;

e   the result of the verification and identity of the signatory are duly displayed;

f   the use of a pseudonym is clearly designated;

g   it is possible to ascertain all changes affecting security.

ARTICLE 18

Fines

1   The Bureau may impose a fine of up to CZK10,000,000 upon an accredited certification service provider or upon a certification service provider issuing qualified certificates which breaches an obligation imposed hereby.

2   If, within a year of the day on which the decision upon the imposition of a fine acquired legal force, an accredited certification service provider or certification service provider issuing qualified certificates has again breached obligations imposed upon it hereby, a fine of up to CZK20,000,000 may be imposed upon it.

3   An accredited certification service provider or certification service provider issuing qualified certificates which thwarts a control procedure performed by the Bureau may be punished, even repeatedly, with an order penalty of up to CZK1,000,000.

4   A fine of up to CZK25,000 may be imposed, even repeatedly, upon a person who, even owing to negligence, fails to provide the Bureau with the necessary co-operation during the performance of a control procedure.

5   During the process of deciding upon the value of a fine, consideration is given to the manner of conduct, degree of fault, seriousness, extent, duration and consequences of the unlawful action.

6   A fine may be imposed within one year of the day on which the relevant organ discovered the breach of obligation, but no later than three years from the day on which the breach of obligation took place.

7   Fines are collected by the Bureau. Fines are enforced by the regional financial organ pursuant to statutory provisions (9).

8   Revenues from fines constitute income of the state budget of the Czech Republic.

ARTICLE 19

untitled

Unless this Act sets out otherwise, statutory legislation shall apply to proceedings hereunder (10).

ARTICLE 20

Authorizing provisions

The Bureau is authorized to issue declarations for the detailed specification of the conditions set out in Articles 6 and 17 and of the method whereby compliance therewith will be documented, and to specify the requirements with which electronic signature product must comply, and for the requirements of the procedure and method of evaluating the compliance of electronic signature product with these requirements.

Finland

Act on Electronic Signatures

(14/2003)

Chapter 1

General provisions

Section 1

Purpose of the Act
The purpose of this Act is to promote the use of electronic signatures and the provision of products and services related to them as well as to promote data protection and data security of electronic commerce and electronic communication.

Section 2

Definitions
For the purposes of this Act:

1) *electronic signature* means data in electronic form which are attached to or logically associated with other electronic data and which serve as a method of authenticating the identity of the signatory;

2) *advanced electronic signature* means an electronic signature

   a) which is uniquely linked to the signatory;

   b) which is capable of identifying the signatory;

   c) which is created using means that the signatory can maintain under his sole control; and

   d) which is linked to other electronic data in such a manner that any subsequent change of the data is detectable.

3)   *signatory* means a natural person who lawfully holds the signature-creation data and who acts either on his own behalf or on behalf of the natural or legal person he represents;

4)   *signature-creation data* means unique data, such as codes or private keys, which are used by the signatory to create an electronic signature;

5)   *signature-creation device* means software or hardware used together with signature-creation data to implement an electronic signature;

6)   *signature-verification data* means data, such as codes or public keys, which are used for the purpose of verifying an electronic signature;

7)   *certificate* means electronic data which links signature-verification data to the signatory and confirms the identity of the signatory;

8)   *certification-service-provider* means a natural or legal person who provides certificates;

9)   *electronic-signature product* means hardware or software, or relevant parts thereof, which are intended to be used by a certification-service-provider for the provision of electronic-signature services or to be used in the creation or verification of electronic signatures; as well as

10) *electronic-signature service* means the provision of certificates as well as that of other products or services related to electronic signatures.

Section 3

Scope of application
This Act shall apply to electronic signatures as well as to service providers who offer products or services related to electronic signatures to the public.

The use of electronic signatures in administration shall further be governed by provisions to be issued separately.

Section 4

Free circulation of services and products
Electronic-signature products and services complying with this Act are permitted to circulate freely in the internal market.

Section 5

Secure signature-creation device
A secure signature-creation device must with sufficient reliability ensure that

1)   the signature-creation data can practically occur only once and that their secrecy is assured;

2)   the signature-creation data cannot be derived from other data;

3)   the signature is protected against forgery;

4) the signatory can protect the signaturecreation data against the use of others; as well as that

5) the creation device does not alter the data to be signed and that it does not prevent such data from being presented to the signatory prior to the signature process.

The signature-creation device shall always be deemed to meet the requirements laid down in paragraph 1 if

1) it complies with the generally accepted standards confirmed by the Commission of the European Communities and published in the Official Journal of the European Communities; or if

2) the secure signature-creation device has been approved by an inspection body designated for the assessment of conformity and located in Finland or in another State belonging to the European Economic Area.

Section 6

The inspection body
The Finnish Communications Regulatory Authority may designate inspection bodies to assess whether a signature-creation device meets the requirements laid down in section 5, paragraph 1. The inspection bodies may be private or public bodies.

The designation of an inspection body shall require that

1) the inspection body is functionally and financially independent;

2) its operations are reliable, appropriate and non-discriminatory;

3) it has sufficient financial resources to arrange its operations appropriately and to cover any liability for damages;

4) it has a sufficient professional and unbiased personnel; and that

5) it has the facilities and equipment necessary for its operations.

The Finnish Communications Regulatory Authority shall designate the inspection bodies upon an application. In addition to the contact information and the Trade Register extract of the applicant, the application shall contain an account of the fulfilment of the requirements referred to in paragraph 2 with respect to the operations of the applicant. Where necessary, the Finnish Communications Regulatory Authority shall issue instructions on the information to be included in the application and on its delivery to the Finnish Communications Regulatory Authority.

The Finnish Communications Regulatory Authority shall supervise the operations of the inspection body. If the inspection body does not meet the requirements laid down or if it violates the provisions, the Finnish Communications Regulatory Authority shall withdraw its designation decision. The inspection body shall notify the Finnish Communications Regulatory Authority of any changes relating to the criteria for designation.

In its assessment work the inspection body may be assisted by outside parties. The work of outside parties assisting it.

Chapter 2

Provision of qualified certificates

Section 7

Qualified certificate
A qualified certificate shall mean a certificate meeting the requirements laid down in paragraph 2 and issued by a certification-service-provider meeting the requirements laid down in sections 10 - 15.

A qualified certificate shall contain:

1) an indication that the certificate is a qualified certificate;

2) the identification of the certificationservice- provider and the State in which it is established;

3) the name of the signatory or a pseudonym, which shall be identified as such;

4) signature-verification data which correspond to the signature-creation data under control of the signatory;

5) the period of validity of the qualified certificate;

6) the identity code of the qualified certificate;

7) the advanced electronic signature of the certification-service-provider;

8) any limitations on the scope of use of the qualified certificate; and

9) specific data relating to the signatory if relevant for the purpose of use of the qualified certificate.

Section 8

Qualified certificate provided by a certification-service-provider established outside Finland
A certificate provided as a qualified certificate by a certification-service-provider not established in Finland shall be deemed to meet the requirements concerning qualified certificates laid down in this Act if

1) the certification-service-provider is established in a State belonging to the European Economic Area and the certificate meets the requirements laid down for a qualified certificate in the State of establishment; or if

2) the certification-service-provider belongs to a voluntary accreditation scheme in a State belonging to the European Economic Area and meets the national requirements laid down in that State for the implementation of Directive 1999/93/EC; or if

3) the certificate is guaranteed by a certification-service-provider that is established in a State belonging to the European Economic Area and who meets the national requirements laid down in that State for the implementation of Directive 1999/93/EC of the European Parliament and of the Council on a Community framework for electronic signatures, hereafter Directive on electronic signatures; or if

4) the certificate or certification-serviceprovider is recognised under a bilateral or multilateral agreement between the European Community and third countries or international organisations.

Section 9

Notification on the start of operations
A certification-service-provider that intends to provide qualified certificates to the public shall, prior to the start of the provision of qualified certificates, submit a written notification to the Finnish Communications Regulatory Authority. The notification shall contain the name and contact information of the certification-service-provider as well as information on the basis of which it is possible to ensure that the requirements laid down in section 7 and sections 10-15 are fulfilled. The Finnish Communications Regulatory Authority may issue orders and recommendations necessary for supervision on the further contents of the information to be provided to the Finnish Communications Regulatory Authority and on the procedure for its notification.

If a certificate does not fulfil the requirements laid down in section 7, paragraph 2, or if the certification-serviceprovider does not fulfil the requirements laid down in sections 10 - 15, the Finnish Communications Regulatory Authority shall without delay after learning of the matter forbid the certification-service-provider from providing its certificates as qualified certificates.

If the information referred to in paragraph 1 has changed, the certification-serviceprovider shall without delay inform the Finnish Communications Regulatory Authority of the changes in writing.

The Finnish Communications Regulatory Authority shall maintain a public register of certification-service-providers providing qualified certificates.

Section 10

General obligations of a certification-service-provider providing qualified certificates to the public
The operations of a certification-serviceprovider providing qualified certificates to the public shall be careful, reliable and appropriate and non-discriminatory towards its customers. The certification-serviceprovider
shall have technical expertise and financial resources sufficient vis-á-vis the scope of operations. The certificationservice- provider shall be liable for all the aspects of the certification operations, including the reliability and functionality of any services and products produced by parties assisting the certification-serviceprovider.

The certification-service-provider shall:

1) ensure that its personnel has sufficient expertise, experience and qualifications;

2) ensure that it has sufficient financial resources to arrange its operations and to cover any liability for damages;

3) have generally available all relevant information on the certificate and certification operations for the assessment of the operations and reliability of the certification-service-provider; and

4) ensure the confidentiality of the certificate-creation data when these data are produced by the certification-serviceprovider.

The certification-service-provider may not store or copy the signature-creation data submitted to the signatory.

Section 11

Trustworthy hardware and software
A certification-service-provider providing qualified certificates to the public shall ensure that the systems, hardware and software it uses are sufficiently trustworthy as well as protected against alterations and forgery.

Hardware or software relating to electronic signatures is deemed to fulfil the requirements laid down in paragraph 1, if it complies with the generally accepted standards confirmed by the Commission of the European Communities and published in the Official Journal of the European Communities.

Section 12

Issuing a qualified certificate
A certification-service-provider providing qualified certificates to the public shall, in a careful and reliable manner, verify the identity of the person applying a qualified certificate as well as any other data relating to the person applying for the certificate necessary for the issuing and maintenance of the qualified certificate.

A certification-service-provider providing qualified certificates to the public shall, before entering into a contract, inform the person applying for a qualified certificate of the terms regarding the use of the qualified certificate, including any limitations on its use, the existence of voluntary accreditation schemes, the supervision of certification operations by the authorities as well as of the procedure for complaints and dispute settlement. The person applying for a
qualified certificate shall be given the information in an easily comprehensible form. The information shall be given at least in Finnish or Swedish according to the applicant's choice.

Section 13

Revocation of a qualified certificate
The signatory shall without delay request the certification-service-provider that has issued the qualified certificate to revoke it if it has justified reason to suspect unlawful use of the signature-creation data.

A certification-service-provider providing qualified certificates to the public shall, without delay, revoke a qualified certificate when so requested by the signatory. A request for the revocation of a qualified certificate shall be deemed received by the certification-service-provider when it has been available to the certification-serviceprovider so that the handling of the request has been possible.

A qualified certificate may also be revoked for another special reason. The signatory shall always be informed of the revocation of a qualified certificate and the time of its revocation.

Section 14

Registers maintained by a certification-service-provider providing qualified certificates to the public

A certification-service-provider providing qualified certificates to the public shall maintain a register of qualified certificates issued by it (certificate register). The following shall be entered in the register:

1)   the data content of a qualified certificate defined in section 7, paragraph 2;

2)   the data relating to the person applying for the certificate and referred to in section 12, paragraph 1, including information on the procedure used to identity the applicant when issuing the qualified certificate, and necessary information of a possible document used in identification; and

3)   the information referred to in section 21 on checking the validity of the certificate from the revocation list, if the certificationservice- provider providing qualified certificates to the public uses the right to store information as referred to in section 21.

A certification-service-provider providing qualified certificates to the public shall ensure that the data content of the certificate defined in section 7, paragraph 2 is available to a party relying on an advanced electronic signature certified with a qualified certificate. However, information referred to above in paragraph 1, subparagraph 3 shall not have to be stored in a certificate register, if the certification-service-provider takes other measures to ensure that the party relying on the certificate is able to reliably show that a revocation list is properly checked.

The certification-service-provider shall also maintain a public register of revoked qualified certificates (revocation list) available to parties relying on qualified certificates. Information on the revocation of a qualified certificate and a specific time of revocation shall appropriately and without delay be entered in the revocation list.

The information referred to in paragraphs 2 and 3 shall be available 24 hours a day.

Section 15

Maintenance of the information in the certificate register

A certification-service-provider providing qualified certificates to the public shall maintain the information of the certificate register in a reliable and appropriate manner for 10 years after the end of the validity of the certificate.

Section 16

Liability for damages of a certification-service-provider providing qualified certificates

A certification-service-provider providing qualified certificates to the public shall be liable for damage caused to a party relying on a qualified certificate due to the following:

1)   the data entered in the qualified certificate have been wrong when the certificate has been issued;

2) the qualified certificate does not contain the data referred to in section 7, paragraph 2;

3) at the time of the issuance of the certificate, the signatory identified in the qualified certificate did not hold the signature-creation data corresponding to the signature-verification data;

4) the signature-creation data and signature-verification data created by the certification-service-provider or the party assisting it are not compatible; or

5) the certification-service-provider or a party assisting it has not revoked the qualified certificate in the manner provided for in section 13.

The certification-service-provider shall be discharged from the liability laid down in paragraph 1 if it proves that the damage was not due to his own negligence or the negligence of a party assisting it.

A certification-service-provider shall not be liable for damage caused by violating a limitation on use contained in a qualified certificate.

In other respects, the liability for damages of a certification-service-provider providing qualified certificates to the public shall be governed by the Damages Act (412/1974).

The provisions of this section shall also apply to a certification-service-provider, who guarantees to the public that a certificate is a qualified certificate.

Section 17

Liability for unauthorised use of signature-creation data
The signatory shall be liable for damage caused by unauthorised use of the signaturecreation data of an advanced electronic signature certified by a qualified certificate until the request to revoke the certificate has been received by the certification-serviceprovider as provided for in section 13, paragraph 2.

However, a consumer shall be subject to the liability laid down in paragraph 1 only if:

1) he has given the creation data to someone else;

2) the creation data have ended in the possession of a person not authorised to use them due to the negligence of the signatory, which is not slight; or if

3) after losing control of the creation data in a manner other than that referred to in subparagraph 2, he has failed to request the revocation of the qualified certificate as provided for in section 13, paragraph 1.

A contract term derogating from the provisions of paragraph 2 to the detriment of the consumer shall be void.

Chapter 3

Legal effect of an electronic signature and the processing of personal data

Section 18

Legal effect of an electronic signature
If the law requires that a signature be attached to a legal act, this requirement shall be fulfilled at least by an advanced signature based on a qualified certificate and created by means of a secure signature-creation
device.

Section 19

Processing of personal data
A certification-service-provider providing
certificates to the public may collect personal data necessary for the issuing and
maintenance of the certificate only directly from the signatory. With regard to a
certification-service-provider providing qualified certificates to the public, further
provisions on the issuing of a qualified certificate, the registers to be maintained and the
information to be maintained are contained in chapter 2 of this Act.

When verifying the identity of a person applying for a certificate, the
certificationservice- provider may require him to provide his personal identity number.
The personal identity number of the signatory may not be included in the certificate.

Personal data may only under the explicit written permission of the signatory:

1) be collected otherwise than directly from the signatory; or

2) be processed for a purpose other than that referred to in paragraph 1.

The processing of personal data shall further be governed by the provisions of the
Personal Data Act (523/1999) thereon.

Section 20

Use of the Population Information System
Upon the express consent of the person applying for a certificate, the certification-service-
provider may obtain and verify the personal data given by the person from the
Population Information System.

The information extracted from the Population Information System shall be delivered
as a public-law performance in accordance with the Act on the Charge Criteria of the State
(150/1992).

Section 21

Storing the information regarding the validity checking of a certificate
The certification-service-provider may store the information regarding the checking of the
validity of a certificate from the revocation list. The information stored may only be used
to invoice for the use of certificates or to verify legal acts performed by using an electronic
signature certified by a certificate.

Chapter 4

General guidance and supervision

Section 22

General guidance and supervision
The general guidance and development of certification operations shall be the
responsibility of the Ministry of Transport and Communications.

The Finnish Communications Regulatory Authority shall be in charge of supervision in compliance with this Act. Where necessary, the Finnish Communications Regulatory Authority shall issue technical orders and recommendations on the requirements of reliability and data security of the operations of certification-service-providers providing qualified certificates relating to electronic signatures.

Provisions of the Act on the Charge Criteria of the State (150/1992) shall apply to charges collected for supervision and other tasks of the Finnish Communications Regulatory Authority.

The Data Protection Ombudsman shall supervise the compliance with the provisions of this Act concerning personal data. When performing his duties, the Data Protection Ombudsman shall have the right to obtain information and to perform inspections referred to in the Personal Data Act. Provisions on appeal regarding the operations of the Data Protection Ombudsman shall be governed by the Personal Data Act.

Section 23

Right to obtain information

Without prejudice to provisions on secrecy, the Finnish Communications Regulatory Authority may obtain information necessary for the tasks laid down in section 22 from certification-service-providers who provide to the public qualified certificates relating to electronic signatures, and from people assisting them.

Section 24

Right of inspection

An inspector appointed to the task by the Finnish Communications Regulatory Authority shall have the right to perform an inspection to supervise compliance with this Act and the orders issued thereunder. The person performing the inspection shall have the right to inspect the hardware and software used by a certification-serviceprovider providing qualified certificates to the public and of a party assisting it if the hardware or software may be relevant for the supervision of compliance with this Act and with orders issued thereunder.

A certification-service-provider providing qualified certificates to the public or a party assisting it shall provide the inspector referred to in paragraph 1 access to its manufacturing, business and storage premises, if these do not fall within the scope of domestic peace.

The Finnish Communications Regulatory Authority shall be entitled to obtain executive assistance from the police to perform an inspection referred to in paragraphs 1 and 2.

Section 25

Secrecy obligation

Those performing duties under this Act shall be subject to a secrecy obligation as provided for in the Act on Openness of Government Activities (621/1999).

Chapter 5

Miscellaneous provisions

Section 26

Provisions on sanctions

Punishment for a personal register crime shall be governed by the provisions of chapter 38, section 9 of the Penal Code (39/1889) and that for a personal register offence by the provisions of section 48, paragraph 2 of the Personal Data Act.

Section 27

Administrative coercive measures

The Finnish Communications Regulatory Authority may order anyone violating this Act or orders issued thereunder to remedy his fault or omission. The decision may be enforced through the imposition of a conditional fine or a threat that either part or all of the operations are suspended or that the omitted measure will be ordered to be performed at the cost of the party in question. The conditional fine, threat of suspension and threat of having a measure performed shall be governed by the provisions of the Act on the Conditional Imposition of a Fine (1113/1990).

The costs of work ordered to be performed shall be paid in advance from State funds and they shall be collected from the neglecting party as provided for in the Act on the Collection of Taxes and Charges through Execution (367/1961).

Section 28

Appeal

Appeal against a decision made by the Finnish Communications Regulatory Authority by virtue of this Act shall be governed by the provisions of the Administrative Judicial Procedure Act (586/1996).

The Finnish Communications Regulatory Authority may in its decision order that the decision shall be complied with before it becomes final. However, the appeal authority may enjoin the enforcement of the decision until the appeal has been decided.

Section 29

Entry into force

This Act shall enter into force on 1 February 2003.

Measures necessary for the implementation of this Act may be taken prior to its entry into force.

Section 30

Transitional provisions

A certification-service-provider that has started to provide qualified certificates to the public prior to the entry into force of the Act shall make a notification referred to in section 9 no later than within three months from the entry into force of the Act.

Germany

Law Governing Framework Conditions for Electronic Signatures and Amending Other Regulations

Part One: General Provisions

Section 1: Purpose and Area of Application

(1)   The purpose of this Law is to create framework conditions for electronic signatures.

(2)   Where electronic signatures are not specifically required by law their use shall be voluntary.

(3)   Legal provisions may require compliance with additional conditions for the use of qualified electronic signatures for public administrative activities. These conditions shall be objective, proportionate, and non-discriminatory, and shall relate only to the specific characteristics of the relevant applications.

Section 2: Definition of Terms

For the purposes of this Law

1.   "Electronic signatures" shall be data in electronic form that are attached to other electronic data or logically linked to them and used for authentication;

2.   "Advanced electronic signatures" shall be electronic signatures as in 1. above that

   a)   are exclusively assigned to the owner of the signature code

   b)   enable the owner of the signature code to be identified

    c)   are produced with means which the owner of the signature code can keep under his sole control and

    d)   are so linked to the data to which they refer that any subsequent alteration of such data may be detected;

3.   "Qualified electronic signatures" shall be electronic signatures as in 2. above that

    a)   are based on a qualified certificate valid at the time of their creation and

    b)   have been produced with a secure signature-creation device;

4.   "Signature codes" shall be unique electronic data such as private cryptographic codes that are used to create an electronic signature;

5.   "Signature test codes" shall be electronic data such as public cryptographic codes that are used to test an electronic signature;

6.   "Certificates" shall be electronic certificates assigning signature test codes to a person and confirming his or her identity;

7.   "Qualified certificates" shall be electronic certificates pursuant to 6. above for natural persons that fulfill the requirements in Section 7 and are issued by certification-service providers who meet at least the requirements under Sections 4 to 14 or Section 23 of this Law and the provisions of the statutory ordinance pursuant to Section 24 that are based on this Law;

8.   "Certification-service providers" shall be natural persons or legal entities who issue qualified certificates or qualified time stamps;

9.   "Signature-code owners" shall be natural persons who own signature codes and to whom the appropriate signature test codes have been assigned in qualified certificates;

10.   "Secure signature-creation devices" shall be software or hardware products used to store and apply the respective signature code, that meet or exceed the requirements of Section 17 or Section 23 of this Law and the provisions of the statutory ordinance pursuant to Section 24 that are based on this Law, and that are designed for qualified electronic signatures;

11.   "Signature-application components" shall be software and hardware products designed to

    a)   assign data to the process of producing or testing qualified electronic signatures or

    b)   test qualified electronic signatures or check qualified certificates and display the results;

12.   "Technical components for certification services" shall be software or hardware products designed to

    a)   create signature codes and transfer them into a secure signature-creation device

    b)   keep qualified certificates available for testing and, if necessary, downloading by the public, or

    c)   produce qualified time stamps;

13. "Products for qualified electronic signatures" shall be secure signature-creation devices, signature-application components, and technical components for certification services;

14. "Qualified time stamps" shall be electronic certificates issued by a certification-service provider that meet or exceed the requirements under Sections 4 to 14 and Section 17 or Section 23 of this Law and the provisions of the statutory ordinance pursuant to Section 24 that are based on this Law, and that confirm that certain electronic data have been presented to it at a certain time;

15. "Voluntary accreditation" shall be a procedure to issue a permit that authorizes the operation of a certification service and confers specific rights and obligations.

Section 3: Competent Authority

The tasks of the competent authority under this Law and the statutory ordinance under Section 24 shall be performed by the authority named in Section 66 of the Telecommunications Act.

Part Two: Certification-Service Providers

Section 4: General Requirements

(1) The operation of a certification service shall not require approval under current law.

(2) Only those who can prove that they have the necessary reliability and specialized knowledge may operate as certification-service providers. They shall also show that they have cover under Section 12 and fulfill the other conditions for the operation of a certification service under this Law and the statutory ordinance under Section 24 (1), (3), and (4). An applicant shall have the necessary reliability if he can guarantee that as certification-service provider he will observe the legal regulations governing this operation. The necessary specialized knowledge shall be available if the persons who will work in the certification-service office have the knowledge, experience, and skills needed for this work. The other conditions for operating a certification service shall be met if the measures to fulfill the security requirements under this Law and the statutory ordinance under Section 24 (1), (3), and (4) have been presented to the competent authority in a secure concept, are appropriate, and have been implemented in practice.

(3) Anyone commencing to operate a certification service shall report this to the competent authority at the latest when commencing operation. The report shall include appropriate proof that the conditions under (2) have been met.

(4) It shall be ensured that the conditions under (2) can be fulfilled throughout the entire duration of operation as certification-service provider. Circumstances that render this impossible shall be reported to the competent authority without delay.

(5) The certification-service provider may transfer work under this Law and the statutory ordinance under Section 24 to third parties if this is included in his security concept under (2) Sentence 4.

Section 5: Issue of Qualified Certificates

(1)　The certification-service provider shall reliably identify persons who apply for a qualified certificate. He shall confirm the assignment of a signature-test code to an identified person with a qualified certificate and ensure that this can be examined and downloaded by anyone at any time using public telecommunication links. A qualified certificate may only be kept accessible for downloading with the approval of the signature-code owner.

(2)　If requested by an applicant, a qualified certificate may contain data on his authorization to act for a third party and occupational or other data on his person (attributes). In regard to the data on the authorization to act for a third party, the approval of this person must be proven; occupational or other data on the person must be confirmed by the office responsible for the occupational or other data. Data on the authorization to act for a third party may only be included in a qualified certificate if proof of this party's approval is given as stated in Sentence 2; occupation or other data on the person from the applicant may be included only if the approval is presented in accordance with Sentence 2. Other personal data may be included in a qualified certificate only with the approval of the person concerned.

(3)　If requested by the applicant the certification-service provider shall use a pseudonym instead of his name in the qualified certificate. If a qualified certificate contains data on the authorization to act for a third party or occupational or other data on the person, the approval of the third party or the office responsible for the occupational or other data shall be required for the pseudonym to be used.

(4)　The certification-service provider shall make arrangements to ensure that data for qualified certificates cannot be falsified or forged without detection. He shall also take steps to ensure that the signature codes are kept secret. Signature codes may not be stored outside the secure signature- creation device.

(5)　For the purposes of certifying qualified electronic signatures, the certification-service provider shall employ reliable personnel and products that meet the requirements under Sections 4 to 14 and Section 17 or Section 23 of this Law and the statutory ordinance pursuant to Section 24.

(6)　The certification-service provider shall obtain suitable proof that the applicant owns the relevant secure signature-creation device.

Section 6: Information Obligations

(1)　The certification-service provider shall inform the applicant under Section 5(1) of the measures needed to increase the security of qualified electronic signatures and to test them reliably. He shall remind the applicant that data with a qualified electronic signature may have to be signed again lest the security value of the current signature be reduced by the passage of time.

(2)　The certification-service provider shall inform the applicant that a qualified electronic signature has the same effect in legal transactions as a handwritten signature unless otherwise specified by law.

(3)   To fulfill the information obligations under (1) and (2), the applicant shall be given a written information sheet and confirm by separate signature that he has read and taken note of this. If an applicant has already been informed pursuant to (1) and (2), further information shall not be necessary.

Section 7: Contents of Qualified Certificates

(1)   A qualified certificate shall contain the following data and bear a qualified electronic signature:

1.   The name of the signature-code owner, to which a supplement shall be added if there is a possibility of confusion with another name, or an unmistakable pseudonym assigned to the signature-code owner and recognizable as such;

2.   The assigned signature-test code;

3.   The designation of the algorithms with which the signature-test code of the signature-code owner and the signature-test code of the certification-service provider may be used;

4.   The current number of the certificate;

5.   The start and end of its validity;

6.   The name of the certification-service provider and the state in which he is domiciled;

7.   Information on whether the use of the signature code is limited to certain applications by nature or extent;

8.   Information that this is a qualified certificate; and

9.   If necessary, attributes of the signature-code owner.

(2)   Attributes may also be included in a separate qualified certificate (qualified attribute certificate). In a qualified attribute certificate, the data under (1) may be replaced with clear reference data from the qualified certificate to which it refers, where this is not needed to use the qualified attribute certificate.

Section 8: Invalidating Qualified Certificates

(1)   The certification-service provider shall invalidate a qualified certificate without delay if a signature-code owner or his representative so demands, if the certificate was issued on the basis of false data on Section 7, if the certification-service provider has ceased to operate and the operation is not being continued by another certification-service provider, or if the competent authority orders the certificate invalidated in accordance with Section 19(4). The invalidation must state the time from which it applies. Invalidation with backdated effect is not permitted. If a qualified certificate was issued with false data, the certification-service provider may also make this known.

(2)   If a qualified certificate contains data under Section 5(2), the third party or the office responsible for the occupational or other data on the person may demand

invalidation of the certificate in question under (1) if the conditions for the occupational or other data on the person cease to apply after being included in the qualified certificate.

Section 9: Qualified Time Stamps

If a certification-service provider issues a qualified time stamp, Section 5(5) shall apply mutatis mutandis.

Section 10: Documentation

(1) The certification-service provider shall document the security measures taken to observe this Law and the statutory ordinance under Section 24 Nos. 1 and 3, and document the qualified certificates issued in accordance with Sentence 2 so that the data and their correctness may be confirmed at any time. The documentation shall be made without delay, and in such a manner that it cannot subsequently be altered without detection. This shall particularly apply to the issuance and invalidation of qualified certificates.

(2) Upon request, the signature-code owner shall be given access to the data and the procedural steps concerning him.

Section 11: Liability

(1) If a certification-service provider infringes the requirements under this Law and the statutory ordinance under Section 24, or if his products for qualified electronic signatures or other technical security facilities fail, he shall reimburse a third party for any damage suffered from relying on the data in a qualified certificate or a qualified time stamp or on information given in accordance with Section 5(1) Sentence 2. Damages shall not be payable if the third party knew, or must have known, that the data was faulty.

(2) Damages need not be reimbursed if the certification-service provider has incurred no culpability.

(3) If a qualified certificate restricts the use of the signature code to certain applications by type or extent, damages shall be payable only within the limits of these restrictions.

(4) The certification-service provider shall be liable for third parties commissioned under Section 4(5) and when guaranteeing foreign certificates under Section 23(1) No. 2 as for his own actions. Section 831(1) Sentence 2 of the German Civil Code shall not apply.

Section 12: Cover

The certification-service provider shall be obliged to make appropriate cover provisions to ensure that he can meet his statutory obligations for reimbursement of damages caused by an infringement by him of the requirements or products of this Law or the statutory ordinance under Section 24, or if his products for qualified electronic signatures or other technical security facilities fail. The minimum amount shall be 500,000 deutschmarks for damages caused by an occurrence of the kind described in Sentence 1 for which he is liable.

Section 13: Cessation of Operations

(1)   The certification-service provider shall report the cessation of his operations to the competent authority without delay. He shall ensure that the qualified certificates that are still valid when he ceases to operate will be taken over by another certification-service provider or invalidate them. He shall inform the signature-code owners concerned that he is ceasing to operate and that the qualified certificates are being taken over by another certification-service provider.

(2)   The certification-service provider shall hand over the documentation under Section 10 to the certification-service provider who is taking over the certificates under (1). If no other certification- service provider takes over the documentation, the competent authority shall do so. In response to legitimate interest, the competent authority shall provide information on the documentation pursuant to Sentence 2 if this is technically possible and does not require an overproportionate amount of effort.

(3)   The certification-service provider shall inform the competent authority without delay of an application to open insolvency proceedings.

Section 14: Data Protection

(1)   The certification-service provider may only obtain data on persons directly from these persons and only to the extent necessary to issue a qualified certificate. Obtaining data from third parties shall only be permitted with the consent of the person concerned. The data may only be used for purposes other than those given in Sentence 1 if this Law permits or the person concerned gives his consent.

(2)   In the case of a signature-code owner with a pseudonym, the certification-service provider shall hand the data on his identity to the competent authority upon request, where this is necessary for the prosecution of criminal acts or infringement of regulations, to avoid risk to public security or order or to fulfill the tasks legally required of the constitutional protection agencies of the federal government and the individual states, the Federal Secret Service, military defense, or the fiscal authorities, or insofar as the courts order this as part of proceedings pending and pursuant to the appropriate statutory provisions. The information shall be documented. The authority requesting the information shall inform the signature-code owner that his pseudonym has been revealed as soon as this will not restrict the performance of its legal duties, or if the interests of the signature-code owner in being informed outweigh the other considerations.

(3)   Where certification-service providers other than those named in Section 2 No. 8 issue certificates for electronic signatures, (1) and (2) shall apply mutatis mutandis.

Part Three: Voluntary Accreditation

Section 15: Voluntary Accreditation of Certification-Service Providers

(1)   Certification-service providers may be accredited by the competent authority upon application; the competent authority may make use of private offices for the accreditation. Accreditation shall be given if the certification-service provider can show that the requirements under this Law and the statutory ordinance under Section 24 are fulfilled. Accredited certification-service providers will be given a quality sign by the competent authority. This shall be proof that the qualified electronic signatures (qualified electronic signatures with provider accreditation) based on their qualified certificates offer security that has been comprehensively tested technically and administratively. They shall be allowed to call themselves accredited certification-service providers and refer to the proven security in legal and business transactions.

(2)   To fulfill the requirements under (1), the security concept under Section 4(2) Sentence 4 shall be comprehensively tested for its suitability and practical implementation and approved by an office under Section 18. The testing and approval shall be repeated after any changes that greatly affect security, and at regular intervals of time.

(3)   The accreditation may be given with conditions attached where this is necessary to ensure fulfillment of the requirements under this Law and the statutory ordinance under Section 24 upon commencement of and during operations.

(4)   The accreditation shall be refused if the conditions under this Law and the statutory ordinance under Section 24 are not fulfilled; Section 19 shall apply mutatis mutandis.

(5)   If the requirements under this Law or the statutory ordinance under Section 24 are not fulfilled, or if there is reason to refuse accreditation under (5), the competent authority shall revoke the accreditation or, if the reasons were already given when the accreditation was accorded, withdraw it if measures under Section 19(2) would not appear likely to succeed.

(6)   If an accreditation is revoked or withdrawn, or if an accredited certification-service provider ceases to operate, the competent authority shall ensure that his operations are taken over by another accredited certification-service provider or that the contracts with the signature-code owners can be handled. This shall also apply if the application is made to open insolvency proceedings, if the operations are not continued. If no other accredited certification-service provider is taking over the documentation in accordance with Section 13(2), the competent authority shall take it over. Section 10(1) Sentence 1 shall apply mutatis mutandis.

(7)   In the case of products for electronic signatures, fulfillment of the requirements under Section 17(1 to 3) and the statutory ordinance under Section 24 shall be

adequately tested with state-of-the-art science and technology and confirmed by an office under Section 18; (1) Sentence 3
shall apply mutatis mutandis. The accredited certification-service provider shall

1.   Only use products and qualified electronic signatures in his certification operations that have been tested and approved pursuant to Sentence 1;

2.   Only issue qualified certificates for persons who can prove that they have secure signaturecreation devices that have been tested and approved in accordance with Sentence 1; and

3.   Inform the signature-code owners of signature-application components that have been tested and confirmed in accordance with Sentence 1, within the framework of Section 6(1).

Section 16: Certificates from the Competent Authority

(1)   The competent authority shall issue the accredited certification-service providers with the qualified certificates they need for their operations. The regulations for the issuance of qualified certificates by accredited certification-service providers shall apply mutatis mutandis for the competent authority. It shall invalidate qualified certificates it has issued if an accredited certification- service provider ceases to operate or if an accreditation is withdrawn or revoked.

(2)   The competent authority shall ensure that

1.   The names, addresses, and communication links of the accredited certification-service providers

2.   The revocation or withdrawal of an accreditation

3.   The qualified certificates it has issued and their invalidation and

4.   The cessation of operations by an accredited certification-service provider and a ban on these

are available to be checked and downloaded at any time by anyone using public communication links.

(3)   If necessary, the competent authority shall also issue the electronic certificates needed by the certification-service providers or producers for the automatic authentication of products under Section 15(7).

Part Four: Technical Security

Section 17: Products for Electronic Signatures

(1)   To store signature codes and to produce qualified electronic signatures, secure signaturecreation devices shall be used that will reliably identify forged signatures and false signed data and offer protection against unauthorized use of the signature codes. If the signature codes are themselves produced on a secure signature-creation device, (3) No. 1 shall apply mutatis mutandis.

(2)   The presentation of data to be signed requires signature-application components that will first clearly indicate the production of a qualified electronic signature and enable the data to which the signature refers to be identified. To check signed data, signature-application components are needed that will show

1.   To which data the signature refers

2.   Whether the signed data are unchanged

3.   To which signature-code owner the signature is to be assigned

4.   The contents of the qualified certificate on which the signature is based, and of the appropriate qualified attribute certificates, and

5.   The results of the subsequent check of certificates under Section 5(1) Sentence 2.

Signature-application components shall, if necessary, also make the contents of the data to be signed or already signed sufficiently evident. The signature-code owners should use these signature- application components or take other suitable steps to secure qualified electronic signatures.

(3)   The technical components for certification services shall contain provisions to

1.   Ensure that signature codes produced and transferred are unique and secret and exclude storage outside the secure signature-creation device

2.   Protect qualified certificates that are available to be tested or downloaded in accordance with Section 5(1) Sentence 2 from unauthorized alteration and unauthorized downloading, and

3.   Exclude the possibility of forgery and falsification in the production of qualified time stamps.

(4)   Confirmation shall be given by an office under Section 18 that the requirements under (1) and (3) No. 1 and the statutory ordinance under Section 24 have been fulfilled. To fulfill the requirements under (2) and (3) Nos. 2 and 3, a declaration by the manufacturer of the product for electronic signatures is sufficient.

Section 18: Recognition of Testing and Confirmation Offices

(1)   The competent authority shall recognize a natural person or a legal entity upon application as confirmation office under Section 17(4) or Section 15(7) Sentence 1 or as a testing and confirmation office under Section 15(2) if it can prove it has the reliability, independence, and specialized knowledge needed to exercise these functions. The recognition may be limited in content, be preliminary, or be given for a limited period of time; conditions may also be attached.

(2)   The offices recognized under (1) shall perform their tasks impartially, free of instruction, and conscientiously. They shall document the tests and confirmations and hand over this documentation to the competent authority if they cease to operate.

Part Five: Supervision

Section 19: Supervision Measures

(1) Supervision of observance of this Law and the statutory ordinance under Section 24 shall be the responsibility of the competent authority; it may use private entities to perform this supervision. A certification-service provider shall be subject to supervision by the competent authority when he commences to operate.

(2) The competent authority may take steps in regard to certification-service providers to ensure observance of this Law and the statutory ordinance under Section 24.

(3) The competent authority shall forbid a certification-service provider to operate temporarily, in part or wholly if facts justify the assumption that it

   1. Does not have the reliability necessary to operate as certification-service provider;

   2. Cannot prove that the specialized knowledge necessary for its operations is available;

   3. Does not have the necessary cover;

   4. Is using unsuitable products for electronic signatures;

   5. Does not fulfill the other conditions to operate as certification-service provider under this Law and the statutory ordinance under Section 24

   and if measures under (2) are not likely to succeed.

(4) The competent authority may order qualified certificates to be invalidated if facts justify the assumption that qualified certificates are forged or are not sufficiently secure against forgery, or that secure signature-creation devices have security defects that would enable qualified electronic signatures to be forged without detection or the falsification of data signed with these to go undetected.

(5) The validity of qualified certificates issued by a certification-service provider shall not be affected by a ban on his operations and cessation of operations or by withdrawal and revocation
of an accreditation.

(6) The competent authority shall keep the names of the certification-service providers registered with it and of the certification-service providers that have ceased to operate under Section 13, or whose operations have been forbidden under Section 19(3), available for downloading through public communication links available to anyone.

Section 20: Obligatory Cooperation

(1) The certification-service providers and the third parties working for them under Section 4(5) shall permit the competent authority and the persons acting on its behalf to enter their premises and workshops during normal operating hours and

upon request present for inspection the relevant books, records, vouchers, written material, and other documents in a suitable manner, including those in electronic form, and give information and the necessary support.

(2)   The person obliged to give information may refuse to answer questions if this would expose him or a person connected with him as described in Section 383(1) Nos. 1 to 3 of the Order on Civil Proceedings to the risk of criminal prosecution or proceedings under the Law on Infringements of Regulations. He shall be informed of this right.

Part Six: Final Regulations

Section 21: Fines

(1)   A person infringes regulations who deliberately or negligently

1.   Operates a certification service in violation of Section 4(2) Sentence 1, or in connection with a statutory ordinance under Section 24 Nos. 1, 3, and 4;

2.   In violation of Section 4(3) Sentence 1 or Section 13(1) Sentence 1 does not report his operation, reports it incorrectly, or not within the required time;

3.   In violation of Section 5(1) Sentence 1 in connection with a statutory ordinance under Section 24 No. 1 does not identify a person, or does so incorrectly, or not within the required time;

4.   In violation of Section 5(1) Sentence 2 and in connection with a statutory ordinance under Section 24 No. 1 does not keep a qualified certificate available for testing;

5.   In violation of Section 5(1) Sentence 3 makes a qualified certificate available for downloading;

6.   Includes information in a qualified certificate in violation of Section 5(2) Sentences 3 or 4;

7.   In violation of Section 5(4) Sentence 2 and in connection with a statutory ordinance under Section 24 No.1 fails to take certain steps or does not take them correctly;

8.   Stores a signature code in violation of Section 5(4) Sentence 3;

9.   In violation of Section 10(1) Sentence 1 and in connection with a statutory ordinance under Section 24 No.1 fails to document a security measure or a qualified certificate or does so incorrectly or not within the required time;

10.   In violation of Section 13(1) Sentence 2 and in connection with a statutory ordinance under Section 24 No.1 fails to ensure that a qualified certificate is taken over by another certification- service provider and fails to invalidate a qualified certificate or does not do so at the right time; or

11.   In violation of Section 13(1) Sentence 3 in connection with a statutory ordinance under Section 24 No.1 fails to inform a signature-code owner or does so incorrectly or not within the required time.

(2)   Violation of the regulations may carry a fine of up to one hundred thousand deutschmarks in cases in (1) Nos.1, 7, and 8, and in the other cases a fine of up to twenty thousand deutschmarks may be imposed.

(3)   The administrative authority as defined under Section 36(1) No.1 of the Law on Infringements of Regulations shall be the Regulatory Authority for Telecommunications and Posts.

Section 22: Costs and Contributions

(1)   The competent authority shall charge costs for the following official duties (fees and expenditure):

  1.   Measures as part of the voluntary accreditation of certification-service providers under Section 15 and the statutory ordinance under Section 24;

  2.   Measures as part of the issue of qualified certificates under Section 16(1) and the issue of certificates under Section 16(3).

  3.   Measures as part of the recognition of testing and confirmation offices under Section 18 and the statutory ordinance under Section 24.

  4.   Measures as part of the supervision under Section 19(1to 4) in conjunction with Section 4(2 to 4) and the statutory ordinance under Section 24.

  Costs shall also be charged for the administration expenditure incurred if the authority uses private offices to perform the supervision. The Law on Administrative Costs shall apply.

(2)   Certification-service providers who have reported the commencement of operations under Section 4(3) shall pay a levy to the competent authority to cover the administrative expenditure for the continuous fulfillment of the conditions under Section 19(6); this shall be charged as an annual contribution. Certification-service providers accredited under Section 15(1) shall pay a levy to the competent authority to cover the administrative expenditure for the continuous fulfillment of the conditions under Section 16(2); this shall be charged as an annual contribution.

Section 23: Foreign Electronic Signatures and Products for Electronic Signatures

(1)   Electronic signatures for which a foreign qualified certificate has been issued by another member state of the European Union or signatory to the Treaty on the European Economic Area shall be the equivalent of qualified electronic signatures if they correspond to Article 5(1) of Directive 1999/93 EC of the European Parliament and of the Council of 13 December 1999 on a Community framework for electronic signatures (OJ EC 2000 No. L 13, p. 2) in the current version. Electronic signatures from third countries shall be the equivalent of qualified electronic signatures if the certificate is issued publicly as a qualified certificate by a certification-service provider in that country and is designed for an electronic signature in the meaning of Article 5(1) of Directive 1999/93 EC, and if

1. The certification-service provider fulfills the requirements of the Directive and is accredited in a member state of the European Union or another signatory to the Treaty on the European Economic area, or if

2. A certification-service provider domiciled in the EU and meeting the requirements of the Directive guarantees the certificate, or if

3. The certificate or the certification-service provider is recognized under a bilateral or multilateral agreement between the European Union and third countries or international organizations.

(2) Electronic signatures under (1) shall be the equivalent of qualified electronic signatures with provider accreditation under Section 15(1) if they can prove that they offer equivalent security.

(3) Products for electronic signatures shall be recognized if it has been established in another EU Member State or another signatory to the Treaty on the European Economic Area that they meet the requirements of Directive 1999/93 EC in its current version. Products for qualified electronic signatures tested under Section 15(8) shall be regarded as the equivalent of products for electronic signatures from a country named in Sentence 1 or a third country if they can prove that they offer the same security.

Section 24: Legal Regulations

The federal government shall be empowered to issue the regulations necessary to implement Sections 3 to 23 by statutory ordinance on

1. The details of the duties of the certification-service providers in regard for the commencement of operations and during operation and upon cessation of operation under Section 4 (2 and 3), Sections 5, 6(1), and Sections 8, 10, 13, and 15

2. The items on which fees are payable and the rates for these fees, and the level of contributions and the procedure for levying these charges by the competent authority; the assessment of the contributions must be based on the administrative expenditure (personnel and material) and the investment where this has not already been covered by a fee

3. The details of the contents and period of validity of qualified certificates under Section 7

4. The reserves permitted to meet the obligations for cover provisions under Section 12, as well as their volume, level, and contents

5. The detailed requirements for products for qualified electronic signatures under Section 17(1 to 3) and the testing of these products, and the confirmation that the requirements have been fulfilled, under Section 17(4) and Section 15(7)

6. The details of the procedure for recognition and the work of testing and confirmation offices under Section 18

7. The period after which data with a qualified electronic signature under Section 6(1) Sentence 2 must be signed again and the procedure for doing this

8.   The procedure to establish the equivalent security of foreign electronic signatures and foreign products for electronic signatures under Section 23.

Section 25: Transitional Regulations

(1)   The certification offices approved under the Signatures Law of 28 July 1997 (BGBl. I, pp. 1870, 1872), amended by Article 5 of the Law of 19 December 1998 (BGBl. I, p. 3836), shall be regarded as accredited within the meaning of Section 15. They shall present proof of cover in accordance with Section 12 to the competent authority within three months of this Law coming into force.

(2)   The certificates issued by certification offices under (1) up to the time when this Law comes into force under Article 5 of the Signatures Law of 28 July 1997 (BGBl. I, pp. 1870, 1872), amended by Article 5 of the Law of 19 December 1998 (BGBl. I, p. 3836), shall be the equivalent of qualified certificates. Owners of certificates under Sentence 1 shall be informed in an appropriate manner within six months of this Law coming into force, by the certification office in accordance with Section 6(2) Sentences 1 and 2.

(3)   The recognition by the competent authority of testing and confirmation offices under Section 4(3) Sentence 3 and Section 14(4) of the Signatures Law of 28 July 1997 (BGBl. I, pp. 1870, 1872), amended by Article 5 of the Law of 19 December 1998 (BGBl. I, p. 3836), shall remain valid if they are in accordance with Section 18 of this Law.

(4)   Technical components whose compliance with the requirements in Section 14(4) of the Signatures Law of 28 July 1997 (BGBl. I, pp. 1870, 1872) has been tested and confirmed shall
be products for qualified electronic signatures under Section 15(7) of this Law.

Article 2

Conversion of Regulations to Euro

The Signatures Law of . . . (BGBl. I, pp. . .) shall be amended as follows:

1.   In Section 12 Sentence 2 "500,000 deutschmarks" shall be replaced by "250,000 euros."

2.   In Section 21 the words "a hundred thousand deutschmarks" shall be replaced by the words "fifty thousand euros" and the words "twenty thousand deutschmarks" by the words "ten thousand euros."

Article 3

Adjustment of Federal Law

(1)   In Section 15 Sentence 2 of the Ordinance on the Issue of Public Orders of 9 January 2001 (BGBl. I, p. 110) the words "signature in the meaning of the

Signatures Law" shall be replaced by the words "a qualified electronic signature under the Signatures Law."

(2) In Section 7(3) of the Ordinance on Social Insurance of 15 July 1999 (BGBl. I, p. 1627) the words "digital signature under Section 2(1) of the Signatures Law (Article 3 of the Law of 22 July 1997, BGBl. I, pp. 1870, 1872)" shall be replaced by the words "a qualified electronic signature under the Signatures Law."

Article 4

Return to a Uniform Order of Regulations

The parts of the statutory ordinance based on Article 3(1 and 2) and amended therein may be amended by statutory ordinance on the basis of the relevant authorizations.

Article 5

Coming into Force / Annulment of Legislation

This Law, with the exception given in Sentence 2, shall enter into force on the day after its publication; at the same time, the Signatures Law of 28 July 1997 (BGBl. I, pp. 1870, 1872), amended by Article 5 of the Law of 19 December 1998 (BGBl. I, p. 3836), shall be annulled. Article 2 shall enter into force on 1 January 2002.

Ordinance on Electronic Signatures[1]

unofficial working translation

for the official version see

the Federal Law Gazette

(Bundesgesetzblatt - BGBl.) p. I 3074

(German language)

1   The notification requirements pursuant to Directive 98/34/EC of the European Parliament and of the Council of 22 June 1998 laying down a procedure for the provision of information in the field of technical standards and regulations (OJ EC No. L 204 p. 37 of 21 July 1998), last amended by Directive 98/48/EC of the European Parliament and of the Council of 20 July 1998 (OJ EC No. L 217 p. 18 of 5 August 1998) have been duly observed.

Ordinance on Electronic Signatures (Signatures Ordinance – SigV) of November 16th, 2001

On the basis of Section 24 of the Signatures Act of 16 May 2001 (Federal Law Gazette I. p. 876) in conjunction with the Second Section of the Administrative Costs Act of 23 June 1970 (Federal Law Gazette I p. 821), the Federal Government decrees as follows:

Contents

Section 1   Form, content and change of notification
Section 2   Content of the security concept
Section 3   Identification verification and attribute proof
Section 4   Maintenance of a register of certificates
Section 5   Individual security precautions taken by certification service providers
Section 6   Provision of information
Section 7   Revocation of qualified certificates

Section 8   Scope of the documentation
Section 9   Details of the financial provision
Section 10   Cessation of operations
Section 11   Voluntary accreditation
Section 12   Stipulation and levying of costs
Section 13   Stipulation and levying of contributions
Section 14   Content and validity periods of qualified certificates
Section 15   Requirements pertaining to products for qualified electronic signatures
Section 16   Procedures for the recognition and the operation of evaluation and certification bodies
Section 17   Period and procedure for long-term data security
Section 18   Procedure for the assessment of equivalent security of foreign electronic signatures and products
Section 19   Entry into force/expiry

Annex 1 (ad Section 11 (3) and ad Section 15 (5))

Provisions on the evaluation of products for qualified electronic signatures

Annex 2 (ad Section 12)

Costs

Section 1 Form, content and change of notification

(1)   A notification pursuant to Section 4 (3) of the Signatures Act shall be submitted to the competent authority in written form or furnished with a qualified electronic signature pursuant to the Signatures Act.

(2)   The notification must contain the following details and documentation:

1.   the name and address of the certification service provider,

2.   the names of the legal representatives,

3.   current certificates of good conduct pursuant to Section 30 (5) of the Federal Central Register Act for the certification service provider and his legal representatives,

4.   a current extract from the commercial register or a comparable document,

5.   documents to prove the necessary technical, administrative and legal specialised knowledge pursuant to Section 4 (2) sentence 3 of the Signatures Act,

6.   a security concept with a precise explanation of how this is implemented, including the delegation of functions to third parties pursuant to Section 4 (5) of the Signatures Act, and

7.   proof of financial cover pursuant to Section 12 of the Signatures Act.

If there is a change in the circumstances pursuant to sentence 1 no. 1 or no. 2 or security-relevant circumstances pursuant to sentence 1 no. 6, the competent authority must be informed in writing or by means of an electronic document furnished with a qualified electronic signature pursuant to the Signatures Act. This shall be without prejudice to Section 2.

(3)   If parts of the certification service are rendered in a country pursuant to Section 23 (1) sentence 1 of the Signatures Act or in a third country under the conditions of Section 23 (1) sentence 2 no. 3 of the Signatures Act, additional documents shall be submitted to prove that the operation is subject to equivalent supervision. The operation of parts of the certification service in a country not covered by sentence 1 shall be permitted only within the framework of a voluntary accreditation if it is documented that the supervision is ensured.

Section 2 Content of the security concept

The security concept pursuant to Section 4 (2) sentence 4 of the Signatures Act shall contain the following:

1.   a description of all necessary technical, structural and organisational security measures and their appropriateness,

2.   a list of the products used for qualified electronic signatures with manufacturer declarations pursuant to Section 17 (4) sentence 2 or certifications pursuant to Section 17 (4) sentence 1 or Section 15 (7) sentence 1 of the Signatures Act,

3.   an overview of the organisation of the establishment and operations and of the certification activities,

4.   the precautions and measures to secure and maintain operations, especially in case of emergencies,

5.   the procedures to assess and secure the reliability of the personnel, and

6.   an assessment and evaluation of the remaining security risks.

Section 3 Identification verification and attribute proof

(1)   The certification service provider shall identify the applicant pursuant to Section 5 (1) of the Signatures Act by means of the national identity card or a passport issued for a person with citizenship of a member state of the European Union or a state of the European Economic Area, or by means of documents offering an equivalent level of security. If an application for a qualified certificate is submitted by means of an electronic document furnished with a qualified electronic signature pursuant to the Signatures Act, the certification service provider may dispense with further identification. The identification shall take place before the issuance of a qualified certificate and before inclusion in the register of certificates pursuant to the provisions of Section 4 (1).

(2)   If a qualified certificate is to contain attributes pursuant to Section 5 (2) of the Signatures Act, the approval or certification required pursuant to Section 5 (2) sentence 2 or 4 or subsection (3) sentence 2 of the Signatures Act must be

submitted by means of an electronic document furnished with a qualified electronic signature pursuant to the Signatures Act or in writing. The third party or the office responsible for the professional or other data relating to the person shall be informed by means of an electronic document furnished with a qualified electronic signature pursuant to the Signatures Act or in writing about the contents of the qualified certificate and about the possibility of revocation.

Section 4 Maintenance of a register of certificates

(1)   The certification service provider shall keep the qualified certificates issued by it in a register pursuant to the provisions of Section 5 (1) sentence 2 of the Signatures Act, unless the time is later pursuant to Section 5 (2) sentence 2, from the time of their issuance for the validity period named in the relevant certificate and at least for another five years from the end of the year in which the validity of the certificate terminates.

(2)   An accredited certification service provider shall keep the qualified certificates issued by it in a register pursuant to the provisions of Section 5 (1) sentence 2 of the Signatures Act, unless the time is later pursuant to Section 5 (2) sentence 2, from the time of their issuance for the validity period named in the relevant certificate and for at least another 30 years from the end of the year in which the validity of the certificate terminates.

(3)   In the case of a takeover of qualified certificates pursuant to Section 13 (1) sentence 2 of the Signatures Act, paragraphs 1 and 2 shall apply accordingly.

Section 5 Individual security precautions taken by certification service providers

(1)   The certification service provider shall ensure by means of appropriate measures that signa-ture keys are produced only on the relevant secure signature creation device or by him or another certification service provider by using technical components pursuant to Section 17 (3) no. 1 of the Signatures Act and transferred to secure signature creation devices. If he also makes available knowledge data on the identification of the signature key holder in relation to a secure signature creation device or technical components to handle biometrical characteristics and to transfer reference data to the secure signature creation device, he shall also take precautions to guarantee the secrecy of the identification data and to exclude their being stored outside the relevant secure signature creation device after inclusion in this device.

(2)   The certification service provider shall personally hand over to the signature key holder the signature keys and identification data provided by him on the secure signature creation device and shall obtain confirmation of the handover from him in writing or as an electronic document furnished with a qualified electronic signature pursuant to the Signatures Act, unless a different handover is arranged in writing or by means of an electronic document furnished with a qualified electronic signature pursuant to the Signatures Act. The relevant qualified certificate must not be verifiable and, if so agreed, available for retrieval pursuant to Section 5 (1) sentences 2 and 3 of the Signatures Act, until after the signature

key holder has confirmed the receipt of the secure signature creation device to the certification service provider.

(3)   In order to fulfil the preconditions pursuant to Section 5 (5) of the Signatures Act, the certification service provider must convince himself in an appropriate manner of the reliability of persons involved in the certification procedure. To this end, he can in particular require the presentation of a certificate of good conduct pursuant to Section 30 (1) of the Federal Central Register Act. Unreliable persons must be excluded from the certification procedure. The certification service provider must also convince himself, using the manufacturer's data or in another appropriate manner, of the appropriateness of the products used by him for qualified electronic signatures and must take precautions in order to protect these against unauthorised access.

Section 6 Provision of information

Information pursuant to Section 6 (1) of the Signatures Act shall be provided to the applicant in a generally understandable language and shall contain at least the following:

1.   the storage and usage of the secure signature creation device and appropriate measures in case of loss or suspicion of misuse,

2.   the confidentiality of personal identification numbers or other data to identify the signature key holder in relation to the secure signature creation device,

3.   the necessary security measures regarding the creation and verification of a qualified elec-tronic signature,

4.   the possibility of limitations in qualified certificates pursuant to Section 7 (1) no. 7 of the Signatures Act,

5.   the need to sign data with a qualified electronic signature once again if the security value of the signature is reduced by the passage of time,

6.   the existence of a voluntary accreditation system,

7.   the complaint and dispute-settlement procedures available to the applicant and the details of how to use such procedures, and

8.   the procedure for revocation pursuant to Section 7.

The information shall also be made available to third parties upon request.

Section 7 Revocation of qualified certificates

(1)   The certification service provider shall, pursuant to Section 8 of the Signatures Act, inform the parties authorised to revoke qualified certificates of a telephone number under which they can cause such certificates to be revoked without delay.

(2)   Prior to the revocation, the certification service provider must ensure himself in an appropriate manner of the identity of the person authorised to revoke the certificate. The revocation of qualified certificates must be clearly recorded in the register of certificates pursuant to Section 4, including the date and the official time pertaining at this time.

Section 8 Scope of the documentation

(1)   The documentation pursuant to Section 10 of the Signatures Act shall comprise the security concept, including any amendments, the documents regarding the specialised knowledge of the persons working in the company and the contractual arrangements with the applicants.

(2)   At least the following data and documents shall be retained with regard to the relevant applicant:

    1.   a photocopy of the submitted identity card or other proof of identity,

    2.   any pseudonym issued,

    3.   proof of the provision of information to the applicant pursuant to Section 6 of the Signatures Act,

    4.   proof of the approval of the authorised persons pursuant to Section 5 (2) sentences 2 and 4 and subsection (3) sentence 2 of the Signatures Act,

    5.   the certifications by the bodies responsible pursuant to Section 5 (2) sentence 2 of the Signatures Act,

    6.   the qualified certificates issued, including the relevant times of issuance and handover as well as the time of inclusion in the register of certificates,

    7.   the revocation of qualified certificates,

    8.   information pursuant to Section 14 (2) sentence 2 of the Signatures Act, and

    9.   the handover confirmations for signature keys and identification data pursuant to Section 5 (2) sentence 1 or the declaration by the signature key holder if he has requested a different handover, and any other proof, if appropriate.

(3)   Subject to sentence 3, the documentation shall be kept at least for the period pursuant to Section 4 (1) and in the case of accredited certification service providers at least for the period pursuant to Section 4 (2). In the case of proceedings in court in which the proof of the certification is relevant, the documentation shall be kept, notwithstanding sentence 1, at least until the final conclusion of the proceedings. The documentation of information pursuant to Section 14 (2) sentence 2 of the Signatures Act shall be kept for twelve months.

Section 9 Details of the financial provision

(1)   The financial provision pursuant to Section 12 of the Signatures Act can be supplied

    1.   by a liability insurance policy with an insurance company authorised to operate in the area covered by this Act or

    2.   by an indemnification or guarantee commitment by a bank authorised to operate in the area covered by this Act if it ensured that it offers security comparable to a liability insurance policy.

(2)   Where the provision is supplied by means of an insurance policy pursuant to subsection (1) no. 1, the following provisions apply:

1.   Section 158b (2) and Sections 158c to 158k of the Insurance Contract Act shall apply to this insurance policy. The competent authority pursuant to Section 158c (2) of the Insurance Contract Act shall be the authority pursuant to Section 66 of the Telecommunications Act.

2.   The minimum sum insured must be 2.5 million euro for each insured event. An insured event shall be each occurrence causing liability related to the individual event pursuant to Section 12 (1) of the Signatures Act, irrespective of the number of resulting cases of damage. Any arrangement according to which an error which affects several certificates, time stamps or the information pursuant to Section 5 (1) sentence 2 of the Signatures Act is regarded as one insured event shall not be permissible. If a maximum annual amount for all damages caused in one year of cover is agreed upon, this amount shall total at least four times the minimum sum insured.

3.   The geographical coverage of the insurance can be restricted to the area of validity of Directive 1999/93/EC of the European Parliament and of the Council of 13 December 1999 on a Community framework for electronic signatures (OJ EC 2000 No. L 13 p. 2).

4.   The insurance policy may exclude payment of benefits only in case of claims for damages resulting from intentional breaches of duty committed by the certification service provider or by the persons for which he is answerable.

5.   The agreement of a deductible of up to 1 per cent of the minimum sum insured is permissible.

Section 10 Cessation of operations

(1)   The certification service provider should inform the competent authority pursuant to Section 13 (1) sentence 1 of the Signatures Act at the latest two months prior to the cessation of operations.

(2)   The certification service provider should inform the signature key holders pursuant to Section 13 (1) sentence 3 of the Signatures Act at least two months prior to the cessation of operations. He must inform the signature key holders whether another certification service provider is taking over the certificates and must name this provider.

Section 11 Voluntary accreditation

(1)   Applications for accreditation pursuant to Section 15 (1) of the Signatures Act shall be made in writing or by means of an electronic document furnished with a qualified electronic signature pursuant to the Signatures Act. Applications for voluntary accreditation shall be regarded as notification pursuant to Section 1 if the requirements contained in that section are fulfilled.

(2)   Proof pursuant to Section 15 (1) sentence 2, subsection (2) sentence 2 and subsection (7) of the Signatures Act shall be provided by submitting the results of

the evaluation and certification body in writing or by means of an electronic document furnished with a qualified electronic signature pursuant to the Signatures Act. The regular evaluations pursuant to Section 15 (2) sentence 2 of the Signatures Act shall take place every three years. The evaluation report and the certification that the requirements of the Signatures Act and of this Ordinance continue to be fully met shall be submitted unsolicited to the competent authority.

(3)   The evaluation and certification of the security of products for qualified electronic signatures pursuant to Section 15 (7) sentence 1 of the Signatures Act shall be carried out in accordance with the provisions of Section 1 of Annex 1 to this Ordinance.

Section 12 Stipulation and levying of costs

(1)   The official acts, the performance of which is subject to fees pursuant to Section 22 of the Signatures Act, are listed in Annex 2 to this Ordinance. Expenses shall be charged pursuant to Section 10 of the Administrative Costs Act. For the cancellation, withdrawal or rejection of an application or an administrative act, fees shall be levied in accordance with Section 15 of the Administrative Costs Act.

(2)   For the hourly rates pursuant to no. 2 of Annex 2 to this Ordinance, a quarter of the hourly rate shall be calculated for each quarter hour begun. If public services are provided by members of the competent authority outside that authority, fees shall also be calculated which are within normal working hours or which are especially settled by the competent authority, as well as for waiting periods caused by the person liable to pay the costs.

Section 13 Stipulation and levying of contributions

(1)   The contributions pursuant to Section 22 (2) sentence 1 of the Signatures Act are calculated on the basis of the spending on staff and materials by the competent authority which is necessary for this, including the expenditure on investment. The contribution rate is 0.48 euro for each qualified certificate issued by the person liable to pay the contributions. The share of the costs accounted for by the general public interest has been taken into account and has resulted in a reduction of the costs. The proportions of the remaining expenditure will be allocated to the persons liable to pay the contributions in line with the number of qualified certificates issued by them, which must be listed in the register of certificates pursuant to Section 4 (1). The persons liable to pay the contributions must inform the competent authority of the number of certificates pursuant to sentence 2 annually, at the latest on 31 January of the following year. If a person liable to pay contributions fails to fulfil his obligation pursuant to sentence 5, the competent authority can estimate the number of qualified certificates issued by a person liable to pay contributions.

(2)   The costs of the expenditure on investment are stipulated in line with the respective tax rules on the depreciation of capital goods in force at the time.

(3)   For the contributions pursuant to Section 22 (2) sentence 2 of the Signatures Act, the rules of subsections (1) and (2), with the exception of subsection (1) sentence

4, shall apply accordingly. The proportions of the remaining expenditure pursuant to subsection (1) sentence 1 shall be allocated to the persons liable to pay contributions in line with the number of qualified certificates issued by them, which must be listed in the register of certificates pursuant to Section 4 (2).

(4)   The requirement to pay contributions pursuant to Section 22 (2) sentence 1 of the Signatures Act shall commence from the month of notification pursuant to Section 4 (3) of the Signatures Act, and the requirement to pay contributions pursuant to Section 22 (2) sentence 2 of the Signatures Act shall commence from the month of accreditation. The requirement to pay contributions shall end at the end of the month of cessation of operations pursuant to Section 13 (1) of the Signatures Act and, in the case of voluntary accreditation, at the end of the month of the cancellation or withdrawal of an accreditation pursuant to Section 15 (5) of the Signatures Act. The contribution shall be levied annually. The basis shall be the calendar year. If the requirement to pay contributions does not exist for the entire calendar year, the contribution shall be calculated on a pro-rata basis; sentences 1 and 2 shall apply accordingly. The contributions shall be levied pursuant to the provisions of the Administrative Enforcement Act.

Section 14 Content and validity periods of qualified certificates

(1)   The data pursuant to Section 7 (1) of the Signatures Act in a qualified certificate must be unambiguous.

(2)   A qualified attribute certificate pursuant to Section 7 (2) of the Signatures Act must contain, apart from an unambiguous reference to the underlying qualified certificate, at least the following data and must bear a qualified electronic signature of the certification service provider:

1.   the designation of the algorithms with which the signature verification key of the certification service provider can be used,

2.   the number of the attribute certificate,

3.   the name of the certification service provider and the state in which he is established,

4.   information that this is a qualified certificate and

5.   one or several attributes pursuant to Section 5 (2) of the Signatures Act.

(3)   The validity period of a qualified certificate shall be no longer than five years and shall not exceed the period during which the applied algorithms and related parameters remain suitable. The validity of a qualified attribute certificate terminates at the latest with the validity of the qualified certificate to which it refers.

Section 15 Requirements pertaining to products for qualified electronic signatures

(1)   Secure signature creation devices pursuant to Section 17 (1) sentence 1 of the Signatures Act must guarantee that the signature key cannot be used until after the identification of the holder through possession and knowledge or through

possession and one or several biometrical characteristics. The signature key must not be disclosed. If biometrical characteristics are used, it must be adequately ensured that unauthorised use of the signature key is not possible and that the level of security is equivalent to the knowledge-based procedure. The technical components required for the production and transfer of signature keys pursuant to Section 17 (1) sentence 2 or subsection (3) no. 1 of the Signatures Act must guarantee that the signature key cannot be derived from the relevant signature verification key or signature and that it is not possible to duplicate the signature keys.

(2)   Signature application components pursuant to Section 17 (2) of the Signatures Act must ensure that

1.   when producing a qualified electronic signature

a)   the identification data are not disclosed and are stored only on the relevant secure signature creation device,

b)   a signature is provided only at the initiation of the authorised signing person,

c)   the production of a signature is clearly indicated in advance, and

2.   when verifying a qualified electronic signature

a)   the correctness of a signature is reliably verified and appropriately displayed and

b)   it can be clearly determined whether the verified qualified certificates were present in the relevant register of certificates at the given time and were not revoked.

(3)   Technical components pursuant to Section 17 (3) of the Signatures Act must ensure that the revocation of a qualified certificate cannot be rescinded without this being noticed and that the information can be checked for genuineness. The information pursuant to sentence 1 must include whether the verified qualified certificates were present in the register of qualified certificates at the given time and were not revoked. Only verifiably held qualified certificates must not be publicly available for retrieval. In the case of Section 17 (3) no. 3 of the Signatures Act it must be ensured that the official time valid at the time of production of the qualified time stamp shall be included in that time stamp without falsification.

(4)   Security-relevant changes in technical components pursuant to subsections (1) to (3) must be apparent for the user.

(5)   A manufacturer declaration pursuant to Section 17 (4) of the Signatures Act must

1.   precisely identify the issuer and the product and

2.   contain precise information about which individual requirements of the Signatures Act and of this Ordinance have been fulfilled.

When evaluating and certifying the security of products pursuant to Section 17 (1) and (3) no. 1 of the Signatures Act, the provisions of Section II of Annex 1 to this Ordinance shall be observed.

(6) If reference numbers of generally recognised standards for products for qualified electronic signatures are established within the framework of the procedure pursuant to Article 3 (5) and Article 9 of Directive 1999/93/EC in the current version and are published in the Official Journal of the European Communities, they shall also apply notwithstanding subsections 1 to 5 except for the products pursuant to Section 15 (7) of the Signatures Act. The competent authority shall publish the current requirements in the Federal Gazette on the basis of the stipulations pursuant to sentence 1.

Section 16 Procedures for the recognition and the operation of evaluation and certification bodies

(1) An application by an evaluation and certification body pursuant to Section 18 (1) of the Signatures Act must include the following:

1. name and address of the applicant and of his legal representative,

2. current certificates of good conduct pursuant to Section 30 (5) of the Federal Central Register Act for the applicant pursuant to no. 1 and for his legal representatives,

3. a current extract from the commercial register or a comparable document,

4. documents to prove financial independence, especially proof of minimum capital and compa-rable collateral,

5. documents to prove the necessary technical, administrative and legal specialised knowledge pursuant to Section 18 (1) sentence 1 of the Signatures Act, and

6. a declaration as to which statutory operations of the Signatures Act the application refers.

(2) For recognition as certification body for operations pursuant to Section 15 (7) and Section 17 (4) sentence 1 of the Signatures Act the applicant must prove that he has sufficient experience in the application of the evaluation criteria pursuant to Annex 1 to this Ordinance. In addition, he must describe how he will guarantee adequate supervision of the evaluation.

(3) The requirements concerning the operation as certification body or evaluation and certification body pursuant to Section 18 (1) of the Signatures Act and Commission decision 2000/709/EC of 6 November 2000 (OJ EC No. L 289 p. 42) on the minimum criteria pursuant to Article 3 (4) of Directive 1999/93/EC shall be met

1. with regard to reliability by persons who due to their personal characteristics, their behaviour and their abilities are suitable for the proper fulfilment of the tasks that they have assumed,

2. with regard to independence by persons who are not under any economic, financial or other pressure which may affect their judgement or endanger confidence in the impartial fulfilment of their tasks,

3. with regard to specialised knowledge by persons who due to their education, vocational training and practical experience are suitable for the proper fulfilment of the tasks that they have assumed.

(4) The operator of a certification body or an evaluation and certification body pursuant to Section 18 of the Signatures Act must satisfy himself in an appropriate manner of the reliability and specialised knowledge of persons involved in the evaluation or certification. He may require these persons to present a certificate of good conduct pursuant to Section 30 (1) of the Federal Central Register Act.

(5) The competent authority shall publish the details of the requirements pursuant to subsections (1) to (4) and the minimum criteria pursuant to Article 3 (1) of Directive 1999/93/EC in the Federal Gazette.

Section 17 Period and procedure for long-term data security

Pursuant to Section 6 (1) sentence 2 of the Signatures Act, data with a qualified electronic signature shall be re-signed if they are required in signed form for a period longer than that for which the algorithms and related parameters used to create and verify them are considered to be suitable. In this case the data shall be furnished with a new qualified electronic signature prior to the time at which the suitability of the algorithms and related parameters ends. This signature shall be furnished with suitable new algorithms or related parameters, include earlier signatures and bear a qualified time stamp.

Section 18 Procedure for the assessment of equivalent security of foreign electronic signatures and products

(1) A certification service provider who, pursuant to Section 23 (1) sentence 2 no. 2 of the Signatures Act, guarantees qualified certificates with legal effect pursuant to Article 5 (1) of Directive 1999/93/EC of a certification service provider established outside the European Economic Area (third country) must notify this in writing or by means of an electronic document furnished with a qualified electronic signature pursuant to the Signatures Act to the competent authority at the latest at the time at which these certificates are intended to become effective in the area of application of the Signatures Act. He must ensure that the qualified certificates of the foreign certification service provider and the qualified electronic signatures that are based on them meet the requirements of the Signatures Act and of this Ordinance and must submit the documentation on the foreign certification service provider in accordance with Section 1 (2). Section 2 shall apply accordingly to the details about the foreign certification service provider. Pursuant to Section 19 (6) of the Signatures Act, the competent authority shall keep available for retrieval the name of the foreign certification service provider, listing also the certification service provider guaranteeing his qualified certifi-cates.

(2) The security of foreign electronic signatures shall be deemed equivalent pursuant to Section 23 (2) of the Signatures Act if the competent authority has established that

1. the security requirements for certification service providers and products for qualified elec-tronic signatures,

2. the evaluation modalities for certification service providers and products for qualified electronic signatures as well as the requirements for the evaluation and certification bodies and

3. the accreditation and supervision systems

offer equivalent security. In order to establish equivalent security, the competent authority may agree with the competent foreign body on the recognition procedures unless otherwise provided in bilateral or multilateral agreements.

(3) Products shall be deemed equivalent pursuant to Section 23 (3) sentence 2 of the Signatures Act if the competent authority has established this after having applied the provisions pursuant to paragraph 2.

(4) The competent authority shall include in its register pursuant to Section 16 (2) of the Signatures Act the qualified certificates for signature verification keys of top-level foreign certification service providers which are recognised as equivalent pursuant to Section 23 (2) of the Signatures Act. It shall certify the recognition by means of a qualified electronic signature with provider accreditation pursuant to Section 15 of the Signatures Act.

Section 19 Entry into force/expiry

This Ordinance shall enter into force on the day following its promulgation; at the same time, the Signatures Ordinance of 27 October 1997 (Federal Law Gazette I p. 2498), amended by the Ordinance of 22 June 2000 (Federal Law Gazette I p. 981), shall expire.

Annex to the Ordinance on Electronic Signatures

Annex 1 (ad Section 11 (3), ad Section 15 (5) and ad section 16 (2))

Provisions on the evaluation of products for qualified electronic signatures

I. Ad Section 11 (3) of this Ordinance and pursuant to Section 15 (7) of the Signatures Act (voluntary accreditation)

1. Provisions on evaluation

1.1. Requirements on level of evaluation

The evaluation of products for qualified electronic signatures in line with Sections 15 (7) and 17 (4) of the Signatures Act shall occur on the basis of the Common Criteria for Information Technology Security Evaluation (Federal Gazette 1999 p. 1945 – ISO/IEC 15408) or the Information Technology Security Evaluation Criteria (ITSEC – Joint Ministerial Bulletin of 8 August 1992 p. 545) in the version currently in force.

The evaluation must

a) cover at least evaluation level EAL 4 or E 3 for technical components pursuant to Section 2 no. 12 a) of the Signatures Act,

b) cover at least evaluation level EAL 4 or E 3 for secure signature creation devices pursuant to Section 2 no. 10 of the Signatures Act,

c) i) cover at least evaluation level ÒEAL 4Ó or ÒE 3Ó for technical components for certification services pursuant to Section 2 no. 12 b) and c) of the Signatures Act which are used outside a specially secured area (Òtrust centreÓ), ii) cover at least evaluation level ÒEAL 3Ó or ÒE 2Ó for technical components for certification services pursuant to Section 2 no. 12 b) and c) of the Signatures Act which are used within a specially secured area,

d) cover at least evaluation level ÒEAL 3Ó or ÒE 2Ó for signature application components pursuant to Section 2 no. 11 of the Signatures Act.

1.2. Requirements on the assessment of weak points/strengths of mechanisms

In the case of evaluation levels ÒEAL 4Ó and in the case of ÒEAL 3Ó pursuant to Section I no. 1.1. a) – c) i) and d), in addition to the measures prescribed for this evaluation level, evaluations shall be conducted against a high attack potential and a full misuse analysis shall be carried out.

The strength of the security mechanisms must be assessed as ÒhighÓ in the case of all products pursuant to Section I no. 1.1. a) – d) in the ÒE 3Ó and ÒE 2Ó case.

In derogation from this, for the identification mechanism using biometrical characteristics, an assessment of the security mechanisms as ÒaverageÓ shall suffice if these are used for identification in addition to knowledge data.

1.3. Requirements regarding algorithms

The algorithms and related parameters must be assessed as suitable pursuant to Section I no. 1.2. of this Annex.

2. Algorithms – publication and redefinition of suitability

The competent authority shall publish in the Federal Bulletin an overview of the algorithms and related parameters which are deemed suitable for creating signature keys, for hashing data that are to be signed or for producing and verifying qualified electronic signatures as well as the time until which the suitability is valid. The time should be at least six years after the time of assessment and publication. The suitability must be determined again annually or as the need arises. Suitability shall be established if within the defined period the possibility of an undetectable forgery of qualified electronic signatures or falsification of signed data can be excluded with near certainty on the basis of state-of-the-art findings. Suitability shall be established by the German Information Security Agency, taking account of international standards. Experts from industry and science shall be involved.

3.   Security certifications for signature products

The certification of the fulfilment of the requirements by products for qualified electronic signatures shall state

a)   to which requirements pursuant to Section 17 of the Signatures Act and pursuant to Section 15 of this Ordinance the certification refers and under which conditions of use,

b)   which algorithms and related parameters pursuant to Section I no. 2 are used and until which time they are at least suitable, and

c)   according to which standard the products were evaluated and which mechanism strength was reached.

Copies of the evaluation report, of the assessment by the certification body and of the certification shall be deposited with the competent authority. Upon request, all other evaluation documents shall also be submitted to this body. In case of indications of shortcomings regarding evaluations or certified products and on a random basis, the competent authority may obtain expert reports by independent third parties as to whether the products were evaluated pursuant to this Annex and whether they meet the requirements of the Signatures Act and the Signatures Ordinance. Manufacturers, distributors and evaluation offices concerned must provide the necessary support. If they fail to do so or if it becomes evident that certified products were not sufficiently evaluated or do not meet requirements, the competent authority may declare issued certifications invalid.

4.   Publication of the security certification for products

The competent authority shall publish in the Federal Gazette products for qualified electronic signatures which have been certified pursuant to Section I no. 3 by a body that is recognised pursuant to Section 18 of the Signatures Act. It shall be stated until which time at least the certification is valid. If a certification is declared invalid, the competent authority shall also publish this in the Federal Gazette and shall name the time from which this measure applies.

II. Ad Section 15 (5) of this Ordinance and pursuant to Section 17 (1) and (3) no. 1 of the Signatures Act (certification service providers notified pursuant to Section 4 (3) of the Signatures Act without voluntary accreditation)

For the evaluation of products pursuant to Section 15 (5), the requirements of Section I apply accordingly.

In derogation from this,

—   products can be used which correspond to the standards pursuant to Section 15 (6),

—   products can be used pursuant to Section 17 (2) and (3) no. 2 and 3 of the Signatures Act (or pursuant to Section I no. 1.1. c) and d) for which, instead of the certification, a manufacturer declaration is provided pursuant to Section 17 (4) of the Signatures Act.

Annex 2 (ad Section 12) – Costs –

Costs for official acts pursuant to Section 22 (1) of the Signatures Act

1.1 Costs pursuant to Section 22 (1) no. 1 of the Signatures Act

Item no.	Official act	€
1	Evaluation and issuance of an accreditation pursuant to Section 15 (1) of the Signatures Act	Time-based fee
2	Rejection of an application for accreditation pursuant to Section 15 (4) of the Signatures Act or cancellation or withdrawal of an accreditation pursuant to Section 15 (5) of the Signatures Act	Time-based fee
3	Full or partial rejection of a challenge in the context of the procedure pursuant to Section 15 (1) – (6) of the Signatures Act	2500
4	Review of evaluation reports and certifications pursuant to Section 15 (2) of the Signatures Act	3500
5	Measures in the case of cancellation or withdrawal of an accreditation or in the case of cessation of operations by an accredited certification service provider pursuant to Section 15 (6) of the Signatures Act	Time-based fee
6	Investigations and other measures pursuant to Section 19 of the Signatures Act	Time-based fee

1.2 Costs pursuant to Section 22 (1) no. 2 of the Signatures Act

Item no.	Official act	€
7	Issuance of a qualified certificate and its revocation pursuant to Section 16 (1) of the Signatures Act	500
8	Issuance of an attestation pursuant to Section 16 (3) of the Signatures Act	500

1.3 Costs pursuant to Section 22 (1) no. 3 of the Signatures Act

Item no.	Official act	€
	Issuance of recognition as a certification body or evaluation and certification body pursuant to Section 18 (1) of the Signatures Act, pursuant to	
9	Section 15 (2) of the Signatures Act,	2500
10	Section 15 (7) of the Signatures Act,	2500
11	Section 17 (3) of the Signatures Act.	1000
	Rejection of an application for recognition or cancellation or withdrawal of a recognition for activities pursuant to	
12	Section 15 (2) of the Signatures Act,	2500
13	Section 15 (7) of the Signatures Act,	2500
14	Section 17 (4) of the Signatures Act	1000
15	Full or partial rejection of a challenge in the context of the procedure pursuant to Section 18 (1) of the Signatures Act	1000

1.4 Costs pursuant to Section 22 (1) no. 4 of Signature Act

Item no.	Official act	€
16	Processing of a notification pursuant to Section 4 (2) and (3) of the Signatures Act and first review of adherence to the Signatures Act and to this Ordinance pursuant to Section 19 of the Signatures Act	Time-based fee
17	Random checks in the context of supervision pursuant to Section 19 (1) of the Signatures Act, in the case of the discovery of a violation of the provisions of the Signatures Act or of this Ordinance which apply to the operation of a certification service	Time-based fee
18	Non-random checks and other measures pursuant to Section 19 (1) of the Signatures Act in the case of a violation of the provisions of the Signatures Act or of this Ordinance which apply to the operation of a certification service	Time-based fee

1.5 Costs pursuant to Section 23 (1) of the Signatures Act

Item no.	Official act	€
19	Processing of a notification pursuant to Section 18 (1) sentence 1 of this Ordinance including the inclusion in the register of certificates pursuant to Section 18 (1) sentence 4 of this Ordinance	Time-based fee

2 Hourly rates and kilometre allowances for use of vehicles

Item no.	Hourly rate/kilometre allowance	€
20	Officials of administrative level or comparable employees	125
21	Officials of executive level or comparable employees	95
22	Officials of secretarial level or comparable employees	69
23	Use of vehicle	0.70 €/km

Ireland

AN BILLE UM THRÁCHTÁIL LEICTREONACH, 2000
ELECTRONIC COMMERCE BILL, 2000

ACTS REFERRED TO

Companies Act, 1990	1990, No. 33
Consumer Credit Act, 1995	1995, No. 24
Criminal Evidence Act, 1992	1992, No. 12
Petty Sessions (Ireland) Act,	1851 14 & 15 Vict., c.93
Succession Act,	1965 1965, No. 27

AN BILLE UM THRÁCHTÁIL LEICTREONACH, 2000
ELECTRONIC COMMERCE BILL, 2000

BILL

AN ACT TO PROVIDE FOR THE LEGAL RECOGNITION OF ELECTRONIC CON-
TRACTS, ELECTRONIC WRITING, ELECTRONIC SIGNATURES AND ORIGINAL

INFORMATION IN ELECTRONIC FORM IN RELATION TO COMMERCIAL AND
NON-COMMERCIAL TRANSACTIONS AND DEALINGS AND OTHER MATTERS,
THE ADMISSIBILITY OF EVIDENCE IN RELATION TO SUCH MATTERS, THE
ACCREDITATION, SUPERVISION AND LIABILITY OF CERTIFICATION SERVICE
PROVIDERS AND THE REGISTRATION OF DOMAIN NAMES, AND TO PROVIDE
FOR RELATED MATTERS. BE IT ENACTED BY THE OIREACHTAS AS FOLLOWS:

PART 1

PRELIMINARY AND GENERAL

Short title and commencement.
1.—

(1)   This Act may be cited as the Electronic Commerce Act, 2000.

(2)   This Act shall come into operation on such day or days as the Minister, after
consultation with the Minister for Enterprise, Trade and Employment, may
appoint by order or orders, either generally or with reference to any particular
purpose or provision, and different days may be so appointed for different
purposes or different
provisions.

Interpretation.
2.—
(1)
In this Act, unless the context otherwise requires—

"accreditation" means an accreditation under *section 29(2)*;

"addressee", in relation to an electronic communication, means a person or public
body intended by the originator to receive the electronic communication, but
does not include a person or public body acting as a service provider in relation
to the processing, receiving or storing of the electronic communication or the
provision of other services in relation to it;

"advanced electronic signature" means an electronic signature—

(*a*)   uniquely linked to the signatory,

(*b*)   capable of identifying the signatory,

(*c*)   created using means that are capable of being maintained by the signatory
under his, her or its sole control, and

(*d*)   linked to the data to which it relates in such a manner that any subsequent
change of the data is detectable;

"certificate" means an electronic attestation which links signature verification
data to a person or public body, and confirms the identity of the person or public
body;

"certification service provider" means a person or public body who issues
certificates or provides other services related to electronic signatures;

"Directive" means the European Parliament and Council Directive 1999/93/EC of 13 December, 1999[1];

"electronic" includes electrical, digital, magnetic, optical, electromagnetic, biometric, photonic and any other form of related technology;

"electronic communication" means information communicated or intended to be communicated to a person or public body, other than its originator, that is generated, communicated, processed, sent, received, recorded, stored or displayed by electronic means or in electronic form, but does not include information communicated in the form of speech unless the speech is processed at its destination by an automatic voice recognition system;

"electronic contract" means a contract concluded wholly or partly by means of an electronic communication;

"electronic signature" means data in electronic form attached to, incorporated in or logically associated with other electronic data and which serves as a method of authenticating the purported originator, and includes an advanced electronic signature;

"excluded law" means a law referred to in *section 10*;

"information" includes data, all forms of writing and other text, images (including maps and cartographic material), sound, codes, computer programmes, software, databases and speech;

"information system" means a system for generating, communicating, processing, sending, receiving, recording, storing or displaying information by electronic means;

"legal proceedings" means civil or criminal proceedings, and includes proceedings before a court, tribunal, appellate body of competent jurisdiction or any other body or individual charged with determining legal rights or obligations;

"Minister" means the Minister for Public Enterprise;

"originator", in relation to an electronic communication, means the person or public body by whom or on whose behalf the electronic communication purports to have been sent or generated before storage, as the case may be, but does not include a person or public body acting as a service provider in relation to the generation, processing, sending or storing of that electronic communication or providing other services in relation to it;

"person" does not include a public body;

"prescribed" means prescribed by regulations made under *section 3*;

"public body" means—

(*a*) a Minister of the Government or a Minister of State,

(*b*) a body (including a Department of State but not including a non-government organisation) wholly or partly funded out of the Central Fund or out of moneys provided by the Oireachtas or moneys raised by local taxation or charges, or

(c) a commission, tribunal, board or body established by an Act or by arrangement of the Government, a Minister of the Government or a Minister of State for a non-commercial public service or purpose;

"qualified certificate" means a certificate which meets the requirements set out in Annex I and is provided by a certification service provider who fulfils the requirements set out in Annex II;

"secure signature creation device" means a signature creation device which meets the requirements set out in Annex III;

"signatory" means a person who, or public body which, holds a signature creation device and acts in the application of a signature by use of the device either on his, her or its own behalf or on behalf of a person or public body he, she or it represents;

"signature creation data" means unique data, such as codes, passwords, algorithms or private cryptographic keys, used by a signatory or other source of the data in generating an electronic signature;

"signature creation device" means a device, such as configured software or hardware used to generate signature creation data;

"signature verification data" means data, such as codes, passwords, algorithms or public cryptographic keys, used for the purposes of verifying an electronic signature;

"signature verification device" means a device, such as configured software or hardware used to generate signature verification data.

(2) In the application of this Act, "writing", where used in any other Act or instrument under an Act (and whether or not qualified by reference to it being or being required to be under the hand of the writer or similar expression) shall be construed as including electronic modes of representing or reproducing words in visible form, and cognate words shall be similarly construed.

(3) In this Act—

(a) a reference to a section is a reference to a section of this Act, unless it is indicated that a reference to some other enactment is intended,

(b) a reference to a subsection, paragraph or subparagraph is a reference to a subsection, paragraph or subparagraph of the provision in which the reference is made, unless it is indicated that a reference to some other provision is intended,

(c) a reference to an enactment shall, except to the extent that the context otherwise requires, be construed as a reference to that enactment as amended by or under any other enactment, and

(d) a reference to an Annex by number is a reference to the Annex so numbered to the Directive and included in the *Schedule* to this Act.

(4) Where in any legal proceedings the question of whether—

(a) a body is a non-government organisation, or

(b)   a body, commission, tribunal or board is or was established by an Act or by arrangement of the Government, a Minister of the Government or a Minister of State for a non-commercial service or purpose,

is in issue then, for the purpose of establishing whether it is or is not a public body as defined in *subsection (1)*, a document signed by the Minister, a Minister of the Government or a Minister of State declaring that—

(i)   he or she is the appropriate Minister for determining whether the body is or is not a non-government organisation, and that in fact it is or is not such an organisation, or

(ii)   he or she is the appropriate Minister for determining whether the body, commission, tribunal or board was or was not so established for a non-commercial service or purpose, and that in fact it was or was not so established,

is sufficient evidence of those facts, until the contrary is shown, and the Minister, Minister of the Government or Minister of State may make such a declaration.

Regulations.
3.—

(1)   The Minister may make regulations prescribing any matter or thing referred to in this Act as prescribed or to be prescribed, or in relation to any matter referred to in this Act as the subject of regulation.

(2)   Regulations under this section may contain such incidental, supplementary and consequential provisions as appear to the Minister to be necessary or expedient for the purposes of the regulations or for giving full effect to this Act.

Laying of orders and regulations before Houses of Oireachtas.
4.—Every order (other than an order made under *section 1(2)*) or regulation made by the Minister under *section 3* shall be laid before each House of the Oireachtas as soon as may be after it is made and, if a resolution annulling the order or regulation is passed by either such House within the next subsequent 21 days on which that House has sat after the order or regulation is laid before it, the order or regulation shall be annulled accordingly but without prejudice to the validity of anything previously done under it.

Expenses of Minister.
5.—Expenses incurred by the Minister in the administration of this Act shall, to such extent as may be sanctioned by the Minister for Finance, be paid out of moneys provided by the Oireachtas.

Prosecution of offences.
6.—

(1)   Summary proceedings for offences under this Act or a regulation made under *section 3* may be brought and prosecuted by the Minister or a person or public body prescribed by the Minister for that purpose.

(2)   Notwithstanding section 10(4) of the Petty Sessions (Ireland) Act, 1851, summary proceedings for an offence under this Act or a regulation made under *section 3*

may be commenced at any time within 12 months from the date on which evidence that, in the opinion of the person or public body by whom the proceedings are brought, is sufficient to justify the bringing of the proceedings, comes to that person's or public body's knowledge.

(3)   For the purpose of *subsection (2)*, a document signed by or on behalf of the person or public body bringing the proceedings as to the date on which the evidence referred to in that subsection came to his, her or its knowledge is *prima facie* evidence thereof and in those or any other legal proceedings a document purporting to be issued for the purpose of this subsection and to be so signed is taken to be so signed and shall be admitted as evidence without further proof of the signature of the person or public body purporting to sign it.

Offences by bodies corporate.

7.—Where an offence under this Act has been committed by a body corporate and is proved to have been committed with the consent or connivance of, or to be attributable to any neglect on the part of, a person being a director, shadow director (as defined in section 3(1) of the Companies Act, 1990), manager, secretary or other officer of the body corporate, or a person who was purporting to act in any such capacity, that person, as well as the body corporate, shall be guilty of an offence and be liable to be proceeded against and punished as if he or she were guilty of the first-mentioned offence.

Penalties.

8.—A person or public body guilty of an offence under this Act for which no penalty other than by this section is provided shall be liable—

(*a*)   on summary conviction, to a fine not exceeding £1,500 or, at the discretion of the court, to imprisonment for a term not exceeding 12 months, or to both the fine and the imprisonment, or

(*b*)   on conviction on indictment, to a fine not exceeding £500,000 or, at the discretion of the court, to imprisonment for a term not exceeding 5 years, or to both the fine and the imprisonment.

PART 2

Legal Recognition and Non-Discrimination in respect of Electronic Signatures, Originals, Contracts and Related Matters

Legal Recognition of Electronic Communications and Information in Electronic Form

Electronic form not to affect legal validity or enforceability.

9.—Information (including information incorporated by reference) shall not be denied legal effect, validity or enforceability solely on the grounds that it is wholly or partly in electronic form, whether as an electronic communication or otherwise.

Excluded laws.

10.—

(1)   *Sections 12* to *23* are without prejudice to—

(*a*)   the law governing the creation, execution, amendment, variation or revocation of—

     (i)   a will, codicil or any other testamentary instrument to which the Succession Act, 1965, applies,

     (ii)   a trust, or

     (iii)   an enduring power of attorney,

(*b*)   the law governing the manner in which an interest in real property (including a leasehold interest in such property) may be created, acquired, disposed of or registered, other than contracts (whether or not under seal) for the creation, acquisition or disposal of such interests,

(*c*)   the law governing the making of an affidavit or a statutory or sworn declaration, or requiring or permitting the use of one for any purpose, or

(*d*)   the rules, practices or procedures of a court or tribunal, except to the extent that regulations under *section 3* may from time to time prescribe.

(2)   Where the Minister is of the opinion that—

(*a*)   technology has advanced to such an extent, and access to it is so widely available, or

(*b*)   adequate procedures and practices have developed in public registration or other services, so as to warrant such action, or

(*c*)   the public interest so requires, he or she may, after consultation with such Minister or Ministers as in the Minister's opinion has or have a sufficient interest or responsibility in relation to the matter, by regulations made under *section 3*, for the purpose of encouraging the efficient use of electronic communication facilities and services in commerce and the community generally while at the same time protecting the public interest, extend the application of this Act or a provision of this Act to or in relation to a matter specified in *subsection (1)* (including a particular aspect of such a matter) subject to such conditions as he or she thinks fit, and the Act as so extended shall apply accordingly.

(3)   Without prejudice to the generality of *subsection (2)*, the regulations may apply to a particular area or subject, or for a particular time, in the nature of a trial of technology and procedures.

Certain laws not to be affected.
11.—Nothing in this Act shall prejudice the operation of—

(*a*)   any law relating to the imposition, collection or recovery of taxation or other Government imposts, including fees, fines and penalties,

(*b*)   the Companies Act, 1990 (Uncertificated Securities) Regulations, 1996 (S.I. No. 68 of 1996) or any regulations made in substitution for those regulations,

(*c*)   the Criminal Evidence Act, 1992, or

(d)   the Consumer Credit Act, 1995, or any regulations made thereunder and the European Communities (Unfair Terms in Consumer Contracts) Regulations, 1995 (S.I. No. 27 of 1995).

Writing.
12.—

(1)   If by law or otherwise a person or public body is required (whether the requirement is in the form of an obligation or consequences flow from the information not being in writing) or permitted to give information in writing (whether or not in a form prescribed by law), then, subject to *subsection (2)*, the person or public body may give the information in electronic form, whether as an electronic communication or otherwise.

(2)   Information may be given as provided in *subsection (1)* only—

   (a)   if at the time the information was given it was reasonable to expect that it would be readily accessible to the person or public body to whom it was directed, for subsequent reference,

   (b)   where the information is required or permitted to be given to a public body or to a person acting on behalf of a public body and the public body consents to the giving of the information in electronic form, whether as an electronic communication or otherwise, but requires—

      (i)   the information to be given in accordance with particular information technology and procedural requirements, or

      (ii)   that a particular action be taken by way of verifying the receipt of the information, if the public body's requirements have been met and those requirements have been made public and are objective, transparent, proportionate and non-discriminatory, and

   (c)   where the information is required or permitted to be given to a person who is neither a public body nor acting on behalf of a public body— if the person to whom the information is required or permitted to be given consents to the information being given in that form.

(3)   *Subsections (1)* and *(2)* are without prejudice to any other law requiring or permitting information to be given—

   (a)   in accordance with particular information technology and procedural requirements,

   (b)   on a particular kind of data storage device, or

   (c)   by means of a particular kind of electronic communication.

(4)   This section applies to a requirement or permission to give information whether the word "give", "send", "forward", "deliver", "serve" or similar word or expression is used.

(5)   In this section, "give information" includes but is not limited to—

   (a)   make an application,

   (b)   make or lodge a claim,

(c)   make or lodge a return,

(d)   make a request,

(e)   make an unsworn declaration,

(f)   lodge or issue a certificate,

(g)   make, vary or cancel an election,

(h)   lodge an objection,

(i)   give a statement of reasons,

(j)   record and disseminate a court order,

(k)   give, send or serve a notification.

Signatures
13.—

(1)   If by law or otherwise the signature of a person or public body is required (whether the requirement is in the form of an obligation or consequences flow from there being no signature) or permitted, then, subject to *subsection (2)*, an electronic signature may be used.

(2)   An electronic signature may be used as provided in *subsection (1)* only—

(a)   where the signature is required or permitted to be given to a public body or to a person acting on behalf of a public body and the public body consents to the use of an electronic signature but requires that it be in accordance with particular information technology and procedural requirements (including that it be an advanced electronic signature, that it be based on a qualified certificate, that it be issued by an accredited certification service provider or that it be created by a secure signature creation device)— if the public body's requirements have been met and those requirements have been made public and are objective, transparent, proportionate and non-discriminatory, and

(b)   where the signature is required or permitted to be given to a person who is neither a public body nor acting on behalf of a public body— if the person to whom the signature is required or permitted to be given consents to the use of an electronic signature.

(3)   *Subsections (1)* and *(2)* are without prejudice to any other provision of this Act or law requiring or permitting an electronic communication to contain an electronic signature, an advanced electronic signature, an electronic signature based on a qualified certificate, an electronic signature created by a secure signature creation device or other technological requirements relating to an electronic signature.

Signatures required to be witnessed.
14.—

(1)   If by law or otherwise a signature to a document is required to be witnessed (whether the requirement is in the form of an obligation or consequences flow from the signature not being witnessed) that requirement is taken to have been met if—

(a)   the signature to be witnessed is an advanced electronic signature, based on a qualified certificate, of the person or public body by whom the document is required to be signed,

(b)   the document contains an indication that the signature of that person or public body is required to be witnessed, and

(c)   the signature of the person purporting to witness the signature to be witnessed is an advanced electronic signature, based on a qualified certificate.

(2)   An advanced electronic signature based on a qualified certificate may be used as provided in *subsection (1)* only—

(a)   where the signature required or permitted to be witnessed is on a document to be given to a public body or to a person acting on behalf of a public body and the public body consents to the use of an electronic signature of both the person attesting the document and witnessing the signature but requires that the document and signatures be in accordance with particular information technology and procedural requirements (including that a qualified certificate on which the signature or signatures are based be issued by an accredited certification service provider)— if the public body's requirements are met and those requirements have been made public and are objective, transparent, proportionate and non-discriminatory, and

(b)   where the document on or in respect of which the signature is to be witnessed is required or permitted to be given to a person who is neither a public body nor acting on behalf of a public body— if the person to whom it is required or permitted to be given consents to the use of an advanced electronic signature based on a qualified certificate for that purpose.

Consumer law to apply.
15.—All electronic contracts within the State shall be subject to all existing consumer law and the role of the Director of Consumer Affairs in such legislation shall apply equally to consumer transactions, whether conducted electronically or non-electronically.

Documents under seal.
16.—

(1)   If by law or otherwise a seal is required to be affixed to a document (whether the requirement is in the form of an obligation or consequences flow from a seal not being affixed) then, subject to *subsection (2)*, that requirement is taken to have been met if the document indicates that it is required to be under seal and it includes an advanced electronic signature, based on a qualified certificate, of the person or public body by whom it is required to be sealed.

(2)   An advanced electronic signature based on a qualified certificate may be used as provided in *subsection (1)* only—

(a)   where the document to be under seal is required or permitted to be given to a public body or to a person acting on
behalf of a public body and the public body consents to the use of an electronic signature but requires that it be in accordance with particular

information technology and procedural requirements (including that a qualified certificate on which it is based be issued by an accredited certification service provider)— if the public body's requirements have been met and those requirements have been made public and are objective, transparent, proportionate and non-discriminatory, and

(b) where the document to be under seal is required or permitted to be given to a person who is neither a public body nor acting on behalf of a public body— if the person to whom it is required or permitted to be given consents to the use of an advanced electronic signature based on a qualified certificate.

Electronic originals.
17.—

(1) If by law or otherwise a person or public body is required (whether the requirement is in the form of an obligation or consequences flow from the information not being presented or retained in its original form) or permitted to present or retain information in its original form, then, subject to *subsection (2)*, the information may be presented or retained, as the case may be, in electronic form, whether as an electronic communication or otherwise.

(2) Information may be presented or retained as provided in *subsection (1)* only—

(a) if there exists a reliable assurance as to the integrity of the information from the time when it was first generated in its final form, whether as an electronic communication or otherwise,

(b) where it is required or permitted that the information be presented— if the information is capable of being displayed in intelligible form to a person or public body to whom it is to be presented,

(c) if, at the time the information was generated in its final form, it was reasonable to expect that it would be readily accessible so as to be useable for subsequent reference,

(d) where the information is required or permitted to be presented to or retained for a public body or for a person acting on behalf of a public body, and the public body consents to the information being presented or retained in electronic form, whether as an electronic communication or otherwise, but requires that it be presented or retained in accordance with particular information technology and procedural requirements— if the public body's requirements have been met and those requirements have been made public and are objective, transparent, proportionate and non-discriminatory, and

(e) where the information is required or permitted to be presented to or retained for a person who is neither a public body nor acting on behalf of a public body— if the person to whom the information is required or permitted to be presented or for whom it is required or permitted to be retained consents to the information being presented or retained in that form.

(3) *Subsections (1)* and *(2)* are without prejudice to any other law requiring or permitting information to be presented or retained—

(a)   in accordance with particular information technology and procedural requirements,

(b)   on a particular kind of data storage device, or

(c)   by means of a particular kind of electronic communication.

(4)   For the purposes of *subsections (1)* and *(2)*—

(a)   the criteria for assessing integrity is whether the information has remained complete and unaltered, apart from the addition of any endorsement or change which arises in the normal course of generating, communicating, processing, sending, receiving, recording, storing or displaying, and

(b)   the standard of reliability shall be assessed in the light of the purpose for which and the circumstances in which the information was generated.

Retention and production.
18.—

(1)   If by law or otherwise a person or public body is required (whether the requirement is in the form of an obligation or consequences flow from the information not being retained or produced in its original form) or permitted to retain for a particular period or produce a document that is in the form of paper or other material on which information may be recorded in written form, then, subject to *subsection (2)*, the person or public body may retain throughout the relevant period or, as the case may be, produce, the document in electronic form, whether as an electronic communication or otherwise.

(2)   A document may be retained throughout the period, or produced, by the person or public body as provided in *subsection (1)* only—

(a)   if there exists a reliable assurance as to the integrity of the information from the time when it was first generated in its final form as an electronic communication,

(b) in the case of a document to be produced— if the information is capable of being displayed in intelligible form to the person or public body to whom it is to be produced,

(c)   in the case of a document to be retained— if, at the time of the generation of the final electronic form of the document, it was reasonable to expect that the information contained in the electronic form of the document would be readily accessible so as to be useable for subsequent reference,

(d)   where the document is required or permitted to be retained for or produced to a public body or for or to a person acting on behalf of a public body, and the public body consents to the document being retained or produced in electronic form, whether as an electronic communication or otherwise, but requires that the electronic form of the document be retained or produced in accordance with particular information technology and procedural requirements— if the public body's requirements have been met and those requirements have been made public and are objective, transparent, proportionate and nondiscriminatory, and (*e*)   where the document is required or permitted to be retained for or produced to a person who is neither a public body nor acting on behalf of a public body— if the person for or to whom the document is required or permitted to be retained or produced consents to it being retained or produced in that form.

(3)   *Subsections (1)* and *(2)* are without prejudice to any other law requiring or permitting documents in the form of paper or other material to be retained or produced—

    (*a*)   in accordance with particular information technology and procedural requirements,

    (*b*)   on a particular kind of data storage device, or

    (*c*)   by means of a particular kind of electronic communication.

(4)   For the purposes of *subsections (1)* and *(2)*—

    (*a*)   the criteria for assessing integrity is whether the information has remained complete and unaltered, apart from the addition of any endorsement or change which arises in the normal course of generating, communicating, processing, sending, receiving, recording, storing or displaying, and

    (*b*)   the standard of reliability shall be assessed in the light of the purpose for which the information was generated and the circumstances in which it was generated.

Contracts.
19.—

(1)   An electronic contract shall not be denied legal effect, validity or enforceability solely on the grounds that it is wholly or partly in electronic form, or has been concluded wholly or partly by way of an electronic communication.

(2)   In the formation of a contract, an offer, acceptance of an offer or any related communication (including any subsequent amendment, cancellation or revocation of the offer or acceptance of the offer) may, unless otherwise agreed by the parties, be communicated by means of an electronic communication.

Acknowledgement of receipt of electronic communications.
20.—

(1)   Subject to any other law, where the originator of an electronic communication indicates that receipt of the electronic communication is required to be acknowledged but does not indicate a particular form or method of acknowledgement, then, unless the originator and the addressee of the electronic communication agree otherwise, the acknowledgement shall be given by way of an electronic communication or any other communication (including any conduct of the addressee) sufficient to indicate to the originator that the electronic communication has been received.

(2)   Where the originator of an electronic communication indicates that receipt of the electronic communication is required to be acknowledged, the electronic communication, in relation to the establishing of legal rights and obligations between parties, shall, until the acknowledgement is received by the originator and unless the parties otherwise agree, be treated as if it had never been sent.

(3)   Where the originator of an electronic communication has indicated that receipt of the electronic communication is required to be acknowledged but has not stated that the electronic communication is conditional on the receipt of acknowledgement and the acknowledgement has not been received by the originator within the time specified or agreed or, if no time has been specified or agreed, within a reasonable time, then the electronic communication, in relation to the establishing of legal rights and obligations between parties, shall, unless the parties otherwise agree, be treated as if it had never been sent.

Time and place of dispatch and receipt of electronic communications.
21.—

(1)   Where an electronic communication enters an information system, or the first information system, outside the control of the originator, then, unless otherwise agreed between the originator and the addressee, it is taken to have been sent when it enters such information system or first information system.

(2)   Where the addressee of an electronic communication has designated an information system for the purpose of receiving electronic communications, then, unless otherwise agreed between the originator and the addressee or the law otherwise provides, the electronic communication is taken to have been received when it enters that information system.

(3)   Where the addressee of an electronic communication has not designated an information system for the purpose of receiving electronic communications, then, unless otherwise agreed between the originator and the addressee, the electronic communication is taken to have been received when it comes to the attention of the addressee.

(4)   *Subsections (1), (2)* and *(3)* apply notwithstanding that the place where the relevant information system is located may be different from the place where the electronic communication is taken to have been sent or received, as the case may be, under those subsections.

(5)   Unless otherwise agreed between the originator and the addressee of an electronic communication, the electronic communication is taken to have been sent from and received at, respectively, the place where the originator and the addressee have their places of business.

(6)   For the purposes of *subsection (5)*, but subject to *subsection (7)*—

   (a)   if the originator or addressee has more than one place of business, the place of business is the place that has the closest relationship to the underlying transaction or, if there is no underlying transaction, the principal place of business, and

   (b)   if the originator or addressee does not have a place of business, the place of business is taken to be the place where he or she ordinarily resides.

(7)   If an electronic communication is or is in connection with a notification or other communication required or permitted by or under an Act to be sent or given to, or served on, a company at its registered office, the registered office is taken to be the place of business of the company in connection with that electronic communication for the purpose of *subsection (5)*.

Admissibility.
22.—In any legal proceedings, nothing in the application of the rules of evidence shall apply so as to deny the admissibility in evidence of—

(a) an electronic communication, an electronic form of a document, an electronic contract, or writing in electronic form—

   (i) on the sole ground that it is an electronic communication, an electronic form of a document, an electronic contract, or writing in electronic form, or

   (ii) if it is the best evidence that the person or public body adducing it could reasonably be expected to obtain, on the grounds that it is not in its original form,

   or

(b) an electronic signature—

   (i) on the sole ground that the signature is in electronic form, or is not an advanced electronic signature, or is not based on a qualified certificate, or is not based on a qualified certificate issued by an accredited certification service provider, or is not created by a secure signature creation device, or

   (ii) if it is the best evidence that the person or public body adducing it could reasonably be expected to obtain, on the grounds that it is not in its original form.

Defamation law to apply.
23.—All provisions of existing defamation law shall apply to all electronic communications within the State, including the retention of information electronically.

General

Electronic form not required.
24.—Nothing in this Act shall be construed as—

(a) requiring a person or public body to generate, communicate, produce, process, send, receive, record, retain, store or display any information, document or signature by or in electronic form, or

(b) prohibiting a person or public body engaging in an electronic transaction from establishing reasonable requirements about the manner in which the person will accept electronic communications, electronic signatures or electronic forms of documents.
Prohibition of fraud and misuse of electronic signatures and signature creation devices.

Prohibition of fraud and misuse of electronic signatures and signature creation devices.
25.—A person or public body who or which—

(a) knowingly accesses, copies or otherwise obtains possession of, or recreates, the signature creation device of another person or a public body, without the authorisation of that other person or public body, for the purpose of creating or allowing, or causing another person or public body to create, an unauthorised electronic signature using the signature creation device,

(b) knowingly alters, discloses or uses the signature creation device of another person or a public body, without the authorisation of that other person or public body or in excess of lawful authorisation, for the purpose of creating or allowing, or causing another person or public body to create, an unauthorised electronic signature using the signature creation device,

(c) knowingly creates, publishes, alters or otherwise uses a certificate or an electronic signature for a fraudulent or other unlawful purpose,

(d) knowingly misrepresents the person's or public body's identity or authorisation in requesting or accepting a certificate or in requesting suspension or revocation of a certificate,

(e) knowingly accesses, alters, discloses or uses the signature creation device of a certification service provider used to issue certificates, without the authorisation of the certification service provider or in excess of lawful authorisation, for the purpose of creating, or allowing or causing another person or a public body to create, an unauthorised electronic signature using the signature creation device, or

(f) knowingly publishes a certificate, or otherwise knowingly makes it available to anyone likely to rely on the certificate or on an electronic signature that is verifiable with reference to data such as codes, passwords, algorithms, public cryptographic keys or other data which are used for the purposes of verifying an electronic signature, listed in the certificate, if the person or public body knows that—

(i) the certification service provider listed in the certificate has not issued it,

(ii) the subscriber listed in the certificate has not accepted it, or

(iii) the certificate has been revoked or suspended, unless its publication is for the purpose of verifying an electronic signature created before such revocation or suspension, or giving notice of revocation or suspension,

is guilty of an offence.

Activities partly outside the State.
26.—The provisions of *section 25* extend to activities that took place partly outside the State.

Investigative procedures.
27.—

(1) Where, on the sworn information of an officer of the Minister or a member of the Garda Síochána not below the rank of Inspector, a judge of the District Court is satisfied that there are reasonable grounds for suspecting that evidence of or relating to an offence under this Act is to be found at a place specified in the information, the judge may issue a warrant for the search of that place and any persons found at that place.

(2)   A warrant issued under this section shall authorise a named officer of the Minister or member of the Garda Síochána, alone or accompanied by such member or other members of the Garda Síochána and such other persons as may be necessary—

(a)   to enter, within 7 days from the date of the warrant, and if necessary by the use of reasonable force, the place named in the warrant,

(b)   to search the place and any person reasonably suspected of being connected with any activities of the place found thereon, and

(c)   to seize anything found there, or anything found in the possession of a person present there at the time of the search, which that officer or member reasonably believes to be evidence of or relating to an offence under this Act and, where the thing seized is or contains information or an electronic communication that cannot readily be accessed or put into intelligible form, to require the disclosure of the information or electronic communication in intelligible form.

(3)   An officer of the Minister or member of the Garda Síochána acting in accordance with a warrant issued under this section may require any person found at the place where the search is carried out to give the officer or member the person's name and address.

(4)   A person who or public body which—

(a)   obstructs or attempts to obstruct an officer of the Minister or member of the Garda Síochána acting in accordance with a warrant issued under *subsection (1)*,

(b)   fails or refuses to comply with a requirement under this section, or

(c)   gives a name or address which is false or misleading, is guilty of a summary offence.

(5)   An officer of the Minister or member of the Garda Síochána may retain anything seized under *subsection (2)(c)* which he or she has reasonable grounds for believing to be evidence of an offence under this Act, for use as evidence in relation to proceedings in relation to any such offence, for such period as is reasonable or, if proceedings are commenced in which the thing is required to be used in evidence, until the conclusion of the proceedings.

(6)   In this section, "place" includes any dwelling, any building or part of a building and any vehicle, vessel or structure.

Confidentiality of deciphering data.
28.—Nothing in this Act shall be construed as requiring the disclosure or enabling the seizure of unique data, such as codes, passwords, algorithms, private cryptographic keys, or other data, that may be necessary to render information or an electronic communication intelligible.

PART 3

Certification Services

Accreditation and supervision of certification service providers.
29.—

(1) A person or public body is not required to obtain the prior authority of any other person or public body to provide certification or other services relating to electronic signatures.

(2)

    (*a*) The Minister, after consultation with the Minister for Enterprise, Trade and Employment, may by regulations made under *section 3* establish a scheme of voluntary accreditation of certification service providers for the purpose of the Directive and to enhance levels of certification service provision in the State, and may designate accreditation authorities and prescribe such matters relating to their designation as the Minister thinks appropriate for the purpose.

    (*b*) A person or public body who or which provides certification or other services in the State relating to electronic signatures may apply as prescribed to the accreditation authority designated under *paragraph (a)* to participate in any scheme of voluntary accreditation established pursuant to that paragraph.

    (*c*) The regulations may prescribe—

        (i) the rights and obligations specific to the provision of certification services of participants in a scheme of voluntary accreditation, and

        (ii) the manner in which the accreditation authority designated under *paragraph (a)* shall elaborate and supervise compliance with those rights and obligations in accordance with the Directive and, in particular, Annex II.

    (*d*) A participant in a scheme referred to in *paragraph (a)* shall not exercise a right under the scheme without the prior permission of the accreditation authority.

(3) The Minister shall prescribe a scheme of supervision of certification service providers established in the State who issue qualified certificates to the public.

(4)

    (*a*) The Minister may, after consultation with the Minister for Enterprise, Trade and Employment, by order, designate persons or public bodies for the purposes of determining whether secure signature creation devices conform with the requirements of Annex III.

    (*b*) The Minister may, by order, amend or revoke an order under this subsection, including an order under this paragraph.

(5) No civil action shall lie or be maintained against a person or public body designated under or for the purposes of *subsection (2), (3)* or *(4)* in

respect of any determination made or thing done by the person or public body, in good faith, in the performance or purported
performance of a function under a scheme referred to in *subsection (2)* or *(3)* or for which he, she or it is designated under *subsection (4)*.

Liability of certification service providers.
30.—

(1) A certification service provider who provides a service to the public of issuing certificates and who as a part of that service issues a certificate as a qualified certificate or guarantees such a certificate, shall be liable for any damage caused to a person who, or public body which, reasonably relies on the certificate unless the certification service provider proves that he, she or it has not acted negligently.

(2) It shall be the duty of every certification service provider who provides to the public a service of issuing certificates and who issues a certificate as a qualified certificate or guarantees such a certificate, to take reasonable steps to ensure—

   (*a*) the accuracy of all information in the qualified certificate as at the time of issue and that the certificate contains all the details required by Annex I to be so contained in a qualified certificate,

   (*b*) that, at the time of the issue of the certificate, the signatory identified in the certificate held the signature creation device corresponding to the signature verification device given or identified in the certificate, and

   (*c*) that the signature creation device and the signature verification device act together in a complementary manner, 10 in cases where the certification service provider generates both.

(3) A certification service provider who provides a service to the public of issuing certificates and who as a part of that service issues a certificate as a qualified certificate, or guarantees such a certificate, is liable for any damage caused to a person who, or public body which, reasonably relies on the certificate, for the certification service provider's failure to register or publish notice of the revocation or suspension of the certificate as prescribed, unless the certification service provider proves that he, she or it has not acted negligently.

(4) A certification service provider who provides a service to the public of issuing certificates and who as a part of that service issues a certificate as a qualified certificate, or guarantees such a certificate, may indicate in the qualified certificate limits on the uses of the certificate (including a limit on the value of transactions for which the certificate can be used) and, if the limits are clear and readily identifiable as limitations, the certification service provider shall not be liable for damages arising from a contrary use of a qualified certificate which includes such limits on its uses.

PART 4

Domain Name Registration

Registration of domain names
31.—

(1) The Minister may, by regulations made for the purpose of easy comprehension, fairness, transparency, avoidance of deception, promotion of fair competition and public confidence under *section 3* after consultation with the Minister for Enterprise, Trade and Employment and such other persons and public bodies, if any, as the Minister thinks fit, including the body known as the Internet Corporation for Assigned Names and Numbers, authorise, prohibit or regulate the registration and use of the ie domain name in the State.

(2) Without prejudice to the generality of *subsection (1)*, the regulations may prescribe—

  (*a*) designated registration authorities,

  (*b*) the form of registration,

  (*c*) the period during which registration continues in force,

  (*d*) the manner in which, the terms on which and the period or periods for which registration may be renewed,

  (*e*) the circumstances and manner in which registrations may be granted, renewed or refused by the registration authorities,

  (*f*) the right of appeal and appeal processes,

  (*g*) the fees, if any, to be paid on the grant or renewal of registration and the time and manner in which such fees are to be paid,

  (*h*) such other matters relating to registration as appear to the Minister to be necessary or desirable to prescribe.

(3) A person who contravenes or fails to comply with a regulation made pursuant to this section is liable on summary conviction to a fine not exceeding £500.

(4) In this section "ie domain name" means the top level of the global domain name system assigned to Ireland according to the twoletter code in the International Standard ISO 3166-1 (Codes for Representation of Names of Countries and their Subdivision) of the International Organisation for Standardisation.

SCHEDULE

Section 2(3)(d).

ANNEXES TO DIRECTIVE OF THE EUROPEAN PARLIAMENT AND OF THE COUNCIL ON A COMMUNITY FRAMEWORK FOR ELECTRONIC SIGNATURES

ANNEX I

Section 30(2)(a).

Requirements for qualified certificates
Qualified certificates must contain:

- (*a*) an indication that the certificate is issued as a qualified certificate;

- (*b*) the identification of the certification-service-provider and the State in which it is established;

- (*c*) the name of the signatory or a pseudonym, which shall be identified as such;

- (*d*) provision for a specific attribute of the signatory to be included if relevant, depending on the purpose for which the certificate is intended;

- (*e*) signature-verification data which correspond to signaturecreation data under the control of the signatory;

- (*f*) an indication of the beginning and end of the period of validity of the certificate;

- (*g*) the identity code of the certificate;

- (*h*) the advanced electronic signature of the certification-service- provider issuing it;

- (*i*) limitations on the scope of use of the certificate, if applicable; and

- (*j*) limits on the value of transactions for which the certificate can be used, if applicable.

ANNEX II

Section 29(2)(c)(ii).

Requirements for certification-service-providers
issuing qualified certificates
Certification-service-providers must:

- (*a*) demonstrate the reliability necessary for providing certification services;

- (*b*) ensure the operation of a prompt and secure directory and a secure and immediate revocation service;

- (*c*) ensure that the date and time when a certificate is issued or revoked can be determined precisely; 10

(*d*)   verify, by appropriate means in accordance with national law, the identity and, if applicable, any specific attributes of the person to which a qualified certificate is issued;

(*e*)   employ personnel who possess the expert knowledge, experience and qualifications necessary for the services provided, in particular competence at managerial level,
expertise in electronic signature technology and familiarity with proper security procedures; they must also apply administrative and managerial procedures which are adequate and correspond to recognised standards;

(*f*)   use trustworthy systems and products which are protected against modification and ensure the technical and cryptographic security of the processes supported by them;

(*g*)   take measures against forgery of certificates, and, in cases where the certification-service-provider generates signature-creation data, guarantee confidentiality during the process of generating such data;

(*h*)   maintain sufficient financial resources to operate in conformity with the requirements laid down in the Directive, in particular to bear the risk of liability for damages, for example by obtaining appropriate insurance;

(*i*)   record all relevant information concerning a qualified certificate for an appropriate period of time, in particular for the purpose of providing evidence of certification for the purposes of legal proceedings. Such recording may be done electronically;

(*j*)   not store or copy signature-creation data of the person to whom the certification-service-provider provides key management services;

(*k*)   before entering into a contractual relationship with a person seeking a certificate to support his electronic signature, inform that person by a durable means of communication of the precise terms and conditions regarding the use of the certificate, including any limitations on its use, the experience of a voluntary accreditation scheme and procedures for complaints and dispute settlement. Such information, which may be transmitted electronically, must be in writing and in readily understandable language. Relevant parts of this information must also be made available on request to third-parties relying on the certificate;

(*l*)   use trustworthy systems to store certificates in a verifiable form so that:

— only authorised persons can make entries and changes,

— information can be checked for authenticity,

— certificates are publicly available for retrieval in only 5 those cases for which the certificate-holder's consent has been obtained, and

— any technical changes comprising these security requirements are apparent to the operator.

ANNEX III

Section 29(4)
Requirements for secure signature-creation devices

1. Secure signature-creation devices must, by appropriate technical and procedural means, ensure at the least that:

    (*a*)   the signature-creation-data used for signature generation can practically occur only once, and that their secrecy is 15 reasonably assured;

    (*b*)   the signature-creation-data used for signature generation cannot, with reasonable assurance, be derived and the signature is protected against forgery using currently available technology; 20

    (*c*)   the signature-creation-data used for signature generation can be reliably protected by the legitimate signatory against the use of others.

2. Secure signature-creation devices must not alter the data to be signed or prevent such data from being presented to the signatory 25 prior to the signature process.

Latvia

Law on Electronic Documents

Chapter I

General Provisions

Article 1

Terms Used for the Purposes of this Law
The following terms are used in this Law:

1) **safe means of creating an electronic signature** – software, hardware and data for creating an electronic signature in compliance with all of the following requirements:

   a) data for creating the electronic signature have been created only once and their confidentiality is ensured;

   b) data for creating the electronic signature cannot be derived and technologies are used to protect the electronic signature against counterfeiting;

   c) data for creating an electronic signature are safely protected against misuse by third persons;

   d) safe means of creating an electronic signature do not alter the electronic document to be signed electronically and do not prevent any person from reading the document prior to its signing;

2) **safe electronic signature** – an electronic signature that complies with all of the following requirements:

   a) it is associated only with the signatory;

   b) it ensures identification of the signatory;

   c) it has been created with safe means of creating an electronic signature that can be controlled only by the signatory;

       d)   it is linked with the signed electronic document in a manner that allows to track subsequent changes in the document;

       e)   it is confirmed with a qualified certificate;

3)   **electronic document** – any data that have been created, stored, sent or received in an electronic form and can be used to perform an activity, enforce or protect the right;

4)   **electronic signature** – electronic data attached to or logically linked to the electronic document that ensure the authenticity of the document and certify the identity of the signatory;

5)   **data of verifying an electronic signature** – data used to verify an electronic signature;

6)   **data for creating an electronic signature** – data created only once that are used by the signatory to create an electronic signature;

7)   **qualified certificate** – a certificate containing the information as established by this Law and has been issued by a trusted certification provider;

8)   **time stamp** – electronically signed verification that the electronic document has been marked by the certification provider on a particular date and time;

9)   **signatory** – a person possessing the means for creating an electronic signature and acting either on its own behalf or on behalf of a natural person, a legal person or an institution it represents;

10)   **certification services** – issuing, canceling, suspending and renewing certificates, registering certificates, maintaining a register of data of verifying electronic signatures, marking electronic documents with a time stamp, consulting on issues relating to an electronic signature;

11)   **certificate** – an electronic approval linking the verification data of an electronic signature and the signatory and is a means of identifying the signatory.

Article 2

Scope of the Law

(1)   This Law shall establish the legal status of an electronic document and an electronic signature.

(2)   This Law shall not apply if an electronic document has been marked with a time stamp by a legal or a natural person other that the provider of certification services.

Chapter II

Electronic Documents and Their Derivatives

Article 3

Electronic Documents

(1)   In relation to an electronic document, the requirement for a document in writing shall be deemed as complied provided that the electronic document bears an electronic signature and complies with other requirements set out in laws and regulations.

(2)   An electronic document shall be deemed as autographed provided that it bears a safe electronic signature.

(3)   Where laws and regulations establish that a document shall bear a seal imprint apart from other corporate or personal information, this requirement shall be deemed as complied provided that an electronic document bears a safe electronic signature and time stamp.

(4)   An electronic signature shall be a legal evidence and the submission of an electronic document to competent authorities as an evidence shall not be restricted by the fact that:

1)   the document is in an electronic form;

2)   it does not bear a safe electronic signature.

(5)   In the flow of electronic documents between governmental and municipal institutions or between those institutions and legal or natural persons, an electronic document shall be deemed as signed provided that it bears a safe electronic signature and a time stamp.

(6)   This Law shall not apply:

1)   to agreements that create or transfer rights to real estate, except the rights to lease;

2)   to agreements that are not effective pursuant to the law unless they are certified in the procedure established by the law;

3)   to guarantee agreements whereby a guarantee is granted and to pledge agreements whereby the pledge is given by a person that performs for purposes other than those related with that person's occupation, business or profession;

4)   to deals that fall within the scope of family rights and heritage rights.

Article 4

Original Electronic Document

(1)   Where laws and regulations establish that original documents shall be stored or presented, as to electronic documents this requirement shall be deemed as

complied provided that the electronic document complies with the requirements set out in Article 3(2) and (3) hereof.

(2) Article 4(1) hereof shall refer to a requirement formulated as an obligation or to cases when laws and regulations establish legal consequences for a failure to store a document or present the original document.

Article 5

Derivatives of Electronic Documents

(1) A copy, duplicate or extract of an electronic document on paper shall have the same legal effect as the original document provided that the copy, duplicate or extract has been certified as correct pursuant to laws and regulations and the person submitting the copy, duplicate or extract on paper is able to present, upon request, the original electronic document that complies with the requirements of this Law.

(2) An electronic copy, duplicate or extract of a document on paper shall have the same legal effect as the original document provided that the person that is entitled to certify copies, duplicates or extracts of original documents pursuant to laws and regulations has certified the copy, duplicate or extract as correct with a safe electronic signature and a time stamp and it complies with the requirements of laws and regulations.

(3) The electronic counterpart of a document on paper shall have the same legal effect as the original document provided that the counterpart has been issued and formatted pursuant to the requirements of this Law and other laws and regulations.

(4) Derivatives on paper of an electronic document shall be made from such electronic documents that can be presented in a readable or graphic form.

Chapter III

Provisions Governing the Flow and Storing of Electronic Documents

Article 6

General Provisions Governing the Flow and Storing of Electronic Documents

(1) Where laws and regulations establish requirements for preparing, formatting and storing a particular type of documents on paper, the same provisions shall apply to electronic documents.

(2) The Cabinet of Ministers shall issue provisions that govern the procedure whereby electronic documents are prepared, formatted, stored and circulated in governmental and municipal institutions and the procedure whereby electronic documents are circulated between governmental and municipal institutions and between such institutions and legal or natural persons.

(3)   The Directorate General of State Archives shall be the responsible institution to assess and select electronic documents for long-term or permanent storing, and to follow that the archives of governmental and municipal institutions ensure the storing and availability of electronic documents.

(4)   Governmental and municipal institutions shall develop instructions for an internal circulation of electronic documents that comply with this Law, the regulations issued by the Cabinet of Ministers as referred to in Article 2(2) hereof and the specific activity of the institution, and provide a possibility for legal and natural persons to submit to and receive from governmental and municipal institutions documents, copies, duplicates, extracts and counterparts of documents in an electronic or other form upon their choice.

(5)   The provisions issued by the Cabinet of Ministers shall establish the manner for assessing electronic documents and timing for their submission to the State Archives for storing.

Article 7

Specific Provisions for Storing Electronic Documents

(1)   Where laws and regulations establish that certain documents, records or data shall be stored, as to electronic documents this requirement shall be deemed as complied where:

1)   data included in the electronic document are available for using;

2)   electronic document is stored in the form it has been originally created, sent or received or in the form disclosing the originally created, sent or received data

3)   stored data allow to establish the origin or destination of the electronic document, its sending or receiving time.

(2)   Article 7(1) 3) hereof shall not apply to data that are created automatically in the process of receiving or sending an electronic document.

(3)   A person shall be entitled to ensure compliance with the requirement set out in Article 7(1) hereof by using the services of another person provided that the provisions of this Law are followed.

Chapter IV

Provider of Certification Services and Reliable Provider of Certification Services

Article 8

Provider of Certification Services

(1)   Provider of certification services is a natural or a legal person that provides certification services without a special permit.

(2)   Accreditation of a provider of certification services is voluntary.

(3) A provider of certification services shall be deemed reliable provided that it complies with all requirements set out in Article 9 hereof.

Article 9

Reliable Provider of Certification Services

A provider of certification services, a natural or a legal person, shall be deemed reliable provided that it complies with all of the following requirements:

1) it uses reliable staff that have the necessary specific knowledge, experience and qualification for the provision of certification services, that know the relevant safety rules for the provision of certification services and have not been found guilty for a deliberate crime;

2) it uses reliable and safe information systems and products that are adequately protected against unauthorized access and change;

3) it has sufficient funds to comply with the requirements set out in this Law and regulations issued with respect to this Law, and it insures its civil liability to be able to cover any loss incurred on persons as a result of malicious intent or negligence;

4) it is accredited by the Data State Inspectorate (hereinafter, "a supervisory authority") pursuant to this Law;

5) it ensures that the register of data of verifying an electronic signature is continuously available on line;

6) it ensures that a certificate is cancelled, suspended or renewed without delay in cases established in this Law;

7) it ensures that it is possible at any time to establish the date and time of issuing, canceling, suspending or renewing a qualified certificate;

8) it uses safe systems to store qualified certificates in a verifiable form and ensures that:

   a) records or amendments thereto can be made only by persons authorized by a reliable provider of certification services;

   b) any changes in information can be verified and detected;

   c) issued qualified certificates are not publicly available except in cases when the signatory has issued its consent to this effect in writing;

   d) any technical changes that relate to safety requirements are obvious to the system administrator;

   e) technology used ensures that the data of creating an electronic signature are never copied when they are used;

9) it marks an electronic document with a time stamp to ensure the possibility to establish the exact date and time of the received electronic document;

10) it ensures that the time stamp does not change the electronic document.

Article 10

Accreditation of a Reliable Provider of Certification Services
In order to be accredited, a provider of certification services shall submit the following documents to the supervisory authority:

1) application in writing;

2) regulations governing the provision of certification services;

3) description of safety of the information systems and procedures used to provide certification services;

4) opinion of the safety test of the information systems and procedures used to provide certification services;

5) document that evidences compliance with the requirements set out in Article 9 3) hereof.

Article 11

Regulations Governing the Provision of Certification Services

(1) The regulations governing the provision of certification services shall include the following:

    1) name of a company and registration number or the name, last name, identity number, address, phone and e-mail address of a reliable provider of certification services;

    2) information on the information systems, hardware, technologies and software used to provide certification services and documents certifying the rights to use them;

    3) sample agreement between a reliable provider of certification services and the signatory;

    4) information on the procedure whereby a qualified certificate is issued and the safety of the procedure;

    5) information on the various possibilities for a signatory to restrict the use of a safe electronic signature;

    6) information on the procedure whereby a qualified certificate is cancelled, suspended or renewed;

    7) information on the technical and technological facilities offered by the provider of certification services to protect the safe means of creating an electronic signature, data of verifying the electronic signature and qualified certificates against illegal using;

    8) information that registers of the data of verifying an electronic signature and of the certificates that have been issued, cancelled, suspended and renewed are continuously freely available on line;

    9) information on the marking of an electronic document with a time stamp and the safety of the procedure;

10) information on the fact that the time stamp register is continuously freely available on line.

(2) Should the information included in the regulations change, a reliable provider of certification services shall without delay submit to the supervisory authority amendments to the regulations.

Article 12

Description of Safety of the Information Systems, Hardware and Procedures Used to Provide Certification Services

(1) The Cabinet of Ministers shall establish the information to be included in the description of safety of the information systems, hardware and procedures used to provide certification services.

(2) Should the information included in the description of safety of the information systems, hardware and procedures used to provide certification services change, a reliable provider of certification services shall submit without delay to the supervisory authority amendments to the description.

Article 13

Safety Test of the Information Systems, Hardware and Procedures Used to Provide Certification Services

(1) An expert that has been included in the list approved by the supervisory authority, shall test the safety of the information systems, hardware and procedures used to provide certification services and prepare an opinion thereof.

(2) A person shall be included in the list approved by the supervisory authority provided that it complies with all of the following requirements:

1) it has technical facilities to establish that the safety of the information systems, hardware and procedures used to provide certification services complies with the requirements of laws and regulations;

2) it is legally and financially independent on reliable providers of certification services and the supervisory authority;

3) its staff has the necessary knowledge;

4) it does not engage in the production and supply of information systems and other information technologies used to provide certification services.

(3) The Cabinet of Ministers shall establish the procedure and timing for testing the safety of the information systems, hardware and procedures used to provide certification services.

Article 14

Insurance of the Civil Liability

(1) A reliable provider of certification services shall be required to insure the potential risk of loss associated with its activity.

(2) Insurance of the activity risk of a reliable provider of certification services shall cover claims that are likely to arise in relation to its activity.

(3) A reliable provider of certification services shall sign insurance agreement prior to accreditation and the insurance agreement shall be valid during the whole period of the provision of certification services.

(4) Where actions or inactions of a reliable provider of certification services incur loss, the insurance company shall cover the loss from the insurance indemnity of the reliable provider of certification services pursuant to the insurance agreement.

(5) The Cabinet of Ministers shall establish the procedure whereby the minimum insurance and the insurance indemnity are calculated.

Article 15

Protection of Natural Person Data

(1) A provider of certification services shall be entitled to get the data on natural persons either directly from the signatory or from the third person provided that the signatory has issued its consent to this effect.

(2) A provider of certification services shall be entitled to process the data on natural persons only with the purpose of issuing and maintaining a certificate.

(3) Without the consent of the signatory a provider of certification services shall not be entitled to process the data on natural persons for other purposes.

Chapter V

Qualified Certificate

Article 16

Information to be Included in a Qualified Certificate

(1) The following information shall be included in a qualified certificate:

    1) indication to the effect that it is a qualified certificate;

    2) name, registration number and domicile or name, last name and identity number of a reliable provider of certification services;

    3) name and last name or pseudonym, indicating it as such, of the signatory;

    4) identity number of the signatory;

    5) expiration date of the qualified certificate;

6)   order number granted to a certificate by a reliable provider of certification services;

7)   data of verifying an electronic signature that comply with the data of creating an electronic signature controlled by the signatory.

(2)   In addition to the information listed in Article 16(1) hereof, a qualified certificate may also include the following information:

1)   the scope of a qualified certificate or other restrictions on the activity of the certificate;

2)   any specific legal fact relating to the signatory (if considered necessary) depending on the purpose of the qualified certificate;

3)   any restrictions on the amount of deals for which the qualified certificate will be used;

4)   personal identification number of the signatory.

(3)   A qualified certificate shall bear a safe electronic signature of a reliable provider of certification services.

Article 17

Granting a Qualified Certificate

(1)   To receive a qualified certificate, the signatory shall submit an application in writing.

(2)   Prior to granting a qualified certificate, a reliable provider of certification services, in the presence of the signatory, shall verify the identity of the signatory with the identification document presented by the signatory.

(3)   On the basis of an application in writing submitted by the signatory, a reliable provider of certification services shall include in the qualified certificate the information on the authority granted to the signatory or any other significant information referred to in Article 16(2) hereof.

(4)   Upon a request in writing submitted by the signatory, a reliable provider of certification services shall be entitled to enter a pseudonym in the space for the signatory's name and last name, indicating this fact in the certificate.

(5)   A qualified certificate shall be issued to the signatory by a reliable provider of certification services.

(6)   Several qualified certificates may be issued to the signatory.

(7)   A reliable provider of certification services, retaining its liability pursuant to this Law, shall be entitled to sign an agreement with another person that will carry out the activities listed in Article 17(2), (3) and (4) hereof provided that the supervisory authority has issued a written consent to this effect.

Article 18

Canceling, Suspending and Renewing a Qualified Certificate

(1) To cancel a qualified certificate shall mean to recognize a certificate void. A cancelled qualified certificate may not be renewed.

(2) A reliable provider of certification services shall cancel without delay a qualified certificate in the following cases:

1) the signatory demands that the certificate be cancelled;

2) a reliable provider of certification services is officially notified of the signatory's death or other information included in the certificate is changed;

3) the signatory has submitted to the reliable provider of certification services false or misleading data to receive a qualified certificate;

4) the reliable provider of certification services executes a court decision to cancel a qualified certificate.

(3) To suspend a qualified certificate shall mean to recognize a certificate temporarily void. A suspended qualified certificate may be renewed.

(4) To renew a qualified certificate shall mean to recognize as valid a qualified certificate that has been suspended.

(5) A qualified certificate shall be suspended and renewed by a reliable provider of certification services that executes a court decision or a demand submitted by the signatory in writing.

(6) A qualified certificate shall not be cancelled and suspended or renewed as of a previous date (retrospectively).

(7) A safe electronic signature shall not be valid as of the cancellation or suspension of a qualified certificate.

(8) In case of the signatory's death, the safe electronic signature shall not be valid as of the date of the signatory's death.

(9) Where a reliable provider of certification services cancels, suspends or renews a qualified certificate without legal justification, as a result of malicious intent or negligence, the reliable provider of certification services shall cover the loss incurred to persons due to canceling, suspending or renewing a qualified certificate without justification.

Chapter VI

Supervision of Reliable Providers of Certification Services

Article 19

Supervisory Authority of Reliable Providers of Certification Services

(1) The Data State Inspectorate shall be the supervisory authority of reliable providers of certification services.

(2)   The supervisory authority shall monitor, on a regular basis, the compliance of the activity of providers of certification services with the requirements of this Law, other laws and regulations.

Article 20

Responsibilities of the Supervisory Authority

(1)   The supervisory authority shall be responsible for the following:

   1)   it shall accredit providers of certification services pursuant to the principle of voluntary accreditation;

   2)   it shall inspect that reliable providers of certification services comply with the regulations governing the provision of certification services;

   3)   it shall monitor that the safety of the information systems and procedures of reliable providers of certification services comply with the requirements set out in this Law, other laws and regulations and the description of the safety of the information systems, hardware and procedures used to provide certification services;

   4)   it shall monitor that registers of the data on qualified certificates issued, cancelled, suspended and renewed and of the data of verifying an electronic signature and time stamp register are continuously available on line;

   5)   it shall ensure that the register of reliable providers of certification services accredited in Latvia, that shall also include information on the providers of certification services of other countries whose qualified certificates are guaranteed by a reliable provider of certification services accredited in the Republic of Latvia are continuously freely available on line.

(2)   The supervisory authority shall maintain a register of reliable providers of certification services that is continuously freely available on line; the register shall make available the following information:

   1)   company name or name and last name of a reliable provider of certification services;

   2)   address, phone and e-mail address of a reliable provider of certification services;

   3)   regulations governing the provision of certification services;

   4)   description of the safety of the information systems, hardware and procedures used to provide certification services;

   5)   opinion of the safety test of the information systems, hardware and procedures used to provide certification services;

   6)   accreditation date;

   7)   information on warnings, reprimands or cancellation of accreditation.

(3)   Where the submitted documents and the provider of certification services comply with the requirements set out in this Law and other laws and regulations, the

supervisory authority shall grant an accreditation certificate to the provider of certification services within ten days of the receipt of documents referred to in Article 10 hereof and include the information listed in Article 20(2) hereof in the register of reliable providers of certification services.

(4)   Where the submitted documents or the provider of certification services fail to comply with the requirements set out in this Law and other laws and regulations, the supervisory authority shall issue a written refusal to accredit the provider within ten days of the receipt of documents referred to in Article 10 hereof.

Article 21

Supervisory Measures

(1)   The supervisory authority shall be entitled to give instructions to a reliable provider of certification services to prevent any failure to comply with this Law, other laws and regulations, regulations governing the provision of certification services as included in the register of reliable providers of certification services or the description of safety of the information systems, hardware and procedures used to provide certification services.

(2)   The supervisory authority shall establish the timing to ensure compliance with the abovementioned.

(3)   Where the provider fails to comply with the timing established by the supervisory authority, the supervisory authority shall issue a warning to the reliable provider of certification services that the accreditation granted to it may be cancelled.

(4)   Where the provider fails to comply with the instructions within ten days of the receipt of the warning from the supervisory authority, the accreditation granted to a reliable provider of certification services shall be cancelled without delay and information to this effect shall be included in the register of reliable providers of certification services.

(5)   Provisions set out in Article 22(2), (3), (4) and (5) hereof shall apply after the accreditation granted to a reliable provider of certification services has been cancelled.

(6)   An official of the supervisory authority shall present a service identity card when performing supervision. The official shall be entitled to the following:

   1)   access freely any uninhabited premises where the information systems and hardware of a reliable provider of certification services are located and test them or carry out other measures in the presence of the provider to establish the compliance of the certification services process with this Law, other laws and regulations, regulations governing the provision of certification services as included in the register of reliable providers of certification services and description of safety of the information systems, hardware and procedures used to provide certification services;

   2)   demand oral or written explanations from the representatives and employees of the reliable provider of certification services;

3) read documents and other information that relate to the provision of certification services;

4) demand that the information systems, hardware and procedures used to provide certification services be tested and establish an independent expertise to examine the verifiable issues.

(7) The supervisory authority shall be entitled to apply to the court and demand that the activity of a reliable provider of certification services be terminated where the respective reliable provider of certification services violates this Law, other laws or regulations.

(8) Decisions of the supervisory authority may be appealed to the court.

Article 22

Termination of the Activity of a Reliable Provider of Certification Services, Recognition of its Insolvency and Suspension of the Provision of Services

(1) A reliable provider of certification services shall without delay notify the supervisory authority and those signatories with which it has signed an agreement on the provision of certification services that its activities have been terminated, it has been recognized insolvent or the provision of certification services has been suspended.

(2) In cases referred to in Article 22(1) hereof a reliable provider of certification services shall ensure that the data, information, data bases, registers, other relevant information, information systems and certification services are preserved and transferred to another reliable provider of certification services upon mutual agreement.

(3) The supervisory authority shall be notified in writing and without delay of all transfers and timings.

(4) Where it is not possible to effect the transfer referred to in Article 22(2) hereof, the reliable provider of certification services shall transfer to the State Archives, under the supervision of the supervisory authority, the data, information, data bases, registers, other relevant information, information systems and certification services.

(5) After the receipt of information on the termination of the activity of a reliable provider of certification services, recognition of its insolvency or suspension of services, the signatory shall be entitled to transfer the data related to the received qualified certificate to another reliable provider of certification services it has chosen.

(6) The supervisory authority shall without delay cancel the accreditation granted to a reliable provider of certification services whose activity has been terminated, that has been recognized insolvent or whose services have been suspended and include information to this effect in the register of reliable providers of certification services.

Chapter VII

Responsibilities and Liability of a Reliable Provider of Certification Services and a Signatory

Article 23

Responsibilities of a Reliable Provider of Certification Services
A reliable provider of certification services shall have the following responsibilities:

1) it shall use safe information systems, hardware and procedures to provide certification services that guarantee an adequate safety of certification services;

2) it shall take the necessary measures to guarantee confidentiality of the data of creating a safe electronic signature, protection of the data of creating an electronic signature against illegal processing, protection of the qualified certificate against counterfeiting and ensuring that qualified certificates are available only upon the consent of signatories;

3) it shall ensure that the information systems, hardware and procedures used to provide certification services comply with this Law, other laws and regulations;

4) it shall ensure that the information that identifies the signatory is included in the qualified certificate only on the basis of an identification document presented in the presence of the signatory;

5) it shall ensure that a qualified certificate is granted after an agreement on the provision of certification services has been signed with the signatory;

6) before the agreement is signed, it shall inform in writing the signatory of the provisions and conditions relating to the application of the qualified certificate, including information on restrictions to use the qualified certificate, the procedures to deal with complaints and disputes and the civil liability of a reliable provider of certification services. Information may be mailed electronically provided that it bears a safe electronic signature of the reliable provider of certification services. The relevant parts of this information shall be made available to those persons, upon their request, that rely on the qualified certificate;

7) before the agreement is signed, it shall inform in writing the signatory on the regulation governing the provision of certification services and safety measures undertaken by the reliable provider of certification services to prevent illegal use of the issued qualified certificates;

8) after a qualified certificate is issued, it shall notify in writing the signatory of the conditions included in the certificate and restrictions to use the certificate;

9) it shall comply with this Law, other laws and regulations, regulations governing the provision of certification services as included in the register of reliable providers of certification services and the description of safety of the information systems and procedures used to provide certification services;

10) it shall notify the supervisory authority without delay of all conditions that prevent its compliance with this Law, other laws and regulations, regulations governing the provision of certification services as included in the register of

reliable providers of certification services and the description of safety of the information systems and procedures used to provide certification services;

11) it shall cancel without delay a qualified certificate in cases referred to in Article 18(2) hereof;

12) if the facts referred to in Article 18(2) 2) and 3) hereof cannot be supported without delay and doubt, it shall suspend the qualified certificate until the underlying truth is established;

13) it shall notify without delay the signatory, persons authorized by the signatory or heirs of a cancelled or suspended qualified certificate;

14) it shall maintain on line continuously, free of charge and freely available the complete registers of the data of verifying an electronic signature, and of the qualified certificates issued, cancelled, suspended and renewed and a complete time stamp register;

15) it shall record the complete procedures whereby qualified certificates are issued, cancelled, suspended or renewed and time stamp is used;

16) it shall store information that is related to the qualified certificates and time stamp for a definite period of time and in accordance with the procedure established in this Law, other laws and regulations;

17) it shall carry out, on a regular basis, safety tests of the information systems, hardware and procedures used to provide certification services and store test records. The test records shall contain all measures that are related with the issuing, canceling, suspending and renewing of a qualified certificate, measures that are related with the marking of an electronic document with a time stamp and all other changes affecting the data. Test records shall be stored permanently. Physical and logical protection as established in laws and regulations shall be ensures to test records;

18) it shall carry our measures to prevent possible counterfeiting of the qualified certificate and time stamp and to guarantee the confidentiality of the data of creating an electronic signature at the time the data are created;

19) it shall not store and copy the data of creating an electronic signature;

20) it shall ensure that the time stamp shows the precise time that is internationally coordinated;

21) it shall submit information pursuant to laws and regulations to the court, prosecutor's office and investigation institutions on the certificates that have been issued, cancelled, suspended and renewed and time stamp;

22) it shall ensure compliance with the Law on the protection of the data on natural persons and other laws and regulations that govern the security of information systems;

23) it shall submit the register of the cancelled and terminated certificates to the State Archives pursuant to the regulations issued by the Cabinet of Ministers that govern the procedure and timing for assessing, storing and transferring of electronic documents to the State Archives;

24) it shall insure its civil liability.

Article 24

Liability of a Reliable Provider of Certification Services

(1)   A reliable provider of certification services shall be responsible for loss incurred on a person that reasonably relies on a qualified certificate in relation to the following:

1)   compliance with this Law, other laws and regulations when issuing qualified certificates, compliance with the regulations governing the provision of certification services as included in the register of reliable providers of certification services and with the description of safety of the information systems, hardware and procedures used to provide certification services;

2)   information included in the qualified certificate;

3)   compliance of the data of creating an electronic signature with the data of verifying an electronic signature as included in the certificate at the time of issuing a qualified certificate;

4)   appropriate utilization of the data of creating an electronic signature and of the data of verifying an electronic signature.

(2)   A reliable provider of certification services shall be responsible for loss incurred on a person that reasonably relies on a qualified certificate as a result of a failure to register the cancellation or suspension of that certificate.

(3)   A reliable provider of certification services shall not be responsible for loss incurred on a person that reasonably relies on a qualified certificate as a result of utilization of such certificate without respecting the conditions or restrictions included in the certificate or exceeding the restricted amount of deals indicated in the certificate.

Article 25

Responsibilities and Liability of the Signatory

(1)   The signatory shall have the following responsibilities:

1)   it shall provide the reliable provider of certification services with truthful information;

2)   before the agreement on the provision of certification services is signed, it shall certify in writing that it has read the regulations governing the provision of certification services as included in the register of reliable providers of certification services, the description of safety of the information systems, hardware and procedures used to provide certification services, other safety measures undertaken by the reliable provider of certification services to prevent illegal application of the qualified certificate;

3)   after the receipt of a qualified certificate, it shall certify in writing that it has read the conditions and restrictions included in the qualified certificate;

4) it shall ensure that the data of creating an electronic signature shall not be used without the knowing of the signatory;

5) it shall demand without delay that the reliable provider of certification services cancel or suspend the qualified certificate where there is a motivated reason to consider that the data of creating an electronic signature have been used without the knowing of the signatory;

6) it shall demand without delay that the reliable provider of certification services cancel the issued qualified certificate if the information contained in it has changed.

(2) The signatory shall be responsible for loss incurred on a person that reasonably relies on a qualified certificate if:

1) the signatory has submitted false information to the reliable provider of certification services;

2) the signatory has been negligent to protect the data of creating an electronic signature against illegal utilization;

3) there is a motivated reason to consider that the data of creating an electronic signature have been used without the knowing of the signatory but the signatory has failed to demand that the reliable provider of certification services cancel or suspend the qualified certificate.

Chapter VIII

Recognition of a Certificate Issued Abroad

Article 26

Recognition of a Certificate Issued Abroad

A qualified certificate issued abroad shall enjoy the legal status and consequences as established in this Law provided that the legal status and the data of verifying the electronic signature the certificate bears can be verified in Latvia; moreover, the qualified certificate shall comply with at least one of the following conditions:

1) it complies with all requirements set out in this Law, other laws and regulations;

2) it has been issued by a provider of certification services accredited voluntarily by the supervisory authority;

3) it is guaranteed by a provider of certification services accredited voluntarily by the supervisory authority;

4) it is recognized in Latvia pursuant to international agreements;

5) it has been issued by a provider of certification services accredited in a EU Member State or is guaranteed by a provider of certification services accredited in a EU Member State.

Transitional provision

Governmental and municipal institutions shall have an obligation to accept electronic documents from natural and legal persons not later than January 1, 2004.

The Law takes effect on January 1, 2003.

The Law was adopted by the Saeima on October 31, 2002.

Luxembourg

ELECTRONIC COMMERCE

Mémorial A no. 96 of 8 September 2000

Law of 14 August 2000 relating to electronic commerce, modifying the Civil Code, the New Code of Civil Procedure, the Commercial Code, the Penal Code, and transposing Directive 1999/93 of 13 December 1999 relating to a Community framework for electronic signatures, Directive 2000/31/EC of 8 June 2000 relating to certain legal aspects of information society services, and certain provisions of Directive 97/7/EC of 20 May 1997 concerning distance selling of goods and services other than financial services

"Only French version binding"

Summary

ELECTRONIC COMMERCE

Law of 14 August 2000 relating to electronic commerce modifying the Civil Code, the New Code of Civil Procedure, the Commercial Code, the Penal Code and transposing Directive 1999/93 relating to a Community framework for electronic signatures, the Directive relating to certain legal aspects of information society services, and certain provisions of Directive 97/7/EC concerning distance selling of goods and services other than financial services

Law of 14 August 2000 relating to electronic commerce, modifying the Civil Code, the New Code of Civil Procedure, the Commercial Code, the Penal Code, and transposing Directive 1999/93 of 13 December 1999 relating to a Community framework for electronic signatures, Directive 2000/31/EC of 8 June 2000 relating to certain legal aspects of information society services, and certain provisions of Directive 97/7/EC of 20 May 1997 concerning distance selling of goods and services other than financial services

I, JEAN, by the grace of God, Grand Duke of Luxembourg, Duke of Nassau;

Having heard my Council of State;

With the assent of the Chamber of Deputies;

Having regard to the decision of the Chamber of Deputies of 12 July 2000 and that of the Council of State of 21 July 2000 that there is no need for a second vote;

Have ordered and order as follows:

SECTION I. GENERAL PROVISIONS

Art. 1. Definitions

Within the meaning of this law, the following term shall bear the following meaning:

"Information society services" shall mean any service provided, normally for a fee, via an electronic means at a distance and at the individual request of a recipient of the services.

For the purposes of this definition, the following terms shall bear the following meanings:

"distance" means a service provided without the simultaneous presence of both parties;

"by electronic means" means a service sent from the place of origin and received at a destination by means of electronic processing equipment (including digital compression) and data storage equipment, and which is entirely transmitted, routed and received by wires, by radio, by optical methods or by other electromagnetic methods;

"at the individual request of a recipient of the services" means a service provided by data transmission upon an individual request;

"service provider" means any natural or legal person providing an information society service;

"established service provider" means a service provider who effectively pursues an economic activity using a fixed installation for an indefinite period. The presence and use of the technical means and technologies required to provide a service do not, in themselves, constitute an establishment of the provider;

"recipient of the service" means any natural or legal person who, for professional ends or otherwise, uses an information society service, in particular for the purposes of seeking information or making the same accessible.

Art. 2. Scope of application

(1)   This law does not apply to:

-        the field of taxation, without prejudice to the provisions of article 16 of this law;

-        to agreements or practices governed by the legislation relating to cartels.

(2)   The provisions of this law do not apply to the representation of a client and the defence of his interests before the courts.

(3)   The provisions of this law apply without prejudice to the provisions relating to the protection of personal data.

(4)   The law of the place at which the information society service provider is established applies to service providers and to the services which they provide, without prejudice to the freedom of the parties to choose the law applicable to their contract.

(5)   Irrespective of the place at which the information society service provider is established, Luxembourg law applies to gambling activities which involve wagering a monetary stake in games of chance, including lotteries and transactions involving bets.

(6)   The National Accreditation and Monitoring Authority referred to in article 17 may restrict the free movement of an information society service originating in another Member State when the said service represents a real and serious risk affecting public policy (ordre public), public security, public health or consumer protection, while also complying with the requirements imposed by Community law in the exercise of this option.

Art. 3. The use of cryptography

Cryptography techniques may be used freely.

Art. 4. Access to the activity of service providers

Without prejudice to the provisions of the law of establishment, access to the activity of a service provider is not, in itself, subject to prior authorisation.

Art. 5. General obligation of providing information to recipients

(1)   The information society service provider shall render easily, directly and permanently accessible to the recipients of the service and the competent authorities, the following information:

   a)   its name;

   b)   the geographic address at which the service provider is established;

   c)   details which allow him to be contacted rapidly and communicated with in a direct and effective manner, including his electronic mail address;

   d)   where appropriate, his professional title and details of the professional body with which he is registered, his registration number on a trade register, his VAT number and the authorisation granted to him to exercise his activity, together with details of the authority granting such authorisation.

(2)   Where information society services refer to prices and conditions of sale or performance of a service, these are to be indicated clearly and unambiguously. It should also be stated whether taxes and additional expenses are included in the

price. These provisions apply without prejudice to consumer protection legislation.

SECTION II. CONCERNING PROOF AND ELECTRONIC SIGNATURE

Chapter 1. - Documentary evidence

Art. 6. Signature

After article 1322 of the Civil Code, an article 1322-1 has been added which states "The signature needed to complete a private deed identifies the person who has placed such signature demonstrates his compliance with the content of the deed.

It may be handwritten or electronic.

An electronic signature consists of a set of data, inseparably associated with the document, which guarantees the integrity thereof and satisfies the conditions stated in the first paragraph of this article."

Art. 7.

After article 1322 of the Civil Code, an article 1322-2 has been added which states: "An electronic private deed is valid as an original when there are reliable guarantees concerning the maintenance of its integrity from the time when it was created for the first time in its definitive form."

Art. 8.

Article 292 of the New Code of Civil Procedure is modified as follows: the words "signed and initialled" are replaced by "signed and, in the case of a handwritten signature, initialled."

Art. 9.

Article 1325 of the Civil Code is completed by the following paragraph: "This article does not apply to private deeds bearing an electronic signature."

Art. 10.

Article 1326 of the Civil Code is modified as follows: "The legal act by which one party undertakes to another to pay him a sum of money or to deliver to him fungible goods must be established in a deed containing the signature of the person making the undertaking together with a statement of the sum or the quantity in words. This statement shall be written in his hand or shall specifically bear an electronic signature; if it is also given in figures, where there is a difference, the private deed shall be valid for the sum written in words unless it can be proved which of the two is in error."

Art. 11.

In the first section of Chapter VI of the Civil Code, the heading of Paragraph III is replaced by the following heading: "Concerning copies of private deeds."

Art. 12.

Article 1333 of the Civil Code is reintroduced with the following text: "When the original deed or a document reproducing the original in accordance with article 1322-2 exists, copies only authenticate what is contained in the deed or document, sight of which may always be required."

Art. 13.

Article 1334 of the Civil Code is inserted in Paragraph III and is replaced by the following provision:

"When the original deed or a document reproducing the original in accordance with article 1322-2 no longer exists, copies made from it, under the auspices of the person who is responsible for safekeeping of the same, have the same probative value as the private documents of which they are presumed to be a faithful copy, unless there is proof to the contrary, when such copies have been produced in the context of a properlymonitored procedure for issue and when they satisfy the conditions determined by Grand-Ducal regulation."

Art. 14.

Article 1348 paragraph 2 of the Civil Code is deleted. The Grand-Ducal regulation of 22 December 1986, in implementation of article 1348 of the Civil Code, continues to apply on the basis of article 13 of this law.

Art. 15.

The first two paragraphs of article 11 of the Commercial Code are replaced by the following paragraph: "With the exception of the balance sheet and the profit and loss account, the documents or information referred to in articles 8 to 10 may be stored in the form of a copy. These copies have the same probative value as the originals of which they are presumed to be a faithful copy, unless there is proof to the contrary, when they have been produced in the context of a properly-monitored procedure for issue and when they satisfy the conditions determined by Grand-Ducal regulation."

Art. 16.

Any person who is obliged by law to deliver or communicate documents and data at the request of an agent of the tax administration must, when these documents and data only exist in electronic form, issue or communicate the same, at the request of an agent of the tax administration, in a legible and directly intelligible form, certified to be in accordance with the original, as hard copy or, by way of derogation, by means of any other technical procedure which the tax administration may determine.

Failure to comply with a request or instructions from the tax administration on the part of the person who is under a duty to issue or communicate such documents and data constitutes a failure in the duty of issue or communication.

Chapter 2.- Electronic signature and certification-service-providers

Section 1. Definitions and legal effect of electronic signature

Art. 17. Definitions

"Signatory" means any person who holds a signature-creation device and acts either on his own behalf or on behalf of the natural or legal person or entity he represents.

"Signature-creation device" means a device which meets the requirements defined in the Grand-Ducal regulation relating to the qualified certificate.

"Secure-signature-creation device" means a signature-creation device which meets the requirements laid down by Grand-Ducal regulation

"Signature-verification device" means a device which meets the requirements defined in the Grand-Ducal regulation relating to the certificate.

"Qualified certificate" means a certificate which meets the requirements determined on the basis of article 25 of this law.

"Certification-service-provider" means an entity or a legal or natural person who issues certificates or provides other services related to electronic signatures.

"Certificate holder" means an entity or a legal or natural person to whom a certification-service-provider has issued a certificate.

"Accreditation" means a procedure by which a body serving as an authority formally recognises that a body or an individual is competent to carry out specific tasks.

"Accreditation system" means a system having its own rules of procedure and management and competent to carry out accreditation.

"Voluntary accreditation" means any permission, setting out rights and obligations specific to the provision of certification services, to be granted upon request by the certification-service-provider concerned, by the National Accreditation and Monitoring Authority charged with the elaboration of, and supervision of compliance with, such rights and obligations, where the certification-service-provider is not entitled to exercise the rights stemming from the permission and until it has received the decision by the body.

"The National Accreditation and Monitoring Authority" is the Minister whose remit includes Economy:

- who, via his offices, organises and manages an accreditation system and who makes pronouncements on accreditation;

- who, via his offices organises and manages the supervision of electronic signature certification-serviceproviders, and more particularly of those who issue qualified certificates.

Art. 18. Legal effects of electronic signature

(1) Without prejudice to articles 1323 ff. of the Civil Code, an electronic signature created by a securesignature- creation device which the signatory is able to keep under his own exclusive control and which is based upon a qualified certificate, constitutes a signature within the meaning of article 1322-1 of the Civil Code.

(2) An electronic signature may not be rejected by a judge for the sole reason that it is presented in electronic form, that it is not based upon a qualified certificate issued by an accredited certification-service-provider, or that it was not created by a secure-signature-creation device.

(3) No person may be required to sign electronically.

Section 2. Certification-service-providers

SUB-SECTION1. COMMON MEASURES

Art. 19. Obligation of professional secrecy

(1) Directors, members of executive and supervisory bodies, managers, employees and other persons in the service of a certification-service-provider, together with all those who themselves exercise the functions of certification-service-provider, are obliged to keep strictly secret all information entrusted to them in the context of their professional activity, with the exception of information which the holder of the certificate has agreed may be published or communicated. Disclosure of such information shall be punished by the sanctions specified in article 458 of the Penal Code.

(2) The obligation of secrecy ceases when the disclosure of information is authorised or imposed by or on the basis of a legislative measure, even prior to this law.

(3) No obligation of secrecy exists with regard to the National Accreditation and Monitoring Authority acting within the framework of its legal powers.

(4) Any person exercising or having exercised an activity for the National Accreditation and Monitoring Authority, together with auditors appointed by the National Accreditation and Monitoring Authority, have an obligation of professional secrecy and are liable to the sanctions specified in article 458 of the Penal Code in the event of violation of secrecy.

(5) Subject to the rules applicable in penal matters, the information referred to in section 1, once disclosed, cannot be used except for the purposes for which the law has permitted it to be disclosed.

(6)   Any person bound by the obligation of secrecy referred to in section 1 and who has legally disclosed information covered by this obligation, cannot incur any penal or civil liability from this fact alone.

Art. 20. Protection of personal data

(1)   The National Accreditation and Monitoring Authority and certification-service-providers are obliged to comply with the legislative measures governing the processing of personal data.

(2)   A certification-service-provider who issues certificates to the public may collect personal data only directly from the person requesting a certificate or, further to the explicit consent of the person requesting a certificate, from a third party. The service provider shall only collect data in so far as it is necessary for the purposes of issuing and maintaining the certificate. Data may not be collected or processed for any other purposes without the explicit consent of the data subject.

(3)   When a pseudonym is used, the true identity of the holder may only be revealed by the certificationservice- provider further to the consent of the holder or in the cases specified in article 19 section 2.

Art. 21. Obligations of the certificate holder

(1)   From the time the signature-creation data is created, the holder of the certificate is solely responsible for the confidentiality and integrity of the data related to creation of the signature he uses. Unless proved otherwise, any use of such data is deemed to have been made by him.

(2)   The certificate holder is required to notify the certification-service-provider as soon as possible of any changes made to the information contained in the certificate.

(3)   If there is any doubt as to maintenance of the confidentiality of signature-creation data, or doubt that information contained in the certificate is still accurate, the holder is required to have the certificate revoked immediately in compliance with article 26 of this law.

(4)   When a certificate has reached its expiry date or has been revoked, its holder can no longer use the corresponding signature-creation data to sign nor cause such data to be certified by another certificationservice- provider.

SUB-SECTION 2. CERTIFICATION-SERVICE-PROVIDERS ISSUING QUALIFIED CERTIFICATES

Art. 22. Obligation of information

(1)   Prior to any contractual relationship with a person applying for a qualified certificate or at the request of a third party who relies on such a certificate, the certification-service-provider shall procure the information needed for the proper

and secure use of his services on a durable medium and in a readily comprehensible language.

The minimum information required is as follows:

a) the procedure to be followed to create and verify an electronic signature;

b) the specific modalities and conditions of use of certificates, including limits imposed on their use, provided that these limits may be discerned by third parties;

c) the obligations which, by virtue of this law, are incumbent upon the certificate-holder and the certificationservice- provider;

d) the existence of a voluntary accreditation system;

e) the contractual conditions for issuing a certificate, including any limitation on the liability of the certification-service-provider;

f) the procedures by which complaints may be made and disputes settled.

(2) The certification-service-provider shall provide one copy of the certificate to the candidate holder.
Once the certificate has been accepted by the candidate holder, the certification-service-provider shall record the certificate in the electronic directory referred to in the Grand-Ducal regulation, provided that the certificateholder has given their consent to such recording.

Art. 23. Obligation of verification

(1) Prior to the issue of a certificate, the service provider shall verify the complementary nature of the signature-creation and signature-verification data.

(2) When a qualified certificate is issued to a corporate entity, the certification-service-provider shall verify beforehand the identity and the authority to represent the natural person applying to him.

Art. 24. Acceptance of certificates

(1) The content and publication of a certificate is subject to the consent of its holder.

(2) The certification-service-provider shall keep an electronic directory which shall include the certificates he issues and their expiry date. As soon as the certificate has been accepted by the candidate holder, the certification-service-provider shall record the certificate in the electronic directory referred to in the Grand-Ducal regulation, provided that the certificate holder has given their consent to such recording.

Art. 25. Issue and content of qualified certificates

(1)   In order to be able to issue qualified certificates, certification-service-providers must have adequate financial resources and material, technical and human resources to guarantee the security, reliability and durability of the certification services offered. These requirements may be specified by means of a Grand-Ducal regulation.

(2)   All qualified certificates shall contain such information as is ordered by Grand-Ducal regulation.

(3)   At the request of the holder, the certificate may contain other information, not certified by the certificationservice- provider, specifying that such information has not been verified by the certification-service-provider.

(4)   A qualified certificate may be issued both by an accredited certification-service-provider or by a nonaccredited certification-service-provider provided the latter meets the conditions required by the law and by the regulations of the Grand Duke enacted by way of implementation.

Art. 26. Revocation of certificates

(1)   The certification-service-provider shall immediately revoke the qualified certificate at the request of the holder, after his identify has been verified.

(2)   The certification-service-provider shall also immediately revoke a certificate when:

a)   after suspension, a more thorough examination shows that the certificate was based on incorrect or falsified information, that the information contained in the certificate is no longer accurate, or that the confidentiality of the signature-creation data has been violated or that the certificate has been used fraudulently;

b)   when the certification-service-provider has been informed of the death of the natural person or the dissolution of the corporate entity holding the certificate.

(3)   The certification-service-provider shall inform the holder that the certificate has been revoked as soon as possible, and give the reasons for his decision.

He shall advise the holder of expiry of the certificate at least one month in advance.

(4)   The revocation of a qualified certificate is final.

(5)   Immediately after a decision to revoke a certificate, the certification-service-provider shall enter a record of the revocation of the certificate in the electronic directory referred to in article 23.

The revocation shall become demurrable in relation to third parties as soon as it has been recorded in the electronic directory.

Art. 27. Liability of qualified certificate service providers

(1) Unless he can prove that he has not been negligent, a certification-service-provider who issues a qualified certificate to the public or who guarantees such a certificate to the public is liable for damage caused to any person who reasonably relies on:

- the accuracy at the time of issuance of the information contained in the qualified certificate;

- an assurance that at the time of issuance of the certificate, the signatory identified in the qualified certificate held the signature-creation data corresponding to the signature-verification data given or identified in the certificate;

- the assurance that the signature-creation device and the signature-verification device can be used in a complementary manner, where the certification-service-provider generates them both.

(2) Unless he can prove that he has not acted negligently, a certification-service-provider who has issued a qualified certificate to the public or who guarantees publicly such a certificate is liable for damage caused to any person who reasonably relies on the certificate for failure to register revocation of the certificate.

(3) The certification-service-provider shall not be liable for damage resulting from the improper use of a qualified certificate exceeding the limits set for its use or the limit value of transactions for which the certificate may be used, in so far as these limits are recorded in the certificate and are recognisable to third parties.

(4) The measures referred to in paragraphs 1 to 3 are without prejudice to the modified law of 25 August 1983 relating to consumer protection legislation.

Art. 28. Recognition of certificates by third countries

Certificates issued as qualified certificates by a certification-service-provider established in a third country within the European Union are legally equivalent in Luxembourg to those issued by a certification-serviceprovider established in Luxembourg:

a) if the certification-service-provider fulfils the requirements laid down in this law and has been accredited under a voluntary accreditation scheme established by a Member State of the European Union; or

b) if a certification-service-provider established in a Member State of the European Union guarantees such certificates; or

c) if the certificate or the certification-service-provider is recognised under a bilateral agreement between Luxembourg and third countries or under a multilateral agreement between the European Union and third countries or international organisations.

Art. 29. Supervision

(1) The National Accreditation and Monitoring Authority shall ensure that service-providers issuing qualified certificates comply with the requirements contained in articles 19 to 27 of this law and in the regulations of the Grand Duke implementing the same.

(2) All service providers issuing qualified certificates are required to notify the National Authority that his activities comply with the requirements of this law and the regulations enacted in execution hereof.

(3) The National Authority shall keep a register of notifications, which will be published at the end of each calendar year in the *Mémorial, Recueil administratif et économique*, without prejudice to the option of the National Authority to publish striking-off from the register at any time, either in the *Mémorial*, or in one or more foreign or national newspapers, if such publicity is required in the public interest.

(4) The National Authority may, either ex officio or at the request of any interested party, verify or arrange for verification that the activities of a certification-service-provider comply with the provisions of this law or the regulations enacted in execution hereof.

The Authority may make use of registered external auditors for such verification. A Grand-Ducal regulation shall determine the procedure for approval, such approval to be issued by the Minister whose remit includes Economy. The subject of such approval may be persons holding an adequate professional qualification and who have knowledge and specialist experience in the domain of electronic-signature technology, and who can offer guarantees of professional repute and independence in relation to the certification-service-providers whose activities they are called on to verify.

(5) In carrying out their mission of verification, once their credentials have been verified, the agents of the National Authority and registered external auditors shall be entitled to access to any establishment and to have any information and documents which they feel to be useful or necessary in accomplishing their mission communicated to them.

Any refusal by a certification-service-provider to co-operate actively shall be punished by a fine of between 10,001 and 800,000 francs. In such a case, the Authority may also strike service-providers off the notification register.

(6) If, upon a report by its agents or the appointed external auditor, the National Authority becomes aware that the activities of the certification-service-provider do not comply with the provisions of this law or the regulations adopted in execution hereof, it shall invite the service provider to comply with the said provisions within a time which it shall determine. If the service provider has not complied at the end of this period, the National Authority will remove the service provider from the notification register.

(7) If a serious violation by a certification-service-provider of the provisions of this law or the regulations adopted in execution hereof is determined, the National Authority may appropriately notify the same to, in particular, the administrative authorities competent in matters of the right of establishment. Reports produced

for the attention of the National Authority may be sent to these authorities, provided that the certificationservice- provider has been made aware of them in the context of its links with the National Authority.

Art. 30. Accreditation

(1)   Certification-service-providers are free to apply for accreditation or not.

(2)   Accreditation covers the issue of certificates relating to identity; it may include the professional or any other durable attribute of the certificate holder, together with any other information which can be certified.

(3)   The certification-service-provider may apply for accreditation for one or more of these elements and for one or more categories of holder.

Art. 31. Conditions for obtaining accreditation

(1)   The conditions for obtaining and keeping accreditation are determined by a Grand-Ducal regulation.

(2)   A Grand-Ducal regulation shall lay down:

   a)   the procedure for the issue, extension, suspension and withdrawal of accreditation;

   b)   the costs of examining and monitoring dossiers;

   c)   time-frames for examination of applications;

   d)   amounts and modalities in respect of financial guarantees;

   e)   the conditions intended to ensure interoperability of certification systems and the interconnection of certificate registers;

   f)   the rules relating to the information which the certification-service-provider must retain concerning its services and the certificates it has issued;

   g)   the guarantees of independence which certification-service-providers must offer to users of the service;

   h)   the period for which data must be kept.

(3)   Further conditions may be determined by Grand-Ducal regulation before a certification-service-provider may issue certificates to persons who wish to use an electronic signature in their exchanges with the public authorities.

(4)   A decision to suspend or withdraw accreditation may be brought before the Administrative Court within one month, failing which the matter shall be statute-barred. The Court shall rule on the merits of the case.

Art. 32. Cessation and transfer of activities

(1) An accredited certification-service-provider shall inform the National Accreditation and Monitoring Authority within a reasonable time of its intention to cease its activities or, if appropriate, of its inability to continue its activities. It shall ensure that these activities are continued by another accredited certificationservice- provider, under the conditions described in section 2 of this article, or, failing this, it shall take the measures required in section 3 of this article.

(2) An accredited certification-service-provider may transfer all or part of its activities to another service
provider. Certificates shall be transferred under the following conditions:

    a)   the certification-service-provider shall notify all holders of a certificate still in force at least one month before the planned transfer of the fact that it intends to transfer the certificates to another certification-serviceprovider;

    b)   the certification-service-provider shall specify the identity of the certification-service-provider to whom it is planned to transfer these certificates;

    c)   the certification-service-provider shall inform all certificate holders of their right to refuse the planned transfer, together with the times within which and modalities by which they may refuse it. If the certificate holder does not expressly accept the transfer within the time allowed, the certificate is revoked.

(3) All accredited certification-service-providers who cease their activities without the same being taken up by another accredited certification-service-provider shall revoke certificates one month after they have notified the holders and shall take the measures required to ensure that data is preserved in accordance with article 25.

(4) The death, incapacity, bankruptcy, voluntary winding-up or liquidation, or any other involuntary reason for cessation of activities, shall be deemed cessation of activity within the meaning of this law.

Art. 33. Control

(1) When the National Accreditation Authority becomes aware that an accredited certification-serviceprovider is not complying with the specifications of this law and with the regulations, it shall determine a time by which the situation must be regularised and, if necessary, shall suspend the accreditation.

(2) If, after the time limit has expired, the accredited certification-service-provider has not regularised his situation, the authority will withdraw his accreditation.

(3) The certification-service-provider shall be under a duty to immediately record the withdrawal of accreditation in his electronic directory and inform certificate holders thereof without delay.

SUB-SECTION 4. ELECTRONIC RECORDED DELIVERY

Art. 34.

A message signed electronically on the basis of a qualified certificate for which the time, date, despatch and, if necessary, receipt are certified by the service provider in accordance with the conditions determined by Grand-Ducal regulation, shall constitute recorded delivery.

SECTION III. SANCTIONS

Art. 35.

Article 196 of the Penal Code is modified as follows: "Imprisonment of between five and ten years shall be the penalty imposed upon other persons who have committed forgery of authentic and public texts, and all persons who commit forgery of commercial, banking or private documents, including electronic private deeds,

Either by false signatures,

Or by counterfeiting or alteration of text or of signatures,

Or by fabrication of agreements, provisions, obligations or discharges, or by the insertion thereof after the event in the documents in question,

Or by the addition or alteration of clauses, declarations or facts which it was the object of such deeds to receive and record."

Art. 36.

Article 197 of the Penal Code is modified as follows: "In all the cases expressed in this section, a person who has made use of a forgery shall be punished as if he were the author of the forgery."

Art. 37.

Article 487 of the Penal Code is modified as follows: "The following are classified as false keys: all picklocks, master keys, copied keys, counterfeit keys or altered keys, including electronic keys;

Keys which have not been designated by the owner, tenant, landlord or lodger, to the locks, padlocks or closures of any kind for which the offender has employed them;

Keys which have been lost, mislaid or removed, including electronic keys, which have been used to commit theft.

However, the use of false keys shall only constitute an aggravating circumstance if such use occurred in order to open objects, the accessing of which would result in a heavier sentence."

Art. 38.

Article 488 of the Penal Code is modified as follows: "Whoever shall have fraudulently counterfeited or altered keys, including electronic keys, shall be sentenced to imprisonment of between three months and two years and to a fine of between 10,001 francs and 80,000 francs."

Art. 39.

Article 498 of the Penal Code is modified as follows: "A person who has deceived a buyer shall be punished by imprisonment of between one month and one year and by a fine of between 20,000 francs and 400,000 francs, or by one of these sanctions only, where deception relates to the following:

The identity of the goods sold, by fraudulently delivering an item other than the specified item which was the subject of the transaction;

The nature or origin of the item sold, by selling or delivering an item similar in appearance to the one which the buyer bought or believed he had bought.

The preceding provisions apply to movables, including intangible assets and real property."

Art. 40.

Article 505 of the Penal Code is modified as follows: "Whoever shall have handled, in whole or in part, objects or intangible assets removed, misappropriated or obtained by means of a crime or misdemeanour shall be punished by imprisonment of between fifteen days and five years and by a fine of between 10,001 francs and 200,000 francs.

Their sentence may also include loss of civil rights, in accordance with article 24.

The fact of having knowingly benefited from the result of a crime or a misdemeanour also constitutes handling."

Art. 41.

Article 509-1 of the Penal Code is modified as follows: "Whoever shall fraudulently have accessed or kept wholly or in part a system for the processing or automatic transmission of data, shall be punished by imprisonment of between two months and two years and by a fine of between 20,000 francs and 1,000,000 francs or by one of these two sanctions.

When data contained in the system shall have been deleted or modified as a result, the period of imprisonment shall be from four months to two years and a fine from 50,000 francs to 1,000,000 francs."

Art. 42.

Article 509-2 of the Penal Code is modified as follows: "Whoever shall, intentionally and in disregard of the rights of others, interfered with or disturbed the operation of a system for the processing or automatic transmission of data, shall be punished by imprisonment of between three months and three years and by a fine of between 50,000 francs and 500,000 francs or by one of these two sanctions."

Art. 43.

Article 509-3 of the Penal Code is modified as follows: "Whoever shall, intentionally and with disregard of the rights of others, directly or indirectly, have introduced data into a processing or automatic data transmission system or have deleted or modified the data it contains or the method of processing or transmission, shall be punished by imprisonment of between three months and three years and by a fine of between 50,000 francs and 500,000 francs or by one of these two sanctions."

Art. 44.

Article 509-4 of the Penal Code is repealed.

Art. 45.

Article 509-5 of the Penal Code is repealed.

SECTION IV. CONCERNING COMMERCIAL COMMUNICATIONS

Art. 46. Definition

"Commercial communication" means any form of communication designed to promote, directly or indirectly, the goods, services or image of a company, organisation or person pursuing a commercial, industrial or craft activity or profession.

The following do not in themselves constitute commercial communications:

- information allowing direct access to the activity of the company, organisation or person, in particular a domain name or an electronic-mail address;

- communications relating to the goods, services or image of the company, organisation or person compiled in an independent manner, particularly when this is without financial consideration.

Art. 47. Transparency requirements

A commercial communication shall comply with the following conditions:

a)   a commercial communication shall be clearly identifiable as such;

b)   the natural or legal person on whose behalf the commercial communication is made shall be clearly identifiable;

c)   promotional competitions or games shall be clearly identifiable as such and their conditions of participation shall be easily accessible and be presented clearly and unambiguously.

Art. 48. Unsolicited commercial communications

(1)   An unsolicited commercial communication sent by electronic mail shall be identifiable clearly and unambiguously as such as soon as it is received by the recipient.

(2)   Commercial communications may only be sent by electronic mail by an information society service provider to a recipient if there is no clear opposition to this by the recipient.

(3)   Service-providers who send unsolicited commercial communications by electronic mail shall regularly consult the "opt out" registers established by Grand-Ducal regulation in which natural persons not wishing to receive such communications can register themselves, and comply with the wishes of these persons. Natural persons may enter their names on one or more opt out registers without cost to themselves.

Any service provider who has not complied with the wishes of persons entered on one or more opt out registers shall be punished by a fine of between 10,001 and 200,000 francs.

SECTION V. CONCERNING CONTRACTS CONCLUDED BY ELECTRONIC MEANS

Chapter 1. - Common measures

Art. 49. Definitions

"Durable medium" means any instrument which allows the consumer to store information addressed personally to him in a manner allowing him to refer easily to it in the future over a period of time which is appropriate for the intended purposes of the information and which allows identical reproduction of the information stored.

"Financial service" means any service provided by a credit establishment, another financial sector professional or an insurance and reinsurance company.

Art. 50. Scope of application

(1)   This section applies to contracts concluded by electronic means between professionals, and between professionals and consumers, with the exception of the following contracts:

-     contracts that create or transfer rights in real estate, except for rental rights;

- contracts requiring by law the involvement of courts, public authorities or professions exercising public authority;

- contracts of suretyship and guarantees furnished by persons acting for ends outside their trade, business or profession;

- contracts governed by family law or by the law of succession.

(2) The provisions of articles 53 to 59 apply only between professionals and consumers.

Art. 51. General technical information to be provided

(1) Without prejudice to the general obligation of information of article 5 of this law and, unless the parties are professionals and have agreed otherwise, the procedures for conclusion of a contract by electronic means shall be transmitted by the service provider clearly and unambiguously and prior to the conclusion of contract. The information to be provided should in particular include:

a) the different technical steps to follow to conclude the contract;

b) whether or not the concluded contract will be filed by the service provider and whether it will be accessible;

c) the technical means for identifying and correcting input errors prior to conclusion of the contract;

d) the languages offered for conclusion of the contract.

(2) The contractual clauses and general terms and conditions must be provided to the recipient in such manner as allows him to store and reproduce the same.

(3) Paragraphs 1 and 2 of this article shall not apply to contracts between persons not acting for purposes within the framework of their trade, business or profession concluded exclusively by exchange of electronic mail or by equivalent individual communications.

Art. 52. Time when the contract is concluded

(1) Except where otherwise agreed by parties who are professionals, in cases where a recipient of the service has been asked to give their consent by using technological means in order to accept the offer of the service provider, the contract is concluded when the recipient of the service has received from the service provider, by electronic means, an acknowledgement of receipt of the acceptance from the recipient of the service.

a) the acknowledgement of receipt of acceptance is deemed to be received when the recipient of the service is able to access it;

b) the service provider must send the acknowledgement of receipt of acceptance immediately.

(2)   The provisions of the first paragraph of this article only apply to contracts between persons not acting for the purposes of their trade, business or profession concluded exclusively by exchange of electronic messages or by equivalent individual communications.

Chapter 2.- Contracts concluded with consumers

Art. 53. Prior information to be given to the consumer

(1)   Without prejudice to the general obligation of information of article 5 of this law and the obligations of information which are specific to financial services, the service provider is obliged to provide the consumer, within sufficient time before conclusion of the contract, the following information in a clear and comprehensible manner:

-    details of the certification-service-provider, who may or may not be accredited, from whom the service provider has obtained a certificate;

-    the main characteristics of the product or service offered;

-    the currency in which bills will be made out;

-    the period for which the offer and price remain valid;

-    payment terms and methods, the consequences of poor performance or non-performance of undertakings by the service provider;

-    if appropriate, the conditions of credit proposed;

-    whether or not there is a right of withdrawal;

-    how sums which may have been paid by the consumer will be reimbursed in the event of his withdrawal;

-    the cost of using an information society service when this is calculated on a basis other than the basic tariff;

-    conditions of existing commercial guarantees and after-sales service;

-    the lack of confirmation of information, if appropriate;

-    for contracts concerning long-term or periodic supply of a product or service, the minimum duration of contract.

(2)   This information must be provided by any method appropriate for the information society service used, and accessible at all stages of the transaction.

When he is able to do so, the service provider must put in place an information society service allowing the consumer to conduct a dialogue directly with him.

(3)   For products and services which are not subject to a right of withdrawal in accordance with article 55 section 4, the following further information should be provided to the consumer:

-    details of the operating system or equipment required to use in an effective manner the product or service ordered;

-     the approximate time and cost of any downloading of a product or service, and any procedures and conditions relating to the licence contract.

Art. 54. Confirmation and recording of information

(1)   The consumer must receive, at the latest at the time of delivery of the product or of the performance of the service provided, on a durable medium available to him and to which he has access, confirmation of the information mentioned in article 53 and, where appropriate, conditions for exercising the right of withdrawal.

(2)   Section 1 does not apply to services for which the performance itself takes place by means of an information society service, if these services are provided on a single occasion and are billed by the service provider.

(3)   The service provider must allow the consumer to obtain on a durable medium, as soon as possible after conclusion of the contract, the content of the transaction, specifying in particular the date and time of conclusion of the contract.

Art. 55. Consumer's right of withdrawal

(1)   For any contract concluded by electronic means, the consumer shall have a period of seven days in which to withdraw, without penalty and without giving any reason.

However, if the consumer has not received the confirmation laid down in article 54, the period of withdrawal is three months.

The period of withdrawal shall be increased to 30 days for contracts relating to insurance policies except for policies laid down in section 4 g) of this article, and to pension operations.

These periods shall run:

-     in the case of services, from the day of conclusion of the contract;

-     in the case of goods, from the day of receipt of the goods.

(2)   If this confirmation is received during the three-month period laid down in section 1, the period of seven days shall recommence, to run from the day of receipt of the information by the consumer.

(3)   The consumer shall exercise his right of withdrawal on any durable medium.

In addition, the consumer must be reimbursed within 30 days in respect of any sums which he may have paid.

(4)   Unless agreed otherwise, the consumer may not exercise the right of withdrawal provided for in section 1 in respect of the following contracts:

a)   for the provision of services if performance has begun, with the consumer's agreement, before the end of the seven-day withdrawal period referred to in section 1;

b)   for the supply of goods made to the consumer's specifications or clearly personalised or which, by their nature, cannot be returned or are likely to deteriorate or expire rapidly;

c)   for the supply of audio or video recordings or computer software which were unsealed or downloaded by the consumer;

d)   for the supply of newspapers, periodicals and magazines;

e)   for gaming and lottery services;

f)   for financial services, the price of which depends on financial market fluctuations outside the control of the service provider, which may take place during the withdrawal period, such as services relating to:

-   foreign exchange operations;

-   money market instruments;

-   transferable securities and other tradable securities;

-   UCITS and other collective investment systems;

-   futures contracts and options;

-   interest-rate guarantee contracts (FRA)

-   swaps on interest rates, currencies or exchange contracts on flows related to equities or equity indices (equity swaps);

-   options on the purchase or sale of any instrument included in this list, including futures contracts and options;

g)   insurance policies lasting for less than one month.

(5)   If the price of the service is fully or partly covered by credit granted to the consumer by the service provider or by a third party, on the basis of an agreement concluded between the third party and the service provider, the credit agreement shall be cancelled, without penalty, if the consumer exercises his right of withdrawal.

Art. 56. Payment for a financial service provided before withdrawal

(1)   When the consumer exercises his right of withdrawal in accordance with article 55, he may only be held liable for payment of that part of the price proportional to the financial service actually provided by the service provider.

(2)   The service provider may not ask the consumer for payment on the basis of section 1 if he has not fulfilled his obligation of information as laid down in article 53, nor if he has begun to execute the contract before the end of the withdrawal period without the consumer having expressly given his consent to such execution.

(3)   As soon as possible, and at the latest within 30 days, the service provider shall return to the consumer all sums that he has received from the latter in accordance with the contract concluded, except the sum to be paid under section 1 of this

article. This period runs from the day when the service provider has received notification of withdrawal by the consumer.

(4)   The consumer shall return to the service provider any sum or property which he has received from the service provider, as soon as possible and at the latest within 30 days. This period runs from the date of despatch of notification of withdrawal by the consumer.

Art. 57. Unsolicited supplies

(1)   Without prejudice to the rules applying in the matter of renewal of contracts by tacit agreement, the supply of an unsolicited product or service to the consumer is prohibited when it is accompanied by a request for payment.

(2)   The consumer is not bound by any undertaking relating to supplies of goods or services which he has not expressly requested, the absence of a response not constituting consent.

Art. 58. Responsibility for proof

Proof of the existence of prior information, confirmation of information, compliance with deadlines and the consent of the consumer is the responsibility of the service-provider. Any clause to the contrary is regarded as improper within the meaning of article 1 of the modified law of 25 August 1983 relating to the legal protection of the consumer.

Art. 59. Exemptions

Articles 53, 54 and 55 do not apply to the following:

- contracts for the supply of foodstuffs, beverages or other household goods for everyday use supplied to the consumer's domicile, residence or place of work;

- contracts for the supply of services of accommodation, transport, catering or leisure, when the service provider undertakes, at the time the contract is concluded, to supply the services on a specific date or for a specified period.

SECTION VI. LIABILITY OF INTERMEDIATE SERVICE PROVIDERS

Art. 60. Mere conduit

(1)   An information society service provider who transmits over a communication network information provided by the recipient of the service or who provides access to a communication network shall not be liable for the information transmitted, on condition that the provider:

a)   does not initiate the transmission;

b)   does not select the receiver of the transmission; and

c)   does not select or modify the information contained in the transmission.

(2)   The acts of transmission and provision of access referred to in paragraph 1 include the automatic, immediate and transient storage of the information transmitted in so far as this takes place for the sole purpose of carrying out the transmission over the communication network, and provided that the information is not stored for any period longer than is reasonably necessary for the transmission.

Art. 61. Caching

A service provider who provides an information society service that consists of the transmission in a communication network of information provided by a recipient of the service shall not be liable for the automatic, intermediate and temporary storage of that information, performed for the sole purpose of making more efficient the information's onward transmission to other recipients of the service on demand, on condition that:

a)   he does not modify the information;

b)   he complies with conditions on access to the information;

c)   he complies with rules regarding the updating of the information, specified in a manner widely recognised and used by industry;

d)   he does not interfere with the lawful use of technology, widely recognised and used by industry, to obtain data on the use of the information; and

e)   he acts expeditiously to remove the information which he has stored or to disable access to the same as soon as he actually gains knowledge of the fact that the information has been removed from its initial source on the network, or of the fact that access to the information has been disabled, or of the fact that a court or an administrative authority has ordered removal of the information or prohibited access thereto.

Art. 62. Hosting

(1)   Without prejudice to the provisions of article 63 section 2, a service provider who provides an information society service that consists of the storage of information provided by the recipient of the service, shall not be liable for the information stored at the request of a recipient of the service, on condition that:

a)   the service provider does not have actual knowledge that the activity or information is illegal and, as regards claims for damages, that he is not aware of facts or circumstances from which the illegal activity or information is apparent; or

b)   the service provider, upon obtaining such knowledge or awareness, acts expeditiously to remove or to disable access to the information.

(2)   Paragraph 1 shall not apply when a recipient of the service is acting under the authority or the control of the service provider.

Art. 63. Obligation to monitor

(1) When providing the services covered by articles 60 to 62, service providers do not have a general obligation to monitor the information which they transmit or store, nor a general obligation to seek facts or circumstances indicating illegal activity.

(2) When providing the services covered by article 62, service providers do however have a specific obligation to monitor in order to detect possible infractions of articles 383, paragraph 2 and 457-1 of the Penal Code.

(3) Paragraphs 1 and 2 of this article are without prejudice to any activity of monitoring, targeted or temporary, requested by the judicial authorities of Luxembourg when this is necessary to protect the security, defence, public security and for the prevention, investigation, detection and prosecution of criminal offences.

SECTION VII. ELECTRONIC PAYMENTS

Art. 64. Definitions

For the application of this section :

(1) "electronic payment instrument" means any system making it possible to effect the following operations by wholly or partially electronic means:

  a) transfers of money;

  b) withdrawals and deposits of cash;

  c) remote access to an account;

  d) the loading and unloading of a reloadable electronic payment instrument.

(2) "reloadable electronic payment instrument" means any electronic payment instrument on which value units are stored electronically.

Art. 65. Scope of application

(1) The provisions of this law do not apply:

  a) to electronic transfers of money made by cheque and to the guaranteeing of transfers of money made by cheque;

  b) to electronic transfers of money made by means of reloadable instruments without direct access to an account for loading and unloading, and which can only be used for a single seller of products or services.

Art. 66. Proof of payments made

The issuer must keep an internal record of operations performed by means of an electronic payment instrument for a period of three years from performing the operations.

Art. 67. Responsibility for proof

In the event of a dispute concerning an operation performed by means of an electronic payment instrument, the issuer must provide proof that the operation was correctly recorded and accounted for, and has not been affected by a technical incident or other failure.

Art. 68. Risks related to the use of an electronic payment instrument

(1)   The holder of an electronic payment instrument has an obligation to notify the issuer – or the body designated by him – as soon as he becomes aware of any loss or theft of this instrument or of ways in which it is possible to use it fraudulently, as well as any loss or theft of a reloadable electronic payment instrument.

The issuer of an electronic payment instrument must make available to the holder appropriate means by which to make this notification and to provide proof that he has done so.

(2)   Unless he has been found guilty of fraud or gross negligence, the holder of an electronic payment instrument covered by article 64 section 1 a), b) and c):

-     shall assume until the notification laid down in the previous paragraph the consequences related to the loss, theft or fraudulent use by a third party, up to a sum determined by Grand-Ducal regulation. This sum may not exceed 150 Euro.

By way of derogation from paragraph 1 of section 2 of this article, the issuer is not liable for loss of value stored on a reloadable electronic payment instrument, when this is a consequence of the use of such instrument by an unauthorised third party, even after the notification laid down in this article.

-     is discharged from any liability for the use of an electronic payment instrument as covered by article 64 section 1a), b) and c) after notification.

(3)   In any event, the use of an electronic payment instrument without physical presentation of the same or electronic identification does not entail the liability of the holder.

Art. 69. Irrevocability of payment instructions

The holder may not revoke an instruction that he has given by means of an electronic payment instrument, except an instruction for which the amount is not known at the time the instruction is given.

SECTION VIII. FINAL PROVISIONS

Art. 70.

The Minister of Economy is authorised to appoint three senior civil servants for the requirements of the National Accreditation and Monitoring Authority, in permanent and full-time posts. Recruitment of personnel permanently employed in the service of the state will be made in excess of the total number of personnel and in addition to the number of additional posts determined in the law of 24 December 1999 concerning the state budget of revenue and expenditure for the financial year 2000.

Art. 71.

(1) By Grand-Ducal regulation, an "electronic commerce" committee may be formed, consisting of users from both the public and private sectors. A Grand-Ducal regulation shall determine the composition of this committee.

(2) The aim of this committee will be to monitor the application of this law, to distribute information on electronic commerce, and to produce opinions for the competent Ministry.

Art. 72.

In any future legal or regulatory provisions, reference may be made to this law in an abbreviated form using the terms of "Law of 14 August 2000 relating to electronic commerce".

We command and order that this law should appear in the *Mémorial* to be executed and observed by all those concerned by the matter.

The Minister of Economy, Cabasson, 14 August 2000.

Henri Grethen On behalf of the Grand Duke:

His Lieutenant and Representative

Henri

Heir to the Grand Duke

Parl. doc. 4641, ord. sess. 1999-2000; Dir. 93/13 and 97/7; Dir. 2000/31/EC.

Luxembourg (cont'd)

Grand-Ducal Regulation of 1 June 2001 relating to electronic signatures, to electronic payment and to the creation of the 'electronic commerce' committee.

English version for information only.

The French original remains the authentic text.

We, Henri, Grand-Duke of Luxembourg, Duke of Nassau;

In view of the law of 14 August 2000 relating to electronic commerce amending the civil code, the new code of civil procedure, the code of commerce, the penal code and transposing Directive 1999/93 of 13 December 1999 on a Community framework for electronic signatures, Directive 2000/31/EC of 8 June 2000 relating to certain legal aspects of the services of the information society, certain provisions of Directive 97/7/EEC of 20 May 1997 concerning distance-selling of goods and services other than financial services and particularly articles 17, 22, 24, 25, 68 and 71;

In view of the opinions of the Chamber of Commerce and of the Professional Chamber;

In agreement with our Council of State;

On the report of Our Minister of the Economy and after deliberation of the Government in Council;

Pronounce:

Art. 1.

For the purposes of the present Regulation, we understand by:

1°   **Data pertaining to signature creation:** unique data, such as private codes or cryptographic keys, which the signatory uses to create an electronic signature.

2°   **Signature creation device:** a software or material device configured to put into application the data pertaining to signature creation.

3°   **Secured signature creation device:** signature creation device that satisfies the requirements provided for by article 4 of the present Grand-Ducal Regulation.

4°   **Data pertaining to signature verification:** data, such as public codes or cryptographic keys, which are used to verify the electronic signature.

5°   **Signature verification device:** a software or material device configured to put into application the data pertaining to signature verification.

6°   **Certificate:** an electronic attestation that connects data pertaining to signature verification to a person and confirms the identity of that person.

7°   **Qualified certificate:** a certificate that satisfies the requirements set out in article 2 of the present Regulation and that is issued by a certification service provider that satisfies the requirements of article 3 of the present Regulation.

8°   **Electronic signature product:** any material or software product, or specific element of that product, intended to be used by a certification service provider for the provision of electronic signature services or intended to be used for the creation or verification of electronic signatures.

9°   **Electronic signature of a certification service provider issuing qualified certificates:** an electronic signature that satisfies the following requirements:

-   is linked only to the signatory;

-   allows identification of the signatory;

-   is created using means over which the signatory has exclusive control; and

-   is linked to the data to which it relates in such a way that any later modification of the data is detectable.

CHAPTER I - REQUIREMENTS RELATING TO THE QUALIFIED CERTIFICATE

Art. 2.

(1)   Any qualified certificate must contain the following information:

1°   a mention specifying that the certificate is issued as a qualified certificate;

2°   identification of the certification service provider, as well as the country in which the latter is established;

3°   name of the signatory or a pseudonym that is identified as such;

4°   data pertaining to signature verification that correspond to the data for signature creation under the control of the signatory;

5°   indication of the beginning and the end of the validity period of the certificate, which may not exceed 3 years;

6°   identity code of the certificate;

7°   electronic signature of the certification service provider issuing qualified certificates as defined by Art.1. point 9°.

(2)   The qualified certificate also contains, where applicable, the following information:

1°   a specific quality of the signatory, as determined by the usage for which the certificate is intended;

2°   the accreditation of the certification service provider;

3° t he usage limits of the certificate, as well as the limits of the value of transactions for which the certificate may be used.

(3)   The Minister responsible for standardization publishes in the *Mémorial* the references of the technical norms or regulations generally admitted, including national ones, relating to the qualified certificate, with reference to the present Regulation.

CHAPTER II - REQUIREMENTS RELATING TO CERTIFICATION SERVICE PROVIDERS ISSUING QUALIFIED CERTIFICATES

Art. 3.

(1)   A certification service provider must:

1°   give evidence that he is sufficiently reliable to provide certification services;

2°   ensure the functioning of a fast and safe directory service and a safe and immediate revocation service;

3°   see to it that the date and time of issuance and revocation of a certificate can be determined with precision;

4°   verify, by inspection of an official identity document, the identity and, where applicable, the specific qualities of the person to whom a qualified certificate is issued;

5°   have recourse to personnel with the specific knowledge, experience and qualifications necessary for the provision of services and, more specifically, competence at the management level, specialized knowledge of electronic signature technology and good practical knowledge of the appropriate security procedures; they must also implement administrative and managerial procedures and methods that are adapted to, and in conformance with, recognized norms;

6°   use reliable systems and products that are protected against tampering and assure the technical and cryptographic security of the functions they perform;

7°   take measures to protect against forgery of the certificates and, in cases where the certification service provider generates data pertaining to signature creation, guarantee confidentiality throughout the process of generating such data;

8°   have at their disposal sufficient financial resources to operate in accordance with the requirements stipulated by the law and by the Grand-Ducal Regulations, in particular as regards the assumption of responsibility for damages;

9°   record all relevant information relating to a qualified certificate for a period of at least ten years following its issuance date, in particular so as to be able to provide proof of the certification before the courts. These records may be made by electronic means;

10°   neither store nor copy the data pertaining to the creation of the signature of a person to whom the certification service provider has provided key-management services;

11°   use reliable systems to store the certificates in a verifiable form such that:

-    only authorized persons can input or modify the data,

-    the authenticity of the information can be controlled,

-    the certificates are only available for public research in those cases where the holder of the certificate has given consent; and

-    any technical modification that compromises these security features is apparent to the operator.

(2)   The Minister responsible for standardization publishes in the *Mémorial* the references of the technical norms or regulations generally admitted, including national ones, relating to certification service providers issuing qualified certificates, with reference to the present Regulation.

Those norms relating to electronic signature products whose reference numbers have been published in the Official Journal of the European Communities are not published in the *Mémorial*.

CHAPTER III - REQUIREMENTS RELATING TO SECURED ELECTRONIC SIGNATURE CREATION DEVICES

Art. 4.

(1)   Secured electronic signature creation devices must guarantee, through appropriate technical means and procedures, that:

1°   the data used for the creation of the signature occur once only, and that their confidentiality is reasonably assured;

2°   there is sufficient assurance that the data used for the creation of the signature cannot be discovered by deduction and that the signature is protected against all currently available technical means of falsification;

3°   use by third parties of the data used for the creation of the signature can be reliably protected against by the legitimate signatory.

(2)   Secured electronic signature creation devices must not modify the data to be signed or prevent these data from being submitted to the signatory before the signing process.

(3)   The Minister responsible for standardization publishes in the *Mémorial* the references of the technical norms or regulations generally admitted, including national ones, relating to electronic signature products, with reference to the present Regulation, except for those norms relating to electronic signature products whose reference numbers have been published in the Official Journal of the European Communities.

References to secured electronic signature creation devices that have been certified as conforming to the requirements set out in the present article by a body designated for this purpose by a Member State of the European Community are also published in the *Mémorial*, with reference to the present Regulation.

CHAPTER IV - ELECTRONIC PAYMENT

Art. 5.

Except in the case where he has been found guilty of fraud or gross negligence, the holder of an electronic payment instrument accepts the consequences resulting from its loss, theft or fraudulent use by a third party, up to the amount of 150 euro, until such time as he complies with the requirement for notification as provided for by article 68 ¤1 of the law of 14 August 2000 on electronic commerce.

CHAPTER V - CREATION OF THE 'ELECTRONIC COMMERCE' COMMITTEE

Art. 6.

A consultative body attached to the Ministry of the Economy is created, called the Electronic Commerce Committee, hereinafter referred to as 'the Committee'.

Art. 7.

The Committee's mission is:

1°   to ensure that all interested parties are involved in the activities of this domain;

2°   to contribute towards clarifying the requirements relating to qualified certificates;

3°   to contribute towards clarifying the requirements relating to providers issuing qualified certificates;

4°   to contribute towards clarifying the requirements relating to secured electronic signature creation devices;

5°   to make recommendations for secured signature verification;

6°   to disseminate information on electronic commerce.

Art. 8.

The Committee comprises the following members:

1°   five members nominated on proposal by the Ministers responsible for the State, the Economy, Justice, the Middle Classes and Finance;

2°   one member nominated on proposal by the *Office Luxembourgeois d'Accréditation et de Surveillance* (OLAS);

3°   one member nominated on proposal by the Luxembourg standardization body;

4°   three members nominated on proposal by the professional employment chambers;

5°   two members selected for their specific competence in the field;

6°   one member representing consumers.

The members are appointed by the Minister of the Economy.

The Minister of the Economy appoints a president and a vice-president from among the members of the Committee.
The mandate is approved for a period of three years. It is renewable.

Art. 9.

Assigned to the Committee is a secretariat, the management of which is assured by an agent designated by the Minister of the Economy.

Art. 10.

The Committee convenes upon convocation by its president.

The president must convoke the Committee upon request by at least three of its members.

Art. 11.

Experts may be called to assist during meetings.

Art. 12.

Unless specifically stated otherwise, the minutes of the meeting stand as the opinion of the Committee. They indicate the majority view of the Committee members. Members who are of a different opinion have the right to have their opinions included in the minutes. The minutes are submitted to the Committee members for approval before being transmitted to the Minister of the Economy.

Art. 13.

The Committee may constitute working groups entrusted with preparing a study or opinion on specific matters to be submitted to the Committee.

Art. 14.

An attendance fee, to be fixed by reasoned decree by the Government in Council, is allocated per meeting to those Committee members who are present, to the working groups, to experts who are present and to the agent who manages the Committee secretariat.

Art. 15.

Our Minister of the Economy is entrusted with the execution of the present Grand-Ducal Regulation, which will be published in the *Mémorial*.

San Marino, 1 June 2001,

Henri

The Minister of the Economy,

Henri Grethen

Malta

CHAPTER 426
ELECTRONIC COMMERCE ACT

AN ACT to provide in relation to electronic commerce and to provide for matters connected therewith or ancillary thereto.

(   )

ACT III of 2001.

PART I

PRELIMINARY

Short title and commencement.

1.   The short title of this Act is Electronic Commerce Act, and shall come into force on such date as the Minister may by notice in the Gazette appoint and different dates may be so appointed for different provisions or different purposes of this Act.

Interpretation.

2.   In this Act, unless the context otherwise requires -

"addressee" in relation to an electronic communication means a person who is intended by the originator to receive the electronic communication, but does not include a person acting as a service provider with respect to the processing, receiving or storing of that electronic communication or providing other services with respect to it;

"advanced electronic signature" means an electronic signature which meets the following requirements:

(*a*)   it is uniquely linked to the signatory;

(*b*)   it is capable of identifying the signatory;

(*c*)   it is created using means that the signatory can maintain under his sole control; and

(*d*)   it is linked to the data to which it relates in such a manner that any subsequent change of the data is detectable;

"certificate" means an electronic attestation, which links signature verification data to a person and confirms the identity of that person;

"competent authority" means the authority so designated in terms of article 20;

"consumer" means any natural person who is acting for purposes which are outside his trade, business or profession;

"data" means a representation of information, knowledge, facts, concepts or instructions that has been prepared or is being prepared in any manner and has been processed, is being processed or is intended to be processed in an information system, a computer system or a computer network. Data may be in any form or derived from any device or source, including computer memory, computer printouts, any storage media, electronic or otherwise and punched cards;

"data storage device" means any thing, including a disk, from which data and information is capable of being reproduced with or without the aid of any thing or device;

"electronic communication" means information generated, communicated, processed, sent, received, recorded, stored or displayed by electronic means;

"electronic contract" means a contract concluded wholly or partly by electronic communications or wholly or partly in an electronic form;

"electronic signature" means data in electronic form which are attached to, incorporated in or logically associated with other electronic data and which serve as a method of authentication;

"information" includes information in the form of data, text, images, sound or speech;

"information society service" means any service which is provided at a distance, by electronic means and at the individual request of a recipient of the service, whether such service is provided for consideration or not, and for the purposes of this definition:

(*a*)   "at a distance" means that the service is provided without the parties being simultaneously present;

(*b*)   "by electronic means" means that the service is sent initially and received at its destination by means of electronic equipment for the processing (including digital compression) and storage of data, and entirely transmitted, conveyed and received by wire, by radio, by optical means or by any electromagnetic means;

(*c*)   "at the individual request of a recipient of the service" means that the service is provided through the transmission of data on individual request;

"information system" means a system for generating, sending, receiving, recording, storing or otherwise processing electronic communications;

"information technology requirements" includes software, network and data storage requirements;

"Minister" means the Minister responsible for communications;

"originator" in relation to an electronic communication means the person by whom, or on whose behalf, the electronic communication purports to have been sent or generated prior to storage, if any, but does not include a person acting as a service provider with respect to the generating, processing, sending or storing of that electronic communication or providing other services with respect to it;

"place of business" in relation to a government, an authority of a government, a public body, a charitable, philanthropic or similar institution means a place where any operations or activities are carried out by that government, authority, body or institution;

"prescribed" means prescribed by regulations made by the Minister in accordance with the provisions of this Act;

"qualified certificate" means a certificate which meets the requirements established by or under this Act and is provided by a signature certification service provider who fulfils the requirements established by or under this Act;

"recipient" means any person who uses an information society service for the purposes of seeking information or making it accessible;

"signature certification service provider" means a person who issues certificates or provides other services related to electronic signatures;

"secure signature creation device" means a signature creation device which meets the requirements laid down in the Fourth Schedule to this Act;

"signature verification data" means data, such as codes or private cryptographic keys, which are used for the purpose of verifying an electronic signature;

"signature verification device" means configured software or hardware used to implement the signature verification data;

"transaction" includes a transaction of a non-commercial nature;

"voluntary accreditation" means any permission, setting out rights and obligations specific to the provision of signature certification services, to be granted upon request by the signature certification service provider concerned, by the public or private body charged with the elaboration of, and supervision of compliance with, such rights and obligations, where the signature certification service provider is not entitled to exercise the rights stemming from the permission until it has received the decision by the body.

PART II

APPLICATION OF LEGAL REQUIREMENTS TO ELECTRONIC COMMUNICATIONS AND TRANSACTIONS

Validity of transactions.

3. For the purposes of any law in Malta and subject to the other provisions of this Act, a transaction is not deemed to be invalid merely because it took place wholly or partly by means of one or more electronic communications.

Excluded laws.

4. (1) Unless otherwise prescribed, the provisions of articles 5 to 15 shall not apply to -

(a) the law governing the creation, execution, amendment, variation or revocation of -

(i) a will or any other testamentary instrument;

(ii) a trust; or

(iii) a power of attorney;

(b) any law governing the manner in which rights over immovable property other than leases may be created, acquired, disposed of or registered;

(c) any law governing the making of an affidavit or a solemn declaration, or requiring or permitting the use of one for any purpose;

(d) any provision of the law of persons;

(e) the rules, practices or procedures of a court or tribunal;

(f) any law relating to the imposition, collection or recovery of taxation and other Government imposts, including fees, fines and penalties;

(g) any law relating to contracts of suretyship and collateral security furnished by persons for the purpose of their trade, business or profession; or

(h) any law relating to the giving of evidence in criminal proceedings.

(2) Where the Minister is of the opinion that -

(a) technology has advanced to such an extent, and access to it is so widely available, or

(b) adequate procedures and practices have developed in public registration or other services, so as to warrant such action, or

(c) the public interest so requires, he may, after consultation with the Minister as in the Minister's opinion has sufficient interest or responsibility in relation to the matter, by Order in the Gazette extend the application of this Act or a provision of this Act to or in relation to a matter specified in subarticle (1) above, including the applicability to a particular area or subject, or for a particular time, for the purposes of a trial of the technology and procedures, subject to such conditions as he thinks fit.

Requirement or permission to give information in writing,

5. (1) If under any law in Malta a person is required or permitted to give information in writing, that requirement shall be deemed to have been satisfied if the person gives the information by means of an electronic communication: Provided that -

(a) at the time the information was given, it was reasonable to expect that the information would be readily accessible so as to be useable for subsequent reference; and

(b) if the information is required to be given to a person, or to another person on his behalf, and the first mentioned person requires that the information be given in accordance with particular information technology requirements, by means of a particular kind of electronic communication, that person's requirement has been met; and

(c) if the information is required to be given to a person, or to another person on his behalf, and the first mentioned person requires that a particular action be taken by way of verifying the receipt of the information, that person's requirement has been met.

(2) For the purposes of this article, giving information includes, but is not limited to, the following:

(a) making an application;

(b) making or lodging a claim;

(c) giving, sending or serving a notification;

(d) lodging a return;

(e) making a request;

(f) making a declaration;

(g) lodging or issuing a certificate;

(h) lodging an objection; and

(i) making a statement.

(3) For the purposes of this article, a requirement or permission in relation to a person to give information shall extend to and shall be equally applicable to the requirement or information which is stated to be sent, filed, submitted, served or otherwise transmitted and includes similar or cognate expressions, thereof. Signature. **6.** If under any law in Malta the signature of a person is required, such requirement is deemed to have been satisfied if such signature is an electronic signature and such signature shall not be denied legal effectiveness on the grounds that it is:

(a) in electronic form; or

(b) not based upon a qualified certificate; or

(c) not based upon a qualified certificate issued by an accredited signature certification service provider; or

(d) not created by a secure signature creation device: Provided that if the electronic signature is in the form of an advanced electronic signature, which is based on a qualified certificate and is created by a secure creation device, it shall for all intents and purposes of law be presumed to be the signature of the signatory.

Requirement or permission for production of document and integrity.

7. (1)   Unless otherwise provided by or under this Act, if under any law in Malta, a person is required to produce a document that is in the form of a paper, or of any other substance or material, that requirement is deemed to have been satisfied if the person produces, by means of an electronic communication, an electronic form of that document: Provided that:

(a)   having regard to all the relevant circumstances at the time of the communication, the method of generating the electronic form of the document provided a reliable means of assuring the maintenance of the integrity of the information contained in the document;

(b)   at the time the communication was sent, it was reasonable to expect that the information contained in the electronic form of the document would be readily accessible so as to be useable for subsequent reference;

(c)   if the document is required to be given to a person, or to another person on his behalf, and the first mentioned person requires that an electronic form of the document be given, in accordance with particular information technology requirements, by means of a particular kind of electronic communication, the person's requirement is satisfied; and

(d)   if the document is required to be given to a person, or to another person on his behalf, and the first mentioned person requires that a particular action be taken by way of verifying the receipt of the information, the person's requirement is satisfied.

(2)   For the purposes of this article, the integrity of information contained in a document is only maintained if the information remains complete and unaltered, save for -

(a)   the addition of any endorsement; or

(b)   any change not being a change to the information, which is necessary in the normal course of communication, storage or display.

(3)   For the purposes of subarticles (1) and (2) and of article 8, the production by means of an electronic communication of an electronic form of a document or the generation of an electronic form of a document shall not give rise to any liability for infringement of the copyright in a work or other subject matter embodied in the document.

Retention of information, documents and communications.

8. (1)   If under any law in Malta, a person is required to record information in writing, that requirement is deemed to have been satisfied if the person records the information in electronic form:

Provided that such information in electronic form is readily accessible so as to be useable for subsequent reference and it complies with such regulations as may be prescribed.

(2) If under any law in Malta, a person is required to retain, for a particular period, a document that is in the form of a paper or of any other substance or material, that requirement is deemed to have been satisfied if the person retains an electronic form of the document throughout that period: Provided that if -

   (a) having regard to all the relevant circumstances at the time of the generation of the electronic form of the document, the method of generating the electronic form of the document, provided a reliable means of assuring the maintenance of the integrity of the information contained in that document; and

   (b) at the time of the generation of the electronic form of the document, it was reasonable to expect that the information contained in the electronic form of the document would be readily accessible so as to be useable for subsequent reference; and

   (c) it complies with such regulations as may be prescribed.

(3) For the purpose of subarticle (2), the integrity of information contained in a document is only maintained if the information has remained complete and unaltered, save for-

   (a) the addition of any endorsement; or

   (b) any change not being a change to the information, which is necessary in the normal course of communication, storage or display.

(4) If under any law in Malta, a person is required to retain, for a particular period, information that was the subject of an electronic communication, that requirement is deemed to have been satisfied if that person retains, or causes another person to retain, in electronic form, that -

   (a) at the time of commencement of the retention of the information, it was reasonable to expect that the information would be readily accessible so as to be useable for subsequent reference; and

   (b) having regard to all the relevant circumstances, at the time of commencement of the retention of the information, the method of retaining the information in electronic form provided a reliable means of assuring the maintenance of the integrity of the information contained in the electronic communication; and

   (c) throughout that period that person also retains, or causes another person to retain, in electronic form, such additional information obtained as is sufficient to enable the identification of the following:

      (i) the origin of the electronic communication;

      (ii) the destination of the electronic communication;

      (iii) the time when the electronic communication was sent;

      (iv) the time when the electronic communication was received; and

   (d) at the time of commencement of the retention of the additional information specified in paragraph (c) it was reasonable to expect that the additional

information would be readily accessible so as to be useable for subsequent reference; and

(e)   it complies with such regulations as may be prescribed.

(5)   For the purposes of subarticle (4), the integrity of the information which is the subject of an electronic communication is only maintained if the information remains complete and unaltered, save for -

(a)   the addition of any endorsement; or

(b)   any change not being a change to the information, which arises in the normal course of communication, storage or display.

PART III

ELECTRONIC CONTRACTS

Electronic contract.
9. (1)   An electronic contract shall not be denied legal effect, validity or enforceability solely on the grounds that it is wholly or partly in electronic form or has been entered into wholly or partly by way of electronic communications or otherwise.

(2)   For the purposes of any law relating to contracts, an offer, an acceptance of an offer and any related communication, including any subsequent amendment, cancellation or revocation of the offer, the acceptance of the contract may, unless otherwise agreed by the contracting parties, be communicated by means of electronic communications.

Formation of electronic contract.
10.(1)   Unless otherwise agreed by parties who are not consumers, where the addressee of an electronic communication is required to give his consent through technological means:

(a)   in accepting the originator's offer, an electronic contract is concluded when the addressee has received from the originator, electronically, an acknowledgement of receipt of the addressee's consent; and

(b)   for the purposes of paragraph (a), an acknowledgement of receipt is deemed to have been received when the addressee is able to access it.

(2)   Unless otherwise agreed by parties who are not consumers, the originator shall provide the addressee with effective and accessible means to identify and correct handling errors and accidental transactions prior to the conclusion of the contract.

(3)   The provisions of subarticle (1)(a) and of subarticle (2) above shall not apply to contracts concluded exclusively by electronic mail or by any other similar technological means.

Information requirements relating to electronic contract.
11.   Unless otherwise agreed by parties who are not consumers, and without prejudice to any consumer rights under the provisions of any other law, the originator shall provide information in clear, comprehensive and unambiguous

terms regarding the matters set out in the First Schedule to the Act. Such information shall be provided prior to the placement of the order by the addressee.

PART IV

TRANSMISSION OF ELECTRONIC COMMUNICATIONS

Time of dispatch.

12.(1)   If an electronic communication enters a single information system outside of the control of the originator, then, save as otherwise agreed between the originator and the addressee of the electronic communication, the dispatch of the electronic communication occurs at the time when it enters the information system.

(2)   If an electronic communication enters successively two or more information systems outside of the control of the originator, then, unless otherwise agreed between the originator and the addressee of the electronic communication, the dispatch of the electronic communication occurs when it enters the first of those information systems.

Time of receipt.

13.(1)   If the addressee of an electronic communication has designated an information system for the purpose of receiving electronic communications, then, save as otherwise agreed between the originator and the addressee of the electronic communication, the time of receipt of the electronic communication is the time when the electronic communication enters the information system.

(2)   If the addressee of an electronic communication has not designated an information system for the purpose of receiving electronic communications, then, save as otherwise agreed between the originator and the addressee of the electronic communication, the time of receipt of the electronic communication is the time when the electronic communication comes to the attention of the addressee.

Place of dispatch and receipt.

14.(1)   Save as may be otherwise agreed between the originator and the addressee of an electronic communication -

    (*a*)   the electronic communication is deemed to have been dispatched at the place where the originator has his place of business; and

    (*b*)   the electronic communication is deemed to have been received at the place where the addressee has his place of business.

(2)   For the purposes of the subarticle (1) -

    (*a*)   if the originator or the addressee has more than one place of business, and one of those places has a closer relationship to the underlying transaction, that place of business shall be deemed to be the originator's or the addressee's place of business; and

(b)   if the originator or the addressee has more than one place of business, but paragraph (a) does not apply, the originator's or the addressee's principal place of business shall be deemed to be the originator's or the addressee's place of business; and

(c)   if the originator or addressee does not have a place of business, the originator's or the addressee's place of business shall be deemed to be the originator's or addressee's ordinary residence.

Attribution of electronic communication.

15.(1)   Save as otherwise agreed between the originator and the addressee of an electronic communication, the originator of an electronic communication is bound by that communication only if the communication was sent by him or under his authority.

(2)   Nothing in subarticle (1) shall affect the operation of any law that makes provision for-

(a)   the conduct engaged by a person within the scope of the person's actual or apparent authority to be attributed to another person; or

(b)   a person to be bound by conduct engaged in by another person within the scope of the other person's actual or apparent authority.

(3)   An electronic communication between an originator and an addressee shall be deemed to be of the originator if it was sent by an information system programmed to operate automatically by or on behalf of the originator.

(4)   An addressee shall have the right to consider each electronic communication received by him as a separate electronic communication and to act on that assumption, except to the extent that such communication is a duplicate of another electronic communication and the addressee knew or should have known, had he exercised reasonable care or used any agreed procedure, that the electronic communication was a duplicate.

PART V

PROVISION OF SIGNATURE CERTIFICATION SERVICES

Accreditation of signature certification service providers.

16.(1)   The provision of signature certification services or services otherwise related to electronic signatures shall not be subject to prior authorisation.

(2)   Without prejudice to the generality of subarticle (1) the Minister may by regulations, introduce and maintain a voluntary accreditation scheme aiming at enhanced levels of signature certification service provision and may designate accreditation authorities and may also make regulations on any other matter relating to such designation as the Minister may deem necessary.

Supervision of signature certification service providers that issue qualified certificates.

17.(1)   The Minister shall by Order designate a competent authority for the supervision of signature certification service providers established in Malta which issue qualified certificates to the public.

(2)   The Minister may prescribe on any of the following matters -

(a)   the powers and functions of the competent authority;

(b)   any other matter relating to the competent authority which may appear to the Minister to be necessary or desirable.

Liability of signature certification service providers.
18.(1)   Signature certification service providers who issue a certificate as a qualified certificate to the public or who guarantee such certificate shall be liable for any damage caused to any person who reasonably relies on such certificate.

(2)   It shall be the duty of the signature certification service provider who issues a certificate as a qualified certificate to the public or who guarantees such certificate to reasonably assure -

(a)   the accuracy of all information in the qualified certificate as of the time of issue and that the certificate contains all the details prescribed in relation to a qualified certificate;

(b)   that at the time of the issue of the certificate, the signatory identified in the qualified certificate held the signature creation device corresponding to the signature verification device given or identified in the certificate;

(c)   that the signature creation device and the signature verification device act together in a complementary manner, in cases where the signature certification service provider generates the two.

(3)   A signature certification service provider who has issued a certificate as a qualified certificate to the public or who has guaranteed such certificate is liable for damage caused to any person who reasonably relies on the certificate for failure to register or publish revocation or suspension of the certificate unless the signature certification service provider proves he has not acted negligently.

(4)   A signature certification service provider who issues a certificate as a qualified certificate to the public or who guarantees such certificate may indicate in the qualified certificate limits on the uses of that certificate: Provided that the limits are clear and readily identifiable as limitations, the signature certification service provider shall not be liable for damages arising from a contrary use of a qualified certificate which includes limits on its user.

(5)   A signature certification service provider who issues a certificate as a qualified certificate to the public or who guarantees such certificate may indicate in the qualified certificate a limit on the value of transactions for which the certificate can be used. Any such indication must be clear and readily identifiable as a limitation.

PART VI

INTERMEDIARY SERVICE PROVIDERS

Mere conduit.
19.(1)   Where an information society service is provided, and such service consists in the transmission, in a communication network, of information provided by the

recipient of the service, or the provision of access to a communication network, the provider of such a service shall not be liable, otherwise than under a prohibitory injunction, for the information transmitted. Provided that such provider:

(a)   does not initiate the transmission;

(b)   does not select the receiver of the transmission; and

(c)   does not select or modify the information contained in the transmission.

(2)   The acts of transmission and of the provision of access referred to in subarticle (1) hereof, include the automatic intermediate and transient storage of the information transmitted in so far as this takes place for the sole purpose of carrying out the transmission in the communication network, and provided that the information is not stored for any period longer than is reasonably necessary for the transmission.

Caching.

20.   Where an information society service is provided, and such service consists in the transmission, in a communication network, of information provided by a recipient of the service, the provider of that service shall not be liable for damages for the automatic, intermediate and temporary storage of that information, performed for the sole purpose of making more efficient the information's onward transmission to other recipients of the service upon their request.

Provided that:

(a)   the provider does not modify the information;

(b)   the provider complies with the conditions on access to the information;

(c)   the provider complies with any conditions regulating the updating of the information;

(d)   the provider does not interfere with the technology used to obtain data on the use of the information; and

(e)   the provider acts expeditiously to remove or to bar access to the information upon obtaining actual knowledge of any of the following:

(i)   the information at the initial source of the transmission has been removed from the network;

(ii)   access to it has been barred;

(iii)   the Court or other competent authority has ordered such removal or barring.

Hosting.

21.(1)   Where an information society service is provided, and such service consists in the storage of information provided by a recipient of the service, the provider of that service shall not be liable for damages for the information stored at the request of a recipient of the service. Provided that:

(a)   the provider does not have actual knowledge that the activity is illegal and is not aware of facts or circumstances from which illegal activity is apparent; or

(b)   the provider, upon obtaining such knowledge or awareness, acts expeditiously to remove or to disable access to the information.

(2)   Subarticle (1) hereof shall not apply when the recipient of the service is acting under the authority or the control of the provider of the service.

Obligations of intermediary service providers.

22.   Information society service providers shall promptly inform the public authorities competent in the matter of any alleged illegal activity undertaken or information provided by recipients of their service and shall grant to any such authority upon request information enabling the identification of recipients of their service with whom they have storage agreements: Provided that nothing in this Part of the Act shall be interpreted as imposing an obligation on information society service providers to monitor the information which they transmit or store or to actively seek facts or circumstances indicating illegal activity in connection with the activities described in articles 19 to 21 above.

PART VII

GENERAL

Prohibition on misuse of electronic signatures, signature creation devices, certificates and fraud.
23.(1)   No person shall access, copy or otherwise obtain possession of or recreate the signature creation device of another person without authorisation, for the purpose of creating, or allowing or causing another person to create an unauthorised electronic signature using such signature device.

(2)   No person shall alter, disclose or use the signature creation device of another person without authorisation, or in excess of lawful authorisation, for the purpose of creating or allowing or causing another person to create an unauthorised electronic signature using such signature creation device.

(3)   No person shall create, publish, alter or otherwise use a certificate or an electronic signature for any fraudulent or other unlawful purpose.

(4)   No person shall misrepresent his identity or authorisation in requesting or accepting a certificate or in requesting suspension or revocation of a certification.

(5)   No person shall access, alter, disclose or use the signature creation device of a signature certification service provider used to issue certificates without the authorisation of the signature certification service provider, or in excess of lawful authorisation, for the purpose of creating, or allowing or causing another person to create, an unauthorised electronic signature using such signature creation device.

(6)   No person shall publish a certificate, or otherwise knowingly make it available to anyone likely to rely on the certificate or on an electronic signature that is

verifiable with reference to data such as codes, passwords, algorithms, public cryptographic keys or other data which are used for the purposes of verifying an electronic signature, listed in the certificate, if such person knows that -

(a)   the signature certification service provider listed in the certificate has not issued it; or

(b)   the subscriber listed in the certificate has not accepted it; or

(c)   the certificate has been revoked or suspended, unless such publication is for the purpose of verifying an electronic signature created prior to such revocation or suspension, or giving notice of revocation or suspension.

(7)   No person shall use cryptographic or other similar techniques for any illegal purpose.

Offences and penalties.

24.   Any person contravening any of the provisions of this Act or of any regulations made thereunder shall be guilty of an offence and shall, on conviction, be liable to a fine (*multa*) not exceeding one hundred thousand liri or to imprisonment not exceeding six months, or to both such fine and imprisonment, and in the case of a continuous offence to a fine not exceeding one thousand liri for each day during which the offence continues.

Power to make regulations,

25.(1)   The Minister may make regulations to provide for any matter related to electronic commerce in order to give fuller effect to the provisions of this Act, and in particular, but without prejudice to the generality of the aforesaid, such regulations may provide for -

(a)   any derogation from or restriction in relation to any cross-border transaction where this is necessary for one of the following reasons -

   (i)   public policy, in particular the protection of minors, or the fight against any incitement to hatred on grounds of race, sex, religion, political opinion or nationality;

   (ii)   the protection of public health;

   (iii)   public security;

   (iv)   consumer protection;

(b)   identifying:

   (i)   transactions;

   (ii)   requirements or permissions to give information in writing;

   (iii)   requirements or permissions to produce documents;

   (iv)   requirements to retain information, documents and communications;

   (v)   signatures; that may be exempt from any provision of this Act;

(c)   additional requirements for the use of signatures in electronic communications in the public sector;

(d)   the recognition of signature certification service providers who had they been operating in Malta would have satisfied the requirements set out for such providers;

(e)   any matter relating to commercial communications, including, but not limited to matters relating to:-

(i)   information to be provided in commercial communications;

(ii)   unsolicited commercial communications;

(iii) commercial communications by regulated professions;

(f)   the authorisation to the competent authority to impose administrative fines or sanctions on any person acting in contravention of any provision of this Act or of any regulation made thereunder:

Provided that -

(i)   any administrative fine provided for by regulations made under this article shall not exceed the amount of ten thousand liri for each offence and one thousand liri for each day during which failure to observe the provisions of this Act or of any regulation made thereunder persists;

(ii)   administrative fines stipulated in paragraph (i) of this proviso may be increased by regulation up to a maximum of fifty thousand liri and five thousand liri for each day during which any contravention persists, respectively; Cap. 12.

(iii) regulations made under this paragraph may prescribe that any such administrative penalty or sanction shall be due to the competent authority as a civil debt constituting an executive title for the purposes of Title VII of Part I of Book Second of the Code of Organization and Civil Procedure as if the payment of the amount of the fine had been ordered by a judgement of a court of civil jurisdiction;

(iv)   such regulations may also prescribe any right of appeal from decisions of the competent authority to impose an administrative sanction;

(g)   procedures to be established for out of court schemes, for the settlement of disputes arising in relation to information society services including appropriate electronic measures.

(2)   The Minister may also by regulations amend the Schedules to this Act and prescribe anything that may or is required to be prescribed under this Act.

English text to prevail.

26.   In the case of conflict between the Maltese and English texts of this Act, the English text shall prevail.

PART VIII

COMPUTER MISUSE

Amendment to the Criminal Code. Cap. 9.

27. Immediately after article 337 of the Criminal Code there shall be inserted the following new Sub-title and articles:

"Sub-title V of Computer Misuse Interpretation **337**(B)(1)For the purposes of this Sub-title the following definitions, unless the context otherwise requires, shall apply:

"computer" means an electronic device that performs logical, arithmetic and memory functions by manipulating electronic or magnetic impulses, and includes all input, output, processing, storage, software and communication facilities that are connected or related to a computer in a computer system or computer network;

"computer network" means the interconnection of communication lines and circuits with a computer through a remote device or a complex consisting of two or more interconnected computers;

"computer output "or" output "means a statement or a representation of data whether in written, printed, pictorial, screen display, photographic or other film, graphical, acoustic or other form produced by a computer;

"computer software" or "software" means a computer program, procedure or associated documentation used in the operation of a computer system;

"computer supplies" means punched cards, paper tape, magnetic tape, disk packs, diskettes, CD-roms, computer output, including paper and microform and any storage media, electronic or otherwise;

"computer system" means a set of related computer equipment, hardware or software;

"function" includes logic, control, arithmetic, deletion, storage, retrieval and communication of data or telecommunication to, from or within a computer;

"supporting documentation" means any documentation used in the computer system in the construction, clarification, implementation, use or modification of the software or data.

(2) A reference in this Sub-title to software includes a reference to a part of the software.

(3) A reference in this Sub-title to a computer includes a reference to a computer network.

(4) A reference in this Sub-title to data, software or supporting documentation held in a computer or computer system includes a reference to data, software or supporting documentation being transmitted through a computer network.

(5) For the purposes of this Sub-title, a person uses software if the function he causes the computer to perform:

(a)   causes the software to be executed; or

(b)   is itself a function of the software.

(6)   A reference in this Sub-title to any software or data held in a computer includes a reference to any software or data held in any removable storage medium which is for the time being in the computer.

Unlawful access to, or use of, information.
337(C)

(1)   A person who without authorisation does any of the following acts shall be guilty of an offence against this article -

(a)   uses a computer or any other device or equipment to access any data, software or supporting documentation held in that computer or on any other computer, or uses, copies or modifies any such data, software or supporting documentation;

(b)   outputs any data, software or supporting documentation from the computer in which it is held, whether by having it displayed or in any other manner whatsoever;

(c)   copies any data, software or supporting documentation to any storage medium other than that in which it is held or to a different location in the storage medium in which it is held;

(d)   prevents or hinders access to any data, software or supporting documentation;

(e)   impairs the operation of any system, software or the integrity or reliability of any data;

(f)   takes possession of or makes use of any data, software or supporting documentation;

(g)   installs, moves, alters, erases, destroys, varies or adds to any data, software or supporting documentation;

(h)   discloses a password or any other means of access, access code or other access information to any unauthorised person;

(i)   uses another person's access code, password, user name, electronic mail address or other means of access or identification information in a computer;

(j)   discloses any data, software or supporting documentation unless this is required in the course of his duties or by any other law.

(2)   For the purposes of this Sub-title:

(a)   a person shall be deemed to act without authorisation if he is not duly authorised by an entitled person;

(b)   a person shall be deemed to be an entitled person if the person himself is entitled to control the activities defined in paragraphs (a) to (j) of subarticle (1) or in paragraphs (a) and (b) of article 4 of this Sub-title.

(3)   For the purposes of subarticle (1):

(a) a person shall be deemed to have committed an offence irrespective of whether in the case of any modification, such modification is intended to be permanent or temporary;

(b) the form in which any software or data is output and in particular whether or not it represents a form in which, in the case of software, it is capable of being executed or, in the case of data, it is capable of being processed by a computer, is immaterial.

(4) For the purposes of paragraph (f) of subarticle (1), a person who for the fact that he has in his custody or under his control any data, computer software or supporting documentation which he is not authorised to have, shall be deemed to have taken possession of it.

Misuse of hardware,
337(D) Any person who without authorisation does any of the following acts shall be guilty of an offence against this article -

(a) modifies computer equipment or supplies that are used or intended to be used in a computer, computer system or computer network;

(b) takes possession of, damages or destroys a computer, computer system, computer network, or computer supplies used or intended to be used in a computer, computer system or computer network or impairs the operation of any of the aforesaid.

Commission of an offence outside Malta.
337(E) If any act is committed outside Malta which, had it been committed in Malta, would have constituted an offence against the provisions of this Sub-title, it shall, if the commission affects any computer, software, data or supporting documentation which is situated in Malta or is in any way linked or connected to a computer in Malta, be deemed to have been committed in Malta.

Offences and penalties.
337(F)

(1) Without prejudice to any other penalty established under this Sub-title, any person who contravenes any of the provisions of this Sub-title shall be guilty of an offence and shall be liable on conviction to a fine (*multa*) not exceeding ten thousand liri or to imprisonment for a term not exceeding four years, or to both such fine and imprisonment.

(2) Where any such offence constitutes an act which is in any way detrimental to any function or activity of Government, or hampers, impairs or interrupts in any manner whatsoever the provision of any public service or utility, whether or not such service or utility is provided or operated by any Government entity, the penalty shall be increased to a fine (*multa*) of not less than one hundred liri and not exceeding fifty thousand liri or to imprisonment for a term from three months to ten years, or to both such fine and imprisonment:

Provided that where a person is found guilty of an offence against this subarticle for a second or subsequent time, the minimum of the penalty for such an offence shall not be less than five hundred liri.

(3) The penalties established under subarticle (2) shall also apply in the case of any offence against any of the provisions of this Sub-title -

(a) where the offence is committed in any place by an employee to the prejudice of his employer or to the prejudice of a third party, if his capacity, real or fictitious, as employee, shall have afforded him facilities in the commission of the offence; and

(b) with the exception of subarticle (2), where the offence committed by a person is the second or subsequent offence against any of the provisions of this Sub-title.

Consequential amendments to the Extradition Act. Cap. 276.

28. The Extradition Act shall be amended by the addition of the following item immediately after item 30 of the Schedule to the said Act -

"31. An offence against the law relating to computer misuse".

(4) A person who produces any material or does any other act preparatory to or in furtherance of the commission of any offence under this Subtitle shall be guilty of that offence and shall on conviction be liable to the same punishment provided for the offence.

(5) Any person who is an accomplice in the commission of an offence against this Sub-title or who in any way aids or abets such commission shall be liable to the same penalties contemplated for such an offence.

(6) It shall not be necessary for the prosecution to negative by evidence any authorisation required under this Sub-title and the burden of proving any such authorisation shall lie with the person alleging such authorisation: Provided that this burden shall not be considered to have been discharged with the mere uncorroborated testimony of the person charged. Search and seizure. 337(G)The Minister may, for the purposes of this Sub-title, by regulations prescribe:

(a) the manner in which the Police may search computers, computer systems or computer supplies and seize data or software stored therein;

(b) procedures and methods for handling evidence that is in an electronic form".

FIRST SCHEDULE

(Article 11)

Information Requirements Relating to Electronic Contracts

(a) the name and address where the originator is established;

(b) the electronic-mail address where the originator can be contracted in a direct manner;

(c) the registration number of the originator in any trade register or of any professional body if applicable;

(d) where the activity of the originator is subject to an authorisation, the activities covered by the authorisation granted to the originator and the particulars of the authority providing such authorisation;

(e) the Value Added Tax (VAT) registration number of the originator where the originator undertakes an activity that is subject to VAT;

(f) the different steps to follow to conclude the contract;

(g) a statement of whether the concluded contract will be filed by the originator and whether it will be accessible.

SECOND SCHEDULE

(Article 2)

Requirements for Qualified Certificates
Qualified certificates must contain:

(a) an indication that the certificate is issued as a qualified certificate;

(b) the identification of the signature certification service provider and the State in which it is established;

(c) the name of the signatory or a pseudonym, which shall be identified as such;

(d) provision for a specific attribute of the signatory to be included if relevant, depending on the purpose for which the certificate is intended;

(e) signature-verification data which correspond to signature-creation data under the control of the signatory;

(f) an indication of the beginning and end of the period of validity of the certificate;

(g) the identity code of the certificate;

(h) the advanced electronic signature of the signature certification service provider issuing it;

(i) limitations on the scope of the use of the certificate, if applicable; and

(j) limits on the value of transactions for which the certificate can be used, if applicable.

THIRD SCHEDULE

(Article 2)

Requirements for Signature Certification Service Providers Issuing Qualified Certificates
Signature Certification service providers must:

(a) demonstrate the reliability necessary for providing signature certification services;

(b) ensure the operation of a prompt and secure directory and a secure and immediate revocation service;

(c) ensure that the date and time when a certificate is issued or revoked can be determined precisely;

(d) verify, by appropriate means in accordance with national law, the identity and, if applicable, any specific attributes of the person to whom a qualified certificate is issued;

(e) employ personnel who possess the expert knowledge, experience, and qualifications necessary for the services provided, in particular competence at managerial level, expertise in electronic signature technology and familiarity with proper security procedures; they must also apply administrative and management procedures which are adequate and correspond to recognised standards;

(f) use trustworthy systems and products which are protected against modification and ensure the technical and cryptographic security of the processes supported by them;

(g) take measures against forgery of certificates, and, in cases where the signature certification service provider generates signature-creation data, guarantee confidentiality during the process of generating such data;

(h) maintain sufficient financial resources to operate in conformity with the requirements laid down in the Act, in particular to bear the risk of liability for damages, for example, by obtaining appropriate insurance;

(i) record all relevant information concerning a qualified certificate for an appropriate period of time, in particular for the purpose of providing evidence of certification for the purposes of legal proceedings. Such recording may be done electronically;

(j) not store copy signature-creation data of the person to whom the signature certification service provider provided key management services;

(k) before entering into a contractual relationship with a person seeking a certificate to support his electronic signature, inform that person by a durable means of communication of the precise terms and conditions regarding the use of the certificate, including any limitations on its use, the existence of a voluntary accreditation scheme and procedures for complains and dispute settlement. Such information, which may be transmitted electronically, must be in writing and in readily understandable language. Relevant parts of this information must also be made available on request to third-parties relying on the certificate;

(l) use trustworthy systems to store certificates in a verifiable form so that:

- only authorised persons can make entries and changes;

- information can be checked for authenticity;

- certificates are publicly available for retrieval in only those cases for which the certificate-holder's consent has been obtained; and

- any technical changes compromising these security requirements are apparent to the operator.

FOURTH SCHEDULE

(Article 2)

Requirements for Secure Signature-Creation Devices

01. Secure signature creation devices must, by appropriate technical and procedural means, ensure at the least that:

(a) the signature creation data used for signature generation can practically occur only once, and that their secrecy is reasonably assured;

(b) the signature creation data used for signature generation cannot, with reasonable assurance, be derived and the signature is protected against forgery using currently available technology;

(c) the signature-creation-data used for signature generation can be reliably protected by the legitimate signatory against the use of others.

02. Secure signature creation devices must not alter the data to be signed or prevent such data from being presented to the signatory prior to the signature process.

Poland

Act on Electronic Signature (Poland) of 18th September 2001

Chapter I

General Provisions

Article 1

This Act specifies conditions of the use of electronic signature, legal effects of its use, the principles of provision of certification services and principles of supervision over certification-service-providers.

Article 2

The provisions of this Act shall apply to certification-service-providers established in Poland or providing services within her territory.

Article 3

For the purposes of this Act:

1) **electronic signature** shall mean data in electronic form which are attached to or logically associated with other electronic data and which serve to confirm the identity of the signatory;

2) **secure electronic signature** shall mean an electronic signature which:

   (a) is uniquely linked to the signatory;

   (b) is created using secure-signature-creation devices and signature-creation data that the signatory can maintain under his/her sole control; and

    (c)   is linked to the data to which it has been attached, in such a manner that any subsequent change of the data is detectable;

3)   **signatory** shall mean a natural person who holds a signature-creation device and acts either on his own behalf or on behalf of the natural or legal person, or an organisational unit other than legal person;

4)   **signature-creation data** shall mean unique data linked to a natural person, which are used by that person to create an electronic signature;

5)   **signature-verification-data** shall mean unique data linked to a natural person, which are used to confirm the identity of the signatory;

6)   **signature-creation device** shall mean software or hardware configured in a manner enabling creation of electronic signature or authentication with the use of signature-creation or authentication-creation data;

7)   **secure-signature-creation device** shall mean a signature-creation device which meets the requirements laid down in the Act;

8)   **signature-verification device** shall mean software or hardware configured in a manner confirming the identity of the signatory being a natural person, with the use of signature-verification-data or in a manner confirming the identity of a certification-service-provider or an authority charged with issuing certification attestations, with the use of electronic-authentication-verification-data;

9)   **secure signature-verification device** shall mean a signature-verification device which meets the requirements laid down in the Act;

10)   **certificate** shall mean an electronic attestation which links signature-verification data to a signatory and confirms his/her identity;

11)   **certification attestation** shall mean an electronic attestation which links authentication-verification data to a certification-service-provider or an authority referred to in Article 30, paragraph 1, and confirms the identity of such provider or authority;

12)   **qualified certificate** shall mean a certificate which meets the requirements laid down in the Act and is provided by a qualified certification-service-provider who fulfils the requirements laid down in the Act;

13)   **certification services** shall mean issuing of certificates, time- stamping or other services related to electronic signatures;

14)   **certification-service-provider** shall mean an entrepreneur within the meaning of the provisions of the Act of 19th November 1999-Economic Activity Law (Dziennik Ustaw No. 101, item 1178; of 2000--No. 86, item 958 and No. 114, item 1193; and of 2001--No. 49, item 509 and No. 67, item 679), the National Bank of Poland, or a public authority, which provides at least one of the services referred to in subparagraph 13;

15)   **qualified certification-service-provider** shall mean a certification-service-provider entered in the register of qualified certification-service-providers;

16)   **timestamping** shall mean the service which consists in the attachment to data in electronic form, logically associated with the data certified with electronic

signature or authentication, of specification of time and electronic authentication (confirmation) of the data generated in such way by the provider of that service;

17)   **certification policy** shall mean detailed solutions, including those of technical and organisational nature, indicating the manner, scope and security conditions for the generation and use of certificates.

18)   **recipient of certification services** shall mean a natural person, a legal person or an organisational unit other than legal person, which:

(a)   have concluded an agreement with a certification-service-provider for the provision of certification services, or

(b)   may act, within the limits specified by certification policy, on the basis of the certificate or other data electronically authenticated by the certification-service-provider,

19)   **electronic authentication** shall mean data in electronic form which are attached to or logically associated with other electronic data and which serve to confirm the identity of the certification-service-provider or the authority issuing certification attestations, and which meet the following requirements:

(a)   are created using secure-signature-creation devices and electronic authentication-creation data that the certification-service-provider or the authority issuing the certification attestation can maintain under its sole control; and

(b)   any subsequent change of the authenticated data is detectable;

20)   **electronic authentication-creation data** shall mean unique data linked to the certification-service-provider or the authority issuing certification attestations which are used by the provider or authority to create an electronic authentication;

21)   **electronic authentication-verification data** shall mean unique data linked to the certification-service-provider or the authority issuing certification attestations which are used to confirm the identity of the provider or authority creating an electronic authentication;

22)   **certification of a secure electronic signature** shall mean activities which confirm identity of the person creating an electronic signature and prove that the signature has been created with the use of signature- creation data linked to that person, and that the data signed with that signature has not been changed after the creation of the electronic signature.

Article 4

A certificate issued by a certification-service-provider not established in the Republic of Poland and which does not provide services within her territory, shall be legally equivalent to qualified certificates issued by a certification-service-provider established or providing services within the territory of the Republic of Poland, if one of the following prerequisites is satisfied:

1)   the certification-service-provider which issued the certificate is accredited,

2)   this is stipulated in an agreement, to which Poland is a party, concerning mutual recognition of certificates,

3)   the certification-service-provider which issued the certificate is entered in the register of qualified certification-service-providers,

4)   a certification-service-provider established in the European Community, which complies with the requirements of the Act, guarantees the certificate,

5)   the certificate is recognised as a qualified certificate under an international agreement between the European Community on the one hand and third countries or international organisations on the other,

6)   the certification-service-provider which issued the certificate is recognised under an international agreement between the European Community on the one hand and third countries or international organisations on the other.

Chapter II

Legal Effects of Electronic Signature

Article 5

1.   A secure electronic signature verified with the use of a qualified certificate shall have the legal effects specified by this Act, provided that it has been made within the period of validity of that certificate. A secure electronic signature made within the period of suspension of a qualified certificate used to verify it, shall take legal effect from the time of the repeal of such suspension.

2.   The electronic data signed with a secure electronic signature verified with the use of a valid qualified certificate shall have legal effects equivalent to documents signed with a hand-written signature, unless separate provisions provide otherwise.

3.   A secure electronic signature verified with the use of a qualified certificate shall ensure integrity of the data signed with that signature, and unique identification of a qualified certificate in such a manner that any change--effected after the creation of the signature--of the data and of the identification of a qualified certificate for the verification of that signature is detectable.

Article 6

1.   A secure electronic signature verified with the use of a qualified certificate shall a be confirmation of the fact that it has been created by a person specified in that certificate as a signatory.

2.   The provisions of paragraph 1 shall nor apply to the certificate after the expiration of its validity date or the date of its revocation, and in the period of its suspension, unless it has been proven that the signature was created before the

date of expiration of validity of the certificate or before its revocation or suspension.

3. No one may claim that the electronic signature verified with the use of a valid qualified certificate has not been created with the use of secure devices and data subjected to an exclusive supervision of the signatory.

Article 7

1. An electronic signature may be timestamped.

2. Timestamping carried out by a qualified certification-service-provider shall, in particular, have the legal effect of the certified date within the meaning of the Civil Code.

3. An electronic signature timestamped by a certification-service-provider shall be assumed to be created no later than at the time of the provision of such service. Such assumption shall exist until the day of expiration of the attestation used for verification of that stamping. Any extension of the assumption shall require a subsequent timestamping of the electronic signature together with the data used to the preceding verification by a qualified provider of that service.

Article 8

The validity and legal effectiveness of an electronic signature shall not be denied solely on the grounds that it is in electronic form, or the signature-verification data have no qualified certificate or that it has not been put with the use of a secure signature-creation device.

Chapter III

Obligations of Certification-Service-Providers

Article 9

1. No licence and concession shall be required from those engaged in the provision of certification services.

2. Public authorities and the National Bank of Poland may provide certification services, subject to paragraph 3, solely for their own purposes or the purposes of other public authorities.

3. Local authority may provide certification services on a non-profit basis also for members of a local community.

Article 10

1. A qualified certification-service-provider issuing qualified certificates shall be obliged to:

    1)   provide technical and organisational means for prompt and reliable issuance, suspension and revocation of certificates and for precise determination of the date and time of such activities,

    2)   verify the identity of the person seeking a certificate,

    3)   take measures against forgery of certificates and other data electronically authenticated by those providers, in particular by guaranteeing protection of the devices and data used in the course of the provision of certification services,

    4)   obtain appropriate civil liability insurance for damages caused to receivers of certification services,

    5)   before entering into a contractual relationship with a person seeking a certificate, inform that person about the terms and conditions regarding the acquisition and use of the certificate, including any limitations on its use,

    6)   use systems to generate and store certificates in such a manner that only authorised persons can enter and change the data,

    7)   if the provider guarantees public access to the certificates, their publication shall require prior consent of the person to which the certificate has been issued,

    8)   make available to the receiver of certification services a complete list of secure signature-creation and verification devices, as well as technical requirements they should meet,

    9)   guarantee, in cases where the certification-service-provider generates signature-creation data, confidentiality during the process of generating them, and not store or copy such data or other data which would be used for their retrieval, and disclose them only to the person who will use them to create an electronic signature,

    10) guarantee, in cases where the certification-service-provider generates signature-creation data, that the likelihood that they will appear only one time is close to certainty,

    11) publish the data needed for verification, which may be done electronically, of the authenticity and validity of certificates and other data subject to electronic authentication by that provider and ensure access without payment to these data to receivers of certification services.

2. The qualified provider of certification services which consist in time- stamping is under an obligation to meet the requirements under paragraph 1 subparagraphs 3, 4 and 8, and to use the systems of time- stamping, making and storing certification attestations in a manner allowing only the authorised persons to feed in and change the relevant data, and also to ensure that the time they define is the time when the electronic authentication was made, and that these systems

impede the stamping with a time different from the one when the timestamping service was performed.

3. The certification-service-provider shall:

   1) have full capacity to enter into legal transactions,

   2) not be validly sentenced for an offence against the reliability of documents, economic relations, money circulation, trading in securities, for a fiscal offence or for offences under chapter VIII of this Act,

   3) have the necessary knowledge and skills with regard to the technology of producing certificates and performing other services related with electronic signature.

4. The Council of Ministers may issue a regulation defining in detail the technical specifications and organisational requirements, including the requirements pertaining to the physical security of the rooms where information under Article 12 paragraph 1 is stored, the qualified certification-service-provider shall meet. The relevant regulation shall allow for the sphere of application of the certificates he/she issues, for the requirement of their security and for the need to protect the interests of persons for whom certification service is intended.

5. The appropriate minister in charge of financial institutions shall, in consultation with the appropriate minister in charge of economy and having sought an opinion of the Polish Chamber of Insurance, issue a regulation explaining in detail the way and conditions how to meet the obligation to obtain insurance under paragraph 1 subparagraph 4. The regulation shall explain in particular the date of the inception of the obligation to conclude an insurance contract and the minimum guarantee sums, allowing for the need to guarantee the fulfilment of the obligation to conclude an insurance contract.

Article 11

1. Certification service receivers shall not hold the certification-service-provider responsible, apart from paragraphs 2 and 3, for any losses arising from his/her failure to meet his/her obligations or from the negligent fulfilment of his/her obligations regarding the services performed unless the failure to meet or the negligent fulfilment of these obligations is due to circumstances for which the certification-service- provider is not responsible and which he/she could not prevent, his/her due diligence notwithstanding.

2. Certification service receivers shall not hold the certification-service-provider responsible for the losses arising from the use of the certificate outside the scope provided for in the certification policy which was determined in the certificate. Particularly he/she will not be held responsible for the losses arising from the exceeding of the greatest boundary value of the relevant transaction, provided that value was indicated in the certificate.

3. Certification service receivers shall not hold the certification-service-provider responsible for the losses arising from the falsity of the data revealed in the certificate at the request of the person to have put his/her electronic signature.

4. Certification service receivers shall hold the certification-service-provider who underwrote the certificate pursuant to Article 4 paragraph 4 responsible for all the losses arising from the use of this certificate unless the loss arises from the use of this certificate outside the scope provided for in the certification policy which was determined in the certificate.

Art. 12

1. Information related to the providing of certification services, the unauthorised disclosure of which might cause the certification-service- provider or the certification service receiver to sustain a loss, and especially the data which serve to make certification authentications, is kept secret. Information about violations of this Act by the certification-service-provider shall not be kept secret.

2. The following persons shall be obliged to keep secret the information under paragraph 1:

    1) those representing the certification-service-provider,

    2) those having an employment, contract or another legal relationship of a similar character with the certification-service-provider,

    3) those having an employment, contract or another legal relationship of a similar character with providers of services for the certification-service-provider,

    4) people and organs who became in the secret under the procedure established under paragraph 3.

3. The persons referred to under paragraph 2 shall be obliged to give information referred to under paragraph 1, with the exception of the data which serve to make certification authentications, exclusively on demand of:

    1) the court or prosecutor--in connection with the action pending,

    2) the appropriate minister in charge of economy--in connection with control he/she exerts under chapter VII over the performance of certification-service-providers,

    3) other state organs authorized under separate acts- in connection with action pending in cases regarding the performance of certification-service-providers,

4. The duty to keep a secret under paragraph 1, subject to the provisions of paragraph 5, is valid for ten years from the end of the legal relationship under paragraph 2.

5. The duty to keep secret the data which serve to make certification authentications shall be for perpetuity.

Article 13

1. Subject to the provisions of paragraph 5 and of Article 10 paragraph 1 subparagraph 9, the certification-service-provider shall store in an archive those documents and data in an electronic form which are directly related with certification services performed in a manner which shall ensure the security of the documents and data stored.

2. In case of qualified certification-service-providers the duty to store documents and data under paragraph 1 shall be valid for 20 years since a given document or data was completed.

3. In case a given qualified certification-service-provider discontinues his activities, the documents and data under paragraph 1 shall be stored by the appropriate minister in charge of economy or by the person he/she shall indicate. For the maintenance of documents and data under paragraph 1 the appropriate minister in charge of economy shall collect charge, which will not exceed, however, the Polish złoty equivalent of 1 euro for each issued certificate whose file is liable to storage, which shall be calculated according to the average rate determined by the National Bank of Poland and going on the day the qualified certification-service-provider discontinues his activities. The charge shall be appropriated for the financing of the acts referred to in the first sentence.

4. The appropriate minister in charge of economy shall issue a regulation

establishing the procedure and the amount of charge referred to in paragraph 3, allowing for the number and the anticipated costs of the storage of the documents and data referred to in paragraph 1

5. The certification-service-provider shall destroy the data which serve to make a certification authentication as soon as the certification attestation shall be annulled or the validity of the certification attestation used for the verification of these authentications shall expire.

Chapter IV

Provision of Certification Services

Article 14

1. The certification-service-provider shall issue a certificate on a contract basis.

2. Prior to the conclusion of a contract referred to in paragraph 1, the certification-service-provider shall in a lucid manner define in writing or in an electronic form the detailed conditions of the use of that certificate, including the way complaints shall be examined and disputes settled, particularly of the important conditions regarding:

   1) the scope of and limits to the use of such certificate,

   2) the legal consequences of putting electronic signatures verified with the use of this certificate,

3)   information about the system of voluntary registration of qualified providers and about their importance.

3.   In case of certificates which shall not be qualified certificates, information referred to in paragraph 2 shall also point out that the electronic signature verified with the use of this certificate shall not produce legal consequences equivalent to the sign manual.

4.   The certification-service-provider shall give anyone who shall request it the significant elements of information referred to in paragraph 2.

5.   The certification-service-provider shall be obliged to acquire a written acknowledgement of his/her having become familiar with the information referred to in paragraph 2, prior to the conclusion of a given contract.

6.   The certification-service-provider may, subject to the provisions of Article 10 paragraph 1 subparagraph 2, use the notary-established identity of the certification service receivers if the relevant certification policy provides for it.

7.   When issuing qualified certificates, the certification-service-provider shall adopt such procedures of issuing them, which shall let him/her get the applicant's written consent to his/her utilising the data used to verify the applicant's electronic signature, which are revealed in the certificate issued.

Article 15

The certification service receiver is obliged to store the signature-creation data in a manner ensuring their protection against their unauthorised use in the validity period of the certificate used for verifying these signatures.

Article 16

1.   The contract for the provision of certification services shall be made in writing under pain of invalidity.

2.   Invalidity of contract for the provision of certification services shall not imply invalidity of the certificate with the proviso that its issuance met the requirements described in Article 14 paragraphs 2 and 5, and that consent referred to in Article 14 paragraph 7 has been given.

Article 17

1.   The qualified certification-service-provider is obliged to define a certification policy. The certification policy comprises in particular:

1)   the scope of its adoption,

2)   the explanation of the way of creating and transmitting the electronic data the qualified certification-service-provider shall attest,

3) maximum validity of the certificates,

4) the way of identifying and authenticating the persons to whom certificates are issued as well as the certification-service-provider,

5) the methods and procedure of producing and making available certificates, lists of revoked and blocked certificates and other electronically attested data,

6) the description of the electronic record of the structure of the data revealed in the certificates and other electronically attested data,

7) the manner of managing the documents relating to the provision of certification services.

2. In consultation with the President of the National Bank of Poland, the Council of Ministers shall issue a regulation which shall describe the basic organisational and technical requirements applying to certification policies with regard to qualified certificates, which shall take into account the scope of these certificates' application, the periods of their validity, the need to ensure joint action of different devices to put and verify electronic signatures, the need to ensure security of legal transactions and to meet the relevant European Union standards.

Article 18

1. The secure-signature-creation device should at least:

1) make impossible the obtainment of signature-creation data or certification attestation,

2) not change the data which are to be signed or attested electronically and make it possible for the person to put an electronic signature to produce these data before he/she shall put his/her electronic signature,

3) guarantee that the warning that the continuing of the operation shall be tantamount to putting the electronic signature shall precede the putting of signature,

4) ensure an easy recognition of changes in the signature-creation device or of the certification authentication with security implications.

2. The secure-signature-verification device shall fulfil the following requirements:

1) the data used to verify the electronic signature shall correspond to the data revealed to the signature verifier,

2) the electronic signature shall be verified reliably, and the verification result pleaded correctly,

3) the verifier can beyond a doubt establish the contents to which the electronic signature relates,

4) the authenticity and validity of the certificates and other data electronically attested shall be verified reliably,

5) the result of the verification of the identity of the person putting an electronic signature shall be pleaded in a correct and persuasive manner,

6) the use of a pseudonym shall be indicated explicitly,

7) changes in the signature-verification device with security implications, shall be indicated.

3. The Council of Ministers shall issue a regulation which shall lay down detailed technical specifications to be followed by secure signature-verification devices and which shall take care of the need to ensure inviolability and confidentiality of the electronically signed data.

4. The compliance of the devices referred to in paragraphs 1 and 2 with the requirements of this Act shall be verified in pursuance of separate provisions.

5. State protection services shall, as understood by the provisions on protection of secret information, assess the usefulness of the devices referred to in 1 and 2 for the protection of secret information, and shall issue the relevant certificates of safety.

Article 19

1. For the transactions referred to in Article 18 paragraphs 4 and 5 costs shall be charged.

2. The costs referred to in paragraph 1 shall be in compliance with the provisions of the Act on protection of secret information of 22nd January 1999 (Dz. U., No. 11, item 95, from the year 2000--No. 12, item 136 and No. 39, item 462; from the year 2001--No. 22, item 247; No. 27, item 298 and No. 56, item 580).

Article 20

1. The qualified certificate shall contain as a minimum such data as:

   1) the certificate number,

   2) an indication that the certificate has been issued as a qualified certificate to be used in accordance with a definite certification policy,

   3) a designation of the certification-service-provider and of the state where he/she is established, his/her number in the register of certification-service-providers,

   4) the name of the signatory or pseudonym which must be indicated as such,

   5) signature-verification-data,

   6) an indication of the beginning and the end of the validity of the certificate,

   7) an electronic authentication by the certification-service-provider concerned,

   8) limitations of the validity of the certificate if provided for in the certification policy,

9) the greatest boundary value of the transaction where the certificate may be used if provided for in the certification policy or in the contract referred to in Article 14 paragraph 1.

2. At the request of the applicant, when issuing a qualified certificate, the certification-service-provider is obliged to include in this certificate other data than those referred to in paragraph 1, and particularly the indication whether the applicant acts-

   1) on his/her own behalf or

   2) on behalf of another natural or legal person or organisational unit with no legal entity or

   3) as a member of an organ or an organ of a natural person or organisational unit with no legal entity or

   4) as an official authority agency.

3. By issuing a qualified certificate, the certification-service-provider shall attest to the truthfulness of the data referred to in paragraph 2, and shall notify the persons referred to in paragraph 2 subparagraphs 2-4 about the certificate contents, and inform them of the possibility for revocation of the certificate at their request.

Chapter V

Validity of Certificates

Article 21

1. The certificate is valid for the period indicated therein.

2. The certification-service-provider shall revoke a qualified certificate before the expiration of its validity if:

   1) the certificate was issued on the grounds of false or obsolete data as referred to in Article 20 paragraph 1 subparagraph 4 and paragraph 2,

   2) he/she did not fulfil the statutory obligations,

   3) the person to have put an electronic signature to be verified on the basis of this certificate did not fulfil the obligations referred to in Article 15,

   4) the certification-service-provider ceases operations and his/her rights and duties are not taken over by another qualified certification-service-provider,

   5) the signatory or the third party indicated in the certificate so requests,

   6) the appropriate minister for economy so requests,

   7) the signatory lost the capacity to enter into legal transaction.

3. The revocation of the certificate pursuant to paragraph 2 subparagraph 2 shall not exclude certification-service-provider's liability for the damage inflicted on the signatory.

4. In case there are grounds for revoking the qualified certificate, the certification-service-provider shall suspend the certificate and take immediate measures to clear the justified doubts.

5. The suspension of the qualified certificate shall not last longer than seven days.

6. Upon lapse of the period referred to in paragraph 5, in case it is impossible to clear doubts, the certification-service-provider shall revoke the qualified certificate immediately.

7. The suspended certificate may next be revoked or its suspension reversed.

8. Once revoked, the certificate cannot be next recognised as valid.

9. The appropriate minister for economy shall file a request referred to in paragraph 2 subparagraph 6 on the grounds specified in paragraph 2 subparagraphs 1-4 and 7.

10. The certificate-service-provider shall notify the person putting an electronic signature to be verified on its grounds of the revocation or suspension of his/her certificate forthwith.

11. Retroactive suspensions or retroactive revocations shall not be permitted.

Article 22

1. The certificate-service-provider shall publish a list of suspended and revoked certificates.

2. The information about the suspension or revocation of a given certificate shall be on the list of suspended and revoked certificates to be published before the expiration of the certificate's validity and on the first list circulated thereafter.

3. The list of suspended and revoked certificates shall include in particular:

    1) the list's consecutive number and an indication that the list is published in conformity with a definite certification policy and that it applies to certificates issued in conformity with this policy,

    2) the date, including the exact time when the list is published--with the accuracy stipulated by the certification policy,

    3) the date of the envisaged circulation of another list,

    4) a depiction of the certification-service-provider who publishes the list and the state where he/she is established, his/her number in the register of qualified certification-service-providers,

    5) the number of every suspended or revoked certificate and an indication whether it was suspended or revoked,

    6) the date and the time how long the specific certificate shall be suspended or revoked--with the accuracy stipulated by the certification policy,

    7) a certification authentication by the certification-service-provider who publishes the list.

4. The certification-service-provider shall release information about the suspension or revocation of a given certificate on the list referred to in paragraph 1, in conformity with a definite certification policy, no later however than within an hour from the revocation or suspension of the certificate.

5. The suspension and revocation of a certificate shall produce legal consequences from the moment referred to in paragraph 3 subparagraph 6, which shall not precede however the date, including the exact time of the publication of the previous list of suspended and revoked certificates.

Chapter VI

Granting Accreditation and Entering into Register of Qualified Certification-Service-Providers

Article 23

1. The qualified certification-service-provider or a person intending to take up such activity may apply for entry into the register of qualified certification-service-providers.

2. The provision of certification services in one's capacity as a qualified certification-service-provider requires that the applicant be entered into the register of qualified certification-service-providers and be issued a certification attestation which shall be used to verify certification authentications by this provider; his certification authentications shall be by the appropriate minister in charge of economy, subject to the provisions of paragraphs 4 and 5.

3. The appropriate minister in charge of economy shall publish, in an electronic form, the list of certification attestations referred to in paragraph 2 and the data to be used to verify the certification attestations by him/herself.

4. The appropriate minister in charge of economy may, under the procedures of the regulations on public orders, entrust a certification-service-provider with making and issuing such certification attestations as referred to in paragraph 2, with a publication of the list referred to in paragraph 3 and of the data to be used to verify the certification attestations issued.

5. At the request of the President of the National Bank of Poland, the appropriate minister in charge of economy shall authorise the National Bank of Poland or a person to have a dependency relationship with the Bank, which was indicated in the request, to provide the services referred to in paragraph 4. By virtue of the law the authorisation given to the dependent person expires with the end of his/her dependency relationship with the National Bank of Poland.

6. The persons referred to in paragraphs 4 and 5 shall fulfil the requirements of the Act regarding qualified certification-service-providers, pertaining to security, issuance, storage and revocation of certificates; these persons may not provide services involving the issuing of certificates.

7. In the cases referred to in paragraphs 4 and 5, when making an entry into the register, referred to in 1, the appropriate minister in charge of economy shall point

out to the certification-service-provider the name and the location of the person authorised to make and issue certification attestations.

Article 24

1. Entry into the register of qualified certification-service-providers shall be made at the request of the person intending to or providing certification services.

2. request for an entry into the register of qualified certification-service-providers shall contain:

    1) the forename and surname or the name (company name) of the applicant,

    2) definition of the certification policy according to which qualified certificates are to be produced or other services relating to electronic signature provided,

    3) the applicant's abode or location and address,

    4) a current excerpt from the registers of entrepreneurs and insolvent debtors,

    5) the forenames and surnames of the persons referred to in Article 10 paragraph 3, the applicant employs or intends to employ,

    6) information about the qualifications and professional experience, and also a certificate stating that the persons referred to in Article 10 paragraph 3 have no criminal record,

    7) an indication of technical and organisational feasibility of performing acts related to the provision of certification services,

    8) an indication of the way how to prevent the revealing of information the use of which might violate the interest of the receivers of certification services,

    9) documents outlining the financial standing, the organisational plan and financial forecast regarding the applicant,

    10) the payment receipt for the considering of an application to be entered in the register of qualified certification-service-providers,

    11) electronic-authentication-verification-data produced by the person within the framework of the certification services provided by him/her,

    12) the applicant's taxpayer's identification number,

    13) the applicant's number in the REGON Register of Units of the National Economy.

3. The provisions of paragraph 2 subparagraphs 4, 9 and 13 shall not apply to the application submitted by an official authority or the National Bank of Poland.

4. In case of any defects in the application, the appropriate minister in charge of economy shall summon the applicant to correct a defect, fixing a time limit no shorter than seven days.

5. At the applicant's substantiated request, the time limit referred to in paragraph 4 may be extended.

6. Non-correction of a defect in the application in the time limit fixed shall cause a dismissal of the application.

7. For the considering of an application to be entered in the register of qualified certification-service-providers a fee shall be charged. Once paid, the fee shall not be refundable.

8. The appropriate minister in charge of economy shall issue a regulation deciding on:

   1) a specimen and the detailed scope of the application, allowing for a possibility of an electronic processing of the data produced on printed sheets,

   2) a detailed procedure of making and issuing a certification attestation, also by the persons authorised on the grounds of Article 23 paragraph 4 or 5, taking into consideration the need to ensure confidentiality of the making and issuing of a certification attestation,

   3) the amount due for the considering of the application to be entered in the register of qualified certification-service-providers, taking into account the reasonable expenses borne in connection with the registration proceedings and the holding of records.

Article 25

1. Upon carrying out an inspection, within a time frame of two months since the submission of the request which fulfilled the requirements referred to in Article 24 paragraph 2, the appropriate minister in charge of economy shall enter the applicant in the register of qualified certification-service-providers or make a decision refusing to enter the applicant in the register of qualified certification-service-providers.

2. The entry into the register, referred to in paragraph 1, of the certification-service-provider acknowledges that he/she is an institution with sufficient essential and technical potential and fulfils the requirements described in this Act.

3. The decision to enter the applicant in the register should, in particular, give the name of the certification policy within the framework of which a given person may issue qualified certificates or provide other services related to electronic signature.

4. The appropriate minister in charge of economy shall deny entry in the register referred to in paragraph 1, provided-

   1) the application and the documents enclosed do not satisfy the conditions set out by this Act,

   2) provisions of the applicant's organisational documents can threaten the security or in some other way violate the interest of the receivers of certification services,

   3) the applicant has been entered into the register of insolvent debtors,

4)   the technical and organisational feasibility of the performing of acts related to the provision of certificate services indicated in the application do not satisfy the conditions set out on the grounds of Article 10 paragraph 4, Article 17 paragraph 2 and Article 18 paragraph 3,

5)   the persons referred to in Article 24 paragraph 2 subparagraph 5 do not fulfil the requirements referred to in Article 10 paragraph 3.

Article 26

1.   Entry into the register of qualified certification-service-providers shall comprise:

   1)   the forename and surname or the name (company name) of the respective qualified certification-service-provider,

   2)   the way the respective qualified certification-service-provider is represented, the entry number in the register of entrepreneurs and the identification of the court that holds this register,

   3)   the forenames and surnames of the persons representing the respective qualified certification-service-provider,

   4)   the name of the certification policy within the framework of which a given person may issue qualified certificates or provide other services related with electronic signature,

   5)   information on the insurance sum and terms of the contract referred to in Article 10 paragraph 1 subparagraph 4, and the name of the respective insurance agency,

   6)   the date of the entry into the register or of the decision on the removal of the given entry.

2.   The person entered into the register of qualified certification-service-providers is obliged, within a time frame of 30 days from the day the decision to enter him/her into the register was delivered to him/her, to supply a proof of the conclusion of a contract referred to in Article 10 paragraph 1 subparagraph 4, and to provide information referred to in paragraph 1 subparagraph 5.

3.   As soon as the appropriate minister in charge of economy shall obtain information referred to in paragraph 1 subparagraph 5, he/she shall add it to the entry into the register of qualified certification-service-providers.

4.   If the person entered into the register of qualified certification-service-providers does not meet the obligation referred to in paragraph 2 in time, the appropriate minister in charge of economy shall decide on the removal of his/her entry from the register of qualified certification-service-providers.

5.   Right upon the entry into the register of qualified certification-service-providers, no earlier however than on the day when the certification-service-provider concerned meets his/her obligation referred to in paragraph 2, the appropriate minister in charge of economy shall issue the certification attestation referred to in Article 23 paragraph 2.

Article 27

1. The register of qualified certification-service-providers shell be kept by the appropriate minister in charge of economy.

2. The register referred to in paragraph 1 and certification attestations referred to in Article 23 paragraph 2 are open and available to the public, the electronic form included.

3. The appropriate minister in charge of economy shall issue a regulation deciding on the way how the register of qualified certification-service-providers shell be kept, on the specimen register and detailed procedure to be adopted in registration proceedings, allowing for the need to ensure the third party's access to the register and the possibility for entering all the data obtained in the course of registration proceedings with regard to qualified certification-service-providers, including the information on the liquidation or bankruptcy of a given certification-service-provider.

Article 28

1. The qualified certification-service-provider is obliged to notify the appropriate minister in charge of economy of every change in the data produced in his/her application referred to in Article 24 paragraph 2 forthwith, no later than within a time frame of seven days since the change of the facts of the case or of the regulatory environment.

2. The person referred to in paragraph 1 is obliged without delay to notify the appropriate minister in charge of economy of the date when he/she plans to cease providing certification services, no later however than three months ahead of the planned date of the cessation of his/her operations.

Article 29

1. In case of the institution of liquidation proceedings concerning a qualified certification-service-provider, the appropriate minister in charge of economy shall decide on the removal of this person's entry from the register of qualified certification-service-providers.

2. In case of the declaration of a qualified certification-service-provider's bankruptcy, the removal of this person's entry from the register of qualified certification-service-providers shall take place by virtue of the law.

3. If separate provisions do not provide for the liquidation of a given certification-service-provider, the appropriate minister in charge of economy shall decide on the removal of this person's entry from the register of qualified certification-service-providers in case this provider ceases operations.

4. The duty to notify the appropriate minister in charge of economy of the declaration of bankruptcy or of the closing of a given liquidation shall rest with the official receiver or liquidator.

5.   In case the bankruptcy petition is dismissed for reasons referred to in Article 13 of the regulation by the President of the Republic, dated 24th October 1934, "Bankruptcy Act" (Dz. U., No. 118, 1991, item 512; No. 1, 1994, item 1; No. 85, 1995, item 426; No. 6, 1996, item 43; No. 43, 1996, item 189; No. 106, 1996, item 496; No. 149, 1996, item 703; No. 28, 1997, item 153; No. 54, 1997, item 349; No. 117, 1997, item 751; No. 121, 1997, item 770; No. 140, 1997, item 940; No. 117, 1998, item 756; No. 26, 2000, item 306; No. 84, 2000, item 948; No. 94, 2000, item 1037; No. 114, 2000, item 1193; No. 3, 2001, item 18) paragraph 2 shall apply respectively. The duty to notify the appropriate minister in charge of economy shall rest with members of the organ of the juridical person, general partners in commercial partnerships or with partners in registered partnerships.

Chapter VII

Supervision over Performance of Certification-Service-Providers

Article 30

1.   The appropriate minister in charge of economy shall supervise compliance with this Act, guaranteeing protection of the interests of the receivers of certification services.

2.   The appropriate minister in charge of economy shall carry out the task referred to in paragraph 1 particularly through:

   1)   keeping a register of qualified certification-service-providers,

   2)   issuing and revoking certification attestations referred to in Article 23 paragraph 2,

   3)   control over the performance of certification-service-providers from the point of view of their performance's compliance with this Act,

   4)   imposing penalties this Act provides for.

3.   The appropriate minister in charge of economy may entrust the keeping of the register of qualified certification-service-providers to the persons referred to in Article 23 paragraphs 4 and 5, who fulfil this Act's requirements with regard to qualified certification-service-providers in the areas of security, the issuance, storage and revocation of certificates and who do not provide certification services consisting in the issuance of certificates.

Article 31

1.   The appropriate minister in charge of economy shall decide on the removal of an entry from the register of qualified certification-service-providers if a given certification-service-provider-

   1)   conducts business contrary to this Act's regulations, to the prejudice of the interests of the receivers of certification services or

2) requests to have his/her entry into the register cancelled or

3) plans to cease operations and notifies the appropriate minister in charge of economy of his/her decision pursuant to Article 28 paragraph 2 or

4) refuses to submit him/herself to inspection referred to in Article 38.

2. In case referred to in paragraph 1 subparagraph 1, the appropriate minister in charge of economy may, instead of taking a decision, summon a given certification-service-provider to correct the faults pointed out to him/her within a definite period of time and to make his/her operations compatible with the provisions of this Act.

3. When taking a decision referred to in paragraph 1, the appropriate minister in charge of economy may revoke the certification attestation referred to in Article 23 paragraph 2 and place it on the list of revoked certification attestations originally issued to qualified certification-service-providers. Regulations concerning the list of revoked certificates referred to in Article 22 shall apply accordingly.

4. The revocation of a certificate attestation referred to in Article 23 paragraph 2, used to verify the certification authentication by qualified certification-service-providers, annuls the relevant authentications unless it has been proved that a given authentication was made prior to the revocation of the certificate attestation concerned.

5. The revocation of the electronic authentication referred to in paragraph 4, used to verify the validity of certifications issued by the qualified certification-service-provider, shall annul these certificates.

6. In case the certification authentication, used to verify the validity of the timestamping service supplied by the qualified certification-service-provider, referred to paragraph 4, has been annulled, Article 7 paragraphs 2 and 3 shall not apply.

Article 32

1. When issuing a summons referred to in Article 31 paragraph 2, the appropriate minister in charge of economy may impose on the certification-service-provider a cash penalty of up to 50,000 złoty if the irregularities revealed were particularly flagrant.

2. In case the irregularities were not corrected within a fixed time limit, the appropriate minister in charge of economy may impose on the certification-service-provider concerned a cash penalty of up to 50,000 złoty.

3. When determining the amount of cash penalties referred to in paragraphs 1 and 2, the appropriate minister in charge of economy is obliged to take into consideration the kind and importance of the irregularities revealed.

4. The cash penalty shall be liable to enforcement under enforcement proceedings taken in the administration.

Article 33

1. In case an electronic authentication was made in flagrant violation of this Act, the decision on the removal of a given entry from the register of qualified certification-service-providers shall be enforceable forthwith.

2. In the case referred to in paragraph 1, Article 40 of The Supreme Administrative Court Act of 11th May 1995 (Dz. U., No. 74, item 368 and No. 104, 1995, item 515; No. 75, 1997, item 471; No. 106, 1997, item 679; No. 114, 1997, item 739; No. 144, 1997, item 971; No. 162, 1998, item 1126; No. 75, 1999, item 853; No. 2, 2000, item 5; No. 48, 2000, item 552; No. 60, 2000, item 704; No. 91, 2000, item 1008; No. 49, 2001, item 508f) shall not apply.

Article 34

From the day the decision on the removal of a given entry from the register of qualified certification-service-providers, the certification-service-provider concerned may not conclude a contract of provision of certification services regarding the certification policy this decision concerns.

Article 35

1. Supervision shall be carried out by employees of an organisational division of a ministry that attends to the appropriate minister in charge of economy, hereinafter referred to as "supervisors," on the basis of their respective identity card and the individual authorisation which shall define the certification-service-provider coming under supervision, the scope of supervision and the legal grounds for supervision.

2. Individual authorisations to carry out supervision shall be given by the appropriate minister in charge of economy or by the director of the organisational division of a ministry that attends to the appropriate minister in charge of economy the minister in charge of economy has authorised to give such authorisations.

3. Supervision referred to in paragraph 1 may be carried out also by the minister in charge of economy-authorised supervisors who work for the person referred to in Article 23 paragraph 5 or for the certifying organ within the meaning of the provisions referred to in Article 18 paragraph 4.

4. In case supervision is carried out under authorisation of the appropriate minister in charge of economy, the person or the certifying organ referred to in paragraph 3 deserves a fee for the supervision carried out.

5. The minister in charge of economy shall issue a regulation establishing the principles of remuneration for carrying out supervision on authorisation from the minister, taking into consideration the scope and kind of supervision and its reasonable expenses.

Article 36

The minister in charge of economy shall carry out supervision-

1) ex officio,

2) on demand of the prosecutor or court, or other state organs authorised to make such demand on the basis of the relevant laws in connection with the proceedings they have instituted with regard to the operations of certification-service-providers.

Article 37

The aim of supervision is to establish whether the operations of a given certification-service-provider is in compliance with this Act. The scope of supervision is outlined by the authorisation referred to in Article 35 paragraph 1 or paragraph 3.

Article 38

In order to carry out supervision properly-

1) the managers of certification-service-providers shall be obliged, on the supervisor's demand, to submit all documents and evidence indispensable to the arrangement for and the carrying out of supervision--subject to the regulations on information protected by law,

2) supervisors have a right to-

   (a) enter the buildings and premises of the certification-service-providers supervised,

   (b) inspect documents and other sources of information except for the data used to put an electronic signature or to make authentication which can serve to reconstruct these data, directly related with the operations supervised, and to secure documents and other evidence subject to the regulations on information protected by law,

   (c) inspect the buildings, other constituents of property and transactions linked with the provision of certification services,

   (d) demand that all employees of the certification-certificate-providers furnish an oral or written explanation,

   (e) receive expert assistance.

Article 39

To supervisory proceedings shall apply provisions of Articles 31, 32, 35-41, 53-55, 57 and 59 of the Act of 23rd December 1994 on the Supreme Chamber of Control (Dz. U., No. 13, 1995, item 59; No. 64, 1996, item 315; No. 89, 1996, item 402; No. 28, 1997, item 153; No. 79, 1997, item 484; No. 96, 1997, item 589; No. 121, 1997, item 770; No. 133, 1997, item 883;

No. 148, 1998, item 966; No. 155, 1998, item 1016; No. 162, 1998, items 1116 and 1126; No. 60, 2000, item 704) respectively, on condition that whenever this Act makes a reference to-

1)   the Supreme Chamber of Control, this shall be construed as meaning a ministry attending to the appropriate minister in charge of economy,

2)   the President of the Supreme Chamber of Control, this shall be construed as meaning the appropriate minister in charge of economy,

3)   the director of the appropriate supervisory agency, this shall be construed as meaning the director of the appropriate organisational division of a ministry that attends to the appropriate minister in charge of economy, referred to in Article 35 paragraph 1,

4)   a supervisor, this shall be construed as meaning the supervisor referred to in Article 35 paragraph 1 or paragraph 3.

Article 40

Upon becoming familiar with the record, reservations and explanations furnished by the certification-service-provider supervised, the appropriate minister in charge of economy shall notify this provider of the supervision results and in case any irregularities were revealed, shall fix a time limit for their emendation, this limit being however not lower than 14 days.

Article 41

1.   The supervisor is obliged to keep secret the information he/she obtained in connection with the performance of his/her on-duty acts.

2.   The obligation to preserve a secret shall last also after the termination of employment.

Article 42

The appropriate minister in charge of economy shall consider complaints against certification-service-providers. Doing this, he/she shall adhere to the rules of the Code of Administrative Procedure.

Article 43

1.   Employees of an organisational division of a ministry that attends to the appropriate minister in charge of economy, who execute tasks specified in statutory law, shall not be engaged in any economic activity, be partners or shareholders or carry out the duties of a representative or member of the supervisory board or the audit committee of the certification-service-provider,

establish employment, contract or any other legal relationship of a similar nature with the certification-service-provider.

2. The regulation of paragraph 1 does not contravene the regulations on limitation of running of a business by persons in government service.

Article 44

Employees of organisational divisions of a ministry that attends to the appropriate minister in charge of economy, who execute tasks specified in statutory law, and also persons performing acts specified in this Act on behalf of these divisions on the basis of contract or another legal relationship of a similar nature are obliged to keep secret the information obtained in connection with the performance of these acts.

Chapter VIII

Criminal Regulations

Article 45

Who provides certification services in his/her capacity as qualified certification-service-provider without having first concluded a contract for civil liability insurance against damages done to the receivers of this service is liable to a fine of up to 1,000,000 złoty.

Article 46

The certification-service-provider who, when providing certification services, in defiance of the obligation specified in statutory law, does not inform the person applying for a certificate about the conditions of obtaining and using the certificate, is liable to a fine of up to 30,000 złoty.

Article 47

Who puts a secure electronic signature by means of data that are linked to another person is liable to a fine or penalty of up to three years' imprisonment or to both.

Article 48

Who, when providing certification services, copies or stores data which serve to put a secure electronic signature or electronic authentication, or other data which might serve their reconstruction is liable to a fine or penalty of up to three years' imprisonment or to both.

Article 49

1. Who, when providing certification services, issues a certificate revealing fictitious data, referred to in Article 20 paragraph 1, is liable to a fine or penalty of up to three years' imprisonment or to both.

2. The person who on behalf of the certification-service-provider enables the issue of the certificate referred to in paragraph 1 is liable to the same penalty.

3. The person who makes use of the certificate referred to in paragraph 1 is liable to the same penalty.

Article 50

Who, when providing certification services, in defiance of the obligation referred to in Article 21 paragraph 2 subparagraphs 5 and 6, desists from revocation of the certificate, is liable to a fine or penalty of up to three years' imprisonment or to both.

Article 51

Who, when providing a timestamping service in his/her capacity as qualified certification-service-provider, enables specification of time different from that when the service was actually provided and authenticates electronically the thus created data is liable to a fine or penalty of up to three years' imprisonment or to both.

Article 52

1. The person obliged to preserve a secret related to the provision of certification services who reveals or exploits secret information in contravention of conditions specified in statutory law is liable to a fine of up to 1,000,000 złoty or penalty of up to three years' imprisonment or to both.

2. If the perpetrator resorts to an act referred to in paragraph 1 in a capacity as a certification-service-provider or as a supervisor or for the purpose of gaining a financial or personal benefit, he/she is liable to a fine of up to 5,000,000 złoty or penalty of up to five years' imprisonment or to both.

Article 53

Who resorts to acts referred to in these regulations, acting on behalf or in the interest of another natural or legal person or organisational division with no legal personality, is liable to penalties specified in Articles 45-51.

Chapter IX

Changes in Provisions in Force, in Transitory and Final Provisions

Article 54

To the Act of 23rd April 1964 on the Civil Code (Dz. U., No. 16, item 93; from 1971--No. 27, item 252; from 1976--No. 19, item 122; from 1982--No. 11, item 81; No. 19, item 147; No. 30, item 210; from 1984--No. 45, item 242; from 1985--No. 22, item 99; from 1989--No. 3, item 11; from 1990--No. 34, item 198; No. 55, item 321; No. 79, item 464; from 1991--No. 107, item 464; No. 115, item 496; from 1993--No. 17, item 78; from 1994--No. 27, item 96; No. 85, item 388; No. 105, item 509; from 1995--No. 83, item 417; from 1996--No. 114, item 542; No. 139, item 646; No. 149, item 703; from 1997--No. 43, item 272; No. 115, item 741; No. 117, item 751; No. 157, item 1040; from 1998--No. 106, item 668; No. 117 item 758; from 1999-No. 52, item 532; from 2000-No. 22, item 271; No. 74, items 855 and 857; No. 114, item 1191; from 2001--No. 11, item 91; No. 71, item 733) introduced are the following amendments:

1)   Article 60 now reads:

"Article 60. Barring the exceptions provided for by statutory law the intention of a person performing an act in law may be expressed by any behaviour of that person which manifests that intention sufficiently, including the manifestation of that intention in an electronic form (declaration of intent)."

2)   Article 78 now reads:

"Article 78. Paragraph 1. For the observance of the written form of an act in law it is sufficient to append one's autograph signature to the document containing the declaration of intent. For the conclusion of the contract it shall suffice to exchange the documents each of which carries the declaration of intent of one of the parties and is signed by it.

Paragraph 2. The declaration of intent made in an electronic form and with a secure electronic signature verified with the aid of a valid qualified certificate affixed to it shall be equivalent to the written form."

Article 55

To the Act of 29th August 1997 on The Banking Law (Dz. U., No. 140, item 939; from 1998--No. 160, item 1063; No. 162, item 1118; from 1999--No. 11, item 95; No. 40, item 399; from 2000--No. 93, item 1027; No. 94, item 1037; No. 114, item 1191; No. 116, item 1216; No. 119, item 1252; No. 122, item 1316; from 2001--No. 8, item 64) introduced are the following amendments:

1)   to Article 6 paragraph 1 introduced is subparagraph 6a which reads:

"6a) provide certification services within the meaning of the provisions on electronic signature, exclusive of the issuance of qualified certificates used by banks when concluding transactions to which they are parties;"

2)   Article 7 paragraph 4 now reads:

"4.   Having sought an opinion of the President of the National Bank of Poland, the Council of Ministers shall issue a regulation establishing the rules of the producing, making accessible, storing and securing, also with the use of electronic signature, of the bank documents referred to in paragraph 2."

Article 56

To the Act of 4th September 1997 on the Branches of Government Administration (Dz. U., No. 82, 1999, item 928: No. 12, 2000, item 136; No. 43, 2000, item 489; No. 48, 2000, item 550; No. 62, 2000, item 718; No. 70, 2000, item 816; No. 73, 2000, item 852; No. 109, 2000, item 1158; No. 122, 2000, items 1314 and 1321; No. 3, 2001, item 18; No. 5, 2001, item 43f; No. 42, 2001, item 475; No. 63, 2001, item 634; No. 73, 2001, item 761), Article 9 paragraph 2, after subparagraph 4, introduced is subparagraph 5 which reads:

"5)   supervision over the provision of services related to electronic signature within the meaning of regulations on electronic signature."

Article 57

Until 31st December 2003, requests referred to in Article 24 paragraph 2, instead of an up-to-date extract from the register of entrepreneurs, may include an extract from the records of economic activity.

Article 58

1.   By 31st December 2002, banks and agencies of official authority shall have brought into line their activities regarding the provision of certification services and the use of electronic information systems related to the provision of these services with the requirements of this Act.

2.   Within a time frame of four years from the date this Act becomes effective, agencies of official authority shall make it possible for receivers of certification services to submit applications and requests and to perform other acts in an electronic form whenever the relevant legal provisions demand that these be submitted in a definite form or after a definite pattern.

3.   The appropriate minister in charge of economy, in agreement with the appropriate minister in charge of public service, shall issue a regulation laying down technical specifications and safety conditions regarding the making of printed forms and patterns, referred to in paragraph 2, available.

4.   Within a time frame of one year from the date this Act becomes effective, the appropriate minister in charge of public finances shall adjust the regulations concerning the payment of charges for acts of administration to the requirements of the conduct of legal transactions with the use of electronic signature.

Article 59

1. This Act shall come into force after the expiry of nine months from the date of its promulgation, with the exception of Article 4 points 3-6 and Article 11 paragraph 4 which shall come into force on the day the Republic of Poland becomes a member of the European Union.

2. The provision of Article 4 point 2 becomes vacated on the day the Republic of Poland becomes a member of the European Union.

PRESIDENT OF THE REPUBLIC OF POLAND

Slovakia

Electronic Signature Act

PART I

SECTION 1

Sphere of application

1   This Act regulates matters relating to the creation and use of electronic signatures, conduct of natural and legal persons using electronic signatures in electronic communication, trustworthiness and protection of electronic documents signed with electronic signatures.

2   Nothing in this Act shall affect the creation and use of an electronic signature with regard to classified information, which matter is regulated by other legislation (1).

3   Within any closed system, the creation and use of electronic signatures is regulated by this Act unless participants of such system vary by agreement.

SECTION 2

Definitions

For the purpose of this Act:

a   'document' means any finite non-empty sequence of characters;

b   'digital document' means a digitally encoded document;

c   'electronic document' means a digital document stored on a tangible medium, transmitted or processed by electrical, magnetic, optical or other means;

d   'signed electronic document' means an electronic document for which an electronic signature has been created provided that the electronic document is available along with the relevant electronic signature;

e 'private key' means cryptographic data used to create an electronic signature for an electronic document;

f 'public key' means data made available to a verifier to verify an electronic signature created with the private key corresponding to the relevant public key;

g 'electronic-signature creation device' means hardware or software, or a configuration thereof, which, based on his private key and an electronic document, is used by a signatory to create an electronic signature;

h 'secure electronic-signature creation device' means an electronic-signature creation device which meets the requirements laid down in this Act and is used to create advanced electronic signatures;

i 'electronic-signature verification device' means hardware or software, or a configuration thereof, which, based on a signed electronic document and the public key corresponding to the private key applied to create an electronic signature, is used by the verifier to verify an electronic signature;

j 'closed system' means a system which serves the purpose of its participants, is formed by agreement between them and is open exclusively to the participants of such system;

k 'certification service' includes, but is not limited to, the issuance of certificates, revocation of certificates, publication of certificate revocation lists, confirmation of the existence and validity of certificates, and provision of directory access to issued certificates for reference;

l 'accredited certification service' includes, but is not limited to, the issuance of qualified certificates, revocation of qualified certificates, publication of qualified certificate revocation lists, confirmation of the existence and validity of qualified certificates, directory access to issued qualified certificates for reference, and issuance and verification of time stamps;

m 'certification function' means the provision of certification services, receipt for processing of certificate issuance requests, record keeping, operation of necessary equipment, as well as, other functions necessary for the provision of certification services;

n 'certificate management' means the issuance, validation and revocation of certificates, maintenance of certificate archives, and related certification functions;

o 'electronic signature product' means hardware or software, or relevant components thereof, which are intended to be used by a certification service provider for certification functions or are intended to be used for the creation and verification of electronic signatures;

p 'certification service provider' means a natural or legal person who performs certification services;

q 'certification authority' means a certification service provider that manages certificates in accordance with paragraph (n);

r 'accredited certification authority' means a certification authority that provides accredited certification services pursuant to this Act and is accredited by the

National Security Bureau (2) (hereinafter referred to as "Bureau") to provide such services;

s   'registration authority' means a certification service provider that performs on behalf of a certification authority specific certification functions and acts as an intermediary providing certification authority services to certificate holders and applicants requesting the issuance of certificates;

t   'signatory' means a natural person who holds a private key and, using the private key, is capable of creating an electronic signature to be affixed to an electronic document;

u   'certificate issuer' means a certification authority or the Bureau;

v   'certificate holder' means

   i   a natural person to whom a certification authority has issued a certificate in accordance with this Act;

   ii   a certification authority;

   iii   the Bureau;

w   'electronic-signature verifier' means a natural or legal person who, using an electronic signature verification device, public key, signed electronic document and related electronic signature, is capable of verifying the validity of the electronic signature;

x   'secure time-stamp creation device' means hardware and software which meet the requirements laid down in this Act and are used, based on the time value, electronic document and private key intended for such purpose, to create a time stamp for the electronic document.

SECTION 3

Electronic signature

1   An electronic signature means data affixed to or logically associated with an electronic document, which shall meet the following requirements:

   a   they are incapable of being created without knowing the private key and electronic document;

   b   they are capable of being used, based on the data and the public key corresponding to the private key used to generate the data, to verify that an electronic document, which they are affixed to or logically associated with, is identical with the electronic document used to generate the data.

2   The technique of creating an electronic signature is such that a signatory, using his private key and electronic document, generates data that meet the requirements of subsection (1).

SECTION 4

Advanced electronic signature

1 An advanced electronic signature means an electronic signature that meets the requirements of section 3; and

   a   is created by the private key which is intended for the creation of an advanced electronic signature;

   b   is capable of being created solely with a secure electronic-signature creation device defined in section 2(h);

   c   the method of creation makes it possible to identify reliably the natural person who has created an advanced electronic signature;

   d   a qualified certificate is issued in support of the public key corresponding to the private key which is used to create an advanced electronic signature.

2 An advanced electronic signature is valid if

   a   there exists a qualified certificate containing the public key corresponding to the private key used to create an electronic signature;

   b   it can be demonstrated that the qualified certificate referred to in point (a) is valid at the time of the creation of such signature;

   c   an electronic document, which an advanced electronic signature is affixed to or logically associated with, is identical with the electronic document used for the creation of such signature, which fact is verified by the public key contained in the qualified certificate referred to in point (a).

3 The technique of creating an advanced electronic signature is such that a signatory, using a private key and electronic document, applies a secure signature creation device to generate data that meet the requirements of subsection (1).

4 The format of an advanced electronic signature and the method of creating an advanced electronic signature shall be prescribed by a binding regulation made by the Bureau.

5 The method of making publicly available the public key corresponding to the private key which is intended to be used by the Bureau to create its own advanced electronic signature shall be prescribed by a binding regulation made by the Bureau.

6 An advanced electronic signature of the Bureau is valid if an electronic document, which the advanced electronic signature is affixed to or logically associated with, is identical with the electronic document used for the creation of the signature, which fact is verified by using the public key of the Bureau made publicly available in accordance with subsection (5).

SECTION 5

Use of electronic signatures

1   If an electronic signature may be used in communication with public authorities, such electronic signature shall be an advanced electronic signature.

2   A verifier verifies an electronic signature, using a signature verification device, signed electronic document and the public key held by the claimed signatory.

3   For the purpose of verifying an electronic signature, the verifier may request the validation of the public key held by the claimant. To that end the verifier may use the public-key certificate of the signatory.

4   In verifying an advanced electronic signature, the verifier determines whether the claimed signatory is the subject named in the qualified public-key certificate which contains the public key used to decrypt the advanced electronic signature.

5   Specifics of the validity conditions of an advanced electronic signature, verification procedures and advanced electronic signature verification conditions shall be prescribed by a binding regulation made by the Bureau.

SECTION 6

Public-key certificate

1   A public-key certificate (hereinafter referred to as "certificate") means an electronic document whereby the certificate issuer affirms the public key in the certificate is related to the recipient of the certificate (hereinafter referred to as "certificate holder").

2   A certificate consists of the main part of the certificate and the electronic signature to be affixed to the main part of the certificate.

3   The main part of a certificate includes, but is not limited to,

    a   identity information on the certificate issuer;

    b   the certificate identification number;

    c   identity information on the certificate holder;

    d   the date and time of the start and expiration of certificate validity;

    e   the public key of a certificate holder;

    f   a public key algorithm identifier;

    g   a certificate signature algorithm identifier.

4   A certificate issuer creates the electronic signature to be affixed to the main part of the certificate with the certificate issuer's private key intended for such purpose.

5   A pseudonym may be used in support of certificate holder identity information in accordance with subsection (3)(c) only if the information obtained by the

certification authority from a certificate applicant uniquely identifies the certificate holder. The certification authority expressly indicates in the certificate that the subject identity information is a pseudonym.

6   A cross-certificate means a certificate issued by one certification authority to another certification authority in support of the public key of the other certification authority. In issuing a cross-certificate, one certification authority makes it possible to verify electronic signatures based on certificates issued and signed by another certification authority using the private key corresponding to the public key in the cross-certificate.

SECTION 7

Qualified certificate

1   A qualified certificate means a certificate of a natural person, a certificate of an accredited certification authority, a cross-certificate of an accredited certification authority or a certificate of the Bureau which meets the requirements imposed in accordance with subsections (2) to (5) and section 6.

2   A qualified certificate of a natural person is a certificate which meets the following requirements:

   a   it is issued to a natural person by an accredited certification authority;

   b   it contains an indication that it is a qualified certificate;

   c   it indicates any limitations on the scope of use of the certificate if such limitations are recognizable to third parties;

   d   to the main part of the certificate there is affixed the advanced electronic signature of an accredited certification authority created by the private key intended for that purpose.

3   A qualified certificate of an accredited certification authority is a certificate which meets the following requirements:

   a   it is issued to an accredited certification authority by the Bureau;

   b   it contains an indication that it is a qualified certificate;

   c   it indicates the purpose the certificate is intended for;

   d   to the main part of the certificate there is affixed the advanced electronic signature of the Bureau.

4   A cross-certificate of an accredited certification authority means a cross-certificate which meets the following requirements:

   a   it is issued to one accredited certification authority by another accredited certification authority;

   b   it contains an indication that it is a cross-certificate;

   c   to the main part of the certificate there is affixed the advanced electronic signature of an accredited certification authority.

5   A qualified certificate of the Bureau means a certificate which meets the requirements laid down in subsection (3)(b) to (d) and is issued in support of the Bureau's own public key.

6   The format and contents of a qualified certificate, as well as, the specifics of qualified-certificate management shall be prescribed by a binding regulation made by the Bureau.

7   A qualified certificate is valid throughout the period in respect of which the qualified certificate is verified if

   a   that period lies between the start and expiration dates of certificate validity;

   b   the advanced electronic signature affixed to the main part of the certificate is valid;

   c   the certificate has not been revoked within such period.

SECTION 8

Certificate revocation list

1   A certificate revocation list means an electronic document generated by the certificate issuer managing certificates so as to publicize the certificates that have been terminated before the expiration date and time of their validity.

2   A certificate revocation list consists of the main part of the certificate revocation list and the electronic signature affixed to the main part.

3   The main part of a certification revocation list is an electronic document which includes, but is not limited to,

   a   identity information on the certificate issuer managing certificates;

   b   the date and time of the publication of a certificate revocation list;

   c   the date and time of the next update of a certificate revocation list;

   d   the date and time, and identification numbers of revoked certificates.

4   A certificate issuer managing certificates creates the electronic signature to be affixed to the main part of a certification revocation list with the private key intended for such purpose.

5   A qualified-certificate revocation list means a certificate revocation list generated by a qualified-certificate issuer managing certificates so as to publicize the qualified certificates that have been terminated before the expiration date and time of their validity. A qualified certificate revocation list shall meet the requirements laid down in subsections (1) to (4); and

   a   it is published by an accredited certification authority or the Bureau;

   b   the electronic signature affixed to the main part of the certification revocation list has been created with the private key intended for that purpose;

c   an accredited certification authority or the Bureau has issued a certificate in support of the public key corresponding to the private key in accordance with point (b).

6   The format, frequency and method of publishing a qualified-certificate revocation list shall be prescribed by a binding regulation made by the Bureau.

SECTION 9

Time stamp

1   A time stamp means data affixed to or logically associated with an electronic document, which shall meet the following requirements:

a   they are incapable of being created without knowing the private key intended for such purpose, and electronic document;

b   they are capable of being used, based on the public key corresponding to the private key used to generate the data, to verify that the electronic document, which they are affixed to or logically associated with, is identical with the electronic document used for the creation of the data;

c   they are created by an accredited certification authority using the private key intended for such purpose;

d   they are capable of being created solely by means of a secure time-stamp creation device in accordance with section 2(x). Specific conditions regarding such device shall be prescribed by a binding regulation made by the Bureau;

e   an accredited certification authority has issued a qualified certificate in support of the public key corresponding to the private key used to generate such data;

f   they make it possible to determine unambiguously the date and time when they were generated.

2   The format of a time stamp, method of generating a time stamp, requirements for the source of the time value to be used in a time stamp, as well as, maintenance of time-stamp documentation shall be prescribed by a binding regulation made by the Bureau.

SECTION 10

The Bureau

1   The Bureau is the central public administration body in charge of the matters regarding electronic signatures.

2   The Bureau shall be responsible for the following:

a   the oversight of compliance with this Act (section 11);

b   the review of requests for accreditation made by certification authorities operating in Slovakia, accreditation grant to and withdrawal from a certification authority, and issuance of accreditation clearances;

c   the issuance of qualified public-key certificates in accordance with section 7(3) to certification authorities accredited by the Bureau;

d   the publication of the public key of the Bureau in accordance with section 4(5) and issuance of the qualified public-key certificate of the Bureau in accordance with section 7(5);

e   the issuance of qualified public-key certificates to foreign-based certification authorities in accordance with section 17(1)(a) and (c);

f   the maintenance of records of certification authorities operating in Slovakia;

g   the maintenance of the register of accredited certification authorities operating in Slovakia, as well as, the register of de-accredited certification authorities. The Bureau makes the registers publicly accessible on a website;

h   the revocation of the qualified certificate issued to an accredited certification authority in cases where the Bureau withdraws an accreditation from the accredited certification authority or the accredited certification authority ceases operation;

i   the maintenance of the register of foreign-based certification authorities whose certificates are recognized by the Bureau;

j   the certification of electronic signature products, including, but not limited to, secure electronic-signature creation devices, secure time-stamp creation devices, as well as, the publication of recommendations, standards, and guidelines regarding electronic signatures;

k   the performance of any commission arising from this Act. To the end of executing such commission, the Bureau may seek assistance of other public authorities, as well as, of natural or legal persons.

3   The requirements for qualified-certificate management by an accredited certification authority shall apply to the Bureau.

SECTION 11

Oversight

1   The Bureau may inspect a certification authority on the day of receipt of notice of commencing operation and ever afterwards. Within the Bureau's scope of oversight falls any registration authority acting on behalf of such certification authority.

2   To the end of effecting an inspection, a certification authority shall allow the authorized personnel of the Bureau as extensive access to its offices and business premises as necessary; show, upon request, all of the documents, records, documentary evidence, files and any other material relating to its business; allow as extensive access to its computer information system as necessary; as well as, provide the authorized personnel with information and requisite assistance.

3   The authorized employees of the Bureau are entitled to request of the personnel of an accredited certification authority, certification authority or registration authority, as the case may be, under inspection assistance and any information relating to the performance of certification functions. Inspectors are bound to non-disclosure of the facts they become aware of in the course of inspection. The obligation of non-disclosure continues even after their employment at the Bureau has been terminated. Such obligation may be rescinded by separate legislation.

4   Where in the course of inspection, the Bureau finds a certification authority in breach of the obligations arising from this Act, it may in particular:

a   suspend for no longer than 3 months, or interdict a certification authority from performing or continuing any certification function or service, provided that the Bureau finds the certification authority

i   untrustworthy enough (3) to conduct the business of a certification authority;

ii   in failure of compliance with statutory requirements or requirements imposed by binding regulations;

b   make an injunction of revoking qualified certificates in cases where

- the Bureau finds them to be forgeries or inadequately proof against forgery, or

- secure electronic-signature creation devices prove deficient in safety, which might result in undetectable forgery of advanced electronic signatures or documents signed by means of such devices.

5   Notwithstanding the suspension or interdiction of a certification authority from operation in accordance with subsection (4), the validity of the certificates that have been issued by the certification authority prior to such act is not prejudiced.

6   Notwithstanding the suspension or interdiction of an accredited certification authority from operation in accordance with subsection (4) or withdrawal of an accreditation from an accredited certification authority, the validity of the qualified certificates that have been issued by the accredited certification authority prior to such act is not prejudiced.

SECTION 12

Certification authority

1   A certification authority is a certification service provider that manages certificates and performs certification functions.

2   The provision of certification services is a business activity (4).

3   The performance of certification functions described in this Act is not subject to prior authorization.

4   The provision of accredited certification services is subject to accreditation granted by the Bureau.

5   Prior to the commencement of providing services, a certification authority shall publish free of charge the following:

   a   certificate guidelines which include, but are not limited to, entities and persons to whom, and conditions under which the certification authority provides services, classes of certificates, rights and obligations of the users of services, sample request form for the use of services, rules regarding the use and revocation of certificates;

   b   technical specifications, formats and standards used to perform operation;

   c   the price list of chargeable services and the listing of free services;

   d   limitations on the provision of services, if applicable;

   e   the procedure of authenticating an applicant requesting the use of services;

   f   status information on accreditation.

6   Furthermore, a certification authority shall:

   a   disclose its own identity information and information regarding certificates under its management;

   b   give the Bureau 30 days' notice of the commencement of operation.

7   In the notice of the commencement of operation, a certification authority shall include the company name and identity information, principal place of business of the applicant; business license; in the case of a legal person a copy of an entry in the Commercial Register no older than 3 months; and information intended for publication in accordance with this Act.

8   A certification authority shall make publicly accessible the information in accordance with subsections (5) and (6)(a) on a website.

SECTION 13

Accreditation

1   A certification authority may apply for accreditation with the Bureau.

2   A certification authority may be a legal or natural person who satisfies the requirements for tangible assets, premises, equipment, personnel, organizational policies and legal conditions necessary for the provision of accredited certification services. Specific conditions regarding the provision of accredited certification services shall be prescribed by a binding regulation made by the Bureau.

3   With a request for accreditation, a certification authority shall furnish the Bureau with

   a   the applicant's name and identity information, and principal place of business;

    b   a copy of an entry in the Commercial Register no older than 3 months;

    c   a statement of criminal records of any authorized representative of a legal person or a statement of criminal records of a natural person, in each case, no older than 3 months;

    d   the public key corresponding to the private key to be used by the applicant to sign issued certificates electronically;

    e   findings of a security audit of its operations;

    f   information made publicly available under the provisions of this Act.

4   If an applicant seeking an accreditation fulfills the conditions of the grant of an accreditation in accordance with this Act, the Bureau shall make an award of an accreditation and issue a certificate to the applicant within 90 days of receipt of the application.

5   If an application for an accreditation is incomplete, the Bureau shall give the applicant notice to produce additional information within 7 days of the notice to produce while staying the accreditation proceedings for such period of time. If the applicant seeking an accreditation fails to produce within such period of time, the Bureau shall dismiss the application.

6   If the Bureau finds any accredited certification authority in failure of compliance with the requirements for the provision of accredited certification services, it may suspend such authority's accreditation for the period of 3 months, ordering such authority to perform corrective arrangements. If the accredited certification authority fails to perform, the Bureau shall withdraw accreditation from the accredited certification authority.

7   A de-accredited certification authority may reapply for accreditation.

8   A request for accreditation is subject to administrative fees (5).

SECTION 14

Conduct of the accredited certification authority

1   A certification authority must

    a   develop security policies and certification practices;

    b   adhere to its security policies and certification practices throughout its operation;

    c   perform its certification functions in such a manner that it is impracticable to make copies of or retain information on the private key of the person to whom the certification authority provides its services, without prejudice to the private key used by the certification authority to perform its certification functions;

    d   notify the Bureau of changes in the scope and contents of provided certification services, no later than 30 days;

    e   issue to applicants certificates based on an agreement which is

        i   in writing and signed in holograph; or

        ii   in the form of an electronic document signed with advanced electronic signatures of each party to the agreement.

    f   inform, prior to entering into an agreement, the person seeking its services of its security policy and certification practices. Such information shall be in writing or in electronic form, in detail and in understandable language. This information shall also be made available, upon request, to any natural or legal person who proves a justified interest in it;

    g   provide the applicant seeking a certificate with information on electronic signature products, and procedures fit to create and verify an electronic signature;

    h   inform a certificate holder of the legal consequences of the procedure applied to create an electronic signature, of the obligations of a certificate holder, and of the liabilities of the certification authority;

    i   ensure throughout its operation:

        i   that the certificates issued by the certification authority satisfy the terms and conditions laid down in this Act;

        ii   that in case where the certificates issued by the certification authority have any limitations on their use, such limitations are readily recognizable to third parties.

        iii   the availability of a certificate revocation service;

        iv   the publication of a certificate revocation list;

        v   that the certificate holder whose certificate has been revoked is informed to that effect, without delay, in written or electronic form;

    j   maintain operation documents regarding certification functions. The scope and contents of such documentation shall be prescribed by a binding regulation made by the Bureau;

    k   maintain archives of the documents relating to issued certificates, so provided by other legislation (6).

2   An accredited certification authority must develop security policies and certification practices in accordance with the guidelines provided by a binding regulation made by the Bureau.

3   Furthermore, an accredited certification authority must:

    a   demonstrate the trustworthiness necessary for the provision of certification services in accordance with the requirements laid down in a binding regulation (section 13(2));

    b   inform the applicant seeking a qualified certificate of the terms and conditions of the use of the certificate, limitations on the use thereof and procedures for dispute settlement. Such information shall also be made available, upon request, to any natural or legal person who proves a justified interest in it;

c   provide the applicant seeking a qualified certificate with information on the hardware and software products, procedures and equipment which have been certified by the Bureau in accordance with section 10(2)(j) to be acceptable electronic signature products for creating and verifying advanced electronic signatures;

d   when issuing a qualified certificate or making a warranty in accordance with section 17(1)(b), ensure:

     i   that any information contained in the qualified certificate is true and accurate at the time of issuance;

     ii   that the person named in the certificate is the holder of the private key corresponding to the public key in the certificate at the time of issuance;

     iii   that the private key and the corresponding public key match upon application of electronic-signature products and procedures, intended to be used for the creation or verification of electronic signatures, which the certification authority supplies or recommends;

     iv   that the certificate shall be revoked by the appointed time upon receipt of a revocation request;

     v   the availability of a certification revocation service.

SECTION 15

Certificate revocation

1   A certification authority shall revoke a certificate under its management if

     a   it finds non-fulfillment of the requirements for certificate issuance laid down in this Act;

     b   it becomes aware that the certificate has been issued upon misrepresentation of information;

     c   the certificate holder or subscriber named in the certificate requests the revocation of the certificate;

     d   certificate revocation is ordered by of a court of law;

     e   it has become aware of the decease or dissolution of the certificate holder as the case may be with a natural or legal person;

     f   it finds the private key corresponding to the public key in the certificate is known to a person other than the certificate subscriber.

2   In the case of revocation in accordance with subsection (1) the certification authority shall revoke the certificate within such period of time as specified by the certification authority's certificate guidelines.

3   Any certificate is deemed to be revoked at and ever after the time of the publication of the first certificate revocation list recording such certificate. The revalidation of a revoked certificate is prohibited.

4   A certification authority shall maintain documentation on requests and motions for certificate revocation. In the documentation there shall be recorded in particular the year, month, day, hours, minutes and seconds of

- receipt of a certificate revocation request, or

- determining the cause of certificate revocation; and information establishing the identity of

- the person requesting certificate revocation, or

- the legal and natural persons moving for certificate revocation.

SECTION 16

Conduct of the certification authority with respect to certificate management

1   In issuing a public-key certificate, a certification authority certifies the genuineness of the public key in the certificate and the fact that the certificate holder has at his disposal the private key for which the public key in the certificate is intended.

2   A certification authority certifies the genuineness of the public key of the certificate holder by, upon authenticating required particulars, issuing to the requester a certificate which the certification authority signs by an electronic signature supported by its private key.

3   A certification authority authenticates required particulars (proof of identity, ownership of the private key corresponding to the presented public key) by itself or using a registration authority that acts on behalf of the certification authority.

4   A certification authority shall create conditions that enable a verifier to verify the validity of a certificate issued by the certification authority. For that purpose, the certification authority shall ensure its public key is retrievable by the verifier from multiple online sources.

SECTION 17

Recognition of foreign certificates

1   A certificate or a qualified certificate that has been issued by a certification authority whose principal place of business is outside of Slovakia (hereinafter referred to as "foreign certification authority"), and whose validity is verifiable in Slovakia, may be recognized in Slovakia if:

a   the foreign certification authority that has issued the certificate is registered with the Bureau, or the foreign certification authority that has issued a qualified certificate is accredited in Slovakia;

b a certification authority that has a place of business in Slovakia and satisfies the requirements laid down in this Act warrants the validity of such certificate, e.g., by having issued a cross public-key certificate to the foreign certification authority, or in the case of an accredited certification authority that has a place of business is in Slovakia and satisfies the requirements laid down in this Act, it warrants the validity of a qualified certificate, e.g., by having issued a qualified cross public-key certificate to the foreign certification authority;

c under a treaty between Slovakia and third countries a foreign qualified certificate is recognized as such, or the foreign certification authority is recognized as an accredited certification authority in Slovakia.

2 On the day of Slovakia's entry into the European Union, any certificate, issued by a certification authority whose principal place of business is in a member state of the Community, whose validity is verifiable in Slovakia shall be an equivalent certificate issued in Slovakia. In the case of any qualified certificate this subsection shall apply mutatis mutandis.

SECTION 18

Archiving

1 A certification authority shall, for at least 10 years, retain:

a documents regarding the organizational and technical security arrangements made to ensure the fulfillment of the requirements laid down in this Act and relevant regulations;

b original requests for the issuance of certificates and respective documents proving the identity of applicants;

c records, in accordance with section 15(4), regarding any revoked certificate.

2 If record integrity and durability are ensured, a certification authority may archive documents mentioned in subsection (1) in electronic form.

SECTION 19

Liability for damage

1 A certification authority is liable, under general regulations governing compensation, for damage arising from a breach of obligations (7).

2 In the case of any limitation on the use of a qualified certificate, an accredited certification authority shall not be held liable for damage arising from the use of the qualified certificate in contravention of such limitation as indicated in the qualified certificate.

3 In the case of any limit as indicated in a qualified certificate on the value of a transaction for which the qualified certificate may be used, an accredited certification authority shall not be held liable for damage arising from such limit being exceeded.

4   An accredited certification authority shall be held liable in accordance with subsection (1) unless it proves to the contrary.

SECTION 20

Impediment and cessation of operation

1   A certification authority shall inform the Bureau of any impediment of performing certification services in accordance with operation guidelines within 30 days of becoming aware of such impediment.

2   An accredited certification authority shall inform, without delay, the Bureau of any impediment of performing certification services in accordance with operation guidelines.

3   If a certification authority contemplates the cessation of performing certification services, it shall give 6 months' notice of its intention to cease to the Bureau and to any holder of a valid certificate that has been issued by the certification authority.

4   If a certification authority intends to cease its operation, it may make arrangements with another certification authority whereby the other certification authority takes custody of the lists of issued and revoked certificates, and operation documents. In case where no other certification authority takes custody of the lists, the validity of any certificate which has been issued by the certification authority ceasing its operation shall expire on the day of the cessation of certification authority operation.

5   If an accredited certification authority intends to cease its operation, it may make arrangements with another accredited certification authority whereby the other accredited certification authority takes custody of the lists of issued and revoked certificates, and operation documents. In case where no other accredited certification authority takes custody of the lists, the Bureau shall do so.

6   Prior to ceasing operation, an authorized representative of the certification authority shall ensure the exercise of an audit of compliance with the provisions laid down in the Act governing personal information protection (8).

SECTION 21

Registration authority

1   A registration authority defined in section 2(s) acts on behalf of a certification authority or under a contract to which it is a party.

2   The performance of certification functions by a registration authority acting on behalf of a certification authority in accordance with this Act or under a contract

between the registration authority and a certification authority shall not be subject to prior authorization.

3   The operation of a registration authority acting on behalf of a certification authority or under a contract to which it is a party shall be governed by the certification authority's certificate guidelines.

4   A registration authority in particular

   a   receives for processing certificate issuance applications;

   b   verifies the conformity of information represented in the certificate issuance applications with information in the document of identification produced by the certificate issuance requester;

   c   sends a certificate issuance request to the certification authority;

   d   hands over a certificate to a certificate issuance requester;

SECTION 22

Conduct of the certificate holder

1   A certificate holder shall:

   a   exercise due care with respect to his private key so as to avoid unauthorized use of his private key;

   b   make accurate, true and complete representations of information in relation to his public-key certificate;

   c   seek, without undue delay, of the certification authority managing his certificate the revocation of his certificate in cases where the certificate holder knows of unauthorized use of his private key or there is a risk of unauthorized use of his private key or there has occurred any change in the information entered in his certificate.

2   A certificate holder shall be held liable for damage resulting from his failure to observe his obligations in accordance with general regulations on compensation (9).

SECTION 23

Personal information protection

Matters of the information system of a certification service provider are governed by other legislation (10).

SECTION 24

Requirements for electronic signature products

1   For the purposes of storing a private key and creating an advanced electronic signature, such secure electronic-signature creation device is required to be used that is capable of reliably protecting the private key stored within it and capable of making forgery of an advanced electronic signature and a signed electronic document reliably detectable.

2   Subsection (1) shall apply, mutatis mutandis, to any secure electronic-signature creation device provided that such device is used to generate a private key.

3   A secure electronic-signature creation device and the process of advanced electronic signature creation shall:

   a   reliably ensure that the electronic document to be signed is not altered at the time of creating an advanced electronic signature;

   b   make the electronic document to be signed perceivable by the signatory prior to the process of advanced electronic signature creation;

   c   ensure that the likelihood of any advanced electronic signature's being created more than once is infinitesimal.

4   For the purposes of issuing and retaining qualified certificates, such facilities and procedures are required to be used that are capable of providing protection against forgery.

5   For the purpose of verifying an advanced electronic signature, such technical means and procedures are required to be used that are capable of ensuring:

   a   that a signed electronic document is not altered at the time of advanced electronic signature verification;

   b   that an advanced electronic signature is reliably verified and the result of verification is correctly displayed;

   c   that it can be determined whether the signed electronic document is the equivalent electronic document for the purpose of which the advanced electronic signature has been created;

   d   that the verifier can identify the person to whom the advanced electronic signature is bound and whose use of a pseudonym is clearly indicated.

6   Subsections (1) to (5) shall apply, mutatis mutandis, to any secure time-stamp creation device mentioned in section 9.

7   The Bureau is responsible for assessing and certifying technical means and procedures of creating advanced electronic signatures or time stamps, as well as, electronic-signature products to be in compliance with the requirements laid down in section 10(2)(j).

8   The requirements for electronic-signature products shall be prescribed by a binding regulation made by the Bureau.

SECTION 25

Security audit

1 An accredited certification authority shall submit to repeated external security audits of providing certification services in such a manner that the audit may be concluded within 12 months after the date of becoming accredited or after the date of the conclusion of the previous audit. The specific requirements for auditing, and details of audit scope and auditor qualifications shall be prescribed by a binding regulation made by the Bureau.

2 An accredited certification authority shall submit a report to the Bureau on the results of an audit, including, if necessary, any corrective arrangements and time limits for the elimination of ascertained deficiencies. The final report on the audit results shall be submitted to the Bureau within 30 days of audit completion.

3 If the Bureau from the final report on the audit results arrives at a conclusion that the accredited certification authority has failed to comply with the obligations laid down in this Act, the Bureau will impose corrective measures and time limits within which the accredited certification authority must eliminate any deficiencies.

SECTION 26

Deterrents

1 For non-compliance with the obligations in accordance with this Act the Bureau will impose a fine of

    a up to SK10 million upon any legal or natural person who provides accredited certification services in the absence of an accreditation;

    b up to SK10 million upon any accredited certification authority that:

        i provides certification services in violation of this Act and security guidelines prescribed by a binding regulation made by the Bureau;

        ii fails to provide a certificate revocation service;

        iii fails to publish a certification revocation list;

        iv fails to make publicly available its identity information or certificates used in the course of providing certification services;

        v fails to comply with the obligation to inform the Bureau of the commencement of operation in accordance with section 12(6)(b);

        vi continues performing any function from which the accredited certification authority has been suspended;

    c up to SK5 million, which may be reimposed, upon any accredited certification authority that fails to disclose or conceals information, or fails to provide assistance to the Bureau in the course of an inspection in accordance with section 11;

d   up to SK1 million, which may be reimposed, upon any certification authority that fails to comply with the obligations laid down in section 14(1)(c);

e   up to SK1 million upon any certification authority that fails to revoke any certificate or fails to maintain documentation required by section 15(4);

f   up to SK1 million upon any certification authority in cases where the registration authority acting on its behalf:

    i   fails to provide services in compliance with the procedures and security policies prescribed by the certification authority;

    ii   fails to ensure that the information collected from subscribers is accurate, true and complete;

    iii   fails to maintain documentation regarding the procedure of providing services and the security of provided services, and fails to protect personal information on subscribers as provided by other legislation;

g   up to SK1 million upon any legal person who has made unauthorized use of the private key of any signatory;

h   up to SK500,000, which may be reimposed, upon any accredited certification authority that fails to comply with the obligation to submit to an audit in accordance with section 25(1) or fails to submit the final report on audit results within such time as prescribed by section 25(2);

i   up to SK500,000 upon any certification authority that:

    i   fails to satisfy the notification requirement prescribed by section 14(1)(d);

    ii   fails to give notice of the cessation of operation to the Bureau within such time as prescribed by this Act;

    iii   fails to comply with the obligations of a certificate holder in accordance with section 22;

    iv   fails to comply with the obligations in respect of archiving in accordance with section 18(1);

j   up to SK100,000 upon any natural person who has made unauthorized use of the private key of the signatory or misrepresented information at the time of filing a request for certificate issuance;

2   Before imposing any fine, the gravity, length of time and consequences of unlawful conduct will be taken into consideration.

3   The Bureau may impose the fine referred to in subsection (1) within one year after the date of finding any violation of obligations and no later than 3 years after the date of such violation being committed.

4   The proceeds of any fine shall be for the public revenue of the Slovak Republic.

5   With the imposition of any fine in accordance with subsection (1), the right of damages shall not be prejudiced.

SECTION 27

Enabling provision

The mode and procedure of the use of electronic signatures in commerce and in communication with public authorities shall be specified in detail by a binding regulation made by the Bureau.

SECTION 28

Common provision

The general regulation on administrative proceedings (11) shall apply to the proceedings of the Bureau unless this Act provides otherwise.

PART II

After the first sentence of subsection (4) of Section 40 of Act 40/1964–Civil Code (Law Gazette), as amended by Act 58/1969 (Law Gazette), Act 131/1982 (Law Gazette), Act 131/1982 (Law Gazette), Act 94/1988 (Law Gazette), Act 188/1988 (Law Gazette), Act 87/1990 (Law Gazette), Act 105/1990 (Law Gazette), Act 116/1990 (Law Gazette), Act 87/1991 (Law Gazette), Act 509/1991 (Law Gazette), Act 264/1992 (Law Gazette), Act 278/1993 (Law Gazette), Act 249/1994 (Law Gazette), Act 153/1997 (Law Gazette), Act 211/1997 (Law Gazette), Act 252/1999 (Law Gazette), Act 218/2000 (Law Gazette), Act 261/2001 (Law Gazette), Act 281/2001 (Law Gazette), Act 23/2002 (Law Gazette) and Act 34/2002 (Law Gazette), there shall be inserted the following sentence:

"Written form is always preserved if any legal act performed by electronic means is signed with an advanced electronic signature.".

PART III

The first sentence of subsection (1) of section 42 of Act 99/1963– Civil Procedure Code, as amended by Act 36/1967 (Law Gazette), Act 158/1969 (Law Gazette), Act 49/1973 (Law Gazette), Act 20/1975 (Law Gazette), Act 133/1982 (Law Gazette), Act 180/1990 (Law Gazette), Act 328/1991 (Law Gazette), Act 519/1991 (Law Gazette), Act 263/1992 (Law Gazette), Act 5/1993 (Law Gazette), Act 46/1994 (Law Gazette), Act 190/1995 (Law Gazette), Act 232/1995 (Law Gazette), Act 233/1995 (Law Gazette), Act 22/1996 (Law Gazette), Act 58/1996 (Law Gazette), Constitutional Court Ruling 281/1996 (Law Gazette), Act 211/1997 (Law Gazette), Constitutional Court Ruling 359/1997 (Law Gazette), Act 124/1998 (Law Gazette), Act 144/1998 (Law Gazette), Act 187/1998 (Law Gazette), Act 169/1998 (Law Gazette), Act 225/1998 (Law Gazette), Act 233/998 (Law Gazette), Act 235/1998 (Law Gazette), Constitutional Court Ruling 318/1998 (Law

Gazette), Act 331/1998 (Law Gazette), Act 46/1999 (Law Gazette), Constitutional Court Ruling 66/1999 (Law Gazette), Constitutional Court Ruling 166/1999 (Law Gazette), Constitutional Court Ruling 185/1999 (Law Gazette), Act 223/1999 (Law Gazette), Act 303/2001 (Law Gazette) and Act 501/2001 (Law Gazette), shall be replaced with the following:

"Filing may be made in writing, orally to be on record, by electronic means signed with an advanced electronic signature as provided by other legislation, by telegraph or by telefacsimile.".

PART IV

In section 31 of Act 511/1992 governing the administration of taxes and charges and changes in the system of the territorial financial authorities, as amended by Act 102/1993 (Law Gazette), Act 165/1993 (Law Gazette), Act 253/1993 (Law Gazette), Act 254/1993 (Law Gazette), Act 172/1994 (Law Gazette), Act 187/1994 (Law Gazette), Act 249/1994 (Law Gazette), Act 367/1994 (Law Gazette), Act 374/1994 (Law Gazette), Act 58/1995 (Law Gazette), Act 146/1995 (Law Gazette), Act 304/1995 (Law Gazette), Act 386/1996 (Law Gazette), Act 12/1998 (Law Gazette), Act 219/1999 (Law Gazette), Act 367/1999 (Law Gazette), Act 240/2000 (Law Gazette) and Act 493/2001 (Law Gazette) °X

1   Subsection (9) shall be replaced with the following:

"(9) Registration or notification made under this Act may be submitted to the tax administrator on a form prescribed by the Ministry in hard copy or by electronic means signed with an advanced electronic signature as provided by other legislation. On the form, the taxpayer shall declare it is his first-time registration or mention any previous registration, in the latter case, he shall list the dates, tax administrators, tax identification number assigned him, name or corporate name under which he has been registered and whether registration has been withdrawn or repealed and any reason for it. The Ministry and the Central Taxation Office may increase the amount of information required for registration in hard copy or in electronic form signed with an advanced electronic signature in case where such information is necessary for the regular administration of respective taxes.".

2   Subsection (17) shall be replaced with the following:

"(17) The payer of a tax on income from employment and emoluments thereof shall submit to the tax administrator, within 30 days after the end of a calendar quarter of a year, a summary of the amounts of such tax and tax subject to a special rate which were deducted and pre-paid in the previous quarter of a year on a form whose format is specified by the Ministry or if the relevant taxation office provides so, the summary may be filed by electronic means, signed with an advanced electronic signature prescribed by other legislation.".

PART V

Subsection (1) of section 19 of Act 71/1967 governing administrative proceedings–Administrative Procedure Act (Law Gazette) shall be replaced with the following subsection:

"(1) Filing may be made in writing or orally to be on record or by electronic means signed with an advanced electronic signature as provided by other legislation. It may also be made by telegraph; such filing containing a motion on the merits shall be made complete in writing or orally to be entered in the report no later than three days after the initial filing.".

PART VI

Subsection (1) of section 59 of Act 141/1961 governing criminal court proceedings–Criminal Procedure Act (Law Gazette), as amended by Act 57/1965 (Law Gazette), Act 58/1969 (Law Gazette), Act 149/1969 (Law Gazette), Act 156/1969 (Law Gazette), Act 48/1973 (Law Gazette), Act 29/1978 (Law Gazette), Act 43/1980 (Law Gazette), Act 159/1989 (Law Gazette), Act 178/1990 (Law Gazette), Act 303/1990 (Law Gazette), Act 558/1991 (Law Gazette), Act 6/1993 (Law Gazette), Act 156/1993 (Law Gazette), Act 178/1993 (Law Gazette), Act 247/1994 (Law Gazette), Constitutional Court Ruling 222/1998 (Law Gazette), Act 256/1998 (Law Gazette), Act 272/1999 (Law Gazette), Act 173/2000 (Law Gazette), Act 366/2000 (Law Gazette) a Act 253/2001 (Law Gazette), shall be replaced with the following subsection:

"(1) Filing shall be always considered in accordance with its contents even if it may be wrongly marked. It may be made in writing, orally to be on record or by electronic means signed with an advanced electronic signature as provided by other legislation, by telegraph, telefacsimile or by teletypewriter. Filing that has been made by telegraph, telefacsimile or by teletypewriter is required to be certified in writing or orally to be entered in the report. The provisions under section 158 shall not be prejudiced.".

PART VII

In the Annex "Administrative fee schedule" to Act 145/1995 governing administrative fees (Law Gazette), as amended by Act 123/1996 (Law Gazette), Act 224/1996 (Law Gazette), Act 70/1997 (Law Gazette), Act 1/1998 (Law Gazette), Act 232/1999 (Law Gazette), Act 3/2000 (Law Gazette), Act 142/2000 (Law Gazette), Act 211/2000 (Law Gazette), Act 468/2000 (Law Gazette) and Act 553/2001 (Law Gazette), there shall be inserted the following part:

"PART XX

Electronic signature

Item 268

(a) Filing an application for the accreditation of a certification services provider SK20,000;

(b) Filing an application for the compliance assessment and certification of technical means of creating and verifying electronic signatures SK10,000.".

PART VIII

This Act shall come into effect on May 1, 2002, except for Part I

section 4,

section 5 (1), (4) and (5),

section 7,

section 8 (5) and (6),

section 9,

section 10 (2) (a) to (e), (g) and (h), and (3),

section 11,

section 12 (4),

section 13,

section 14 (2) and (3),

section 24,

section 25,

section 26,

which provisions shall come into effect on September 1, 2002.

REFERENCES

(1) Act 241/2001 governing classified information protection and amending other legislation (Law Gazette).
(2) Section 1(2) of Act 241/2001 (Law Gazette). Section 34 of Act 575/2001 governing the organization of the activities of the Government and the organization of central administration (Law Gazette).
(3) Section 6(8) and section 48 of Act 241/2001 governing classified information protection and amending other legislation (Law Gazette).
(4) Section 2 of the Commercial Code.
(5) Act 145/1995 governing administrative fees (Law Gazette) as amended.
(6) Act 149/1975 governing the maintenance of archives (Law Gazette) as amended.
(7) Sections 420 and 420(a) of the Civil Code.
(8) Act 52/1998 governing personal information protection in information systems.
(9) Sections 420 and 420(a) of the Civil Code.
(10) Act 52/1998 governing personal information protection in information systems.
(11) Act 71/1967 governing administrative proceedings– Administrative Procedure Act (Law Gazette).

Spain

Law on Electronic Signatures of June 2003

PART I

General provisions

Article 1. Subject matter

1. This Law governs electronic signatures, their legal efficacy and the provision of certification services.

2. The provisions contained in this Law do not alter the rules relating to the conclusion, formalisation, validity and efficacy of contracts and any other legal acts, nor those relating to the constituent documents of either category.

Article 2. Providers of certification services subject to the Law

1. This Law will apply to providers of certification services established in Spain and certification services that providers residing or domiciled in another State offer through a permanent establishment situated in Spain.

2. Provider of certification services means a physical or legal person that issues electronic certificates or provides other services in connection with electronic signatures.

3. A provider of certification services will be deemed to be established in Spain in cases where its residence or corporate domicile is situated within Spanish territory, provided that these coincide with the location where the administrative running and the management of its business is effectively centralised, otherwise the ruling location will be that where said running or management is conducted.

4.   A provider will be deemed to operate via a permanent establishment situated within Spanish territory in cases where that establishment includes installations or workplaces in which it continuously or habitually conducts the whole or part of its activity.

5.   A provider of certification services will be presumed to be established in Spain in cases where said provider or any of its subsidiaries are entered in the Mercantile Register or in another Spanish public Register in which it is necessary to be entered in order to acquire legal status.

The mere use of technological means situated in Spain for the provision of or access to the service will not of itself alone imply the establishment of the provider in Spain.

Article 3. Concept, classes and effects of electronic signatures

1.   An electronic signature is a combination of data in electronic form, set out together with others or associated with them, which may be used as the signatory's means of identification.

2.   An advanced electronic signature is an electronic signature which makes it possible to identify the signatory and verify the integrity of the data signed, through being related exclusively to the signatory and to the data referred to and through having been created by means which the signatory can maintain under his exclusive control.

3.   A recognised electronic signature is taken to be an advanced electronic signature based on a recognised certificate and generated by a secure signature creation device.

4.   A recognised electronic signature will have, with respect to data set out electronically, the same legal value as a manuscript signature in connection with those set out on paper.

Legal effects will not be denied to an electronic signature which does not meet the requirements of a recognised electronic signature in relation to data with which it is associated through the mere fact of being presented electronically.

5.   A support on which electronically signed data appear will be admissible as documentary evidence in court.

Article 4. Use of electronic signatures within the scope of Public Administrations

1.   This Law will apply to the use of electronic signatures within Public Administrations, their public agencies and within entities dependent on or related to Public Administrations, and in relations which the former and the latter maintain among themselves or with private individuals, without prejudice to additional conditions that may be established for safeguarding the guarantees of each procedure.

Additional conditions established may include inter alia the imposing of electronic dates on electronic documents integrated in an administrative file. Electronic date means a combination of data in electronic form used as means of recording when an operation is performed on other electronic data with which they are associated.

2. The additional conditions referred to in the foregoing paragraph may only refer to the specific characteristics of the application concerned and must guarantee compliance with the provisions of Article 45 of Law 30/1992 of 26 November 1992 on the Legal Regime of Public Administrations and the Common Administrative Procedure.

   Such conditions will be objective, proportionate, transparent and non-discriminatory and must not hinder the provision of certification services to citizens in cases where such provision involves various different national or foreign Public Administrations.

3. The rules that establish additional general conditions for the use of electronic signatures vis-a-vis the general Administration of the State, its public agencies and vis-a-vis entities which are subordinate or related to them will be enacted on joint proposal from the Ministries of Public Administrations and of Science and Technology and after report from the Higher Council on Information Technology and for the encouragement of Electronic Administration.

4. The use of electronic signatures in communications that affect classified information, public safety/security or national defence will be governed by specific regulations.

Article 5. Regime of provision of certification services

1. The provision of certification services is not subject to prior authorisation and will be conducted in a regime of free competition. No restrictions may be established for certification services which originate from another member State of the European Economic Area.

2. The competition protection bodies will see to the maintenance of conditions of effective competition in the provision of certification services to the public by exercising the functions legally attributed to them.

3. The provision to the public of certification services by Public Administrations, their public agencies or by entities subordinate or related to Public Administrations will be conducted in accordance with the principles of objectivity, transparency and no discrimination.

PART II

Electronic certificates

CHAPTER I

General provisions

Article 6. Electronic certificates

1. An electronic certificate is a document signed electronically by a provider of certification services which relates some signature verification data to a signatory and confirms his identity.

2. A signatory is a person that possesses a signature creation device and acts in his own name or in the name of a physical or legal person that he represents.

Article 7. Electronic certificates of legal persons

1. Electronic certificates of legal persons may be applied for by their directors, legal and voluntary representatives with sufficient power for these purposes. Electronic certificates of legal persons may not affect the organic or voluntary representation regime governed by the civil or mercantile legislation applicable to each legal person.

2. The custody of the signature creation data associated with each electronic certificate of a legal person will be the responsibility of the applicant physical person, whose identification will be included in the electronic certificate.

3. Signature creation data may only be used where so allowed in relations which the legal person maintains with public Administrations or in the contracting of goods and services which pertain to or concern its ordinary trade or run of business. A legal person may also impose additional limits, by reason of quantity or subject matter, for the use of said data which must in any case appear in the electronic certificate.

4. Acts or contracts in which the signature of a legal person is used within the limits referred to in the foregoing subsection will be deemed to be done/made by that legal person. If its signature is used beyond the aforesaid limits, the legal person will only be bound vis-a-vis third parties if it assumes them as its own or if they are concluded in its interest, otherwise the effects of said acts will apply to the physical person responsible for the custody of the signature creation data, who may take action as appropriate against whoever has used them.

5. The provisions of this Article will not apply to certificates that serve to verify the electronic signature of the provider of certification services, which signature is used to sign the electronic certificates that it issues.

6. The provisions of this Article will not apply to certificates issued in favour of Public Administrations, which certificates will be subject to specific regulations.

Article 8. Extinction of validity of electronic certificates

1.   The following are causes of extinction of the validity of an electronic certificate:

   a)   Expiry of the period of validity of the certificate.

   b)   Revocation formulated by the signatory, the physical or legal person represented by the signatory, an authorised third party or a physical person applicant for an electronic certificate of a legal person.

   c)   Violation or jeopardising of the secrecy of the signature creation data of the signatory or the provider of certification services, or improper use of said data by a third party.

   d)   Judicial or administrative decision that so orders.

   e)   Bankruptcy or extinction of the signatory's legal status; bankruptcy or extinction of the principal's legal status; occurrence of the signatory's or his principal's total or partial incapacity; termination of representation; dissolution of the legal person represented or alteration of the signature creation data use or custody conditions that are reflected in certificates issued to a legal person.

   f)   Cessation of activity of the provider of certification services unless, after the signatory's express prior consent, the management of the electronic certificates issued by said provider is transferred to another provider of certification services.

   g)   Alteration of data furnished for obtaining a certificate, or modification of circumstances verified for the issue of a certificate, e.g. those relating to responsibilities or to powers of representation, such that the certificate no longer conforms to reality.

2.   The period of validity of electronic certificates will be appropriate to the characteristics and technology used for generating the signature creation data. In the case of recognised certificates, this period may not exceed four years.

3.   Extinction of the validity of an electronic certificate will produce effects vis-a-vis third parties, in cases of expiry of the period of validity, from when this circumstance occurs, and in other cases from when the indication of said extinction is included in the service consultable about the validity of certificates from the provider of certification services.

Article 9. Suspension of validity of electronic certificates

1.   Providers of certification services will suspend the validity of electronic certificates issued if any of the following causes arises:

   a)   Request from the signatory, the physical or legal person represented by the signatory, an authorised third party or a physical person applicant for a legal person's electronic certificate.

   b)   Judicial or administrative decision that so orders.

c)   The existence of founded doubts about the occurrence of the certificate validity extinction causes contemplated in items c) and g) of Article 8.

d)   Any other cause referred to in the declaration of certification practices that affects the security of systems used by the provider of certification services or affects the reliability of certificates issued or in general affects the certification service.

2.   Suspension of the validity of an electronic certificate will produce effects vis-a-vis third parties from when it is included in the service consultable about the validity of certificates from the provider of certification services.

Article 10. Provisions common to the extinction and suspension of validity of electronic certificates

1.   Providers of certification services will immediately place on record in a clear and undoubted manner the extinction or suspension of validity of electronic certificates in the service consultable about the validity of certificates when they have well-founded knowledge of any of the events that determine the extinction or suspension of their validity.

2.   Providers of certification services will notify this circumstance to the signatory prior to or simultaneously with the extinction or suspension of validity of the electronic certificate, specifying the reasons and the date and time at which the certificate will become inoperative. In cases of suspension it will also indicate its maximum duration, with extinction of validity of the certificate if that period passes without the suspension having been lifted.

3.   Extinction or suspension of validity of an electronic certificate will not have retrospective effects.

4.   Extinction or suspension of validity of an electronic certificate will be kept accessible in the service consultable about the validity of certificates at least up to the date on which its initial period of validity would have ended.

CHAPTER II

Recognised certificates

Article 11. Concept and content of recognised certificates

1.   Recognised certificates means electronic certificates issued by a provider of certification services that meets the requirements stated in this Law as to verification of the identity and other circumstances of applicants and as regards the reliability and guarantees of the certification services which they provide.

2.   Recognised certificates will include at least the following data:

a)   Indication that they are issued as such.

b)   Each certificate's unique identifying code.

c)   Identification of the provider of certification services that issues the certificate and its domicile.

d)   Advanced electronic signature of the provider of certification services that issues the certificate.

e)   Identification of the signatory, in the case of physical persons, by his forename and surnames and National Identity Document number or by means of a pseudonym set out unambiguously as such and, in the case of legal persons, by their name or corporate style and their Tax Identification Code.

f)   Signature verification data corresponding to signature creation data which are under the signatory's control.

g)   Beginning and end of the certificate's period of validity.

h)   Certificate use limits, if any are set.

i)   Limits on the values of transactions for which the certificate may be used, if any limits are set.

3.   Recognised certificates may also contain any other circumstance or specific attribute of the signatory in cases where it may be significant as a function of the actual purpose of the certificate and provided that the signatory so requests.

4.   If recognised certificates allow a representation relationship, they will include indication of the public document that authentically substantiates the signatory's powers to act in the name of the person or entity that he represents and, in cases where registration is obligatory, indication of the registration data, in accordance with the second subsection of Article 13.

Article 12. Obligations prior to the issue of recognised certificates

Before the issue of a recognised certificate, providers of certification services must comply with the following obligations:

a)   Check the identity and personal circumstances of applicants for certificates in accordance with the provisions of the next Article.

b)   Verify that all information contained in the certificate is accurate.

c)   Make sure that the signatory is in possession of signature creation data corresponding to the verification data set out in the certificate.

d)   Guarantee complementarity of the signature creation and verification data, provided that both are generated by the provider of certification services.

Article 13. Checking the identity and other personal circumstances of applicants for a recognised certificate

1.   Identification of the physical person applying for a recognised certificate will require his personal appearance before those responsible for verifying it and will

be substantiated by means of National Identity Document, passport or other means recognised in law. Personal appearance may be dispensed with if his signature on the application for issue of a recognised certificate has been legitimated in the presence of a notary.

The regime of personal appearance when applying for certificates that are issued after identification of the applicant to Public Administrations will be governed by the provisions of the administrative regulations.

2. In the case of recognised certificates of legal persons, providers of certification services will also check the data relating to the formation and legal status and to the extent and validity of the powers of representation of the applicant, either by consulting the public Register in which the documents of formation and empowerment are entered or by means of public documents that serve to substantiate the aforesaid particulars authentically in cases where their registration is not compulsory.

3. If recognised certificates reflect a voluntary representation relationship, providers of certification services will check the data relating to the principal's legal status and to the extent and validity of the representative's powers, either by consulting the public Register in which they are entered or by means of public documents that serve to substantiate the aforesaid particulars authentically in cases where their registration is not compulsory. If recognised certificates allow other forms of representation, providers of certification services must require substantiation of the circumstances on which they are based, in the same manner as stated above.

A recognised certificate may mention other attributes or personal circumstances of the applicant, such as his status as holder of a public position, his membership of a professional body or his academic qualifications, provided that these can be checked by means of public documents that substantiate them.

4. The provisions of the foregoing subsections may not be enforceable in the following cases:

   a) Where the identity or other permanent circumstances of applicants for certificates have already been recorded by the provider of certification services by virtue of a pre-existing relationship in which the means referred to in this Article were used for identifying the person concerned and the period of time that has passed since identification is less than five years.

   b) Where in order to apply for a certificate, use is made of another for the issue of which the signatory was identified in the manner prescribed in this Article and the provider of services finds that the period of time that has passed since identification is less than five years.

5. Providers of certification services may carry out the checking operations referred to in this Article for themselves or through other physical or legal persons, public or private, but in all cases the provider of certification services will be responsible.

Article 14. International equivalence of recognised certificates

Electronic certificates which providers of certification services established in a State that is not a member of the European Economic Area issue to the public as recognised certificates according to the legislation applicable in said State will be deemed equivalent to those issued by those established in Spain, provided that any of the following conditions is fulfilled:

a) That the provider of certification services meets the requirements stated in the Community regulations concerning electronic signatures for the issue of recognised certificates and has been certified in accordance with a voluntary certification system established in a member State of the European Economic Area.

b) That the certificate is guaranteed by a provider of certification services established within the European Economic Area that fulfils the requirements stated in the Community regulations concerning electronic signatures for the issue of recognised certificates.

c) That the certificate or the provider of certification services are recognised by virtue of a bilateral or multilateral agreement between the European Community and third countries or international organisations.

CHAPTER III

Electronic National Identity Documents

Article 15. Electronic National Identity Documents

1. An electronic National Identity Document is a National Identity Document that substantiates electronically its holder's personal identity and makes possible the electronic signing of documents.

2. All physical or legal persons, public or private, will recognise the efficacy of an electronic National Identity Document for substantiating the holder's identity and other personal data which appear therein, and for substantiating the signatory's identity and the integrity of documents signed with electronic signature devices included in it.

Article 16. Requirements and characteristics of electronic National Identity Documents

1. The competent agencies of the Ministry of the Interior for the issue of electronic National Identity Documents will fulfil the obligations which this Law imposes upon providers of certification services that issue recognised certificates, with the exception of the obligation relating to the furnishing the guarantee referred to in subsection 2 of Article 20.

2. The General Administration of the State will as far as possible use systems that guarantee compatibility of electronic signature instruments included in electronic National Identity Documents with the various generally accepted electronic signature products and devices.

PART III

Provision of certification services

CHAPTER I

Obligations

Article 17. Protection of personal data

1. The processing of personal data which providers of certification services require for conducting their activity and administrative bodies require for exercising the functions attributed by this Law will be subject to the provisions of Organic Law 15/1999 of 13 December 1999 on the Protection of Data of a Personal Character, and its development rules.

2. For the issue of electronic certificates to the public, providers of certification services may only gather personal data directly from signatories or after the latter's prior consent.

    The data required will be exclusively those needed for issuing and maintaining electronic certificates and for providing other services in connection with electronic signatures, and may not be processed for other purposes without the signatory's express consent.

3. Providers of certification services that set out a pseudonym in an electronic certificate at the signatory's request must record his true identity and retain the documentation that substantiates it.

    Said providers of certification services will be obliged to reveal the identity of signatories when so requested by judicial bodies in pursuance of the functions attributed to them and in the other cases referred to in Article 11.2 of the Organic Law on the Protection of Data of a Personal Character in which this is required.

Article 18. Obligations of providers of certification services that issue electronic certificates

Providers of certification services that issue electronic certificates must fulfil the following obligations:

a) Not to store or copy signature creation data of persons to whom they provide their services.

b) To provide the applicant, before issuing a certificate, with at least the following information, which must be transmitted, free of charge, in writing or by electronic means:

    1st The signatory's obligations, the manner in which the signatory creation data have to be kept safe, the procedure to be followed for notifying any loss or possible improper use of said data, and specified electronic signature creation and verification devices that are compatible with the signature data and with the certificate issued.

2nd   Mechanisms for guaranteeing the reliability of the electronic signature of a document over time.

3rd   Method used by the provider for checking the signatory's identity or other data that appear in the certificate.

4th   Precise conditions of use of the certificate, its possible limits of use and the manner in which the provider guarantees its asset responsibility.

5th   Any certifications that have been obtained by the provider of certification services and the procedures applicable for extrajudicial resolving of any conflicts that may arise in the course of its activity.

6th   Other information contained in the declaration of certification practices which it is promised will be applied in the course of its activity.

Any information mentioned above that is relevant to third parties affected by certificates must be available at their request.

c)   To maintain an up-to-date Directory of Certificates which will identify certificates issued and indicate whether they are in force or whether their validity has been suspended or extinguished. The Directory's integrity will be protected by using appropriate security mechanisms.

d)   To guarantee the availability of a rapid and secure service consultable about the validity of certificates.

Article 19. Declaration of certification practices

1.   All providers of certification services will formulate a declaration of certification practices which details, within the framework of this Law and its development provisions, the obligations whose fulfilment is promised in connection with the management of signature creation and verification data and electronic certificates, the conditions applicable to applications for and the issue, use, suspension and extinction of validity of certificates and, where applicable, the existence of procedures of coordination with corresponding public Registers that enable immediate interchange of information about the validity of powers indicated in certificates and which have compulsorily to be entered in said Registers.

2.   Each provider's declaration of certification practices will be available to the public by electronic means and free of charge.

Article 20. Obligations of providers of certification services that issue recognised certificates

1.   In addition to the obligations set out in this Chapter I, providers of certification services that issue recognised certificates must fulfil the following obligations:

a)   Prove the reliability needed for providing certification services.

b)   Guarantee that the date and time when a certificate is issued or its validity is extinguished or suspended can be determined with precision.

c) Employ personnel with the qualifications, know-how and experience needed for the provision of the certification services offered and the appropriate security and management procedures within the scope of electronic signatures.

d) Use reliable products and systems which are protected against any alteration and which guarantee technical and, where applicable, cryptographic security of the certification processes which they serve to support.

e) Take measures to prevent falsification of certificates and, in cases where the provider of certification services generates signature creation data, guarantee their confidentiality during the generation process and their delivery by a secure procedure to the signatory.

f) Keep recorded by any secure means all information and documentation relating to a recognised certificate and relevant aspects of the declaration of certification practices that apply at each time, for at least fifteen years from the date of its issue, in such a way that the signatures effected with it can be verified.

g) Use reliable systems for storing recognised certificates that make it possible to check their authenticity and prevent any possibility of unauthorised persons altering data, restrict their accessibility in such cases or to such persons as the signatory has indicated, and make it possible to detect any change that affects these security conditions.

2. Providers of certification services that issues recognised certificates must furnish a guarantee by means of bank guarantee or bond insurance in the amount of at least 3,000,000 euros to meet the risk of liability for damages that may arise from the use of certificates issued by them.

The aforesaid guarantee may be replaced in whole or in part by civil liability insurance such that the aggregate of the sums insured is at least 3,000,000 euros.

The sums and the means of insurance and guarantee stated in the two foregoing paragraphs may be modified by Royal Decree.

Article 21. Cessation of activity of a provider of certification services

1. A provider of certification services that is to cease its activity must so notify the signatories who use electronic certificates that have been issued by it, as also applicants for certificates issued in favour of legal persons; and it may transfer, with their express consent, the management of those which continue to be valid at the date on which the cessation occurs to another provider of certification services which takes them on or else extinguishes their validity. The aforesaid notification will be at least two months ahead of the effective cessation of activity and will where applicable provide information about the characteristics of the provider to which the transfer of management of the certificates is proposed.

2. A provider of certification services that issues electronic certificates to the public must notify the Ministry of Science and Technology, with the prior notice period indicated in the foregoing subsection, of the cessation of its activity and the

intended fate of the certificates, specifying where applicable whether their management is to be transferred and to whom or whether their validity will be extinguished.

It will also notify any other relevant circumstance that may prevent continuation of its activity. In particular it must notify, as soon as it becomes aware of it, the opening of any bankruptcy procedure conducted against it.

3. Providers of certification services will present the Ministry of Science and Technology, prior to definitive cessation of activity, with information relating to electronic certificates whose validity has been extinguished so that that Ministry may take over their custody for the purposes referred to in item f) of the first subsection of Article 20. That Ministry will maintain accessible to the public a specific consultable service which gives an indication about the aforesaid certificates for a period which it considers sufficient as a function of the consultations thereof that take place.

CHAPTER II

Responsibility

Article 22. Responsibility of providers of certification services

1. Providers of certification services will be liable for damages that they cause to any person in the course of their activity in cases where they fail to fulfil the obligations imposed upon them by this Law.

    The liability upon providers of certification services that is governed by this Law will apply according to the general rules concerning contractual or extracontractual fault, as appropriate, and it will be up to the provider of certification services to prove that it acted with the professional diligence requirable of it.

2. If a provider of certification services does not fulfil the obligations referred to in items b) to d) of Article 12 to guarantee an electronic certificate issued by a provider of certification services established in a State not belonging to the European Economic Area, it will be liable for damages caused by use of said certificate.

3. In particular, a provider of certification services will be liable for losses caused to the signatory or to third parties in good faith through failure to include or delay in including the extinction or suspension of validity of the electronic certificate in the service consultable about the validity of certificates. .

4. Providers of certification services will assume full responsibility to third parties for the actions of persons to whom they delegate the performance of one or more of the functions needed for the provision of certification services.

5. The rules contained in this Law concerning the responsibility of providers of certification services are without prejudice to the provisions of legislation on improper clauses in contracts concluded with consumers.

Article 23. Limitation of liability of providers of certification services

1. A provider of certification services will not be liable for damages caused to the signatory or third parties in good faith if the signatory falls within any of the following cases:

    a) Not having provided the provider of certification services with true, complete and accurate information about data that have to appear in an electronic certificate or are necessary for its issue or for extinction or suspension of its validity, in cases where it was not possible for their inaccuracy to be detected by the provider of certification services.

    b) Failure to notify without delay to the provider of certification services any modification to circumstances reflected in an electronic certificate.

    c) Negligence in preservation of his signature creation data, in ensuring their confidentiality and in the protection of any access or disclosure.

    d) Failing to ask for suspension or revocation of an electronic certificate in cases of doubt about the maintenance of confidentiality of his signature creation data.

    e) Using signature creation data when the period of validity of an electronic certificate has expired or the provider of certification services notifies him of the extinction or suspension of its validity.

    f) Exceeding the limits which appear in an electronic certificate as to its possible uses and as to the individualised amount of transactions that may be effected with it, or failing to use it in accordance with the conditions stated and notified to the signatory by the provider of certification services.

2. In the case of electronic certificates that incorporate a power to represent the signatory, both the latter and the person or entity represented are obliged to ask for revocation or suspension of validity of the certificate within the terms set out in this Law.

3. Where the signatory is a legal person, the applicant for the electronic certificate will assume the obligations indicated in the first subsection.

4. A provider of certification services will likewise not be liable for damages caused to the signatory or to third parties in good faith if the intended recipient of electronically signed documents acts negligently. The intended recipient will in particular be deemed to act negligently in the following cases:

    a) Where he does not check and disregards the restrictions which appear in the electronic certificate as to its possible uses and as to the individualised amount of transactions that may be effected with it.

    b) Where he disregards a suspension or loss of validity of the electronic certificate published in the service consultable about the validity of certificates, or fails to verify the electronic signature.

5. A provider of certification services will not be liable for damages caused to the signatory or third parties in good faith through inaccuracy of data set out in the electronic certificate if those data were substantiated to it by public document. In

cases where said data have to be entered in a public register, the provider of certification services must check them in the aforesaid register immediately before issuing the certificate, possibly using, where applicable, data communication means.

6.   Exemption from liability to third parties requires the provider of certification services to prove that it did in any case act with due diligence.

PART IV

Electronic signatures devices and certification systems of providers of certification services and of electronic signature devices

CHAPTER I

Electronic signatures

Article 24. Electronic signature creation devices

1.   Electronic creation data are unique data, such as codes or private cryptographic keys, which the signatory uses for creating an electronic signature.

2.   A signature creation device is an information technology system or programme which serves for applying signature creation data.

3.   A secure signature creation device is a signature creation device which affords at least the following guarantees:

   a)   That data used for signature generation can be produced only once and it reasonably ensures their secrecy.

   b)   That there is reasonable security that data used for signature generation cannot be derived from signature verification data or from the actual signature and that the signature is protected against falsification with the technology existing at each time.

   c)   That signature creation data can be protected reliably by the signatory against their use by third parties.

   d)   That the device used does not alter data and the document to be signed nor prevent the latter's being shown to the signatory before the signing process.

Article 25. Electronic signature verification devices

1.   Signature verification data are data, such as codes or public cryptographic keys, that are used for verifying an electronic signature.

2.   A signature verification device is an information technology system or programme which serves for applying signature verification data.

3. Electronic signature verification devices guarantee, wherever technically possible, that the process of verification of an electronic signature satisfies at least the following requirements:

a) That the data used for verifying the signature correspond to the data shown to the person who verifies the signature.

b) That the signature is verified reliably and the results of its verification are presented properly.

c) That the person who verifies the electronic signature can where necessary establish reliably the content of the data signed and detect whether they have been modified.

d) That there is proper showing not only of the signatory's identity or, where applicable, clear placing on record of the use of a pseudonym, but also the results of the verification.

e) That the authenticity and validity of the corresponding electronic certificate are reliably verified.

f) That any change relating to its security can be detected.

4. Also, the data referring to verification of signature, such as when it takes place or ascertainment of the validity of the electronic certificate at the time, will be storable by the person who verifies the electronic signature or by trusted third parties.

CHAPTER II

Certification of providers of certification services and of electronic signature creation devices

Article 26. Certification of providers of certification services

1. Certification of a provider of certification services is a voluntary procedure whereby a qualified public or private entity issues a declaration in favour of a provider of certification services which implies recognition of the fulfilment of specific requirements in the provision of services offered to the public.

2. Certification of a provider of certification services may be requested by the latter and may be carried out inter alia by certification entities recognised by an accreditation entity designated in accordance with the provisions of Law 21/1992 of 16 July 1992 on Industry, and its development provisions.

3. Certification procedures will involve the use of technical rules that enjoy broad recognition and are approved by European standardisation organisations and, failing such, other international and Spanish rules.

4. Certification of a provider of certification services will not be necessary for recognising the legal efficacy of an electronic signature.

Article 27. Certification of secure electronic signature creation devices

1. Certification of secure electronic signature creation devices is a voluntary procedure for checking that device fulfils the requirements stated in this Law for it to be deemed a secure signature creation device.

2. Certification may be applied for by manufacturers or importers of signature creation devices and will be carried out by certification entities recognised by an accreditation entity designated in accordance with the provisions of Law 21/1992 of 16 July 1992 on Industry, and its development provisions.

3. Certification procedures will involve using technical rules whose reference numbers are published in the "Official Journal of the European Union" and, exceptionally, those approved by the Ministry of Science and Technology that will be published at that Ministry's Internet address.

4. Certificates of conformity of secure signature creation devices will be modified or, where applicable, revoked in cases where their holders cease to fulfil conditions laid down for obtaining them.

   Certification bodies will ensure the dissemination of decisions revoking certificates of signature creation devices.

Article 28. Recognition of conformity to regulations applicable to electronic signature products

1. The electronic signature products referred to in item d) of the first subsection of Article 20 and the third subsection of Article 24 will be presumed to conform to the requirements stated in those Articles if they comply with the corresponding technical rules whose reference numbers are published in the "Official Journal of the European Union".

2. Efficacy will be recognised in the case of certificates of conformity concerning secure signature creation devices that are granted by organisations designated for the purpose in any member State of the European Economic Area.

PART V

Supervision and control

Article 29. Supervision and control

1. The Ministry of Science and Technology will monitor the fulfilment by providers of certification services that issue electronic certificates to the public of the obligations stated in this Law and in its development provisions. It will also supervise the functioning of the system and of the organisations involved in certification of secure electronic signature creation devices.

2.   The Ministry of Science and Technology will carry out inspection operations as necessary for exercising its control function.

Officials assigned to the Ministry of Science and Technology who carry out the inspection referred to in the foregoing subsection will have the consideration of public authority in the performance of their tasks.

3.   The Ministry of Science and Technology may agree appropriate measures for the fulfilment of this Law and its development provisions.

4.   The Ministry of Science and Technology may resort to technically qualified independent entities to assist it in the work of supervision and control of providers of certification services which this Law assigns to it.

Article 30. Duty to inform and collaborate

1.   Providers of certification services, the independent accreditation entity and the certification organisations have the obligation to provide the Ministry of Science and Technology with all the information and collaboration needed for performing its functions.

In particular, they must enable its agents or the inspecting personnel to have access to their installations and to consult any documentation relevant to the inspection concerned, with application where appropriate of the provisions of Article 8.5 of Law 29/1998 of 13 July 1998 governing Administrative Litigation Jurisdiction.

2.   Providers of certification services must notify to Ministry of Science and Technology the commencement of their activity, their identification data, including fiscal and registration data, where applicable, data which make it possible to establish communication with the provider, including Internet domain number, the public attention data, the characteristics of the services they are to provide, the accreditations obtained for their services and the certifications of the devices they use. This information must be properly updated by the providers and will be published at the aforesaid Ministry's Internet address with a view to disseminating and making it known as widely as possible.

3.   In cases where an inspection operation reveals facts that may constitute offences defined in other laws, those facts will be reported to the agencies or organisations competent to supervise and sanction them.

PART VI

Offences and sanctions

Article 31. Offences

1.   Offences against the precepts of this Law are classified as very serious, serious and minor.

2. The following are very serious offences:

   a) Default on any of the obligations stated in Articles 18 and 20 in the issue of recognised certificates, provided that serious harm has been caused to users or the security of certification services has been serious affected.

   The provisions of this subsection do not apply with respect to default on the obligation to furnish the economic guarantee referred to in the second subsection of Article 20.

   b) Issue of recognised certificates without carrying out all the prior checks referred to in Article 12, in cases where this affects the majority of the recognised certificates issued in the three years prior to commencement of the sanctioning procedure or from commencement of the provider's activity, if this latter period is shorter.

3. The following are serious offences:

   a) Default on any of the obligations stated in Articles 18 and 20 in the issue of recognised certificates, except the obligation to furnish the guarantee referred to in the second subsection of Article 20, in cases not constituting a very serious offence.

   b) Failure by providers issuing recognised certificates to furnish the economic guarantee contemplated in the second subsection of Article 20.

   c) Issue of recognised certificates without carrying out all the prior checks indicated in Article 12, in cases not constituting a very serious offence.

   d) Failure by providers of certification services that do not issue recognised certificates to fulfil the obligations stated in Article 18, if serious harm has been caused to users or the security of certification services has been seriously affected.

   e) Default by providers of certification services on the obligations stated in Article 21 regarding cessation of their activity or the production of circumstances that prevent continuation of their activity.

   f) Unjustified resistance, obstruction, excuse or refusal with respect to inspection operations by agencies empowered to carry them out under this Law, and deficient or no presentation of information requested by the Ministry of Science and Technology in its inspection and control function.

   g) Failure to comply with decisions adopted by the Ministry of Science and Technology for ensuring that providers of certification services conform to this Law.

4. The following constitute minor offences:

   Failure by providers of certification services that do not issue recognised certificate to fulfil the obligations stated in Article 18 and other Articles of this Law, in cases not constituting a serious or very serious offence.

Article 32. Sanctions

1. The following sanctions will be imposed for committing offences referred to in the foregoing Article:

    a) Fine of 150,001 to 600,000 euros for an offender committing a very serious offence.

    Committing two or more very serious offences within a period of three years may give rise, as a function of the grading criteria of the next Article, to the sanction of being barred from operating in Spain for a maximum period of two years.

    b) Fine of 30,001 to 150,000 euros for an offender committing a serious offence.

    c) A fine of up to 30,000 euros for an offender committing a minor offence.

2. Serious and very serious offences may give rise, at the expense of the person sanctioned, to publication of the sanctioning decision in the Spanish official gazette *"Boletín Oficial del Estado"* and in two nationally distributed newspapers or on the opening page of the provider's Internet site and, where applicable, on the Ministry of Science and Technology's Internet site, once the decision has become final.

    For imposing this sanction, there will be consideration of the social repercussions of the offence committed, the number of users affected and the seriousness of the unlawfulness.

Article 33. Grading of the amount of sanctions

The amount of fines imposed within the limits indicated will be graded taking the following into account:

a) Any intentionality or reiteration.

b) Recurrence, by committing offences of the same nature, that are sanctioned by a final decision.

c) Nature and amount of losses caused.

d) Period of time during which the offence was committed.

e) Benefit that committing the offence brought the offender.

f) Volume of billing affected by the offence committed.

Article 34. Provisional measures

1. In procedures sanctioning serious or very serious offences, the Ministry of Science and Technology may adopt, under Law 30/1992 of 26 November 1992 on the Legal Regime of Public Administrations and the Common Administrative Procedure, and its development rules, such provisional measures as are deemed necessary for ensuring the effectiveness of the decision to be finally adopted, the

completion of the procedure, to prevent continuation of the effects of the offence, and the requirements of the general interest.

In particular, the following may be ordered:

a) Temporary suspension of activity of the provider of certification services and, where applicable, provisional closure of its establishments.

b) Sealing, deposit or seizure of information technology archives, supports and records, and documents in general, as also information technology equipment and apparatus of every kind.

c) Warning to the public of the existence of possible offending forms of conduct and the opening of the sanctioning proceedings concerned, as also of the measures adopted for ensuring the cessation of such conduct.

In the adoption and fulfilment of the restrictive measures referred to in this subsection, there will in all cases be observance of the guarantees, rules and procedures referred to in the legal system for protecting the right to personal privacy and to protection of personal data, in cases where these might be affected.

2. In cases of harm of exceptional seriousness to the security of systems used by the provider of certification services that seriously decreases the confidence of users in the services offered, the Ministry of Science and Technology may order suspension or loss of validity of the certificates affected, possibly permanently.

3. In any case, the principle of proportionality of the measure to be adopted to the objectives in view will be observed in each case.

4. In cases of urgency and for immediate protection of the interests involved, the provisional measures referred to in this Article may be ordered before initiation of sanctioning proceedings.

The measures must be confirmed, modified or withdrawn in the order initiating the procedure, which must be made within fifteen days following their adoption, which may be subject to appeal as appropriate.

In any case, said measures will remain inoperative unless the sanctioning procedure is commenced within that time limit or if the initiating order does not contain an express pronouncement concerning those measures.

Article 35. Coercive fine

The administrative body competent to rule in the sanctioning procedure may impose coercive fines not exceeding in amount 6,000 euros per day that passes without fulfilment of any provisional measures that have been ordered.

Article 36. Competence and sanctioning procedure

1. The imposing of sanctions for failure to comply with the provisions of this Law will be incumbent, in the case of very serious offences, upon the Ministry of Science and Technology, and in the case of serious and minor offences, upon the Secretary of State for Telecommunications and for the Information Society.

2.   The sanctioning power governed by this Law will be exercised in accordance with the relevant provisions of the Law on the Legal Regime of Public Administrations and the Common Administrative Procedure and its development rules.

First additional provision. Public attestation and use of electronic signature by Notaries and Property, Mercantile and Personalty Registrars

The provisions of this Law are without prejudice to those of legislation governing the incorporation of electronic, information technology and data communications techniques in preventive legal security. They likewise neither replace nor modify the rules governing the functions pertaining to Notaries for attesting documents or authorising them, intervening or raising them to public documents, and the qualification functions of Property, Mercantile and Personalty Registrars; nor the rules that govern the operation of the General Council of the Notarial Profession and the Professional Body of Property, Mercantile and Personalty Registrars, in their function as providers of certification services for the exclusive purposes of electronic signature attribution to such officials.

Second additional provision. Exercising sanctioning power over the accreditation entity and organisations that certify electronic signature creation devices

1.   Within the scope of the certification of signature creation devices, it will be incumbent upon the Ministry of Science and Technology's Secretary of State for Telecommunications and for the Information Society to impose sanctions for the committing by organisations that certify secure electronic signature creation devices, or by the entity accrediting them, of the serious offences referred to in items e), f) and g) of the second subsection of Article 31 of Law 21/1992 of 16 July 1992 on Industry, and the minor offences indicated in item a) of the third subsection of Article 31 of that Law which they commit in the course of activities relating to electronic signature certification.

2.   Such offences that merit classification as very serious offences will be sanctioned by the Ministry of Science and Technology.

Third additional provision. Issue of electronic certificates to entities without legal status for the fulfilment of tax obligations

Electronic certificates may be issued to the entities without legal status referred to in Article 33 of the General Tax Law for the sole purposes of their use within the scope of taxation, within terms laid down by the Minister of Finance.

Fourth additional provision. Provision of services by the currency agency *Fabrica Nacional de Moneda y Timbre-Real Casa de la Moneda*

The provisions of the present Law are without prejudice to those of Article 81 of Law 66/1997 of 30 December 1997 on Fiscal, Administrative and Social Measures.

Fifth additional provision. Modification of Article 81 of Law 66/1997 of 30 December 1997 on Fiscal, Administrative and Social Measures.

A subsection Twelve is added to Article 81 of Law 66/1997 of 30 December 1997 on Fiscal, Administrative and Social Measures, with the following wording:

"In the exercise of the functions attributed to it by the present Article, *Fabrica Nacional de Moneda y Timbre-Real Casa de la Moneda* will be exempt from furnishing the guarantee referred to in subsection 2 of Article 20 of the Law (. . .) on Electronic Signatures."

Sixth additional provision. Legal regime of electronic National Identity Documents

1.   Without prejudice to applying the prevailing regulations on National Identity Documents in all respects appropriate to their particular characteristics, electronic National Identity Documents will be governed by specific regulations.

2.   The Ministry of Science and Technology may contact the Ministry of the Interior with a view to the latter adopting the measures needed for ensuring fulfilment of the obligations incumbent upon it as a provider of certification services in relation to electronic National Identity Documents.

Seventh additional provision. Issue of invoices by electronic means

The provisions of this Law are without prejudice to the requirements arising from the tax rules regarding the issuing of invoices by electronic means.

First transitional provision. Validity of electronic certificates issued prior to the effective date of this Law

Electronic certificates issued by providers of certification services within the framework of Royal Decree-Law 14/1999 of 17 September 1999 concerning electronic signatures will maintain their validity.

Second transitional provision. Providers of certification services established in Spain before the effective date of this Law

Providers of certification services established in Spain before the effective date of this Law must notify to the Ministry of Science and Technology their activity and the characteristics of the services they provide within the time limit of one month from the aforesaid effective date. That information will be published at the aforesaid Ministry's Internet address with a view to disseminating and making it known as widely as possible.

Sole repealing provision. Repeal of enactment

Royal Decree-Law 14/1999 of 17 September 1999 concerning electronic signatures and any provisions of equal or inferior rank that conflict with the provisions of the present Law are repealed.

First final provision. Constitutional basis

This Law is issued under Article 149.18.a, 18.a, 21.a and 29.a of the Constitution.

Second final provision. Regulatory development

1.   The Government will adapt the regulations governing National Identity Documents to the provisions of the present Law.

2.   The Government is also empowered to issue such other regulatory provisions as may be necessary for the development and application of this Law.

Third final provision. Effective date

The present Law will come into force three months from its publication in the Spanish official gazette *"Boletín Oficial del Estado"*.

United Kingdom

Electronic Communications 2000

2000 Chapter c.7

Acts of Parliament printed from this website are printed under the superintendence and authority of the Controller of HMSO being the Queen's Printer of Acts of Parliament.

The text of this Internet version of the Act is published by the Queen's Printer of Acts of Parliament and has been prepared to reflect the text as it received Royal Assent. A print version is also available and is published by The Stationery Office Limited as the Electronic **Communications Act 2000**, ISBN 0 10 540700 3. The print version may be purchased by clicking . Braille copies of this Act can also be purchased at the same price as the print edition by contacting TSO Customer Services on 0870 600 5522 or e-mail: SHOW PHIL-- customer.services@tso.co.uk.

Further information about the publication of legislation on this website can be found by referring to the Frequently Asked Questions.

To ensure fast access over slow connections, large documents have been segmented into "chunks". Where you see a "continue" button at the bottom of the page of text, this indicates that there is another chunk of text available.

Electronic Communications Act 2000

2000 Chapter c.7

ARRANGEMENT OF SECTIONS

PART I

CRYPTOGRAPHY SERVICE PROVIDERS

Section

1.   Register of approved providers.

2.   Arrangements for the grant of approvals.

3.   Delegation of approval functions.

4.   Restrictions on disclosure of information.

5.   Regulations under Part I.

6.   Provision of cryptography support services.

PART II

FACILITATION OF ELECTRONIC COMMERCE, DATA STORAGE, ETC.

7.   ELECTRONIC SIGNATURES AND RELATED CERTIFICATES

8.   POWER TO MODIFY LEGISLATION

9.   SECTION 8 ORDERS

10. MODIFICATIONS IN RELATION TO WELSH MATTERS

PART III

MISCELLANEOUS AND SUPPLEMENTAL

Telecommunications licences

11. Modification of licences by the Director.

12. Appeals against modifications of licence conditions.

Supplemental

13. Ministerial expenditure etc.

14. Prohibition on key escrow requirements.

15. General interpretation.

16.   Short title, commencement, extent.

An Act to make provision to facilitate the use of electronic communications and electronic data storage; to make provision about the modification of licences granted under section 7 of the Telecommunications Act 1984; and for connected purposes.

[25th May 2000]

BE IT ENACTED by the Queen's most Excellent Majesty, by and with the advice and consent of the Lords Spiritual and Temporal, and Commons, in this present Parliament assembled, and by the authority of the same, as follows:-

PART I

RYPTOGRAPHY SERVICE PROVIDERS

Register of approved providers.

1.

    (1)   It shall be the duty of the Secretary of State to establish and maintain a register of approved providers of cryptography support services.

    (2)   The Secretary of State shall secure that the register contains particulars of every person who is for the time being approved under any arrangements in force under section 2.

    (3)   The particulars that must be recorded in every entry in the register relating to an approved person are-

        (a)   the name and address of that person;

        (b)   the services in respect of which that person is approved; and

        (c)   the conditions of the approval.

    (4)   It shall be the duty of the Secretary of State to ensure that such arrangements are in force as he considers appropriate for-

        (a)   allowing members of the public to inspect the contents of the register; and

        (b)   securing that such publicity is given to any withdrawal or modification of an approval as will bring it to the attention of persons likely to be interested in it.

Arrangements for the grant of approvals.

2.

    (1)   It shall be the duty of the Secretary of State to secure that there are arrangements in force for granting approvals to persons who-

        (a)   are providing cryptography support services in the United Kingdom or are proposing to do so; and

(b)   seek approval in respect of any such services that they are providing, or are proposing to provide, whether in the United Kingdom or elsewhere.

(2)   The arrangements must-

    (a)   allow for an approval to be granted either in respect of all the services in respect of which it is sought or in respect of only some of them;

    (b)   ensure that an approval is granted to a person in respect of any services only if the condition for the grant of an approval to that person is fulfilled in accordance with subsection (3);

    (c)   provide for an approval granted to any person to have effect subject to such conditions (whether or not connected with the provision of the services in respect of which the approval is granted) as may be contained in the approval;

    (d)   enable a person to whom the Secretary of State is proposing to grant an approval to refuse it if the proposal is in different terms from the approval which was sought;

    (e)   make provision for the handling of complaints and disputes which-

        (i)   are required by the conditions of an approved person's approval to be dealt with in accordance with a procedure maintained by him in pursuance of those conditions; but

        (ii)   are not disposed of by the application of that procedure;

    (f)   provide for the modification and withdrawal of approvals.

(3)   The condition that must be fulfilled before an approval is granted to any person is that the Secretary of State is satisfied that that person-

    (a)   will comply, in providing the services in respect of which he is approved, with such technical and other requirements as may be prescribed;

    (b)   is a person in relation to whom such other requirements as may be prescribed are, and will continue to be, satisfied;

    (c)   is, and will continue to be, able and willing to comply with any requirements that the Secretary of State is proposing to impose by means of conditions of the approval; and

    (d)   is otherwise a fit and proper person to be approved in respect of those services.

(4)   Regulations made by virtue of paragraph (a) or (b) of subsection (3) may frame a requirement for the purposes of that subsection by reference to the opinion of a person specified in the regulations, or of a person chosen in a manner determined in accordance with the regulations.

(5)   The requirements which (subject to subsection (6)) may be imposed by conditions contained in an approval in accordance with the arrangements include-

    (a)   requirements to provide information to such persons, in such form, at such times and in response to such requests as may be specified in or determined under the terms of the condition;

(b) requirements that impose obligations that will continue or recur notwith-standing the withdrawal (in whole or in part) of the approval;

(c) requirements framed by reference to the opinion or directions of a person specified in or chosen in accordance with provision contained in the conditions.

(6) Nothing in the arrangements shall authorise the imposition, by conditions contained in an approval, of any requirements for-

(a) the provision of information, or

(b) the maintenance of a procedure for handling complaints or disputes,

in relation to any matter other than one appearing to the Secretary of State to be relevant to the matters mentioned in subsection (3)(a) to (d).

(7) Any requirement to provide information that is imposed in accordance with the arrangements on any person by the conditions of his approval shall be enforceable at the suit or instance of the Secretary of State.

(8) Where any arrangements under this section so provide, a person who-

(a) seeks an approval under the arrangements,

(b) applies for a modification of such an approval,

(c) is for the time being approved under the arrangements, or

(d) has his approval under the arrangements modified wholly or partly in consequence of an application made by him,

shall pay to the Secretary of State, at such time or times as may be prescribed, such fee or fees as may be prescribed in relation to that time or those times.

(9) Sums received by the Secretary of State by virtue of subsection (8) shall be paid into the Consolidated Fund.

(10) For the purposes of subsection (1) cryptography support services are provided in the United Kingdom if-

(a) they are provided from premises in the United Kingdom;

(b) they are provided to a person who is in the United Kingdom when he makes use of the services; or

(c) they are provided to a person who makes use of the services for the purposes of a business carried on in the United Kingdom or from premises in the United Kingdom.

Delegation of approval functions.

3.

(1) The Secretary of State may appoint any person to carry out, in his place, such of his functions under the preceding provisions of this Part (other than any power of his to make regulations) as may be specified in the appointment.

(2) An appointment under this section-

(a) shall have effect only to such extent, and subject to such conditions, as may be set out in the appointment; and

(b) may be revoked or varied at any time by a notice given by the Secretary of State to the appointed person.

(3) A person appointed under this section shall, in the carrying out of the functions specified in his appointment, comply with all such general directions as may be given to him from time to time by the Secretary of State.

(4) Subject to any order under subsection (5) and to any directions given by the Secretary of State, where a body established by or under any enactment or the holder of any office created by or under any enactment is appointed to carry out any functions of the Secretary of State under this Part-

(a) the enactments relating to the functions of that body or office shall have effect as if the functions of that body or office included the functions specified in the appointment; and

(b) the body or office-holder shall be taken to have power to do anything which is calculated to facilitate, or is incidental or conducive to, the carrying out of the functions so specified.

(5) The Secretary of State may, by order made by statutory instrument, provide for enactments relating to any such body or office as is mentioned in subsection (4) to have effect, so far as appears to him appropriate for purposes connected with the carrying out of functions that have been or may be conferred on the body or office-holder under this section, with such modifications as may be provided for in the order.

(6) An order shall not be made under subsection (5) unless a draft of it has first been laid before Parliament and approved by a resolution of each House.

(7) It shall be the duty of the Secretary of State to secure-

(a) that any appointment made under this section is published in such manner as he considers best calculated to bring it to the attention of persons likely to be interested in it;

(b) that any variation or revocation of such an appointment is also so published; and

(c) that the time fixed for any notice varying or revoking such an appointment to take effect allows a reasonable period after the giving of the notice for the making of any necessary incidental or transitional arrangements.

(8) Nothing in this section, or in anything done under this section, shall prejudice-

(a) any power of the Secretary of State, apart from this Act, to exercise functions through a Minister or official in his department;

(b) any power of any person by virtue of subsection (4), or by virtue of an order under subsection (5), to act on behalf of a body or office-holder in connection with the carrying out of any function;

(c) any provision by virtue of section 2(4) or (5)(c) that imposes a requirement by reference to the opinion of any person or determines the manner of

choosing a person whose opinion is to be referred to.
Restrictions on disclosure of information.

4.

(1)   Subject to the following provisions of this section, no information which-

    (a)   has been obtained under or by virtue of the provisions of this Part, and

    (b)   relates to the private affairs of any individual or to any particular business,

shall, during the lifetime of that individual or so long as that business continues to be carried on, be disclosed without the consent of that individual or the person for the time being carrying on that business.

(2)   Subsection (1) does not apply to any disclosure of information which is made-

    (a)   for the purpose of facilitating the carrying out of any functions under this Part, or any prescribed functions, of the Secretary of State or a person appointed under section 3;

    (b)   for the purpose of facilitating the carrying out of any functions of a local weights and measures authority in Great Britain;

    (c)   for the purpose of facilitating the carrying out of prescribed public functions of any person;

    (d)   in connection with the investigation of any criminal offence or for the purposes of any criminal proceedings;

    (e)   for the purposes of any civil proceedings which-

        (i)   relate to the provision of cryptography support services; and

        (ii)   are proceedings to which a person approved in accordance with arrangements under section 2 is a party; or

    (f)   in pursuance of a Community obligation.

(3)   In subsection (2)(a) the reference to functions under this Part does not include a reference to any power of the Secretary of State to make regulations.

(4)   In subsection (2)(c) "public functions" includes any function conferred by or in accordance with any provision contained in or made under any enactment or Community legislation.

(5)   If information is disclosed to the public in circumstances in which the disclosure does not contravene this section, this section shall not prevent its further disclosure by any person.

(6)   Any person who discloses any information in contravention of this section shall be guilty of an offence and liable-

    (a)   on summary conviction, to a fine not exceeding the statutory maximum;

    (b)   on conviction on indictment, to imprisonment for a term not exceeding two years or a fine, or to both.

Regulations under Part I.

5.

(1) In this Part "prescribed" means prescribed by regulations made by the Secretary of State, or determined in such manner as may be provided for in any such regulations.

(2) The powers of the Secretary of State to make regulations under this Part shall be exercisable by statutory instrument, which (except in the case of the initial regulations) shall be subject to annulment in pursuance of a resolution of either House of Parliament.

(3) The initial regulations shall not be made unless a draft of them has been laid before Parliament and approved by a resolution of each House.

(4) In this section "the initial regulations" means the regulations made on the first occasion on which the Secretary of State exercises his powers to make regulations under this Part.

(5) Before making any regulations by virtue of section 2(3)(a) or (b) the Secretary of State shall consult-

   (a) such persons appearing to him to be likely to be affected by those regulations, and

   (b) such persons appearing to him to be representative of persons likely to be so affected,

as he thinks fit.

(6) Regulations made by the Secretary of State under any provision of this Part-

   (a) may make different provision for different cases; and

   (b) may contain such incidental, supplemental, consequential and transitional provision as the Secretary of State thinks fit.

Provision of cryptography support services.

6.

(1) In this Part "cryptography support service" means any service which is provided to the senders or recipients of electronic communications, or to those storing electronic data, and is designed to facilitate the use of cryptographic techniques for the purpose of-

   (a) securing that such communications or data can be accessed, or can be put into an intelligible form, only by certain persons; or

   (b) securing that the authenticity or integrity of such communications or data is capable of being ascertained.

(2) References in this Part to the provision of a cryptography support service do not include references to the supply of, or of any right to use, computer software or computer hardware except where the supply is integral to the provision of cryptography support services not consisting in such a supply.

PART II

FACILITATION OF ELECTRONIC COMMERCE, DATA STORAGE, ETC.

Electronic signatures and related certificates.

7.

(1)   In any legal proceedings-

(a)   an electronic signature incorporated into or logically associated with a particular electronic communication or particular electronic data, and

(b)   the certification by any person of such a signature,

shall each be admissible in evidence in relation to any question as to the authenticity of the communication or data or as to the integrity of the communication or data.

(2)   For the purposes of this section an electronic signature is so much of anything in electronic form as-

(a)   is incorporated into or otherwise logically associated with any electronic communication or electronic data; and

(b)   purports to be so incorporated or associated for the purpose of being used in establishing the authenticity of the communication or data, the integrity of the communication or data, or both.

(3)   For the purposes of this section an electronic signature incorporated into or associated with a particular electronic communication or particular electronic data is certified by any person if that person (whether before or after the making of the communication) has made a statement confirming that-

(a)   the signature,

(b)   a means of producing, communicating or verifying the signature, or

(c)   a procedure applied to the signature,

is (either alone or in combination with other factors) a valid means of establishing the authenticity of the communication or data, the integrity of the communication or data, or both.

Power to modify legislation.

8.

(1)   Subject to subsection (3), the appropriate Minister may by order made by statutory instrument modify the provisions of-

(a)   any enactment or subordinate legislation, or

(b)   any scheme, licence, authorisation or approval issued, granted or given by or under any enactment or subordinate legislation,

in such manner as he may think fit for the purpose of authorising or facilitating the use of electronic communications or electronic storage (instead of other forms of communication or storage) for any purpose mentioned in subsection (2).

(2) Those purposes are-

(a) the doing of anything which under any such provisions is required to be or may be done or evidenced in writing or otherwise using a document, notice or instrument;

(b) the doing of anything which under any such provisions is required to be or may be done by post or other specified means of delivery;

(c) the doing of anything which under any such provisions is required to be or may be authorised by a person's signature or seal, or is required to be delivered as a deed or witnessed;

(d) the making of any statement or declaration which under any such provisions is required to be made under oath or to be contained in a statutory declaration;

(e) the keeping, maintenance or preservation, for the purposes or in pursuance of any such provisions, of any account, record, notice, instrument or other document;

(f) the provision, production or publication under any such provisions of any information or other matter;

(g) the making of any payment that is required to be or may be made under any such provisions.

(3) The appropriate Minister shall not make an order under this section authorising the use of electronic communications or electronic storage for any purpose, unless he considers that the authorisation is such that the extent (if any) to which records of things done for that purpose will be available will be no less satisfactory in cases where use is made of electronic communications or electronic storage than in other cases.

(4) Without prejudice to the generality of subsection (1), the power to make an order under this section shall include power to make an order containing any of the following provisions-

(a) provision as to the electronic form to be taken by any electronic communications or electronic storage the use of which is authorised by an order under this section;

(b) provision imposing conditions subject to which the use of electronic communications or electronic storage is so authorised;

(c) provision, in relation to cases in which any such conditions are not satisfied, for treating anything for the purposes of which the use of such communications or storage is so authorised as not having been done;

(d) provision, in connection with anything so authorised, for a person to be able to refuse to accept receipt of something in electronic form except in such circumstances as may be specified in or determined under the order;

(e)   provision, in connection with any use of electronic communications so authorised, for intermediaries to be used, or to be capable of being used, for the transmission of any data or for establishing the authenticity or integrity of any data;

(f)   provision, in connection with any use of electronic storage so authorised, for persons satisfying such conditions as may be specified in or determined under the regulations to carry out functions in relation to the storage;

(g)   provision, in relation to cases in which the use of electronic communications or electronic storage is so authorised, for the determination of any of the matters mentioned in subsection (5), or as to the manner in which they may be proved in legal proceedings;

(h)   provision, in relation to cases in which fees or charges are or may be imposed in connection with anything for the purposes of which the use of electronic communications or electronic storage is so authorised, for different fees or charges to apply where use is made of such communications or storage;

(i)   provision, in relation to any criminal or other liabilities that may arise (in respect of the making of false or misleading statements or otherwise) in connection with anything for the purposes of which the use of electronic communications or electronic storage is so authorised, for corresponding liabilities to arise in corresponding circumstances where use is made of such communications or storage;

(j)   provision requiring persons to prepare and keep records in connection with any use of electronic communications or electronic storage which is so authorised;

(k)   provision requiring the production of the contents of any records kept in accordance with an order under this section;

(l)   provision for a requirement imposed by virtue of paragraph (j) or (k) to be enforceable at the suit or instance of such person as may be specified in or determined in accordance with the order;

(m)   any such provision, in relation to electronic communications or electronic storage the use of which is authorised otherwise than by an order under this section, as corresponds to any provision falling within any of the preceding paragraphs that may be made where it is such an order that authorises the use of the communications or storage.

(5)   The matters referred to in subsection (4)(g) are-

(a)   whether a thing has been done using an electronic communication or electronic storage;

(b)   the time at which, or date on which, a thing done using any such communication or storage was done;

(c)   the place where a thing done using such communication or storage was done;

(d)   the person by whom such a thing was done; and

(e)   the contents, authenticity or integrity of any electronic data.

(6)   An order under this section-

   (a)   shall not (subject to paragraph (b)) require the use of electronic communications or electronic storage for any purpose; but

   (b)   may make provision that a period of notice specified in the order must expire before effect is given to a variation or withdrawal of an election or other decision which-

      (i)   has been made for the purposes of such an order; and

      (ii)   is an election or decision to make use of electronic communications or electronic storage.

(7)   The matters in relation to which provision may be made by an order under this section do not include any matter under the care and management of the Commissioners of Inland Revenue or any matter under the care and management of the Commissioners of Customs and Excise.

(8)   In this section references to doing anything under the provisions of any enactment include references to doing it under the provisions of any subordinate legislation the power to make which is conferred by that enactment.
Section 8 orders.
9.

(1)   In this Part "the appropriate Minister" means (subject to subsections (2) and (7) and section 10(1))-

   (a)   in relation to any matter with which a department of the Secretary of State is concerned, the Secretary of State;

   (b)   in relation to any matter with which the Treasury is concerned, the Treasury; and

   (c)   in relation to any matter with which any Government department other than a department of the Secretary of State or the Treasury is concerned, the Minister in charge of the other department.

(2)   Where in the case of any matter-

   (a)   that matter falls within more than one paragraph of subsection (1),

   (b)   there is more than one such department as is mentioned in paragraph (c) of that subsection that is concerned with that matter, or

   (c)   both paragraphs (a) and (b) of this subsection apply,

references, in relation to that matter, to the appropriate Minister are references to any one or more of the appropriate Ministers acting (in the case of more than one) jointly.

(3)   Subject to subsection (4) and section 10(6), a statutory instrument containing an order under section 8 shall be subject to annulment in pursuance of a resolution of either House of Parliament.

(4)   Subsection (3) does not apply in the case of an order a draft of which has been laid before Parliament and approved by a resolution of each House.

(5)   An order under section 8 may-

    (a)   provide for any conditions or requirements imposed by such an order to be framed by reference to the directions of such persons as may be specified in or determined in accordance with the order;

    (b)   provide that any such condition or requirement is to be satisfied only where a person so specified or determined is satisfied as to specified matters.

(6)   The provision made by such an order may include-

    (a)   different provision for different cases;

    (b)   such exceptions and exclusions as the person making the order may think fit; and

    (c)   any such incidental, supplemental, consequential and transitional provision as he may think fit;

and the provision that may be made by virtue of paragraph (c) includes provision modifying any enactment or subordinate legislation or any scheme, licence, authorisation or approval issued, granted or given by or under any enactment or subordinate legislation.

(7)   In the case of any matter which is not one of the reserved matters within the meaning of the Scotland Act 1998 or in respect of which functions are, by virtue of section 63 of that Act, exercisable by the Scottish Ministers instead of by or concurrently with a Minister of the Crown, this section and section 8 shall apply to Scotland subject to the following modifications-

    (a)   subsections (1) and (2) of this section are omitted;

    (b)   any reference to the appropriate Minister is to be read as a reference to the Secretary of State;

    (c)   any power of the Secretary of State, by virtue of paragraph (b), to make an order under section 8 may also be exercised by the Scottish Ministers with the consent of the Secretary of State; and

    (d)   where the Scottish Ministers make an order under section 8-

        (i)   any reference to the Secretary of State (other than a reference in this subsection) shall be construed as a reference to the Scottish Ministers; and

        (ii)   any reference to Parliament or to a House of Parliament shall be construed as a reference to the Scottish Parliament.

Modifications in relation to Welsh matters.

10.

(1)   For the purposes of the exercise of the powers conferred by section 8 in relation to any matter the functions in respect of which are exercisable by the National Assembly for Wales, the appropriate Minister is the Secretary of State.

(2)   Subject to the following provisions of this section, the powers conferred by section 8, so far as they fall within subsection (3), shall be exercisable by the National Assembly for Wales, as well as by the appropriate Minister.

(3)   The powers conferred by section 8 fall within this subsection to the extent that they are exercisable in relation to-

   (a)   the provisions of any subordinate legislation made by the National Assembly for Wales;

   (b)   so much of any other subordinate legislation as makes provision the power to make which is exercisable by that Assembly;

   (c)   any power under any enactment to make provision the power to make which is so exercisable;

   (d)   the giving, sending or production of any notice, account, record or other document or of any information to or by a body mentioned in subsection (4); or

   (e)   the publication of anything by a body mentioned in subsection (4).

(4)   Those bodies are-

   (a)   the National Assembly for Wales;

   (b)   any body specified in Schedule 4 to the Government of Wales Act 1998 (Welsh public bodies subject to reform by that Assembly);

   (c)   any other such body as may be specified for the purposes of this section by an order made by the Secretary of State with the consent of that Assembly.

(5)   The National Assembly for Wales shall not make an order under section 8 except with the consent of the Secretary of State.

(6)   Section 9(3) shall not apply to any order made under section 8 by the National Assembly for Wales.

(7)   Nothing in this section shall confer any power on the National Assembly for Wales to modify any provision of the Government of Wales Act 1998.

(8)   The power of the Secretary of State to make an order under subsection (4)(c)-

   (a)   shall include power to make any such incidental, supplemental, consequential and transitional provision as he may think fit; and

   (b)   shall be exercisable by statutory instrument subject to annulment in pursuance of a resolution of either House of Parliament.

PART III

MISCELLANEOUS AND SUPPLEMENTAL

Telecommunications licences

Modification of licences by the Director.

11.

(1) In subsection (3) of section 12 of the Telecommunications Act 1984 (which requires notice of a proposed modification of the conditions of a licence under section 7 of that Act to be served on the licensee), for "that person" there shall be substituted "every relevant licensee".

(2) For subsection (4) of that section (circumstances in which a proposal by the Director General of Telecommunications for the modification of the conditions of a licence is made by agreement) there shall be substituted the following subsections-

"(4A)In the case of a licence granted to all persons, or to all persons of a particular class, the Director shall not make any modification unless-

   (a) he has considered every representation made to him about the modification; and

   (b) there has not been any objection by a person running a telecommunication system under the authority of the licence to the making of the modification.

(4B) In the case of a licence granted to a particular person, the Director shall not make any modification unless-

   (a) he has considered every representation made to him about the modification or any modification in the same or similar terms that he is at the same time proposing to make in the case of other licences; and

   (b) the requirements of section 12A below are satisfied in the case of the modification and also in the case of every such modification in the same or similar terms."

(3) After subsection (6) of that section there shall be inserted the following subsections-

"(6A)Where the Director makes a modification under this section, he shall, as soon as reasonably practicable after making the modification, give notice of his reasons for doing so.

(6B) Subsection (3) above shall apply in the case of a notice under subsection (6A) above as it applies in the case of a notice under subsection (2) above.

(6C) Where the Director has given notice under subsection (2) above of a proposal to modify the conditions of a licence, he may in such manner and at such time as he considers appropriate publish-

   (a) the identities of any or all of the persons who objected to the making of the modification; and

(b)   to the extent that confidentiality for representations or objections in relation to the proposal for the modification has not been claimed by the persons making them, such other particulars of the representations or objections as he thinks fit.

(6D) In this section and section 12A below (except in subsection (6C) above), a reference to a representation or objection, in relation to a modification, is a reference only to a representation or objection which-

(a)   was duly made to the Director within a time limit specified in the case of that modification under subsection (2)(c) above or section 12A(5)(d) below; and

(b)   has not subsequently been withdrawn;

and for the purposes of this section and section 12A below representations against a modification shall be taken to constitute an objection only if they are accompanied by a written statement that they are to be so taken.

(6E) In this section and section 12A below "relevant licensee", in relation to a modification, means-

(a)   in a case where the same or a similar modification is being proposed at the same time in relation to different licences granted to different persons, each of the persons who, at the time when notice of the proposals is given, is authorised by one or more of those licences to run a telecommunication system; and

(b)   in any other case, the person authorised by the licence in question to run such a system.

(6F) In this section references to a modification of the conditions of a licence do not include references to any modification to which effect is given by the exercise of a power under the terms of any licence to revoke it and by the grant of a new licence."

(4)   After that section there shall be inserted the following section-

"Agreement required for the purposes of section 12.

12A.

(1)   The requirements of this section are satisfied in the case of a modification if any of subsections (2) to (4) below applies.

(2)   This subsection applies if-

(a)   it appears to the Director that the relevant licensee or, as the case may be, each of the relevant licensees has been given a reminder, at least seven days before the making of the modification, of the Director's powers in the absence of objections; and

(b)   there has not been an objection by a relevant licensee to the making of the modification.

(3)   This subsection applies if-

(a) the modification is one which in the opinion of the Director is deregulatory; and

(b) the notice given under section 12(2) above in the case of the proposal for the modification contained a statement of that opinion and of the Director's reasons for it.

(4) This subsection applies if-

(a) the modification is in the same or similar terms as modifications that the Director has already proposed but not yet made in the case of other licences;

(b) the licence in question is one issued since the making of the proposal for the modification of the conditions of the other licences;

(c) subsection (2) or (3) above applies in the case of the modifications of the conditions of the other licences;

(d) it appears to the Director that the person holding the licence in question has been given a reasonable opportunity of stating whether he objects to the modification; and

(e) that person has not objected.

(5) A reminder for the purposes of subsection (2)(a) above-

(a) must be contained in a notice given by the Director and, in the case of a relevant licensee which is a company with a registered office in the United Kingdom, must have been given to that company by being sent to that office;

(b) must remind the licensee of the contents of the notice which was copied to the licensee under section 12(3) above in the case of the modification in question;

(c) must state that the Director will be able to make the modification if no relevant licensee objects; and

(d) must specify a time (not being less than seven days from the date of the giving of the notice) at the end of which the final opportunity for the making of representations and objections will expire.

(6) Nothing in subsection (2) above shall require a reminder to be sent to a person who has consented to the making of the modification in question.

(7) For the purposes of this section a modification is deregulatory if-

(a) the effect of the conditions to be modified is to impose a burden affecting the holder of the licence in which those conditions are included;

(b) the modification would remove or reduce the burden without removing any necessary protection;

(c) the modification is such that no person holding a licence granted under section 7 above to a particular person would be unduly disadvantaged by the modification in competing with the holder of the licence in which those conditions are included."

(5) In section 12 of that Act-

    (a) in subsection (2), the words after paragraph (c) (duty to consider representations and objections) shall be omitted; and

    (b) in subsection (7) (references to modification not to include modifications relating to the telecommunications code), for "sections 13 to 15" there shall be substituted "sections 12A to 15".

Appeals against modifications of licence conditions.

12. In subsection (1) of section 46B of the Telecommunications Act 1984 (appeals against decisions of the Secretary of State or the Director), after paragraph (d) there shall be inserted-

"(da) a decision with regard to the modification under section 12 of a condition of a licence granted under section 7 above to a particular person;".

Supplemental

Ministerial expenditure etc.

13. There shall be paid out of money provided by Parliament-

    (a) any expenditure incurred by the Secretary of State for or in connection with the carrying out of his functions under this Act; and

    (b) any increase attributable to this Act in the sums which are payable out of money so provided under any other Act.

Prohibition on key escrow requirements.

14.

    (1) Subject to subsection (2), nothing in this Act shall confer any power on any Minister of the Crown, on the Scottish Ministers, on the National Assembly for Wales or on any person appointed under section 3-

        (a) by conditions of an approval under Part I, or

        (b) by any regulations or order under this Act,

    to impose a requirement on any person to deposit a key for electronic data with another person.

    (2) Subsection (1) shall not prohibit the imposition by an order under section 8 of-

        (a) a requirement to deposit a key for electronic data with the intended recipient of electronic communications comprising the data; or

(b)   a requirement for arrangements to be made, in cases where a key for data is not deposited with another person, which otherwise secure that the loss of a key, or its becoming unusable, does not have the effect that the information contained in a record kept in pursuance of any provision made by or under any enactment or subordinate legislation becomes inaccessible or incapable of being put into an intelligible form.

(3)   In this section "key", in relation to electronic data, means any code, password, algorithm, key or other data the use of which (with or without other keys)-

(a)   allows access to the electronic data, or

(b)   facilitates the putting of the electronic data into an intelligible form;

and references in this section to depositing a key for electronic data with a person include references to doing anything that has the effect of making the key available to that person. nHead2General interpretation.

15.

(1)   In this Act, except in so far as the context otherwise requires-

"document" includes a map, plan, design, drawing, picture or other image;

"communication" includes a communication comprising sounds or images or both and a communication effecting a payment;

"electronic communication" means a communication transmitted (whether from one person to another, from one device to another or from a person to a device or vice versa)-

(a)   by means of a telecommunication system (within the meaning of the Telecommunications Act 1984); or

(b)   by other means but while in an electronic form;

"enactment" includes-

(a)   an enactment passed after the passing of this Act,

(b)   an enactment comprised in an Act of the Scottish Parliament, and

(c)   an enactment contained in Northern Ireland legislation,

but does not include an enactment contained in Part I or II of this Act;

"modification" includes any alteration, addition or omission, and cognate expressions shall be construed accordingly;

"record" includes an electronic record; and

"subordinate legislation" means-

(a)   any subordinate legislation (within the meaning of the Interpretation Act 1978);

(b)   any instrument made under an Act of the Scottish Parliament; or

(c)   any statutory rules (within the meaning of the Statutory Rules (Northern Ireland) Order 1979).

(2)   In this Act-

(a) references to the authenticity of any communication or data are references to any one or more of the following-

   (i)   whether the communication or data comes from a particular person or other source;

   (ii) whether it is accurately timed and dated;

   (iii) whether it is intended to have legal effect; and

(b) references to the integrity of any communication or data are references to whether there has been any tampering with or other modification of the communication or data.

(3) References in this Act to something's being put into an intelligible form include references to its being restored to the condition in which it was before any encryption or similar process was applied to it.

Short title, commencement, extent.

16.

(1) This Act may be cited as the Electronic Communications Act 2000.

(2) Part I of this Act and sections 7, 11 and 12 shall come into force on such day as the Secretary of State may by order made by statutory instrument appoint; and different days may be appointed under this subsection for different purposes.

(3) An order shall not be made for bringing any of Part I of this Act into force for any purpose unless a draft of the order has been laid before Parliament and approved by a resolution of each House.

(4) If no order for bringing Part I of this Act into force has been made under subsection (2) by the end of the period of five years beginning with the day on which this Act is passed, that Part shall, by virtue of this subsection, be repealed at the end of that period.

(5) This Act extends to Northern Ireland.

Other UK Acts/Home/Scotland Legislation/Wales Legislation/Northern Ireland Legislation/Her Majesty's Stationery Office

We welcome your comments on this site

© Crown copyright 2000

Prepared 19 June 2000

Statutory Instrument 2002 No. 318

The Electronic Signatures Regulations 2002

The text of this Internet version of the Statutory Instrument which is published by the Queen's Printer of Acts of Parliament has been prepared to reflect the text as it was Made. A print version is also available and is published by The Stationery Office Limited as the **The Electronic Signatures Regulations 2002**, ISBN 0 11 039401 1. The print version may be purchased by clicking here. Braille copies of this Statutory Instrument can also be purchased at the same price as the print edition by contacting TSO Customer Services on 0870 600 5522 or e-mail: customer.service@tso.co.uk.

Further information about the publication of legislation on this website can be found by referring to the Frequently Asked Questions.

To ensure fast access over slow connections, large documents have been segmented into "chunks". Where you see a "continue" button at the bottom of the page of text, this indicates that there is another chunk of text available.

STATUTORY INSTRUMENTS

2002 No. 318

ELECTRONIC COMMUNICATIONS

The Electronic Signatures Regulations 2002

Made

13th February 2002

Laid before Parliament

14th February 2002

Coming into force

8th March 2002

The Secretary of State, being designated for the purpose of section 2(2) of the European Communities Act 1972 in relation to electronic signatures, in exercise of the powers conferred on her by the said section 2(2), hereby makes the following Regulations:

Citation and commencement

1. These Regulations may be cited as the Electronic Signatures Regulations 2002 and shall come into force on 8th March 2002.

Interpretation

2. In these Regulations-

"advanced electronic signature" means an electronic signature-

    (a)   which is uniquely linked to the signatory,

    (b)   which is capable of identifying the signatory,

    (c)   which is created using means that the signatory can maintain under his sole control, and

    (d)   which is linked to the data to which it relates in such a manner that any subsequent change of the data is detectable;

"certificate" means an electronic attestation which links signature-verification data to a person and confirms the identity of that person;

"certification-service-provider" means a person who issues certificates or provides other services related to electronic signatures;

"Directive" means Directive 1999/93/EC of the European Parliament and of the Council on a Community framework for electronic signatures;

"electronic signature" means data in electronic form which are attached to or logically associated with other electronic data and which serve as a method of authentication;

"qualified certificate" means a certificate which meets the requirements in Schedule 1 and is provided by a certification-service-provider who fulfils the requirements in Schedule 2;

"signatory" means a person who holds a signature-creation device and acts either on his own behalf or on behalf of the person he represents;

"signature-creation data" means unique data (including, but not limited to, codes or private cryptographic keys) which are used by the signatory to create an electronic signature;

"signature-creation device" means configured software or hardware used to implement the signature-creation data;

"signature-vertification data" means data (including, but not limited to, codes or public cryptographic keys) which are used for the purpose of verifying an electronic signature;

"signature-vertification device" means configured software or hardware used to implement the signature-verification data;

"voluntary accreditation" means any permission, setting out rights and obligations specific to the provision of certification services, to be granted upon request by the certification-service-provider concerned by the person charged with the elaboration of, and supervision of compliance with, such rights and obligations, where the certification-service-provider is not entitled to exercise the rights stemming from the permission until he has received the decision of that person.

Supervision of certification-service-providers

3.

(1) It shall be the duty of the Secretary of State to keep under review the carrying on of activities of certification-service-providers who are established in the United Kingdom and who issue qualified certificates to the public and the persons by whom they are carried on with a view to her becoming aware of the identity of those persons and the circumstances relating to the carrying on of those activities.

(2) It shall also be the duty of the Secretary of State to establish and maintain a register of certification-service-providers who are established in the United Kingdom and who issue qualified certificates to the public.

(3) The Secretary of State shall record in the register the names and addresses of those certification-service-providers of whom she is aware who are established in the United Kingdom and who issue qualified certificates to the public.

(4) The Secretary of State shall publish the register in such manner as she considers appropriate.

(5) The Secretary of State shall have regard to evidence becoming available to her with respect to any course of conduct of a certification-service-provider who is established in the United Kingdom and who issues qualified certificates to the public and which appears to her to be conduct detrimental to the interests of those persons who use or rely on those certificates with a view to making any of

this evidence as she considers expedient available to the public in such manner as she considers appropriate.

Liability of certification-service-providers

4.

(1) Where-

    (a)   a certification-service-provider either-

        (i)   issues a certificate as a qualified certificate to the public, or

        (ii)   guarantees a qualified certificate to the public,

    (b)   a person reasonably relies on that certificate for any of the following matters-

        (i)   the accuracy of any of the information contained in the qualified certificate at the time of issue,

        (ii)   the inclusion in the qualified certificate of all the details referred to in Schedule 1,

        (iii)   the holding by the signatory identified in the qualified certificate at the time of its issue of the signature-creation data corresponding to the signature-verification data given or identified in the certificate, or

        (iv)   the ability of the signature-creation data and the signature-verification data to be used in a complementary manner in cases where the certification-service-provider generates them both,

    (c)   that person suffers loss as a result of such reliance, and

    (d)   the certification-service-provider would be liable in damages in respect of any extent of the loss-

        (i)   had a duty of care existed between him and the person referred to in sub-paragraph (b) above, and

        (ii)   had the certification-service-provider been negligent,

    then that certification-service-provider shall be so liable to the same extent notwithstanding that there is no proof that the certification-service-provider was negligent unless the certification-service-provider proves that he was not negligent.

(2) For the purposes of the certification-service-provider's liability under paragraph (1) above there shall be a duty of care between that certification-service-provider and the person referred to in paragraph (1)(b) above.

(3) Where-

    (a)   a certification-service-provider issues a certificate as a qualified certificate to the public,

    (b)   a person reasonably relies on that certificate,

(c) that person suffers loss as a result of any failure by the certification-service-provider to register revocation of the certificate, and

(d) the certification-service-provider would be liable in damages in respect of any extent of the loss-

    (i) had a duty of care existed between him and the person referred to in sub-paragraph (b) above, and

    (ii) had the certification-service-provider been negligent,

then that certification-service-provider shall be so liable to the same extent notwithstanding that there is no proof that the certification-service-provider was negligent unless the certification-service-provider proves that he was not negligent.

(4) For the purposes of the certification-service-provider's liability under paragraph (3) above there shall be a duty of care between that certification-service-provider and the person referred to in paragraph (3)(b) above.

Data Protection

5.

(1) A certification-service-provider who issues a certificate to the public and to whom this paragraph applies in accordance with paragraph (6) below-

(a) shall not obtain personal data for the purpose of issuing or maintaining that certificate otherwise than directly from the data subject or after the explicit consent of the data subject, and

(b) shall not process the personal data referred to in sub-paragraph (a) above-

    (i) to a greater extent than is necessary for the purpose of issuing or maintaining that certificate, or

    (ii) to a greater extent than is necessary for any other purpose to which the data subject has explicitly consented,

unless the processing is necessary for compliance with any legal obligation, to which the certification-service-provider is subject, other than an obligation imposed by contract.

(2) The obligation to comply with paragraph (1) above shall be a duty owed to any data subject who may be affected by a contravention of paragraph (1).

(3) Where a duty is owed by virtue of paragraph (2) above to any data subject, any breach of that duty which causes that data subject to sustain loss or damage shall be actionable by him.

(4) Compliance with paragraph (1) above shall also be enforceable by civil proceedings brought by the Crown for an injunction or for an interdict or for any other appropriate relief or remedy.

(5) Paragraph (4) above shall not prejudice any right that a data subject may have by virtue of paragraph (3) above to bring civil proceedings for the contravention or apprehended contravention of paragraph (1) above.

(6) Paragraph (1) above applies to a certification-service-provider in respect of personal data only if the certification-service-provider is established in the United Kingdom and the personal data are processed in the context of that establishment.

(7) For the purposes of paragraph (6) above, each of the following is to be treated as established in the United Kingdom-

(a) an individual who is ordinarily resident in the United Kingdom,

(b) a body incorporated under the law of, or in any part of, the United Kingdom,

(c) a partnership or other unincorporated association formed under the law of any part of the United Kingdom, and

(d) any person who does not fall within sub-paragraph (a), (b) or (c) above but maintains in the United Kingdom-

(i) an office, branch or agency through which he carries on any activity, or

(ii) a regular practice.

(8) In this regulation-

"data subject" and "personal data" and "processing" shall have the same meanings as in section 1(1) of the Data Protection Act 1998, and

"obtain" shall bear the same interpretation as "obtaining" in section 1(2) of the Data Protection Act 1998.

Douglas Alexander

Minister of E-Commerce and Competitiveness in Europe, Department of Trade and Industry

13th February 2002

SCHEDULE 1

(Regulation 2)

(Annex I to the Directive)

REQUIREMENTS FOR QUALIFIED CERTIFICATES

Qualified certificates must contain:

(a) an indication that the certificate is issued as a qualified certificate;

(b) the identification of the certification-service-provider and the State in which it is established;

(c) the name of the signatory or a pseudonym, which shall be identified as such;

(d) provision for a specific attribute of the signatory to be included if relevant, depending on the purpose for which the certificate is intended;

(e) signature-verification data which correspond to signature-creation data under the control of the signatory;

(f) an indication of the beginning and end of the period of validity of the certificate;

(g) the identity code of the certificate;

(h) the advanced electronic signature of the certification-service-provider issuing it;

(i) limitations on the scope of use of the certificate, if applicable; and

(j) limits on the value of transactions for which the certificate can be used, if applicable.

SCHEDULE 2

(Regulation 2)

(Annex II to the Directive)

REQUIREMENTS FOR CERTIFICATION-SERVICE-PROVIDERS ISSUING QUALIFIED CERTIFICATES

Certification-service-providers must:

(a) demonstrate the reliability necessary for providing certification services;

(b) ensure the operation of a prompt and secure directory and a secure and immediate revocation service;

(c) ensure that the date and time when a certificate is issued or revoked can be determined precisely;

(d) verify, by appropriate means in accordance with national law, the identity and, if applicable, any specific attributes of the person to which a qualified certificate is issued;

(e) employ personnel who possess the expert knowledge, experience, and qualifications necessary for the services provided, in particular competence at managerial level, expertise in electronic signature technology and familiarity with proper security procedures; they must also apply administrative and management procedures which are adequate and correspond to recognised standards;

(f) use trustworthy systems and products which are protected against modification and ensure the technical and cryptographic security of the process supported by them;

(g) take measures against forgery of certificates, and, in cases where the certification-service-provider generates signature-creation data, guarantee confidentiality during the process of generating such data;

(h) maintain sufficient financial resources to operate in conformity with the requirements laid down in the Directive, in particular to bear the risk of liability for damages, for example, by obtaining appropriate insurance;

    (i) record all relevant information concerning a qualified certificate for an appropriate period of time, in particular for the purpose of providing evidence of certification for the purposes of legal proceedings. Such recording may be done electronically;

(j) not store or copy signature-creation data of the person to whom the certification-service-provider provided key management services;

(k) before entering into a contractual relationship with a person seeking a certificate to support his electronic signature inform that person by a durable means of communication of the precise terms and conditions regarding the use of the certificate, including any limitations on its use, the existence of a voluntary accreditation scheme and procedures for complaints and dispute settlement. Such information, which may be transmitted electronically, must be in writing and in readily understandable language. Relevant parts of this information must also be made available on request to third parties relying on the certificate;

(l) use trustworthy systems to store certificates in a verifiable form so that:

— only authorised persons can make entries and changes,

— information can be checked for authenticity,

— certificates are publicly available for retrieval in only those cases for which the certificate-holder's consent has been obtained, and

— any technical changes compromising these security requirements are apparent to the operator.

EXPLANATORY NOTE

(This note is not part of the Regulations)

These Regulations implement Directive 1999/93/EC of the European Parliament and of the Council on a Community framework for electronic signatures. The provisions of this Directive which are implemented relate to the supervision of certification-service-providers, their liability in certain circumstances and data protection requirements concerning them; provisions in the Directive relating to the admissibility of electronic signatures as evidence in legal proceedings were implemented by section 7 of the Electronic Communications Act 2000 (2000 c. 7).

Regulation 3 imposes a duty on the Secretary of State to keep under review the carrying on of activities of certain certification-service-providers, to establish, maintain and publish a register of these certification-service-providers and to have regard to any evidence of their conduct which is detrimental to users of qualified certificates with a view to publication of any of this evidence.

Regulation 4 imposes liability on certification-service-providers in certain circumstances even though there is no proof of negligence unless the certification-service-provider in question proves he was not negligent.

Regulation 5 imposes a duty on certification-service-providers in certain circumstances to comply with specified data protection requirements. Breach of that duty is actionable by a data subject who suffers loss and compliance with the requirements can also be enforced by civil proceedings by the Crown.

A transposition note setting out how the main elements of the Directive are transposed into law has been placed in the libraries of both Houses of Parliament. Copies are also available from Information Security Policy Group, Communications and Information Industries Directorate, Department of Trade and Industry, Bay 226, 151 Buckingham Palace Road, London SW1W 9SS.

Notes:

[1]   S.I. 2000/738.
[2]   1972 c. 68.
[3]   OJ No. L13, 19.1.00, p. 12.
[4]   1998 c. 29.
[5]   OJ No. L13, 19.1.00, p. 12.

ISBN 0 11 039401 1

Other UK SIs/Home/National Assembly for Wales Statutory Instruments/Scottish Statutory Instruments/Statutory Rules of Northern Ireland/Her Majesty's Stationery Office

We welcome your comments on this site

© Crown copyright 2002

Prepared 4 March 2002

INDEX

Access to data
  data protection, 9–099
Accreditation of certification service providers
  and see **Regulation**
  Electronic Signatures Directive, 5–053
Addressees
  UNCITRAL Model Law on Electronic Commerce, 5–011
Admissibility of evidence
  electronic transactions, 8–011
  real-world transactions, 8–003—8–005
Advanced electronic signatures
  Electronic Signatures Directive, 5–045—5–046
Agents, signature by
  signatures, 2–027
Algorithms
  generally, 3–038—3–039
  RSA, 3–044
Archival services
  public key infrastructure (PKI), 4–016
Argentina
  law, 6–138—6–139
  regulation, 9–079—9–080
Asymmetric encryption
  certification service providers, 1–005—1–007
  generally, 1–004
  public key infrastructure (PKI), 1–005—1–007
  technologies, 3–038—3–039
Attacks on security
  brute force
    encryption keys, 3–044

Attacks on security – *contd*
  capture and replay
    biometrics, 3–013
  dictionary
    passwords, 3–005—3–006
  key-search
    encryption keys, 3–039
  side-channel
    information security, 7–019
Attribute authority services
  registration authorities, 4–013
Australia
  dual-use goods, export controls on, 9–110
  Gatekeeper PKI
    Australian Capital Territory, 4–033
    Australian Customs Service, 4–029
    Australian Taxation Office, 4–026
    banking, 4–034
    Canberra Connect, 4–033
    Fedlink, 4–027
    government, central, 4–025
    government, state, 4–030—4–032
    Government Electronic Market (Western Australia), 4–032
    Health Insurance Commission, 4–028
    introduction, 4–023—4–024
    Project Angus, 4–034
    Transport Accident Commission (Victoria), 4–030
  law on electronic signatures
    Commonwealth legislation, 6–066—6–068
    introduction, 6–064—6–065
    state and territory legislation, 6–069—6–070

Australia – *contd*
public key infrastructure (PKI) standards, 10–007
regulation, 9–053

Austria
law, 6–007—6–008
regulation, 9–005—9–006

Authentication
OECD Ministerial Declaration, 1–014
signatures, 2–003—2–004
technologies, 3–048

Automated transactions
Uniform Electronic Transactions Act (UETA) (US), 6–109

Bangladesh
law, 6–071
regulation, 9–054

Banking
infrastructure, 4–006

BAPI (Biometric Application Programming Interface)
biometrics, 3–034

Belgium
law, 6–009
regulation, 9–007—9–008

Biometrics
Biometric Application Programming Interface (BAPI), 3–034
body salt identification, 3–032
capture and replay attacks, 3–013
Common Biometric Exchange File Format (CBEF), 3–034
conclusion, 3–033—3–034
digitisation, 3–011
DNA matching, 3–029
ear lobes, 3–026
face recognition, 3–018
facial thermograms, 3–027
fingerprints, 3–019—3–020
hand/finger geometry, 3–021
handprints, 3–019—3–020
handwritten signature dynamics, 3–022
introduction, 3–011—3–013
iris scans, 3–016—3–017
keystroke dynamics, 3–028
odour recognition, 3–030
palm-prints, 3–031
proposed forms of, 3–025—3–032
retina scans, 3–014—3–015

Biometrics – *contd*
standards, 3–034
vein patterns, 3–024
voice recognition, 3–023

Bitmap scans of signatures
technologies, 3–007

Body salt identification
biometrics, 3–032

Brazil
law, 6–140
regulation, 9–081

British Standards Institute (BSI)
generally, 1–016
standards, 10–015

Brute force attacks
encryption, 3–044

Bulgaria
law, 6–010—6–012
regulation, 9–009—9–010

Burden of proof
electronic transactions, 8–013
generally, 8–002

Business transactions
generally, 2–037
with individuals, 2–035

Buttons, on-screen
generally, 1–016
technologies, 3–009

Canada
law, 6–096—6–098
public key infrastructure (PKI) standards, 10–007
regulation, 9–072

Canberra Connect (Australia)
infrastructure, 4–033

Capture and replay attacks
biometrics, 3–013

CBEF (Common Biometric Exchange File Format)
biometrics, 3–034

Ceremony
technologies, 3–050

Certificate policies
infrastructure, 4–022

Certificates
Electronic Signatures Directive
generally, 5–047—5–049
qualified, 5–048—5–049
invalid, 8–017

invalid, 8–017 – *contd*
  revocation or suspension of
      certification service providers, 4–014
      certification practice statements,
        4–018—4–019
  transactions outside scope of, 8–017
Certification
  UNCITRAL Model Law on Electronic
  Signatures, 5–014
Certification authorities
  see **Certification service providers**
Certification practice statements
  generally, 4–017—4–020
  limitations, 4–021
  RFC 2527, 4–017—4–020
  VeriSign, 4–021
Certification service providers
  Electronic Signatures Directive,
  5–050—5–053
  generally, 1–005—1–007
  GUIDEC, 5–029
  public key infrastructure (PKI), 4–014
  revocation or suspension of certificates,
  4–014
  standards
      ISO 9000, 10–012
      QMS (Quality Management System),
        10–012—10–013
      qualified certificates, 10–014
  transactions with
      duty of care, 7–015
      errors, 7–010—7–011
      generally, 7–010—7–011
      liability, 7–010—7–011
      relying party, 7–015
      relying party agreements, 7–016—7–
        017
      subscribers, 7–012—7–014
      unfair contract terms, 7–012
  UNCITRAL Model Law on Electronic
  Signatures, 5–020—5–026
Chile
  law, 6–141—6–142
  regulation, 9–082—9–083
China
  law, 6–072—6–073
  regulation, 9–055
Choice of law clauses
  generally, 7–003—7–005

Choice of law clauses – *contd*
  reliability, 7–007—7–009
  signature policies, 7–006—7–009
Ciphers
  encryption, 3–036
Clicking on-screen buttons
  generally, 1–016
  technologies, 3–009
Colombia
  law, 6–143—6–144
  regulation, 9–084—9–085
Common Biometric Exchange File Format (CBEF)
  biometrics, 3–034
Common Criteria for Information Technology Security Evaluation (US)
  EALs (Evaluation Assurance Levels),
  10–005
  protection profiles, 10–005—10–006
Companies
  signatures, 2–005—2–006
Compensation
  data protection, 9–099
Compliance assessment standards
  Common Criteria for Information Technology Security Evaluation (US),
    10–005—10–006
  introduction, 10–005
  ITSEC (Information Security Evaluation
  Criteria), 10–005
Compliance audits
  certification practice statements, 4–017
Conditional access devices
  export controls on dual-use goods,
  9–109
Confidentiality
  and see **Data protection**
  certification practice statements, 4–017
Consent of data subject
  data protection, 9–098
Consumer consent
  E-Sign (US), 6–124—6–128
Contracts, formation of
  generally, 1–003
  UNCITRAL Model Law on Electronic
  Commerce, 5–007
Controllers of data
  data protection, 9–096
Correction of data

Correction of data – *contd*
data protection, 9–099
Crime
information security, 7–021
regulation
disclosure of information, 9–105—9–106
introduction, 9–102
key escrow, 9–103—9–104
trusted first parties, 9–104
trusted third parties, 9–103
Cross-border transactions
choice of law and jurisdiction clauses
generally, 7–003—7–005
reliability, 7–007—7–009
signature policies, 7–006—7–009
introduction, 7–001—7–002
Cryptanalysis
encryption, 3–036
Cryptographic keys
generally, 1–004
Cryptography
see **Encryption**
Cryptography Guidelines, OECD
generally, 1–012—1–013
Cybercrime
information security, 7–021
regulation
disclosure of information, 9–105—9–106
introduction, 9–102
key escrow, 9–103—9–104
trusted first parties, 9–104
trusted third parties, 9–103
Cyprus
law, 6–013
regulation, 9–011
Czech Republic
law, 6–014
regulation, 9–012—9–014
DAAM (Dynamic Associative Access Memory)
encryption, 3–044
Data Encryption Standard (DES)
encryption, 3–044
Data protection
access, right of, 9–099
compensation, right to, 9–099
consent of data subject, 9–098

Data protection – *contd*
controller, 9–096
correction of data, right to, 9–099
EU Directive, 5–059—5–061
introduction, 9–095
personal data, 9–096
processing, 9–096—9–097
quality of data, 9–097
remedies of data subjects, 9–099
rights of data subjects, 9–099
sensitive data, 9–097
third parties, data collected from, 9–098
Data subjects, rights and remedies of
data protection, 9–099
Decryption
encryption, 3–036
Denmark
law, 6–015—6–016
regulation, 9–015
DES (Data Encryption Standard)
encryption, 3–044
Dictionary attacks
passwords, 3–005—3–006
Digital signatures
advantages, 3–041—3–042
functions, 2–043
hash functions, 3–040—3–041
identity of parties, 1–004
limitations, 3–043
message digest functions, 3–040—3–041
nature, 3–040—3–041
time stamping, 3–042
Digitisation
biometrics, 3–011
Directory services
certification service providers, 4–014
Disclosure of information
regulation of encryption technologies, 9–105—9–106
Distinguished names
standards, 10–011
DNA matching
biometrics, 3–029
Document retention
E-Sign (US), 6–120
Driving licences
electronic identity, 2–042
Dual-use goods, export controls on
Australia, 9–110

Dual-use goods, export controls on – *contd*
conditional access devices, 9–109
European Union, 9–108—9–109
internationally, 9–107
United Kingdom, 9–111—9–112
United States, 9–113
Wassenaar Arrangement, 9–107

Duress
signatures, 2–030

Duty of care
certification service providers, 7–015

Dynamic Associative Access Memory (DAAM)
encryption, 3–044

EALs (Evaluation Assurance Levels) (US)
standards, 10–005

Ear lobes
biometrics, 3–026

Ecuador
law, 6–145—6–147
regulation, 9–086

EDI (Electronic Data Interchange)
generally, 1–001

EESSI (European Electronic Signature Standardisation Initiative)
generally, 1–016
standards
public key infrastructure (PKI), 10–008
technologies, 10–009

Electronic agents
E-Sign (US), 6–123
Uniform Electronic Transactions Act (UETA) (US), 6–109

Electronic commerce
generally, 1–001—1–002
UNCITRAL Convention, 1–009
UNCITRAL Model Law
addressees, 5–011
contracts, formation of, 5–007
electronic signatures, definition of, 5–005
errors in transmission, 5–011
form, 5–004
generally, 1–009
guidance, 5–006
introduction, 5–002—5–003
liability, 5–010

Electronic commerce – *contd*
UNCITRAL Model Law – *contd*
originators, 5–008—5–009
reliability, 5–005

Electronic Data Interchange (EDI)
generally, 1–001

Electronic identity
signatures, 2–038—2–044

Electronic records
E-Sign (US), 6–121
Uniform Electronic Transactions Act (UETA) (US), 6–106

Electronic signatures
and see under individual headings
advanced, 5–045—5–046
certification service providers, 1–005—1–007
contracts, formation of, 1–003
definitions
Electronic Signatures Directive, 5–042—5–044
UNCITRAL Model Law on Electronic Commerce, 5–005
UNCITRAL Model Law on Electronic Signatures, 5–013
E-Sign (US), 6–122
functions, 2–043
GUIDEC, 1–010—1–011
historical development, 1–008—1–014
identity, 1–004—1–007
introduction, 1–001—1–003
liability, 1–004—1–007
OECD Guidelines, 1–012—1–014
public key infrastructure (PKI), 1–005—1–007
standards, 1–016
technology, 1–015—1–016
UNCITRAL Model Law
certification, 5–014
certification service providers, 5–020—5–026
electronic signatures, definition of, 5–013
generally, 1–009
introduction, 5–012
reliability, 5–015—5–016
relying party, 5–018—5–019
signatory, 5–017
Uniform Electronic Transactions Act (UETA) (US), 6–107

Electronic Signatures Directive
  data protection, 5–059—5–061
  electronic signatures
    accreditation of certification service
      providers, 5–053
    advanced, 5–045—5–046
    certificates, 5–047—5–049
    certification service providers,
      5–050—5–053
    definition, 5–042—5–044
    legal effect, 5–041
    qualified certificates, 5–048—5–049
    secure signature-creation devices,
      5–056—5–058
    secure signature verification,
      5–065—5–067
    signatory, 5–054
    signature-creation data and devices,
      5–055
    signature-verification data and
      devices, 5–055
  final form, 5–038—5–039
  historical development, 5–035—5–037
  internal market, 5–059—5–061
  international aspects, 5–064
  introduction, 5–033—5–034
  liability, 5–062—5–063
  market access, 5–059—5–061
  scope, 5–040
  secure signature verification, 5–065—5–
    067
  technologies, 3–001—3–003
Encryption
  algorithms, 3–038—3–039
  Data Encryption Standard (DES), 3–044
  decryption, 3–036
  digital signatures, 3–040—3–043
  introduction, 3–035
  key length, 3–044
  methods, 3–037—3–044
  one-time pads, 3–037
  private key, 3–038—3–039
  public key, 3–038—3–039
  steganography, 3–036
  terminology, 3–036
Encryption technologies, regulation of
  cybercrime
    disclosure of information, 9–105—9–
      106

**Encryption technologies, regulation
  of** – *contd*
  cybercrime – *contd*
    introduction, 9–102
      key escrow, 9–103—9–104
      trusted first parties, 9–104
      trusted third parties, 9–103
    dual-use goods, export controls on
      Australia, 9–110
      conditional access devices, 9–109
      European Union, 9–108—9–109
      internationally, 9–107
      United Kingdom, 9–111—9–112
      United States, 9–113
      Wassenaar Arrangement, 9–107
    introduction, 9–100
    military roots of cryptography, 9–101
    terrorism, 9–102—9–106
E-notary services
  public key infrastructure (PKI), 4–016
"Entitlement" cards
  electronic identity, 2–039—2–043
Errors
  certification service providers,
    7–010—7–011
  UNCITRAL Model Law on Electronic
    Commerce, 5–011
Escrow, key
  regulation of encryption technologies,
    9–103—9–104
E-Sign (US)
  conclusion, 6–136
  consumer consent, 6–124—6–128
  document retention, 6–120
  electronic agents, 6–123
  electronic records, 6–121
  electronic signatures, 6–122
  exclusions, 6–118—6–119
  government regulations, 6–129
  inclusions, 6–116—6–117
  introduction, 6–112
  scope, 6–113
  state law, and, 6–130—6–135
  validity, 6–114—6–115
  voluntariness, 6–114—6–115
Estonia
  law, 6–017—6–019
  regulation, 9–016—9–018
**European Electronic Signature Stand-
  ardisation Initiative (EESSI)**

European Electronic Signature Standardisation Initiative (EESSI) – *contd*
generally, 1–016
standards
public key infrastructure (PKI),
10–008
technologies, 10–009
European Union
export controls on dual-use goods,
9–108—9–109
Evaluation Assurance Levels (EALs) (US)
standards, 10–005
Evidence
and see under individual headings
burden of proof, 8–002
electronic transactions
admissibility, 8–011
burden of proof, 8–013
introduction, 8–010
relying party, 8–019
repudiation of electronic signatures,
8–014—8–018
weight, 8–012
introduction, 8–001
preservation of, 10–018—10–019
real-world transactions
admissibility, 8–003—8–005
burden of proof, 8–002
hearsay evidence, 8–005
weight, 8–006—8–007
signatures, 8–008—8–009
standard of proof, 8–002
Face recognition
biometrics, 3–018
Facial thermograms
biometrics, 3–027
Facsimile signatures
generally, 2–023—2–029
False signatures
repudiation of electronic signatures,
8–018
Faxed signatures
generally, 2–023—2–029
Federal Electronic Signatures in Global and National Commerce Act (E-Sign) (US)
conclusion, 6–136
consumer consent, 6–124—6–128
document retention, 6–120

Sign) (US) – *contd*
electronic agents, 6–123
electronic records, 6–121
electronic signatures, 6–122
exclusions, 6–118—6–119
government regulations, 6–129
inclusions, 6–116—6–117
introduction, 6–112
scope, 6–113
state law, and, 6–130—6–135
validity, 6–114—6–115
voluntariness, 6–114—6–115
Federal Information Processing Standards (FIPS) (US)
generally, 1–016
standards, 10–009
Fedlink (Australia)
infrastructure, 4–027
Finger/hand geometry
biometrics, 3–021
Fingerprints
biometrics, 3–019—3–020
Finland
law, 6–020—6–021
regulation, 9–019
FIPS (Federal Information Processing Standards) (US)
generally, 1–016
standards, 10–009
Formation of contracts
generally, 1–003
UNCITRAL Model Law on Electronic
Commerce, 5–007
France
law, 6–022—6–023
regulation, 9–020
Fraud
signatures, 2–030
Gatekeeper PKI (Australia)
Australian Capital Territory, 4–033
Australian Customs Service, 4–029
Australian Taxation Office, 4–026
banking, 4–034
Canberra Connect, 4–033
Fedlink, 4–027
government, central, 4–025
government, state, 4–030—4–032
Government Electronic Market (Western Australia), 4–032

Gatekeeper PKI (Australia) – *contd*
  Health Insurance Commission, 4–028
  introduction, 4–023—4–024
  Project Angus, 4–034
  Transport Accident Commission (Victoria), 4–030
General Usage for International Digitally Ensured Commerce (GUIDEC)
  certification service provider, 5–029
  generally, 1–010—1–011
  introduction, 5–027
  relying party, 5–030
  signatory, 5–028
Germany
  law, 6–024—6–025
  regulation, 9–021—9–022
Government Electronic Market (Western Australia)
  infrastructure, 4–032
Government transactions
  personal identity, 2–036
Greece
  law, 6–026
  regulation, 9–023
Guernsey
  law on electronic signatures, 6–027
GUIDEC (General Usage for International Digitally Ensured Commerce)
  certification service provider, 5–029
  generally, 1–010—1–011
  introduction, 5–027
  relying party, 5–030
  signatory, 5–028
Hand/finger geometry
  biometrics, 3–021
Handprints
  biometrics, 3–019—3–020
Handwritten signature dynamics
  biometrics, 3–022
Handwritten signatures
  generally, 2–019—2–022
  technologies, and
    authentication, 3–048
    ceremony, 3–050
    identification, 3–047
    intention, 3–049
    introduction, 3–045—3–046
    non-repudiation, 3–052
    originality of document, 3–051

Hash functions
  digital signatures, 3–040—3–041
Hearsay evidence
  generally, 8–005
Hong Kong
  law, 6–074—6–075
  regulation, 9–056—9–057
Hungary
  law, 6–028—6–029
  regulation, 9–024—9–025
Identity
  certification service providers, 1–005—1–007
  cross-border transactions
    banking, 4–006
    Identrus, 4–006
    introduction, 4–001—4–003
    notarisation, 4–001—4–002
    public key infrastructure (PKI), 4–005—4–009
    simple distributed security infrastructure (SDSI), 4–010
    webs of trust, 4–004
  electronic, 2–038—2–044
  introduction, 1–004
  personal
    business transactions, 2–037
    business transactions with individuals, 2–035
    government transactions with individuals, 2–036
    introduction, 2–032
    names, 2–032—2–034
    private transactions, 2–033—2–034
    technologies, 3–047
  public key infrastructure (PKI), 1–005—1–007
Identity cards
  electronic identity, 2–039—2–043
Identrus
  infrastructure, 4–006
IETF (Internet Engineering Task Force)
  generally, 1–016
Indemnities
  regulation of certification service providers (US), 9–076
India
  law, 6–076—6–077
  regulation, 9–058

Indonesia
  law, 6–078
  regulation, 9–059
Information security
  cybercrime, 7–021
  introduction, 7–018
  OECD Guidelines, 7–020—7–021
  offences, 7–021
  side-channel attacks, 7–019
  standards
    introduction, 10–015
    ISO 17799 (Code of Practice for
    Information Security Management),
    10–015—10–017
    trustworthiness of systems, 10–017
Infrastructure
  and see under individual headings
  certificate policies, 4–022
  certification practice statements
    generally, 4–017—4–020
    limitations, 4–021
    RFC 2527, 4–017—4–020
    VeriSign, 4–021
  Gatekeeper PKI (Australia)
    Australian Capital Territory, 4–033
    Australian Customs Service, 4–029
    Australian Taxation Office, 4–026
    banking, 4–034
    Canberra Connect, 4–033
    Fedlink, 4–027
    government, central, 4–025
    government, state, 4–030—4–032
    Government Electronic Market
    (Western Australia), 4–032
    Health Insurance Commission, 4–028
    introduction, 4–023—4–024
    Project Angus, 4–034
    Transport Accident Commission
    (Victoria), 4–030
  identity in cross-border transactions
    banking, 4–006
    Identrus, 4–006
    introduction, 4–001—4–003
    notarisation, 4–001—4–002
    public key infrastructure (PKI),
    4–005—4–009
    simple distributed security infra-
    structure (SDSI), 4–010
    webs of trust, 4–004

Infrastructure – *contd*
  introduction, 4–001
  public key infrastructure (PKI), roles
  within
    archival services, 4–016
    certification service providers, 4–014
    e-notary services, 4–016
    introduction, 4–011
    registration authorities, 4–012—4–013
    time stamping, 4–015
Intention
  signatures, 2–004
  technologies, 3–049
Intention to be legally bound
  repudiation of electronic signatures,
  8–016
Internal market
  Electronic Signatures Directive,
  5–059—5–061
International initiatives
  and see under individual headings
  Electronic Signatures Directive
    data protection, 5–059—5–061
    electronic signatures, 5–041—5–058
    final form, 5–038—5–039
    historical development, 5–035—5–
    037
    internal market, 5–059—5–061
    international aspects, 5–064
    introduction, 5–033—5–034
    liability, 5–062—5–063
    market access, 5–059—5–061
    scope, 5–040
    secure signature verification,
    5–065—5–067
  GUIDEC
    certification service provider, 5–029
    introduction, 5–027
    relying party, 5–030
    signatory, 5–028
  introduction, 5–001
  OECD Ministerial Declaration on
  Authentication for Electronic Com-
  merce,
  5–031—5–032
  UNCITRAL Model Laws
    Electronic Commerce, 5–003—5–011
    Electronic Signatures, 5–012—5–026
    introduction, 5–002

International Standards Organisation (ISO)
generally, 1–016
International Telecommunications Union
generally, 1–016
Internet
generally, 1–001
influence of, 1–015—1–016
Internet Engineering Task Force (IETF)
generally, 1–016
Internet Protocol (IP) addresses
electronic identity, 2–038
Internet Public Key Infrastructure Certificate Policy and Certification Practices Framework (RFC 2527)
certification practice statements, 4–017—4–020
Invalid certificates
repudiation of electronic signatures, 8–017
Investigation
regulation of certification service providers (US), 9–075
Invoices, electronic
generally, 1–014
IP (Internet Protocol) addresses
electronic identity, 2–038
Ireland
law, 6–030—6–031
regulation, 9–026
Iris scans
biometrics, 3–016—3–017
ISO (International Standards Organisation)
generally, 1–016
Israel
law, 6–155—6–156
regulation, 9–092—9–093
Italy
law, 6–032—6–034
regulation, 9–027
Japan
law, 6–079
regulation, 9–060
Jurisdiction clauses
generally, 7–003—7–005
reliability, 7–007—7–009
signature policies, 7–006—7–009
Key escrow

Key escrow – *contd*
regulation of encryption technologies, 9–103—9–104
Key length
encryption, 3–044
Keys, cryptographic
generally, 1–004
Key-search attacks
encryption, 3–039
Keystroke dynamics
biometrics, 3–028
Latvia
law, 6–035—6–036
regulation, 9–028—9–029
Laws on electronic signatures
and see under individual headings
Asia/Pacific
Australia, 6–064—6–070
Bangladesh, 6–071
China, 6–072—6–073
Hong Kong, 6–074—6–075
India, 6–076—6–077
Indonesia, 6–078
Japan, 6–079
Malaysia, 6–080
New Zealand, 6–081—6–083
Pakistan, 6–084—6–085
Philippines, 6–086—6–088
Singapore, 6–089—6–090
South Korea, 6–091
Sri Lanka, 6–092
Thailand, 6–093—6–095
Europe
Austria, 6–007—6–008
Belgium, 6–009
Bulgaria, 6–010—6–012
Cyprus, 6–013
Czech Republic, 6–014
Denmark, 6–015—6–016
Estonia, 6–017—6–019
Finland, 6–020—6–021
France, 6–022—6–023
Germany, 6–024—6–025
Greece, 6–026
Guernsey, 6–027
Hungary, 6–028—6–029
introduction, 6–006
Ireland, 6–030—6–031
Italy, 6–032—6–034

Laws on electronic signatures – *contd*
  Europe – *contd*
    Latvia, 6–035—6–036
      Lithuania, 6–037—6–038
      Luxembourg, 6–039—6–040
      Malta, 6–041—6–042
      Netherlands, 6–043—6–044
      Poland, 6–045—6–046
      Portugal, 6–047—6–050
      Romania, 6–051—6–052
      Slovakia, 6–053—6–054
      Slovenia, 6–055—6–057
      Spain, 6–058—6–059
      Sweden, 6–060
      Switzerland, 6–061
      United Kingdom, 6–062—6–063
    introduction, 6–001—6–005
  Latin America
    Argentina, 6–138—6–139
    Brazil, 6–140
    Chile, 6–141—6–142
    Colombia, 6–143—6–144
    Ecuador, 6–145—6–147
    Peru, 6–148
    Venezuela, 6–149—6–150
  North and Central America
    Canada, 6–096—6–098
    Mexico, 6–099—6–100
    United States, 6–101—6–137
  rest of the world
    Israel, 6–155—6–156
    Russian Federation, 6–151—6–152
    South Africa, 6–153—6–154
    Turkey, 6–157
Liability
  certification practice statements,
  4–017—4–018
  certification service providers
    generally, 7–010—7–011
    information security, 7–019
  Electronic Signatures Directive,
  5–062—5–063
  introduction, 1–004
  public key infrastructure (PKI),
  1–005—1–007
  UNCITRAL Model Law on Electronic
  Commerce, 5–010
Licensing
  regulation of certification service providers (US), 9–075—9–076

Light pens
  technologies, 3–008
Lithuania
  law, 6–037—6–038
  regulation, 9–030
Luxembourg
  law, 6–039—6–040
  regulation, 9–031—9–032
Malaysia
  law, 6–080
  regulation, 9–061—9–062
Malta
  law, 6–041—6–042
  regulation, 9–033
Market access
  Electronic Signatures Directive,
  5–059—5–061
Marks
  signatures, 2–017—2–021
Message digest functions
  digital signatures, 3–040—3–041
Mexico
  law, 6–099—6–100
  regulation, 9–073
Military technologies, regulation of
  cryptography, 9–101
  cybercrime
    disclosure of information, 9–105—9–106
    introduction, 9–102
    key escrow, 9–103—9–104
    trusted first parties, 9–104
    trusted third parties, 9–103
  dual-use goods, export controls on
    Australia, 9–110
    conditional access devices, 9–109
    European Union, 9–108—9–109
    internationally, 9–107
    United Kingdom, 9–111—9–112
    United States, 9–113
    Wassenaar Arrangement, 9–107
  introduction, 9–100
  terrorism, 9–102—9–106
Misrepresentation
  signatures, 2–030
Mistake
  signatures, 2–030
  Uniform Electronic Transactions Act
  (UETA) (US), 6–110

Model Laws, UNCITRAL
Electronic Commerce
addressees, 5–011
contracts, formation of, 5–007
electronic signatures, definition of, 5–005
errors in transmission, 5–011
form, 5–004
generally, 1–009
guidance, 5–006
introduction, 5–002—5–003
liability, 5–010
originators, 5–008—5–009
reliability, 5–005
Electronic Signatures
certification, 5–014
certification service providers, 5–020—5–026
electronic signatures, definition of, 5–013
generally, 1–009
introduction, 5–012
reliability, 5–015—5–016
relying party, 5–018—5–019
signatory, 5–017
Names
personal identity, 2–032—2–034
Netherlands
law, 6–043—6–044
regulation, 9–034—9–035
New Zealand
law, 6–081—6–083
regulation, 9–063
Non est factum
signatures, 2–030
Non-repudiation of electronic signatures
technologies, 3–052
Notarisation
infrastructure
e-notary services, 4–016
generally, 4–001—4–002
signatures, 2–006
Odour recognition
biometrics, 3–030
OECD (Organisation for Economic Co-operation and Development)
Cryptography Guidelines, 1–012—1–013
Ministerial Declaration on Authentication for Electronic Commerce

OECD (Organisation for Economic Co-operation and Development) – *contd*
Ministerial Declaration on Authentication for Electronic Commerce – *contd*
generally, 1–014
international initiatives, 5–031—5–032
Security Guidelines (Guidelines for the Security of Information Systems and Networks)
generally, 1–012
information security, 7–020—7–021
Offences
information security, 7–021
One-time pads
encryption, 3–037
Organisation for Economic Co-operation and Development (OECD)
Authentication for Electronic Commerce, Ministerial Declaration on, 1–014
Cryptography Guidelines, 1–012—1–013
Security Guidelines, 1–012
Originality of document
technologies, 3–051
Originators
UNCITRAL Model Law on Electronic Commerce, 5–008—5–009
Pakistan
law, 6–084—6–085
regulation, 9–064
Palm-prints
biometrics, 3–031
Passwords
technologies, 3–005—3–006
Personal data
data protection, 9–096
Personal Identification Numbers (PINs)
technologies, 3–005—3–006
Peru
law, 6–148
regulation, 9–087
Philippines
law, 6–086—6–088
regulation, 9–065
PINs (Personal Identification Numbers)
technologies, 3–005—3–006

PKI (public key infrastructure)
  identity
    cross-border transactions, 4–005—4–009
    generally, 1–005—1–007
  roles within
    archival services, 4–016
    certification service providers, 4–014
    e-notary services, 4–016
    introduction, 4–011
    registration authorities, 4–012—4–013
    time stamping, 4–015
  standards
    Australia, 10–007—10–008
    EESSI (European Electronic Signature Standardisation Initiative), 10–008
    introduction, 10–007
    Public Key Authentication Framework (PKAF) (Australia), 10–008
PKIX (PKI X.509)
  standards, 10–001
"Plaintext"
  encryption, 3–036
Poland
  law, 6–045—6–046
  regulation, 9–036—9–038
Portugal
  law, 6–047—6–050
  regulation, 9–039—9–040
Porvoo Group
  electronic identity, 2–042—2–043
Printed signatures
  generally, 2–018—2–023
Privacy
  and see **Data protection**
  certification practice statements, 4–017
Private cryptographic keys
  generally, 1–004
Private key encryption
  technologies, 3–038—3–039
Private transactions
  personal identity, 2–033—2–034
Processing of data
  data protection, 9–096—9–097
Project Angus (Australia)
  infrastructure, 4–034
Protection profiles (US)
  standards, 10–005—10–006

Public Key Authentication Framework (PKAF) (Australia)
  standards, 10–008
Public key encryption
  certification service providers, 1–005—1–007
  generally, 1–004
  public key infrastructure (PKI), 1–005—1–007
  technologies, 3–038—3–039
Public key infrastructure (PKI)
  identity
    cross-border transactions, 4–005—4–009
    generally, 1–005—1–007
  roles within
    archival services, 4–016
    certification service providers, 4–014
    e-notary services, 4–016
    introduction, 4–011
    registration authorities, 4–012—4–013
    time stamping, 4–015
  standards
    Australia, 10–007—10–008
    EESSI (European Electronic Signature Standardisation Initiative), 10–008
    introduction, 10–007
    Public Key Authentication Framework (PKAF) (Australia), 10–008
Qualified certificates
  Electronic Signatures Directive, 5–048—5–049
  standards, 10–010—10–011
Quality of data
  data protection, 9–097
Record keeping
  generally, 7–022—7–023
  public key infrastructure (PKI), 4–016
  regulation of certification service providers (US), 9–077
Registration authorities
  public key infrastructure (PKI), 4–012—4–013
Regulation
  and see under individual headings
  certification service providers
    Argentina, 9–079—9–080
    Australia, 9–053

Regulation – *contd*
  certification service providers – *contd*
    Austria, 9–005—9–006
     Bangladesh, 9–054
     Belgium, 9–007—9–008
     Brazil, 9–081
     Bulgaria, 9–009—9–010
     Canada, 9–072
     Chile, 9–082—9–083
     China, 9–055
     Colombia, 9–084—9–085
     Cyprus, 9–011
     Czech Republic, 9–012—9–014
     Denmark, 9–015
     Ecuador, 9–086
     Electronic Signatures Directive, 9–004
     Estonia, 9–016—9–018
     Finland, 9–019
     France, 9–020
     Germany, 9–021—9–022
     Greece, 9–023
     Hong Kong, 9–056—9–057
     Hungary, 9–024—9–025
     India, 9–058
     Indonesia, 9–059
     introduction, 9–002—9–003
     Ireland, 9–026
     Israel, 9–092—9–093
     Italy, 9–027
     Japan, 9–060
     Latvia, 9–028—9–029
     Lithuania, 9–030
     Luxembourg, 9–031—9–032
     Malaysia, 9–061—9–062
     Malta, 9–033
     Mexico, 9–073
     Netherlands, 9–034—9–035
     New Zealand, 9–063
     Pakistan, 9–064
     Peru, 9–087
     Philippines, 9–065
     Poland, 9–036—9–038
     Portugal, 9–039—9–040
     Romania, 9–041—9–042
     Russian Federation, 9–090
     Singapore, 9–066—9–067
     Slovakia, 9–043—9–044
     Slovenia, 9–045—9–046

Regulation – *contd*
  certification service providers – *contd*
    South Africa, 9–091
     South Korea, 9–068—9–069
     Spain, 9–047—9–048
     Sri Lanka, 9–070
     Sweden, 9–049
     Switzerland, 9–050
     Thailand, 9–071
     Turkey, 9–094
     United Kingdom, 9–051—9–052
     United States, 9–074—9–078
     Venezuela, 9–088—9–089
  data protection
    access, right of, 9–099
    compensation, right to, 9–099
    consent of data subject, 9–098
    controller, 9–096
    correction of data, right to, 9–099
    EU Directive, 9–096—9–098
    introduction, 9–095
    personal data, 9–096
    processing, 9–096—9–097
    quality of data, 9–097
    remedies of data subjects, 9–099
    rights of data subjects, 9–099
    sensitive data, 9–097
    third parties, data collected from, 9–098
  dual-use goods, export controls on
    Australia, 9–110
    conditional access devices, 9–109
    European Union, 9–108—9–109
    internationally, 9–107
    United Kingdom, 9–111—9–112
    United States, 9–113
    Wassenaar Arrangement, 9–107
  encryption technologies
    cybercrime, 9–102—9–106
    dual-use goods, as, 9–100
    introduction, 9–100
    military roots of cryptography, 9–101
    terrorism, 9–102—9–106
  introduction, 9–001
Reliability
  choice of law and jurisdiction clauses, 7–007—7–009
  UNCITRAL Model Laws
    Electronic Commerce, 5–005

Reliability – *contd*
UNCITRAL Model Laws – *contd*
Electronic Signatures, 5–015—5–016
Relying party
evidence, 8–019
GUIDEC, 5–030
transactions with certification service
providers, 7–015
UNCITRAL Model Law on Electronic
Signatures, 5–018—5–019
Relying party agreements
transactions with certification service
providers, 7–016—7–017
Repositories
regulation of certification service providers (US), 9–078
Repudiation of electronic signatures
false signatures, 8–018
intention to be legally bound, 8–016
invalid certificates, 8–017
transactions outside scope of certificate,
8–017
unauthorised use of genuine signatures, 8–014—8–015
Retention of documents
E-Sign (US), 6–120
Retina scans
biometrics, 3–014—3–015
Revocation of certificates
certification practice statements,
4–018—4–019
certification service providers, 4–014
RFC 2527
certification practice statements,
4–017—4–020
Romania
law, 6–051—6–052
regulation, 9–041—9–042
RSA algorithm
encryption, 3–044
Russian Federation
law, 6–151—6–152
regulation, 9–090
Scanned handwritten signatures
technologies, 3–007
**SDSI (simple distributed security infra-
structure)**
infrastructure, 4–010
Sealing

Sealing – *contd*
signatures, 2–006
Secure signature verification
Electronic Signatures Directive,
5–065—5–067
Secure signature-creation devices
Electronic Signatures Directive,
5–056—5–058
Security attacks
brute force
encryption keys, 3–044
capture and replay
biometrics, 3–013
dictionary
passwords, 3–005—3–006
key-search
encryption keys, 3–039
side-channel
information security, 7–019
Security Guidelines, OECD
generally, 1–012
Security of information
cybercrime, 7–021
introduction, 7–018
OECD Guidelines, 7–020—7–021
offences, 7–021
side-channel attacks, 7–019
Sensitive data
data protection, 9–097
Side-channel attacks
information security, 7–019
Signatory
Electronic Signatures Directive, 5–054
GUIDEC, 5–028
UNCITRAL Model Law on Electronic
Signatures, 5–017
Signature policies
choice of law and jurisdiction clauses,
7–006—7–009
Signature-creation data and devices
Electronic Signatures Directive, 5–055
Signatures
and see under individual headings
companies, 2–005—2–006
contracts, formation of, 1–003
definition, 2–019
effect, 2–030—2–031
electronic, 2–044
evidence, 8–008—8–009

Signatures – *contd*
  false, 8–018
  formalities
    agents, signature by, 2–027
    facsimile signatures, 2–023—2–029
    handwritten signatures, 2–019—2–022
    introduction, 2–016
    marks, 2–017—2–021
    printed signatures, 2–018—2–023
    sound recordings, 2–027
    stamped signatures, 2–017—2–022
    typewritten signatures, 2–018—2–023
    wills, 2–016—2–017
  functions
    authentication, 2–003—2–004
    giving of legal effect, 2–007
    identification, 2–002
    intention, 2–004
    introduction, 2–001
  identity, electronic, 2–038—2–044
  identity, personal
    business transactions, 2–037
    business transactions with individuals, 2–035
    government transactions with individuals, 2–036
    introduction, 2–032
    names, 2–032—2–034
    private transactions, 2–033—2–034
  introduction, 2–001—2–006
  legal effect, 2–030—2–031
  requirements, 2–016—2–029
  Statutes of Frauds
    civil law jurisdictions, 2–015
    common law jurisdictions, 2–014
    England, 2–008—2–011
    United States, 2–012—2–013
  unauthorised use, 8–014—8–015
Signature-verification data and devices
  Electronic Signatures Directive, 5–055
Simple distributed security infrastructure (SDSI)
  infrastructure, 4–010
Singapore
  law, 6–089—6–090
  regulation, 9–066—9–067
Slovakia
  law, 6–053—6–054

Slovakia – *contd*
  regulation, 9–043—9–044
Slovenia
  law, 6–055—6–057
  regulation, 9–045—9–046
Sound recordings
  signatures, 2–027
South Africa
  law, 6–153—6–154
  regulation, 9–091
South Korea
  law, 6–091
  regulation, 9–068—9–069
Spain
  law, 6–058—6–059
  regulation, 9–047—9–048
Sri Lanka
  law, 6–092
  regulation, 9–070
Stamped signatures
  generally, 2–017—2–022
Standard of proof
  evidence, 8–002
Standards
  and see under individual headings
  biometrics, 3–034
  certification services
    ISO 9000, 10–012
    QMS (Quality Management System), 10–012—10–013
    qualified certificates, 10–014
  compliance assessment
    Common Criteria for Information Technology Security Evaluation (US), 10–005—10–006
    introduction, 10–005
    ITSEC (Information Security Evaluation Criteria), 10–005
  evidence, preservation of, 10–018—10–019
  historical development, 1–016
  information security
    introduction, 10–015
    ISO 17799 (Code of Practice for Information Security Management), 10–015—10–017
    trustworthiness of systems, 10–017
  introduction, 10–001—10–004
  overview, 10–001—10–004

Standards – *contd*
  public key infrastructure (PKI)
    Australia, 10–007—10–008
    EESSI (European Electronic Signature Standardisation Initiative),
      10–008
    introduction, 10–007
    Public Key Authentication Framework (PKAF) (Australia), 10–008
  technologies
    distinguished names, 10–011
    EESSI (European Electronic Signature Standardisation Initiative),
      10–009
    FIPS (Federal Information Processing Standards) (US), 10–009
    qualified certificates, 10–010—10–011
    X.509, 10–010—10–011
Statutes of Frauds
  civil law jurisdictions, 2–015
  common law jurisdictions, 2–014
  England, 2–008—2–011
  United States, 2–012—2–013
Steganography
  encryption, 3–036
Subscribers
  transactions with certification service providers, 7–012—7–014
Suspension of certificates
  certification practice statements, 4–018—4–019
  certification service providers, 4–014
Sweden
  law, 6–060
  regulation, 9–049
Switzerland
  law, 6–061
  regulation, 9–050
Symmetric encryption
  technologies, 3–038—3–039
Technologies
  and see under individual headings
  biometrics
    Biometric Application Programming Interface (BAPI), 3–034
    body salt identification, 3–032
    capture and replay attacks, 3–013
    Common Biometric Exchange File Format (CBEF), 3–034

Technologies – *contd*
  biometrics – *contd*
    conclusion, 3–033—3–034
    digitisation, 3–011
    DNA matching, 3–029
    ear lobes, 3–026
    face recognition, 3–018
    facial thermograms, 3–027
    fingerprints, 3–019—3–020
    hand/finger geometry, 3–021
    handprints, 3–019—3–020
    handwritten signature dynamics, 3–022
    introduction, 3–011—3–013
    iris scans, 3–016—3–017
    keystroke dynamics, 3–028
    odour recognition, 3–030
    palm-prints, 3–031
    proposed forms of, 3–025—3–032
    retina scans, 3–014—3–015
    standards, 3–034
    vein patterns, 3–024
    voice recognition, 3–023
  Electronic Signatures Directive, 3–001—3–003
  encryption
    algorithms, 3–038—3–039
    Data Encryption Standard (DES), 3–044
    decryption, 3–036
    digital signatures, 3–040—3–043
    introduction, 3–035
    key length, 3–044
    methods, 3–037—3–044
    one-time pads, 3–037
    private key, 3–038—3–039
    public key, 3–038—3–039
    steganography, 3–036
    terminology, 3–036
  handwritten signatures, and
    authentication, 3–048
    ceremony, 3–050
    identification, 3–047
    intention, 3–049
    introduction, 3–045—3–046
    non-repudiation, 3–052
    originality of document, 3–051
  historical development, 1–015—1–016
  introduction, 3–001—3–003

Technologies – *contd*
  'low-tech' solutions
      bitmap scans of signatures, 3–007
      buttons, on-screen, 3–009
      conclusion, 3–010
      introduction, 3–004
      light pens, 3–008
      miscellaneous, 3–009
      passwords, 3–005—3–006
      PINs (Personal Identification Numbers), 3–005—3–006
      scanned handwritten signatures, 3–007
      typewritten signatures, 3–004
  standards
      distinguished names, 10–011
      EESSI (European Electronic Signature Standardisation Initiative), 10–009
      FIPS (Federal Information Processing Standards) (US), 10–009
      qualified certificates, 10–010—10–011
      X.509, 10–010—10–011
Terrorism
  see **Cybercrime**
Thailand
  law, 6–093—6–095
  regulation, 9–071
Third Generation (3G) mobile services
  generally, 1–002
Third parties, data collected from
  data protection, 9–098
Third parties, trusted
  regulation of encryption technologies, 9–103
3G (Third Generation) mobile services
  generally, 1–002
Time stamping
  digital signatures, 3–042
  public key infrastructure (PKI), 4–015
Trading Partner Agreements
  generally, 1–001
Triple DES (Data Encryption Standard)
  encryption, 3–044
Trusted first parties
  regulation of encryption technologies, 9–104
Trusted third parties
  regulation of encryption technologies, 9–103

Turkey
  law, 6–157
  regulation, 9–094
Typewritten signatures
  generally, 2–018—2–023
  technologies, 3–004
UCC (Uniform Commercial Code) (US)
  signatures, 2–012
UETA (Uniform Electronic Transactions Act) (US)
  automated transactions, 6–109
  electronic agents, 6–109
  electronic records, 6–106
  electronic signatures, 6–107
  exclusions, 6–105
  government records, 6–111
  introduction, 6–102—6–103
  mistake, 6–110
  scope, 6–104
  voluntariness, 6–108
Unauthorised use of signatures
  generally, 8–014—8–015
UNCITRAL (United Nations Commission on International Trade Law)
  Convention on Electronic Commerce, 1–009
  Model Law on Electronic Commerce
      addressees, 5–011
      contracts, formation of, 5–007
      electronic signatures, definition of, 5–005
      errors in transmission, 5–011
      form, 5–004
      generally, 1–009
      guidance, 5–006
      introduction, 5–002—5–003
      liability, 5–010
      originators, 5–008—5–009
      reliability, 5–005
  Model Law on Electronic Signatures
      certification, 5–014
      certification service providers, 5–020—5–026
      electronic signatures, definition of, 5–013
      generally, 1–009
      introduction, 5–012
      reliability, 5–015—5–016
      relying party, 5–018—5–019

UNCITRAL (United Nations Commission on International Trade Law) – *contd*
Model Law on Electronic Signatures – *contd*
signatory, 5–017
Unconscionable bargains
signatures, 2–030
Undue influence
signatures, 2–030
Unfair contract terms
transactions with certification service providers, 7–012
Uniform Commercial Code (UCC) (US)
signatures, 2–012
Uniform Electronic Transactions Act (UETA) (US)
automated transactions, 6–109
electronic agents, 6–109
electronic records, 6–106
electronic signatures, 6–107
exclusions, 6–105
government records, 6–111
introduction, 6–102—6–103
mistake, 6–110
scope, 6–104
voluntariness, 6–108
United Kingdom
dual-use goods, export controls on, 9–111—9–112
law on electronic signatures, 6–062—6–063
regulation of certification service providers, 9–051—9–052
United Nations Commission on International Trade Law (UNCITRAL)
Convention on Electronic Commerce, 1–009
Model Law on Electronic Commerce
addressees, 5–011
contracts, formation of, 5–007
electronic signatures, definition of, 5–005
errors in transmission, 5–011
form, 5–004
generally, 1–009
guidance, 5–006
introduction, 5–002—5–003
liability, 5–010

United Nations Commission on International Trade Law (UNCITRAL) – *contd*
Model Law on Electronic Commerce – *contd*
originators, 5–008—5–009
reliability, 5–005
Model Law on Electronic Signatures
certification, 5–014
certification service providers, 5–020—5–026
electronic signatures, definition of, 5–013
generally, 1–009
introduction, 5–012
reliability, 5–015—5–016
relying party, 5–018—5–019
signatory, 5–017
United States
dual-use goods, export controls on, 9–113
Federal Electronic Signatures in Global and National Commerce Act (E-Sign)
conclusion, 6–136
consumer consent, 6–124—6–128
document retention, 6–120
electronic agents, 6–123
electronic records, 6–121
electronic signatures, 6–122
exclusions, 6–118—6–119
government regulations, 6–129
inclusions, 6–116—6–117
introduction, 6–112
scope, 6–113
state law, and, 6–130—6–135
validity, 6–114—6–115
voluntariness, 6–114—6–115
FIPS (Federal Information Processing Standards), 1–016
general law, 6–101
historical development, 1–008
regulation of certification service providers
indemnities, 9–076
investigation, 9–075
licensing, 9–075—9–076
record keeping, 9–077
repositories, 9–078

United States – *contd*
  regulation of certification service
  providers – *contd*
    Utah Act, 9–074—9–076
     Utah Rules, 9–077
     warranties, 9–076
  regulations, 6–137
  Statues of Frauds, 2–012—2–013
  Uniform Electronic Transactions Act
  (UETA)
    automated transactions, 6–109
    electronic agents, 6–109
    electronic records, 6–106
    electronic signatures, 6–107
    exclusions, 6–105
    government records, 6–111
    introduction, 6–102—6–103
    mistake, 6–110
    scope, 6–104
    voluntariness, 6–108
Utah Digital Signature Act (Utah Act)
(US)
  historical development, 1–008
  regulation of certification service pro-
  viders, 9–074—9–076
Utah Digital Signature Administration
Rules (Utah Rules) (US)
  regulation of certification service pro-
  viders, 9–077
Validity
  E-Sign (US), 6–114—6–115
Vein patterns
  biometrics, 3–024

Venezuela
  law, 6–149—6–150
  regulation, 9–088—9–089
VeriSign
  certification practice statements, 4–021
Voice recognition
  biometrics, 3–023
Voluntariness
  E-Sign (US), 6–114—6–115
  Uniform Electronic Transactions Act
  (UETA) (US), 6–108
WAP (Wireless Application Protocol)
  generally, 1–002
Warranties
  regulation of certification service providers (US), 9–076
Wassenaar Arrangement
  export controls on dual-use goods,
  9–107
Webs of trust
  infrastructure, 4–004
Weight of evidence
  electronic transactions, 8–012
  real-world transactions, 8–006—8–007
Wills
  signatures, 2–016—2–017
Wireless Application Protocol (WAP)
  generally, 1–002
Witnessing
  signatures, 2–006
World Wide Web (WWW)
  generally, 1–001
X.509
  standards, 10–010—10–011

Acknowledgements

Sweet and Maxwell would like to acknowledge the following sources for providing permission to use their materials in the appendices and accompanying CD-Rom to *Electronic Signatures Law and Regulation* by Lorna Brazell.

Sweet and Maxwell have attempted to trace the copyright owners (including copyright owners of translations) of these materials. Where we have been unable to do so, we will be happy to publish the appropriate acknowledgement on the website referred to below. Copyright owners should contact the publishers at 100 Avenue Road, London NW3 3PF, United Kingdom.

Sweet and Maxwell may from time to time provide updates to the CD-Rom or additional country legislation not on the CD at http://www.sweetandmaxwell.co.uk/online/intreg/index.html

Appendices Materials

Czech Republic

Electronic Signature Act. This is a translation of the Act, the original of which is found on the official website of the Bureau of Personal Data Protection (www.uoou.cz). The translation has been obtained from and reproduced with the permission of the proprietors of the website www.e-podpis.sk. The proprietor states that: "Every effort has been made to preserve the accuracy of the information in and ensure fidelity to the said text. However, neither the e-podpis.sk website, nor the persons associated with it will be held liable for any inaccuracies in the said text or in this document. The circulation or reproduction of this document is permitted on condition the document is circulated or reproduced in its entirety, including this note." E-PODPIS.SK © 2002 – 2003. All rights reserved.

Finland

Act on Electronic Signatures (14/2003), unofficial translation, reproduced with the permission of the Ministry of Transport and Communications Finland.

Germany

Law Governing Framework Conditions for Electronic Signatures and Amending Other Regulations. This is an unofficial working version for industry consultation. For the official German text please refer to the Official Journal (Bundesgesetzblatt – BGBl. Teil I S. 876 vom 21. Mai 2001).

Ordinance on Electronic Signatures. This is an unofficial working translation (2001). For the official German version see the Federal Law Gazette (Bundesgesetzblatt - BGBl.) p. I 3074.

These materials are reproduced with the permission of the German Ministry of Research.

Ireland

Electronic Commerce Bill 2000, reproduced with the permission of the House of the Oireachtas, Parliament of Ireland.

Slovakia

Electronic Signature Act: Copyright © 2002 by Ivar Elznic. This is a translation of the Act. It has been obtained from and reproduced with the permission of the translator and proprietors of the website www.e-podpis.sk. The translator and proprietors state that: "Every effort has been made to preserve the accuracy of the information in and ensure fidelity to the original. However, neither the translator, nor the E-PODPIS.SK website or the persons associated with it will be held liable for any inaccuracies in the original or in the translated document. The circulation or reproduction of this document is permitted on condition the document be circulated or reproduced in its entirety, including this note; when quoting the document, the translator and the source, (www.e-podpis.sk) should be acknowledged.

Slovenia

Electronic Commerce and Electronic Signature Act. This is a translation of the Act, the original of which is on the official website of the Government of the Republic of Slovenia Center for Informatics (www.sigov.si). The translation has been obtained from and reproduced with the permission of the proprietors of the website www.e-podpis.sk. The proprietors state that: "Every effort has been made to preserve the accuracy of the information in and ensure fidelity to the said text. However, neither the e-podpis.sk website, nor the persons associated with it will be held liable for any inaccuracies in the said text or in this document. The circulation or reproduction of this document is permitted on condition the document be circulated or reproduced in its entirety, including this note." E-PODPIS.SK © 2002 – 2003. All rights reserved.

United Kingdom
E-Commerce Act ss. 7 and 15: Electronic Signatures Legislation: © Crown Copyright 2002.

CD Materials

Sweet and Maxwell would also like to acknowledge the following sources for providing permission to use their materials in the CD-Rom:

Australia
Electronic Transactions Act 1999. "All legislation herein is reproduced by permission but does not purport to be the official or authorised version. It is subject to Commonwealth of Australia copyright. The *Copyright Act 1968* permits certain reproduction and publication of Commonwealth legislation. In particular, section 182A of the Act enables a complete copy to be made by or on behalf of a particular person. For reproduction or publication beyond that permitted by the Act, permission should be sought in writing. Requests should be addressed to Commonwealth Copyright Administration, Australian Government Department of Communications, Information Technology and the Arts, GPO Box 2154, Canberra ACT 2601, or posted at http://www.dcita.gov.au/cca."

Bulgaria
Bulgarian Law on Electronic Document and Electronic Signature (2001) reproduced with the permission of the Centre for the Study of Democracy (www.csd.bg).

Canada
Uniform Electronic Commerce Act reproduced with the permission of the Uniform Law Conference of Canada.

Czech Republic
Electronic Signature Act: This is a translation of the Act, the original of which is on the official website of the Bureau of Personal Data Protection (www.uoou.cz). The translation has been obtained from and reproduced with the permission of the proprietors of the website www.e-podpis.sk. The proprietors state that: "Every effort has been made to preserve the accuracy of the information in and ensure fidelity to the said text. However, neither the e-podpis.sk website, nor the persons associated with it will be held liable for any inaccuracies in the said text or in this document. The circulation or reproduction of this document is permitted on condition the document is circulated or reproduced in its entirety, including this note." E-PODPIS.SK © 2002 – 2003. All rights reserved.

Denmark
Bill on Electronic Signatures (2000) published with the permission of the Ministry of Research and Information Technology.

EC
Directive 1999/93/EC of the European Parliament and of the Council of 13 December 1999 on a Community Framework for Electronic Signatures © European Communities, 1995-2003. Only European Community legislation printed in the paper edition of the Official Journal of the European Union is deemed authentic.

Estonia
Estonian Digital Signatures Act (2000): This is a translation of the Act which is on the website of the Estonian Legal Translation Centre (www.riik.ee).

Finland
Act on Electronic Signatures (14/2003), unofficial translation, published with the permission of the Ministry of Transport and Communications Finland.

The Companion CD

Instructions for Use

Introduction

These notes are provided for guidance only. They should be read and interpreted in the context of your own computer system and operational procedures. It is assumed that you have a basic knowledge of Windows. However, if there is any problem please contact our help line on 020 7393 7266 who will be happy to help you.

CD Format and Contents

To run this CD you need at least:
- IBM compatible PC with Pentium processor
- 8MB RAM
- CD-ROM drive
- Microsoft Windows 95
- Adobe Reader

The CD contains legislation some of which appears in this book. It does not contain software or commentary

Installation

The following instructions make the assumption that you will copy the data files to a single directory on you hard disk (e.g. C:\Electronic Signatures)

Open your **CD ROM drive**, select and double click on the **setup.exe** and follow the instructions. The files will be unzipped to your **C drive** and you will be able to open them up from the new **C:\Electronic Signatures** folder there.

LICENCE AGREEMENT

Definitions

1. The following terms will have the following meanings:
"The PUBLISHERS" means SWEET AND MAXWELL LIMITED of 100 Avenue Road, London NW3 3PF on behalf of Thomson Legal & Regulatory Europe Limited of 100 Avenue Road, London NW3 3PF (which expression shall, where the context admits, include Publisher's assigns or successors in business as the case may be);
"The LICENSEE" means the purchaser of the Work
"Licensed Material" means the data included on the CD ROM;
"Work" means the book entitled "Electronic Signatures Law and Regulation of which the enclosed CD ROM (to which this Licence Agreement related) forms a part and which contains the Licensed Material.

Grant of Licence; Back-up Copies

2.(1) The PUBLISHERS hereby grant to the LICENSEE, a non-exclusive, non-transferable licence to access the Licensed Material in accordance with the terms and conditions of this Licence Agreement.
(2) The LICENSEE may install the Licensed Material for access from one computer only at any one time.
(3) The LICENSEE may make one back-up copy of the Licensed Material only, to be kept in the LICENSEE's control and possession.

Proprietary Rights

3.(1) Copyright in the Licensed Material is owned by the relevant copyright owner and not the Publishers and accordingly permission to reproduce the Licensed Material cannot be granted by the Publishers and permission requests should be made to the relevant copyright owner.
(2)The Licensed Material is not sold to the LICENSEE who shall not acquire any right, sale or interest in the Licensed Material or in the media upon which the Licensed Material is supplied.
(3) The LICENSEE, shall not erase, remove, deface or cover any trademark, copyright notice, guarantee or other statement on any media containing the Licensed Material.
(4) The LICENSEE shall only access the Licensed Material in the normal course of its business and shall not use the Licensed Material for the purpose of operating a bureau or similar service or any online service whatsoever.
(5) The LICENSEE shall not sublicensee the Licensed Material to others and this Licence Agreement may not be transferred, sublicensed, assigned or otherwise disposed of in whole or in part.
(6) The LICENSEE shall inform the PUBLISHERS on becoming aware of any unauthorised access to or use of the Licensed Material.

Warranties

4. (1) Whilst reasonable care is taken to ensure the accuracy of the Licensed Material supplied, the PUBLISHERS make no representations or warranties, express or implied, that the Licensed Material is free from errors or omissions.
(2) The LICENSEE acknowledges that some of the Licensed Material is not published in full and it is the sole responsibility of the LICENSEE to satisfy itself that such materials are suitable for the LICENSEE'S requirements.
(3) The Licensed Material is supplied to the LICENSEE on an "as is" basis and has not been supplied to meet the LICENSEE's individual requirements. It is the sole responsibility of the LICENSEE to satisfy itself prior to entering this Licence Agreement that the Licensed Material will meet the LICENSEE's requirements and be compatible with the LICENSEE's hardware/software configuration. No failure of any part of the Licensed Material to be suitable for the LICENSEE's requirements will give rise to any claim against the PUBLISHERS.
(4) In the event of any material inherent defects in the physical media on which the Licensed Material may be supplied, other than caused by accident abuse or misuse by the LICENSEE, the PUBLISHERS will replace the defective original media free of charge provided it is returned to the place of purchase within 90 days of the purchase date. The PUBLISHERS' entire liability and the LICENSEE's exclusive remedy shall be the replacement of such defective media.
(5) Whilst all reasonable care has been taken to exclude computer viruses, no warranty is made that the Licensed Material is virus free. The LICENSEE shall be responsible to ensure that no virus is introduced to any computer or network and shall not hold the PUBLISHERS responsible.
(6) The warranties set out herein are exclusive of and in lieu of all other conditions and warranties, either express or implied, statutory or otherwise.
(7) All other conditions and warranties, either express or implied, statutory or otherwise, which relate in the condition and fitness for any purpose of the Licensed Material are hereby excluded and the PUBLISHERS shall not be liable in contract or in tort for any loss of any kind suffered by reason of any defect in the Licensed Material (whether or not caused by the negligence of the PUBLISHERS).

Limitation of Liability and Indemnity

5.(1) The LICENSEE shall accept sole responsibility for and the PUBLISHERS shall not be liable for the access to or use of the Licensed Material by the LICENSEE, its agents and employees and the LICENSEE shall hold the PUBLISHERS harmless and fully indemnified against any claims, costs, damages, loss and liabilities arising out of any such access and/or use.
(2) The PUBLISHERS shall not be liable for any indirect or consequential loss suffered by the LICENSEE' (including without limitation loss of profits, goodwill or data) in connection with the Licensed Material howsoever arising.
(3) The PUBLISHERS will have no liability whatsoever for any liability of the LICENSEE or any third party which might arise.
(4) The LICENSEE hereby agrees that:
(a) the LICENSEE is best placed to foresee and evaluate any loss that might be suffered in connection with this Licence Agreement;
(b) that the cost of supply of the Licensed Material has been calculated on the basis of the limitations and exclusions contained herein; and
(c) the LICENSEE will effect such insurance as is suitable having regard to the LICENSEE's circumstances.
(5) The aggregate maximum liability of the PUBLISHERS in respect of any direct loss or any other loss (to the extent that such loss is not excluded by this Licence Agreement or otherwise) whether such a claim arises in contract or tort shall not exceed a sum equal to that paid as the price for the Work.

Termination

6.(1) In the event of any breach of this Licence Agreement including any violation of any copyright in the Licensed Material, whether held by the PUBLISHERS or third parties, this Licence Agreement shall automatically terminate immediately, without notice and without prejudice to any claim which the PUBLISHERS may have either for moneys due and/or damages and/or otherwise.
(2) Clauses 3 to 5 shall survive the termination for whatsoever reason of this Licence Agreement.
(3) In the event of termination of this Licence Agreement the LICENSEE will remove the Licensed Material from any computer on which it has been stored and destroy or return any CD ROM in its possession on which the Licensed Material is contained

Miscellaneous

7.(1) Any delay or forbearance by the PUBLISHERS in enforcing any provisions of this License Agreement shall not be construed as a waiver of such provision or an agreement thereafter not to enforce the said provision.
(2) This Licence Agreement shall be governed by the laws of England and Wales. If any difference shall arise between the Parties touching the meaning of this Licence Agreement or the rights and liabilities of the parties thereto, the same shall be referred to arbitration in accordance with the, provisions of the Arbitration Act 1996, or any amending or substituting statute for the time being in force.